Life in Biblical Israel

LIBRARY OF ANCIENT ISRAEL

Douglas A. Knight, *General Editor*

Other books in the *Library of Ancient Israel* series

Sage, Priest, Prophet: Religious and Intellectual Leadership in Ancient Israel
Joseph Blenkinsopp

Oral World and Written Word: Ancient Israelite Literature
Susan Niditch

Scribes and Schools: The Canonization of the Hebrew Scriptures
Philip R. Davies

The Israelites in History and Tradition
Niels Peter Lemche

Reconstructing the Society of Ancient Israel
Paula M. McNutt

The Religion of Ancient Israel
Patrick D. Miller

The Politics of Ancient Israel
Norman K. Gottwald

Life in Biblical Israel

PHILIP J. KING
LAWRENCE E. STAGER

Westminster John Knox Press
LOUISVILLE • LONDON

Unless otherwise indicated, scripture translations are those of the authors.

Book design by Sharon Adams
Cover design by Mark Abrams
Cover illustration: Catherine S. Alexander

First edition
Published by Westminster John Knox Press
Louisville, Kentucky

This book is printed on acid-free paper that meets the American National Standards Institute Z39.48 standard. ∞

PRINTED IN CHINA

08 09 10 — 10 9 8 7 6 5

Library of Congress Cataloging-in-Publication Data

King, Philip J.
  Life in biblical Israel / Philip J. King, Lawrence E. Stager.
     p. cm. — (Library of ancient Israel)
  Includes bibliographical references and index.
  ISBN-10: 0-664-22148-3 (alk. paper)
  ISBN-13: 978-0-664-22148-5 (alk. paper)
    1. Jews—Social life and customs—To 70 A.D. 2. Palestine—Social life and customs—To 70 A.D. 3. Bible—Antiquities. I. Stager, Lawrence E. II. Title. III. Series.

DS112.K48 2001
221.9'5—dc21

                                                                    2001026334

To Leon Levy and Shelby White
for their enduring friendship and generosity

Contents

Illustrations

Foreword

The historical and literary questions preoccupying biblical scholars since the Enlightenment have focused primarily on events and leaders in ancient Israel, the practices and beliefs of Yahwistic religion, and the oral and written stages in the development of the people's literature. Considering how little was known just three centuries ago about early Israel and indeed the whole ancient Near East, the gains achieved to date have been extraordinary, due in no small part to the unanticipated discovery by archaeologists of innumerable texts and artifacts.

Recent years have witnessed a new turn in biblical studies, occasioned largely by a growing lack of confidence in the "assured results" of past generations of scholars. At the same time, an increased openness to the methods and issues of other disciplines such as anthropology, sociology, linguistics, and literary criticism has allowed new questions to be posed regarding the old materials. Social history, a well-established area within the field of historical studies, has proved especially fruitful as a means of analyzing specific segments of the society. Instead of concentrating predominantly on national events, leading individuals, political institutions, and "high culture," social historians attend to broader and more basic issues such as social organization, conditions in cities and villages, life stages, environmental contexts, power distribution according to class and status, and social stability and instability. To inquire into such matters regarding ancient Israel shifts the focus away from those with power and the events they instigated and onto the everyday realities and social subtleties experienced by the vast majority of the population. Such exploration has now gained new force with the application of various forms of ideological criticism and other methods designed to ferret out the political, economic, and social interests concealed in the sources.

This series represents a collaborative effort to investigate several specific topics—societal structure, politics, economics, religion, literature, material culture, law, intellectual leadership, ethnic identity, social marginalization, the international context, and canon formation—each in terms of its social dimensions and processes within ancient Israel. Some of these subjects have not been explored in depth until now; others are familiar areas currently in need of reexamination. While the sociohistorical approach provides the general perspective for most volumes of the series, each author has the latitude to determine the most appropriate means for dealing with the topic at hand. Individually and collectively, the volumes aim to expand our vision of the culture and society of ancient Israel and thereby generate new appreciation for its impact on subsequent history.

The present volume, by Philip J. King and Lawrence E. Stager, is devoted to precisely that level of social existence that was scarcely known to students of the Bible until the advent of archaeology. In fact, only in recent decades have archaeologists trained their sights on this most fundamental aspect in the history of antiquity—the everyday life of the Israelites, from commoner to king, rustic to urbanite, young to old. Even if many lacunae remain, we are now in possession of a vast store of details about their settlement patterns, living arrangements, kinship structures, domestic life, food production and preparation, health and illness, attire, song and dance, and writing materials. Substantial information is also available about cities, the life of royalty and the elite, the military and the machines of warfare, and cultic places, practices, and paraphernalia. In fact, thanks to the determined efforts of so many archaeologists, the details on most of these points have proliferated to the extent that only the specialists can now be in command of them. Drawing on their years of experience in archaeological work, King and Stager have masterfully constructed a multidimensional picture of everyday life in ancient Israel. Both material artifacts and texts, biblical as well as other ancient writings, serve as their sources, juxtaposed in a manner such that each illumines the other. The frequent use of illustrations and photographs, many previously unpublished, enhances our understanding of these details of life. The result brings us much closer than previously possible to an immersion into the ancient Israelites' culture and context.

DOUGLAS A. KNIGHT
General Editor

Preface

Utilizing an array of texts and artifacts, the authors have attempted to outline the main features of life in the biblical world. While focusing on the Iron Age, in order to contextualize a vast amount of material, we also called upon the ambient cultures of the ancient Near East. The Israelites did not live in isolation, but were deeply influenced by their neighbors, as the Bible attests. Since the Bible takes many aspects of daily life for granted, for elucidation, recourse to contemporary extrabiblical texts and archaeology is essential.

The subject of this book is so vast—stretching over many generations—that we can offer only an encapsulation of the primary aspects of everyday life. As the select bibliography indicates, each topic is a book in itself. Consequently, the research involved was more time consuming than the writing. The project took much longer than anticipated, but upon finishing, we realized we had just begun. The footnotes attest to our dependence on the expertise of colleagues. Aiming the book at both the specialist and nonspecialist, we hope that in the process we do not miss both.

Although this is a two-person project, we still depended heavily upon the assistance of others. In addition to colleagues acknowledged in the footnotes, we wish to express our indebtedness to the following: Douglas A. Knight of Vanderbilt University, editor of the series *Library of Ancient Israel*, without whom this book would never have appeared, and whose contributions of his time and talent far exceeded what editors ordinarily do; and Ephraim Stern of the Hebrew University, Jerusalem, who read the complete manuscript with the greatest care. Also, we want to acknowledge with gratitude four members of the younger generation who gave so generously of their time and talent: Christine Dungan, for organizing and formatting the bibliography; Kevin McGuire, for his professional computer assistance; Jeremy Hutton, for transliterating so carefully the Hebrew texts; and especially Kristen Vagliardo, for arranging and digitizing all the illustrations as well as for performing a host of other tasks. Without their assistance the project would not have reached completion.

Finally, were it not for Leon Levy and Shelby White, to whom this book is sincerely dedicated, this project, like several others undertaken by the authors over many years, would not have become a reality. To keep the book within the financial reach of potential readers, they generously subsidized the publication of *Life in Biblical Israel*.

Abbreviations

AASOR	Annual of the American Schools of Oriental Research
AB	Anchor Bible
ABD	*The Anchor Bible Dictionary*. Edited by D. N. Freedman. 6 vols. New York: Doubleday, 1992.
AnBib	Analecta Biblica
ANEP	*The Ancient Near East in Pictures Relating to the Old Testament.* Edited by James B. Pritchard. Princeton: Princeton University Press, 1969.
ANET	*Ancient Near Eastern Texts Relating to the Old Testament.* Edited by James B. Pritchard. Princeton: Princeton University Press, 1969.
AJA	*American Journal of Archaeology*
BA	*Biblical Archaeologist*
BAR	*Biblical Archaeology Review*
BASOR	*Bulletin of the American Schools of Oriental Research*
CAD	*The Assyrian Dictionary of the Oriental Institute of the University of Chicago.* Edited by Ignace J. Gelb et al. Chicago: The Oriental Institute of Chicago, 1956ff.
CANE	*Civilizations of the Ancient Near East.* Edited by J. M. Sasson. 4 vols. New York: Simon & Schuster, 1995.
CTA	*Corpus des tablettes en cunéiformes alphabétiques découvertes à Ras Shamra-Ugarit de 1929 à 1939.* Edited by A. Herdner. Mission de Ras Shamra 10. Paris, 1963.
CBQ	*Catholic Biblical Quarterly*
E.T.	English translation
HSM	Harvard Semitic Monographs
HTR	*Harvard Theological Review*
HUCA	*Hebrew Union College Annual*
IB	*The Interpreter's Bible*
ICC	International Critical Commentary
IDB	*The Interpreter's Dictionary of the Bible.* Edited by George A. Buttrick et al. 4 vols. New York: Abingdon Press, 1962.

IEJ	*Israel Exploration Journal*
JANES	*Journal of the Ancient Near Eastern Society of Columbia University*
JBL	*Journal of Biblical Literature*
JAOS	*Journal of the American Oriental Society*
JCS	*Journal of Cuneiform Studies*
JNES	*Journal of Near Eastern Studies*
JSOTSup	Supplement to *Journal for the Study of the Old Testament*
JSS	*Journal of Semitic Studies*
KAI	*Kanaanäische und aramäische Inschriften.* H. Donner and W. Röllig. 2d ed. Wiesbaden, 1966–1969.
KTU	*Die keilalphabetischen Texte aus Ugarit.* Edited by M. Dietrich, O. Loretz, and J. Sanmartín. AOAT 24/1. Neukirchen-Vluyn, 1976. 2d enlarged ed. of *KTU: The Cuneiform Alphabetic Texts from Ugarit, Ras Ibn Hani, and Other Places.* Edited by M. Dietrich, O. Loretz, and J. Sanmartín. Munster, 1995 (-*CTU*).
LAI	Library of Ancient Israel
LXX	Septuagint
MT	Masoretic Text
NAB	New American Bible
NEA	*Near Eastern Archaeology*
NEAEHL	*The New Encyclopedia of Archaeological Excavations in the Holy Land.* Edited by E. Stern. Jerusalem: Israel Exploration Society & Carta; New York: Simon & Schuster, 1993.
NJPS	New Jewish Publication Society
NRSV	New Revised Standard Version
OBO	Orbis Biblicus et Orientalis
OEANE	*Oxford Encyclopedia of Archaeology in the Near East.* Edited by E. M. Meyers. 5 vols. New York: Oxford University Press, 1997.
OIP	Oriental Institute Publications, University of Chicago
OTL	Old Testament Library
PEQ	*Palestine Exploration Quarterly*
RB	*Revue Biblique*
SBLWAW	Society of Biblical Literature Writings of the Ancient World
TA	*Tel Aviv*
TDOT	*Theological Dictionary of the Old Testament.* Edited by G. J. Botterweck and H. Ringgren. Grand Rapids: Eerdmans, 1974ff.
UF	*Ugarit-Forschungen*
VT	*Vetus Testamentum*
VTSup	Supplement to *Vetus Testamentum*

Chronology of the Levant

Neolithic	8500–4500 B.C.E.
Pre-Pottery Neolithic A (PPNA)	8500–7300
Pre-Pottery Neolithic B (PPNB)	7300–6300
Pottery Neolithic A (PNA)	6300–5000
Pottery Neolithic B (PNB)	5000–4500
Chalcolithic	4500–3500 B.C.E.
Early Bronze	3500–2250 B.C.E.
EB I	3500–3100
EB II	3100–2650
EB III	2650–2250
Early Bronze IV/Middle Bronze I	2250–1925 B.C.E.
Middle Bronze II	1925–1550 B.C.E.
MB IIA	1925–1700
MB IIB	1700–1600
MB IIC	1600–1550
Late Bronze	1550–1200 B.C.E.
LB I	1550–1400
LB IIA	1400–1300
LB IIB	1300–1200
Iron Age	1200–586 B.C.E.
Iron I	1200–1000
Iron IIA	1000–900
Iron IIB	900–700
Iron IIC	700–586
Neo-Babylonian	586–539 B.C.E.
Persian	539–332 B.C.E.
Hellenistic	332–53 B.C.E.

CHAPTER 1

Introduction:
The Importance of the Everyday Life

The task undertaken in the present book is to recreate the lifeways and mental attitudes of the ancient Israelites, from the courtyards of commoners to the courts of kings. It is no easy enterprise, since we lack ready-made ancient documents dealing directly with the issues of social, economic, and cultural history. To create dioramas of the daily life of a world that disappeared more than 2,500 years ago requires a search for data in a myriad of sources: ancient texts of various genres (including the Bible), inscriptions, an incalculable number of "ordinary things" that archaeologists continually dig up (potsherds, bone fragments, and other broken bric-a-brac), iconography (from the wall paintings and reliefs of Mesopotamia and Egypt to finely engraved seals), and ethnography. In mining these many different sources to retrieve something of that normative complex of values, customs, and meanings that constituted Israelite culture, we have not neglected the ordinary things, "the small things forgotten"[1]—architecture, tableware, furniture, furnishings, clothing, and personal adornments—that express that culture as well.[2]

Although we must take care not to lose sight of the unified structure of their lifeways, the various aspects become more readily comprehensible if we view their culture through a prism of topical headings.[3] For each of the following topics, the parenthetical reference indicates the pages where it is treated:

---

1. James Deetz, *In Small Things Forgotten: An Archaeology of Early American Life*, Anchor Books (New York: Doubleday, 1996).

2. Other general discussions of life in ancient Israel include Roland de Vaux, *Ancient Israel* (New York: McGraw-Hill, 1965); Johannes Pedersen, *Israel: Its Life and Culture*, 4 vols. (London: Oxford University Press, 1926–1940); Victor H. Matthews and Don C. Benjamin, *Social World of Ancient Israel 1250–587 B.C.E.* (Peabody, Mass.: Hendrickson, 1993); and Daniel C. Snell, *Life in the Ancient Near East 3100–332 B.C.E.* (New Haven, Conn.: Yale University Press, 1997).

3. This list was gleaned from David Hackett Fischer's *Albion's Seed: Four British Folkways in America* (New York: Oxford University Press, 1989), 8–9.

Family ways: the structure and function of household and family (pp. 36–40)

Gender ways: customs that regulate social relations between men and women (pp. 49–53)

Marriage ways: courtship, marriage, and divorce (pp. 54–57)

Child-rearing ways: nature and nurture of children (pp. 40–49)

Sex ways: conventional sexual attitudes and acts, and treatment of sexual deviance (pp. 59–61)

Age ways: attitudes toward aging and age relationships (pp. 58–59)

Death ways: mourning practices and mortuary rituals (pp. 363–81)

Building ways: dominant forms of vernacular and high architecture and their organization in planned and unplanned settlements (pp. 21–35, 201–10, 319–38)

Social ways: patterns of association and affiliation (pp. 36–84, 210)

Food ways: patterns of diet, nutrition, cooking, eating, feasting, and fasting (pp. 61–84, 93–107, 353–57)

Dress ways: customs of dress, demeanor, and personal adornment (pp. 259–85)

Work ways: nature of and attitudes toward work (pp. 85–122, 129–76)

Leisure ways: attitudes toward recreation and leisure; games and sports (pp. 210, 285–300)

Learning ways: patterns of education; attitudes toward literacy and learning (pp. 300–317)

Religious ways: religious architecture and patterns of worship (pp. 319–81)

Order ways: ideas of order and disorder, enforcement of order and treatment of disorderly conduct (pp. 36–40, 59–61, 201–58)

Power ways: attitudes toward authority and power (pp. 36–53, 201–58)

THE PROBLEM WITH TEXTS

When we try to recreate aspects of life in biblical Israel, we immediately come face to face with a profound dilemma: What periods are represented by that complex document known as the Hebrew Bible?

The earliest poetry, such as Judges 5 and Exodus 15, and the ancestral stories involving the peregrinations of Abraham, Isaac, and Jacob and their families in Canaan and elsewhere should in our view be attributed to the formative period of Israelite religion, the biblical "period of the judges," or the archaeological period known as Iron Age I (1200–1000 B.C.E.). We accept the early dating of the Yahwistic source, known as (J = Jahweh) of the Pentateuch in the tenth century B.C.E.; the combined epic source of J and E (E = Elohim) in the ninth century; the Priestly (P) source collated in the exilic period but containing many earlier traditions; the

Deuteronomistic Historian(s), who edited the books of Deuteronomy through 2 Kings, first in the late seventh century (Dtr 1) and later in the sixth century (Dtr 2). The bulk of the Chronicler (1 and 2 Chronicles, Ezra, Nehemiah) is postexilic and is based on earlier historical accounts (such as the Deuteronomistic History), although it also contains even earlier data (such as Hezekiah's building activities in Jerusalem) absent from 1 and 2 Kings.[4] Both the Deuteronomistic Historian and the Chronicler were interested in reinterpreting and reshaping older and contemporary sources in order to create a new past relevant to their present times and comprehensible to new generations.

In many ways the Bible resembles a highly stratified tell that gradually accumulated, layer upon layer, tradition upon tradition, through the ages. In some cases materials from earlier strata were reused and reshaped into new and different configurations and contexts. As we probe into the various strata of myths, legends, chronicles, odes, and prophecies preserved in this mound of many meanings, it will become apparent that we would situate most of the lifeways expressed in the Bible at various periods within the Iron Age (1200–586 B.C.E.). There, in the cultures of that era, in an area about the size of New Jersey, we find a number of correlations of biblical lore, contemporary extrabiblical inscriptions, and archaeology that cumulatively lead us to reject the current notions of those critics who consider "biblical Israel" to be a late fiction created in the fourth–second centuries B.C.E. as an expression of the Jewish experience of that era.[5]

The Bible has been preserved and protected because it is a document of faith at the very core of Judaism and Christianity. As heirs to this biblical legacy and its ongoing interpretations by communities of faith, our task of disaggregating and appropriating parts of the Bible for historical purposes—purposes quite unintended by its authors and editors—becomes doubly difficult.

Because of our biblical heritage, we probably assume a rather easy, widespread familiarity with the ancient Israelites that is not entirely warranted and is sometimes quite misleading. One need only recall the anachronistic portraits of the biblical world promulgated in Sunday school classes or in the high art of the Middle Ages

---

4. Frank M. Cross, *Canaanite Myth and Hebrew Epic* (Cambridge: Harvard University Press, 1973); Richard E. Friedman, *Who Wrote the Bible?* (San Francisco: Harper, 1987); Theodore Hiebert, *The Yahwist's Landscape: Nature and Religion in Early Israel* (New York: Oxford University Press, 1996).

5. For example, Thomas L. Thompson, *The Mythic Past: Biblical Archaeology and the Myth of Israel* (New York: Basic Books, 1999); Niels Peter Lemche, "Early Israel Revisited," *Currents in Research: Biblical Studies* 4 (1996): 9–34; idem, *Prelude to Israel's Past: Background and Beginnings of Israelite History and Identity* (Peabody, Mass.: Hendrickson, 1998); Philip R. Davies, *In Search of "Ancient Israel,"* JSOTSup 148 (Sheffield: Sheffield Academic Press, 1992). For excellent critiques of their position, see Iain W. Provan, "Ideologies, Literacy, and Critical Reflections on Recent Writing on the History of Israel," *JBL* 114 (1995): 585–606; and more recently and comprehensively, William G. Dever, *What Did the Biblical Writers Know and When Did They Know It?: What Archaeology Can Tell Us about Ancient Israel* (Grand Rapids: Wm. B. Eerdmans, 2001); also, James Barr, *History and Ideology in the Old Testament: Biblical Studies at the End of a Millennium* (New York: Oxford University Press, 2000).

and the Renaissance, when biblical themes were painted with the apparel, environment, and attitudes of the artists, not of the ancient protagonists. Our easy familiarity with these ancient traditions as seen through the lenses of Judaism and Christianity has often blurred the differences between them—the Israelites—and us. As David Lowenthal has emphasized, the "past is a foreign country" where they do things differently from us.[6] It is exotic and alien, with thought and work patterns far removed from those of our world.

THE STRUCTURE OF ISRAELITE SOCIETY

As we shall see, the lives of the ancient Israelites seem to focus on a social order that modern people no longer much experience. For the Israelites, family and kin groups organized around agrarian activities provided the basic elements of daily life and generated the symbols by which the higher levels of order—the political and the cosmological spheres—were understood and represented.[7]

Max Weber's theory of patrimonial authority, when combined with Israelite terminology of self-understanding, provides a powerful lens through which to view the overall structure of their society and their lifeways.[8] We see a three-tiered structure based on a series of nested households. At ground level is the ancestral, or patriarchal, household known in the Bible as *bêt 'āb*, literally "house of the father." At the level of the state or, better, tribal kingdom, in ancient Israel and in neighboring polities, the king functions as paterfamilias, his subjects dependent on personal relationships and loyalty to him, in return for which allegiance they expect protection and succor. As sovereign and proprietor of the land, the king presides over his house (*bayit*), which includes the families and households of the whole kingdom. Thus in a ninth-century B.C.E. stela found at Dan and in another from Moab, the southern kingdom of Judah is referred to as the "house of David" (*byt dwd*), just as the northern kingdom of Israel is known as the "house of Omri" (*bīt Ḥumrî*) in Assyrian annals.

The king, however, does not represent the apex of this societal model; rather, it is

---

6. David Lowenthal, *The Past Is a Foreign Country* (Cambridge: Cambridge University Press, 1985).

7. For a recent discussion of the elements of the Israelite social structure during various periods, as well as the difficulties in recovering and assembling them, see Paula M. McNutt, *Reconstructing the Society of Ancient Israel*, LAI (Louisville, Ky.: Westminster John Knox; London: SPCK, 1999).

8. See Lawrence E. Stager, "The Archaeology of the Family in Ancient Israel," *BASOR* 260 (1985): 25–28; idem, "Forging an Identity: The Emergence of Ancient Israel," in *The Oxford History of the Biblical World*, ed. M. D. Coogan (New York: Oxford University Press, 1998), 149–51, 171–72. For the most elegant development of the Patrimonial Household Model and its application to cultures throughout the ancient world, see J. David Schloen, *The House of the Father as Fact and Symbol: Patrimonialism in Ugarit and the Ancient Near East* (Cambridge: Harvard Semitic Museum, 2001).

Yahweh (in the case of Israel) who is the supreme patrimonial lord. He is the ultimate patrimonial authority over the children of Israel, who are bound to him through
covenant as his kindred (*'am*) or kindred-in-law.[9] Human kingship and divine kingship are, then, simply more inclusive forms of patrimonial domination. Thus we find
households nested within households on up the scale of the social hierarchy, each tier
becoming more inclusive as one moves from domestic to royal to divine levels. At the
same time, this entire structure reinforces and legitimates the authority of the paterfamilias at each of the three levels.

However, while this structure is replicated throughout the social hierarchy, the
domains differ in scale and function as various tiers of patrimonialism are reached.
The family and household provide the central symbol about which the ancient
Israelites created their cosmion, the world in which members of that society expressed
their relationships to each other, to their leaders (whether "judge" or, later, "king"),
and to the deity.

Through this lens we see that the Israelite monarchy was not some kind of "alien"
(read: "Canaanite") urban institution grafted onto a reluctant egalitarian, kin-based
tribal society, which through internal conflict and contradiction became a class-riven
society dominated by an oppressive urban elite. This fantasy in which kingship can-
cels kinship and gives rise to class consciousness is little more than Karl Marx's dialec-
tic in modern guise, in which society evolves from "primitive communalism" to
"slave society" with their masters holding the means of production.

Through the three-tiered patrimonial model of Israelite society, we can understand
how kingship in Israel, as elsewhere, could be a compatible institution along with other
forms of patriarchal dominance. Viewed from this perspective the rural-urban
dichotomy looks more like a mirage than a reality in ancient Israel. There were inequal-
ities to be sure, both in premonarchic and monarchic Israel, but social stratification
along class lines and class consciousness did not exist. The vertical, dyadic relationships
of superior to inferior were of a different sort and far more variegated than class concepts allow. The term *'ebed* can refer to anyone from a slave to a high government official, as on certain seals which refer to *'ebed hammelek*, "servant of the king."[10] The
social context of these referents must be known in order to understand the terminology.
In a society in which countless variations within the patrimonial order were possible,
it is not so difficult to imagine a farmer such as Saul or a shepherd such as David
becoming king. Because kingship was not an alien institution, it could be idealized
into messianic eschatology long after the demise of the monarchy.

---

9. Frank M. Cross, *From Epic to Canon: History and Literature in Ancient Israel* (Baltimore: Johns
Hopkins University Press, 1998), 3–21.
10. For example, seals nos. 6–11 in Nahman Avigad and Benjamin Sass, *Corpus of West Semitic Stamp
Seals* (Jerusalem: Israel Exploration Society, 1997).

THE WORK OF ARCHAEOLOGISTS

Once upon a time biblical archaeologists found it unnecessary to collect human and animal bones, plant remains, or geological specimens. Excavating, collecting, and analyzing these things was an expensive and redundant way of learning what many archaeologists presumed they already knew from reading the Bible. Archaeology—in particular, biblical archaeology—was to serve higher purposes: it should not only illuminate the manuscript but also validate the historicity of events and personages chronicled in the Bible, with the subtle (or not so subtle) assumption that to do so is to affirm the truth of its theological message and claims. The great biblical archaeologist G. Ernest Wright once defined the discipline this way:

> Biblical archaeology is a special "armchair" variety of general archaeology. The Biblical archaeologist may or may not be an archaeologist himself, but he studies the discoveries of the excavations in order to glean from them every fact that throws a direct, indirect or even diffused light upon the Bible. He must be intelligently concerned with stratigraphy and typology, upon which the methodology of modern archaeology rests. . . . Yet his chief concern is not with methods or pots or weapons in themselves alone. His central and absorbing interest is the understanding and exposition of the Scriptures. The intensive study of the Biblical archaeologist is thus the fruit of the vital concern for history which the Bible has instilled in us. We cannot, therefore, assume that the knowledge of Biblical history is unessential to the faith. Biblical theology and Biblical archaeology must go hand in hand, if we are to comprehend the Bible's meaning.[11]

Biblical archaeology, according to this view, was intended to shed light on the great persons and events that shaped Israelite history. Of course, such a goal was an even more expensive enterprise—searching for the "golden calf" in the midst of all that rubble—than making the most of the "ordinary things" that constitute the bulk of the archaeological yield. Only now and then could the great events and peoples of narrative history be correlated with archaeology. And then it was usually the catastrophic event—the archaeology of destruction—that made this possible: for example, the synchronous destructions of Pharaoh Shishak (Sheshonq) in 925 B.C.E.; the destruction of Lachish (Level III) by the Assyrian emperor Sennacherib in 701 B.C.E.; and the scorched-earth policy of King Nebuchadrezzar of Babylon throughout Philistia in 604 B.C.E. and in Judah and Jerusalem in 586 B.C.E.

   Until relatively recent times in the history of modern archaeology, patriarchs, warlords, kings, their armies and their enemies, the Israelite community in direct and special relationship to the deity, and the career of that collective have occupied center stage.

---

11. G. Ernest Wright, *Biblical Archaeology* (Philadelphia: Westminster, 1957), 17. For his latest view on biblical archaeology, in which he provided a prescient post-processual analysis, see "The 'New' Archaeology," *BA* 38 (1975): 104–15.

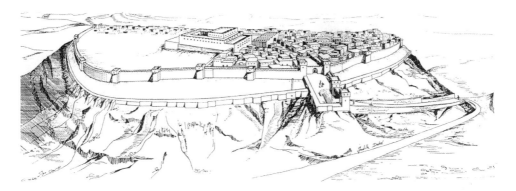

Ill. 1: Reconstruction of Lachish, Level III. (Courtesy of the Expedition to Lachish, David Ussishkin, Director; Drawing: Judith Dekel)

Great men, cosmic events, and special groups have been the focus of attention and analysis. To be sure, political, military, and religious histories are not to be gainsaid, what Fernand Braudel denigrated as *"l'histoire événementielle,"* the short-term, fast-changing history of events—"surface disturbances, crests of foam that the tides of history carry on their strong backs."[12] Nonetheless, our concerns in the present book will be more with his *"conjoncture"*—a middle-term duration, which includes demographic, social, and economic history—and *"la longue durée"*—long-term history, involving unchanging or slowly changing conditions of geography, climate, and environment, as well as our human relationship to them. Of course, there are those *kairotic* moments when these different durations or timescales intersect, when long-term causes precipitate short-term events and personages who have long-term consequences.

For our purposes, then, it matters little whether the biblical accounts are "true" in the positivistic sense of some historians and biblical scholars. It is enough to know that the ancient Israelites believed them to be so. The stories must have passed some test of verisimilitude, that is, having the appearance of being true or real. In this sense the biblical account and many other ancient accounts, however self-serving and tendentious, become grist for the cultural historian's mill. As the first great cultural historian, Jacob Burckhardt, writing in the nineteenth century about the Greeks, reminds us: "Material conveyed in an unintentional, disinterested or even involuntary way by sources and monuments . . . betray their secret unconsciously and even, paradoxically, through fictitious elaborations, quite apart from the material details they set out to record and glorify, and are thus doubly instructive for the cultural historian."[13]

---

12. Fernand Braudel, *The Mediterranean and the Mediterranean World in the Age of Philip II*, 2 vols., trans. Sean Reynolds, rev. ed. (London: Collins, 1972), 21.

13. Jacob Burckhardt, *The Greeks and Greek Civilization*, trans. Sheila Stern and ed., with an introduction by Oswyn Murray (New York: St. Martin's Press, 1998), 5.

In the introduction to Burckhardt's work, the classicist Oswyn Murray, paraphrasing Burckhardt, says:

> It does not matter whether the stories which it uses are true, as long as they are believed to be true. And even a forgery is an important piece of evidence for the period that perpetrated it, since it reveals more clearly than a genuine article the conceptions and beliefs about the past of the age that created it. This principle of unconscious revelation through representation . . . is one of the most powerful tools in the modern historian's study of mentalities. As Burckhardt saw very clearly, it offers a solution to the sterile disputes of positivism as to whether a fact is true or false, and how such a proposition can be established; cultural history is primarily interested in beliefs and attitudes, rather than events—and falsehoods are therefore often more valuable than truths.[14]

THE RHYTHMS OF LIFE

The gap between us and ancient peoples continues to widen as we become further removed from our agrarian roots. Today less than two percent of the population in the United States are farmers. In ancient Israel, it was just the opposite. Nearly everyone, even those living in royal cities such as Jerusalem and Samaria, was involved in some form of agriculture and had encounters with animals wherever they went. Two of the main city gates leading into Iron Age Jerusalem took their names from the creatures being bought and sold there: the Sheep Gate (Neh. 3:1, 32; 12:39) and the Fish Gate (2 Chron. 33:14; Neh. 3:3; 12:39; Zeph. 1:10).

Agricultural life was conducted by a "calendar" very different from ours. Our engagement [appointment] and planning books mark the day, month, year, and even the hour when something is to be done. There were many durations in premodern times: the diurnal in which one rises with the sun and retires when it sets; or the seasons of activities revolving about farming and herding. They did not make use of watches to fine-tune time down to the hour and minute. Ancient time was of a "different texture."[15]

As will be seen in chapter 3, the Gezer calendar highlights the seasonal patterns of the agricultural year, presumably when such festivals as the wine festival (note the example at Shiloh in Judges 21), Weeks (*šābuʿôt*), Tabernacles (*sukkôt*), Passover (*pesaḥ-maṣṣôt*), or sheepshearing took place. One of the most important festal meals was the annual sacrifice, known as *zebaḥ hayyāmîm*, that was

---

14. Oswyn Murray, in Burckhardt, *The Greeks and Greek Civilization*, xxxi.
15. Jacques Barzun and Henry F. Graff, "A Medley of Mysteries: A Number of Dogs That Didn't Bark," in *The Historian as Detective: Essays on Evidence*, ed. Robin W. Winks (New York: Harper, 1970), 213–31; see esp. 229.

designed to strengthen the solidarity of the clan (*mišpāḥâ*). This occasion of sacrifice and feasting "served to legitimate and sustain a social order based on patrilineal descent; to provide a public, observable verification of clan membership; and to confirm hierarchical status within the group by a graded distribution of portions or 'cuts' of the sacrificial animal."[16] It was understood that dead ancestors also participated. The importance of this clan bake can be seen from the story of David, who passes up King Saul's invitation and returns to his clan center in Bethlehem to celebrate there during this two-day feast at the new moon (1 Sam. 20:5–6, 28–29).

Agrarian life, kinship relations, domestic objects, the routines of the day and the year, and other such details of the mundane world play a far greater role on the pages of the Hebrew Bible than we might initially realize. They figure into stories, laws, historical accounts, songs, prophetic critiques, and wisdom sayings—sometimes as prominent features, but just as often as background minutiae. Typically readers will scarcely notice them, perhaps because they are alien to our own contexts or because they seem to fit our stereotyped notions of the character of life in antiquity. In chapters 2–6 we will be elucidating details of the everyday life and organizing them schematically for easier discussion. At this point, though, we will take one specific narrative as an example of the wide range of social, domestic, economic, political, religious, and environmental elements that can come together in a single story. Following the initial discussion, we will then indulge in a fictional portrayal of a "typical" day in the life of this family, in order to convey a sense of the terms of living faced by many of the ancient Israelites. To do so, we will draw on the same types of sources essential for all social history of ancient times—literary texts from roughly the same period, material finds discovered by archaeologists, knowledge of the environment, information about more recent means of living in the same context, and an informed imagination.

Micah and the Levite

A fertile narrative for the premonarchic family and its societal setting, and indeed for some of the elements of domestic life in other periods as well, is Judges 17–18, where the action focuses on the household of Micah, a wealthy landowner in Mount Ephraim. His large household comprises his widowed mother, his sons, their wives and children, and a young priest, who is an itinerant Levite (referred to as *na'ar*, probably as yet unmarried) from Bethlehem, whom Micah adopted and installed as priest of the household shrine (*bêt 'ĕlōhîm*). This shrine was equipped with such cultic paraphernalia as an ephod and teraphim, as well as a cult image with silver overlay. Micah

---

16. Joseph Blenkinsopp, "The Family in First Temple Israel," in L. G. Perdue et al., eds., *Families in Ancient Israel* (Louisville, Ky.: Westminster John Knox, 1997), 79.

paid this ritual specialist an annual salary of ten pieces of silver, gave him a wardrobe, and supplied him with subsistence.

The reference to an ephod and teraphim is obscure. The ephod may be a sacred garment or a ritual object, such as a box. In later sources, the ephod was the apron-like garment worn by the high priest (Ex. 28:6). Attached to the ephod was a breast-plate containing the Urim and Thummim, perhaps sacred dice used for divination. The priests may have used this device for predicting the future. Teraphim or "house-hold gods" served as cult objects. Sometimes they appear to be life-size: "Michal took the teraphim and, placing a tangle of goats' hair at its head, laid it on the bed and covered it with a blanket" (1 Sam. 19:13, 16). At other times they seem to be small and portable: "Now Laban had gone to shear his sheep, and Rachel stole her father's teraphim . . . and put them in the camel saddle and sat on them" (Gen. 31:19, 34).

The main point of the Micah story is to tell how a priest from Bethlehem in Judah, King David's birthplace and ancestral home, came to officiate at the main northern religious center at Dan. It is an etiology to legitimate this sacred center and give it a Levitical priesthood that claimed not only a southern Davidic connection but also a Mushite one. That this story served the interests of the northern kingdom after the division of the monarchy is clear; nevertheless, embedded in the narrative are family relations and arrangements that accurately reflect highland realities of the twelfth through tenth centuries.

According to the story, the Danites stole Micah's shrine and took the Levite to their newly acquired territory of Laish in the north, where they established the cult of Yahweh. The original Danite tribal territory was located in the southwest, bounded by Ephraim to the north, Benjamin to the east, Judah to the south, and the coastal plain to the west. The Danites migrated from the southwest to the northeastern corner of Canaan in the hill country. The Stratum VI destruction at Tel Dan is identified with the Danite conquest of Laish, renamed Dan, in the beginning of the twelfth century. Collared-rim pithoi appear for the first time in Stratum VI at Dan. These pithoi, pottery jars used to store water, wine, oil, and grain, are characteristic of Iron Age Israelite material culture. William F. Albright, followed by Yohanan Aharoni (see chapter 3), attributed this jar-type exclusively to the Israelites, but the pithoi have been discovered in the Jordan Valley, in the Ammonite region, as well as in the north. The East Jordanian sites where the collared-rim pithoi were found include Sahab, Tell Deir 'Alla, Tell el-Mazar, and the Amman citadel. A large number of these pithoi were also uncovered at Canaanite Megiddo.

Micah as the paterfamilias presided over other coresidents in the family com-pound, including his sons (and their families) who occupied houses within the com-pound and were under Micah's authority, that is, "the men who were in the houses within (or under the authority of) Micah's household" (*babbāttîm 'ăšer 'im-bêt mîkâ*,

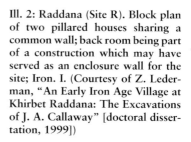

KHIRBET RADDANA   SITE R

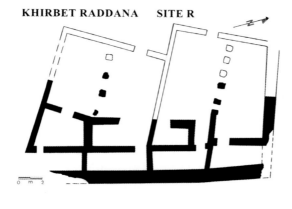

0 m 2

Ill. 2: Raddana (Site R). Block plan of two pillared houses sharing a common wall; back room being part of a construction which may have served as an enclosure wall for the site; Iron. I. (Courtesy of Z. Lederman, "An Early Iron Age Village at Khirbet Raddana: The Excavations of J. A. Callaway" [doctoral dissertation, 1999])

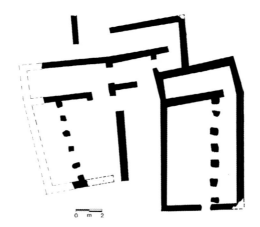

0 m 2

**KHIRBET RADDANA
SITE S**

Ill. 3: Raddana (Site S). Block plan of joint family compound, composed of two three-room houses with pillars, dated Iron I. (Courtesy of Z. Lederman, "An Early Iron Age Village at Khirbet Raddana: The Excavations of J. A. Callaway" [doctoral dissertation, 1999])

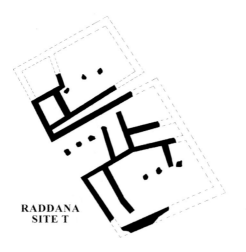

**RADDANA
SITE T**

Ill. 4: Raddana (Site T). Block plan of three or more pillared houses, dated late twelfth or early eleventh century B.C.E. (Courtesy of Z. Lederman, "An Early Iron Age Village at Khirbet Raddana: The Excavations of J. A. Callaway" [doctoral dissertation, 1999])

Judg. 18:22).[17] As will be discussed in more detail in chapter 2, the compound consisted of a cluster of houses within a walled or fenced-off portion of the village (Ill. 2, 3, 4). The same socially inspired architectural configuration seems to persist into New Testament times, as Jesus proclaims, "In my father's house(hold) are many houses" (traditionally, and erroneously, translated "mansions") (John 14:2).

Also living in the family compound was Micah's mother, a widow. Because women were often ten or fifteen years younger than their husbands, it would not be surprising to find more widows than widowers in ancient Israelite society, provided the women survived the rigors of childbirth. It was, of course, one of the primary duties of the son to care not only for his spouse and children but also for his widowed mother. Some of the subdivisions or annexes archaeologists find in the houses of Iron Age villages were probably the "widow's quarters." Other individual houses within the compound might belong to brothers or sons with their families, or serve as living quarters for the young Levite, a *gēr* ("client," usually translated "sojourner" or "stranger"), who "became to him like one of his sons" (Judg 17:11).

A Day in Micah's Household

Micah's father died at the old age of three score and ten, leaving his eldest son, now forty-seven years old, to care for his mother and to become the head of household, a joint family numbering seventeen persons, including two servants and a young priest (unmarried).[18] Micah's household occupies the largest compound in this sizable village of 250 people, all from the same clan, divided into two lineages. Micah's *bêt 'āb* (ancestral household), or compound, consists of three pillared houses arranged around a large walled-off open-air courtyard. It is one of twenty such compounds located on top of this terraced hill in Mount Ephraim.

This village, like many other settlements in the ancient (and modern) Near East, puzzles Western urbanologists. It seems to lack rational organization, consisting of densely packed houses hidden behind featureless courtyard walls, with streets and alleys that lead nowhere—a series of blind alleys and cul-de-sacs. To outsiders (including Western urbanologists) it appears to be a maze of houses and dead-end

---

17. For *'im* as "authority," see Ephraim A. Speiser, *Genesis*, AB 1 (Garden City, N.Y.: Doubleday, 1964), 170, 247.

18. This imaginative account of Micah's household is based on Judges 17–18. The details are drawn from biblical and other ancient Near Eastern sources, archaeological documents, and ethnographic studies of Middle Eastern communities. The following have been especially helpful in creating this imaginary day in an Israelite highland village: Gustaf Hermann Dalman's grand work, *Arbeit und Sitte in Palästina* (Gütersloh: C. Bertelsmann, 1928–42), in eight volumes, relating to Palestine at the turn of the twentieth century; and the ethnographies of Louise E. Sweet, *Tell Toqaan: A Syrian Village* (Ann Arbor: University of Michigan, 1974), and of A. M. Lutfiyya, *Baytin, a Jordanian Village: A Study of Social Institutions and Social Change in a Folk Community* (The Hague: Mouton, 1966). Many of the details of this day and the sources about them can be found in chapters 2–6 below.

Ill. 5: Plan of Tell en-Naṣbeh (ancient Mizpeh). Example of an organic town which grew according to social determinants such as kinship patterns; Iron II. (Courtesy of Z. Herzog; *Archaeology of the City*, Fig. 5.26, p. 238)

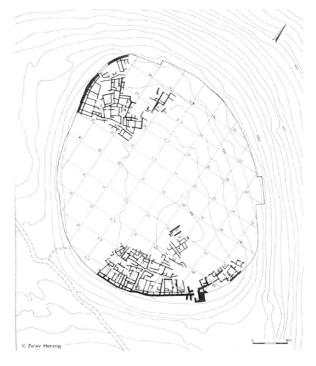

Ill. 6: Plan of Tell Beit Mirsim. Example of an organic town which grew according to social determinants such as kinship patterns; Iron II. (Courtesy of Z. Herzog; *Archaeology of the City*, Fig. 5.29, p. 243)

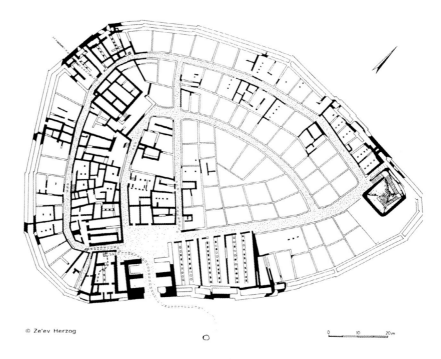

© Ze'ev Herzog

0   10   20 m

Ill. 7: Town layout of Tel Sheva, eighth century B.C.E., Stratum II. Example of planned settlement. (After Z. Herzog, *Archaeology of the City*, Fig. 5.31)

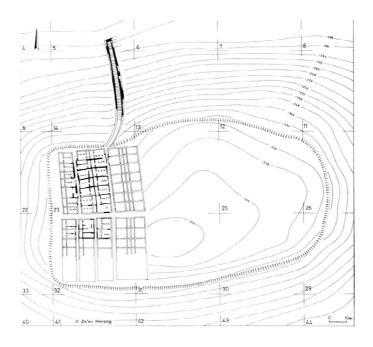

© Ze'ev Herzog

0   10m

Ill. 8: Block plan of Tell es-Saʿidiyeh, latter half of the eighth century B.C.E., illustrating orthogonal planning as a result of Assyrian impact. (Courtesy of Z. Herzog; *Archaeology of the City*, Fig. 5.24, p. 233)

streets, but to insiders it represents a clear map of kinship groups. It is not spatial order derived from some external principles but order emanating from internal social organization, based on neighborhoods coalescing around families and larger units of kinship, patron-client relationships, and other forms of alliance. What looks like utter chaos to an outsider makes a great deal of sense to those who belong there (Ill. 5, 6, 7, 8).

Within his compound, Micah has become the head of this patriarchal household. In his two-story house he lives with his wife, his sixty-year-old mother, and an unmarried paternal aunt. Each of his two married sons lives in a separate two-story pillared house within the compound. Together they have five children, two girls and three boys, ranging in age from three to ten years. The third house in the compound is occupied by an unmarried twenty-year-old son of Micah, two servants, and the Levitical priest, an unmarried teenager who is skilled in divination by consulting Urim and Thummim and in religious rituals and instruction (cf. Deut. 33:8–11).

In the hill country of Mount Ephraim the most pleasant time of year is spring, just after the heavy rains of winter and before the long, hot summer brings swarms of flies and gnats. The New Year's festival, which renews the bonds of belonging to clans and tribes throughout Israel, has been celebrated and sacrifices made. It is the season when lambs, kids, and calves are born and a green carpet of winter wheat spreads over the terraced hills and valley bottoms. Wild flowers of red, yellow, and blue turn the countryside into an impressionist's canvas. Yet it is still cold enough that the most vulnerable and precious livestock must be quartered on the ground floor of the house—their warmth and aromas radiating to the upper story, where most of the family sleeps.

As dawn breaks, the household starts to stir. Micah and his three sons go downstairs to release the livestock from the stables. Other animals are already in the courtyard. The family "breaks its fast" (John 21:12) by eating a "morning morsel" of bread, with a few olives. But morning was not the time for a real meal; that came later in the day (Eccl. 10:16–17).

The lambs and kids born earlier in the spring are separated from their mothers. Micah's unmarried son is the shepherd for one lineage in the village. He takes not only Micah's sheep and goats but also those of related families to graze on the plants and grasses of distant hills, covered with verdant pasturage. He will not return to the compound at midday. He carries his noonday meal with him: some dried figs, parched wheat, pita bread, and a flask of wine (cf. Ruth 2:14; 1 Sam. 25:18).

Since the grandchildren have no schools to attend, they are given many responsibilities in and around the busy compound. One of their chores is to look after the lambs and kids born earlier in the spring and separated from the ewes and nanny goats for most of the day. The young animals are just learning to graze on grass and weeds not far from the compound. They and the children get into all sorts of trouble that requires adult intervention.

Ill. 9: Yoked oxen in a wooden bowl (new) on left, and on right, a terracotta bowl. Tell el-Farʿah (N), probably Early Bronze Age. (Courtesy of the Israel Museum; Photo: A. Hay)

One of the married sons is off to do spring plowing, a time when peas, broad beans, lentils, and garden vegetables are planted. He yokes the two oxen (Amos 6:12) together, throws the wooden plow over the back of one of the large animals, and heads for the nearest unplowed field. His plow, the most important implement in an ancient farmer's repertoire of machinery, is really quite simple: a sturdy section of oak wood, curved toward a sharpened point or toe and shod with a bronze or iron sheath.

This simple machine is ideal for the crusty, terra rossa soils, often consisting of more stones than earth, that form the soil mantle of the highlands. Where the soil is stony and moisture at a premium, the deep-furrowing moldboard plow, with a sod-busting share, would be counterproductive. All that is needed is an implement to loosen the crust and to cover the seeds by cross-plowing, as soon as they are sown. The plow-man also carries a goad with which to jab the oxen. It consists of a two-pronged metal fork at one end and a metal spatula to clean the plow at the other.

Meanwhile, back at the compound, Micah and one of his servants are cleaning out the house stables. They scoop out the straw bedding, now saturated with urine and manure from last night's lodging. There are no separate barns or stables in the village; one would have to go to royal cities for such facilities. Oxen, donkeys, cattle, and some sheep are commonly stabled on the ground floor of village houses. Troughs between the pillars and cobbled side aisles are constructed more for livestock than humans; nevertheless, since no toilets, either indoors or outdoors, exist in most communities, it is convenient for the upstairs inhabitants to relieve themselves during the night in the stables below. Using wooden forks and shovels, Micah and his servant clean the stables while two of the daughters carry the refuse in large straw baskets to the southeastern part of the courtyard, downwind from the prevalent westerlies, where they pile the dung into an already formidable midden. Later in the day, some members of the compound will shape part of the pile into round or square cakes, to be stacked and dried in the sun like mud bricks. Dung cakes will provide excellent fuel for heating and cooking.

Although Micah has the last word in the household, his wife organizes and oversees the myriad of activities taking place in the houses and the courtyard. She and the other women are responsible for food processing and preparation, as well as many other domestic chores. Among those, first and foremost is the preparation of daily bread, the staple of the family. On the other side of the courtyard, opposite the midden heap, stands a beehive-shaped oven (*tannûr*, Ex. 7:28), built of clay and insulated with potsherds. Straw and sticks (never dung) are kindled in the bottom of the oven, sometimes sunk slightly into the ground. When the fire has been reduced to a bed of hot coals in the bottom and the sides of the oven are quite hot, it is time to bake the bread on the interior of the *tannûr*.

Shortly after sunrise, Micah's wife is busy rolling the dough into balls, using a bit of leavening from the last batch of bread dough. After the dough balls have risen, she flattens them out on a stone and then, using both hands, twirls the cake into a flat disc, some twenty-five centimeters in diameter. In one motion she throws the cake through a large opening in the top of the beehive oven so that it sticks to the interior and bakes in minutes. She uses the most common manner of making bread in the village, but there are other ways as well. Some make griddle cakes by baking pita on a ceramic tray or griddle heated over an open fire. Others make fritters by frying the dough in a cooking pot of bubbling olive oil or lard from a fat-tailed sheep (Lev. 2:4–7).

Meanwhile, the daughters-in-law are doing a number of other tasks under the eye of Micah's wife. One is opening the last of the grain silos (*'ăsāmîm*) sunk beneath the floor of the courtyard and filled with wheat from the last harvest ten months ago. The wheat is brought to the handmill operated by another daughter-in-law. She grinds the grain between two coarse basalt slabs: the lower is called the "saddle"; upon it sits the upper stone, known as the "rider." Wheat placed between the two stones is husked and ground as the rider moves across the saddle in a back-and-forth motion. The other daughter-in-law pours the coarsely ground grain into a three-legged mortar made of basalt and, using a pestle, pulverizes the grain into a fine flour, ready for tomorrow's bread. The remaining cracked wheat is made into couscous (bulgur, in Turkish).

After bread making, as noon approaches, it is time to milk the ewes and nannies

Ill. 10: Israelite joint family compound with two pillared houses and various courtyard activities. (Reconstruction: © L. E. Stager, Illustration: C. S. Alexander)

pasturing on a distant hillside. Two of the women take deep earthen bowls with them to bring back the milk. At the compound the fresh milk is poured into a goatskin churn suspended by ropes from a fig tree. The churning bag has been specially cured with pomegranate peel. One of the younger girls shakes the churn back and forth until the milk curdles.

Several members of the family have returned to the compound for the midday meal. Micah's wife puts out fresh pita, onions, and leban (curdled milk) for lunch. Afterward, during the hottest part of the day, Micah and some others take a siesta under the pergola in the courtyard. By mid-afternoon the unmarried son returns from plowing with the oxen. He removes the yoke and harness and waters the team at the stone trough in the middle of the courtyard. Another son takes the oxen out to graze for the remainder of the afternoon. With a hoe Micah is loosening the soil of a small plot near the house (Isa. 7:25) where his wife will plant a vegetable garden of cucumbers, melons, leeks, garlic, onions, and herbs during the coming week.

Meanwhile she has put a large cooking pot of couscous (parched cracked wheat) on a tripod of three stones arranged around an open fire. The main dish of the evening, couscous spiced with onions, coriander, and black cumin, simmers in the pot until sunset. The boys spread the straw bedding throughout the house stables just as the herdsmen return to the village with the livestock. Before the evening meal is served, the boys lead the animals into their evening quarters. Then members of the joint family gather in the upper story of Micah's house, where supper is laid out for them. The couscous is heaped high on a large tray in the middle of the dining room floor. Fresh-baked pita bread sits in a wicker basket. The head of the household offers a blessing for the food and then hands a portion of bread to each of the adults sitting in the family circle on the floor.

After yogurt is poured over the couscous, it has the consistency of "cream of wheat." There are no knives, forks, or spoons. With bread they scoop up the creamy couscous from the pottery tray, careful to use only the fingers of the right hand for eating. A decanter of red wine and raisin cakes accompany the main course.

The plowman and the children unroll their straw-filled mattresses and line them up along the walls of the second floor. They are very tired and have to get up early. Others in the central room continue to chat into the evening. Before retiring, Micah and his sons make sure that the gate to the compound is closed and locked, as well as the doors to the individual houses.

CHAPTER 2

The Israelite House and Household

The foundation of Israelite society was the family. The everyday world of the vast majority of the population was played out in its context—certainly in the many hundreds of small villages spread throughout the countryside where 80–90 percent of the population dwelled, but also in the towns and cities among the elite and the resident work force. For most, the family served as the primary economic, social, and religious center. In narratives, laws, prophetic utterances, and wisdom sayings, the biblical literature touches frequently on aspects of family life. Fortunately, archaeological efforts have succeeded in uncovering a wealth of information to explain and to supplement the details of family life described in the text.

DOMESTIC ARCHITECTURE

Building Materials

The most commonly used building materials in ancient Israel were stone, wood, reeds, and mud. Stone and wood served a range of purposes—from the natural, undressed stone and rough-cut local wood used for the commoner's dwelling to the expertly dressed stone and finely carved wood for the palaces, temples, and manor homes. The monumental buildings of the city far outstripped in elegance the structures found in the many villages and towns scattered throughout the landscape, yet the materials were the same, except for specially imported wood and stone for those who could afford or could mandate it. Skilled labor was also employed in more well-to-do contexts, while villagers relied on native traditions and group effort for meeting their needs for shelter and storage.

Stone, being more durable than wood and mud brick, was the most popular building material. Palestine has an abundance of limestone, a sedimentary rock consisting mostly of calcium carbonate; it was the common building stone, especially in the hill country. *nari*, found in the area east of Jerusalem, is a soft, porous, friable limestone. Easily quarried and dressed, it was the stone used for preparing ashlars and Israelite palmette capitals in the construction of monumental buildings. This elegant architecture reflects the elite status in Iron II (tenth–seventh centuries) in Israel and Judah.[1]

Ashlar masonry, which is Canaanite-Phoenician in origin, designates stones cut and dressed on all six sides, usually cuboid in shape. The use of ashlar for building construction did not appear before LB. Canaan's first example was the LB temple and city gate at Megiddo. In the Iron Age, as a rule, ashlar masonry was utilized on sites that functioned as royal centers in Judah and Israel. Note Amos' denunciation of the powerful: "You have built houses of hewn stone (*bāttê gāzît*), but you shall not live in them" (Amos 5:11). Large-scale use of ashlars dates to Solomon, whose building activities reflect a strong Phoenician influence.

Ashlar was employed more extensively in Israel than in Judah. Northern sites include Hazor, Samaria, Megiddo, and Gezer, as well as Dan, Ta'anach, and Beth-Shean. Southern sites are Jerusalem, Lachish, and Ramat Raḥel, as well as Tel Sera' and Ashkelon (MB IIA gate). The most impressive examples of this finely dressed and squared masonry are found at Samaria, where Omri and Ahab built their royal city in the ninth century. Among recently discovered examples of limestone ashlars are the following. At Dor the ashlar tower is connected to the four-chambered gate house.[2] At Ekron there is an ashlar-faced mudbrick tower in a header-and-stretcher construction on the northeast acropolis, Str III-IB.[3] There are limestone ashlars in the gatehouse at Jezreel.[4]

kurkar, a type of sandstone found along the Mediterranean coast, is often used as building stone. Examples of sandstone ashlars are found at Tel Sera' (ashlar foundations with mud brick superstructure, Str VI [eighth century]). Also, the Ashdod gate (tenth–eighth century) has ashlars on the corners. The Ashkelon royal winery is built of ashlars.[5] Eliezer Oren suggests that ashlar masonry was introduced into the coastal area "by the Phoenicians during the period of Assyrian domination."[6] This would account for construction at Tel Sera' but not for tenth-century Ashdod. The Phoeni-

---

1. Ronny Reich, "Building Materials and Architectural Elements in Ancient Israel," in A. Kempinski and R. Reich, eds., *The Architecture of Ancient Israel from the Prehistoric to the Persian Periods* (Jerusalem: Israel Exploration Society, 1992), 1–2; Ze'ev Herzog, "Building Materials and Techniques," *OEANE*, 1:360–63.

2. Ephraim Stern and Ilan Sharon, "Tel Dor, 1992: Preliminary Report," *IEJ* 43 (1993): 138–39.

3. Seymour Gitin, "Tel Miqne: A Type-Site for the Inner Coastal Plain in the Iron Age II Period," in S. Gitin and W. G. Dever, eds., *Recent Excavations in Israel: Studies in Iron Age Archaeology*, AASOR 49 (Winona Lake, Ind.: Eisenbrauns, 1989), 25–26.

4. David Ussishkin and John Woodhead, "Excavations at Tel Jezreel 1994–1996: Third Preliminary Report," *TA* 24 (1997): 20–22.

5. Lawrence E. Stager, "Ashkelon and the Archaeology of Destruction: Kislev 604 B.C.E.," in A. Biran et al., eds., *Eretz-Israel* 25 [Joseph Aviram Volume] (Jerusalem: Israel Exploration Society, 1996), 62–63.

6. Eliezer Oren, "Sera', Tel," *NEAEHL*, 4:1333.

cians could have introduced ashlar to Ashdod, but it would have been several centuries prior to Assyrian occupation there.

Artisans used chisel and hammer to dress the stones whose surfaces they finished smooth or with bosses, which are the rounded masses of stone in the center of the ashlar face. In the Iron Age, bosses were limited to the lowest foundation levels so as not to be visible. Among the techniques of stone finishing are margins designating the smooth edges along the sides of the ashlars. Ashlars with dressed margins, trimmed on the construction site, fitted so tightly that no spaces were left between the stones. No mortar was used for binding the stones. As a means of strengthening the walls, the ashlar stones were positioned in alternating headers and stretchers manner. Headers were placed perpendicular to the wall's length, with the short side toward the face of the wall. Stretchers were laid parallel to the wall's length, with the long side extending along the face of the wall.[7]

Basalt, a hard, dense, dark volcanic rock with a glassy appearance, is found commonly in Upper Galilee, the Golan, and Bashan. Because it is wear-resistant, basalt is excellent for constructing steps, door sockets, thresholds, drain pipes, and stelae, as well as orthostats (large stone slabs), which frequently flank entrances to monumental buildings, or the lower part of walls (e.g., the Hazor temples) (Ill. 11). In the Golan the superstructures of buildings are made of basalt.[8]

Timber, more plentiful in ancient Israel than it is today, was the principal material for roof beams (*qōrôt*) and joists, as well as window frames, lintels, doors, and

Ill. 11: Basalt lion orthostat, dated between fourteenth and thirteenth centuries B.C.E., Hazor. (Courtesy of Israel Museum; photo: D. Harris)

7. Yigal Shiloh, *The Proto-Aeolic Capital and Israelite Ashlar Masonry*, Qedem 11 (Jerusalem: Institute of Archaeology, Hebrew University, 1979).

8. Claire Epstein, *The Chalcolithic Culture of the Golan* (Jerusalem: Israel Antiquities Authority, 1998) Report #4.

Ill. 12: Cedars of Lebanon

door jambs. To serve as beams in ceiling or roof construction, the timbers need be no more than four to five meters long. With rows of pillars the span is usually two and one-half to four meters for the main room and one and one-half to three meters for the side rooms.[9] Flat roofs (*gaggôt*) of buildings were constructed by laying wooden beams across the open area, their ends supported by the walls at either side. Intermediate vertical posts or columns were usually inserted to shore up these roof beams. Reeds or branches were also used in roof construction by being placed on the wooden rafters (*rāhîṭîm*) to serve as a base for a plaster covering. The brushwood was overlaid with mud and straw, which had to be compacted regularly with a stone roller to maintain its solidity and thus prevent damage from rainwater.

Paleobotanists are sometimes able to identify the timber utilized in construction, although translators and commentators unfamiliar with the flora of Palestine often cause confusion. Among the specific trees and shrubs identified are the tamarisk, acacia, cedar, Phoenician juniper, terebinth, oak, and Aleppo pine.

The tamarisk (*'ēšel*), an evergreen achieving a height of ten meters, is indigenous to the Aravah Valley. It may also be found in the maritime plain, the Jordan Valley, and the Negev.

---

9. Lawrence E. Stager, "The Archaeology of the Family in Ancient Israel," *BASOR* 260 (1985): 15.

Ill. 13: Procession of Assyrian servants carrying exotic potted plants to be transplanted in Sennacherib's palace garden. (Drawing: A. M. Appa after S. Dalley, *Garden History* 12 [1993], p. 10, fig. 2)

The acacia (*šiṭṭâ*), a desert tree, grows five to eight meters high. Found in barren regions like the Sinai Peninsula and the Arabian Desert, its durable wood makes it ideal for building furniture. It is also used for doors in the Iron II city gate at Lachish, where acacia was found adhering to a bronze hinge. Acacia had to be imported to Lachish for the gate doors.[10]

The cedar (*'erez*) is an evergreen that attains a great age and may grow as high as thirty-five meters. This mountain tree was used copiously in constructing both the First and Second Temples. Because it is well suited for beams, boards, pillars, and

10. David Ussishkin, "Lachish," *NEAEHL*, 3:906.

ceilings, cedar was used in all kinds of construction, including boats: "They took a cedar from Lebanon to make a mast for you [Tyre]" (Ezek. 27:5). In biblical times cedar forests covered large areas of Lebanon and the Cilician Taurus (Ill.12). Cedar can be transplanted to other areas for use in protected environments such as pleasure gardens or cemeteries.[11] The answer to Hezekiah's prayer concerning the menacing Sennacherib takes the form of a taunt spoken by Isaiah: "Through your servants you [Sennacherib] have insulted the Lord (*'ădōnāy*). You said: 'With my many chariots I climbed the mountain heights, the recesses of Lebanon; I cut down its lofty cedars (*'ărāzâw*), its choice junipers (*běrôšâw*); I reached the remotest heights, its forest park'" (2 Kings 19:23).

The majestic juniper (*Juniperus excelsa;* Heb. *běrôš*) still grows on Mount Hermon, the Senir of the Bible (Ezek. 27:5). It is a large resinous tree with berries, used in con-

Ill. 14: Bronze Bands, Gates of Balawat. Campaign in Syria, 854 B.C.E. (Upper Register) Assyrians in chariots and on horseback slaughter the men of Hamath. (Lower Register) City of Qarqar is in flames while the Assyrian officers watch the conflagration from a nearby orchard of fruit trees, through which runs an irrigation stream. This is perhaps an example of a royal garden, just outside the city walls. (Courtesy of the Trustees of the British Museum)

---

11. Lawrence E. Stager, "Jerusalem and the Garden of Eden," in B. A. Levine et al., eds., *Eretz-Israel* 26 [Frank Moore Cross Volume] (Jerusalem: Israel Exploration Society, 1999), 185.

struction, especially for roofing beams and furniture, as well as for shipping planks. Hiram of Tyre provided the timbers of cedar and juniper for building the palace and Temple of Solomon (1 Kings 5:21–24).

Translators unfamiliar with the local flora often confuse the terebinth and the oak, using the similar Hebrew names interchangeably or inconsistently. The problem of nomenclature is compounded by the fact that hundreds of species of terebinth and oak have been attested. The root of all these words is *'ēl* (god), suggesting divinity, power, and strength.

'ēlâ and *'allâ*, designating the terebinth (*Pistacia palestina*), also known as the turpentine tree, reaches a height of ten meters. It is found in the Negev, Lower Galilee, and the Dan Valley.[12] Several biblical events are associated with the terebinth (*'ēlâ*). The call of Gideon took place under the terebinth at Ophrah (Judg. 6:11).

'allôn and *'ēlôn* refer to the oak in the Bible. The Tabor oak (*Quercus ithaburensis*), a deciduous tree that attains an age of 300–500 years and a height of twenty-five meters, grows in the forests of the Coastal Plain, Lower Galilee, the Dan Valley, the Hulah Plain, and the Golan Heights. The evergreen oak (*Quercus calliprinos*) is the most common oak in Palestine.[13] Several references to the oak appear in the Bible: "Abraham moved his tent, and came and settled by the oaks of Mamre (*'ēlōnê mamrē'*), which are at Hebron; and there he built an altar to Yahweh" (Gen. 13:18). "Deborah, Rebekah's nurse, died, and she was buried under an oak (*'allôn*) below Bethel. So it was called Allon-bacuth [oak of weeping]" (Gen. 35:8). The oak is used in construction and shipbuilding, and the wood of the oak (*'allôn*) could be crafted into images (Isa. 44:14–17).

The Aleppo pine (*Pinus halepensis*) is the *'ēṣ šemen* (lit. "oil tree") of the Bible, where it is mentioned five times. The only pine native to Palestine, it reaches twenty meters in height and can live for 100–150 years. Pine forests were abundant in biblical times. *'ēṣ šemen* is sometimes wrongly translated "olive wood."[14] The massive figures of cherubim flanking the Ark in the Holy of Holies were carved in pine, not olive wood. It is likely these statues were sculpted not from one large piece of pine but from many smaller pieces combined, as would have been the case had olive wood been used.

In the construction of both public buildings and brick walls, wooden beams (sometimes referred to as sleeper beams) were inserted horizontally between the courses of ashlar to strengthen the masonry or to give it flexibility in earthquakes. "He [Solomon] built the inner court [of the Temple] with three courses of dressed stone (*gāzît*) to one course of cedar beams (*kĕrutōt 'ărāzîm*)" (1 Kings 6:36; also 7:12).

---

12. Cf. Michael Zohary, *Plants of the Bible* (Cambridge: Cambridge University Press, 1982), 110–11.

13. Stager, "The Archaeology of the Family," 4; F. Nigel Hepper, *Baker Encyclopedia of Bible Plants* (Grand Rapids: Baker Book House, 1992), 33.

14. Zohary, *Plants of the Bible*, 114.

Mud brick was the primary construction material for buildings and walls in the coastal plain and in the valleys, where clay was readily at hand and timber and hard stone scarce. Mud brick used in construction was often founded on a stone socle (a plain, low block serving as a support for a pedestal, statue, etc.). In the hill country, stone was used for foundations and superstructures.

Mud was utilized in making both bricks and mortar. Raw mud functioned as mortar; mud poured into molds (square or rectangular) was dried in the sun and formed into bricks (*lĕbēnîm*, from *lābān*, "white"). The sun-dried mud brick was the most common building material in the ancient Near East. Unbaked mud brick was used in the construction of above-ground walls of buildings. Every year brick construction had to be coated on the outside with plaster as a form of weatherproofing (Ezek. 13:10–15).

Chopped straw was mixed with clay and sand to make the mud more cohesive and to prevent the mud from adhering to the mold when poured into rectangular blocks. To make the labor of the Israelites in Egypt more arduous, Pharaoh commanded their taskmasters: "You shall no longer give the people straw (*teben*) to make bricks, as before; let them go and gather straw for themselves" (Ex. 5:7). Bricks began to be made in molds from the beginning of the Bronze Age. There is no evidence of firing clay bricks in a kiln in Israel before the Early Roman period, although there are some earlier cases in Mesopotamia.

Another technique for building exterior walls of monumental buildings was borrowed by the Israelites from the Phoenicians. It is the ashlar pier-and-rubble-panel masonry designed to absorb shock waves from earthquakes or tremors. This pillar-rubble construction was utilized in Solomonic Megiddo, for example, Building 338 (Str IVA), and Palace 1723 (Str VA-IVB), as well as in other Israelite, Phoenician, and Punic architecture.[15]

Pillared House

The typical Israelite house in the Iron Age was rectilinear and consisted of two, three, or four rooms, entered through a wooden door (analogous to wooden city-gates) from an exterior courtyard (Ill. 15). A mud-brick oven for baking and cooking was located in the open courtyard. Two rows of stone pillars separated the central, larger room from the two parallel side rooms. These three parallel rooms extended from a perpendicular "broadroom" running the width of the building. This back room formed one of the four main exterior walls of the rectangular house. The entrance to the house was on the short side and led from the exterior courtyard into the large

---

15. Shiloh, *The Proto-Aeolic Capital*, 52; Stager, "The Archaeology of the Family," 13.

Ill. 15: Typical pillared house of the Israelites, Iron Age I; with stables, storage, food processing, and cistern on ground floor. The upper story is for sleeping, dining, and entertaining. A man with a roof roller keeps the plastered roof intact. (© Lawrence E. Stager)

central room. The broadroom across the back served mainly for storage. The "four-room house" plan was at times extended to larger buildings, such as the so-called Granary at Shechem, now restored as a four-room plan of a public building.[16] It is more likely an administrative center.

In a somewhat obscure verse, the prophet Amos alludes to the broadroom (*yarkâ,*

---

16. Lawrence E. Stager, "The Fortress-Temple at Shechem and the 'House of El, Lord of the Covenant,'" in Prescott H. Williams Jr. and Theodore Hiebert, eds., *Realia Dei: Essays in Archaeology and Biblical Interpretation in Honor of Edward F. Campbell Jr. at His Retirement* (Atlanta: Scholars Press, 1999), 234.

"inmost part") at the rear of a house where a kinsman had gone to see whether any family member was left. "When one's kinsman calls to the one at the rear of the house (*yarkĕtê habbayit*), 'Are there any more with you?' He will reply, 'None'" (Amos 6:10). On the analogy of the Temple, the room in question appears to be on the first floor: "At the rear of the house (*yarkĕtê habbayit*) [Temple] a space of twenty cubits was set off by cedar partitions from the floor to the rafters, enclosing the sanctuary, the Holy of Holies" (1 Kings 6:16). Similarly, "Your wife will be like a fruitful vine in the rear [the innermost parts] of your house (*yarkĕtê bêtekā*)" (Ps. 128:3).

While there were differences from place to place and culture to culture, the typical house was constructed of sun-dried mud bricks sealed and plastered outside to prevent deterioration. The dirt floors consisted of beaten earth. The walls were erected on two or three courses of foundation stones. The first story averaged less than two meters in height, which would seem to us quite low.

Since the original walls of these houses have not been preserved to a height sufficient to determine the details of any windows, archaeologists reconstruct the windows from depictions on ivory plaques. According to the account in Joshua 2:15, the two Israelite spies sent by Joshua were let down by a rope through the window of Rahab's house. Windows (*ḥallônîm*, from the root *ḥll*, "perforate") were simply slits in the wall; they were deliberately made small, both for security and for keeping the house cool in summer and warm in winter. With no chimneys present, windows (and open doors) were indispensable outlets for smoke from fire pits located within the house. "Therefore they [Ephraim] shall be . . . like chaff that swirls from the threshing floor or like smoke from a window" (*'ărubbâ*) [a hole in the wall for smoke to escape]) (Hos. 13:3). The windows did not contain glass. Since the central room was not an open courtyard, as once thought by most archaeologists, windows (and open doors) provided the sole source of natural light in the house.

In palaces and houses of the elite the windows were more ornate, conforming to the "woman-in-the-window" motif depicted on carved ivory plaques at Samaria, at Nimrud and Khorsabad in Assyria, at Arslan Tash in Syria, and in Cyprus. Adorned with an Egyptian-style wig or headdress, the woman peers through a window within recessed frames overlooking a balcony balustrade supported by voluted columns (Ill.16). This scene is reminiscent of Jezebel, who "dressed her hair, and looked out of the window (*ḥallôn*)" when Jehu came to Jezreel (2 Kings 9:30).

Since the Chalcolithic period, bowls and, later, ceramic lamps, fitted with wicks of flax and fueled with olive oil, provided lighting. They were commonly placed in wall niches. The only reference to a household lampstand (*mĕnôrâ*) is included in a list of furnishings in Elisha's quarters (2 Kings 4:10). Ordinarily lampstands were used in cultic rather than domestic contexts.

The door (*delet*, *petaḥ*, "opening") of the house pivoted on sockets fitted into both the lintel and threshold. The door, which opened inward, was sometimes fastened

Ill. 16: Phoenician ivory of so-called "woman in the window," perhaps a goddess; Nimrud. Compare balustrade of the window with the examples from Ramat Raḥel (Ill. 100). (Courtesy of the Trustees of the British Museum)

Ill. 17: A Janus-form capital with female heads; limestone with inlaid eyes, dated Iron II. Compare "woman in the window" ivories. (Courtesy of P. Bienkowski)

with bolts and locks for security. The doorway (*petaḥ*) consisted of a lintel (*mašqôp*) resting on two upright doorposts (*mězûzôt*), and a threshold/platform or sill (*sap, miptān*). Ordinarily made of a single block of stone, the threshold was laid higher than the floor to prevent water from flooding the interior of the building. The horizontal lintel above the doorway lent structural support. According to the Exodus narrative, the Israelites smeared the blood of the Passover lamb on both the lintel and the doorposts of their houses, an apotropaic ritual intended to ward off evil (Ex. 12:7 [P], 22–23 [JE]). Also, they were instructed to write the *Shema* (profession of faith) on the doorposts (*mězûzôt*), which were considered sacred (Deut. 6:9).

In ancient Israel the doors of palaces, temples, granaries, and domestic dwellings were locked with a wooden bolt and tumbler lock mounted on the inside of the door (Judg. 3:25; Isa. 22:22; 1 Chr. 9:27) (Ill. 18). Metal keys, which resemble modern ones, were used in rotary locks no earlier than the Roman period. The prophet Isaiah alludes to a large wooden key when he says: "I will place the key of the house of David on his shoulder" (Isa. 22:22). These large keys are still used in tumbler locks in the Middle East, where they are known as "Egyptian" locks, and the keys are carried over the shoulder. Some are twenty-five to fifty centimeters long and are bent near the end where the teeth are fixed. It looks rather like a large toothbrush. A wooden box containing loose pins was attached to the inside of the door above the wooden bolt, or lock case, into which the pins drop when the bar is moved to locked position. To unlock the door the key is inserted into a slot in the bolt until the matching teeth of the key push up the moveable pins so that the sliding bolt can be drawn. When the key is withdrawn, the bolt can be secured by sliding it horizontally into a position in which the pins drop from the box into the slots of the bolt. To make the tumbler locks more difficult to pick, they were mounted on the inside of the door and reached by passing one's hand and key through a hole in the door.

Such a keyhole is mentioned in the love poem known as the Song of Solomon, dating to the Persian period. The female partner grows sexually excited as her lover approaches her locked domicile:

> My lover thrust his hand (*yādô*)
>   through the hole (*haḥōr*) (in the door),
> and my belly yearned for him.
> I rose to open to my lover,
>   with my hands dripping myrrh;
> with my fingers dripping choice myrrh
>   upon the sockets (*kappôt*) of the bolt (*hamman'ûl*).
> I opened (the door) for my lover,
>   but my lover had turned and gone.
>   (Song of Solomon 5:4–6)

Of course the poet's double entendre is transparent throughout this passage.

Finally, a story set in the "period of the Judges" takes on new meaning with the tumbler lock in mind. Ehud, the left-handed Benjaminite, assassinated Eglon, the obese king of Moab, by driving a dagger, hilt and all, into his belly, while he was in the "throne-room," one of several rooms located on the second floor of the palace. Ehud then fled through the *misdĕrôn*, a pillared portico, or loggia (cf. *sĕdĕrōt* in 1 Kings 6:9; 2 Kings 11:8, 15; 2 Chr. 23:14), locked the double doors of the second story behind him, and left unsuspected by the palace guard.

> When he [Ehud] had left and the servants came, they saw that the doors of the second story were locked, and said, "He [Eglon] must be relieving himself in the throne room." They waited until they finally grew suspicious. Since he did not open the doors of the upper story, they took the key (*hammaptēaḥ*) and opened them. There on the floor, dead, lay their lord.
>   (Judg. 3:24–25)

If the doors to the upper chambers of Eglon's palace were secured with tumbler locks, such as we have described, it would not be necessary for Ehud to escape via the toilet shaft, such as Baruch Halpern imagines, in his reconstruction of the story, bursting with scatological imagery. By putting his hand through the keyhole in the door,

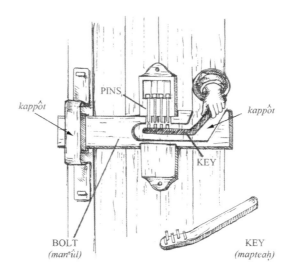

Ill. 18: A tumbler (or "Egyptian") lock with slot and key in the bolt. This type of key is mentioned in Judges 3:25, and is large enough to be slung over the shoulder (Isa. 22:22). The fist-sized keyhole in the door is alluded to in Song of Solomon 5:4. (Drawing: C. Vagliardo after V. J. M. Eras, *Locks and Keys Throughout the Ages*, 1957)

Ehud could have slid the bolt of the tumbler lock into place from outside. The servants, then, would have had to fetch the key to unlock the doors.[17]

The threshold/platform (*sap, miptān*), found in both public and private buildings, marked the boundary with the outside world. Most references are to the entrance of the Temple, where the threshold has a symbolic meaning designating a sacred place. "I [Jeremiah] brought them [Rechabites] to the house of Yahweh into the chamber of the sons of Hanan . . . which was near the chamber of the officials, above the chamber of Maaseiah son of Shallum, keeper of the threshold (*šōmēr hassap*)" (Jer. 35:4). "Keeper of the threshold" is the title of a specially designated priest of the Temple. As for private dwellings, the "threshold" also serves as a boundary marker between the inside (domestic) and the outside world. "In the morning her [the concubine's] master got up, opened the doors of the house, and when he went out to start again on his journey, there was his concubine lying at the door of the house, with her hands on the threshold (*sap*)" (Judg. 19:27).[18]

Most of the cooking was done in the outdoor courtyard, where the baking oven was ordinarily located, although sometimes the oven was situated in the central room of the house. Archaeologists have found cooking pots and ovens in the central room, which was used for food processing. Fire pits were found in ordinary homes. The hearth (*'āḥ*) was sometimes simply a hole in the ground where a fire was kindled for

17. For locks and keys in general, see Vincent J. M. Eras, *Locks and Keys Throughout the Ages* (New York: Lips' Safe and Lock Manufacturing Co., 1957), 18–23. Peter James and Nick Thorpe, *Ancient Inventions* (New York: Ballantine Books, 1994). For a different view of Judg. 3:15–30, see Baruch Halpern, *The First Historians* (San Francisco: Harper & Row, 1988), 39–75, and ch. 4 (in this volume).

18. Carol Meyers, "Threshold," *ABD*, 6:544–45.

cooking or for warmth; at other times, it was a raised feature. "Now the king [Jehoiakim] was sitting in his winter house (it was the ninth month), and there was a fire burning in the hearth (*'āḥ*) before him" (Jer. 36:22). This was probably a copper or bronze, three-legged hearth. House 1727 (Iron II) at Shechem had a large oval hearth in the central space. At Raddana there was a large fire pit in the center of the largest room of House XIV (Iron I); outside in the courtyard was a small "furnace" for metalworking.

The furnishings of the houses were simple, consisting, for the most part, of bedding, kitchen utensils (storage jars, water jugs, cooking pots, serving bowls), looms, and vessels for grinding and crushing. Provisions were kept in large storage jars. The description of Elisha's second floor flat in a wealthy woman's house in Shunem (modern Solem, opposite the town of Jezreel) informs us about household furnishings in the Iron Age. "Let us make a small second story flat [apartment] (*'ăliyyat-qîr*) and put there for him a bed, a table, a chair, and a lampstand, so that he can stay there whenever he comes to us" (2 Kings 4:10). The house of the Shunammite woman appears to have been built over a casemate in the town wall.[19] Private houses were sometimes built into a casemate wall, the outer wall of which served as the back wall of the house (e.g., Tell Beit Mirsim, Tel Sheva). A casemate, typical of Iron II in Israel and Judah, is a fortification wall consisting of two parallel walls with the spaces between them divided into rooms by cross walls or partitions.

Storage, livestock, and workshops occupied the space on the ground floor of the pillared house. The narrower side rooms functioned as stables and shelters for livestock. The medium at Endor whom Saul consulted "had a fatted calf in the house (*'ēgel-marbēq babbayit*)" which she slaughtered and served to Saul (1 Sam. 28:24; see also Amos 6:4). The floors of the side rooms were frequently paved with cobbles or flagstones, whereas the floors of the central room were composed of plaster or beaten earth. These domestic stables served as models for public stables. Mangers for the feeding of animals were located between the pillars, which functioned as room dividers as well as supports for the roof or upper story, their most important function.

Pillared houses were completely roofed. Where a second story existed, pillars supported the flat roof or ceiling. The upper floor (*'ăliyyâ*) could be reached by an exterior stone staircase or an interior wooden ladder. Stairs are sometimes indicated by a square "pillar" in the middle of a room. Wooden steps were attached to small wood supports jutting out of each side of the stone pillar. From this a rectangular stairway could lead to the upper story. At Mareshah (Marisa) in the Shephelah, the excavators uncovered a central pillar (2.8 meters long by 2.3 meters wide), associated with the "southern house" (mid-third century B.C.E.), around which a staircase was built. Similar structures were found at other Persian period and Hellenistic sites.

---

19. Stager, "The Archaeology of the Family," 16.

At Dor this central pillar had appeared already in the Persian period (fifth century B.C.E.).

The "Mosaic" building code required that the roof of a house be enclosed by a parapet (*ma'ăqeh*), lest anyone fall off: "When you build a new house, you shall make a parapet (*ma'ăqeh*) for your roof; otherwise you might have bloodguilt on your house, if anyone should fall from it" (Deut. 22:8).

The roof (*gāg*) and upper story (*'ăliyyâ*) of a house satisfied several purposes, including serving as the main living area. During the warm months, the occupants had the option of sleeping out of doors on the rooftops, as indicated in several biblical stories. When Samuel and Saul came down from the shrine (*bāmâ*), Saul slept on the roof in the town (1 Sam. 9:25–26). Elijah revived the widow's son whom he carried to the upper story where he (Elijah) was lodging, "and laid him on his own bed" (1 Kings 17:19). After David awoke from a nap, while walking on the roof of the palace, he looked over the terraced slopes of Jerusalem and spotted from the roof a woman bathing, who turned out to be Bathsheba (2 Sam. 11:2). The roof could also serve as a place for worship: "And the houses of Jerusalem and the houses of the kings of Judah shall be defiled like the place of Tophet—all the houses upon whose roofs offerings have been made to the whole host of heaven, and libations have been poured out to other gods" (Jer. 19:13; also 32:29; 2 Kings 23:12).

A typical four-room pillared house (labeled 1727, Field VII), dating to the eighth century, was excavated at Shechem, the first capital of the northern kingdom of Israel. The remains of a timber ceiling were found. Domestic objects discovered in the central room illuminate the family's daily routine. They included a small storage bin, a large open hearth in the center, a large saddle-quern (a primitive hand mill for grinding grain), clay jars (to hold the ground flour or feed), and stone grinders. The long back room apparently functioned in part as a pantry, since it had a stone-lined pit at the northern end, as well as a grain silo.

This Shechem house was a two-story construction, with the living quarters upstairs, where a loom was discovered. It was initially assumed that the central room of House 1727 was open to the sky, but recent evidence from the collapse of the roof now indicates that all the rooms of these pillared houses, including the so-called courtyard, were covered by a roof.[20] Further confirmation comes from an Iron I pillared house at Tell el-'Umeiri near Amman (Jordan), where the remnants of the second floor were recovered in the central room, proving once again it was not an open courtyard.[21]

---

20. Stager, "The Archaeology of the Family," 16; Edward F. Campbell, "Archaeological Reflections on Amos's Targets," in M. D. Coogan et al., eds., *Scripture and Other Artifacts* (Louisville, Ky.: Westminster John Knox, 1994), 39.

21. Elizabeth Bloch-Smith and Beth Alpert Nakhai, "A Landscape Comes to Life: The Iron Age I," *NEA* 62 (1999): 113. Larry G. Herr and Douglas R. Clark, "Excavating the Tribe of Rueben," *BAR* 27 (2001): 36–47, 64–66.

FAMILY AND KINSHIP

Family and household constituted the basic social unit in ancient Israel, as well as the most widely used literary metaphor. As a social unit, the extended or joint family, not the biological family, was most important. Sometimes as many as three generations lived in a large family compound, comprising a minimal *bêt 'āb*—"ancestral house or household." *bayit* serves in Hebrew to designate "house," "household," and "dynasty." The further back one traced the ancestry, the larger the lineage or household. Very large families formed the *mišpāḥâ*, a term usually translated "clan." Later in Iron II, the state constituted the largest family of all in ancient Israel: the northern kingdom, Israel, was known as the "house(hold) of Omri"; the southern kingdom, Judah, as the "house(hold) of David."

Many more than just immediate kin made up the residential unit of the small family. The Decalogue (Exodus 20 and Deuteronomy 5) provides a succinct definition of the Israelite household in its prohibition about coveting the neighbor's house(hold): "You shall not covet your neighbor's wife, or male or female slave, or ox, or donkey, or anything that belongs to your neighbor" (Ex. 20:17). In this household, the chattels of which included the wives, slaves, and livestock, there was no mistaking that the ultimate authority was the father, the paterfamilias. His word had the authority of command, subject only to the constraints of customary rules that governed Israelite society and provided a traditional framework in which his word was to be understood.

As to kin included in the joint family, we need look no further than the village of modern Beitin, the biblical site of the religious center Bethel ("house/temple of El"). There, in the late tenth century, according to 1 Kings 12:29–33, the northern kingdom, Israel, located its southern ceremonial center, after the bifurcation of the united kingdom under David and Solomon. In modern Beitin the joint family is still the core constituency of the village. Today the Arab inhabitants refer to what in the Bible was the "ancestral household" (*bêt 'āb*) as *za'ila*.

> It consists of the father, mother, and unwed children as well as the wedded sons and their wives and children, unwed paternal aunts, and sometimes even unwed paternal uncles. In short, this unit is composed of blood relatives plus women who were brought into the kinship through marriage. Large as it may be, this unit tends to occupy one dwelling or a compound of dwellings built close together or often attached to one another. It is an economic as well as a social unit and is governed by the grandfather or the eldest male. The joint family normally dissolves upon the death of the grandfather. The land, which until then had been held by the grandfather, is divided among the heirs, and the male children separately, each to become the nucleus of a new *za'ila*.[22]

---

22. A. M. Lutfiyya, *Baytin, A Jordanian Village: A Study of Social Institutions and Social Change in a Folk Community* (The Hague: Mouton, 1966), 142–43.

In the Bible, the firstborn male (*bĕkôr*) is granted a double portion of the father's possessions (Deut. 21:17) and is accorded special status and authority, as is evident in the blessing Isaac mistakenly bestowed on Jacob in lieu of Esau: "Be lord over your brothers, and may your mother's sons bow down to you" (Gen. 27:29).

Authority over the household resides with the paterfamilias, who in the case of a three-generation household would be the grandfather. How often one would have a three-generation joint family compound in an ancient Israelite village can only be estimated when life expectancy is known and when the age of marriage for males and females is documented. In neither case do we possess adequate statistics for ancient Israel. The average age of royalty can be estimated; however, its general applicability to the non-elite population remains open. According to David Noel Freedman's calculations based on biblical reports, the king acceded to the throne at age twenty-two, on average, and was twenty-six when his son/successor was born. Having reigned for twenty-four years, this typical king died when he was forty-six.[23] In comparison, the common person had to survive under harsher conditions than those enjoyed by the kings and quite probably had a life expectancy of less than 40, lower even for women, who had to survive multiple pregnancies and deliveries.

For the other parameter, age at marriage, no real statistics exist for ancient Israel. A few anecdotal incidents, and a wealth of later documentation, suggest that women married young, while still in their teens, sometimes early teens, in fact; men waited until well into their twenties or even early thirties before marrying. In Egypt, girls were married between twelve and fourteen; boys, between fourteen and twenty. The late-age marriage for Israelite males explains why they were allowed to exempt themselves from military service during their first nuptial year (Deut. 24:5): procreation was a more valuable defense than swordsmanship.

Genealogies figure prominently in biblical history because kinship is the foundation of Israelite society. Classified in descending order, the social units are *šēbeṭ/matṭeh*, commonly translated "tribe" but literally "staff/scepter"; *mišpāḥâ*, rendered as "clan," literally "family," comprising several families; *bêt 'āb*, "the father's house" or "family household," the joint family or lineage. Another kinship term is *'am* (as in *'am* Yahweh), which Frank M. Cross translates "the kindred of Yahweh."[24] This encompassing unit designates the covenanted community or, to use Cross's phrase, "kinship-in-law." This system of social classification is evident in the story about the sin of Achan, where Yahweh instructs Joshua: "In the morning you shall come forward by tribes. The tribe (*šēbeṭ*) that Yahweh takes shall come forward by clans; the

---

23. David N. Freedman, "Kingly Chronologies: Then and Later (with an appendix by A. Dean Forbes)," in S. Ahituv and B. A. Levine, eds., *Eretz-Israel* 24 [Avraham Malamat Volume] (Jerusalem: Israel Exploration Society, 1993), 41*–65*. Cf. the average age of 44, calculated by Hans Walter Wolff, *Anthropology of the Old Testament* (Philadelphia: Fortress, 1974), 119–20; J. Gordon Harris, "Old Age," *ABD*, 5:11.

24. Frank M. Cross, *From Epic to Canon: History and Literature in Ancient Israel* (Baltimore: Johns Hopkins University Press, 1998), 12–14.

clan (*mišpāḥâ*) that Yahweh takes shall come forward by households (*bayit*); and the household that Yahweh takes shall come forward one by one (*gĕbārîm*)" (Josh. 7:14). Note that the least in order is *geber*, "individual."

The biblical family has six main features: it is endogamous, patrilineal, patriarchal, patrilocal, joint, and polygynous.[25] *Endogamy*, in contrast to exogamy, is a preference for marriage between close blood relatives. Exogamy was sometimes practiced among the political elite, not the commoners, especially to seal a diplomatic alliance; an example is Solomon and pharaoh's daughter, about whom the text reads, literally, "Solomon became the son-in-law (*ḥātān*) of Pharaoh, king of Egypt" (1 Kings 3:1).[26] *Patrilineage* regulates descent and inheritance, meaning that descent is reckoned in the father's line, not the mother's. *Patriarchy* signifies that the father (paterfamilias) is head of the family; addressed as *ba'al*, "lord," and has authority over the household, protecting and providing for his wife or wives and children. The father, however, did not have absolute power over his children, nor legal right of execution. The *patria potestas* (paternal authority) is limited (see Deut. 21:18–21). Abraham's sacrifice of Isaac is not applicable because it is a religious rite rather than an exercise of legal power. *Patrilocality* indicates that the man brings his bride into his father's family and household, where she becomes a member and he continues to be a member. This act constituted the main rite of the marriage ceremony. *Joint family* suggests more than one generation, but probably never more than three generations, in view of limited longevity in biblical times. Whereas the "nuclear" or "biological" family consists of father, mother, and minor children, the extended family encompasses the father, his wife or wives, sons with their wives and children, and unmarried daughters, as well as the slaves. All lived in the same house or in several adjoining houses. Property was held in common under the control of the male head. *Polygyny* indicates the practice of having several wives. While monogamy was the ideal, polygyny was possible, though more often among the elite than the commoners. The ancestors are depicted as having had several wives, just as the kings of Israel had their harems. Israelite law took polygyny for granted.

Kinsman-Redeemer

Integral to the family structure and indicative of its solidarity in biblical times is the concept of *gō'ēl*, often translated "redeemer." Cross suggests that the verb *gā'al*, "to redeem," is best translated "to act as kinsman."[27] The *gō'ēl* is the next of kin whose

---

25. Raphael Patai, *Sex and Family in the Bible and the Middle East* (Garden City, N.Y.: Doubleday, 1959), 17–19.

26. Jon D. Levenson and Baruch Halpern, "The Political Import of David's Marriages," *JBL* 99 (1980): 507–18.

27. Cross, *From Epic to Canon*, 4.

duty it is to vindicate a family member within the *mišpāḥâ*. The responsibility of the *gō'ēl* extends to brothers, uncles, cousins, and any other blood relative. He was bound to avenge the murder of a kinsman (Num. 35:19–27), in which role he was known as the "avenger of blood" (*gō'ēl haddām*). Blood revenge is intimately involved with kinship and genealogy. It may also relate to the importance of blood sacrifice among West Semites; in contrast, blood is not important in ritual offerings among East Semites, according to Leo Oppenheim and other scholars.[28]

The levirate (Ruth 3:9, 12–13) required the *gō'ēl* to beget a child for a deceased family member so as to preserve the latter's name and inheritance (*naḥălâ*). He was also to redeem a relative sold into slavery for defaulting on a debt (Lev 25:48–49). If a kinsman had to sell property out of penury, the *gō'ēl* was required to buy it back in order to keep it within the family (Lev. 25:25–33). A notable example is Jeremiah's purchase of the ancestral estate in Anathoth, which was not to be alienated since property was to remain in the family. When Jeremiah's cousin Hanamel was forced to sell his field in the hometown, Jeremiah was obliged to buy it back. While the Babylonians were besieging Jerusalem (588–586 B.C.E.), Hanamel said to Jeremiah: "Buy my field that is at Anathoth in the land of Benjamin, for the right of possession and redemption (*haggě'ullâ*) is yours; buy it for yourself" (Jer. 32:8).

Father's House

The joint family (*bêt 'āb*, literally "father's house"), a multiple-family household consisting of blood relatives as well as the women connected through marriage, formed the basic unit of Israelite society.[29] It was the focus of the religious, social, and economic spheres of Israelite life and was at the center of Israel's history, faith, and traditions. Each joint family had its own land inheritance (*naḥălâ*). Such a group of families with descent from the same paterfamilias and dwelling in the same region or village formed a *bêt 'āb*. Several joint families constituted a "large family," called *mišpāḥâ*, or "clan" in anthropological language. In the joint family or lineage genealogical relations can be demonstrated, but the "clan" is too large to prove that all are related by blood. At this level fictive genealogies enter in. And of course this continues up to the *'am* ("kindred") level.

As all of the social terms are contextual, these traditional definitions are inadequate. The terms are not rigid but fluid. For example, the *bêt 'āb* might be no larger

---

28. A. Leo Oppenheim, *Ancient Mesopotamia: Portrait of a Dead Civilization*, rev. ed. (Chicago: University of Chicago, 1964).

29. Stager, "The Archaeology of the Family," 29. "Nuclear" family equals father, mother, their children, plus live-in servants. "Extended" family equals nuclear family plus married relatives, but only one married couple lives in the household. "Multiple" family equals two or more nuclear families.

than an extended or joint family if the paterfamilias is still living (rarely should this group exceed three generations). However, if the *bêt 'āb* is reckoned by a deceased ancestor, then it could include offspring of up to six generations.[30] When genealogical connections can be demonstrated, the grouping is considered by anthropologists as a "lineage." Beyond this size, the next broad term, "clan," is invoked. At that level, there is no assurance that blood relations are real, although it is possible.

Besides the parents and unmarried children, the *bêt 'āb* might include several generations of family members, depending on who is claimed as the paterfamilias, along with his wife or wives, sons and their wives, grandsons and their wives, the unmarried sons and daughters, slaves, servants, *gērîm*, aunts, uncles, widows, orphans, and Levites who might be members of the household. The *gērîm* were included in the "protective" network, even though not within the gentilic unit. A *gēr*, who was outside the protective unit, often became a "client" or "servant" of the patron who protected him. For example, the household of Micah in the hill country of Ephraim was occupied by Micah, probably his wife or wives, his widowed mother, his sons, probably their wives, a hired priest (the Levite), and servants (Judges 17–18). To obtain a wife for Isaac, Abraham directed his servant, "You shall go to my father's house (*bêt 'āb*) [in Syria], to my clan (*mišpāḥâ*), and get a wife for my son" (Gen. 24:38).

The Israelite family, both large and small, was a cohesive group playing a vital role in the education and socialization of its members. Ideally a strong patriarchal bond held the family together, as the psalmist declares, "Your wife will be like a fruitful vine within your household; your children will be like olive shoots around your table" (Ps. 128:3). Obviously this idyllic relationship was not realized in the many stories about kings and palace intrigue, conspiracy, fratricide, and patricide.

Children

In his history of childhood, Philippe Ariès concludes that childhood in the premodern period was an unimportant phase of life, merely a period of transition from infancy to adulthood, a time when children were considered "small-scale adults."[31] With respect to children in Israel during the monarchy, Joseph Blenkinsopp finds Ariès's thesis somewhat appealing as he examines briefly the pertinent vocabulary, for example, *yeled* and *na'ar* (an unmarried male not yet a head of household), showing the wide range of meanings these terms have. He concludes that childhood in biblical times was not a distinct phase of life and that Ecclesiastes (300–200 B.C.E.) was

---

30. Of course, it is possible for fictive kinship to take over during six generations.
31. Philippe Ariès, *Centuries of Childhood: A Social History of Family Life*, trans. R. Baldick (New York: Vintage Books, 1962), 58.

the first to refer to childhood or youth (*yaldût*) in the abstract (Eccl. 11:9–10).[32] The issue as to whether the Israelites treated their children as children or as "small-scale adults" remains unresolved.

Children were valued in the Israelite family, considered a gift of God and a blessing. Israelite society was pronatalist, taking seriously Yahweh's command, "Be fruitful and multiply" (Gen. 1:28). *Coitus interruptus* is condemned, as in the case of Onan who by withdrawal refused to impregnate Tamar (Gen. 38:8–10). Birth control, abortion, and infanticide are not dealt with directly in the Bible but may nonetheless have been considered contrary to the divine law. Apparently they were practiced by some of the neighboring peoples; at least the Middle Assyrian Laws (twelfth century B.C.E.) have sanctions against the practice of aborting fetuses: "If a woman has had a miscarriage by her own act, when they have prosecuted her (and) convicted her, they shall impale her on stakes without burying her. If she died in having the miscarriage, they shall impale her on stakes without burying her" (*ANET*, 185). The Ebers Papyrus, a medical document from the sixteenth century B.C.E., lists substances that were supposed to abort pregnancies in the first, second, or third trimester, but most of them were probably ineffective. In the discussion of abortion, an oft-cited biblical law concerns injury inflicted on a pregnant woman that results in miscarriage (Ex. 21:22–25), but the texts are not sufficiently clear to be helpful.

At the time of birth a midwife (*měyalledet*) assisted the mother, who nursed the child until it was weaned at the age of three or later. It appears that Hannah nursed Samuel for a period of three years (1 Sam. 1:22–24). Since breast-feeding may delay the return of ovulation after birth, natural nursing is sometimes an effective contraceptive. It is estimated that as a result of nursing babies for as long as three years, Israelite women gave birth to an average of four children.[33] This estimate translates into a standard nuclear-family size of six, which Stager believes is too large.[34] If four were born, only two children reached adulthood due to the high rate of infant and child mortality. Middle Eastern family data must be used with care because families have become much larger in modern times, since the introduction of penicillin.[35]

A personal name, frequently derived from flora and fauna, was conferred on the child immediately after birth. Children were sometimes given theophoric names (names containing divine elements). Some names were patronymics; that is, the child

---

32. Joseph Blenkinsopp, "The Family in First Temple Israel," in L. G. Perdue et al., eds., *Families in Ancient Israel* (Louisville, Ky.: Westminster John Knox, 1997), 66–69.

33. Mayer I. Gruber, "Breast-Feeding Practices in Biblical Israel and in Old Babylonian Mesopotamia," *JANES* 19 (1989): 61–83.

34. Stager, "The Archaeology of the Family," 21.

35. Israel Finkelstein, "A Few Notes on Demographic Data from Recent Generations and Ethnoarchaeology," *PEQ* 122 (1990): 49.

was called after the grandfather or great-grandfather. Two biblical texts suggest that women decided on the child's name: It was Hannah who named her son Samuel (1 Sam. 1:20), and in the Ruth story the women of the neighborhood gave the newly born Obed his name (Ruth 4:17).

For economic reasons a large family was desirable. Boys were favored over girls, since they would perpetuate the family name. When Jacob blessed Joseph's sons, he said, "The angel who has redeemed me from all harm, bless the boys [Manasseh and Ephraim]; and in them let my name be perpetuated, and the name of my ancestors Abraham and Isaac; and let them grow into a multitude on the earth" (Gen. 48:16). Also, boys were better help on the family farm than girls, who would assist their mothers around the house.

"Honor (*kabbēd*) your father and your mother, so that your days may be long in the land that Yahweh your God is giving you" (Ex. 20:12; also 21:15, 17; Lev. 19:3). At first sight, the fifth commandment seems simple and straightforward, but the implications are extensive. The obligation to honor ("show respect to") parents continued beyond their death, requiring children to inter them in the ancestral grave and to oversee the rituals of mourning, as Joseph did when he buried Jacob in Canaan at the cave of Machpelah (Gen. 50:1–14). Herbert Brichto emphasizes the importance of "honoring" parents in their afterlife as the time when they are in even greater need of it. In short, children's care for their parents must be exercised not only in life, but also after death.[36] Brevard Childs understands this commandment as a protection for parents from being expelled from their home or from being abused by their offspring when they are no longer able to work.[37]

An unruly son (a young adult) whose defiant conduct jeopardized the family's well-being (*šālôm*) was to be dealt with severely. There was a hearing in the "court" room of the city gate, presided over by the elders representing the community, before whom the aggrieved parents appeared as plaintiffs. Whether the stipulated punishment was ever imposed is uncertain:

> If someone has a stubborn and rebellious son who will not obey his father and mother, who does not heed them when they discipline him, then his father and his mother shall take hold of him and bring him out to the elders of his town at the gate of that place. They shall say to the elders of his town, "This son of ours is stubborn and rebellious. He will not obey us. He is a glutton and a drunkard." Then all the men of the town shall stone him to death. So you shall purge the evil from your midst: and all Israel will hear, and be afraid. (Deut. 21:18–21)

The law concerning rebellious children underscores the importance of showing gratitude to parents for the care they have shown their children. Addressing the issue of

---

36. Herbert C. Brichto, "Kin, Cult, Land, and Afterlife—A Biblical Complex," *HUCA* 44 (1973): 27–33.
37. Brevard S. Childs, *Book of Exodus* (Philadelphia: Westminster, 1974), 418.

how parents could execute a child upon whom their own future life hinges, Brichto states, "A son who will deny his parents the death or memorial honors they require might as well be dead—or better, executed."[38] Modeling the respect and veneration due parents, Barzillai, the Gileadite who had befriended David, declined the king's invitation to live in the royal court, instead requesting: "Please let your servant return, so that I may die in my own town [Rogelim], near the tomb of my father and my mother" (2 Sam. 19:38 [E.T. 19:37]). The implication is that he would be buried with both his parents in the family tomb within the community necropolis.

Circumcision

The practice of circumcision was widespread in antiquity, but its origin and purpose remain uncertain. Bas-reliefs from Egypt, dating from the third millennium, attest to the practice among the Egyptians (Ill. 19). In biblical times, West Semitic peoples, comprising Israelites, Ammonites, Moabites, and Edomites, were circumcised, but not the East Semitic peoples of Mesopotamia, such as the Akkadians, Assyrians, and Babylonians. The non-Semitic Philistines, probably of Aegean or early Greek origin, did not practice this form of genital mutilation. Consequently, they were derogated by the Israelites as the "uncircumcised" ('ărēlîm) (Judg. 14:3; 15:18; 1 Sam. 18:25; Herodotus, *History*, ii.104).

Whether the Canaanites were circumcised is indeterminable. The painful story told about the Shechemites suggests that at least this group of Canaanites was not circumcised. The sons of Jacob required that the Shechemites be circumcised before they would give their daughters to them in marriage. "On the third day, when they [Shechemites] were still in pain . . . Simeon and Levi . . . took their swords and came against the city unawares, and killed all the males" (Gen. 34:25).

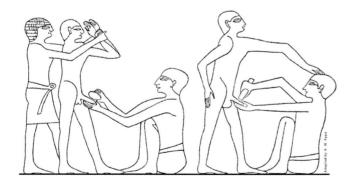

Ill. 19: Priests perform circumcisions on Egyptian boys. A relief of the sixth dynasty from Saqqara. (Drawing: A. M. Appa after H. Gressmann, *Altorientalische Texte und Bilder zum Alten Testament* [Berlin, 1927])

---

38. Brichto, "Kin, Cult, Land, and Afterlife," 32.

The Midianites probably were circumcised, since Zipporah, wife of Moses, cut off (*kārat*) her son's foreskin with a flint knife, if that is the correct interpretation of this obscure passage about a "bridegroom of blood" (Ex. 4:24–26). It is not clear whom she touched with the foreskin—her son or her husband. Despite ambiguity in the account, it underscores the importance of circumcision and the blood rite associated with it, as attested by Zipporah's statement, "A bridegroom of blood by circumcision" (*ḥătan dāmîm lammûlōt*) (Ex. 4:26).

An Israelite infant was circumcised eight days after birth (Gen. 17:12; Lev. 12:3). The procedure was performed by the father (Gen. 21:4), not by a priest, and never in the sanctuary. Indicative of the antiquity of the practice, circumcision in early Israel was done with a flint or stone knife (Ex. 4:25; Josh. 5:2–3). The male children of Israel's neighbors were more apt to be circumcised during childhood or at puberty, instead of eight days after birth.

For the Israelites circumcision was a sign of covenant-kinship between Yahweh and Israel (Gen. 17:10–14). Accordingly, *běrît* (or *bris*), "covenant," is the term Jews use today for circumcision. The Hebrew idiom for making a covenant was *kārat běrît*, "cut a covenant," and literal cutting occurs in some texts as well: The book of Genesis describes a rite of covenant making in which Abram (Abraham) cut in two (*battēr*) a heifer (*'eglâ*), goat, and a ram; afterward a smoking fire pot and a flaming torch, both representing God, passed between those pieces. Whoever violated the covenant would incur the same fate as the animals (Gen. 15:9–19). Jeremiah alludes to this rite: "And those who transgressed my covenant and did not keep the terms of the covenant that they made before me, I will make like the calf (*'ēgel*) when they cut (*kārat*) it in two and passed between its parts" (Jer. 34:18). Parallels to the covenant rite appear among the Amorites, who slew donkeys, goats, and puppies. This was an essential part of treaty making during the Mari period. Killing an animal to seal a treaty between two parties probably gave rise to the Hebrew idiom, *kārat běrît*, meaning "to make a treaty." In the courtyard of the fortress at Haror (MB II), Eliezer Oren has discovered sacrificial remains in pits of birds and puppies (killed by breaking their necks; Isa. 66:3). One large pit contained a pair of donkey burials, the articulated skeleton of one outfitted with a bronze bridle bit.[39]

Even adults had to undergo circumcision to become members of the community, as they do today. In addition to male infants, the household slaves and the *gērîm* living with the Israelites had to be circumcised. Only a circumcised male was qualified to participate in the Passover ritual (Ex. 12:48–49). There is a rather puzzling text in Joshua 5:2–9, set during the wilderness wanderings, in which Yahweh instructs Joshua to circumcise the Israelites "a second time" prior to their celebration of the

---

39. Eliezer D. Oren, "The Kingdom of Sharuhen and the Hyksos Kingdom," in E. D. Oren, ed., *The Hyksos: New Historical and Archaeological Perspectives* (Philadelphia: University Museum, University of Pennsylvania, 1997), 253–83.

Passover. Jack Sasson has clarified this text by comparing the Egyptian and the Israelite styles of circumcision:

> Thus one can note a basic difference between the Israelites and the Egyptians in the surgical process involved in circumcision. Whereas the Hebrews amputated the prepuce and thus exposed the corona of the penis, the Egyptian practice consisted of a dorsal incision upon the foreskin which liberated the glans penis. Two passages from Joshua 5 are relevant to this problem. V. 2 consists of a command issued to Joshua: "Make for yourselves knives of flint and circumcise again the children of Israel the second time." Some have thought that this passage has been altered by a later editor to harmonize it with other references in the Bible. But in the light of the foregoing, this can now be explained as an injunction for those who have accepted an Egyptian circumcision to "improve" on the ritual by undergoing a thorough removal of the foreskin. In this context, God's remark in v. 9 becomes clearer. When the deed was accomplished, he states: "This day I have rolled away the reproach of Egypt from off you."[40]

At the same time, there is a clear biblical sense that the external rite of circumcision was worthless without interior conversion. With metaphorical language, Deuteronomy 10:16 orders, "Circumcise, then, the foreskin of your heart, and do not be stubborn any longer" (see also Lev. 26:41; Jer. 4:4). And Jeremiah cautions that: "The days are surely coming, says Yahweh, when I will attend to all those who are circumcised only in the foreskin: Egypt, Judah, Edom, the Ammonites, Moab" (Jer. 9:24–25 [E.T. 9:25–26]).

Philo was the first Jewish writer to advocate hygiene as a reason for circumcision (*De circumcisione* 11:210). Herodotus (*History*, ii.37) also suggests sanitary considerations as the basis for the procedure among the Egyptians.

Education of Children

The education and socialization of Israelite children fall into several categories, notably religious, vocational, and military.[41] The biblical writers refer frequently to the obligation of parents to instruct their children about the meaning of *pĕ'ullôt YHWH*, "the mighty acts of God" (*magnalia Dei*) in history. Regarding the plague of locusts in Egypt, Yahweh directed: "Tell your children and grandchildren how I have made fools of the Egyptians and what signs I have done among them—so that you may know that I am Yahweh" (Ex. 10:2). Again, with respect to the festival of unleavened bread: "You shall tell your children on that day, 'It is because of what Yahweh did for me when I came out of Egypt'" (Ex. 13:8). So, too, concerning the

---

40. Jack M. Sasson, "Circumcision in the Ancient Near East," *JBL* 85 (1966): 474.
41. Regarding the question of more formalized institutions for schooling, see "Literacy and Schools" in chapter 5.

twelve stones that Joshua set up in Gilgal: when the children ask the parents the meaning of these stones, they are to explain: "Israel crossed over the Jordan here on dry ground" (Josh. 4:21–22). The psalmists refer to transmitting instruction (*tôrâ*) about Yahweh's saving deeds: "Give ear, O my people, to my teaching; incline your ears to the words of my mouth. I will open my mouth in a parable; I will utter dark sayings from of old, things that we have heard and known, that our ancestors have told us" (Ps. 78:1–3; also Ps. 44:2).

Children accompanied their parents to the sanctuary and the Temple. The story of Samuel's birth and dedication relates that it was Hannah, not her husband Elkanah, who brought him to the house of Yahweh at Shiloh, where she offered him as a Nazirite, consecrated to the service of Yahweh (1 Sam. 1:22–28). Samuel was apprenticed to Eli, the high priest of the shrine at Shiloh, where he was instructed in worship: "Now the boy (*na'ar*) Samuel was ministering to Yahweh under Eli" (1 Sam. 3:1). Later, when Israel asked for a king, Samuel replied that later generations would be pressed into quite a different type of training and service: "He [the king] will take your sons and appoint them to his chariots and to be his horsemen, and to run before his chariots . . . and some to plow his ground and to reap his harvest, and to make his implements of war and the equipment of his chariots. He will take your daughters to be perfumers and cooks and bakers" (1 Sam. 8:11–13).[42]

Frequently the parents and children of both genders took part together in the domestic chores. David was a shepherd (1 Sam. 16:11); Rachel, too, tended her father's [Laban's] sheep (Gen. 29:9). The sons were under the tutelage of the father who apprenticed them in farming, shepherding, and nonspecified crafts. Since most Israelites were farmers, it was only natural that "when the child [son of the Shunammite woman] was older, he went out one day to his father among the reapers" (2 Kings 4:18).

Accompanying the father in such activities as warfare and hunting, the boys learned how to handle weaponry—the bow, sling, and sword. Jether, Gideon's firstborn, was commanded by his father to kill the enemies Zebah and Zalmunna, the kings of Midian: "But the boy (*na'ar*) did not draw his sword, for he was afraid because he was still a boy (*na'ar*)" (Judg. 8:20). This incident has nothing to do with childhood as such but with comparative status: the *na'ar*, according to John Mac-Donald, was not of sufficient rank to slay kings.[43] The three eldest sons of Jesse (Eliab, Abinadab, and Shammah) followed Saul to battle against the Philistines (1 Sam. 17:13). The biblical writers describe military training: "He [Yahweh] trains my

---

42. P. Kyle McCarter Jr., *I Samuel*, AB 8 (Garden City, N.Y.: Doubleday, 1980), 161. "Many scholars have tried to find substantial Deuteronomistic reworking in c[hapter] 8. . . . Our own findings with respect to Deuteronomistic supplementation here are minimal."

43. John MacDonald, "The Status and Role of the Na'ar in Israelite Society," *JNES* 35 (1976): 158.

[David's] hands for war, so that my arms can bend a bow of bronze" (2 Sam. 22:35). They also depict hand-to-hand combat between young men of David's army and those of Ishbaal at the battle of Gibeon: "They [the soldiers (*hannĕ'ārîm*)] took hold of each other's heads, their swords at each other's sides, and fell dead together" (2 Sam. 2:16).

A Late Bronze Age text from Ugarit (Ras Shamra) delineates the duties of the "ideal son" 'Aqhat toward his father Danel, a legendary Canaanite king:

> A son ['Aqhat] will be born to me, like my brothers, an heir, like my cousins, who will set up a stele for my divine ancestor, a family shrine in the sanctuary; who will free my spirit from the earth, guard my footsteps from the Slime; who will crush those who rebel against me; drive off my oppressors; who will hold my hand when I am drunk, support me when I am full of wine; who will eat my offering in the temple of Baal, my portion in the temple of El; who will patch my roof when it leaks, wash my clothes when they are dirty.[44]

The mother was the daughter's primary teacher, as the proverb suggests: "Like mother, like daughter" (Ezek. 16:44). Besides religious duties, daughters would learn domestic chores required to run the household. Girls also shared the duties at harvest time, as when Boaz directed Ruth: "Now, listen, my daughter, do not go to glean in another field or leave this one, but keep close to my young women" (Ruth 2:8).

Primogeniture

The practice of primogeniture (*bĕkōrâ*), whereby certain privileges were bestowed on the firstborn son, was common in ancient Israel. The firstborn of humans and animals was regarded as the property of God, as indicated in Yahweh's charge to Moses, "Consecrate to me all the firstborn (*bĕkôr*); whatever is the first to open the womb among the Israelites, of human beings and animals, is mine" (Ex. 13:2). The firstborn son (i.e., the eldest son of the father) enjoyed preferential status. He inherited a double portion of his father's property, received a special blessing from his father, and succeeded his father as head of the household, exercising authority over the other members. At their mother Rebekah's instigation, Jacob tricked his older brother Esau out of this blessing by deceiving their father Isaac (Genesis 27). According to the "last words" to his sons (Gen. 49:1–28), Jacob withdrew the status of firstborn from Reuben and conferred it upon Judah, the fourth son, because Reuben had lain with Bilhah, his father's concubine (Gen. 35:22).[45] Primogeniture determines one's rank and status in kin-based society and in right of succession, whether as property owner,

---

44. Michael D. Coogan, ed. and trans., *Stories from Ancient Canaan* (Philadelphia: Westminster, 1978), 34.
45. It is important to bear in mind that for political purposes the patriarchal narratives are retrojected.

as head of household (paterfamilias), or even as head of the state household ("king"), inasmuch as dynastic succession is patterned after domestic succession.

For a family to be childless was viewed as a curse. Abraham expresses to God his anxiety about an heir: "O Yahweh God, what will you give me, for I continue childless, and the heir of my house is Eliezer of Damascus?" (Gen. 15:2). A stigma was attached to a woman unable to bear children; in such a case, her husband could obtain another wife who could produce children. This explains why Abram (Abraham) took Hagar as his wife when Sarai (Sarah) was unable to conceive (Genesis 16). Hagar, Sarai's Egyptian slave girl, bore Abram a son whom he named Ishmael. However, when Sarai, at the age of ninety-nine, miraculously bore Isaac, he became the preferred heir. But as firstborn to Abram and Sarai, he was also in danger of being "offered" to God as a human sacrifice, just as first fruits and first offspring of other animals were offered. Of course, were this a frequent practice, no firstborns would have survived in society. Fortunately for Isaac, a young ram was found to serve as a suitable substitute. In the case of Jesus, who is described as the firstborn and only son of God in the New Testament, he was sacrificed in place of the paschal lamb. Mesha, king of Moab, "took his eldest son (*běkôr*) who was to succeed him and offered him as a sacrifice (*'ōlâ*) on the (city) wall (*ḥōmâ*)" (2 Kings 3:27). Mesha offered this human sacrifice to the deity as an act of propitiation.

In Israelite society, the Levites served as replacements for the firstborn: "I [Yahweh] hereby accept the Levites from among the Israelites as substitutes for all the firstborn that open the womb among the Israelites. The Levites shall be mine, for all the firstborn are mine" (Num. 3:12–13). Note, however, that the Levitical substitutes were not sacrificed but were ordained for service to Yahweh.

Inheritance

The law governing land tenure provides that ownership remain within a family and not be alienated. The *bêt 'āb* was the basic unit of the land-tenure system, each family and lineage having its own inheritance (*naḥălâ*) (Num. 27:8–11). When a man had only daughters and no sons, his daughters could inherit their father's land to guarantee that it remain in the same family. But they must marry within the clan (*mišpāḥâ*) (Num. 27:1–11; 36:1–12). This provision, resulting from the appeal of the daughters of Zelophehad to Moses, supersedes the law stipulating that only males inherit property.

The classic example of inheritance concerns Naboth's vineyard, adjacent to the royal estate in Jezreel, which King Ahab wished to acquire and annex to royal property in exchange for another vineyard. But Naboth refused to sell it out of duty to his ancestors, so as to keep the patrimonial property (*naḥălâ*) in his own family (1 Kings 21). Ultimately it cost Naboth his life. The important point, however, is that Jezebel and Ahab had to accede enough to customary law (probably developed as early as the "period of the Judges") to trump up charges of blasphemy ratified by the council of elders. This, like the story of Machpelah (Genesis 23), suggests that under extraordinary circumstances the local assembly or council could agree to alienation of family property, with future right of redemption by next of kin.

Women

It is regularly asserted that in patriarchal society women were considered to be property. Christopher Wright challenges this view on the basis of a study of the laws and narratives about wives in the Bible. Phyllis Bird states that, although wives were included among a man's possessions, they were not reckoned as property.[46] In Exodus 20:17 the commandment against coveting (*ḥāmad*) includes the wife as part of the household, along with slave, ox, and donkey. In Deuteronomy 5:21 she is not incorporated among the domestic property but is in a separate category, which may reflect an advance in Israelite thinking.

Nonetheless, the Bible was written and compiled by males who had no special interest in women's roles. They focused principally on the male aspects of life, such as warfare, governing, economy, and worship, in which women were not directly involved or to which they contributed only minimally. In addition, Israel's laws were addressed only to men. The domain of a woman's activities was the household, where she exercised authority in her role as mother.

The creation stories in Genesis make clear that both men and women are created in God's image (Gen. 1:27), with no suggestion of subordination (Gen. 5:2). The woman is designated "a helper as his [Adam's] partner" (*'ēzer kĕnegdô*), that is, "complementary to him" (Gen. 2:20). Curiously, the masculine form *'ēzer* appears in the text; why not *'ezrâ*, the feminine noun? James Kugel, citing the suggestion of a Jewish scholar, mentions that *'ēzer* here is the Hebrew equivalent of Arabic *'adhra'*, "virgin" or "young woman."[47] Other biblical uses of "helper" imply equality between the parties, not inferiority. Even God is referred to as the "helper" of human beings (Ps. 70:6 [E.T. Ps. 70:5] and Ps. 121:2). Alluding to the maternal bond, the Bible uses female imagery to portray God's love for the exiled people of Judah: "As a mother comforts her child, so I [God] will comfort you; you shall be comforted in Jerusalem" (Isa. 66:13; also Isa. 49:15).

"Woman" comes from the rib of "man," and the man says: "This at last is bone of my bones and flesh of my flesh" (Gen. 2:23). In other words, kinship is based on

---

46. Christopher J. H. Wright, "Family," *ABD*, 2:766. Also, Phyllis A. Bird, "Women (OT)," *ABD*, 6:956; Carol Meyers, *Discovering Eve: Ancient Israelite Women in Context* (New York: Oxford University Press, 1988); and Phyllis Trible, *Texts of Terror: Literary-Feminist Reading of Biblical Narratives* (Philadelphia: Fortress, 1984).

47. James L. Kugel, *The Great Poems of the Bible* (New York: Free Press, 1999), 143–45.

Ill. 20: Terracotta figurine fragment of Philistine mother and child, dated Iron II. (Courtesy of the Leon Levy Expedition to Ashkelon; Photo: I. Sztulman)

a bond of blood.[48] However, the legal system of the patriarchal society placed women at a distinct disadvantage. Before marriage a woman was subject to her father; in his absence, to an older brother; and after marriage, to her husband. The laws of inheritance worked to her detriment, too. According to Israel's patrilineal system, only males could inherit property, because it was passed from father to son. As mentioned above, if the father left no sons, the real estate was inherited in the first instance by his daughters, who were then obligated to marry within the circle that perpetuated the father's name.

Women played a prominent role in the context of family life, first as mother and second as wife. Indicative of the importance of these roles, both motherhood and marriage are common biblical metaphors describing the relationship between God and Israel (e.g., Hosea 1–3). The care, discipline, and training of young children were the responsibility of the mother. Childbearing conferred status on the woman, especially in times when the need to produce more children was critical, owing to war, famine, disease, and epidemics.

The mother's authority was exercised in the household. Sarah cast out Hagar and her son Ishmael (Gen. 21:10). The Shunammite woman extended kindness and hospitality to Elisha (2 Kings 4:8–10). Rebekah perpetrated Jacob's deception of his blind father Isaac, which resulted in the wrongful bestowal of his brother Esau's blessing on Jacob (Gen. 27:11–17). This latter example and others like it suggest that trickery and deception may have been necessary, even admirable, qualities in a woman living in a male-dominated society.[49]

Besides raising children, women were responsible for providing food and clothing. They engaged in crafts that could be managed while caring for the children, such as basketry, spinning, and weaving tapestries and mats. Tamar is portrayed as kneading dough, making cakes, and baking them (2 Sam. 13:8). The priest of Midian had

48. Cross, *From Epic to Canon*, 4.
49. Toni Craven, "Women Who Lied for the Faith," in Douglas A. Knight and Peter J. Paris, eds., *Justice and the Holy: Essays in Honor of Walter Harrelson* (Atlanta: Scholars Press, 1989), 35–49.

seven daughters who filled the troughs to water their father's flock (Ex. 2:16). By custom women drew water for the needs of both the household and the livestock (Gen. 24:11). Among their other chores, women built fires, made cheese and yogurt, milked the sheep and goats. They also ground grain into flour on the handmill, and condiments with mortar and pestle. Their other contributions outside the household included working in the fields (Ruth 2:21–23), tending flocks (Gen. 29:9), and acting as professional mourners (Jer. 9:17). The famous description of the "ideal wife" in Proverbs (31:10–29) concerns the variety of women's roles in the household, especially their economic role. It is clear, however, that this litany applies only to elite, noble women. Note the elegant garments: "All her household are clothed in crimson (*šānîm*). She makes herself coverings; her clothing is fine linen (*šēš*) and purple ('*argāmān*)" (Prov. 31:21–22).

Women participated in the daily activities of the community, including worship. In proclaiming the Law, Moses states: "You shall rejoice before Yahweh your God, you together with your sons and your daughters, your male and female slaves" (Deut. 12:12; also 16:10–11; 29:10–13; 31:12). The biblical writers describe women as dancing, singing, and playing musical instruments. After the successful crossing of the Reed Sea, Miriam "took a tambourine in her hand; and all the women went out after her with tambourines and with dancing" (Ex. 15:20; also Judg. 21:21). Women took part in the harvest festivals as they treaded out the grapes. There are references to women sharing in sacrificial meals. After David brought the Ark of Yahweh to the City of David (Jerusalem), he "distributed food among all the people, the whole mul-

titude of Israel, both men and women, to each a cake of bread, a portion of meat, and a cake of raisins" (2 Sam. 6:19).

In the description of Judah's worship of the Queen of Heaven, "The children gather wood, the fathers kindle fire, and the women knead dough, to make cakes (*kawwānîm*) for the Queen of Heaven; and they pour out drink offerings to other gods, to provoke me [Yahweh] to anger" (Jer. 7:18). Worship of the Queen of Heaven was a cult in which women played the leading role. *kawwānîm* (Akk. *kamānū*)

Ill. 21: An ivory pyxis with a carved scene of an ensemble of female musicians playing, from right to left, the double flute, hand drum, and the third with ten strings on a rectangular frame resembling a zither. From Nimrud; Syrian style. Pyxis is 6.7 cm in height, ninth century B.C.E. (Courtesy of the Trustees of the British Museum)

denote cakes used in the cult of the goddess Ishtar, as practiced in Syria and Mesopotamia. The cakes were made in the image of a nude goddess, with emphasis on the breasts and the pudendum[50] (Ill. 23).

There are notable examples, too, of women who served in less traditional roles: for example, Deborah as judge (Judges 4–5), Huldah as prophet (2 Kings 22:14–20), and the medium at Endor (1 Sam. 28:7–25). A traditional role, yet one that is outside the family context, prostitution is frequently mentioned in biblical texts, although it is impossible to know how widespread it was actually practiced. While prostitution seems to have been tolerated in the society, the biblical writers have ambivalent views about it, and the laws are inconsistent. Rahab, who befriended the Israelite spies at Jericho, may be the most renowned of the prostitutes in the Bible, and at the same time she exemplifies the independence that the prostitute could probably maintain from the usual social and economic structures based in the family (Josh. 2:14–16). Gomer, the wife of Hosea, was a prostitute before their marriage. Prostitutes may have worn clothing that distinguished them; Judah thought Tamar was a prostitute "for she had covered her face" with a veil (ṣā'îp) (Gen. 38:14–15).

Birth and the Midwife

In biblical times the midwife (měyalledet) was an important health-care practitioner. In the absence of a midwife, the expectant mother was assisted by relatives and neighbors. At the birth of Benjamin, "when she [Rachel] was in her hard labor, the midwife said to her, 'Do not be afraid; for now you will have another son'" (Gen. 35:17). The most memorable mention of midwives' service occurs in the narrative about birth during the period of oppression in Egypt: "The king of Egypt said to the midwives, one of whom was named Shiphrah and the other Puah, 'When you act as midwives to the Hebrew women, and see them on the birthstool ('obnāyim), if it is a boy, kill him; but if it is a girl, she shall live'" (Ex. 1:15–16).

At the time of delivery Israelite women assumed a crouched position on a birthstool ('obnāyim). Since the Hebrew word is dual in form, apparently the birthstool consisted of two parts. The only other use of the word 'obnāyim designates a potter's wheel, a fast wheel constructed of two parts (Jer 18:3). After the delivery of the child, the umbilical cord was cut, and the infant was bathed, rubbed with salt, and wrapped in strips of cloth. Ezekiel depicts this standard birth ritual in an extended metaphor of Jerusalem as God's adulterous spouse: "As for your birth, the day you were born

---

50. Walter Rast, "Cakes for the Queen of Heaven," in A. L. Merrill and T. W. Overholt, eds., *Scripture in History and Theology: Essays in Honor of J. Coert Rylaarsdam* (Pittsburgh: Pickwick Press, 1977), 167–80. Lawrence E. Stager, "Another Mould for Cakes from Cyprus: In the Queen's Image," *Rivista di Studi Fenici*, 28/1 (2000): 7.

your navel cord was not cut, nor were you washed with water to cleanse you, nor rubbed with salt, nor wrapped in cloths" (Ezek. 16:4).

Widows

By definition, a widow (*'almānâ*) was outside the normal social structure of the community and could therefore be easily victimized and quickly reduced to destitution. There may have been many widows because of age differences at the first marriage, since men usually married later in life and were therefore considerably older than their wives. Without male protection the widow found it hard to survive; her position in the community was considered inferior. A widow was set apart by her distinctive dress: "Then she [Tamar] got up and went away, and taking off her veil she put on the garments of her widowhood" (Gen. 38:19).

Although the widow was free to remarry and to derive security from the levirate legislation, she was disdained in the community and sometimes oppressed: "Ah, you who make iniquitous decrees, who write oppressive statutes, to turn aside the needy from justice and to rob the poor of my people of their right, that widows may be your spoil, and that you may make the orphans your prey!" (Isa. 10:1–2). A widow without an adult son could inherit the property of her deceased husband. If she had a son, he would inherit the father's property, with the responsibility to care for his mother. The Assyrian laws were explicit in prescribing that sons take their widowed mother into their house.

The widow is often linked in the Bible with others who are in need, such as the resident alien or client (*gēr*) and the orphan (*yātôm*) (Deut. 10:17–19; 24:17–22; 27:19). Powerless and often stigmatized, they served as personifications of a misfortunate state because they had no family to protect them. Isaiah, speaking in Yahweh's name about Jerusalem's restoration after the Babylonian exile, announces: "Do not fear, for you will not be ashamed; do not be discouraged, for you will not suffer disgrace; for you will forget the shame of your youth, and the disgrace of your widowhood (*'almānût*) you will remember no more" (Isa. 54:4). The state of the orphaned daughter was even more perilous. As these dependent groups did not fit into the normal social structure of the community, both the king and community were expected to provide for them. Israelite law required that the widow and orphan be treated with kindness: "The Levites, because they have no allotment or inheritance with you, as well as the resident aliens [clients], the orphans and the widows in your towns, may come and eat their fill" (Deut. 14:29). The biblical writers make frequent pleas for the care of the widow and the orphan. Speaking in the name of Yahweh, Isaiah exhorts the Israelites: "Learn to do good; seek justice, rescue the oppressed, defend the orphan, plead for the widow" (Isa. 1:17; also Jer. 22:3). Ultimately, they were dependent on Yahweh, "who executes justice for the orphan (*yātôm*) and the widow (*'almānâ*)" (Deut. 10:18; also Jer. 49:11).

Marriage

In marriage the economic motivation was more important than the romantic. The chief goal of marriage was to have and raise children, especially boys. In ancient Israel, marriage, like the society itself, was patriarchal, with authority residing in the father and different social statuses assigned to men and women. Women were subordinate; in fact, the wife addressed her husband as *ba'al*, "master," or *'ādôn*, "lord." Note the distinction in the text of Hosea: "On that day, says Yahweh, you will call me, 'My husband' (*'îšî*), and no longer will you call me, 'My Ba'al' (*ba'lî*)" (Hos. 2:18 [E.T. 2:16]). At times the two terms seem interchangeable: "When Uriah's wife heard that her husband (*'îšāh*) was dead, she lamented over her husband (*ba'lāh*)" (2 Sam. 11:26). Apparently the husband addressed his wife as *'ištî* ("my wife"), which is the counterpart of *'îšî* ("my husband").

In giving his daughter in marriage, the father received a "bride-price," *mōhar*, the amount of money or equivalent in kind to be paid by the prospective husband to the bride's father (Gen. 34:12; Ex. 22:15–17; 1 Sam. 18:25). It was considered a form of compensation for the loss of the daughter. The custom is still practiced in the Arab world, where it is known as *mahr*. The practice of the bride's father making a gift of a dowry (money or property) is uncertain for lack of information. Israelite legal codes contain no mention of it, although 1 Kings 9:16 recounts how the pharaoh of Egypt gave the city of Gezer, in the central coastal region, to his daughter on her marriage to Solomon.

It is difficult to determine the age of the bride and groom at the time of marriage. The Bible provides no specific information on this subject. As indicated above, it is safe to assume the bride was considerably younger than the groom, and childbearing would have begun soon after puberty.

The first stage in forging the marriage relationship was the betrothal or engagement, which lasted several months. Made sometime before the wedding, this promise of marriage was practically as binding as the marriage itself. Some texts, in fact, treat betrothal and marriage almost the same (Deut. 28:30; 2 Sam. 3:14; Hos. 2:21–22 [E.T. 2:19–21]). There was no opportunity for sexual relations before marriage because the bride was not to be seen by her intended husband until their entry into the wedding chamber. This accounts for Rebekah covering herself with her veil (*ṣā'îp*) when she inadvertently met Isaac in the field before marriage (Gen. 24:65). The woman was expected to be a virgin at the time of marriage, but the man was exempt from the requirement.

Monogamy was the ideal, but polygyny was practiced, especially by the affluent and royalty, as in the case of "political marriages" (e.g., David married Maacah, the daughter of the Aramean king of Geshur [2 Sam. 3:3]; the Egyptian pharaoh gave his daughter in marriage to Solomon [1 Kings 9:16]; Omri arranged the marriage of his son Ahab to Jezebel, daughter of the king of Sidon [1 Kings 16:31]). In effect, the creation story supports monogamy: "Therefore a man leaves his father and his mother and clings to his wife, and they become one flesh" (Gen. 2:24). Nevertheless, the Bible has several accounts of polygyny (one husband with more than one wife) although never polyandry (one wife with more than one husband). A pragmatic reason may account for the custom of acquiring multiple wives: having many children to tend the flocks and sow the fields was an advantage in an agricultural society. As a rule, endogamy (marriage within the clan or tribe) was observed, but the Bible gives several examples of exogamy (marriage to a member outside the kinship group) that threatened the land holdings. Marriage between cousins was not unusual in the Bible: Isaac married his cousin's daughter Rebekah (Gen. 24:15, 24, 47); Jacob married his maternal uncle's daughter Rachel (Gen. 28:2, 5; 29:9–10).

Marriages were ordinarily arranged by the parents according to Near Eastern custom, although this practice is not required by biblical law. In the Genesis story, Hagar arranged the marriage of her son Ishmael to an Egyptian woman: "He [Ishmael] lived in the wilderness of Paran [south of Judah]; and his mother [Hagar] got a wife for him from the land of Egypt" (Gen. 21:21). Abraham arranged the marriage of his son Isaac to Rebekah by sending his servant to secure a wife for Isaac from among his kin in Aram-naharaim (Genesis 24). However, Esau chose his own wife from among his kin without parental consent (Gen. 28:6–9). Samson, too, selected his own wife (Judg. 14:1–10).

Certain biblical songs, notably the Song of Solomon and Psalm 45, may provide clues about aspects of the wedding ritual. While the Song of Solomon has been variously interpreted, it is perhaps best to regard it as a kind of erotic poetry known from Mesopotamian sacred marriage songs and Egyptian love songs. Psalm 45, a royal ode composed for the wedding of a king, reflects several features of the marriage ritual. In the first half of the psalm (vss. 3–9) the king is adulated for his physical appearance, military prowess, and heroic virtue. In the second half (vss. 10–16) the queen is praised for her beauty and for her wedding attire.

The ceremony may have begun with the groom and his friends approaching the house of the bride (Song of Sol. 3:6–11), who is veiled and adorned with jewelry and ceremonial attire (Ps. 45:15–16; Isa. 49:18; 61:10; Jer. 2:32; Ezek. 16:12–13). She was escorted to the groom's home to the accompaniment of singing and dancing (Jer. 7:34; 16:9; 25:10). The bride's entry into the bridegroom's household was the significant moment: at that point they were considered to be husband and wife. "Then Isaac brought her [Rebekah] into his mother Sarah's tent. He took Rebekah, and she became his wife [i.e., the marriage was consummated]; and he loved her" (Gen. 24:67). Oddly, in the case of Gideon and his Shechemite wife, the mother of Abimelech, Gideon lived in Ophrah, and she in Shechem (Judg. 8:31).

A sumptuous repast was served (Gen. 29:22), followed by festivities lasting one or two weeks. On the occasion of Samson's marriage he refers to "the seven days of the feast" (Judg. 14:12). And in the case of Jacob, "Jacob said to Laban, 'Give me my wife that I may consort with her, for my time is completed.' So Laban gathered together all the people of the place, and made a feast. But in the evening he took his daughter Leah and brought her to Jacob; and he cohabited with her" (Gen. 29:21–23). A special nuptial chamber (*ḥuppâ*) was designated, and the bride was escorted there by her parents. This practice finds its way into metaphor as well: "In the heavens he [Yahweh] has set a tent for the sun, which comes out like a bridegroom from his wedding canopy (*ḥuppâ*)" (Ps. 19:5–6, E.T. 19:4–5; also Joel 2:16).

Marriage was not considered a religious rite but a "civil contract." It was the normal way of life: in Israel celibacy had no status, and not to be married was considered a humiliation. "Seven women shall take hold of one man in that day, saying, 'We will eat our own bread and wear our own clothes; just let us be called by your name; take away our disgrace'" (Isa. 4:1). In biblical history, Jeremiah alone was enjoined by Yahweh not to take a wife and have a family: "You [Jeremiah] shall not take a wife, nor shall you have sons or daughters in this place" (Jer. 16:2). By complying with this stricture, Jeremiah was to symbolize the impending death and destruction confronting parents and children before the fall of Judah and the exile.

Levirate

The importance of procreation and the preservation of patrimony are evident in the practice of "levirate" marriages. As Brichto indicates, the duties of the *gōʾēl* went well beyond blood vengeance and the redemption of property: "The *gōʾēl* is he who redeems the dead from the danger to his [the dead's] afterlife by continuing his line."[51] If a married man died without children, his brother was to cohabit with the widow for several reasons: to prevent the widow from marrying an outsider (exogamy), to perpetuate the name of the deceased, and to preserve within the family the inherited land of the deceased. The first son borne by the widow was to be considered the offspring of the deceased husband. This custom is known as the levirate (from Latin *levir*, "husband's brother"; in Heb *yābām*; Deut. 25:5–10).

The classic case of the levirate law concerns Judah and Tamar (Gen. 38:6–26). Tamar prevailed upon her father-in-law Judah to provide a levirate for her after Er, her husband and Judah's eldest son, died. Onan, Judah's second son, failed to fulfill the *levir*'s obligation: "he spilled his semen on the ground whenever he had relations with his brother's wife" (Gen. 38:9). This act of *coitus interruptus* has become known as "onanism" and is mistakenly applied to masturbation. The story should be understood, however, in light of its context—to curb or avoid propagation of the family

---

51. Brichto, "Kin, Cult, Land, and Afterlife," 21.

line—directly the opposite of sex for procreation, that is, "Be fruitful and multiply" (Gen. 1:28). Judah then withheld Shelah, his youngest son, from fulfilling the levirate "for he feared that he too would die, like his brothers" (Gen. 38:11). Ultimately Tamar, disguising herself as a prostitute (*zônâ*), and covering her face with a veil (*ṣā'îp*),[52] tricked her father-in-law Judah into having sexual intercourse (Gen. 38:14). As a result, she bore twins, Perez and Zerah; in an example of fictive kinship, Perez is later identified as an ancestor of David (Ruth 4:12, 18–22) and Jesus (Matt. 1:3).

A less clear case of the levirate involves Boaz and Ruth, for there was a closer (anonymous) relative of her husband who eventually declined to fulfill the role of *levir*. In this story there is a confluence of three key biblical concepts: levirate, genealogy, and inheritance. As noted, the levirate marriage ensures the continuation of the family line (genealogy) and the preservation of property within the family (inheritance). Boaz, a remote kinsman, accomplished the levirate by marrying Ruth so as to perpetuate the name of her deceased husband Mahlon. At the same time Boaz redeemed the family property: "I [Boaz] have also acquired Ruth the Moabite, the wife of Mahlon, to be my wife, to maintain the dead man's name on his inheritance, in order that the name of the dead man may not be cut off from his kindred and from the gate of his native place" (Ruth 4:10). Obed, the son of Boaz and Ruth, was the grandfather of David, as the genealogical appendix makes clear (Ruth 4:18–22). For a long time, scholars considered these concluding verses of Ruth as a priestly addition; today they are looked upon as an integral part of the book, especially since genealogy and inheritance are its main themes. This genealogy begins with Perez (son of Judah and Tamar) and ends with Boaz, Obed, Jesse, and David.[53]

Divorce

Owing to the importance of family life, divorce was presumably not a frequent occurrence. Although divorce was condoned, it was a serious matter and was not considered ordinary. The law of Deuteronomy 24:1–4 gives only to the husband, not the wife, the power to initiate divorce proceedings—and at any time and for any reason, without an obligation to provide for her support. He was required to give her a written document of divorce, lest she be accused of adultery upon remarriage, which was permitted to her. The laws of divorce are to be interpreted in terms of the Israelite social structure, which was agnatic (descended from the father's side), not cognatic (having common ancestors).

---

52. Veils were worn by prostitutes, as well as by women on their wedding day (Gen. 24:65).
53. Brichto, "Kin, Cult, Land, and Afterlife," 11–23. Katharine D. Sakenfeld, *Ruth*, Interpretation (Louisville, Ky.: John Knox, 1999), 70–76.

Old Age

The biblical tradition from the creation accounts onward underscores the centrality of the community in Israelite society as compared with a solitary way of life. Everyone participates in the community, which is comprised of people at every stage of life—infancy, adolescence, maturity, and advanced age. Everyone, including the elderly, has a special role to play in the community. Because of their wisdom, the elderly are entitled to respect; at the same time, it is their responsibility to transmit the tradition to the community: "Remember the days of old, consider the years long past; ask your father, and he will inform you; your elders (*zĕqēnîm*), and they will tell you" (Deut. 32:7). The Holiness Code enjoins honor and respect for the senior members of the community: "You shall rise before the aged, and defer to the old; and you shall fear your God: I am Yahweh" (Lev. 19:32). Isaiah, on the other hand, proclaims that the divine judgment against Judah will be manifest in lawlessness degenerating into social chaos: "The people will be oppressed, everyone by another and everyone by a neighbor; the youth will be insolent to the elder (*zāqēn*), and the base to the honorable" (Isa. 3:5). The divine oracle on the marvelous restoration of Zion (Jerusalem) contains an idyllic description of old age: "Old men and old women shall again sit in the streets of Jerusalem, each with staff in hand because of their great age" (Zech. 8:4). Joseph is a model of devotion toward his elderly parent. His final act of piety was to honor his father Jacob's wish to be buried with his ancestors in Canaan, rather than in Egypt. Joseph responded, "I will do as you have said" (Gen. 47:30). The concluding remarks after Joshua's conquest of Canaan describe the community's fulfillment of this pledge (Josh. 24:32).

The most common biblical terms designating one of advanced age are *śêbâ* ("gray head") and *zāqēn* ("elder", literally "bearded one"). Long life is a sign of accomplishment, prominence, and divine blessing. Isaiah describes poetically how God's people will enjoy long life: "For one who dies at a hundred years will be considered a youth, and one who falls short of a hundred will be considered accursed" (Isa. 65:20). Abraham (Gen. 25:8), Gideon (Judg. 8:32), and David (1 Chron. 29:28) experienced a "good old age" (*śêbâ ṭôbâ*) as a sign of God's blessing.

The psalmist defines the maximum life span: "The days of our life are seventy years, or perhaps eighty, if we are strong" (Ps. 90:10). With life expectancy in biblical times closer to forty, very few, if any, would have attained the psalmist's maximum life span. The preposterous patriarchal ages are the ideal, certainly not the reality. Although it is portrayed as a sign of divine favor, old age is, by contrast, a time of physical deterioration, when the quality of life inevitably diminishes. Some biblical portrayals of old age are rather bleak. Barzillai, who befriended David when he arrived at Mahanaim (in Gilead) after fleeing Jerusalem, declined the king's invitation to join the royal court because of infirmity associated with old age, including sexual impotency:[54] "Today I [Barzillai] am eighty years old; do I know right from wrong? Can your servant taste what he eats or what he drinks? Can I still listen to the voice of singing men and singing women?" (2 Sam. 19:35)

A variety of physical disabilities are associated with advanced age, such as hearing impairment, failing eyesight, and waning vitality: "When Isaac was old and his eyes were dim so that he could not see, he called his elder son Esau and said to him, . . . 'See, I am old; I do not know the day of my death'" (Gen. 27:1–2). When David was old and feeble, suffering from hypothermia, his servants said to him: "Let a young virgin [Abishag] be sought for my lord the king; . . . let her lie in your bosom, so that my lord the king may be warm" (1 Kings 1:2). An additional sign of old age was the inability of the male to father a child and of the female to give birth, illustrated in the account of a son promised to Abraham and Sarah: "Now Abraham and Sarah were old, advanced in age; it had ceased to be with Sarah after the manner of women [menstrual periods]. So Sarah laughed to herself, saying, 'After I have grown old, and my husband is old, shall I have [sexual] pleasure?'" (Gen. 18:11–12). Nonetheless the psalmist, even though he had reached old age, continued to look expectantly to the future: "Even though I am old and gray, do not forsake me, O God, until I proclaim your strength to the next generation, your mighty acts to all who are to come" (Ps. 71:18).

Crimes and Punishments in the Family Context

Illicit sexual relationships are divided between public and private offenses. In the first category are incest, bestiality, and homosexuality; in the latter are rape and adultery. Marriage to the children of one's father was forbidden, punishable by death (Lev. 18:9, 11). Amnon has sexual relations with his half-sister Tamar and is eventually killed for it at the command of her full brother Absalom (2 Sam. 13:14, 28–29). In fact, Amnon may have been guilty of both rape and incest. This case is complicated by the words of Tamar: "Speak to the king; for he will not withhold me from you [Amnon]" (2 Sam. 13:13).

Bestiality is condemned as a perversion (*tebel*) (Lev. 18:23; 20:15–16). Blood guilt was incurred by both human and nonhuman, and the penalty was execution of both. The fact that young men had no social contacts with women might occasion bestiality in an agricultural society, as has been attested in more recent studies.

Homosexuality is also called sodomy from the story of "Sodom," where the townspeople desired sexual relations with Lot's male visitors (*mal'ākîm*, literally "messengers" or "angels") (Gen. 19:1–11). Biblical laws proscribe homosexual relations between males and prescribe capital punishment for both parties (Lev. 18:22; 20:13). Lesbianism is not mentioned in the Bible.

---

54. McCarter, *II Samuel*, 422.

Rape is referred to only in Deuteronomy, but with no sharp distinction between rape and seduction. The rapist "shall give fifty shekels of silver to the young woman's father, and she shall become his wife. Because he violated her, he shall not be permitted to divorce her as long as he lives" (Deut. 22:29). The payment in this case represents the *mōhar*. Dinah, the daughter of Jacob and Leah, was raped by a Canaanite named Shechem, son of Hamor, who was a local chief. Jacob's sons Simeon and Levi, as mentioned above, avenged the rape of their sister by slaying all the male Shechemites (Genesis 34).

Adultery is in a different category from fornication. The seventh commandment forbids a married person from having sexual relations with one who is not his or her spouse, under the penalty of death (Ex. 20:14; Deut. 5:18). If a married man commits adultery with a married woman, both the adulterer and the adulteress shall be put to death (Lev. 20:10; Deut. 22:22). In practice, adultery was a crime when committed by a betrothed or married woman, but not so when committed by the man. Sexual intercourse between a married man and an unmarried woman was not considered adultery. The purpose of the commandment was to protect the inheritance (*naḥălâ*) from falling into the hands of an illegitimate heir. Apparently the commandment against adultery was not always observed; David certainly transgressed (2 Samuel 11).

Council of Elders

Legal arrangements were founded upon a system of village or clan elders.[55] Each village had its council of elders (*zĕqēnîm*). "Samuel did what Yahweh commanded, and came to Bethlehem. The elders of the village came to meet him trembling, and said, 'Do you come peaceably?'" (1 Sam. 16:4). The elders gathered at the gate or in the courtyard, where they sat in a circle to deliberate the political and religious affairs of the community; they also decided legal cases. In the village the notables would come from the leading family or families of the village itself. At clan district headquarters, the notables selected from various villages would meet. Some from the regional councils would then be chosen to represent the clan districts at tribal councils. Tribal elders would in turn be appointed as representatives at the level of confederated tribes or, in the case of kingship, at the "state" level. These may be the notables who sit at the king's table. It is a nested system representing a hierarchy of different functions. For example, councils at the village level would have different juridical and other functions from those at clan district level or at the tribal level. Going to war, as in the Song

55. John S. Holladay, "The Kingdoms of Israel and Judah: Political and Economic Centralization in the Iron IIA-B (ca. 1000–750 B.C.E.)," in T. E. Levy, ed., *The Archaeology of Society in the Holy Land* (New York: Facts on File, 1995), 387.

of Deborah, and sending up militia would have been a pan-tribal decision by the council of elders representing various tribes, who also select the warlord to lead them into battle. The council of elders was known in many Near Eastern societies long before Israel was formed.[56]

MEALS FOR FAMILY AND GUESTS

Hospitality

Hospitality is rooted in kinship. The *gēr* (plural *gērîm*), usually translated "sojourner" or "resident alien" or "client," is anyone outside the kin group or solidarity unit and, therefore, defenseless. *gērîm* had to be under the protection of a host or patron who was a member of the community. Hospitality was a sacred duty for the Israelites, according to the Mosaic law: "When a *gēr* resides with you in your land, you shall not oppress the *gēr*. The *gēr* who resides with you shall be to you as the citizen among you; you shall love the *gēr* as yourself, for you were *gērîm* in the land of Egypt: I am Yahweh your God" (Lev. 19:33–34). Hospitality was preferred to fasting, as Isaiah declares when distinguishing false and true worship. The fast that God desires consists in reaching out to those who are in need: "Is not this the fast that I choose? . . . Is it not to share your bread with the hungry, and bring the homeless poor into your house?" (Isa. 58:6–7). Because table fellowship founded on hospitality implied mutual trust, the psalmist complains bitterly: "Even my bosom friend (*'îš šĕlômî*) [lit. "the man of my peace"] in whom I trusted, who ate of my bread, has lifted the heel against me" (Ps. 41:10 [E.T. 41:9]).

Psalm 23 is a hymn of trust rooted in the conviction *kî-'attâ 'immādî* ("for you [Yahweh] are with me" [v. 4]). This psalm is also a locus classicus of biblical hospitality. It is a diptych, employing two distinct metaphors to describe God. In the first part (vv. 1–4), Yahweh is the solicitous shepherd; in the second (vv. 5–6), God is the gracious host. The shepherd and the host both provide the three essentials—food, drink, protection. The shepherd leads the sheep to lush pasturage and water holes and guides them through treacherous valleys. So, too, the host sets a table for the guest, with ample food and drink, under the protection of his abode. "You [God] prepare a table (*šulḥān*) before me in the presence of my enemies; you anoint my head with oil; my cup overflows" (Ps. 23:5). *šulḥān* is a cognate of the Ugaritic *lḥn*, "table," and not of Arabic *slḥ*, "to strip off the hide," mistakenly interpreted as a mat or piece

---

56. Thorkild Jacobsen, *Toward the Image of Tammuz and Other Essays on Mesopotamian History and Culture*, ed. W. L. Moran (Cambridge: Harvard University, 1970), 157–72.

of leather spread on the ground.[57] On the basis of the final verse, "I shall dwell in the house of Yahweh for days without end," we can assume that the psalm's original setting was cultic, a joyful banquet associated with a sacrifice of thanksgiving.[58]

The narrative in Genesis 18 relates how Abraham and Sarah extend prodigious hospitality to the strangers who visit them at Hebron in the heat of the day. In keeping with the conventions of hospitality, Abraham offers his guests water to wash the dust from their feet. Then the couple prepares an elaborate feast of both animal and vegetable foods, including cakes, a roasted calf, curds, and milk—all this food, despite Abraham's disclaimer, "Let me bring a little bread (*pat-leḥem*), that you may refresh yourselves" (Gen. 18:5). Guests were given freshly baked bread as a sign of hospitality and as a way to honor the guest. The bread was not cut but was always broken into pieces.

There are any number of other biblical examples of this custom. Job vaunts his own spirit of hospitality, saying: "The *gēr* has not lodged in the street; I have opened my door to the traveler" (Job 31:32). The widow of Zarephath (in Phoenicia) shared food with Elijah despite her limited provisions: "When he [Elijah] came to the gate of the town [Zarephath], a widow was there gathering sticks; he called to her and said, 'Bring me a little water in a vessel, so that I may drink.' As she was going to bring it, he called to her and said, 'Bring me a morsel of bread in your hand'" (1 Kings 17:10–11). After the widow informed Elijah that she had only a small amount of meal and oil, he asked her to make him a "little cake" (*'ugâ qĕṭannâ*) (1 Kings 17:13). Oil was stirred into the flour, and the mix was formed into a cake before being baked in an oven. The result was the round, flat bread called "pita." Reuel, the priest of Midian, was astonished when his daughters failed to extend hospitality to the stranger (Moses) who had watered their flock for them: "He [Reuel] said to his daughters, 'Where is he [Moses]? Why did you leave the man? Invite him to break bread'" (Ex. 2:20).

Dining together created a bond among the participants to which a moral obligation was attached. On the occasion of a common meal, friendships were often sealed. After Abram's (Abraham's) victorious return from battle, the king of Salem (Jerusalem?) and priest of El Elyon, Melchizedek, brought out bread and wine, and blessed Abram (Gen. 14:17–20). On the other hand, punishment was meted out to those who failed in hospitality. "No Ammonite or Moabite shall be admitted to the assembly of the Lord . . . because they did not meet you with food and water on your journey out of Egypt" (Deut. 23:3–4). The same principle is applied in the story of Nabal who refused to share food and drink with David and his men. Nabal protested:

---

57. Mitchell Dahood, *Psalms I*, AB 16 (Garden City, N.Y.: Doubleday, 1966), 147.
58. Ernest Vogt, "The 'Place in Life' of Ps 23," *Biblica* 34 (1953): 195–211.

"Shall I take my bread and my water and the meat that I have butchered for my shearers, and give it to men who come from I do not know where?" (1 Sam. 25:11).

Furniture

Furniture is a sign of permanent settlement; nomads have no need for furnishings too cumbersome to carry with them. All ancient furniture was crafted from wood; but like all organic materials, wood deteriorates, leaving at most only remnants. The wooden furnishings preserved in the late Middle Bronze tomb at Jericho are an unusual find.

Festive meals required appropriate furniture. Besides biblical and other contemporary texts, banqueting scenes on reliefs, ivories, and elsewhere provide information about the furniture used for dining, at least among the elite. A relief found in the palace at Nineveh represents Ashurbanipal, king of Assyria, reclining on a high couch in a garden while feasting with his queen (Ill. 22). This reclining position is a unique depiction in Neo-Assyrian art. Until this time, whenever a king celebrated a victory he was represented in a seated position. In front of the queen stands a table; another table to the right holds the king's bow, sword, and quiver. A banquet scene on an eighth-century relief from Carchemish pictures a bearded figure, with attendants, sitting before a table and holding a cup (*ANEP*, 637).

The Israelite practice was to sit or recline during meals. Tables, ordinarily used for serving meals, were also utilized for rituals, money changing, and writing. The table

Ill. 22: Wall relief from Ashurbanipal's palace in Nineveh, seventh century B.C.E. Banqueting scene under the pergola of a formal garden. In this garden scene the king is reclining on a couch and the queen is sitting on a throne with her feet on a footstool. Attendants stand to right and left of the royal couple. To the left are more attendants with trays of delicacies, and a lyre player accompanies the banquet. The king and queen drink wine from bowl/cups typical of the *marzēaḥ*. Next to the musician, from a conifer tree, hangs the head of a defeated Elamite king. (Courtesy of the Trustees of the British Museum)

must have stood low since diners usually squatted or reclined on rugs. Tables found in Egypt were seldom more than thirty centimeters in height. The psalmist depicts parents and their children seated around a dinner table: "Your wife will be like a fruitful vine within your house; your children will be like olive shoots around your table (*šulḥān*)" (Ps. 128:3). A biblical reference to *šulḥān* concerns Adoni-Bezek, a Canaanite king defeated by the tribe of Judah. When the victors cut off his thumbs and his big toes, Adoni-Bezek is quoted as saying: "Seventy kings with their thumbs and big toes cut off used to pick up scraps under my table (*šulḥān*); as I have done, so God has paid me back" (Judg. 1:7), although the story sounds apocryphal. In a vision of the fall of Babylon, the nobles are seated at a banquet. "They prepare the table (*šulḥān*), they spread the rugs, they eat, they drink" (Isa. 21:5). "Preparing a table" sometimes symbolizes the virtue of trust, especially in the Psalter: "You prepare a table before me in the presence of my enemies" (Ps. 23:5). "They [Israelites] spoke against God, saying, 'Can God spread a table in the wilderness?'" (Ps. 78:19).

The chair was no doubt the rectangular stool commonly depicted in Near Eastern art. By contrast, in the scene mentioned above, depicting King Ashurbanipal and his queen feasting in their garden, while the king reclines on a high couch, the queen sits on a high, ornate throne at the foot of the couch. Also, Sennacherib's catalogue of tribute received from Hezekiah includes both couches and chairs (*ANET*, 288).

Amos denounces the indolent upper class who sleep on wooden beds adorned with ivory plaques (*miṭṭôt šēn*) (Amos 6:4). Only the affluent enjoyed the luxury of beds; ordinary folk slept on a rush mat.

Food Preparation

The Bible provides little detail about cooking techniques. The courtyard functioned as the kitchen, where the women of the household or the servants did the cooking. Boiling was the ordinary way to prepare meat. The Hebrew word *bāšal* designates cooking in the general sense. When Tamar went to the house of her brother Amnon, she boiled (*bāšal*) dumplings (*lĕbibôt*) for him (2 Sam. 13:8).[59] Sometimes meat was roasted when it was to be eaten by commoners on festive occasions. With reference to the corrupt sons of Eli, the chief priest of Shiloh, it is said that "the priest's servant would come and say to the one who was sacrificing, 'Give meat (*bāśār*) for the priest to roast (*liṣlôt*); for he will not accept boiled meat (*bāśār mĕbuššāl*) from you, but only raw'" (1 Sam. 2:15).

The ritual laws provide details about the preparation of animals before cooking. After the throat was cut and the blood drained, the animal was flayed and dissected. Small animals, such as the paschal lamb, were roasted whole (*ṣĕli-'ēš*) on a spit over

---

59. McCarter, *II Samuel*, 322.

an open wood fire (Ex. 12:8). In his denunciation of the *marzēaḥ*, a sumptuous banquet of the upper class accompanied by music and entertainment, Amos describes the consumption of "lambs from the flock, and calves from the stall." The latter refers to veal from stall-fattened, tender calves, an epicurean delight (Amos 6:4).

The Bible mentions several vessels for cooking. Describing the priest Eli's greedy sons, the biblical writer lists four types of cooking vessels: "When anyone offered sacrifice, the priest's servant would come, while the meat was boiling, with a three-pronged fork in his hand, and he would thrust it into the basin (*kiyyôr*), or kettle (*dûd*), or cooking jug (*qallaḥat*), or cooking pot (*pārûr*); all that the fork brought up the priest would take for himself" (1 Sam. 2:13–14; see Ill. 71b). In the cult, unlike most domestic households, the vessels were probably metal, as in the Jerusalem Temple. Distinguishing these vessels is difficult, since the same vessel is sometimes given more than one name, and the listing here appears to be conflated. The *kiyyôr* is a shallow, wide-mouth vessel. The *dûd* is a deep, round-bottomed, two-handled cooking pot. The *qallaḥat* is a one-handled cooking jug; so, too, the *pārûr*. There are other containers such as the *sîr*, which is a wide-mouth cooking pot. In the Iron Age, meals were eaten from smaller bowls. In sum, wide-mouthed cooking pots were used for meats and stews and narrow-necked, one-handled cooking jugs for soup and gruel.

Bread Making

Bread making is an ancient art, dating from prehistoric times. The Hebrew word *leḥem* designates "bread," but it may also mean food in general. Ordinarily the women of the household made the bread, most likely a daily chore. Describing the division of labor involved in preparing *kawwānîm*, cakes for the cult of the Queen of Heaven (commonly identified with the goddess Ishtar), Jeremiah notes, "The children gather wood, the fathers kindle fire, and the women knead dough" (Jer. 7:18). The flour[60] was mixed with water and then kneaded into dough in a bowl or trough. A small quantity of fermented dough was added as leavening, and the batter seasoned with salt. Some think *kawwānîm* were ash or ember cakes.[61] Actually, they were flour cakes sweetened with honey or figs. The verb "to knead" (*lûš*) appears in three other well-known biblical stories: Sarah kneaded flour in preparing the cakes for the three strangers (Gen. 18:6). The medium at Endor kneaded flour for the cakes she baked for Saul on the eve of his defeat by the Philistines at Mount Gilboa (1 Sam. 28:24). Tamar kneaded dough and made cakes in the house of her half-brother Amnon before he raped her (2 Sam. 13:8).

---

60. See chapter 3 regarding the processing of grains into flour.
61. Moshe Greenberg, *Ezekiel 1–20*, AB 22 (Garden City, N.Y.: Doubleday, 1983), 107. See his citation of Edward Robinson's description of ember cakes baked in dung fire.

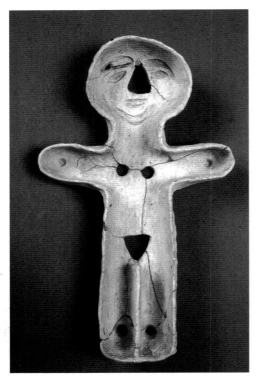

Ill. 23: Cypriot terracotta cake mold (30.4 cm high, 18.5 cm wide, 4.2 cm thick), probably representing Heavenly Aphrodite-Astarte, Ishtar, the Queen of Heaven. The cake from the mold emphasizes the nose, breast, and pudendum. Probably from Iron II or Cypro-Archaic period. (Courtesy of V. Karageorghis, Cyprus Museum, Nicosia)

"Cakes" ('ugôt) are not the same as present-day pastry. The ancient Israelites had honey and dibs, a syrup made from the juice of grapes, dates, or figs. 'ugâ, derived from the Hebrew root "to be round," may denote an ancient version of a griddle cake, since it had to be turned, lest it burn or be only half-baked. Note the metaphorical use: "Ephraim is a cake not turned ('ugâ bĕlî hăpûkâ)" (Hos. 7:8). As a symbol of the siege of Jerusalem and the impending Babylonian exile, Ezekiel is directed to take six vegetables and cereals and mix them for food in a bowl. "And you [Ezekiel], take wheat and barley, fava beans and lentils, millet (dōhan) and emmer (kussĕmîm). Put them into one vessel and bake bread (lehem) for yourself" (Ezek. 4:9). This unusual mixture of foodstuffs, which is legally unclean (Lev. 19:19; Deut. 22:9) and may reflect a scarcity of food, is described as siege food.[62] Ezekiel is then directed to eat this conglomeration as a "barley cake" ('ugat šĕ'ōrîm) (Ezek. 4:12).

In biblical times, a variety of methods was used for baking bread. The simplest and the earliest way was to build a fire on top of a flat stone; after the ashes were removed, the dough was placed on the heated stone and then covered with the ashes. Afterward the ashes were removed, and the bread was ready to eat. This may have been the method intended in the description of the Israelites' flight from Egypt (Ex. 12:39). So, too, in the case of the medium of Endor who had to bake bread in haste (1 Sam. 28:24). As for Elijah, the cake ('ugâ) of dough was baked on heated stones covered with ashes. While lying under the broom tree Elijah looked, "And there at his head was a cake ('ugâ) baked on hot stones" (1 Kings 19:6).[63] When a griddle (mahăbat) of clay or iron (Ezek. 4:3) was used, it was set on stones over a pit in which a fire was kindled; then the dough was baked directly on the griddle. "If your offer-

62. Greenberg, *Ezekiel 1–20*, 106.
63. Greenberg, *Ezekiel 1–20*, 107.

ing is grain prepared on a griddle (*ḥammaḥăbat*), it shall be of choice flour mixed with oil, unleavened" (Lev. 2:5; see Ill. 70b).

Bread ovens are frequently found in domestic quarters, ordinarily located in courtyards. Two kinds of ovens, designated *tabun* and *tannûr*, were used; each had several variations. *tabun*, a Palestinian Arabic word, is not found in the Bible; *tannûr* is the common biblical word for "oven." Both were made from a mixture of clay and chopped straw and shaped like a beehive. The opening on top was capped with a lid. Fuel in the form of flat cakes of dried manure kneaded with straw was heaped against the *tabun* on the exterior, which heated the stone pebble floor inside the oven on which the bread was baked. Dung, even human excrement, served as fuel in extreme situations. Referring to the food Ezekiel is to eat, Yahweh instructs: "Eat it as a barley cake; you shall bake it on human excrement before their eyes" (Ezek. 4:12). A *tannûr* was fueled by a wood fire on the bottom of the oven, and the loaves were placed on the hot interior walls to bake (see p. 17). Dung fuel was not normally used in this oven. According to some lexicographers, biblical references (Ezek. 5:16; Lev. 26:26) to the *maṭṭeh-leḥem* ("staff of bread") do not connote "staff of life" (= bread) in our understanding of the term; rather, the Hebrew phrase refers to the bread pole or stick for stacking or hanging ring-shaped bread to protect it from rodents.[64]

Daily Meals

Small bowls were used for eating and drinking. In biblical times the people ate three daily meals, differing noticeably in quantity. Breakfast was quite meager, consisting of only bread or fruit. The midday meal was light, composed of bread, grain, olives, and figs. Ruth's noon meal, for example, was made up of bread dipped into a vinegar-based wine (*ḥōmeṣ*) and some parched grain (*qālî*) (Ruth 2:14). The main meal was eaten in the evening after sunset, following the day's work, and the whole family participated.[65] The amount of food served depended upon the economic circumstances of the household. The meal was basically a one-pot stew served in a common bowl and sopped up with bread. A thick porridge (*nāzîd)* or stew of vegetables, sometimes containing meat, is mentioned several times in the Bible. Usually made with lentils (*'ădāšîm*) or other vegetables, the pottage was seasoned with herbs. In his deception of Esau to win the birthright, Jacob prepared lentil stew (*nězîd 'ădāšîm*),

---

64. Ludwig Koehler and Walter Baumgartner, *Hebräisches und aramäisches Lexikon zum Alten Testament*, 3d ed. (Leiden: E. J. Brill, 1974), 2:543.

65. In traditional Arab households today, the women do not eat with the men but wait until later. On the basis of Gen. 18:8–9, a similar practice may have obtained in biblical times, or perhaps only when entertaining guests: While the "three men" visiting Abraham by the oaks of Mamre ate, he stood by them, but Sarah remained in the tent.

which Esau described as "that red stuff" (*hā'ādōm hazzeh*) (Gen. 25:29–34). The reference to "red" appears to be a wordplay on the land of Edom ("red") with which Esau was associated. Elisha served a similar stew (*nāzîd*) to the company of prophets, which they ate from the pot (*sîr*) in which it was boiled (and they were almost poisoned) (2 Kings 4:38–41).

The average family ate meat only on festive occasions. The arrival of prominent guests warranted serving meat, as in the case of the three strangers who visited Abraham and Sarah. When Saul consulted the medium at Endor, she slaughtered a stall-fed calf (*'ēgel marbēq*) and baked unleavened cakes (*maṣṣôt*) (1 Sam. 28:24–25). The Hebrew *marbēq* ("stall") designates an enclosure where animals were restrained for fattening. Apparently the "prodigal son" of Luke's Gospel was served the same dish upon his return home (Luke 15:23–27). "Calves from the stall" (*'ăgālîm mittôk marbēq*) were also featured at the *marzēaḥ* (Amos 6:4).

Several other biblical texts provide information about the foods the Israelites ate. When David was in flight from Absalom, provisions brought to him at Mahanaim (in Transjordan) consisted of "wheat, barley, meal, parched grain, beans and lentils, honey and curds, sheep, and cheese from the herd" (2 Sam. 17:28–29). The inventory of daily provisions for Solomon's court consisted of 30 cors [195 bushels] of semolina (*sōlet*), 60 cors [390 bushels] of meal (*qāmaḥ*), 10 fat oxen (*bāqār bĕri'îm*), 20 pasture-fed cattle (*bāqār rĕ'î*), 100 sheep (*ṣō'n*), as well as deer (*mē'ayyāl*), gazelles (*ṣĕbî*), roebucks (*yaḥmûr*), and fatted fowl (*barburîm 'ăbûsîm*) (1 Kings 5:2–3 [E.T. 4:22–23]). When, on the festive occasion of sheepshearing, Nabal refused to share food with David and his retinue, Abigail intervened by providing generously "two hundred loaves, two skins of wine, five sheep ready dressed, five measures of parched grain, one hundred clusters of raisins, and two hundred cakes of figs" (1 Sam. 25:18). This was not the typical Israelite daily menu, but it indicates the kinds of foods they ate.

On at least three occasions cited in the biblical text, common meals are associated with creating covenants. Isaac and King Abimelech of Gerar sealed a pact of nonaggression at a common meal prepared by Isaac (Gen. 26:26–33). Similarly, an agreement was secured between Jacob and Laban by a sacrificial meal (Gen. 31:43–54). As part of the ratification of the Sinai covenant, seventy elders of Israel ascended the mountain, accompanied by Moses, Aaron, Nadab, and Abihu, to eat and drink in the presence of Yahweh (Ex. 24:9–11). In addition, Jethro, Moses' father-in-law, shared a meal with Aaron and the elders of Israel as a sign of the bond between them (Ex. 18:12).

ILLNESS AND HEALING

Clinical descriptions of illnesses in prescientific literature are so inexact that it is impossible to determine the precise diseases being described. Suffice it to say, the ancients had nearly every illness we have and more, because of lack of sanitation and hygiene. Several epidemics are mentioned in the Bible, for example, the fifth plague of Egypt affecting the livestock (Ex. 9:3–7) and the illness of Sennacherib's army (2 Kings 19:35; Isa. 37:36), which was probably dysentery, a common ailment with soldiers in the field.

The practice of medicine was already well advanced in Mesopotamia and Egypt by the third millennium B.C.E. In Mesopotamia there was a goddess of healing named Gula, whose emblem was the dog and whose temple was known as the "dog house." During the Old Kingdom in Egypt, professional physicians were practicing the medical arts. Both Egypt and Mesopotamia remained far ahead of ancient Israel, where the practice was rather primitive throughout the Iron Age, with diagnoses left to the priests and healing rites to the prophets.

Archaeology provides little in the way of buildings or artifacts specifically related to medicine. Most fatal illnesses do not leave traces upon the bones or register symptoms on the skeleton itself. However, a few diseases—arthritis, tuberculosis, septic infection, malignancies—have been detected by physical anthropologists. The skeletal remains do provide evidence of the age, sex, and stature of the deceased, information about diet and nutrition, and indications of trauma and mutilation.[66]

While art and artifacts are quite useful, the biblical texts are not of much help, since the ancient writers' system of classification (which in the P source is concerned primarily with ritual purity) bears no resemblance to scientific terminology and modern classification of diseases and illness. This lack of technical detail makes identification of ailments mentioned in the Bible very difficult, if not impossible. The most common Hebrew words for illness in general are *ḥŏlî*, "sickness," and *ḥālâ*, "to be weak." The opposite state or condition is *šālôm*, "wholeness, well-being."

Hygiene

Directives for maintaining personal hygiene in the medical sections of Leviticus are concerned with ritual purity rather than physical cleanliness. On the Day of Atonement, the high priest Aaron "shall bathe his body in water in a holy place, and put on his vestments" (Lev. 16:24). The cleanliness of the military camp needed also to be maintained, insofar as Yahweh accompanied the army; hence the regulation in Deuteronomy:

> With your utensils you shall have a stick (*yātēd*); when you relieve yourself outside, you shall dig a hole with it and then cover up your excrement.

---

66. Richard N. Jones, "Paleopathology," *ABD*, 5:62; and Robert North, *Medicine in the Biblical Background*, AnBib (Roma: Editrice Pontificio Istituto Biblico, 2000).

> Because Yahweh your God travels along with your camp, to save you and to hand over your enemies to you, therefore your camp must be holy, so that he may not see anything indecent among you and turn away from you. (Deut. 23:13–14)

In antiquity, hygiene was quite primitive. Waste was generally deposited in the streets and eventually disposed of by foraging animals and the rains. Certain Iron Age gates, such as those at Megiddo and Gezer, had sewers running under the street, but house drains were rare. Cisterns were common but susceptible to contamination. Refuse of all kinds, polluted water, and contaminated food all created unsanitary conditions, which were responsible for a high rate of infant mortality as well as deadly diseases. "I [David] beat them [enemies] fine like the dust of the earth, I crushed them and stamped them down like the mire (ṭîṭ) of the streets" (2 Sam. 22:43; also Micah 7:10).[67] Relieving oneself outdoors, as was common practice, could easily lead to the spread of disease. In most cases, there were no outhouses or toilets. Several biblical texts refer to a male as "one who urinates against a wall" (1 Sam. 25:22, 34; 1 Kings 14:10).

The Bible has some examples of bathing unrelated to ritual purity. While walking on the palace roof, David spied Bathsheba bathing; subsequently he had an adulterous affair with her (2 Sam. 11:2). Archaeology, too, attests to the practice of bathing. A tomb in the er-Ras cemetery, at Achzib on the Mediterranean coast north of Acco, contained a clay figurine (probably eighth–seventh century B.C.E.) of a woman bathing in an oval bathtub (Ill. 24). Sometimes the bather probably stood while water was poured from a jar over the head and body.

Foot washing was emphasized in biblical times. Foot baths have been recovered from several sites, among them Samaria, Megiddo, and Lachish. These are pottery basins equipped with footrests and a spout at the bottom for draining the soiled water. Washing the feet was both a convention of hospitality

Ill. 24: Terracotta figurine of a woman bathing in a tub. Achzib, dated to seventh century B.C.E. (Courtesy of the Israel Museum)

---

67. Edward Neufeld, "Hygiene Conditions in Ancient Israel," *BA* 34 (1971): 42–66.

in antiquity and a necessity since people walked barefoot, in sandals, or in slippers with turned-up toes (see Ill. 134). Abraham addressed the three visiting strangers in Hebron: "Let a little water be brought, and wash your feet, and rest yourselves under the tree" (Gen. 18:4; also 19:2). "The man [Abraham's servant] came into the house; and Laban unloaded the camels, and gave him straw and fodder for the camels, and water to wash his feet and the feet of the men who were with him" (Gen. 24:32).

Yahweh, speaking through Jeremiah, charged the Judahites: "Though you wash yourself with natron (*neter*) and use much soap (*bōrît*), the stain of your guilt is still before me" (Jer. 2:22). Detergents were derived from plants, containing mainly potash and soda, grown in Palestine, especially in the Arabah, the Negev, and along the seashore. The detergents of biblical times probably looked like modern-day cakes of soap. *neter* was potassium mixed with alkalis and fats. "Soap" in this translation is an anachronism, since it came into use only in the Hellenistic period (ca. 300 B.C.E.). *bōrît*, a vegetable alkali, was made from simple wood or plant ashes containing potassium carbonate.[68] Hands were washed before and after meals, and most likely at other times during the day. Food was prepared and eaten under what would be considered today unsanitary conditions. Utensils were cleaned by rubbing them with sand.

It was common practice to smear olive oil on the body to prevent the skin from drying and cracking in the arid climate. Generally the oil was applied after bathing. Naomi directed her daughter-in-law Ruth, "Now wash, smear yourself with oil (*sûk*), and put on your best clothes" (Ruth 3:3). Upon hearing of the death of his child, "David rose from the ground, washed, smeared himself with oil (*sûk*), and changed his clothes" (2 Sam. 12:20).

Threats to Health

Parasites

The combination of hot climate, poor hygiene, and polluted water created a breeding ground for parasitic diseases. Archaeologists excavating in the City of David (Jerusalem) uncovered two latrines that were in use just before Nebuchadrezzar destroyed the city and the kingdom. One toilet seat was found in a cubicle associated with the "House of Aḥiel" in Area G (Ill. 25, 26, 28). This seat, constructed from local limestone,

---

68. At Tell el-Hesi, W. M. Flinders Petrie identified a thick deposit of alternating layers of ash and sand as belonging to "alkali burners." Albright considered this the destruction of Eglon by the Israelites. More recent excavators claim that the thin ash layers resulted from burnt-off threshing floors. This rather widespread phenomenon, at the end of the Bronze Age, has not been convincingly explained, although Petrie's "alkali burners" cannot be totally dismissed.

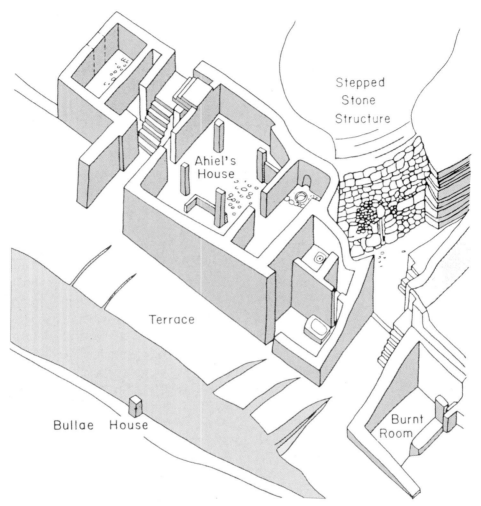

Ill. 25: Isometric drawing of Iron Age II house at base of Stepped Structure: Aḥiel's house and Burnt Room on upper terrace and Bullae House on lower terrace. (Courtesy of Alon de Groot, City of David Archaeological Project)

was located over a cesspit lined with plaster. It has two openings on top: the larger one for defecation; the smaller one for male urination. It is doubtful there were separate facilities for men and women.[69] Ordinary people did not have the luxury of toilets, but some Jerusalemites obviously enjoyed a higher level of sanitation. Iron II toilets, fashioned from slabs with apertures situated over shallow pits, were uncovered also at Bozrah in Edom and Tell es-Saʿidiyeh in Transjordan.

---

69. Jane Cahill et al., "It Had to Happen—Scientists Examine Remains of Ancient Bathrooms," *BAR* 17 (1991): 64–69.

Ill. 26: Area G, restored Stepped Stone Structure built in Jebusite Jerusalem, with Iron II House of Aḥiel. (Courtesy of Z. Radovan, Jerusalem)

Human parasites found in coprolites (fossilized excrement) provide valuable information on disease, diet, and nutrition in antiquity, while also pointing to a low level, by modern standards, of sanitation and hygiene in biblical times. Analysis of coprolites revealed eggs from two types of human intestinal parasites—beef or pork tapeworm and whipworm. Undercooked or raw beef is the likely culprit, since bovine bones are associated with these latrines. No pig bones were found. Pork, a taboo according to ritual laws, is rarely found at Israelite sites. Tapeworm, according to Joseph Zias, is associated with the unsanitary practice of irrigating fields with raw

Ill. 27: Louse

Ill. 28: Limestone toilet seat with two holes, large and small, the latter for male urination. From City of David, house of Ahiel; dates to the destruction of Jerusalem by Nebuchadrezzar in 586 B.C.E. (Courtesy of Z. Radovan, Jerusalem)

sewage. This may be explained by the "runoff" of sewers from the City of David into surrounding valleys. Whipworm infection is contracted by ingesting fecally contaminated food or from generally unsanitary conditions.[70] Fecal remains in the ancient cesspits of the City of David were mixed with ash to sanitize and deodorize the latrines. While the city was under Babylonian siege, it would have been impossible to maintain adequate sanitation.

Predicting Nebuchadrezzar's conquest of Egypt, Jeremiah announces that "as a shepherd delouses his cloak, he [Nebuchadrezzar] shall delouse [pillage] the land of Egypt and depart victorious" (Jer. 43:12). The oldest known remains of head lice (*Pediculi capitis*) date to PPNB (7300–6300 B.C.E.) in the Nahal Hemar cave at the southern edge of the Judean Desert.[71] There is evidence of a widespread problem of lice infestation in biblical times (Ill. 27). The most convincing witness is the fine-tooth combs with eggs of lice clinging to the teeth. Hair combs as delousing implements were both effective and ancient. The comb itself dates as early as the Natufian period, according to M. Dayagi-Mendels, and its design has changed very little over the millennia. In earliest times combs were made of ivory and bone; in the historical period some were made of boxwood, while bone and ivory combs continued in use. Like present-day combs, they consisted of both closely spaced and widely spaced teeth. At Ashkelon a beautiful ivory comb with hunting scenes, dating to the Persian period, was found (Ill. 29a, b). Combs found from a later period at Qumran and Masada contain numerous head lice and their eggs.[72]

Another means of eliminating lice was smearing the hair with oil; this treatment prevented oxygen from penetrating the head and caused the lice to suffocate. Thorkild

70. Joseph Zias, "Health and Healing in the Land of Israel—A Paleopathological Perspective," in O. Rimon, ed., *Illness and Healing in Ancient Times*, Reuben and Edith Hecht Museum Catalogue 13 (Haifa: University of Haifa, 1996), 14*.

71. Joseph Zias and Kostas Mumcuoglu, "Pre-Pottery Neolithic B Head Lice from Nahal Hemar Cave," '*Atiqot* 20 (1991): 167–68.

72. Kostas Mumcuoglu and Joseph Zias, "How the Ancients De-Loused Themselves," *BAR* 15 (1989): 66–69; Michal Dayagi-Mendels, *Perfumes and Cosmetics in the Ancient World*, Israel Museum Catalogue 395 (Jerusalem: Israel Museum, 1993), 74–86.

Ill. 29a: Carved ivory comb from Ashkelon, Persian period, showing a hunter on horseback. Below horse is a reclining ibex. The lions march across the register at the bottom just above the teeth of the comb. (Courtesy of the Leon Levy Expedition to Ashkelon; Photo: C. Andrews)

Ill. 29b: Carved ivory comb from Ashkelon, the other side. Two heroes thrust swords into a lion. The comb is broken at the top and the edges have been pared down in antiquity. (Courtesy of the Leon Levy Expedition to Ashkelon; Photo: C. Andrews)

Jacobsen traced the origin of ritual anointing of the head of kings (messiahs) to this remedy for head lice, which was available primarily to the wealthy. Extolling harmony among kin, the psalmist draws a comparison: "It is like the precious oil (*še-men*) on the head, running down upon the beard, on the beard of Aaron, running down over the collar (*pî*, literally "mouth," the opening through which the head passes) of his robes" (Ps. 133:2).

Blindness, one of the commonest maladies in the Bible, is probably associated with trachoma, an infection of the conjunctiva and cornea, which is transmitted by poor hygiene and especially by flies. One of the oldest diseases in the world, trachoma is readily curable today with antibiotics.

Infertility

In biblical society infertility (barrenness) was looked upon as a malady, by definition a dysfunction of a bodily organ and a reason for lament, humiliation, and despair.

Prominent ancestors such as Sarah (Gen. 16:1), Rebekah (Gen. 25:21), and Rachel (Gen. 30:1), wives of the three patriarchs, were temporarily infertile. Prayer was a trusted means for overcoming infertility, since God was held to be the one who both closed and opened the womb. Isaac, for example, prayed to Yahweh for his wife Rebekah because she was barren, and subsequently she conceived.

In another account, King Abimelech of Gerar took Sarah into his house after Abraham deceived him by saying that Sarah was his sister and not his wife. Learning the truth, Abimelech returned Sarah to Abraham and at the same time lavished gifts upon him. Thereupon the patriarch prayed to God, "and God healed (*rāpā'*) Abimelech, and . . . his wife and female slaves so that they bore children" (Gen. 20:17).

Such beliefs are not limited to the patriarchal literature alone. We read, for example, how Hannah, wife of Elkanah, remained barren for a long time. Deeply troubled by this affliction, she made a vow (*neder*) that if Yahweh would grant her a child she would dedicate him (as a Nazirite) to the service of the shrine at Shiloh. Hannah prayed for fertility at the Shiloh sanctuary "before Yahweh" (*lipnê YHWH*) (1 Sam. 1:12). Later, after bearing Samuel, she went up to Shiloh to fulfill her vow: "I [Hannah] have dedicated him [Samuel] to Yahweh; as long as he lives, he is dedicated to Yahweh" (1 Sam. 1:28).

Health Consultants

Physicians

For many of the biblical writers, especially the Deuteronomist, illness is God's punishment for sin, that is, for breaking the commandments of the covenant between Yahweh and the people of Israel: "Yahweh will afflict you with consumption, fever, inflammation, with fiery heat and drought, and with blight and mildew; they shall pursue you until you perish" (Deut. 28:22). For the righteous sufferer Job, illness is a divine instrument whose purpose remains a mystery to the victim.[73]

For those who view illness as divine retribution for sin and for those who do not, God, like the Canaanite deity Resheph, is both the bearer of disease and pestilence and the healer of these maladies. Job laments that he must "drink the poison" of the "arrows of the Almighty" (Job 6:4), even though he has done no wrong. Previously, his friend Eliphaz had remarked that "man is born to trouble as surely as the 'sons of Resheph' [i.e., flaming arrows] fly upward" (Job 5:7). But in Psalm 76:4 (E.T. 76:3) it is God who "breaks the flaming arrows (*rišpê-qešet*) . . . and the weapons of war." In Habakkuk 3:5 Resheph again appears in thin disguise as an angel of death. March-

---

73. Hector Avalos, *Illness and Health Care in the Ancient Near East*, HSM 54 (Atlanta: Scholars Press, 1995), 372–74.

ing before Yahweh, the divine warrior, is "Pestilence" (*Deber*) and "Plague" (*Resheph*).[74] After the Israelites crossed the Reed Sea and entered the wilderness of Shur (site of an oasis), Yahweh promised to cure all their illnesses with the assurance: "I will not bring upon you any of the diseases that I brought upon the Egyptians, for I Yahweh am your healer (*rōpē'*)" (Ex. 15:26). So, too, in a hymn of praise the psalmist describes Yahweh as the one "who heals (*rāpā'*) all your diseases" (Ps. 103:3).

rōpē' designates "physician," but in ancient Israel, unlike Egypt, medicine as a profession was held in low esteem. With regard to healing, the common verb is *rāpā'*, "to make whole," and the noun is *marpē'*, "healing." "We look for peace (*šālôm*), but find no good, for a time of healing (*marpē'*), but there is terror instead" (Jer. 8:15). Note here the parallelism *šālôm/rāpā'*. Jeremiah refers frequently to God as the true physician or healer, as in the prayer: "Heal (*rāpā'*) me, Yahweh, and I shall be healed (*rāpā'*)" (Jer. 17:14). Through Jeremiah Yahweh promises restoration to Israel and Judah: "For I will restore health to you, and your wounds I will heal (*rāpā'*)" (Jer. 30:17; also 33:6). For Jeremiah, Yahweh is the only authentic healer (*rōpē'*), and human physicians are ineffectual.

Only when the prophetic office came to an end in the postexilic period did professional physicians become prominent and respected. By the second century B.C.E., the physician was the primary provider of health care. Ben Sira reflects the attitude of the time in his tribute to physicians: "Honor physicians for their services, for Yahweh created them; for their gift of healing comes from the Most High, and they are rewarded by the king" (Sir. 38:1–2). The fact that Yahweh was regarded by the earlier biblical writers as sole healer (*rōpē'*) accounted in part for the negative attitude toward human physicians.

Legitimate Health Consultants

The only legitimate health consultants mentioned in the Bible are priests and prophets. However, like many other cultures Israel probably had its unofficial practitioners of "folk medicine." Because medicine and religion were completely intertwined, it is not surprising that the sick turned to priests and prophets for help. The ritual code of Israel linked disease with ritual impurity. Priests diagnosed diseases according to a system of purity, which determined whether or not a person should be quarantined from the community and administered purification rites for the malady.

In Leviticus 13–14, the symptoms of *ṣāra'at* (commonly mistranslated "leprosy") are diagnosed, and the purification rites for cleansing or purifying the victim are prescribed: "As for the person stricken with scale disease (*haṣṣārûa'*), he shall wear torn

---

74. William F. Albright, *Yahweh and the Gods of Canaan* (Garden City, N.Y.: Doubleday, 1968), 136. Frank M. Cross, *Canaanite Myth and Hebrew Epic* (Cambridge: Harvard University, 1973), 102–3.

clothes and let the hair of his head be disheveled; and he shall cover his moustache and cry out 'Impure, impure!' He shall remain impure as long as he has the disease; he is impure. He shall dwell apart; his dwelling shall be outside the camp" (Lev. 13:45–46).[75]

ṣāraʿat has no connection with leprosy as it is diagnosed today. In Leviticus it includes a variety of skin diseases considered cultically unclean. True leprosy is known to cause erosion of the bones of the hands, feet, and face.[76] Analysis of skeletal remains from biblical times shows no indications of leprosy in the technical sense. ṣāraʿat was considered by P to be a divine punishment, an impurity that precluded participation in the Israelite cult. Although no one is certain about which or how many skin diseases this term includes, it does not include "leprosy," which was unknown in Palestine before the Hellenistic era. The closest fit that dermatologists can find with skin disorders and the biblical description of ṣāraʿat is psoriasis—but that is far from exact. It is probably best to translate ṣāraʿat as "scale disease" (following Milgrom).[77] Elisha's healing powers were manifested in the case of the Syrian commander Naaman who was afflicted with "scale disease" (ṣāraʿat). However, instead of performing a ritual, Elisha simply ordered Naaman: "Go and bathe seven times in the Jordan, and your flesh shall be restored and you shall be clean" (2 Kings 5:10).[78] The prophet Isaiah was instrumental in healing King Hezekiah, lying mortally ill from a "boil" (šĕḥîn) in his Jerusalem palace, by applying a cake of figs (a poultice), which was deemed to have therapeutic properties (2 Kings 20:1–7).

Musicians were also consulted on health care. When Saul was troubled by an "evil spirit (rûaḥ rāʿâ) from Yahweh," perhaps a reference to mental illness, a musician was enlisted to relieve his depression: "Whenever the spirit of God would come upon Saul, David would take up the lyre and play, and Saul would find relief and be well, and the evil spirit would depart from him" (1 Sam. 16:23; also 18:10; 19:9).

Home Healings

In ancient Israel health care took place mainly in the home. There were no hospitals, although there may have been healing wards associated with temples. When Amnon lay on his bed at home pretending to be ill, he said to King David: "Please let my sister Tamar come and make a couple of cakes in my sight, so that I may eat from her hand" (2 Sam. 13:6).

---

75. Jacob Milgrom, *Leviticus 1–16*, AB 3 (New York: Doubleday, 1991), 771, 802–9.

76. Claudine Dauphin, "Leprosy, Lust, and Lice: Health Care and Hygiene in Byzantine Palestine," *Bulletin of the Anglo-Israel Archaeological Society* 15 (1996–97): 55.

77. Milgrom, *Leviticus 1–16*, 771–826; E. V. Hulse, "The Nature of Biblical 'Leprosy' and the Use of Alternative Medical Terms in Modern Translations of the Bible," *PEQ* 107 (1975): 87–105.

78. Today, bathing in the Dead Sea and using mudpacks from the area are aids in ameliorating psoriasis and other skin disorders.

Two stories of miraculous healing by Elijah and Elisha are set in the home. Elijah revives the son of a widow in Zarephath on the Phoenician coast. He carried the child to the upper story where he (Elijah) lived and laid him on his bed. "Then he stretched himself upon the child three times, and cried out to Yahweh, 'Yahweh my God, let this child's life come into him again'" (1 Kings 17:21). The healing described here is known as "contactual magic," which was commonly practiced in the ancient Near East. The same story is told of Elisha, who was summoned by the mother of a child who had died, apparently from the symptoms of sunstroke. Going to the upper chamber where the child lay, and using the same procedure as Elijah, Elisha restored the child to health (2 Kings 4:18–37).

Medical Procedures

Surgical and Medical Procedures

Among ancient surgical procedures is trephination, in which part of the skull is removed without penetrating the soft tissue of the brain. Various techniques included scraping the bone, cutting a rectangular hole, or boring a hole. The operation was performed to relieve pressure caused by intracranial infection, to extract an object imbedded in the skull, or to provide evil spirits with a means of escape. Evidence is that the patient could survive for some time (two years or more) after the surgery, since there are indications of healing. If necessary, the procedure could be repeated. Trephination was a rare procedure in the ancient Near East, where the earliest attested date is the fourth millennium. A trephined skull was found in a cemetery at Wadi Hebran, South Sinai. Chalcolithic skeletal remains at Azor bear the scars from trephination. In a tomb cave in the EB II city at Arad a male skull with a large symmetric depression was found. Three

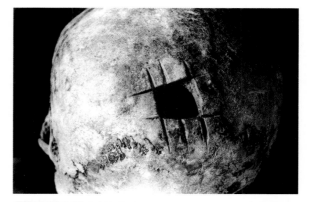
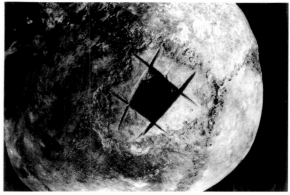

Ill. 30a–b: Two trephined crania with rectangular holes recovered from a mass grave of Iron II (Level III), Lachish. (Courtesy of David Ussishkin; with permission of the Trustees of the British Museum)

trephined crania with rectangular holes were recovered from a mass grave of Iron II (Level III) Lachish[79] (Ill. 30a, b).

In an indictment for violating the Mosaic covenant, Yahweh describes faithless Judah in terms of a victim of deadly assault: "From the sole of the foot to the head, there is no sound spot: wound and welt and gaping gash, not drained, or bandaged, or eased with salve" (Isa. 1:6). This is probably a graphic allusion to certain medical procedures practiced in antiquity. Referring to Nebuchadrezzar's military defeat of Pharaoh Hophra in 588 B.C.E., Yahweh proclaims: "Mortal, I have broken the arm of Pharaoh king of Egypt; it has not been bound up for healing or wrapped with a bandage, so that it may become strong to wield the sword" (Ezek. 30:21). The allusion is to medical treatment, or lack thereof.

Natural Remedies

The Bible describes several natural remedies used in healing. The word *ṣŏrî* (ordinarily "balm," preferably "terebinth resin") appears six times in the Bible, three associated with Gilead in Transjordan (Gen. 37:25; Jer. 8:22; 46:11). It is clear from the six texts that *ṣŏrî* is an export product and a medicine. When Joseph's brothers sat down to eat, "Looking up they saw a caravan of Ishmaelites coming from Gilead, their camels laden with *nĕkō't* ("tragacanth"), *ṣŏrî* ("terebinth resin"), and *lōṭ* ("laudanum"), with which they were on their way down to Egypt" (Gen. 37:25; also 43:11). *ṣŏrî* may have been exported from Gilead to Egypt and Phoenicia, hence the name "balm of Gilead." Then, too, if *ṣŏrî* is terebinth resin from *Pistacia atlantica*, or *palaestina*, this tree grows in Gilead as well as elsewhere. According to Ezekiel 27:17, Israel and Judah exported *ṣŏrî* to Tyre. It was also a highly desirable export to Egypt. For example, the queen of Ugarit sent a jar of *ṣŏrî* to the queen of Egypt, i.e., a "jar of aromatics" (DUG *riq-qu*), *ṣu-ur-wa* (balsam/terebinth resin?). The gloss *ṣu-ur-wa* is cognate with Hebrew *ṣŏrî*.[80] The ton of terebinth resin found in the LB shipwreck at Uluburun (Great Cape) was sent in jars 7.8 liters and 13 liters in size.

Jeremiah associates *ṣŏrî* with Gilead: "Is there no *ṣŏrî* in Gilead? Is there no physician (*rōpē'*) there? Why then has the health of my poor people not been restored?" (Jer. 8:22). This apparently is a sarcastic or rhetorical question. In a judgment on

79. Israel Hershkovitz, "Trephination: The Earliest Case in the Middle East," *Mitekufat Haeven* 20 (1987): 128*–35*. Patricia Smith, "The Trephined Skull from the Early Bronze Age Period at Arad," in A. Eitan, R. Gophna, M. Kochavi, eds., *Eretz-Israel* 21 [Ruth Amiran Volume] (Jerusalem: Israel Exploration Society, 1990), 89*–93*. Joseph Zias, "Three Trephinated Skulls from Jericho," *BASOR* 246 (1982): 55–58.
80. William L. Moran, *The Amarna Letters* (Baltimore: Johns Hopkins University, 1992), 120.

Ill. 31: Colocynth (*Citrullus colocynthis*). A kind of gourd after which some of the architectural designs on the interior of the Solomonic Temple are patterned; also the column bases of the canopy in the gate at Tel Dan. (Courtesy of D. Darom)

Egypt, Yahweh taunts: "Go up to Gilead, and take ṣŏrî, virgin daughter Egypt! In vain you have used many medicines; there is no healing for you" (Jer. 46:11). In an oracle on the destruction of Babylon, Yahweh says: "Suddenly Babylon has fallen and is shattered; wail for her! Bring ṣŏrî for her wound; perhaps she may be healed" (Jer. 51:8). These verses, conjoined with Job's epithet "worthless physicians" (rōp'ê 'ĕlil) (Job 13:4), strongly suggest that in the biblical world physicians and their medications were considered ineffective and that Yahweh was the only true physician (rōpē').[81]

Frankincense (lĕbōnâ, "whiteness") and myrrh (mōr) were used in health care in antiquity; more frequently, however, they were employed in the manufacture of cosmetics and perfumes, and mostly in religious contexts (Ex. 30:34). Frankincense (from Old French *franc encens*, "pure incense") is an aromatic gum resin exuded from Boswellia trees grown in southern Arabia, India, and elsewhere. Imported into Judah from Sheba (Isa. 60:6; Jer. 6:20), frankincense is related to terebinth and to shrubs producing balsam and myrrh. Myrrh is a resin obtained by incising the bark

---

81. Avalos, *Illness and Health Care*, 287–90.

of various trees of the genus *Commiphora*. Besides being a cosmetic, myrrh was used as an ingredient in medicine.

Wild gourds (*paqqu'ōt śādeh*), related to the pumpkin family, are small, melon-like fruits of *Citrullus colocynthis*, a vine that trails in the sand (Ill. 31). This gourd grows in the desert by the Dead Sea, and is probably known as "apple of Sodom." The fruit is poisonous, but the seeds are edible. In small doses the pulp is an effective purgative, but in large doses it can be fatal. There is an intriguing story about Elisha's "company of junior prophets," who in the midst of a famine unknowingly prepared a pot of stew (*sîr hannāzîd*) from wild gourds. It happened after one of them, while gathering herbs for the stew, mistakenly collected the wild gourds (bitter apples) and added them to the stew. "They poured it for the men to eat, and as they were eating the stew they shouted, 'There is death in the pot (*sîr*), man of God!' They could not eat it. Elisha said, 'Then bring some flour (*qemaḥ*).' He threw it into the pot and said, 'Pour out for the men and let them eat.' And now there was nothing harmful in the pot" (2 Kings 4:40–41). By adding *qemaḥ* (flour mixed with water, salt, and leaven) to the already existing stew (lentils or whatever), Elisha was diluting it to the point that each prophet's portion of "bitter apples" would be reduced to a mere purgative rather than a fatal dose.[82]

Religion and Healing

Prayer and Healing

The association of prayer with healing is evident in the Bible. Several of the psalms are petitions for healing; especially the laments attest to the efficacy of prayer in illness. In Psalm 30, a thanksgiving for recovery from serious illness, the connection between prayer and sickness is clear: "Yahweh my God, I cried to you for help, and you have healed me (*rāpā'*)" (v. 3 [E.T. v. 2]). Psalm 38 is a plea for healing by one whose sickness is real, not merely metaphorical: "There is no soundness in my flesh because of your indignation; there is no health in my bones because of my sin" (v. 4 [E.T. v. 3]); "my wounds grow foul and fester because of my foolishness" (v. 6 [E.T. v. 5]); "for my loins are filled with burning, and there is no soundness in my flesh" (v. 8 [E.T. v. 7]).

Isaiah's description of Hezekiah's illness and his prayer for healing is classic. When Hezekiah became sick and was near death, Yahweh through Isaiah told him to get his affairs in order, "for you shall die; you shall not recover." Then Hezekiah prayed to Yahweh, who answered him: "I have heard your prayer, I have seen your tears; I will add fifteen years to your life" (Isa. 38:1–5).

---

82. Hepper, *Baker Encyclopedia of Bible Plants*, 152.

Healing Cults

In several ancient cultures, dogs were associated with a healing cult. At Ashkelon excavators uncovered a dog cemetery containing 1,500 partial or complete dog burials, perhaps associated with Phoenician deities. Each dog was interred with care, placed on its side in a shallow pit (Ill. 32). The pottery in the matrix into which the dogs were interred reveals a fifth-century B.C.E. date for these burials. These dogs, resembling today's Bedouin sheepdogs, were honored as sacred animals. The instinct of dogs to lick their wounds as a way of promoting the healing process suggests their association with curative powers. Stager suggests that the Ashkelon cult had dogs like

the Mesopotamian Gula (goddess of healing) cult and the Phoenician cult at Kition. "Dogs" (*klbm*) and "puppies" (*grm*) were part of a Phoenician healing cult. The latter are mentioned on a mid-fifth-century B.C.E. limestone plaque, found at Kition on Cyprus, inscribed in Phoenician (*Corpus Inscriptionum Semiticarum* 86–90). These "healing" dogs roamed freely about the premises of the Phoenician temple there.[83] Deuteronomy may be condemning a cult similar to the one practiced at Kition. "You shall not bring the 'price of a harlot,' or the 'wages of a dog' into the house of Yahweh your God in payment of any vow; for both of these are an abomination to Yahweh your God"

Ill. 32: Dog burial from Phoenician Ashkelon, from fifth century B.C.E. (Courtesy of the Leon Levy Expedition to Ashkelon; Photo: L. Stager)

---

83. Lawrence E. Stager, "Why Were Hundreds of Dogs Buried at Ashkelon?" *BAR* 17 (1991): 26–42.

(Deut. 23:19 [E.T. 18]). This censure suggests that some sort of cult featured healing dogs that roamed about the premises of the Jerusalem Temple.

Another type of healing cult is implied in the story of Hezekiah's reform of religious practices in Judah: [Hezekiah] "removed the high places (*bāmôt*), broke down the pillars (*maṣṣēbōt*), and cut down the sacred pole (*'ăšērâ*). He smashed (*kittat*) the bronze snake (*nĕḥaš hannĕḥōšet*) that Moses had made, for until those days the people of Israel were offering sacrifices (*mĕqaṭṭĕrîm*) to it; it was called Nehuštan" (2 Kings 18:4).

The purpose of the bronze snake was therapeutic. Before Hezekiah's religious reform, healing rituals were held in the Jerusalem Temple. The Israelites offered sacrifices to Nehuštan, the name Hezekiah gave to the bronze snake. "Nehuštan" is a play on words: *nĕḥōšet*, "bronze/copper," and *nāḥāš*, "snake." It had to be destroyed after becoming an object of worship. Nehuštan was identified in Judahite tradition with the standard crafted by Moses in the wilderness as an antidote to snake bites (Num. 21:4–9). According to the latter account, when the Israelites were bitten by poisonous (fiery) snakes (*nĕḥāšîm śĕrāpîm*), they would look at the bronze snake (*nĕḥaš nĕḥōšet*) formed by Moses at Yahweh's direction and would live.

The "poisonous" snakes are the *śĕrāpîm* (from *śārap*, "to burn"). In Isaiah 14:29 and 30:6, the *śārāp* is a flying snake. Othmar Keel rightly identifies *śĕrāpîm* with uraei with wings, that is, flying cobras.[84] Isaiah 6 refers to *śĕrāpîm* as flying cobras stationed above the cherubim throne of God (*mimma'al lô*) and singing, "Holy, holy, holy is Yahweh of hosts" (Isa. 6:3). They protect themselves from the aura of the deity with their wings. Each seraph has six wings: with one pair he covers his face; with another pair he covers his genitalia ("feet"); and with a third pair he flies. Thus, as Jon Levenson notes, the "call" of Isaiah involves a visionary experience in which Temple imagery comes alive—uraei with wings are *śĕrāpîm*, and probably *śārāp* and Nehuštan (bronze snake with wings) are related.[85] If *śārāp* equals "winged cobra" equals "Nehuštan," then the snake (*nāḥāš*) in the Garden of Eden story was originally winged and, like the *śĕrāpîm*, could talk or sing. When God demotes the snake, he clips his wings and makes him crawl on his belly. Nehuštan was there in the garden sanctuary of the Temple until Hezekiah smashed (*kittat*) it.

---

84. Othmar Keel, *Jahwe-Visionen und Siegelkunst* (Stuttgart: Verlag Katholisches Bibelwerk, 1977), 70–115.

85. Jon D. Levenson, *Sinai and Zion* (Minneapolis: Winston, 1985), 122–24.

CHAPTER 3

The Means of Existence

The Bible portrays Canaan as "a land of wheat and barley, of vines and fig trees and pomegranates, a land of olive trees and honey, a land where you [Israelites] may eat bread without scarcity" (Deut. 8:8–9). According to Ezekiel 27:17, Judah and the "land of Israel" exported wheat, figs, fruit honey,[1] olive oil, and ṣŏrî ("turpentine resin" or "turpentine"). Genesis 43:11 reports that the land's best products were brought by Joseph's brothers as gifts to Egypt: ṣŏrî, děbaš ("honey"), nĕkō't ("tragacanth"), lōṭ ("laudanum"), boṭnîm ("pistachios"), and šĕqēdîm ("almonds").[2]

This description of the fruits of the Promised Land has a striking parallel in the story of Sinuhe and the fruits of the land of Yaa. Sinuhe, an Egyptian official in the court of Amenemhet I, left his country voluntarily to settle in the fertile land of Yaa (probably Canaan). He provides information on the political and social conditions about 2000–1900 B.C.E.: "It was a good land, named Yaa. Figs were in it, and grapes. It had more wine than water. Plentiful was its honey, abundant its olives. Every (kind of) fruit was on its trees. Barley was there, and emmer" (*ANET*, 19).

The Bible affirms that the land of Israel belonged to God, but it was entrusted to the kings and their subjects. As the representative of the heavenly king, the earthly king was looked upon as the owner of the agricultural land. Agriculture, the basis of the economy in ancient Israel, influenced practically every facet of daily life, especially the religious, economic, legal, and social spheres. To describe the various aspects of daily life, biblical texts refer constantly to agriculture in the literal sense, and almost as often to agriculture in the figurative, allegorical, or symbolic sense. Amos describes the new age in terms of the fertility of the land when the crops will be so abundant that the agricultural activities of one season will hardly be finished in time for the next. "The time is surely coming, says Yahweh, when the one who

---

1. Jacob Milgrom, *Leviticus 1–16*, AB 3 (New York: Doubleday, 1991), 189–90.
2. Harold N. Moldenke and Alma L. Moldenke, *Plants of the Bible* (New York: Ronald Press, 1952), 51–52, 77. F. Nigel Hepper, *Baker Encyclopedia of Bible Plants* (Grand Rapids: Baker Book House, 1992), 147–48.

plows shall overtake the one who reaps, and the vintager the one who sows the seed. Grape juice (*'āsîs*) will drip down the mountains, and all the hills will run with it" (Amos 9:13).

Israel's cultic calendar appears in the Pentateuch with substantial variations, but basically the traditional calendar of feasts is associated with agricultural life. The revised liturgical calendar of Deuteronomy (16:16–17) stipulates the pilgrim character of the festivals. Passover (*pesaḥ*) and the feast of Unleavened Bread, originally two separate rites, celebrated the barley harvest. The feast of Weeks or Pentecost (*šābu'ôt*) marked the completion of the wheat harvest. Tabernacles (*sukkôt*), an autumnal festival, celebrated the completion of agricultural work; the early name of this feast was Ingathering (Ex. 23:16). The designations "Tabernacles" or "Booths" derive from the practice of living in booths close at hand during the seven days of the festival. In addition to these annual observances, many of the sacrifices and offerings associated with the cult were agricultural in nature (Num. 18:8–32).

FARMING AND ANIMAL HUSBANDRY

Physical Geography and Climate

Climate has a significant impact on the activities of daily life, especially on agriculture. The climate of Palestine is subtropical and has not changed notably since biblical times. Winds in Palestine come prevailingly from the west, the Mediterranean westerlies. As a general rule, rainfall decreases from north to south, and from west to east. Yet, while rainfall generally decreases the greater the distance from the sea, there are Mediterranean zones east of the Jordan Valley, such as parts of Gilead, Ammon, and Moab, that have as much rainfall as areas to the west of the Jordan.

In an agricultural society at the mercy of the vagaries of rainfall, the timing of the rain is as significant as the amount. That it rained at the proper time from the perspective of the farmer was critical, as indicated in Jeremiah's charge: "They [rebellious people] do not say in their hearts, 'Let us fear Yahweh our God, who gives the rain in its season, the autumn rain and the spring rain, and keeps for us the weeks appointed for the harvest'" (Jer. 5:24). Palestine has only two seasons—the dry season in summer, from May–June through September, when there is usually no rain; and the wet season from mid-October through March, with most of Palestine's rainfall occurring between November and February.

Indicative of the vital importance of rainfall for agriculture is the fact that Hebrew has several words for rain. *māṭār* denotes rain in general. *yôreh* and *malqôš* bracket the beginning and end of the rainy season. "Then he [Yahweh] will give the rain (*měṭar*) for your land in its season, the early rain (*yôreh*) and the later rain (*malqôš*), and you will gather in your grain, your wine, and your oil" (Deut. 11:14). *yôreh*, the early rain arriving in the autumn, softens the ground, preparing the soil for plowing and sowing. *gešem*, the heavy winter rain, soaks the ground and replenishes the cisterns. *malqôš*, the later spring rain, fosters the growth of wheat and barley.

Dew (*ṭal*), the condensation of atmospheric moisture, provides a valuable supplement to rainfall, especially where there is no rain or where rainfall is inadequate. Biblical texts and scientific experiments conducted in the Negev attest that plants benefit from dew. Deuteronomy 33:28 acknowledges its importance: "So Israel lives in safety, untroubled is Jacob's abode in a land of grain and wine, where the heavens drop down dew."

Despite ample rain, the crops were subject to failure from drought, diseases, or locusts, as the prophets frequently mention. Locusts consume almost every plant in their path, and their carcasses obstruct wells and streams.[3] Both Amos (7:1) and Joel (1:4; 2:5) speak of the devastating results of a locust plague; it was the occasion of Joel's oracle: "What the cutting locust (*gāzām*) left, the swarming locust ('*arbeh*) has eaten. What the swarming locust left, the hopping locust (*yāleq*) has eaten, and what the hopping locust left, the destroying locust (*ḥāsîl*) has eaten" (Joel 1:4). The Bible has a dozen words for "locust," '*arbeh* being the generic term; but their specific identification is mostly conjecture. For example, commentators disagree on whether the four words in Joel (above) refer to different growth stages of the insect or to different species.

When allocating the land of Canaan among the tribes of Israel, Joshua assigned the "hill country" (*har*) to the "house of Joseph" (Josh. 17:18). This topographical designation refers to the central ridge or backbone of Palestine, situated between the Coastal Plain and the Jordan Valley. When the Israelites settled in the hilly terrain, they had to deforest the slopes and replace the trees with artificial terraces in order to create enough arable land. Labor-intensive to construct and maintain, terraces serve to retain soil and at the same time to conserve the rain water. Trees and vines are better suited to these narrow terraced slopes; cereals, to the broader plains and valleys.

The Agricultural Year

Archaeology and paleobotany together provide valuable information about the agricultural life of ancient Israel. During his excavations at Gezer, R. A. S. Macalister discovered a small limestone plaque, which has become known as the Gezer Calendar (Ill. 33). Dating to the second half of the tenth century (Solomon's reign), it is one of the oldest Hebrew inscriptions. This seven-line tablet describes agricultural operations

---

3. Certain species of locust are edible, and even considered a delicacy eaten raw or roasted.

Ill. 33: Gezer Calendar. Inscribed limestone in Hebrew found at Gezer, tenth century B.C.E. (Courtesy of Z. Radovan)

during the course of twelve months, with time subdivided by the seasonal farming activities. Referring to the months of the year not by their names but by the harvest associated with them, the Gezer Calendar is based on a twelve-month cycle beginning in the autumn. Eight periods are enumerated, starting with the ingathering of autumn fruits. Four of the seasons extend for two-month periods, and four are of one-month duration.

In addition to linguistic problems, scholars continue to dispute the purpose of the Gezer Calendar. On the basis of Egyptian and Mesopotamian parallels, William Albright described the Gezer Calendar as a "school exercise," arguing that the plaque was just large enough to fit into the hand of an adolescent. He also suggested that the rounded edges of the tablet resulted from regular use and that the scribe's hand was slow and awkward.[4] Albright's translation of the text reads:

> His two months are (olive) harvest,
> His two months are planting (grain),
> His two months are late planting;
> His month is hoeing up of flax,
> His month is harvest of barley,
> His month is harvest and feasting;
> His two months are vine-tending,
> His month is summer fruit. (*ANET*, 320)

The use of "his month" to refer to the month when one works at a specific occupation is idiomatic in Hebrew, according to Albright. As an example: "Those officials supplied provisions for King Solomon and for all who came to King Solomon's table, each one in his month (*ḥodšô*)" (1 Kings 5:7 [E.T. 4:27]). Note that the calendar begins in the fall with the olive harvest (cf. the New Year's festival).

When the first rain came in October–November and the ground was sufficiently softened, the farmer began to break up the soil with a scratch plow. At the same time he would broadcast the seed from a basket, followed then by a second plowing to cover the grain. At harvest time the farmer would grasp the stalks of grain by hand and cut them with a curved hand-sickle fitted with several flint blades. In later times

4. William F. Albright, "The Gezer Calendar," *BASOR* 92 (1943): 16–26.

Ill. 34: Threshing sledge with basalt teeth in a wooden frame, still being used at Tell el-Far'ah (N). (Courtesy of L. E. Stager)

an iron sickle with a wooden handle was used. Allusions to the process occur in various texts: "Begin to count the seven weeks from the time the sickle (*ḥermēš*) is first put to the standing grain" (Deut. 16:9). "Cut off from Babylon the sower, and the wielder of the sickle (*maggāl*) in time of harvest" (Jer. 50:16).

At harvest time the stalks (*'ŏmārîm*) were stacked in sheaves (*'ălummîm*) and brought by cart to the threshing floor. Describing his dream to his brothers, Joseph said: "There we were, binding sheaves (*'ălummîm*) in the field" (Gen. 37:7). The psalmist rhapsodizes: "Those who go out weeping, bearing the seed for sowing, shall come home with shouts of joy, carrying their sheaves (*'ălummōtâw*)" (Ps. 126:6). The threshing of the cereal took place on open, level surfaces, often elevated to catch the breeze needed for winnowing. Sometimes the threshing floor (*gōren*) was located near the city gate: "Now the king of Israel and King Jehoshaphat of Judah were sitting on their thrones, arrayed in their robes, at the threshing floor (*gōren*) at the entrance of the gate of Samaria" (1 Kings 22:10). Threshing sledges fitted with flint studs or basalt embedded in wooden boards and drawn by oxen or donkeys were used to thresh the grain from the stalks (Deut. 25:4). The straw and chaff were separated from the grain by winnowing, that is, tossing the threshed grain into the air so the wind would carry away the chaff. Isaiah describes how Israel would figuratively thresh its enemies: "I [Yahweh] will make of you a threshing sledge, sharp, new, and having teeth; you shall thresh the mountains and crush them, and you shall make the hills like chaff" (Isa. 41:15). According to tradition, David bought a threshing floor on Mount Moriah from the Jebusite Araunah as a site for an altar (2 Sam. 24:16–25), and later Solomon built the Temple there (2 Chron. 3:1).

Ill. 35: Wheat-threshing scene with oxen pulling threshing sled; the hill-top village in background. (Reconstruction: © L. E. Stager; Illustration: C. S. Alexander)

Granaries and silos were used for grain storage. Constructed below or above ground, some were owned publicly and others privately. Storage pits, stone-lined or plastered, were common in the LB and Iron Ages. Food, both liquid and dry commodities, in Iron I was also stored in collared pithoi and other large vessels. Small, plastered subterranean granaries were uncovered at Gezer in the Bronze and Iron Ages. A large subterranean silo with a pair of winding stairs was found at Megiddo in Str III (ca. 725 B.C.E.), a time when the city was under Assyrian rule. John Holladay estimates that this storage pit (no. 1414) contained 346 metric tons of wheat, capable of sustaining 1,178 people for a year.[5] Such a large silo at Megiddo may reflect "Assyrian" government storage, not local Israelite practice. For the silos at Tell Beit Mirsim, Holladay estimates a capacity of one metric ton each. If the household located in SE 12-22-13-33 or 23 controlled thirty-four of these sunken silos, and they were all in use at the same time, it would amount to a total potential storage capacity of thirty-four metric tons of grain. Large, brick-lined pits up to two meters in diameter and two meters deep containing the remnants of wheat were uncovered in the Persian period level (Str VA) at Tell el-Hesi. At Tell Jemmeh, a vast grain-storage depot dating to the Hellenistic period was found. Of the more than ten large, circular mud-brick granaries at Jemmeh, the estimated capacity of one granary was 132 metric tons.

Tripartite pillared buildings dating to Iron II have been excavated at several sites, including Tell el-Hesi, Megiddo, Hazor, Beth-Shemesh, and Tel Sheva. They have been variously interpreted as storehouses, stables, bazaars, or barracks. In Stager's opinion, the reason there are so many different interpretations of their function is that they all might be correct. The two rows of pillars are needed for structural purposes. To span greater widths found between aisles of pillared buildings would require very tall timbers. Thus the function of these three-aisled buildings can be determined only on a case-by-case basis. A recent discovery supporting pillared buildings as mercantile bazaars, according to excavator Moshe Kochavi, was made at Tel Hadar ("splendid hill") on the eastern bank of the Sea of Galilee in the biblical land of Geshur.[6] Kochavi excavated two public buildings (eleventh century B.C.E.) that shared one wall: a tripartite, pillared structure and a solid-wall, tripartite building containing carbonized wheat grains, presumably a granary. A common entrance

---

5. John S. Holladay, "The Kingdoms of Israel and Judah: Political and Economic Centralization in the Iron IIA-B (ca. 1000–750 B.C.E.)," in T. E. Levy, ed. *The Archaeology of Society in the Holy Land* (New York: Facts on File, 1995), 377–78, 398.

6. Larry G. Herr, "Tripartite Pillared Buildings and the Market Place in Iron Age Palestine." *BASOR* 272 (1988): 47–67. Moshe Kochavi, "Divided Structures Divide Scholars," *BAR* 25 (1999): 44–50. Compare Moshe Kochavi, "The Eleventh Century B.C.E. Tripartite Pillar Building at Tel Hadar," in S. Gitin, A. Mazar, and E. Stern, eds., *Mediterranean Peoples in Transition* (Jerusalem: Israel Exploration Society, 1998), 468–78.

served the two adjacent buildings. A second tripartite building with solid internal walls instead of pillars was also found, presumably a storehouse. Kochavi estimates thirty-five tripartite pillared buildings at twelve sites and suggests that they were the "ancient equivalent of shopping malls."

Agricultural Tools

The farmer's most important tool was the plow (*maḥărēšâ* or *maḥărešet*), which was invented more than 5,000 years ago. Its construction style, well known in Palestine at the turn of the twentieth century C.E., probably changed very little from the time of its invention until then. The ancient plow consisted of a pole made from a tree of hard wood such as the oak, a stick for the handle, a blade or share with a metal tip (*'ēt*), and a horizontal yoke. Referred to as a "scratch plow" (from the root *ḥāraš*, "to engrave"), it was ideally suited to the Near Eastern and Mediterranean environment and soils, particularly where the soil was shallow in the hill country. Plowing prepared the ground for sowing in late October–November, after the first rain (*yôreh*) had softened the earth. A field was plowed twice, once to loosen the crusty soil before the seed was broadcast, and then at right angles to the first plowing to cover the seed. The metal-tipped scratch plow did not turn over the soil the way a moldboard plow does but simply scratched a shallow furrow by breaking and loosening the soil. Iron plowpoints dating to the eleventh century have been discovered in Gibeah (Tell el-Ful), and iron plowshares dating to the tenth century were found at Tell Jemmeh, Beth-Shemesh, and Tell en-Naṣbeh.[7]

Oxen, the ordinary draft animals in biblical times, were connected to the plow by a yoke (*môṭâ*; *'ōl*), a wooden crossbar attached with ropes to the neck of the oxen. The two-oxen team was customary in the Levant, although some teams were larger. We read that Elijah came upon Elisha when he was plowing, and "there were twelve yoke of oxen ahead of him [Elisha], and he was with the twelfth" (1 Kings 19:19). The Mosaic law forbade yoking an ox (*šôr*) and a donkey (*ḥămôr*) (Deut. 22:10); apparently commingling dissimilar things was considered contrary to the created order. An ox goad made of wood, sometimes with a metal spur on one end and a plow cleaner on the other, served as a prod for the cattle. Oxen were castrated to make them more docile as draft animals.

Plowing is the source of many metaphors in the Bible. The best known concerns the conversion of swords into "plowpoints" as a sign of peace (Isa. 2:4); and the

---

7. Jane C. Waldbaum, *From Bronze to Iron* (Göteborg: Paul Åströms Förlag, 1978), 27: "A total of over 290 examples of iron come from Iron I sites in Palestine. Of these, over 20 are of 12th century date, 78 from the 11th century, and over 192 are of 10th century date. This represents almost a fourfold increase from the 11th century over the 12th, and a more than twofold increase again in the 10th century."

Ill. 36: Cache of six iron agricultural tools, including a pair of two-pronged plow points, left and center rear. A single-pronged plow point, right rear, a knife with rivets leaning against the single-pronged plow point, a sickle blade, right, in front of the knife; a second sickle blade behind meter stick. In 604 B.C.E. destruction, Tel Miqne-Ekron, Str IB. (Courtesy of Tel Miqne-Ekron Excavation/Publication Project; Photo: I. Sztulman)

opposite as a sign of war (Joel 4:10 [E.T. 3:10]). Note also Samson's response replete with sexual innuendo: "If you had not plowed with my heifer, you would not have guessed my riddle" (Judg. 14:18).

Cultivation and Processing of Edibles

The Israelite diet consisted mainly of grains, vegetables, fruits, and condiments. The chief crops in biblical times were wheat (*ḥiṭṭâ*), barley (*śĕʿōrâ*), olives (*zêtîm*), and grapes (*ʿănābîm*). Cereal cultivation preceded cultivation of fruit trees; cereals, the main part of the diet, were among the earliest domesticated plants. Grain could be eaten parched or raw, mostly in the form of bread or porridge (e.g., cream of wheat). "You shall eat no bread (*leḥem*) or parched grain (*qālî*) or fresh ears (*karmel*) until that very day, until you have brought the offering of your God" (Lev. 23:14; also 2 Kings 4:42). *qālî* designates wheat or barley roasted on a griddle and eaten without additional preparation. "Jesse said to his son David, 'Take for your brothers an ephah of this parched grain (*qālî*) and these ten loaves (*leḥem*), and carry them quickly to the camp to your brothers'" (1 Sam. 17:17).

The legumes consist mainly of lentils (*ʿădāšîm*), fava beans (*pôl*), and chickpeas (ḥimmĕṣîm [Arab. ḥummuṣ]). The vegetables include cucumbers (qiššu'îm), watermelon ('ăbaṭṭîḥîm), onions (bĕṣālîm), leeks (ḥāṣîr), and garlic (šûmîm).

The principal fruit trees are the olive (zayit) and the grapevine (gepen), both playing a key role in the economy. Other fruit trees include the date palm (tāmār), pomegranate (rimmôn), fig (tĕ'ēnâ), and sycamore (šiqmâ).

Grains

Several species of wheat, the staple of the diet, were cultivated: einkorn (*Triticum monococcum*); emmer (*Triticum dicoccum* equals biblical *kussemet*); bread wheat (*Triticum aestivum*); and hard wheat (*Triticum durum*). Bread wheat, a hybrid derived from emmer, was commonly grown in Iron II. Hard wheat became the primary wheat of the Mediterranean basin. The various words for wheat and their specific meaning are difficult to define, since the Bible provides so little detail, compared with the well-known cuisine of Mesopotamia with its extant recipes. Barley (*Hordeum vulgare*), coarser than wheat and inferior, was considered the bread of the poor; it was also fed to animals (1 Kings 5:8; [E.T. 4:28]). This plentiful cereal was harvested two weeks before wheat, in late April and early May. Barley was more salt resistant and could be grown in more marginal, semiarid zones; also it matures early and is more adaptable to environmental fluctuations. Wheat requires more water and soil that is less saline than barley.

The processing of grain was a chore performed by women, servants, or slaves. "Take the millstones and grind (ṭāḥan) meal, remove your veil, strip off your robe, uncover your legs" (Isa. 47:2). "Every firstborn in the land of Egypt shall die, from the firstborn of the Pharaoh who sits on his throne to the firstborn of the female slave who is behind the handmill (rēḥayim)" (Ex. 11:5). After the Philistines seized Samson and gouged out his eyes, they brought him down to Gaza and shackled him, "and he was put to grinding (ṭāḥan) in the prison" (Judg. 16:21). It was common practice to humiliate prisoners of war by forcing them to grind with a handmill. Lamentations 5:13 describes how the Babylonians treated Jerusalem captives in the same manner after the conquest of 586 B.C.E.: "Young men carry the millstones (ṭĕḥôn), boys stagger under loads of wood."

In Iron Age houses, an area was reserved on the ground floor for the preparation and storage of food. The grain was ground daily into flour in preparation for cooking and baking. Grinding grain for bread was so essential for daily life that biblical law stipulated that the grinding stone could not be taken in pledge: "No one shall take a mill (rēḥayim) or an upper millstone (rākeb) in pledge, for that would be taking a life in pledge" (Deut. 24:6). It was foretold that during the Babylonian captivity there would no longer be "the sound of the millstones (qôl rēḥayim) and the light of the lamp" (Jer. 25:10). In other words, bread and light—basic necessities of life—would be lacking.

The handmill or saddle-quern (*rēḥāyim* [dual ending]) consists of two stone slabs: *pelaḥ taḥtît* is the bottom, larger stone; *pelaḥ rekeb* is the upper, smaller, grinding stone, which fits into the hand of the miller and is sometimes known as the "rider." The lower stone is rectangular and slightly concave (hence the term "saddle-quern"). The grain is placed upon the bottom stone, and the grinder kneeling in front of the quern moves the upper stone back and forth over the fixed horizontal stone. Grinding stones were commonly crafted from black basalt. The millstone could also become a lethal weapon; a woman deliberately dropped an upper millstone (*pelaḥ rekeb*) on Abimelech's head, crushing his skull (Judg. 9:53).

qemaḥ designates the ordinary flour produced from the grinding of the grains of cereal plants. This meal is normally made from wheat, but sometimes from barley. *sōlet*, according to commentators, signifies the more costly fine flour made from the inner kernels of wheat and used for sacrifices and special occasions. Milgrom, however, makes a sound argument when he identifies *sōlet* with semolina or grits, the coarse particles of wheat left after the sifting process.[8] Sarah used *qemaḥ sōlet* (*sōlet* is a gloss on *qemaḥ*) to make the cakes (*'ugôt*) for the three strangers who visited Abraham by the oaks of Mamre in Hebron (Gen. 18:6). Solomon's daily provisions also included *sōlet* and *qemaḥ* (1 Kings 5:2 [E.T. 1 Kings 4:22]). According to the account of the Aramean siege of Samaria, *sōlet* was twice as expensive as barley: a *sĕ'â* (ca. 7 liters) of *sōlet* sold for a shekel, and two *sā'tāyim* of barley for a shekel (2 Kings 7:16, 18). Hildegard Lewy, commenting on Old Assyrian cereal names, notes: "In the Near East, ancient as well as modern, wheat and wheat products serve as food of the privileged, whereas barley and barley products are consumed by the lower income groups."[9]

Olive Tree

In Abimelech's parable (Judg. 9:8–9) the olive tree was the first to be asked to rule over all the trees. The hardy, long-lived olive tree is an evergreen growing five to eight meters high and with a trunk up to one meter wide. Found mainly in the highlands and in the foothills between the coastal plain and the central mountain range, the olive tree thrives in the rocky, shallow soil of the hillsides during the Mediterranean's hot, dry summers and cool, rainy winters. It requires an average annual temperature of fifteen degrees centigrade (fifty-nine degrees fahrenheit). Because olives can be grown on mountain slopes with very little soil, the tree does not compete with cereals for fertile, arable soil. The olive tree grows in the Levant but not in Egypt or Mesopotamia, because a certain chill, needed to cause the olives to mature, cannot

---

8. Milgrom, *Leviticus*, 3, 179.
9. Hildegard Lewy, "On Some Old Assyrian Cereal Names," *JAOS* 76 (1956): 203.

be achieved in the warmer climes. It takes years for olive trees to mature to full, producing trees, and then they bear fruit only every other year. It is commonly said that one plants an olive yard not for one's self but for one's grandchildren. Trees begin to flower only after five or six years.

Evidence for a wild olive processing site from the PPN has been found on the sea floor at Maritime 'Atlit south of Haifa, inundated in the mid-sixth millennium, probably by a worldwide flood, after the olives had been processed.[10] Fossilized stones of domesticated olive have been found as early as the Chalcolithic period at Teleilat el-Ghassul, close to Jericho. Olives are handpicked, shaken, or beaten from the tree with a long pole. "When you beat (*ḥābaṭ*) your olive trees, do not strip what is left; it shall be for the alien, the orphan, and the widow" (Deut. 24:20). The olive presses, often rock-hewn, are commonly located in the vicinity of the olive groves.

The production of olive oil was a major industry, accounting for much of the economic prosperity of the region. Surplus oil was exported to Egypt, Phoenicia, and perhaps even to Greece. Hosea refers to the export of oil to Egypt, where the olive tree does not grow (Hos. 12:2 [E.T. 12:1]). Excavations at two important Philistine sites—Ekron (Tel Miqne) and Timnah (Tel Batash)—have shed considerable light on the production of olive oil in Iron II. Occupants of both cities were engaged in the olive-oil industry. The Philistine city-state of Ekron, situated in the inner coastal plain of Philistia on the border of Judah, was perhaps the premier producer of olive oil in the ancient Near East.[11] Having discovered there more than a hundred presses for extracting the olive oil, archaeologists speculate that Ekron produced a thousand tons of oil annually, mostly for export (Ill. 37, 38). Pierced stone drums (once mistakenly identified as dyeing vats for textiles at Tell Beit Mirsim) are now known to be connected with olive-oil pressing.

The picked olives are first crushed and then pressed. In the case of virgin oil they are crushed, not pulverized, to avoid getting pulp-paste into the oil. Crushing is achieved by rolling a large stone (the crushing stone, or *memel*, which could also be used as a roof-roller) over the olives spread on a flat rock-cut installation or on the floor of a rectangular crushing basin (*yām*). Oil from the first crushing produces virgin oil known as *šmn rḥṣ* (literally "washed oil"), mentioned several times in the Samaria ostraca. The oil was extracted by pouring hot water over the crushed olives, stirring the mixture, and then skimming the floating oil off by hand. *šemen rāḥūṣ* equals "crush and wash"; whereas *šemen zayit zāk kātît* (Ex. 27:20; Lev. 24:2) equals "crush only": both equal virgin oil. The first oil from the batch of olives is superior; the quality declines with successive pressings.

---

10. Ehud Galili, "Prehistoric Site on the Sea Floor," *NEAEHL*, 1:120–22.

11. Seymour Gitin, "Ekron of the Philistines, Part II: Olive Oil Suppliers to the World," *BAR* 16/2 (1990): 32–42, 59.

Ill. 37: Olive oil press, composed of crushing basin flanked by two pressing vats, opposite each of which are four perforated stone weights. (Courtesy of Tel Miqne-Ekron Excavation/Publication Project; Photo: D. Guthrie)

After the virgin oil is extracted by cracking and crushing, the second-grade oil is produced by pressing the pulp with a beam-press. The crushed olives are placed in woven baskets (*'ăqālîm*) with holes in the bottom. The baskets are then covered with a stone and placed on the pressing surface. Pressure is exerted on the olives by means of a long beam weighted with stones and secured in a wall niche. The olive oil flows initially through the basket openings into a groove. Cylindrical vats (*gittôt*) are directly below baskets piled high. This type of oil press was used extensively in Iron II.

Practically every aspect of daily life of both rich and poor was affected by the olive tree. Olive oil was utilized in a variety of ways: as a dietary staple, medicine, and fuel for ceramic lamps; as a base for cosmetics, perfumes, and oils; and in ritual contexts, such as the anointing of kings at their coronation, as libation offerings, and as fuel for sanctuary lamps. The olive press in the sacred precinct at Tel Dan provided oil

Ill. 38: Reconstruction of olive oil press, Tel Miqne-Ekron. Note straw baskets stacked on pressing vat with wooden lever and stone weights. (Courtesy of Tel Miqne-Ekron Excavation/Publication Project; Drawing: E. Cohen)

for lighting the lamps and for votive offerings in the temple. Olive wood was used, as today, for making furniture, paneling, and statues.

Grapevine

The earliest evidence for the cultivation of the vine dates from EB I. Grape presses carved in bedrock in the Levant date as early as the third millennium.

The story of Noah describes him as the first to plant a vineyard (Gen. 9:20), suggesting Anatolia, the traditional location of the mountains of Ararat, as the site where viticulture originated. In fact, the Levant and the Aegean were two of the earliest centers of grape cultivation. The Assyrian records make no mention of wine in the Bronze Age. In contrast, wine culture was well developed in the period of the Neo-Assyrian empire during the first half of the first millennium, where by the ninth century wine was popular but expensive.[12] During the first millennium there is evidence of "a well developed wine culture not only in Syria but all along the borderlands between Turkey in the north and Syria and Iraq to the south."[13] A hot, dry climate is not conducive to the cultivation of grapes. In Mesopotamia, grapevines could be nurtured only in the north, notably in the region of Carchemish. With the exception of some oases, vineyards do not grow well in Egypt; therefore the Egyptians imported much of their wine from the Levant and Greece.

Because it requires several years before vines yield grapes of high quality, only a stable society can successfully engage in productive viticulture and exploit its economic advantages, especially in export. Some continuity over time is also required for the labor-intensive task of building and maintaining the hillside terraces on which the vineyards thrive and grow during the summer drought. Stone watchtowers (*migdālîm*) were constructed in the vineyards to guard the ripening fruit. During the harvest season the Israelites lodged in booths made from branches and vines, from which practice the feast of Booths developed.

'*ēnāb* (pl. '*ănābîm*) is the common Hebrew word for "grape." *śōrēq* designates a special kind of dark red grape from the vines of the Soreq Valley in the foothills southwest of Jerusalem (Isa. 5:2; Jer. 2:21). '*āsîs* may be the juice that is naturally exuded by the weight of the grape pile; thus the comment that it "flows down the mountain side" (Amos 9:13; see above). It would be the grape counterpart of virgin oil.

Vine cultivation is done not from seeds but from plant cuttings and shoots, and grapevines were manipulated in several ways. The vines could be draped over a trellis, or trained to climb trees, or allowed to trail on the ground, or worked in a vine-

---

12. David Stronach, "The Imagery of the Wine Bowl: Wine in Assyria in the Early First Millennium B.C.," in P. E. McGovern, S. J. Fleming, and S. H. Katz, eds., *The Origins and Ancient History of Wine* (Amsterdam: Overseas Publishers Association, 1995), 192.

13. Marvin A. Powell, "Wine and the Vine in Ancient Mesopotamia: The Cuneiform Evidence," in McGovern, Fleming, and Katz, eds., *The Origins and Ancient History of Wine*, 121.

Ill. 39: Tomb of Nakht of Thebes, dated late fifteenth century B.C.E. Trapping, plucking, and butchering the geese (lower right), gathering grapes, treading and storing wine in "Canaanite jars" with stoppers (scene above). (Courtesy of the Egyptian Expedition of the Metropolitan Museum of Art, Rogers Fund, 1915)

yard (*kerem*). To plant a vineyard was a sign of permanent settlement. As assurance of restoration to Judah, Yahweh predicts that "houses and fields and vineyards shall again be bought in this land" (Jer. 32:15). Isaiah provides a detailed picture of viti-culture as he recounts a parable about a vineyard planted with "choice vines" (*śōrēq*), although in this case it proved to be unfruitful (Isa. 5:1–7). Despite careful cultiva-tion, the vineyard produced only "wild grapes" (*bě'ušîm*, literally "rotten grapes," from the root *b'š*, "to stink"). The prophet reveals that the useless vineyard in this parable represents the faithless house of Israel, which failed to respond to the tender love of the vineyard keeper, pictured here as Yahweh.

The early grapes ripen in June or July, and the vintage season occurs in August and September. In ancient Israel, harvesting the grapes was apparently a joyous occasion accompanied by celebrating, feasting, shouting, and rejoicing as the family members treaded the grapes, slipping and sliding in their bare feet. In a lament over the destruc-tion of the vineyards of Moab, Isaiah says: "Joy and gladness are taken away from the fruitful field; and in the vineyard no songs are sung, no shouts are raised" (Isa. 16:10; also Jer. 48:33). The story recorded in Judges 21 suggests that during the

Ill. 40: Terracotta portable wine press (*'arevah*) from Ashdod, eighth century B.C.E. (Courtesy of the Israel Museum; Photo: A. Hay)

Ill. 41: Plastered wine press, dated seventh century B.C.E., Ashkelon. Pressing platform to right with later wall over it; receiving vats to left. (Courtesy of the Leon Levy Expedition to Ashkelon; Photo: I. Sztulman)

vintage harvest at Shiloh the young women of the town danced around the vineyards. At such a celebration Shiloh became the scene of the abduction and rape of the young women by the Benjaminites, who were hidden in the nearby vineyards: "As soon as you see the young men of Shiloh coming out to join the dances, come out from the vineyards; let each of you seize a wife from among the young women of Shiloh" (Judg. 21:21).

Harvesting was done by cutting clusters of grapes from the vine with pruning knives. Then the grapes were placed in baskets and carried to the winepress, ordinarily situated within the vineyard but sometimes in the city. Winepresses were hewn from bedrock to form a flat surface for treading. They consisted of a pair of square or circular vats (called *gat* and *yeqeb* in Hebrew) arranged at different levels and connected by a channel. The grapes were trodden by bare feet in the treading platform (*gat*), which was higher and larger than the deeper *yeqeb*, the receptacle into which the new wine flowed from the press. In a judgment on Moab Yahweh declares through Jeremiah: "I have stopped the wine from the wine presses (*yĕqābîm [pars pro toto]*);

no one treads them with shouts of joy" (Jer. 48:33). The grape beam-press came later, a Greek invention dating to the sixth century B.C.E. One end of the beam was secured to a wall, the other end weighted with stones, and the baskets of grapes placed beneath. The earliest evidence of the use of the beam-press in Israel dates to the Hellenistic period (third century B.C.E.). The only apparent difference between the olive and grape beam-presses is that less pressure needs to be exerted on the grapes.

After the grapes were treaded, the expressed juice ran into vats carved in the bedrock or constructed and lined with plaster. The juice collected in these vats was then set in a cool place for fermentation. In Iron II at Ashkelon fat-bellied jars were used for fermentation and storage. Here pressing was done in rooms within a large, centrally located ashlar building, or winery. Press rooms alternated with storerooms in this large complex (Ill. 41).

While grapes were used primarily for wine making, some were spread on mats to dry in the sun and to be made into raisin cakes (ṣimmuqîm or ’ăšîšôt). Others were used to make "dibs," a fruit honey produced by boiling the juice of the grapes, which served as an ingredient for sweetening cakes.

Beverages

Hebrew mišteh, derived from šātâ, "to drink," is commonly translated "festival" or "banquet," suggesting that the essence of a feast was the consumption of alcoholic beverages. Yahweh prohibited Jeremiah from entering the "house of mourning" (bêt marzēaḥ) to participate in a mourning rite (marzēaḥ) that consisted of eating and drinking: "You shall not go into the house of feasting (bêt mišteh) to sit with them [Judahites], to eat (le’ĕkōl) and drink (lištôt)" (Jer. 16:8). Here the "house of mourning" and the "house of feasting" are parallel (Jer. 16:5–9).

Mentioned 185 times in the Hebrew Bible, wine served as the commonly consumed beverage in ancient Israel, since water was often contaminated. Nine names for "wine" appear in the Hebrew Bible, although they do not necessarily designate different kinds of wine. Some names may be derived from the wine's place of origin or from certain characteristics of the wine, as the "dark wine" from Judah is called kāḥôl, from kḥl meaning "to paint the eyes"; some of the various names may merely be synonyms. The most common word for wine is yayin, appearing more than 140 times in the Bible. The root of yayin, perhaps a non-Semitic loan word, is found in several languages of the East Mediterranean. The Hebrew tîrôš ("new wine" or simply "wine") appears thirty-eight times. ’asîs (from ’āsas, "to crush"), literally "juice," is unfermented; tîrôš is newly fermented. ḥemer (Aramaic), a poetic term for "red wine," appears only in Deuteronomy 32:14. The Septuagint uses only oinos for wine.

The pomace of the grape was "distilled" into grappa, a brandy. The simple technology for its production was available in the Bronze Age. It is probably this brandy, with an alcoholic content of 20 to 60 percent, that was known in Hebrew as *šēkar*, giving rise to the verb *šākar*, "to be drunk," which occurs nineteen times in the Bible. "Nazirite" (from *nāzar*, "to consecrate, separate") designates a man or woman who vows to abstain from (1) wine or any other intoxicants (*yayin wĕšēkar*); (2) cutting the hair; and (3) contact with dead bodies (Num. 6:1–8). This vow could be taken permanently or only temporarily. Based on this passage in Numbers, *šēkar* cannot refer to "beer" (as it does in Mesopotamia) but can only be a grape product. *šēkar* is usually parallel with "wine" in the Bible. At Ashkelon it is second on a list of beverages after "red wine" (*yayin 'ādōm*).[14]

Wine was stored in large jars, and a juglet was used for dipping from the store jar. Pitchers and carafes served for pouring wine into drinking cup-bowls (*kōsôt*). It was strained to keep the drinker from ingesting the dregs or other foreign matter, and archaeologists have uncovered various types of strainer jugs for this purpose. In the early seventh century in Phrygia, the strainer was built into the spout of the jugs used to transfer the liquid from the large bowls to the drinking bowls. These strainer jugs were actually composite carafes, serving as decanter and strainer. These wine sets were important vessels in the Philistine repertoire, illustrating that the Philistines drank wine and not beer, as generally assumed. The Philistine wine set, of Iron I, was composed of krater, *skyphos* (drinking cup), and side-strainer spouted jug (Ill. 65). The Canaanite and Egyptian bronze wine sets consisted of three pieces—bowl, juglet, and strainer. A typical example came to light at Tell es-Sa'idiyeh in Jordan, dating to the thirteenth century, and also in a Persian period tomb at Tell el-Far'ah (S), where strainer, ladle, and bowl were uncovered. A small sheet-metal strainer was sometimes fitted to the bottom of the reed.

Besides being a common table beverage, wine was offered as a libation in sacrifice (Ex. 29:40) and was used medicinally. In Egypt and Mesopotamia, beer was the predominant drink, wine being restricted to religious purposes and banqueting among the affluent. On the basis of the biblical warnings against abuse, drunkenness (*šikkārôn*) was considered a disgrace: "Wine (*yayin*) and new wine (*tîrôš*) take away the understanding" (Hos. 4:11). Isaiah denounces those "who rise early in the morning in pursuit of *šēkar* [usually mistranslated by the vague locution 'strong drink'], who linger in the evening to be inflamed by wine (*yayin*)" (Isa. 5:11).

Beer (probably from Latin *bibere*, "to drink") is one of the oldest beverages in the region, dating to the fourth millennium or earlier. Made mainly from barley and wheat, it was the common drink in Mesopotamia and Egypt. The earliest written sources from Mesopotamia mention beer and provide elaborate descriptions of the brewing process. Plaques and cylinders from early Mesopotamia illustrate that beer was drunk through a reed or tube with a sieve on the end to keep it free of straw and

---

14. Lawrence E. Stager, "The Fury of Babylon: Ashkelon and the Archaeology of Destruction," *BAR* 22 (1996): 66. For a significant treatment of viticulture, see Carey Ellen Walsh, *The Fruit of the Vine: Viticulture in Ancient Israel*, HSM 60 (Winona Lake, Ind.: Eisenbrauns, 2000).

chaff. In Mesopotamia, there were many types of beer. "Babylonia like Bavaria was essentially a beer drinking culture."[15] In Israel, on the other hand, it was not a popular beverage; there is not even an ancient Hebrew word for beer if *šēkar* refers to a grape product, such as grappa.

Milk (*ḥālāb*) was part of the staple diet, consumed in the form of curds and cheese and occasionally drunk with meals in biblical times. Goats were the primary milk producers in the ancient Near East; goat milk is richer in protein and fat than sheep and cow's milk. The milk was kept in a leather skin (*no'd*, Judg. 4:19), as the story of Sisera, commander of the Canaanite forces, and Jael, a Kenite woman, illustrates. After feigning hospitality by offering Sisera milk in a bowl (*sēpel*) as a thirst-quencher, she slew him by crushing his skull:

> Water he asked,
> Milk (*ḥālāb*) she gave,
> In a majestic bowl,
> She brought ghee (*ḥem'â*).
> (Judg. 5:25)[16]

Ghee (*ḥem'â*) and milk (*ḥālāb*) appear together several other times in the Bible. They were served to the three strangers who visited Abraham and Sarah (Gen. 18:8; also Deut. 32:14; Judg. 5:25). *ḥem'â*, variously described as curdled milk resembling yogurt, was prepared by churning fresh milk. Churning consists in rocking a skin of milk (*nō'd heḥālāb*), or by beating a suspended skin of milk with a stick. Wine and milk are mentioned together in Isaiah's eloquent invitation to the messianic banquet for all peoples: "Everyone who thirsts, come to the waters; and you who have no money, come, buy and eat! Come, buy wine (*yayin*) and milk (*ḥālāb*) without money and without price" (Isa. 55:1).

Cheese was a common food made from the milk of the ewe or the nanny. In the David and Goliath story, Jesse orders David to "take these ten cuts of cheese (*ḥărisê heḥālāb*) [lit. "slices of milk"] to the commander of their thousands" (1 Sam. 17:18). "Slices of milk" designates a soft cheese that can be sliced.

Other Fruits

tāmār, "date palm," is a Hebrew name often given both to women and to places. Grace and elegance characterize the date palm tree, which with its immense fronds can reach a height of eighteen to twenty-four meters. Jericho is known as the "city of palm trees" (*'îr hattĕmārîm*, Deut. 34:3). The dense growth of the date palm is evident in the Jordan Valley, the Arabah, and parts of the Coastal Plain. The palmette

---

15. Powell, "Wine and the Vine in Ancient Mesopotamia," 106.
16. Frank M. Cross, *From Epic to Canon: History and Literature in Ancient Israel* (Garden City, N.Y.: Doubleday, 1959), 142–43.

(*timōrâ*, diminutive of *tāmār*) is a favorite motif—the sacred tree flanked by cherubim in the Jerusalem Temple (1 Kings 6:29, 32, 35, and Ezek. 41:18–20). The famous capitals for columns and pilasters used in royal buildings in the Iron Age at Hazor, Megiddo, Jerusalem, Samaria, Dan, and Ramat Raḥel derive their form from the heart of the date palm.[17] Also based on the date palm, the stylized cosmic tree—the biblical "tree of life" (Gen. 2:9)—is a favorite symbol of fertility (and of the deity Asherah) found on Phoenician ivories, cult stands, amulets, scarabs, cylinder seals, wall paintings, and pottery. Practically every part of the palm tree is utilized in daily life—the trunk for timber, the leaves for roofing and basket weaving, the fruit for sweets, and the seeds for animal fodder. A basic food and a high-energy source, dates ripen at the end of summer and may be eaten fresh or dried in the form of small cakes. The date palm is also used in the manufacture of wine and honey. Date honey is a sweet syrup called dibs, parallel to the dibs of the grape (grape honey), and can ferment into date palm wine, a common drink in Egypt and Mesopotamia.[18]

The pomegranate (*rimmôn*) is a beautiful, symmetrical fruit, scarlet in color. Filled with small seeds surrounded by juicy pulp, the fruit became an obvious symbol of fertility. The magnificent pomegranate inspired the ornamentation of the Temple capitals (1 Kings 7:20). "The height of one capital [of the Temple] was five cubits; latticework and pomegranates, all of bronze, encircled the top of the capital. And the second pillar had the same, with pomegranates" (Jer. 52:22). Pomegranates and bells also decorated the priestly garments (Ex. 28:33–34).

After the grape, the most valued fruit was the fig (*tě'ēnâ*), mentioned fifty-three times in the Bible. With its dense foliage and broad leaves measuring as much as eight meters in diameter, the fig tree (*tě'ēnâ*) is well known for the copious shade it provides. Remarkable for long life, the fig tree stands at least five meters high. The fig's high sugar content makes it especially nutritious. Figs produce several crops each year: the first in June is especially sweet, the summer figs ripen in August and September, and the winter figs reach fruition at the end of November. Figs may be eaten fresh, dried, or made into cakes (*děbēlîm*). Cakes of dried figs were a convenient provision for travelers and warriors. As related in 1 Samuel 25:18, "one hundred clusters of raisins (*ṣimmuqîm*) and two hundred cakes of figs (*děbēlîm*)" were among the supplies that Abigail, Nabal's spouse, presented to David as an appeasement. An Egyptian who had neither eaten nor drunk for three days was given, in addition to water, "a piece of fig cake (*děbēlâ*) and two clusters of raisins (*ṣimmuqîm*)," and he was revived (1 Sam. 30:12). At Ekron an inscription was found on an Iron II store jar indicating its contents—*dbl*, "cluster of figs." An actual string of dried figs was uncovered in an LB

---

17. Yigal Shiloh, *The Proto-Aeolic Capital and Israelite Ashlar Masonry*, Qedem 11 (Jerusalem: Institute of Archaeology, Hebrew University, 1979), 26–30.

18. Benno Landsberger, *The Date Palm and Its By-Products according to the Cuneiform Sources* (Graz: Weidner, 1967).

store jar, where they had been carbonized in a fire that destroyed Ekron early in the twelfth century B.C.E. (Ill. 42).

The sycamore (*šiqmâ*), which grows wild in the Coastal Plain, is a type of fig tree bearing fruit several times a year. Its small, bluish-purple figs, quite inferior to the domesticated fig, were the food of the poor. The fact that its wood is light and porous makes it suitable for certain kinds of construction. The biblical sycamore (*Ficus sycomorus*) is not to be confused

Ill. 42: Store jar filled with hundreds of carbonized figs, found in a large storage facility, together with other jars containing carbonized grains. The storage facility was sealed by a meter of destruction debris, which brought an end to Str VII, Late Bronze Age II, in the first quarter of the twelfth century B.C.E., Tel Miqne-Ekron. (Courtesy of Tel Miqne-Ekron Excavation/Publication Project; Photo: I. Sztulman)

with the North American sycamore, which is a plane tree (*Platanus occidentalis*), nor with the English maple tree (*Acer pseudoplatanus*). *Ficus sycomorus* is also known as the "Egyptian fig," where it grows abundantly and was used for making mummy cases.[19] This tree, which may attain a height of fifteen meters, is associated in the Hebrew Bible especially with the prophet Amos, who describes his own profession as *bôlēs šiqmîm* (Amos 7:14), that is, one who incises the fig to hasten the ripening process. Gashing the fruit increases the production of ethylene gas responsible for ripening. This technique is still practiced in the Middle East.

Pistachios (*boṭnîm*) and almonds (*šĕqēdîm*) are the principal nuts mentioned in the Bible, but references are scarce. They were among the choice gifts Jacob sent to Joseph in Egypt (Gen. 43:11). The pistachio tree grows as high as ten meters. *šĕqēdîm* comes from the Heb root *šqd*, "to watch, wake," so-called because its splendid white blossoms appear as early as the end of January, a true harbinger of spring. Jeremiah plays on *šqd*: "The word of Yahweh came to me [Jeremiah], saying, 'Jeremiah, what do you see?' And I said, 'I see a branch of an almond tree (*šāqēd*).' Then Yahweh said to me, 'You have seen well, for I am watching (*šōqēd*) over my word to perform it'" (Jer. 1:11–12).

In the midst of their wilderness wanderings, the Israelites, bored with eating only manna, craved the leeks (*ḥāṣîr*), onions (*bĕṣālîm*), and garlic (*šûmîm*) that they had relished in Egypt (Num. 11:5–6). Leeks (*ḥāṣîr* from the root *ḥṣr*, "to be green"), more

---

19. Hogah Hareuveni, *Nature in our Biblical Heritage* (Kiryat Ono: Neot Kedumim, 1980), 128.

pungent than onions, were cultivated in Egypt, and garlic was known in Egypt from 3200 B.C.E. These three vegetables also had medicinal uses.

Condiments

The cargo of the trading vessel shipwrecked about 1300 B.C.E. near Uluburun, Turkey, included, in addition to olives, figs, and pomegranates, various spices and nuts (almonds, acorns, pine nuts, wild pistachios), coriander, black cumin, caper berries, and sumac seeds. The Mari records also mention large quantities of coriander, black and white cumin, saffron, ammi (mint?), fenugreek (fennel), and cloves.[20] The main dishes at meals were ordinarily accompanied by other foods, all well seasoned with a variety of condiments. Salt (*melaḥ*), both a seasoning and a preservative, was also used in sacrifices: "With all your offerings you shall offer salt" (Lev. 2:13). Salt was produced by evaporating sea water or by extracting it from the salt beds of the Dead Sea. In the last days, that is, the eschatological vision of paradise, Ezekiel sees a stream of water issuing up and flowing over the threshold/platform of the Temple, becoming a great river of life as it flows toward the Dead Sea to sweeten its salty waters; however, "its swamps and saltpans will not become fresh; they are to be left for salt" (Ezek. 47:11).

In biblical times honey (*děbaš*) as a sweetener was derived from several sources—from the juices of grapes, dates, and figs, as well as from bees (in the Samson saga, Judg. 14:8, the bees' honey was found in a lion's carcass). Honey was also included among the exports to Tyre described in Ezekiel 27:17.

Vinegar made from fermented wine was used as a condiment, as when Boaz invited Ruth to dip her morsel of bread into the vinegar (*ḥōmeṣ*) (Ruth 2:14). A diluted form of vinegar resembling sour wine was sometimes drunk by the poor and by soldiers.

Cumin is a small plant bearing aromatic seeds which are used to season bread, cake, and other foods. Black cumin seeds are a bit sweeter than white cumin seeds. Because of its pungency cumin is used in highly spiced cuisine—soups, stews, lamb dishes. Cumin oil is used in perfumes. The seeds are also taken as medicine to ease colic, flatulence, stomach disorders, and diarrhea. In a parable on planting and harvesting delicate seeds, Isaiah refers to both black cumin (*qeṣaḥ*) and white cumin (*kammōn*): "Black cumin is not threshed with a threshing sledge, nor is a cart wheel rolled over white cumin; but black cumin is beaten out with a stick (*maṭṭeh*), and white cumin with a rod (*šābeṭ*)" (Isa. 28:27). The point is that the proper implement must always be used, in this case, a stick or a rod.

Cinnamon (*qinnāmôn*) is an ingredient of the holy, perfumed oil for the priests (Ex. 30:23). The cinnamon of the Bible, indigenous to Ceylon (Sri Lanka) and the

---

20. Stephanie Dalley, *Mari and Karana: Two Old Babylonian Cities* (London: Longman, 1984), 83.

coast of India, has many uses: in food, in incense, in perfume. Cassia, rendered by two Hebrew words, *qĕṣî'ôt* (Ps. 45:9) and *qiddâ* (Ex. 30:24), is an aromatic bark resembling, but inferior to, cinnamon, used as a spice and a perfume. *qiddâ*, too, is an ingredient of the holy anointing oil. In the Psalter's only wedding song the king's robes are perfumed with "myrrh and aloes and cassia (*qĕṣî'ôt*)" (Ps. 45:9 [E.T. 45:8]). Cassia was imported from East Asia.

Coriander (*gad*), native to Israel, is a bitter Passover herb, and has a strong smell. Its leaves are used for flavoring soups and wines, and its seeds for seasoning food and vegetables.

Caper (*'ăbiyyônâ*), a pungent condiment mentioned in the Hebrew Bible only in Ecclesiastes 12:5, is variously described as an aphrodisiac and a stimulant to appetite. The capers are flower buds of a bush with round, thick leaves. They like the warm, Mediterranean climate. After picking, the capers are allowed to wilt for a day and then they are preserved in wine vinegar (*ḥōmeṣ*) or olive oil. To retain flavor they must be pickled.

Saffron (*karkōm*), highly prized as a yellow dye, medication, and culinary spice, is from *Crocus sativus* (the yellow autumn crocus). The sole biblical reference to saffron appears in the Song of Solomon (4:14), written in the Persian period, where it is associated with calamus and cinnamon. Saffron is thought to be native to Asia Minor.

Clove is a flower bud of the evergreen clove tree native to the Moluccas (Spice Islands) of Indonesia. It is used to flavor meats and sweets, and oil of cloves serves as a mouthwash and an anesthetic for toothache. Cloves were found at Terqa (modern Ashara) on the banks of the Euphrates.

Fennel, native to the Mediterranean, is an aromatic perennial of the parsley family. Having the flavor of mild anise, it is used in bread, dough, and cakes, and also as a spice for meat, such as lamb and pork. Fennel seeds and oil are also utilized in medicine.

Other Flora

The precise identification of flora is a complex problem, arising from incomplete descriptions in the Bible or from systems of classification quite different from those of botanical science. Lack of consensus about plant references is evident when one compares various translations of the Bible. Isaiah uses the richest vocabulary of plant names in the Bible. Floral imagery abounds in a magnificent poem in praise of Wisdom written by Ben Sira, a teacher in Jerusalem, between 200 and 180 B.C.E.:

> Like a cedar on Lebanon I [Wisdom] am raised aloft, like a cypress on Mount Hermon, like a palm tree in En-Gedi, like a rosebush in Jericho, like a fair olive tree in the field, like a plane tree growing beside the water. Like cinnamon, or

> fragrant balm, or precious myrrh I give forth perfume, like galbanum and ony-
> cha and sweet spices, like the odor of incense in the Holy Place. I spread out
> my branches like a terebinth, my branches so bright and so graceful. I bud
> forth delights like the vine; my blossoms become fruit fair and rich (Sir.
> 24:13–17).

More than fifteen species of trees are mentioned in the Bible, some more prominently than others. Among the most common are the oak, terebinth, pine, cypress, juniper, and cedar. Several species of the oak and terebinth alone flourish in the Levant, and translators unfamiliar with the local flora frequently fail to render the differences accurately, often confusing them or employing terms interchangeably. Isaiah (6:13) uses *'ēlâ/'allâ* and *'allôn/'ēlôn* in the same verse, the former meaning "terebinth" and the latter "oak." These four words, all etymologically related to *'ēl*, *'ēla(t)* ("god" and "goddess"), are associated with worship of the deity. Not only in external appearance, but also in other respects, these two types of trees are different: for example, the oak bears acorns while the terebinth produces pistachio nutlets (*boṭnîm*) and "turpentine" (the resinous sap).

Among the many species of oak in Palestine are the evergreen, or Kermes, oak (*Quercus calliprinos*) and the Tabor oak (*Quercus ithaburensis*). The former is present in the hill country from the Carmel to Hebron and is also found today in Upper Galilee and in Gilead. Tabor oak (*Quercus ithaburensis*), which attains a height up to twenty-five meters, once covered the Coastal Plain, Lower Galilee, the Dan Valley, the Hulah Plain, and the Golan Heights.[21] The central Coastal Plain consists principally of the evergreen, or Kermes, oak and only secondarily of the Tabor oak.[22] The evergreen, or Kermes, oak attains a height of twenty-five meters and may live for three hundred years. Oak is used for construction and shipbuilding and for tools and weapons.

Its imposing stature, longevity, and hardness of wood have lent the oak an auspicious significance, resulting in its frequent association with religious phenomena and cultic settings. There was a Canaanite temple at Avaris, the Hyksos capital of Egypt, with an altar and two evergreen oaks in the courtyard. The acorns on the altar and the sunken pits on both sides of the altar attest to sacred trees growing there—trees that had to be transplants to Egypt. The oak/terebinth is the sacred tree frequently associated with Elat/Asherah.[23] The Lachish Ewer, dating to the thirteenth century B.C.E., was found in refuse outside the so-called Fosse Temple. It is decorated with a row of stylized animals and trees accompanied by an archaic inscription reading "Mattan. An offering to my Lady Elat" (Ill. 43). Presumably the Ewer was presented as a gift

---

21. Michael Zohary, *Plants of the Bible* (Cambridge: Cambridge University Press, 1982), 108.
22. Nili Liphschitz, Simcha Lev-Yadun, and Ram Gophna, "The Dominance of *Quercus Calliprinos* (Kermes Oak) in the Central Coastal Plain in Antiquity," *IEJ* 37 (1987): 43–50.
23. Manfred Bietak, *Avaris: The Capital of the Hyksos* (London: British Museum Press, 1996).

to the goddess Elat, the consort of El.[24] Farther afield, Dodona, located in the northwestern part of Greece, became a famous site in ancient Greece for the oracle of Zeus, who was believed to speak through the branches of an oak tree growing there.

The biblical writers describe open-air sanctuaries in the days of the ancestors—just a few sacred trees and stones—by which they lay claim, through "patriarchal precedence," to the holy ground on which Old Canaanite temples had stood. Thus, Abraham settled by the "oaks of Mamre (*'ēlōnê mamrē'*), which are at Hebron" (Gen. 13:18), where he experienced a theophany of the "three visitors" (Gen. 18:1–22). These cult sites were furnished with *maṣṣēbôt* ("standing stones") and altars. Although temple buildings are not explicitly mentioned in the ancestral narratives, there are many indications that the sacred trees, altars, and *maṣṣēbôt* stood in the courtyards of such temples. The MB II-

Ill. 43: Lachish Ewer, dated thirteenth century B.C.E. Inscription is above the sacred tree flanked by two quadrupeds and reads: "Mattan. An offering to my Lady Elat (the goddess Asherah)." (Courtesy of the Israel Museum; Photo: A. Hay)

Iron I Fortress Temple at Shechem (temple of El, Lord of the Covenant) had sacred tree(s), an altar, and *maṣṣēbôt*. The sanctuary at Bethel had standing stone(s) and a monumental stairway (of the temple) that led up to heaven's gate (*ša'ar haššāmāyim*), that is, to the sacred portals through which one enters the temple, the similitude of heaven on earth. Such outdoor contexts proved conducive as settings for theophanies and rituals.

The terebinth, sometimes standing as high as ten meters, gave its name to the Valley of Elah, where David slew Goliath (1 Sam. 17:19). The terebinth (*Pistacia palaestina*) is the species found in the Negev, Lower Galilee, the Dan Valley, and the hill country. The terebinth is also the source of turpentine, a brownish-yellow viscous resin that had a variety of uses—as a mastic, for caulking, for mummification, and for "shellacking" wall paintings. Turpentine is harvested by slashing the tree's stem (trunk) and branches and collecting the resin in a container.[25] The cargo of the Uluburun

24. Ruth Hestrin, "The Lachish Ewer and the 'Asherah," *IEJ* 37 (1987): 212–23.

25. John A. Selbie, "Terebinth," in J. Hastings, ed., *A Dictionary of the Bible* (Edinburgh: T. & T. Clark, 1898; reprinted by Hendrickson), 4:718–19.

shipwreck included a ton of terebinth resin in more than a hundred Canaanite amphoras.[26] The small stone fruits of this tree, which have been found in Iron Age levels at Tel Sheva and Arad, also emit the pungent odor of turpentine. The terebinth figures frequently in biblical accounts: Under the sacred terebinth at Shechem Jacob hid the foreign gods and earrings of his household (Gen. 35:4). One of the gifts brought by Jacob's sons to Egypt was wild pistachio nuts (*boṭnîm*) of the terebinth (Gen. 43:11). Joshua set up a *maṣṣēbâ* under the terebinth at Shechem (Josh. 24:26). Absalom's long hair became entangled in the branches of a terebinth (*'ēlâ*), and there he was left hanging (2 Sam. 18:9).

The cypress has been identified with various Hebrew words, for example, *tĕ'aššûr* and *bĕrôš*. *tĕ'aššûr* is almost certainly the cypress (*Cupressus sempervirens*). Zohary suggests *bĕrôš* may be a collective term for all these species; while Diakonoff prefers to identify *bĕrôš* with the *Juniperus excelsa*, a conifer resembling the cedar (see chap. 2).[27]

The Aleppo pine (*Pinus halepensis*) was far more abundant in biblical times than it is today. *tĕ'aššûr* is sometimes translated both "pine" and "cypress." *'ēṣ šemen* (literally "oil tree"), occurring five times in the Bible (Isa. 41:19 and elsewhere), should be translated "pine tree" and not "olive wood," as often happens, according to George Post and Zohary.[28] Solomon used *'ēṣ šemen* for crafting certain of the Temple furnishings. In the Holy of Holies he constructed two cherubim of *'ēṣ šemen*, each ten cubits (ca. five meters) high (1 Kings 6:23). Doors and doorposts of the Temple were made of *'ēṣ šemen* (1 Kings 6:31–33).

The magnificent cedar (*'erez*), a mountain tree with a pleasant scent and shaped like a pyramid, is mentioned more than seventy times in the Bible. The biblical reference is usually to the stately "cedar of Lebanon" (*Cedrus libani*), which may grow as high as thirty-five meters. The mountains of Lebanon were the main source of this timber in biblical times (Ezek. 31:3–7). This species of cedar also flourishes in the Taurus and Amanus Mountains. Despite the lore that cedars live thousands of years, the most ancient ones found so far are between three hundred and five hundred years old. With its massive trunk and horizontal branches, it symbolized strength, fecundity, prosperity, and eternity. Cedar wood, famous for durability, was used in the construction of both the First and Second Temples. Its resin and oil were utilized in embalming and perfume. This resinous quality prevented rotting and repelled insects. King Hiram of Tyre supplied David and Solomon with cedar wood. The cedar logs were floated down the Mediterranean to Joppa, a distance of three hundred twenty

---

26. Çemal Pulak, "The Uluburun Shipwreck" in S. Swiny, R. L. Hohlfelder, and H. W. Swiny, eds., *Res Maritimae: Cyprus and the Eastern Mediterranean from Prehistory to Late Antiquity* (Atlanta: Scholars Press, 1997), 233–62.

27. Zohary, *Plants of the Bible*, 106–7.

28. George Post, "Oil Tree," in Hastings, ed., *A Dictionary of the Bible*, 3:592–93. Zohary, *Plants of the Bible*, 114.

kilometers, and then transported overland to Jerusalem, an additional forty kilometers (2 Chron. 2:16). Both David (2 Sam. 5:11) and Solomon had palaces constructed of Lebanon cedar. Solomon's famous "House of the Forest of Lebanon," constructed from imported cedar wood (1 Kings 7:2–5), was so called because its forty-five cedar pillars arranged in three rows of fifteen (four rows according to the Septuagint) created the impression of a cedar forest.

The timber trade between Phoenicia (Lebanon) and Israel in Iron II sheds light not only on the architecture of the period but also on the economy, wealth, commerce, and administrative sophistication of ancient Israel, which was able to locate and acquire substantial amounts of this valuable wood. Remnants of the cedar tree appear at several sites in Israel: Tel Aphek, Tel Gerisa, Jerusalem, and Lachish. Furthermore, significant remains have been uncovered in peripheral sites in the Negev at 'Uza, Tel Sheva, Masos, Arad, and Tel Sera'.[29] Ordinarily cedar is the sign of an elite or state-sponsored building project. The trees were also transplanted and raised under protected conditions in special gardens for divinity and royalty in ancient Israel. "The righteous flourish like the palm tree, and grow like a cedar of Lebanon. They are planted in the house of Yahweh; they flourish in the courts of our God" (Ps. 92:13–14 [E.T. 92:12–13]).

It is unusual to find at archaeological sites well-preserved organic materials, such as wood, leather, and ivory. Kathleen Kenyon recovered pieces of wooden furniture in a good state of preservation in the MB II Jericho tombs. Included were a long, narrow table with two legs at one end and one at the other, as well as stools and a bed. Three-legged furniture is well adapted to uneven floors. There was also a cache of wooden vessels consisting of platters, bowls, cups, and bottles. The larger articles were crafted from imported cedar, and the smaller objects from tamarisk ('ēšel) and poplar ('ărābâ), wood from local trees.[30]

Forestation/Deforestation

Forests in ancient Israel were much more extensive than they are today.[31] The natural forestation of the highlands consisted principally of three of the trees mentioned above, the evergreen oak (*Quercus calliprinos*), the Aleppo pine (*Pinus halepensis*), and the terebinth (*Pistacia palaestina*). No barren hills existed before the human habitation of the area. It must be acknowledged, however, that the Hebrew word for forest (ya'ar), occurring in names like Kiriath-jearim ("town of forests"), is sometimes ambiguous. Several forests are mentioned explicitly in the biblical text—Lebanon,

---

29. Nili Liphshitz and Gideon Biger, "Cedar of Lebanon (*Cedrus libani*) in Israel during Antiquity," *IEJ* 41 (1991): 167–75.
30. Kathleen Kenyon, *Digging Up Jericho* (London: Ernest Benn, 1975), 240–52.
31. John D. Currid, "The Deforestation of the Foothills of Palestine," *PEQ* 116 (1984): 1–11.

Carmel, and Hereth (in Judah). For the psalmist, even trees could praise God: "Then shall all the trees of the forest exult before Yahweh" (Ps. 96:12).

As time went on and the society changed, there were many reasons for the degradation of forests. With the growth of the population, wooded areas had to be cleared for habitation. The marked rise in population after 1200 B.C.E. increased the need for wood charcoal for various pyrotechnologies, such as pottery making, lime slaking, and metallurgy. Indeed, it seems the transition from bronze to iron came about in part, not only because of the superiority in the hardness of iron to bronze, but also because iron is the more fuel efficient.

Probably even more important for the degradation of the primeval forest in the highlands was the need for arable land, which was created on the many slopes of the hill country in the form of stepped terraces. Converting the hillsides into agricultural terraces in order to sustain agriculturally based villages dates as early as 1200 B.C.E. Ecological equilibrium was achieved in the hill country by constructing agricultural terraces that increased the subsistence base. In sum, as population increased, the creation of arable land and the increase in the various pyrotechnologies brought pressure on natural resources in this region.

With the transition from bronze to iron, pyrotechnology continued to need wood for fuel, which led to the depletion of the forests. Iron-tipped scratch plows, iron axes, and weapons of warfare were responsible in part for deforestation. Shipbuilding and the construction of dwellings using wood materials also accounted for the enormous reduction in forests. In addition, flocks of sheep and especially goats contributed to the decline of the wooded land. The pressures that led to broad deforestation during the Iron Age are appropriately depicted in a dialogue between Joshua and the Josephites:

> The sons of Joseph said: "The highlands are not enough for us; yet the Canaanites living in the lowlands all have iron chariots, particularly those in Beth-Shean and its satellite villages (bānôt, lit. "daughters") and those in the Jezreel Valley." Joshua replied to the house of Joseph, that is, to Ephraim and Manasseh: "You are a numerous people and very strong. You shall not have one allotment only. The highlands shall be yours as well; true, it is a forest (ya'ar), but you will clear it and possess it to its farthest limits. And you shall also dispossess the Canaanites, despite their iron chariots and their strength." (Josh. 17:16–18)

Animal Husbandry

In the Levant, a combination of farming and pastoralism (agropastoralism) was typical of village economies from Neolithic times to the present. Families lived together in villages where they farmed, while some members tended the flocks, often at some distance from the homestead. However, this was not true transhumant pastoralism in which whole households move with seasonal migrations.

The domestication of plants preceded the domestication of animals. The former began in PPNA, with cereals and legumes; the latter in PPNB, with sheep, goats, and pigs. This sequence makes eminently good sense, because the domesticated grains would attract certain types of herbivores, such as wild sheep and goats, which could then be eventually domesticated. More than a hundred animal names appear in the Bible, but incomplete descriptions make it difficult to identify fauna with certainty, just as was the case regarding flora. The most frequent domesticated animals found in the Bronze and Iron Age archaeological sites are sheep and goats, usually followed by *Bos* (large cattle). The *ṣō'n* (collective for small cattle, namely, sheep and goats), the most important domestic animals in Palestine and an index of their owner's economic status, are well suited to the dry, hot climate of the Near East. In winter and spring they graze on grass produced by the rains, and in summer and autumn they feed on plants and husks.

Sheep were raised primarily for their wool. The production of wool was a valuable commodity in commerce, as illustrated by the tribute of King Mesha of Moab, who "used to deliver to the king of Israel one hundred thousand lambs, and the wool of one hundred thousand rams" (2 Kings 3:4). Sheepshearing, in the spring of the year, was the occasion of festivities, as is evident in the story about Nabal, the rich rancher who was visited by David's followers on their feast day: "He had three thousand sheep and a thousand goats. He was shearing his sheep in Carmel" (1 Sam. 25:2), a site southeast of Hebron. Wool production went hand in hand with weaving and dyeing.

In addition, sheep provide meat and hides. Slaughtering a sheep to honor a guest was a sign of hospitality. In his condemnation of David's sin with Bathsheba, Nathan confronted him with a parable about a rich man who, to fulfill the law of hospitality,

Ill. 44: Lower Register – Bronze Bands, Gates of Balawat. Campaign in Northern Syria, 850 B.C.E. Syrian flocks and cattle being driven into Syrian camp. (Courtesy of the Trustees of the British Museum)

butchered a poor neighbor's only ewe lamb, instead of one of his own flock (2 Sam. 12:1–7). Sheep have to be carefully tended, since they are easy prey for wild animals. The shepherd is their sole provider and protector. To assure Saul that he could challenge Goliath, the shepherd David told the king that "whenever a lion or a bear came, and took a lamb from the flock, I went after it and struck it down, rescuing the lamb from its mouth" (1 Sam. 17:34–35). In Egypt and in other Near Eastern cultures, the king was considered the "good shepherd" who looks after his subjects—the sheep. In some literature the good shepherd is identified with the Deity, as in Psalm 23.

Goats can provide meat, clothing, and milk (also curds and cheese). Their milk yield is twice that of sheep. As goats tend to destroy crops, overgrazing was a problem for replenishing vegetation. Goat hair and hides were valued for tentmaking and clothing. Coarse goat hair was used for the manufacture of sacks and tent cloth, was woven into carpets, and was fashioned into churns for making ghee. Goat skins functioned as containers for liquids such as water and oil. Like sheep, goats were acceptable sacrificial animals. When Yahweh established his covenant with Abraham, he said: "Bring me a heifer three years old, a female goat three years old, a ram three years old, a turtledove, and a young pigeon" (Gen. 15:9). In the eighteenth century B.C.E., a donkey, a puppy, and a goat were considered acceptable sacrifices for cutting a covenant.

The horse (*sûs*) became prominent in Canaan early in the second millennium, and the development of the chariot followed soon. The Canaanites introduced the horse and chariot into Egypt during the "Hyksos" era, where during the New Kingdom horse and chariot became the most prestigious form of parade in war and in cultic procession. In the Bible, the horse is a symbol of superiority and luxury, utilized in war and hunting, but not in agriculture and transport (Deut. 17:16).

If, as John S. Holladay[32] suggests, many of the pillared public buildings in ancient Israel were really stables, then horses played an extremely prominent role in the economy. Horses were probably more highly prized than people. However, consider the contrasting attitudes of David and Solomon toward horses. David took from the Aramean ruler King Hadadezer 1,700 horsemen and 20,000 foot soldiers: "David hamstrung all the chariot horses, but left enough for a hundred chariots" (2 Sam. 8:4). Barring another explanation for this unusual action, it appears that David was averse to the proliferation of horses for use in battle. According to the biblical report, Solomon had 1,400 chariots and 12,000 horses imported from Egypt and Kue (ancient Adana), "which he stationed in the chariot cities and with the king in Jerusalem" (1 Kings 10:26). Horses and chariots enhanced Solomon's military power.

---

32. John S. Holladay, "The Stables of Ancient Israel: Functional Determinants of Stable Reconstruction and the Interpretation of Pillared Building Remains of the Palestinian Iron Age," in L. T. Geraty and L. G. Herr, eds., *Archaeology of Jordan and Other Studies* (Berrien Springs: Andrews University Press, 1986).

King Ahab of Israel contributed 2,000 chariots to the coalition of the Syrian-Palestinian states in its battle against Assyrian King Shalmaneser III at Qarqar on the Orontes in 853 (*ANET*, 279).

Ill. 45: Terracotta horsehead figurines, found in 604 B.C.E. destruction of Ashkelon. (Courtesy of the Leon Levy Expedition to Ashkelon; Photo: I. Sztulman)

The prophets and the psalmists had a negative attitude toward horses. Yahweh, through Hosea, promises to save Judah but then, contemptuous of human armament, adds, "I will not save them by bow, or by sword, or by war, or by horses, or by horsemen" (Hos. 1:7; also Amos 2:15).[33] "The war horse is a vain hope for victory, and by its great might it cannot save" (Ps. 33:17; also Ps. 147:10). The "Amorite" aversion to horses is expressed in the official correspondence from the Mari archives. The king of Qatna sent horses valued at six hundred shekels of silver to the king of Assyria in the eighteenth century. The latter "reciprocated" with a paltry gift of nine kilograms of tin. But the Qatna king knew that the six hundred shekels should have been worth five to seven times that (forty-five to sixty-three kilograms of tin).[34]

The kings of Israel rode on donkeys or mules instead of horses when performing official functions. A letter of admonition to King Zimri-Lim from the prefect of the Mari palace conveys the impression it was a long-standing custom: "Since you [Zimri-Lim] are the king of the Khana tribesmen . . . my lord ought not to ride horses; rather, it is upon a palanquin or on mules that my lord ought to ride."[35] Jesus's triumphal entry into Jerusalem is described in terms of the coming ruler of God's people by Matthew (21:5) and John (12:15), who cite Zechariah: "See, your king shall come to you . . . meek and riding on a donkey (ḥămôr), on a colt ('ayir), the foal of a donkey" (Zech. 9:9). Matthew mistakenly assumes that the Old Testament parallel refers to two animals.

In antiquity the primary use of the horse was for drawing war chariots. Mounted

---

33. Shalom M. Paul, *Amos*, Hermeneia (Minneapolis: Fortress, 1991), 98.
34. Niels Peter Lemche, "The History of Ancient Syria and Palestine: An Overview," *CANE*, 2:1204.
35. Ibid.

side   front

Ill. 46: Bronze linchpin for a chariot wheel, with the head of a Philistine goddess (so-called "Ashdoda") from Ashkelon; dated Iron I. (Courtesy of the Leon Levy Expedition to Ashkelon; Photo: I. Sztulman)

cavalry appeared in Egypt in the tenth century. By the end of the ninth century, cavalry increased in importance in Mesopotamia among the Assyrians and Urartians, although the horses were ridden without a saddle or stirrups. From the time of the monarchy in Israel, the horse was commonly associated with chariots, not with cavalry. Linchpins to keep chariot wheels on axles were found at Ashkelon and Ekron, two Philistine sites (Ill. 46).

Bits, bridles, and harnesses were developed to gain more control over horses in warfare (Ill. 47). The stirrup was unknown in the ancient Near East. It appeared in India during the late second century B.C.E. and was introduced into the Arab world only in the seventh century C.E. Without the stirrup, the rider ran the risk of being dismounted in combat. The invention of the horseshoe dates only to the ninth century C.E.

In biblical Israel the donkey, the main beast of burden, was used for transport, and the ox for agriculture. The donkey was first domesticated about 3500 B.C.E. The onager (*pereh/pere'*), sometimes another name for the "wild ass" (*Equus hemionus*), is the only equid indigenous to the Near

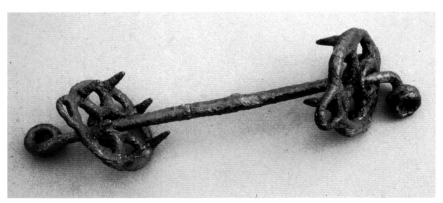

Ill. 47: Bronze donkey bit found with donkey burials in the courtyard of MBII fortress temple at Tel Haror. (Courtesy of E. Oren)

East. Owing to its temperament, the onager, like the gazelle, was never domesticated.[36] However, a copper quadriga (a two-wheeled chariot drawn by four onagers abreast) driven by a bearded charioteer and dating ca. 2800 B.C.E. was found at the Shara temple at Tell Agrab in Iraq.[37] Slim phalanx bones found at Tell Hesban during the Iron Age suggest the presence there of the onager.[38] Using the onager as an ironic metaphor for Israel, Jeremiah declares: "A wild ass (*pereh*) at home in the wilderness, in her heat sniffing the wind! Who can restrain her lust? None who seek her need weary themselves; in her month they will find her" (Jer. 2:24).

The mule (*pered*) is a hybrid, the offspring of a male donkey (jackass) and a female horse (mare). More sure-footed than either horse or donkey, the mule is known for stamina and its ability to carry heavy loads. It was the riding animal of choice for royalty in the biblical world. Absalom was riding on his mule when his head got caught in the terebinth (2 Sam. 18:9). Solomon rode on David's mule on the occasion of his accession to the throne (1 Kings 1:38).

There are two species of camel—the two-humped Bactrian and the single-humped (dromedary) Arabian. The domestication of camels is thought to have taken place in southeastern Arabia in the third millennium, but the evidence for this early date is indecisive. Among the West Semites, the camel is nowhere attested in the Mari and Amarna archives, and in LB camels were still rare in the region. Therefore, Albright[39] concluded that it was either not domesticated or not required among West Semites until late in the second millennium, not long before the twelfth century. His hypothesis still stands. Thus the references to camels in the ancestral stories of Genesis are anachronistic, or the stories do not antedate the twelfth–eleventh centuries. Camels become more numerous in the Iron Age, as attested by remains at Kadesh Barnea, 'Izbet Ṣarṭah, Ashkelon, and Tell Jemmeh. A camel as a domestic beast of burden is represented on the Lachish reliefs in the palace of Sennacherib at Nineveh (Ill. 48). Judahite refugees are pictured departing from Lachish with a camel loaded with water jars. Richard Barnett concludes that from the eighth century onward, the camel served as a beast of burden in the south and southwest of Palestine.[40]

In the late second millennium camels were used to carry spices and incense up the west coast of Arabia through Saba and Yemen.[41] Camels are valued as producers of

---

36. Juliet Clutton-Brock, *A Natural History of Domesticated Mammals* (Cambridge: Cambridge University Press, 1987), 97–101.

37. Seton Lloyd, "Excavating the Land between the Two Rivers," *CANE*, 4:2739–40.

38. Joachim Boessneck and Angela von Den Driesch, "Preliminary Analysis of the Animal Bones from Tell Hesban," *Andrews University Seminary Studies* 16 (1978): 259–287, esp. 275.

39. William F. Albright, "Midianite Donkey Caravans" in H. T. Frank and W. L. Reed, eds., *Translating and Understanding the Old Testament* (Nashville: Abingdon, 1970), 197–205.

40. Richard D. Barnett, "Lachish, Ashkelon and the Camel: A Discussion of Its Use in Southern Palestine," in J. N. Tubb, ed., *Palestine in the Bronze and Iron Ages* (London: Institute of Archaeology, 1985), 15–28.

41. Ibid.

Ill. 48: Lachish Relief from Nineveh: Judahites being deported from Lachish, their belongings placed on the camel's back. (Courtesy of the Expedition to Lachish, D. Ussishkin, Director; Photo: A. Hay)

milk, food, and wool (camel's hair). But their main advantage is their ability to store sufficient water, allowing persons to cross much larger tracts of desert than could be done with donkeys. A camel can drink twenty-eight gallons of water at one time, and a riding camel can travel between ninety-five and one hundred twenty kilometers in a day. This ability opened up overland transport of spices and aromatics (especially myrrh and frankincense) through the vast Arabian deserts and allowed first Midianite, and later Arabian, and later still Nabataean merchants to grow rich from this most lucrative trade in antiquity. As "ships of the desert," camels traversed the trade routes leading from southern Arabia to the markets of Canaan and Mesopotamia.

While the donkey was the principal pack animal for local and regional transport in ancient Israel, the Assyrian army used camels as pack animals. The camel transported warriors to the scene of battle but was not used in the actual battle, because maneuvering a camel in a tight spot was too difficult and its height and bulk made it an easy target.[42] Regarding the common observation that camel-riding raiders are depicted on wall reliefs, a close look indicates they are fleeing from battle.

Dogs evolved from the wolf and were domesticated more than eleven thousand years ago. Because dogs are scavengers, they are held in contempt by the biblical authors. David asked rhetorically of Saul, "Against whom has the king of Israel come

42. M. C. A. Macdonald, "North Arabia in the First Millennium B.C.E.," *CANE*, 2:1363.

out? Whom do you pursue? A dead dog?" (1 Sam. 24:15). Ecclesiastes (Qoheleth) gives faint praise when he concedes: "A living dog is better than a dead lion" (9:4). Job, once revered but later held in public contempt, alludes in his lament to the sheepdogs who guard his flocks: "Now they deride me, men younger than I, whose fathers I had disdained to put with the dogs of my flock" (Job 30:1). The sheepdogs of the Bible and the Iron Age have their closest modern counterparts in the pariah dogs of the Bedouin, who endure great physical hardships as they herd the flocks. Dogs in Mesopotamia were associated with the goddess Gula and healing rites. This association may furnish a clue to the interment of more than 1,500 dogs in a cemetery dated to the fifth century B.C.E. at Ashkelon (Ill. 32). The Phoenicians responsible for the burials may have considered the dogs sacred because of their association with a healing cult.

The Bible has an extensive vocabulary for "cattle," including *běhēmâ*, *miqneh*, *bāqār*, which embraces cattle (*Bos*), sheep, goats, horses, donkeys, and camels. Cattle were domesticated in Anatolia in the late seventh or early sixth millennium. The cow was used in the main for supplying milk, from which other dairy products were made. Ordinarily cattle were not utilized for meat. Certain ungulates were raised for sacrificial rites, notably young bulls, sheep, and goats. Again, in ancient Israel, the size of one's herd was the index of one's wealth, as indicated in Genesis: "Now Abram was very rich in livestock (*miqneh*), in silver, and in gold" (Gen. 13:2).

Pigs were domesticated by the end of the seventh millennium and were raised in Syria and Palestine in antiquity. Unlike sheep, they provide neither milk nor wool but an abundance of meat, making them a rich source of protein. Because of the absence of sweat glands, pigs require either shady environments or marshlands, or they can die from heat. The highland home of the Israelites was the perfect environment for pigs—shady oak trees and acorns that pigs relish. Several arguments from religion, hygiene, ecology, and culture are proffered to explain the pork taboo among the Israelites. Marvin Harris espouses the ecological argument that the prohibition stemmed from the costliness of raising pigs.[43] It seems more probable, however, that the contrast between Philistines and Israelites, between the uncircumcised and the circumcised, between pork eaters and nonpork eaters, established cultural boundaries between the two peoples and "distanced" one from the other. The Philistines had an appreciable number of pigs in Iron I, whereas the Israelites did not.

Chicken husbandry is associated with the Persian and Hellenistic periods, but there are some earlier indications of it as well. Rooster (*Gallus domesticus*) bones were identified at Lachish, dating to early Iron II. The most likely strata are V and IV, although Ussishkin does not rule out VI as the earliest possible date, i.e., the twelfth century. Pigeon and duck were found in the LB II stratum of Lachish but not

---

43. Marvin Harris, *Cows, Pigs, Wars, and Witches: The Riddles of Culture* (New York: Random House, 1975), 35–57.

Ill. 49: Onyx stamp seal and seal impression: stamp seal, left; modern seal impression, right. Engraved with a fighting cock and the inscription *ly'znyhw 'bd ḥmlk* ("belonging to Ya'azanyahu, servant of the king"). Tell en-Naṣbeh, 600 B.C.E.; see 2 Kings 25:23. (Courtesy of Z. Radovan, Jerusalem)

in the Iron Age.[44] The remains of domestic chicken (*Gallus gallus domesticus*) were found at Tell Hesban, dating to the seventh–sixth century B.C.E.[45] Two seals, perhaps a family emblem, have also come to light that are engraved with the figure of the same fighting cock. The first, dating to the late seventh century, was found at Tell en-Naṣbeh (Mizpeh) (Ill. 49). This dome-shaped seal is inscribed with the name of the owner and his title, "Ya'azanyahu, servant of the king." Very similar is a scaraboid seal of unknown provenance, dating to the last half of the seventh century, which reads "Yeho'ahaz, son of the king." Both officials may have been members of the same family.[46] The Hebrew word for "chicken" does not appear in the Bible.

Among the fancy dishes served at Solomon's table are "geese," literally "fatted fowls" (*barburîm 'ăbûsîm*) (1 Kings 5:3 [E.T. 4:23]). However, some guess "cuckoo" or "young chicken" instead of "geese."[47]

On the basis of skeletal evidence from Tell Jemmeh, Brian Hesse reports that the ostrich was present in the northern Negev in LB. He concludes from butchering

44. David Ussishkin, "Excavations at Tel Lachish—1973–1977, Preliminary Report," *TA* 5 (1978): 88–89.

45. Boessneck and von Den Driesch, "Preliminary Analysis of the Animal Bones from Tell Hesban," 266.

46. P. Kyle McCarter, *Ancient Inscriptions* (Washington, D.C.: Biblical Archaeology Society, 1996) 144–45.

47. William L. Holladay, *A Concise Hebrew and Aramaic Lexicon of the Old Testament* (Grand Rapids: Wm. B. Eerdmans, 1971), 47.

marks on the bones that the ostrich was served as food. Ostrich eggs are used for making beads and other jewelry.[48] Decorated eggs have been found at Phoenician and Punic sites. With the introduction of the Ethiopian ostrich, this bird once again became present in modern Israel.

"We remember the fish we used to eat in Egypt" (Num. 11:5) was one of the Israelites' complaints in the wilderness. Fish provided an important source of protein for the ancient Israelites. Information about fish in the biblical period is scarce, because written texts are few, as are analyses of fish bones, at least until recently. Also, the biblical authors use only the generic term *dāg/dāgîm* (pl.) for "fish," failing to differentiate among the species of fish.

During the First Temple period, one of the main gates leading into Jerusalem was known as the Fish Gate, where presumably fish were bought and sold (Zeph. 1:10). The Fish Gate was also built into the reconstructed city wall of the postexilic period (Neh. 3:3). Recent excavations in the City of David have yielded enough fish bones from the Iron Age to support the notion of a fish market there.[49] At that time marine fish from the Mediterranean, more than fifty kilometers to the west, and freshwater fish from the Jordan, thirty kilometers to the east, reached Jerusalem. For fresh fish, the fishermen would have to transport and sell their catch there the same day. It seems more likely that most of the fish brought to the Jerusalem market were preserved by drying, salting, or some other method.

Jerusalemites served up at least seven different species of fish (one of which, the catfish, was not kosher) during the monarchy. From freshwater rivers and lagoons on the coast came the large Nile perch (*Lates niloticus*). It was at home in Egypt but probably inhabited the coastal waters of Palestine during the Iron Age. Also from

Ill. 50: Bronze fishhook from Ashkelon. (Courtesy of the Leon Levy Expedition to Ashkelon; Photo: Carl Andrews)

---

48. Brian Hesse, "Animal Husbandry and Human Diet in the Ancient Near East," *CANE*, 1:220. See Othmar Keel and Christoph Uehlinger, *Gods, Goddesses, and Images of God in Ancient Israel* (Minneapolis: Fortress, 1998), 384–85, for images of ostriches at Ḥorvat Qitmit; 139–40, for images of the inland region of Israel/Judah.

49. H. Lernau and O. Lernau, "Fish Remains," in A. de Groot and D. T. Ariel, eds., *City of David Excavations Final Report III* (Jerusalem: Institute of Archaeology, Hebrew University, 1992), 131–48.

Ill. 51: Bone netting needle. (Courtesy of the
Leon Levy Expedition to
Ashkelon; Photo: I. Sztulman)

these waters and the Jordan River came the Nile catfish (*Clarias gariepinus*).[50] A third freshwater species was the *Tilapia*, still a favorite food dish. Saltwater, or marine, species exported to Jerusalem from Philistia include white grouper (*Epinephelus aeneus*) and sea bream (*Sparus aurata*). Gray mullet (*Mugil cephalus*) and meager (*Argyrosomus regius*) round out the list of fish eaten in Jerusalem during the First Temple period.

In his indictment of the elite women of northern Israel, the prophet Amos states: "The days are coming upon you when you shall be carried off in baskets (*ṣinnôt*), and the very last of you in fishermen's pots (*sîrôt dûgâ*)" (Amos 4:2). "Baskets" were commonly used for catching and transporting fish. This verse presents serious lexical difficulties, which are carefully analyzed by Shalom Paul.[51] The author of Job alludes to the Phoenicians who cut up Leviathan and "load his skin on boats, his head on fishing smacks" (*hatěmallē' běšukkôt 'ôrô / ûběṣilṣal dā(ya)gîm rō'šô*) (Job 40:30–31 [E.T. 41:6–7]).[52] The dragnet (*ḥērem*) and other devices for fishing are mentioned in the Bible, and excavated remains of these implements have been discovered.

WATER SOURCES

Water is so basic to life that it is one of the commonest metaphors in the Bible. Its necessity for the subsistence of humans and animals, and the limited sources available in biblical lands, make water and water conservation primary considerations in the daily life of Israel. In a society whose economy is so dependent upon agriculture, conservation of water is critical. Unlike Egypt, whose agriculture is based on irriga-

---

50. Ibid., 135. This nonkosher fish was probably eaten. No heads were found. Because the head of this fish constitutes a third of its body weight and is not eaten, the fishermen discarded the heavy head before carrying it to Jerusalem.

51. Paul, *Amos*, 129–35.

52. Lawrence E. Stager, "Haggling over Leviathan" (unpublished manuscript).

tion from the Nile, Canaan depends upon the seasonal rains. The relatively short rainy season is followed by a long dry season. The annual rainfall, between November and March, averages about 750 millimeters in the Mediterranean zone, and decreases sharply as one moves to steppe and desert. A key point is not just the rather low annual rainfall, but its concentration in a period of four to six months in winter. Owing to the scarcity of water, resources of all kinds are utilized to supplement the water supply. The primary sources of water are streams, springs, wells, cisterns, and reservoirs.[53]

As for the figurative use of water, the range of the metaphor is evident in the book of Jeremiah, where he at one moment refers to God as "the fountain of living water (*mayim ḥayyîm*)," that is, the flowing water of a spring (Jer. 2:13), and then somewhat later counters: "You [God] are to me like a deceitful brook (*'akzāb*)," a dry stream bed (Jer. 15:18). In the words of Amos, the prophet of social justice: "Let justice roll down like waters (*mayim*), and righteousness like an ever-flowing stream (*naḥal 'êtān*)" (Amos 5:24).

Springs

A spring (*'ayin*) or fountain is the work of nature, in contrast to a constructed well or cistern. The porous limestone of Palestine favored the formation of springs, as attested by the large number of places named for springs; for example, 'Ein-Gedi ("spring of the wild goat"), an oasis on the west shore of the Dead Sea. According to the psalmist, springs are a manifestation of God's graciousness: "You make springs gush forth in the valleys; they flow between the hills, giving drink to every wild animal; the wild asses quench their thirst" (Ps. 104:10–11). In preparation for Sennacherib's invasion of Jerusalem, Hezekiah blocked all the springs in the vicinity: "He [Hezekiah] planned with his officers and his mighty men to stopper the waters of the springs (*mêmê ha'ăyānôt*) that were outside the city; and they helped him. A great many people gathered, and they stopped all the springs (*hamma'yānôt*) and the brook (*naḥal*) that flowed through the land, saying, 'Why should the Assyrian kings come and find much water (*mayim rabbîm*)?'" (2 Chron. 32:3–4).

The Jerusalem springs are the Gihon and 'En-Rogel, the latter commonly identified with the so-called Bir Ayyub, "Job's Well." Springs often determined the location of settlements, which explains why many tells are situated near springs.

Wells

A well is an artificial shaft sunk into the ground to tap into the water table. In a prophecy of judgment on the imminent conquest of Jerusalem, Jeremiah says: "As a

---

53. Tsvika Tsuk, "Hydrology," *OEANE,* 3:132–33.

Ill. 52: Iron Age well at Lachish. (Courtesy of the Expedition to Lachish, D. Ussishkin, Director)

well (*bĕ'ēr*) keeps its water fresh, so she [Jerusalem] keeps fresh her wickedness" (Jer. 6:7). Owing to the scarcity of rainfall, wells were very common and vitally important in the life of ancient Israel. Wells are very ancient; the well at 'Atlit, for example, dates as early as the sixth millennium, while the deep stone-lined wells at Lachish and Tel Sheva are from the biblical period (Ill. 52). The most common Hebrew word for "well" is *bĕ'ēr*, occurring frequently in place-names such as Beersheba. Water shafts connect directly to springs at Hazor, Gezer, Megiddo, Gibeon, and Jerusalem. Ashkelon has more than a hundred wells dating from the Philistine period to the present.

It was easier to dig the shaft to the water table than to determine the location of a promising site. Sinking a well in a wadi bed holds good chances for tapping an aquifer. It is less clear how the ancient well diggers knew where to sink the shaft leading to an aquifer when the well lay within the ancient city. Of course, later diggers would have the precedent of earlier ones to guide them. The actual digging of the well is not unlike the manner in which a well is excavated on an archaeological dig. By sinking a shaft to the water table, an aquifer or underground spring can be reached. To get there, workers make a circular hole about one and a half to two meters wide and begin to dig. To prevent collapse on the way down, the shaft must be lined by chocking in rough fieldstones. Often well houses or wellheads in the form of stone slabs cover the opening to prevent people and animals from falling in and to protect the water from contamination.

The well was the customary gathering place of the village, the center of the social and economic life of the community. Perhaps driven less by thirst than by longing for the well of his hometown, David said, "O that someone would give me water to drink from the well of Bethlehem that is by the gate!" (2 Sam. 23:15). Women apparently had the daily task of drawing water from the well, using a vessel attached to a rope and then carrying the water from the well in jars (*kaddîm*) on their head or shoulder. Wells and events connected with them are prominent in the ancestral and other narratives. The story of Isaac and Rebekah (Gen. 24:1–67) concerns an encounter at a well; similarly the account of Jacob and Rachel (Gen. 29:1–14). When Abraham sends his servant to secure a wife for his son Isaac in Aram-naharaim, the servant meets Rebekah at the well outside the city of Nahor. She responds graciously and generously to his request for water, even watering his ten camels, an unwieldy and time-consuming process, especially when done with a jar (*kad*). The meeting of Jacob and Rachel is not unlike this encounter of Abraham's servant and Rebekah: "Now when Jacob saw Rachel, the daughter of his mother's brother Laban, and the sheep of his mother's brother Laban, Jacob went up and rolled the stone from the well's (*bĕ'ēr*) mouth, and watered the flock of his mother's brother Laban" (Gen. 29:10). A similar encounter with girls coming out to draw water at a well is told about Saul who was searching for Samuel: "As they [Saul and his male servant] went up the hill to the town, they met some female servants coming out to draw water" (1 Sam. 9:11). The betrothal of Moses and Zipporah is situated at a well, when Moses settled in the land of Midian. He sat down by a well, and the seven daughters of the priest of Midian came to draw water. Moses defended them against rude shepherds and watered their flock (Ex. 2:15–22). The use of wells was frequently the occasion of dispute. When Abimelech and Abraham contended about the water rights involving a well, the two made a covenant: "Therefore that place was called Beersheba ["well of the oath"], because there both of them swore an oath" (Gen. 21:31).

Besides providing water for human consumption, wells were needed for watering the herds and flocks. To facilitate the watering of animals, pools were constructed adjacent to the wells. Pools functioned much like cisterns and reservoirs by collecting and holding rainwater as well as spring overflow. "Pool" translates a number of Hebrew words, such as *bĕrēkâ* and *'ăgam*. After King Ahab had been mortally wounded in battle at Ramoth-gilead, east of the Jordan River, he was buried in Samaria, and there his chariot was washed by the pool (*bĕrēkâ*) of Samaria (1 Kings 22:38). The "Pool of Samaria" was identified by excavators George Reisner and Clarence Fisher as the large reservoir for water[54] constructed inside and against the

---

54. George A. Reisner, Clarence S. Fisher, and David G. Lyon, *Harvard Excavations at Samaria* (Cambridge: Harvard University Press, 1924), I. Text, 112–13. The internal measurements of the "Pool of Samaria" in its initial phase equal about ten meters by five meters. If, at a minimum, we suppose a depth of one meter at one end increasing to 1.75 meters at the other, this gives us a volume of 68.75 cubic meters, which equals 18,150 gallons of water. This seems to be a minimum volume for the pool. Of course, if the walls surrounding the pool rose a meter more above Ahab's court, then the total volume would be doubled; however, it would be unlikely that the pool would be filled to the brim, and unlikely that the side walls of the pool rose more than a meter above the court.

casemate wall in the northwest corner of the royal quarter on the acropolis. Its long axis was parallel to the north wall. In a later occupation of the palace the pool was rebuilt on a smaller scale.

Several wells were discovered at Lachish; one at the northeast corner of the mound had been dug to a depth of forty-four meters. Providing the city with water, these wells were partially responsible for making Lachish the second most important city in Judah.

Cisterns

Cisterns (*bôr*, *bō'r*), mentioned frequently in the Bible, are artificial reservoirs, usually cut into bedrock, for collecting and conserving rain runoff from roofs and courtyards. Water is also stored in dams and pools. Cisterns had to be kept covered and were cleaned annually of accumulated sediment. The porous nature of the native bedrock often required that cisterns be waterproofed with lime plaster to prevent leakage. However, cisterns cut into hard limestone, such as the Cenomanian deposits in the hill country of Palestine, were usually impermeable, requiring no special lining. Jeremiah mentions "cracked cisterns that can hold no water" (Jer. 2:13). Apparently these cisterns were hewn into porous rock that required a lime-plaster lining to be watertight, but the plaster had cracked and the cistern had leaked.

Cisterns were of various sizes and shapes. Many were bottle-shaped, with a stone covering the small opening at the top. The neck was a narrow shaft through which vessels were lowered by rope into the cistern. Other cisterns were bell-shaped. Bottle-shaped cisterns of MB were present at Hazor. At Raddana, sixteen kilometers north of Jerusalem, bell-shaped cisterns for water storage were associated with the pillared houses of the Iron I settlement. Iron II saw an increase in the number of cisterns at such sites as Gezer, Beth-Shemesh, and Tell Beit Mirsim. At Tell en-Naṣbeh, fifty cisterns were uncovered. The water supply at Umm al-Biyara ("mother of cisterns"), located in central Edom inside what became the Nabataean city of Petra, was dependent upon a number of deep cisterns cut into the summit. In his description of the Promised Land, Moses indicates that the Israelites will be able to take possession of "hewn cisterns that you [Israelites] did not hew" (Deut. 6:11). Cisterns have been discovered at many other sites as well, including Samaria, Ai, and Jerusalem.

Cisterns were a necessity for settlements lacking natural springs or other water sources. In Iron II, most Israelite households had their own cistern. We are told that, after his invasion of Judah in 701 B.C.E., Sennacherib assured the people of Jerusalem in a propaganda speech that if they would make peace with him, "then every one of you will eat from your own vine and your own fig tree and drink water from your own cistern (*bôr*)" (2 Kings 18:31; Isa. 36:16). In addition, public cisterns were located within the city walls.

In times of drought, cisterns, as well as other water sources, dry up. In this context, the word *gēbîm* is used twice, namely in Jeremiah 14:3 and 2 Kings 3:16; translators render it in a variety of ways, several using "cisterns." The following explanation seems to be the most plausible: "*gēbîm* are the natural depressions in the wadi bed which fill up when the torrent flows and remain full after the surrounding area dries up."[55] Three biblical texts fit this interpretation. Jeremiah proclaims: "Her [Judah's] nobles send their servants for water; they come to the *gēbîm*, they find no water, they return with their vessels empty" (Jer. 14:3). When King Jehoram of Israel was engaged in a military campaign against Mesha, king of Moab, and there was no drinking water for the army and the animals, Elisha promised water, saying, "Thus says Yahweh, 'This wadi shall produce *gēbîm* upon *gēbîm*'" (2 Kings 3:16). And in Ezekiel's description of the eschatological stream flowing out from beneath the Jerusalem Temple and descending toward the Dead Sea, the prophet observes: "But its [the Dead Sea's] swamps and saltpans (*gĕbā'âw*) will not become fresh; they are to be left for salt" (Ezek. 47:11). The reference is to saline wetlands along the Dead (Salt) Sea and the salt collected from evaporation pans.

Occasionally a cistern could serve purposes other than water storage, as in the incident when Jeremiah was imprisoned in one: "So they took Jeremiah and threw him into the cistern (*bôr*) of Malchiah, the king's son, which was in the court of the guard, letting Jeremiah down by ropes. Now there was no water in the cistern (*bôr*), but only mud (*ṭîṭ*), and Jeremiah sank in the mud (*ṭîṭ*)" (Jer. 38:6). According to the biblical account, four men were required to extricate Jeremiah from the accumulated sediment of the cistern (Jer. 38:11–13). Cisterns were sometimes used also for burials, although they were not legitimate burial sites. "Now the cistern (*bôr*) into which Ishmael had thrown all the bodies of the men whom he had struck down was the large cistern that King Asa had made for defense against King Baasha of Israel" (Jer. 41:9).

Underground Reservoirs

A cistern and an underground reservoir provided water for the Iron Age inhabitants of Arad. A circular, stone-lined cistern (once thought to be a well) was sunk in the valley at the bottom of the hill where the citadel stood. The cylindrical cistern collected runoff and rainwater. Water was carried from the cistern to a feeder channel, which cut through the wall of the fortress. From there the water flowed into a large underground reservoir, hewn out of the bedrock beneath the courtyard of the citadel. The reservoir has a capacity of 250 cubic meters, or about 66,000 gallons, of water.[56]

---

55. Mordechai Cogan and Hayim Tadmor, *II Kings*, AB 11 (New York: Doubleday, 1988), 45.
56. Ruth Amiran and Ornit Ilan, "Arad," *NEAEHL* 1:79.

Tel Sheva also has an impressive reservoir built in Iron II, which was designed to capture runoff and floodwater from tributary wadis.

The largest and most elaborate underground reservoir has been recently revealed by the excavations at Beth-Shemesh, directed by Zvi Lederman and Shlomo Bunimovitz. When the town was rebuilt as one of Solomon's provincial capitals (1 Kings 4:9), the town planners dug a huge reservoir in the bedrock beneath the houses, to collect rainwater and runoff from the roofs, streets, and piazzas. Channels from all over the town directed runoff into the cruciform reservoir, with a capacity of about 800 cubic meters, or 211,000 gallons. Three flights of stairs led down a vertical shaft to four halls carved out of the bedrock and lined with plaster.[57]

This type of underground reservoir located beneath royal cities is referred to as *šwḥ* in the Mesha Stela (Moabite Stone, Ill. 53), a victory inscription erected in Dibon (modern Dhiban in Jordan) by Mesha, a Moabite king; and as *šḥt* in the Tell Siran bronze bottle inscription of 'Amminadab, an Ammonite king, reigning about 600 b.c.e.[58]

Among the many building projects mentioned by King Mesha are those in "Qarhoh" (*qrḥh*), usually understood by most translators to refer to a town in the vicinity or in the district of his capital Dibon.[59] We prefer to derive the word from *qrḥ*, relating to "baldness," and see it as the "bald pate" within Dibon; that is, the acropolis on which the king built a temple ("high place" = *bmt*) dedicated to Chemosh, head of the Moabite pantheon; a royal palace (*bt mlk*); the wall of the park (*ḥy'rn*; cf. Eccl. 2:6); the wall of the citadel (*ḥ'pl*; cf. the "Ophel" in Jerusalem, Isa. 32:14, and in Samaria, 2 Kings 5:24); its gates and towers as well as the retaining channels of the underground reservoir (*kl'y h'šw[ḥ]*; cf. Gen. 8:2; Ezek. 31:15).

From the Mesha Stela it is clear that the Moabites distinguished the public underground reservoir (*šwḥ*) from the smaller cistern (*br*), which belonged to each household.[60] Mesha reports: "Now there was no cistern inside the town on the acropolis,

57. Shlomo Bunimovitz and Zvi Lederman, "Beth-shemesh: Culture Conflict on Judah's Frontier," *BAR* 23/1 (1997): 46–47. Zvi Lederman and Shlomo Bunimovitz, "The State at Beth-Shemesh: the Rise and Fall of an Iron II Border Town at the Philistine Frontier of Judah." Paper given at the Annual Meeting (November 16, 2000) of the American Schools of Oriental Research in Nashville, Tennessee.

58. McCarter, *Ancient Inscriptions*, 98–99. Henry O. Thompson and Fawzi Zayadine, "The Tell Siran Inscription," *BASOR* 212 (1973): 5–11, translate *'šḥt* as "cisterns."

59. Andrew Dearman, ed., *Studies in the Mesha Inscription and Moab* (Atlanta: Scholars Press, 1989). The name of Mesha's father, Chemosh-yat, appears on a fragmentary inscription probably part of a dedicatory stela. See John C. L. Gibson, *Textbook of Syrian Semitic Inscriptions* (Oxford: Clarendon Press, 1973), I:83.

60. Kent P. Jackson, "The Language of the Mesha' Inscription," *Studies in the Mesha Inscription and Moab*, 110: *šwḥ* (line 9): "This probably means 'reservoir,' in contrast to *br*, 'cistern,' (line 24). It comes from a root similar or identical to Hebrew *šwḥ*, meaning (in Hebrew) 'sink down.' The Biblical Hebrew cognate is *šûḥâ* (Jer 2:6). See also *'šyḥ* (Sir. 50:3)." Yigael Yadin linked *šwḥ* to the water systems of Megiddo, Hazor, and Gibeon; however, these waterworks tap into groundwater. *šwḥ* seems better suited to collecting basins, or underground reservoirs. Yigael Yadin, "Excavations at Hazor, 1968–1969: Preliminary Communique," *IEJ* 19 (1969): 18.

so I said to all the people, 'Let each of you make a cistern for himself in his house.' I cut the rock channels for the acropolis with Israelite captives." Mesha also made an *šwḥ* inside the town of Ba'al-Meon.

The Ammonite king 'Amminadab extols his accomplishments as builder in the Tell Siran inscription. Among the royal building projects he celebrates are "the vineyard (*ḥkrm*), the gardens (*ḥgnt*), the park (*ḥ'sḥr*), and underground reservoir(s) (*'šḥt*)."

ARTS AND CRAFTS

Besides written records, fruitful sources of information on arts and crafts are archaeology, architecture, and iconography. The Egyptians, especially, have preserved countless reliefs and paintings depicting the arts and crafts. Egyptian models of artisans at their specialties are very illuminating. Ben Sira, the author of Sirach (Ecclesiasticus), pays tribute to those who worked with their hands in antiquity, specifically the artisan, farmer, engraver, smith, and potter: "All these rely on their hands, and all are skillful in their own work. Without them no city can

Ill. 53: Moabite Stela of King Mesha discovered in 1888 at modern Dhiban, dating approximately 840 B.C.E.; black basalt. (Courtesy of Z. Radovan, Jerusalem)

be inhabited, and wherever they live, they will not go hungry. . . . But they maintain the fabric of the world, and their concern is for the exercise of their trade" (Sir. 38:31–32, 34).

Compared with their neighbors, the Israelites contributed little in the way of originality to the arts and crafts. Borrowers for the most part, they produced works hardly distinguishable from those of neighboring peoples. The proscription of the Second Commandment about making graven images (*pesel*) (Ex. 20:4; Deut. 5:8, as well as all the legal codes of ancient Israel), reflecting official Israelite religion, may have discouraged creativity in the arts and crafts. Nonetheless, images existed throughout the history of Israel until the postexilic period. The biblical authors attest to the practice; for example, Gideon made an ephod out of gold (Judg. 8:27), and

Ill. 54: A funerary stela of Neswy with the Ba-Bird perched on top, Ptolemaic period. A winged sun disc spreads over a scarab beetle which represents the rising sun, two winged uraei (cobras) hang from the disc and are flanked by two crouching jackals. These winged cobras are probably the seraphim of the Bible. (Courtesy of the Trustees of the British Museum)

Micah's mother contributed silver for a carved idol (*pesel*) (Judg. 17:3).[61] As Joseph Gutmann points out, Solomon's Temple with its graven images (cherubim and the like) was a direct contravention of the literal understanding of the Second Commandment, yet the biblical writers did not denounce the Temple.[62]

A *pesel* (verb *psl*, "to hew into shape") is an anthropomorphic or theriomorphic representation fashioned from wood or stone (also metal). The biblical injunction does not include painted images. The prohibition was not against art itself but against idolatry (crafting an image as an object of worship), to which the art could lead. The Israelites did, in fact, fashion images, which the prophets and other Yahwists regarded as "idols," a concept unique to Israel. "Then you [Israelites] shall consider unclean your silver-plated statues (*pĕsîlîm*) and your gold-covered images (*massēkōt*)" (Isa. 30:22). "And now they [Israelites] keep on sinning and make an image (*massēkâ*) for themselves, idols (*'ăṣabbîm*) of silver made according to their understanding, all of them the work of artisans (*ḥārāšîm*)" (Hos. 13:2).

---

61. Moshe Weinfeld, *Deuteronomy 1–11*, AB 5 (New York: Doubleday, 1991), 291.
62. Joseph Gutmann, "The 'Second Commandment' and the Image of Judaism," in J. Gutmann, ed., *No Graven Images* (New York: KTAV, 1971), 3–14.

The prohibition against images requires qualification. Obviously, cherubim, seraphim, and other images of "nature" and "mythology" were *at times* excepted from the prohibition. What seems to be forbidden is more often than not depiction of the male deity, for example, the winged sun-disc symbol for Yahweh on the Ta'anach cult stand above the bull calf, and the winged disc/beetle on the *lmlk* ("belonging to the king") seal impressions on the handles of the royal Judahite storage jars.

A proper distinction between aniconism and iconoclasm helps to clarify the issue of graven images. Tryggve Mettinger uses the term "aniconism" to refer to "cults where there is no iconic representation of the deity (anthropomorphic or theriomorphic [animal form]) serving as the dominant or central cultic symbol."[63] Hubert Cancik defines "iconoclasm" as "the religiously motivated, active hatred of images (*Bilderfeindschaft*), that is, the injunction against making or venerating religious images . . . within a given religion, . . . as well as the damaging and demolition of images of another religion."[64]

The Israelites had some of their own craftsmen (*ḥārāšîm*), a word occurring more than thirty times in the Bible. It appears particularly in connection with the building and decorating of the Temple and Tabernacle, as in Exodus 31:1–11 and 35:30–35, where Bezalel and Oholiab were chosen to construct the Tabernacle and its furnishings. The verb *ḥāraš*, "to cut, plow, engrave," was originally associated with woodworkers and later with metallurgists. The verb is often accompanied by a modifier designating a particular craft: "Zillah bore Tubal-cain, who forged vessels of bronze and iron (*lōṭēš kol-ḥōrēš nĕḥōšet ûbarzel*)" (Gen. 4:22). "King Hiram of Tyre sent messengers to David, along with cedar trees, and carpenters (*ḥārāšê 'ēṣ*) and masons (*ḥārāšê 'eben*) who built David a house" (2 Sam. 5:11).

There are far more examples of Phoenicians than Israelites who crafted these items. Among the artisans were carpenters, carvers in bone and ivory, smiths, weavers, tanners, leather workers, basket weavers, woodworkers, metallurgists, potters, glassmakers, and stone masons.[65] Little is known about the status and role of artisans in Israelite society, even though their handiwork was highly regarded, as attested by the report that Nebuchadrezzar II deported a thousand skilled workers to Babylon in 597 when he exiled King Jehoiachin of Judah: "The king of Babylon [Nebuchadrezzar II] brought captive to Babylon all the men of valor, seven thousand, the artisans and the smiths, one thousand (*heḥārāš wĕhammasgēr 'elep*)" (2 Kings 24:16). The conqueror considered the craftsmen valuable booty, although they were

---

63. Tryggve Mettinger, *No Graven Image?* (Stockholm: Almqvist & Wiksell International, 1995), 19, 195.

64. Hubert Cancik, "Ikonoklasmus," in H. Cancik et al., eds., *Handbuch religionswissenschaftlicher Grundbegriffe* (Stuttgart: W. Kohlhammer, 1993), 217–18: "Die religiös motivierte, aktive Bilderfeindschaft . . . (a) (im engeren Sinne) das Verbot der Herstellung und Verehrung religiöser Bilder . . . innerhalb einer bestimmten Religion sowie die Beschädigung oder Zerstörung derartiger Bilder . . .; (b) (im weiteren Sinne) die Beschädigung oder Zerstörung von Bildern . . . einer anderen Religion."

65. Only a limited number of crafts are treated in this chapter, because for the most part they were more highly developed among Israel's neighbors, such as the Canaanites or Phoenicians.

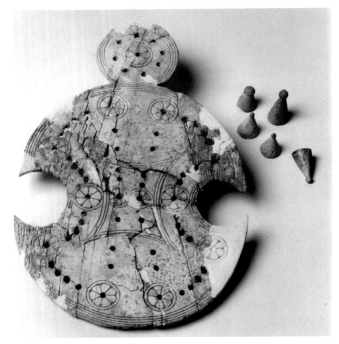

Ill. 56: A perforated ivory stopper, shaped like a male ibex, found in a Judahite house (Level IV) at Lachish. (Courtesy of the Expedition to Lachish, D. Ussishkin, Director)

Ill. 55: Ivory game board from Megiddo, dated Late Bronze II. (Courtesy of the Israel Museum; Photo: A. Hay)

Ill. 57: Worked ivory from hippopotamus tusk from Ashkelon. (Courtesy of the Leon Levy Expedition to Ashkelon; Photo: I. Sztulman)

Ill. 58: Bone gaming piece from Ashkelon, dated Iron II. (Courtesy of the Leon Levy Expedition to Ashkelon; Photo: C. Andrews)

not slaves. However, they may not have been Judahites but foreign craftsmen working in Judah.

Since minimal evidence is available about craftsmen except in the postexilic period, only the following generalizations can be made. Crafts were ordinarily hereditary in families. A village may have specialized in one industry, depending upon the availability of the raw material needed for a craft, such as clay or wool. Artisans of the same trade were located in their own quarter of the town. Jeremiah, for example, refs to the "bakers' street" (Jer. 37:21), and texts from Mari, Ugarit, and Nuzi also mention craft quarters. Remains of workshops have been found. It makes a great deal of difference economically whether craftsmen work in a cottage industry or in a factory—that is, whether they are full-time or part-time craftsmen. In many cases, artisans practiced their crafts at home, usually out of doors. Textiles, for example, were ordinarily made in the home. Certain crafts, especially those emitting unpleasant odors, were relegated to the edge of town.

Pottery

Pottery[66] made its appearance in the Levant before 6000 B.C.E.[67] The need for earthenware vessels in practically every aspect of daily life made the potter's craft one of the oldest in Palestine. Pottery (*ḥereś*) is a synthetic stone produced by firing clay to a sufficiently high temperature to change its physical characteristics and its chemical composition. Despite its antiquity, pottery technology changed relatively little over time. Pottery includes all the objects modeled from clay and hardened by fire, such as vessels, terracotta figurines, spindle whorls, loom weights, bricks, and tiles. The ubiquitous find in archaeological surveys and excavations from the sixth millennium to modern times is pottery, usually in the form of nonfriable sherds, an almost indestructible artifact.[68]

The potter's raw material is earthenware clay: *ḥōmer* is "worked clay," and *ṭîṭ* is "unworked clay" (wet clay). Second Isaiah remarks: "He [Cyrus] shall trample the rulers down like worked clay (*ḥōmer*), as the potter treads the unworked clay (*ṭîṭ*)" (Isa. 41:25). Two qualities make clay suitable for ceramic ware: first, it is plastic, meaning that when mixed with water, it can be molded into a permanent shape; second, it becomes hard when fired.[69] Sometimes "temper" is added to give clay the right consistency or plasticity. Quartz, calcite, and grog are the most common inclusions in the clay as temper. Robert Johnston lists various tempering ingredients: "threshing-floor straw, animal dung, cat-o-nine tail fuzz, shell or sand."[70] Straw is often but not always mixed with the clay as a binder in making sun-dried bricks. "That same day Pharaoh commanded the taskmasters of the people, as well as their supervisors, 'You shall no longer give the people straw to make bricks, as

---

66. The following sources were especially helpful: Robert H. Johnston, "The Biblical Potter," *BA* 37 (1974): 86–106; Nancy L. Lapp, "Pottery Chronology of Palestine," *ABD*, 5:433–44; and Anna O. Shepard, *Ceramics for the Archaeologist* (Washington, D.C.: Carnegie Institution, 1956).

67. Yosef Garfinkel, *Neolithic and Chalcolithic Pottery of the Southern Levant*, Qedem 39 (Jerusalem: Hebrew University, 1999), 16–18, 307. Lawrence E. Stager, "The Periodization of Palestine from the Neolithic to EB Times," in R. W. Ehrich, ed., *Chronologies in Old World Archaeology*, 3d ed. (Chicago: University of Chicago Press, 1992), 1:22–41; 2:17–60.

68. Undoubtedly, the most abundant remnant of today's culture will be undegradable plastic.

69. Shepard, *Ceramics for the Archaeologist*, 370.

70. Johnston, "The Biblical Potter," 90–91.

before; let them go and gather straw for themselves'" (Ex. 5:6–7). Animal dung also acts as a binder.

The earliest handmade pottery, dating to the Neolithic period, was simple and coarse, but it underwent development during the Mid- to Late-Neolithic period. The Chalcolithic period produced a greater variety of pottery forms, some of them painted. Plastic decoration and appliqué became more common. Pottery (handmade) of the Chalcolithic period was often made on a rush/reed or grass mat (also known as a "bat," see p. 136) on which the vessel is turned, and mat impressions are frequently found on the base of this pottery. Clay ossuaries have produced a great variety of anthropomorphic features, for example, the Piqi'im Cave and its many face types.

Ceramic vessels consist of a body (the main part), base or foot, neck, rim, and handles. The earliest vessels were bowls and jars. There were many regional variants in EB I, probably indicating a variety of potting centers. With the introduction of the kiln in EB II, the ceramics show greater uniformity than before. Even after the potter's wheel had been invented, the pottery was still mostly handmade. Large vessels (e.g., pithoi) were formed by the "coil" process, that is, by stacking strands of clay on top of one another. Handles were also added by using coils of clay.

Potters required a spacious area to ply their trade. Associated with their workshop were the wheel, a space for treading, a kiln, a field for storing fuel and vessels, a dump for the rejects, and a water source, either a cistern or a stream. An extensive pottery workshop dating to LB and the Iron Age was excavated at Megiddo. The eastern slope of the city was the site of a ceramic industry. Caves in the area made ideal workshops for the potters, especially since the lower temperature of a cave permits slower drying. Caves serving as potters' workshops were also discovered at Lachish and Hazor. Two shallow pits (C and D) in Cave 4034 at Lachish, dating to Early Iron I (twelfth century), were "possible emplacements for the potter's wheel."[71]

At Hazor (Area C), in Room 6225, the central courtyard of Building 6225, an installation was built in the form of a double wall. On the installation, about forty centimeters above floor level, a pair of potter's wheels (the upper and the lower) was found, consisting of two basalt stones, one pivoted above the other, with the upper cone-shaped stone (male) socketed into the recess cut in the lower stone (female). "It seems that this installation was used as a potter's working place, and that the entire Locus (6225) was a potter's workshop." Additional evidence for this assumption is a "much-rubbed sherd" found nearby, used for smoothing surfaces of the earthenware.[72] Lawrence Stager and Samuel Wolff cite Areas C and H at Hazor as examples of production and commerce in temple courtyards. In Area C, the potters' workshops

---

71. Olga Tufnell, *Lachish IV: The Bronze Age* (London: Oxford University, 1958), 292: "The irregular Pit C, for instance, about a metre deep, was probably caused by use of the stone seat or slab set in the wall, on which the potter sat."

72. Yigael Yadin, *Hazor II* (Jerusalem: Hebrew University, 1960), 101–2.

(Buildings 6063 and 6225), both located near the "Stelae Temple," most likely were associated with the temple activities. In Area H, there was a pottery workshop in the outdoor courtyard of the LB I temple. A bilobate potter's kiln (Locus 2160) with twenty-two miniature bowls in one of the firing chambers stood to the west of the altar.[73]

The preparation of the clay is a critical matter for the potter. First the potter must search for the proper clay sources and then collect the clay. Afterward the clay is wedged (de-aired) to expel air bubbles. This is accomplished by kneading or treading. Potters ordinarily tread their own clay to be certain it is prepared properly for throwing and firing.

Ill. 59: An early Egyptian potter using the tournette; dating around the fifth or sixth dynasty (circa 2500–2200 B.C.E.). (Courtesy of the Oriental Institute of the University of Chicago)

Then the clay is placed in a pit, water is added, and it is allowed to settle.

The potter's wheel is of two kinds: the slow or hand-turned wheel and the fast or kick wheel, also known as the double wheel (*'obnāyim*), which is rotated by foot. The slow wheel, made of clay, wood, or stone and used for finishing vessels, was introduced into Syria-Palestine in EB. The slow wheel is known as a tournette, that is, a horizontal revolving table mounted on a vertical shaft (Ill. 59). When the throwing process is complete, a piece of string is drawn through the vessel to detach it from the wheel.

It cannot be said with certainty when and where the fast or "kick" wheel was invented. The fast wheel came into widespread use early in the second millennium, when an approximation of "mass production" (or, better, factory production) began; the uniformity in pottery becomes even more obvious in the MB IIB-C period. The fast wheel consists of two parts: a lower pivot with a socket in the center, and an upper pivot with a projection in the center, the upper rotating on the lower. Pottery

---

73. Lawrence E. Stager and Samuel R. Wolff, "Production and Commerce in Temple Courtyards: An Olive Press in the Sacred Precinct at Tel Dan," *BASOR* 243 (1981): 97–98.

was thrown on a fast wheel, that is, a wheel with enough centrifugal force to form a vessel. In the course of his prophetic oracles, Jeremiah alludes frequently to potters and their craft. In a classic passage he furnishes the only reference in the Bible to the potter's wheel (*'obnāyim*), a dual form in Hebrew meaning literally "a pair of stones": "The word that came to Jeremiah from Yahweh: 'Come, go down to the potter's house [workshop] (*bêt hayyôṣēr*), and there I will let you hear my words.' So I went down to the potter's house [workshop], and there he was working at his [fast] wheel (*'al-hā'obnāyim*)" (Jer. 18:1–3).

A bat is a mat of woven reeds, rushes or grass, on which the vessel is formed, allowing the potter to move the piece around while shaping it. A bat

Ill. 60: Traditional potter in a workshop near Jericho. (Courtesy of D. Knight)

is for a slow wheel/tournette and is not used with a fast wheel in which centrifugal force causes the vessel to rise on the wheel when the pot is "thrown." Pottery made on a bat is slowly turned by hand, with centrifugal force playing no role in the process.

The potter manipulates the clay by hand on the smaller, revolving stone located on top. It is socketed into the lower stone disc, which, being larger and heavier, supplies the momentum and accelerates the turning. The potter, ordinarily seated at the edge of a shallow pit where the wheel is located, rotates the lower disc by foot. These stone discs could not be kicked fast enough to create centrifugal force, so a larger rim of wood was needed for that purpose. In other words, the stone discs formed the hub of the axle of the fast wheel. Ben Sira describes the potter who, while sitting, revolves the fast/kick wheel (*trochos*) with his feet: "He is always concerned for his products, and turns them out in quantity. With his hands he molds the clay, and with his feet softens it. His care is for proper coloring, and he keeps watch on the fire of his kiln" (Sir. 38:29–30).

Pottery vessels at times were embellished with decoration in several ways. The potter in some cases might apply a slip, defined as a liquid of fine-grained clay suspended in water. Red ochre had to be added for orange-red slip, which is characteristic of Iron II pottery vessels in Israel (Ill. 62). Burnishing, which seals the pores of a vessel, describes the smoothing or polishing of the pot's surface with a hard, smooth tool (stone, shell, bone) usually before the firing of the vessel. Wheel burnishing came into vogue in Iron II. Painting is another method for decorating pottery, for example, Philistine pottery of the early Iron Age, with its stylized water birds and geometric patterns.

From the Late Neolithic cultures through the Iron Age, there are periods when the ceramics were made to imitate metal vessels. The metal prototypes are often obvious from the carination, slip, and burnish of the ceramic vessel. Copper or bronze tableware is imitated by applying a surface slip of red, orange, or brown color and by burnishing

Ill. 61: Clay pool outside potter's workshop—near Jericho. (Courtesy of D. Knight)

or polishing the surface (Ill. 63). Gold, silver, and iron wares also have their lower-status counterparts in variously colored, slipped pottery. Metal rivets, handles, and attachments are imitated in clay. The periods when skeuomorphs (from Greek *skeuos*, "vessel," forms representing utensils) of precious metals in clay appear most frequently are EB II-III, MB II, and Iron II.

Painted or incised geometric decorations appear on pottery in the Neolithic, Chalcolithic, EB I, and LB periods, when the ceramic skeuomorph is related to textile and basket weaving. Stager studied a corpus of EB I painted pottery in the Jordan Valley

Ill. 62: Red ochre found inside a basket with circular weave from Ashkelon. (Courtesy of the Leon Levy Expedition to Ashkelon; Photo: I. Sztulman)

Ill. 63: Phoenician pitcher (*oinochoe*) with red slip burnish, imitating bronze vessel, dated eighth or seventh century B.C.E. (Courtesy of H. Seeden)

and central hill country. Characteristic of this pottery are groups of parallel lines painted in red or brown over the natural clay surfaces of several vessels. He demonstrated that this painted style of pottery (Line-Group Painted Ware) took its inspiration from basket and mat weaving.[74]

Kilns

At first, pottery was fired in a pit, later in a kiln, which reaches much higher temperatures than an open firepit. Firing is the drying process and welds the clay particles. The Hebrew words *tannûr* ("oven") and *kibšān* ("furnace") may designate a kiln; *tannûr* may signify both a small bread oven and a large pottery kiln.[75] Early kilns were mere firepits in the ground, with fuel piled over the pots and then lighted. The two conventional types of kilns are the more common vertical or updraft, and the horizontal or downdraft. They consist of three parts: a fire box where the fuel is burned; a grate above the firing chamber, where the vessels are placed; and a flue for emitting the gases. The usual fuels are dry grass, thorn bushes, dung cakes, wood, and olive pits (cracked or crushed), which have enough oil in them to stoke the fire. The firing process, at about 800 degrees centigrade (1,472 degrees fahrenheit), requires two to three days.

The earliest unmistakable factory for pottery is at Sarepta. In the excavations at Sarepta (modern Sarafand, biblical Zarephath), a Phoenician port city midway between Tyre and Sidon, James Pritchard recovered the remains of twenty-two bilobate-shaped kilns for pottery, varying in size from 1.3 meters to 3.8 meters. He speculated there may have been as many as a hundred kilns in the industrial area. The kilns were found in the Iron Age "Industrial Quarter" of the city, which served not only potters but also pressers of oil, dyers, and metal workers.[76] William Anderson describes the kilns of Sarepta's ceramic industry as "bilevel in form and bilobate in plan, with an ovate lower chamber divided into two kidney-shaped lobes by a baffle

---

74. Lawrence E. Stager, "Painted Pottery and Its Relationship to the Weaving Crafts in Canaan during the Early Bronze Age I," in A. Eitan et al., eds., *Eretz-Israel* 21 [Ruth Amiran Volume] (Jerusalem: Israel Exploration Society, 1990), 83*–88*.

75. For further discussion, see "Bread Making." A *tannûr* is also distinguished from a *tabun*. The *tannûr*, more popular in the north, has the fuel and heat on the inside; the *tabun*, more popular in the south, has the heat on the outside. Neither is closed on top.

76. James B. Pritchard, *Recovering Sarepta, a Phoenician City* (Princeton: Princeton University Press, 1978).

wall or tongue."[77] To retain heat, part of the firing chamber was located below ground and insulated with clay. The "grill" (a perforated floor/ceiling made of clay) of the firing chamber also functioned as the floor of the stacking chamber for the pots.

Sarepta was a major center for the production of Phoenician pottery. The excavators identified more than fifteen pottery workshops dating from the beginning of LB II (1400 B.C.E.) to the Persian period. Storage jars, bichrome and burnished bowls, plates, and jugs were found in the ceramic repertoire. The presence of settling basins, kilns, and workshops at Sarepta is evidence of large-scale production, not simply cottage industry. Throughout the Iron Age, production levels were probably at an all-time high, as the potters supplied clay shipping containers, known as amphoras, for the large-scale export of commodities, especially wine and olive oil.[78]

Iron Age Pottery

By the end of LB, ceramic imports from the Cypriot and Mycenaean worlds no longer appear in Levantine contexts. However, Egyptian garrisons either inside larger Canaanite cities or in outposts near Canaanite centers continued to exist throughout much of the twelfth century B.C.E. The presence of Egyptians is indicated by their special pottery, such as "beer bottles" and terracotta anthropoid coffins[79] (Ill. 224).

New and different ceramic repertoires appear during Iron I in southwest Canaan in the territory conquered by the Philistines. During the first generation, the Philistines produced, from local clays in Canaan, pottery types that closely resembled their earlier prototypes in their original homeland—somewhere in the Mycenaean world. These vessels included an Aegean-style cooking jug with one handle, craters decorated with water bird and geometric designs in black paint, stirrup jars, large and small bell-shaped bowls, and carinated dishes also painted in black monochrome (Ill. 67). By the third generation the Philistines had adapted several local styles of pottery to their repertoire; they painted their geometric and animal motifs in both red and black paint (the traditional Philistine Bichrome Ware)(Ill. 64, 65).

Meanwhile, in the highlands the Israelites were using relatively few ceramic forms in their small agrarian communities: two-handled cooking pots with triangular or flanged rims, collared-rim store jars (or pithoi), and undecorated bowls and juglets.

By about 1000 B.C.E. or earlier, a new fashion in pottery began to appear, first in coastal communities in Phoenicia and Philistia: red-slipped and hand-burnished pottery in the form of bowls and jugs. Clearly the potters were attempting to imitate in clay the more luxurious copper and bronze vessels of their day. The pottery, wheel-made and

---

77. William P. Anderson, "The Kilns and Workshops of Sarepta (Sarafand, Lebanon): Remnants of a Phoenician Ceramic Industry," *Berytus* 35 (1987): 42.
78. For eighth-century B.C.E examples of such ships, see "Phoenicians Ships."
79. Lawrence E. Stager, "Forging an Identity: The Emergence of Ancient Israel," in M. D. Coogan, ed., *The Oxford History of the Biblical World* (New York: Oxford University Press, 1998), 160–61.

Ill. 64: An assemblage of Philistine Bichrome pottery from Ashdod; it dates around 1150 B.C.E.; see also Ill. 113. (Courtesy of Trude Dothan, Hebrew University)

Ill. 65: Assemblage of Philistine Bichrome pottery; three of the vessels forming a wine set. The krater (far left) for mixing the wine with water; the drinking bowl/cup in front of krater and the strainer jug/carafe (far right) for pouring the wine. The stirrup jar (center left) for olive-oil based perfumes and ointments. Bottles (center right) also for perfumes and scented oils. Items from twelfth or eleventh century B.C.E. (Courtesy of Israel Museum)

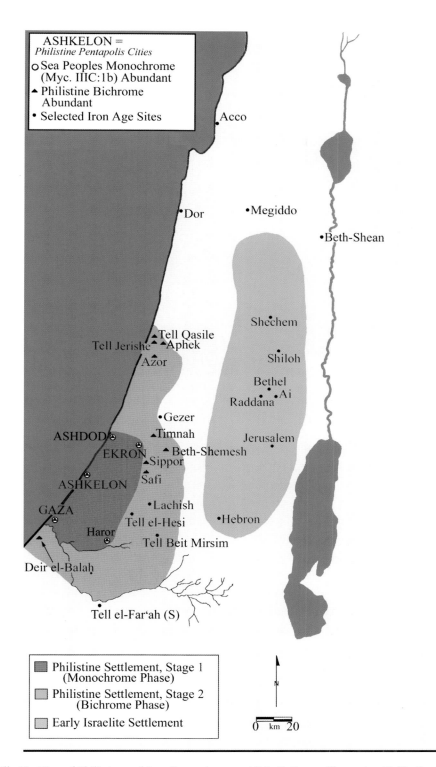

Ill. 66: Map of Philistine and Israelite settlements. (© L. E. Stager, illustration K. Vagliardo)

Ill. 67: An assemblage of Monochrome (Mycenaean IIIC:1b) Sea Peoples/Philistine pottery. From Tel Miqne-Ekron, Str VII, first third of the twelfth century B.C.E. (Courtesy of Tel Miqne-Ekron Excavation/Publication Project; Photo: I. Sztulman)

well fired, was of superior quality. "Phoenician Fine Ware" was the elegant pottery of this period; for example, the so-called "Samaria Ware," a type of bowl found in Phoenicia, Philistia, and the northern kingdom of Israel has a high-quality red slip and burnish. Besides household vessels, other items made of clay included mud bricks, figurines, jewelry, lids, toys, lamps, cult objects, pottery stands, bread ovens, loom weights, spindle whorls, and writing materials (sealings).

When attempting to match pottery vessels named in the Bible with corresponding types found in excavations, it is difficult to determine the vessel type from the text alone. A few common pottery vessels can be linked to Hebrew terms with some certainty (Ill. 70a, b). The earthenware jug (*baqbuq*) is a burnished decanter that functioned as a carafe. *gabîaʿ*, a ceramic pitcher, twenty to twenty-five centimeters high, held either wine or water. *kôs* denotes a drinking vessel, either a cup or a bowl, shaped like a shallow bowl in a variety of sizes, with or without handles. Assyrian reliefs depict scenes with the king drinking from such a bowl. A *nēbel* is the large storage jar, used especially for wine (*nēbel* means "wineskin"), oil, and grains. The largest size of this ovoid store jar holds a bath (thirty-two and one-half liters) and has four handles for carrying. The *kad* is a smaller and shorter version of a storage jar used for both flour and water. In the Elijah saga (1 Kings 17:12) the *kad* held the

Ill. 68: Iron Age I pottery assemblage from Israelite Shiloh with collared-rim store jars in the background. (Courtesy of I. Finkelstein)

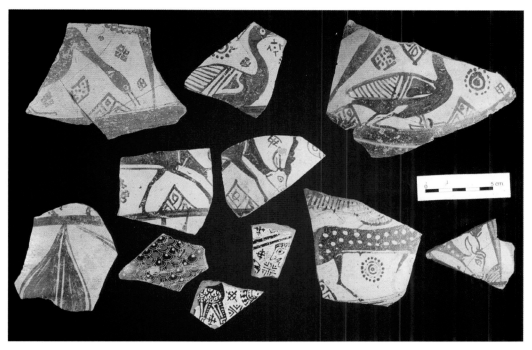

Ill. 69: East Greek pottery of Wild Goat style including stags and geese, except for two fragments from Chios with sphinx face and legs and except for fragment with scallop pattern from Corinth. From 604 B.C.E. destruction layer at Ashkelon. (Courtesy of the Leon Levy Expedition to Ashkelon; Photo: I. Sztulman)

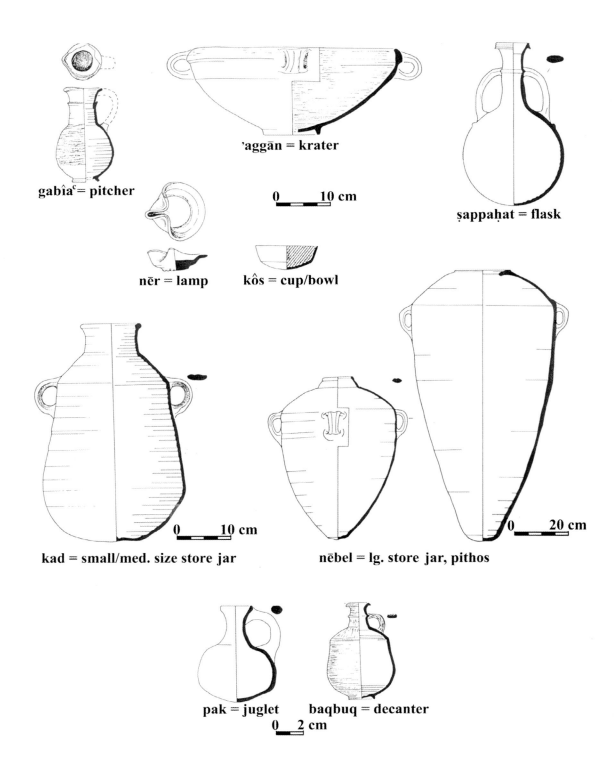

gabîaᶜ = pitcher

'aggān = krater

ṣappaḥat = flask

0 _____ 10 cm

nēr = lamp   kôs = cup/bowl

kad = small/med. size store jar

nēbel = lg. store jar, pithos

0 _____ 10 cm

0 _____ 20 cm

pak = juglet   baqbuq = decanter

0 __ 2 cm

Ill. 70a: Palestinian pottery with possible identification with terms in biblical Hebrew.

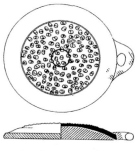

maḥăbat = griddle

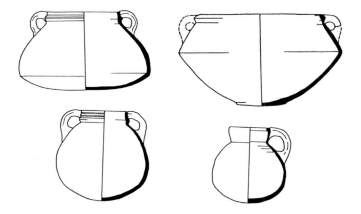

**Variety of Iron Age II cooking pots
among which should be dûd,
sîr, qallaḥat, parûr**

0 ___ 10 cm

Ill. 70b: Palestinian pottery with possible identification with terms in biblical Hebrew.

"handful of flour" of the widow of Zarephath (Sarepta). The water jar Rebekah carried on her shoulder to the well is designated as a *kad* (Gen. 24:15).[80]

Patrick McGovern and Garman Harbottle define the "Canaanite Jar," so-called because it most likely originated in ancient Canaan (the Syro-Palestinian coast), as "an ovoid-shaped amphora with two handles, a rounded or slightly flattened base,

---

80. James L. Kelso, "The Ceramic Vocabulary of the Old Testament," *BASOR* Supplementary Studies (New Haven: ASOR, 1948).

Ill. 71: "Canaanite Jar" from Ashkelon dated around 1700 B.C.E. This was the transport amphora for shipping wine and olive oil throughout the Mediterranean. (Courtesy of the Leon Levy Expedition to Ashkelon; Photo: I. Sztulman)

and a narrow mouth" (Ill. 71). They observe that it had a capacity of thirty liters and was "remarkably standardized" in size, shape, rim, base, and ware. They call it "the export pottery vessel par excellence for Mediterranean Sea trade," which continued in use "for thousands of years." It was utilized for the transportation and storage of wine, olive oil, tree resins, incense, and honey. Already between 1800 and 1600 B.C.E. the "Canaanite Jar," filled with wine or olive oil, was being shipped from the Levant to the Hyksos capital Avaris (Tell el-Dab'a) by the millions.[81]

Phoenician amphoras of the Iron Age are the descendants of the "Canaanite Jar." Amphoras were used for shipping; having "toes," they could be "stacked" or "nested" in holds of ships. These storage jars served as containers for food and liquids.

It seems likely that a very specialized industry was producing on a massive scale the standardized amphoras found on the two Phoenician ships laden with hundreds of these vessels, all holding seventeen to nineteen liters (Ill. 89a, b). This means that such mass-produced, special-purpose pottery was manufactured within 10 percent variation in volume, which approaches modern standards of production. Such potteries would have been especially designed to meet the needs of those who bottled commodities, such as wine or olive oil, for commercial shipping abroad.

Textiles

The textile industry is second in importance only to agriculture. Textiles, that is, fabrics formed by twisted or spun threads, reveal much about daily life, cult, economy,

---

81. Patrick E. McGovern and Garman Harbottle, "'Hyksos' Trade Connections between Tell el-Dab'a (Avaris) and the Levant: A Neutron Activation Study of the Canaanite Jar," in E. D. Oren, ed., *The Hyksos: New Historical and Archaeological Perspectives* (Philadelphia: University Museum, 1997), 143. The term "Canaanite Jar" was first applied to these amphoras by Virginia R. Grace, "The Canaanite Jar," in S. S. Weinberg, ed., *The Aegean and the Near East: Studies Presented to Hetty Goldman on the Occasion of Her 75th Birthday* (Locust Valley, N.Y.: Augustin, 1956), 80–109. Peter Parr added further details to the concept: Peter Parr, "The Origin of the Canaanite Jar" in D. E. Strong, ed., *Archaeological Theory and Practice* (London: Seminar Press, 1973), 173–81.

and trade.[82] Textiles were used for clothing, curtains, decorations, basketry, sackcloth, tents, rugs, wall hangings, shrouds, and other purposes. In contrast to Egypt's dry climate, the wet climate of the eastern Mediterranean was not conducive to preservation of these perishable substances, and few textiles have survived from ancient Palestine. Wool was the primary animal fiber in antiquity; flax and cotton the main vegetable (plant) fibers. While flax and cotton were imported from Egypt, they were also cultivated in Palestine. Cotton, however, is not attested earlier than the 8th–7th century B.C.E.[83] Wool (*ṣemer*), flax (*pištâ*), and, to a less extent, goats' hair were the fibers most often used in spinning. They were also the leading materials for weaving cloth for apparel and linen. "I [Yahweh] will snatch away my wool (*ṣamrî*) and my flax (*pištî*) that serve to cover her [unfaithful Israel's] nakedness" (Hos. 2:11 [E.T. 2:9]). The wool of white sheep served everyday purposes as well as luxury uses. The goats' hair was utilized in making rough covers, ropes, and tents.

The biblical law codes (Lev. 19:19; Deut. 22:9–11) prohibit the mixing of two fibers, such as wool and linen. The rationale for this ancient regulation is uncertain, but Martin Noth traces it to the general law against crossbreeding as a contravention of divine ordinance. The blending of fibers was forbidden, just as the yoking of different animals was proscribed. Menahem Haran notes that in biblical tradition mixing is forbidden in ordinary use, but in cultic contexts the appearance of heterogeneous combinations is regarded as a "hallmark of holiness."[84]

Wool

Wool (*ṣemer*) is a major class of fiber. The economies of the biblical world were, to a large extent, based on wool. It was also the principal fiber in Mesopotamia, comparable to flax in Egypt. Each sheep produces about one kilogram of wool, according to texts from Larsa (modern Senkereh), one of the ancient capital cities of Babylonia, thirty-two kilometers southeast of Uruk. Faunal remains of "old sheep" found in excavations indicate that sheep were raised not for their meat but for their fibers and to lesser extent for milk.[85] *Ovis* (sheep) or *Capra* (goat) are the most

---

82. The following have been particularly helpful: Elizabeth W. Barber, *Prehistoric Textiles: The Development of Cloth in the Neolithic and Bronze Ages with Special Reference to the Aegean* (Princeton: Princeton University Press, 1991); id., *Women's Work: The First 20,000 Years* (New York: W. W. Norton, 1994); Carol Bier, "Textile Arts in Ancient Western Asia," *CANE*, 3:1567–88; Grace M. Crowfoot, "Textiles, Basketry, and Mats," in C. J. Singer, E. J. Holmyard, and A. R. Hall, eds., *A History of Technology* (Oxford: Clarendon Press, 1954), 1:413–55.

83. Zohary, *Plants of the Bible*, 78

84. Menahem Haran, *Temples and Temple-Service in Ancient Israel* (Winona Lake, Ind.: Eisenbrauns, 1985), 160–62.

85. Hesse, "Animal Husbandry and Human Diet in the Ancient Near East," *CANE*, 1:203–22. The articles of Brian Hesse and Paula Wapnish are an invaluable resource.

plentiful bone remains by far. They are followed in importance by *Bos* (cattle). From Late Neolithic to the Iron Age, there was a growing dependence on sheep and goats.[86]

"White wool" (*ṣemer ṣāḥar*, Ezek. 27:18) seems to be the best type of wool. Its lustre certainly added to its appeal. The "white wool" of Damascus was prized merchandise. Ezekiel (27:18) included *ṣemer ṣāḥar* (conjecturally translated "white wool" or "wool of Zachar") among the choice commodities Tyre imported from Damascus. Commentators suggest Zachar may be located in the desert plateau *eṣ-ṣaḥra* northwest of Damascus.[87]

The frequent biblical references and metaphors regarding sheep and shepherds reveal the important place of wool in the economic life of ancient Palestine. "The first of the fleece of your sheep" is included among the first fruits to be offered by the priests (Deut. 18:4). King Ahab of Israel accepted wool as tribute from King Mesha of Moab: "Now King Mesha of Moab was a sheep breeder (*nōqēd*), who used to deliver to the king of Israel one hundred thousand lambs, and the wool of one hundred thousand rams" (2 Kings 3:4). These numbers appear to be inflated. David tended the sheep of his father Jesse (1 Sam. 16:11). Nabal became rich from raising sheep and goats in Carmel (modern Tell el-Kirmil, a small town in Judah about eleven kilometers south of Hebron). "He [Nabal] had three thousand sheep and a thousand goats. He was shearing his sheep in Carmel" (1 Sam. 25:2). The Carmel region is good pasturage, lying as it does near Ziph (of *lmlk* fame) and Maon. While this area is good grazing ground, it is not so productive for farming.

Linen

Flax (*Linum usitatissimum*), a wetland plant, is probably the oldest known textile fiber, domesticated at least by the eighth millennium. Fabrics from fine linen yarn found in the Naḥal Ḥemar Cave in the Judean Desert date to PPNB (7300–6300 B.C.E.). Perhaps there was simple loom weaving in the Neolithic period in the Naḥal Ḥemar Cave.[88] Linen fragments dating to Chalcolithic (ca. 3500) were retrieved from the Cave of the Treasure in Naḥal Mishmar. Flax was probably domesticated in Egypt by 4500 B.C.E.

In the Bible *pištâ/pēšet* (plural *pistîm*) refers to the flax plant, its fibers, and the linen that it produced. The flax plant is mentioned only once in the Bible, in connection with the devastation wrought in Egypt by the plagues: "Now the flax (*pištâ*) and the barley were ruined, for the barley was in the ear and the flax (*pištâ*) was in bud" (Ex. 9:31).

---

86. Caroline Grigson, "Plough and Pasture in the Early Economy of the Southern Levant," in T. E. Levy, ed., *The Archaeology of Society in the Holy Land* (New York: Facts on File, 1995), 250.

87. Walther Zimmerli, *Ezekiel 2*, Hermeneia (Philadelphia: Fortress, 1983), 67.

88. Ofer Bar-Yosef, Tamar Schick, and David Alon, "Naḥal Ḥemar Cave," *NEAEHL*, 3:1082–84.

Flax was grown extensively along the Nile in Egypt, as attested in Egyptian and other extrabiblical literature, and various sources tell us that the most prized linen came from Egypt. The book of Proverbs mentions the fine imported linen: "I [a prostitute] have decked my couch with covers of dyed Egyptian linen ('ēṭûn)" (Prov. 7:16). Where there is little rainfall, irrigation is required to raise flax. Irrigated flax seems to produce better linen than rain-fed flax. Using the imagery of the drying up of the Nile and the withering of the flax, Isaiah depicts the collapse of Egypt: "The workers in flax (pištîm) will be in despair, and the carders and those at the loom will grow pale" (Isa. 19:9). This was a great disaster, because the fields along the Nile had to be irrigated to produce flax.

Flax was grown and linen was made not only in Egypt but in Canaan/Israel as well. Flax was produced in Neolithic Jericho for oil, and probably also for linen. Many organic artifacts, including fabrics, cordage, and basketry, dating to PPNB, were preserved in the Naḥal Ḥemar Cave. (See below.) For the most part the fabrics were made from fine linen yarn. Among the remains of linen textiles was an exquisite net headdress. Jericho may have been the source of flax for the fabrics found in the Naḥal Ḥemar Cave. In the Cave of the Treasure in Naḥal Mishmar, situated in cliffs above the shores of the Dead Sea, Chalcolithic textile remains were recovered. They consist of thirty-seven linen and eight woolen samples. The colors represented are yellow, red, green, and black. Remnants of a horizontal loom and loom weights were also present. Archaeologists speculate that the flax from which the textiles were made may have been grown at 'Ein-Gedi, where there is an adequate supply of water for flax cultivation.

The Gezer Calendar (ca. 900 B.C.E.) mentions "the month (Adar-Nisan) of the uprooting of flax." Paleobotanical studies of Deir 'Alla in the Jordan Valley, east of the river, reveal that flax was grown there as early as Iron Age I and became an important crop plant by the seventh century B.C.E. Willem van Zeist and Johanna Heeres conclude that "all the flax from Deir 'Alla was grown on irrigated fields and that consequently irrigation was practiced at least since ca. 1200 B.C. onwards."[89]

Flax was cultivated both for its fiber and for its seeds. The fiber produced linen yarn and fabric; the seed was the raw material for linseed oil. Flax was the leading source of oil before the olive was domesticated.

In processing the flax, the fiber was obtained from the stalks that first had to be retted (soaked in order to soften and separate the fibers), dried, crushed, and beaten before the flax was spun into yarn and woven into linen cloth. After retting, the flax stems were set out to dry and to bleach, usually on rooftops, where the stems could be spread out. Then the flax was combed and spun into thread that, in turn, was

---

89. Willem van Zeist and Johanna A. Heeres, "Paleobotanical Studies of Deir 'Alla, Jordan," *Paleorient* 1 (1973): 27.

woven into linen. A glimpse of one stage in this process is provided in the story about the spies sent by Joshua to gather intelligence on Jericho. When they entered the house of the prostitute Rahab, she concealed them from the men of Jericho's king: She had "brought them up to the roof and hidden them within the stalks of flax (*pištê hā'ēṣ*) that she had laid out on the roof" (Josh. 2:6). These "stalks of flax" were undressed flax fibers.

Linen production was a prominent industry in ancient Palestine. The Chronicler refers to the "families of the linen factory (*mišpĕḥôt bêt-'ăbōdat habbuṣ*) at Beth-ashbea" [town or ethnic affiliation] (1 Chron. 4:21). Flax had many uses, depending upon the quality of the flax plants. The long fibers of flax made the best thread, while the broken fibers (tow) were used for lampwicks. Describing the gentle nature of the Servant of Yahweh, the prophet observes: "A dimly burning wick (*pištâ*) he will not quench" (Isa. 42:3).

There were several kinds and qualities of linen. Hebrew has three main words for "linen"—*bād*, *bûṣ*, and *šēš*—to designate varieties of linen, the finest worn mostly by royalty and religious personnel; but it is not easy to grade them with respect to quality. *bād*, linen cloth mentioned more than twenty times in the Bible, is probably ordinary linen. It was used in the linen vestments (*bigdê habbād*) of the high priest, which had to be of pure white linen (Lev. 16:23, 32).

Both *šēš* and *bûṣ* mean "fine linen." *šēš* is earlier, preexilic Hebrew, probably a loan word from Egypt, designating Egyptian linen.[90] "He [Pharaoh] arrayed him [Joseph] in garments of fine linen (*bigdê-šēš*)" (Gen. 41:42). The Tabernacle and its furnishings were woven from this same kind of "fine linen" (*šēš*) (Ex. 25:4), as were the sacred garments (Ex. 35:25). *bûṣ*, a late Hebrew word and probably an Aramaic or an Akkadian loanword, is a fine quality of linen. It is restricted to late biblical writings. When bringing the Ark to Jerusalem, David "was clothed with a robe of fine linen (*mĕ'îl bûṣ*), as also were all the Levites who were carrying the ark" (1 Chron. 15:27). On that occasion, David is described as performing a ritual dance before Yahweh while girded in a linen ephod (*'ēpôd bād*) (2 Sam. 6:14). Commentators dispute whether the "linen ephod" was a simple linen cloth or a special priestly garment. They point out that in the Chronicler's era, only priests wore the linen ephod, thereby accounting for the difference between 2 Samuel and 1 Chronicles. At any rate, in each case there is no question that the garment was made of linen, whether *bûṣ* or *bād*.

Linen was used for clothing of all kinds. Owing to its costliness, it was ordinarily worn only by the wealthy and the elite. The description of the virtues of a capable wife according to the wisdom tradition includes these: "She seeks wool and flax

---

90. Avi Hurvitz, "The Usage of *šēš* and *bûṣ* in the Bible and Its Implication for the Date of P," *HTR* 60 (1967): 117–21; "The Evidence of Language in Dating the Priestly Code," *RB* 81 (1974): 33–35.

(*pištîm*), and works with willing hands. . . . She makes linen garments (*sādîn*) and sells them" (Prov. 31:13, 24). Comparing Jerusalem to God's faithless bride, Ezekiel states that the bride's clothing includes "fine linen" (*šēš*) (Ezek. 16:10, 13). Anticipating Tyre's destruction by the Babylonians, Ezekiel compares the Phoenician city to a stately sailing ship. Describing the ship, he says: "Of fine embroidered linen (*šēš-bĕriqmâ*) from Egypt was your (Tyre's) sail, serving as your ensign" (Ezek. 27:7). Also, Ezekiel lists "fine linen" (*bûṣ*) among the wares Edom traded with Tyre" (Ezek. 27:16).

Israelite priests wore linen garments, including linen underwear: "The priest shall dress in linen raiment (*middô bad*), with linen underwear (*miknĕsê-bad*) next to his body" (*bĕśārô*) [euphemism for the genitals] (Lev. 6:3 [E.T. 6:10]). Ezekiel describes explicitly the exclusive use of linen garments by the priests: "They [the priests] shall not gird themselves with anything that causes sweat" (Ezek. 44:18). Linen was also used in priestly appurtenances: the ephod or long vest was made of "fine linen" (*šēš*) (Ex. 28:6); the checkered tunic was also made of "fine linen" (*šēš*), likewise the turban (*šēš*) (Ex. 28:6, 39).

Owing to the dry desert conditions surrounding Kuntillet ʿAjrud (Ḥorvat Teman), a fortress sanctuary and caravanserai in Northern Sinai where Yahweh and "his asherah" were worshiped, about a hundred cloth fragments from the period of the monarchy were preserved. There were several linen fabrics and a few pieces of woolen fabrics. Loom weights and worked wooden beams (probably for a loom), as well as flax fibers, spun yarn, and twisted thread, indicate that this was the site of textile manufacturing. The remains, including the textiles, date to about 800 B.C.E. Contrary to the prohibition of mixing fabrics of linen and wool (Lev. 19:19; Deut. 22:11), some fabrics at Kuntillet ʿAjrud were made by interweaving red-dyed woolen threads and light-blue linen threads. The mixed fabric (wool and linen) suggests sacerdotal garments, since mixing is prohibited in everyday clothing.[91] We know from other remains that Kuntillet ʿAjrud had cultic connections.[92]

Weaving was sometimes done at cultic places: "He [Josiah] broke down the houses of the sacred males (*qĕdēšîm*) who were in the house of Yahweh where the women weave linen garments (*baddîm*) for Asherah" (2 Kings 23:7). Stager and Wolff read *baddîm*, "linen garments," for *bāttîm*, "houses."[93] The meaning is to clothe a cult

---

91. When entering the Holy of Holies the high priest had to dress entirely in linen. Priestly garments made of plain linen were called "holy garments" (*bigdê-qōdeš*, Lev. 16:4).

92. Zeʾev Meshel, *Kuntillet ʿAjrud: A Religious Centre from the Time of the Judean Monarchy on the Border of Sinai* (addendum: Sheffer, Avigail, "The Textiles"), Catalogue 175 (Jerusalem: Israel Museum, 1978), no page numbers: "The abundance of written material at this site indicates its unique character and importance and suggests some cultic function. The drawings of figures and the decorative designs point in the same direction."

93. Stager and Wolff, "Production and Commerce in Temple Courtyards," 100, n. 5.

statue or an icon in a manner similar to the garments adorning the statues of the gods in Mesopotamia, as attested in the ninth and eighth centuries (Jer. 10:1–16).[94]

Linen could also be utilized for wrapping scrolls, as in the case of the Dead Sea (Qumran) Scrolls. Cave I at Qumran contained a large number of linen fragments, some used to enclose the scrolls.

Cotton

The cotton plant (*karpas*) was first domesticated in India about 3000 B.C.E. It was present in Mesopotamia after 1000 B.C.E. and in the Aegean in the sixth–fifth centuries B.C.E. There is evidence of cotton in the seventh century B.C.E. at Ḥorvat ʿUza, situated at the eastern end of the Arad Valley. Cotton is mentioned only once in the Bible; the book of Esther (1:6) refers to "white cotton (*karpas*) curtains" hanging in King Ahasuerus's palace at Susa (Persia). The Annals of Sennacherib (OIP 2 116 viii 64) note that the Assyrian king planted "the trees bearing wool" in the Amanus "which the people pluck and weave into clothing." These strange trees were cotton plants. Apparently there is no Akkadian word for cotton plants.

Spinning and Weaving

Textile techniques include spinning and weaving, which go back to at least PPNB (7300–6300 B.C.E.). They were typically women's work performed at home while tending the children. Their skills were used in making hangings and coverings for the Tabernacle: "All the women who were expert spinners (*ṭāwû*) brought hand-spun blue-purple, red-purple, and scarlet yarn, and fine linen. All the women who possessed the skill spun (*ṭāwû*) goat hair" (Ex. 35:25–26). Spinning is an ancient process for making threads by drawing out and twisting fibers, usually wool, goats' hair, and flax. Flax was the easiest fiber to spin. Drawing consists of pulling out the fibers lengthwise, and twisting serves the indispensable purpose of making the threads continuous for weaving. Spun thread is used for weaving cloth, whereas to produce matting or basketry unspun fibers are woven.

Spinning is done by means of the distaff and spindle. The distaff (a large stick) holds on its cleft end the unspun flax or wool from which the thread is drawn (Ill. 72). The hand-held spindle, which is used to this day, is the rotating rod or shaft on which the fibers are twisted to form thread and are then wound. The spindle may be weighted by pierced, circular objects known as spindle whorls, which have been recovered in large quantity at practically every excavation in Palestine. They are made of various materials, such as rounded and perforated fragments of pottery, bone, ivory, and

---

94. A. Leo Oppenheim, "The Golden Garments of the Gods," *JNES* 8 (1949): 172–93.

wood. Spindle whorls, dating as early as the Neolithic period, were found at 'Ein el-Jarba in the southwestern area of the Jezreel Valley. Spinning with spindle whorls was well known at Jericho about the same time. The book of Proverbs includes a brief description: "She [the capable wife] puts her hands to the distaff (*kîšôr*), and her hands hold the spindle (*pālek*)" (Prov. 31:19).

Ill. 72: Woman spinning wool into yarn using a distaff. Note spindle whorl on staff. (Courtesy of L. E. Stager)

Weaving ('*ōrēg*, *ḥōšēb*, "weaver") is the interlacing of a series of spun threads or yarns, one called the warp (vertical yarns) and the other the woof or weft (horizontal yarns), so that they cross at right angles to form a textile. The warp threads are stretched on a loom for weaving; the woof threads are then

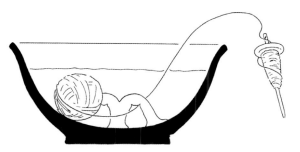

Ill. 73: Spinning bowl for flax/linen yarn. (Drawing: Catherine S. Alexander)

passed over and under them. A shuttle is a device for passing the horizontal threads of the woof between the vertical threads of the warp. Shuttles have been found at several sites. The heddle rod (*mānôr*) consists of parallel wires in a loom used to separate and guide the warp threads and raise and lower them in weaving. The heddle rod is another name for the weaver's beam. 1 Samuel 17:7 (also 2 Sam. 21:19) compares the staff of Goliath's spear with a weaver's beam (*měnôr 'ōrgîm*). Like the heddle rod, the shaft of the spear had a thong attached to a ring for slinging. The purpose of the thong was to increase the velocity of the spear when thrown. The comparison is to the shape and appearance of the spear, not to its size; the heddle rod was not the largest part of the loom.[95] Since there was no name for this exotic weapon in Hebrew, the writer had to describe it analogously with what was known in the material culture of the Israelites, namely the weaver's beam (Ill. 74).

Looms are basically of two kinds, the horizontal and the vertical. The horizontal ground loom, the more prevalent and older (end of Neolithic) of the two and also the more portable, consists of two beams fastened to four pegs driven into the ground,

95. Yigael Yadin, "Goliath's Javelin and the *menor 'orgim*," *PEQ* 86 (1955): 58–69.

Ill. 74: Greek kylix from fifth century B.C.E, depicting the Greek warrior throwing the javelin, the thong of which was likened to a "weaver's beam," when the biblical authors were describing Goliath's weapons (1 Sam. 17:7). The thong and cord wound around the shaft of the javelin so that it could be hurled a greater distance with greater accuracy. (Courtesy of the Trustees of the British Museum)

with the warp stretched between them. The oldest horizontal looms were found at Naḥal Mishmar and Naḥal Ḥemar.[96] The earliest known representation appears on a bowl (late fourth millennium) from Badari in Upper Egypt. Nomadic pastoralists still use the horizontal ground loom.

The vertical loom is basically a wooden frame used for making thread into cloth by weaving strands together at right angles. The vertical-framed loom consists of two vertical beams and a horizontal beam. The warp is strung from the horizontal beam and held taut at the bottom by perforated loom weights of clay or stone. Clay loom weights found in straight rows indicate the position of vertical looms, sometimes located near walls. The warp-weighted (longitudinal threads stretched and held in tension) loom was already known in the mid-third millennium (Ill. 76). The weavers in antiquity are always depicted sitting directly in front of the vertical loom.

Weaving was a familiar home craft at Timnah (Tel Batash) and several other Iron Age sites where large numbers of loom weights were found within the houses. The various weights were attached to the ends of the warp threads to keep them taut. In the Levant, these loom weights, pierced for attaching the warp thread, came in varied shapes: pyramidal, pierced near the apex; circular, pierced through the center; also, a cylindrical loom weight of unbaked clay, unpierced (Ill. 75). In the last case, the thread was tied around the "pinched waist" of the loom weights, found at the Philistine sites of Ashkelon, Ekron, and Ashdod.[97] These are the Aegean spool weights.

---

96. Pessah Bar-Adon, *The Cave of the Treasure* (Jerusalem: Israel Exploration Society, 1980), 177–85.
97. Stager, "Forging an Identity: The Emergence of Ancient Israel," 165–66. Margaret Wheeler, "Loomweights and Spindle Whorls," in K. M. Kenyon and T. A. Holland, eds., *Excavations at Jericho* (London: British School of Archaeology in Jerusalem), 4:623: "The clay loomweights found at Jericho fall into two distinct types: pierced conical or globular forms often showing grooves where the coils of yarn have worn into them, and pierced, circular forms."

Ill. 75: Unbaked spherical clay loomweights from Ashkelon; also used as jar stoppers, dated to Iron Age II. (Courtesy of the Leon Levy Expedition to Ashkelon; Photo: C. Andrews)

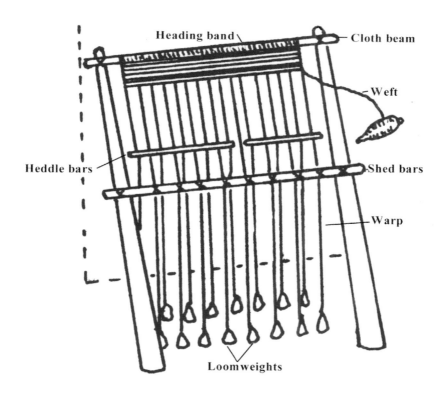

Ill. 76: Sketch of warp-weighted loom. (Drawing: M. Vostral, after E. J. W. Barber, *Prehistoric Textiles*)

Ill. 77: Tomb of Khnumhotep at Beni Hasan, dated around 1900 B.C.E. At left: horizontal loom (as seen from above) operated by two women. At right: women spinning yarn using the spindle with whorl; overseer stands in background. (Courtesy of the Metropolitan Museum of Art, Rogers Fund, 1933)

The Samson-Delilah story illustrates the weaving process: Delilah tries to dissipate Samson's strength by weaving his hair into the warp of her loom. Samson confided to Delilah: "If you weave (*ta'argî*) the seven locks of my hair into the web and fasten them with the [loom] pin, I shall be as weak as any other man" (Judg. 16:13 [compare Greek]). Seated on the ground beside a vertical loom with Samson's head in her lap, Delilah found it easy to weave his long hair into the warp of the loom while he slept.

Weaving and spinning took place near the tenth-century Cultic Structure at Ta'anach. Sixty ceramic loom weights, a spindle whorl, 140 sheep astragali, and store jars containing grain have been recovered from there.[98] In a cult room at Megiddo (Str VA-IVB, Locus 2081), parallel to Ta'anach in type and date, a bowl full of sheep/goat astragali, incense altars, whorls or loom weights, all indicative of weaving, were preserved.[99]

In the Chalcolithic layer of the Cave of the Treasure in Naḥal Mishmar were objects associated with weaving, for example, two-edged bone needle-shuttles and parts of a horizontal ground loom.[100]

Tamar Schick reports that hundreds of examples of cordage, matting, and basketry, dating to PPNB, were found in the Naḥal Ḥemar Cave. The cordage consists of ropes of unspun fibrous material. Containers built of cordage coated with layers of asphalt (*ḥēmār*), both inside and outside, to serve as the binding are also represented. Examples of both twined and coiled basketry are present.[101]

The crafts of weaving and basket and mat making are represented in the Cave of the Warrior, a fourth-millennium burial in the Judean Desert, in the Jericho area. The primary assemblage consists of three objects: a large wrapping sheet, a medium-sized rectangular cloth, and a long, narrow sash. The so-called "wrapping sheet" is a shroud about seven meters long and two meters wide woven from linen yarn, embellished with decorative bands and warp fringes. The "sash," two meters long and twenty centimeters wide, is made of linen threads.[102] It could be an EB I prototype of the

---

98. Paul W. Lapp, "The 1963 Excavations at Ta'annek," *BASOR* 173 (1964): 4–44; "The 1966 Excavations at Tell Ta'annek," *BASOR* 185 (1967): 2–39; "Taanach by the Waters of Megiddo," *BA* 30 (1967): 2–27; "The 1968 Excavations at Tell Ta'annek," *BASOR* 195 (1969): 2–49. For the identification of astragali as sheep/goat rather than those of pig, see Lawrence E. Stager and Sam Wolff in "Production and Commerce in Temple Courtyards," 100, n. 7.

99. Gordon Loud, *Megiddo II: Seasons of 1935–39* (Chicago: Oriental Institute, University of Chicago Press, 1948), 44–45, 161–62.

100. Bar-Adon, *The Cave of the Treasure*, 185: "The presence of the loom seems to indicate that at least some of the textiles found in the cave were produced there. Perhaps the flax, from which most of the textiles were made, grew at 'En-gedi, as it is the only place in the vicinity [Naḥal Mishmar is ten kilometers south of the oasis of 'En-gedi] where there is sufficient water for the cultivation of this plant."

101. Tamar Schick, "Cordage, Basketry and Fabrics," in O. Bar-Yosef and D. Alon, *Nahal Hemar Cave*, 'Atiqot 18 (Jerusalem: Israel Exploration Society, 1988), 31–43. Compare Elizabeth Crowfoot, "Textiles, Matting and Basketry," in Kenyon and Holland, eds., *Excavations at Jericho*, 2:662–63. Also, Bar-Adon, *The Cave of the Treasure*, 190: "The finds from both the early and the later strata include mats, trays, baskets, and ropes. The Chalcolithic material is particularly rich and varied, and is exceptional in the number of objects found, their size and their state of preservation."

102. Tamar Schick, *The Cave of the Warrior* (Jerusalem: Israel Antiquities Authority, 1998).

biblical "belt" or "sash." Although the evidence is flimsy, irrigated flax grown around Jericho may be the source from which these beautiful textiles were woven. In summation, the "warrior" had kilt, sash, and a large shroud buried with him along with his sandals, a wooden offering bowl, his bow, and plaited mats.[103]

Embroidery

Embroidery (*rōqēm*, "embroiderer") or decorative needlework consists of interweaving threads of various colors in specific patterns, as with the Tabernacle hangings. The needles were made from bronze, bone, and ivory. Ezekiel mentions that Egypt and Edom produced embroidery (Ezek. 27:7, 16). Embroidered garments were a sign of luxury, worn by royalty and by the high priest (Ex. 28:39). In Psalm 45, a royal psalm composed for the wedding of a king, it is said of the queen: "In embroidery (*rĕqāmôt*) she is led to the king" (Ps. 45:15; E.T. 45:14). "I [Yahweh] clothed you [Jerusalem, the harlot] with an embroidered (*riqmâ*) gown" (Ezek. 16:10; also Ezek. 26:16).

The design of the Tabernacle curtains is described in detail. "Moreover you shall make the Tabernacle with ten curtains of fine twisted linen, and blue-purple, red-purple, and scarlet yarns; you shall make them with cherubim skillfully worked into them (*maʿăśēh ḥōšēb* [lit. "the work of a weaver"]) (Ex. 26:1). Bezalel and Oholiab, craftsmen designated to construct the Tabernacle, were noted for embroidery among their other skills. "He [Yahweh] has endowed them [Bezalel and Oholiab] with skill to execute all types of work: engraving, embroidering, the making of variegated cloth of blue-purple, red-purple, scarlet yarn, and fine linen thread, weaving, and all other arts and crafts" (Ex. 35:35; also Ex. 38:23).

Considerable value was attached to fine embroidery. Awaiting Sisera's triumphant return, his anxious mother speculates that the reason for his delay has to do with gathering the booty of war: "Are they not finding and dividing the spoil?—A girl or two for every man; spoil of dyed stuffs (*ṣĕbāʿîm*) for Sisera, spoil of dyed stuffs embroidered (*ṣĕbāʿîm riqmâ*), two pieces of dyed work embroidered (*ṣebaʿ riqmātayim*) for my neck as spoil?" (Judg. 5:30).

Fulling

Fulling denotes the shrinking, cleaning, and thickening of new cloth to make it attractive. The cleaning process consists of trampling, beating, or rubbing the fabric. The participle *kōbēs*, designating the "fuller," comes from the Hebrew root *kbs*, "to clean cloth by treading, kneading, and beating." Washing was accomplished by

---

103. Perhaps the "shroud" was an outer garment, the kilt an undergarment, and the sash/belt around the complete dress.

treading on the cloth in tubs, a process that required an abundant water source such as a spring, cistern, or pool.

Isaiah was directed by Yahweh to meet King Ahaz of Judah "at the end of the conduit of the Upper Pool (*tĕ'ālat habbĕrēkâ*) on the highway to the Fuller's Field (*śĕdēh kôbēs*)" (Isa. 7:3). There the prophet was to encourage the king not to fear the impending attack of Rezin and Pekah. This same location was the meeting place between the Assyrian commanders and the officers of King Hezekiah (Isa. 36:2; 2 Kings 18:17). The lack of geographical detail precludes identification of the "Upper Pool" or the "Fuller's Field," although there are many conjectures. Dan Bahat (also David Ussishkin) locates the Fuller's Field and the conduit on the northern side of Jerusalem.[104]

The fulling process preceded dyeing in order to cleanse the wool and woven cloth of natural oils and gummy substances adhering to the raw fibers. Various substances, not soap, were used for washing; soap was a later invention. Jeremiah specifies two detergents—*neter* and *bōrît* (from *bārar* "to cleanse"): "Though you wash yourself with natron (*neter*) and use much lye (*bōrît*), the stain of your guilt is still before me, says Yahweh" (Jer. 2:22). *neter* ("natron") is a mineral of hydrous sodium carbonate. Lye is a solution of potash (potassium carbonate) and soda (sodium carbonate) in water. Potash is obtained by burning saliferous desert plants. *bōrît* designates a vegetable alkali, not soap in the strict sense. Both *neter* and *bōrît* have detergent properties. Petrie described "the widespread bed of ashes" across the mound of Tell el-Hesi, which he mistakenly identified with Lachish, and attributed the phenomenon to the burning of plants for alkali. Bliss associated this bed of ashes with the "fourth city," which he dated about 1300 B.C.E., and assigned the ashes to furnaces, but he did not know their use.[105]

Dyeing

Dyeing of cloth was practiced in Egypt about 2500 B.C.E., as evidenced in linen mummy wrappings.[106] In Akkadian, *gabu* ("alum") apparently comes from Egypt and is used in dyeing, tanning, and glassmaking.[107] The sources for dyeing are mineral, plant, and animal matter. Since colors are a mark of status, dyeing was a major industry. The simplest dyeing method was immersion of the finished cloth in a dye bath. The basins and vats were very small. Pierced stone vats have been mistakenly

---

104. Dan Bahat, "The Fuller's Field and the 'Conduit of the Upper Pool,'" in A. Ben-Tor, J. C. Greenfield, and A. Malamat, eds., *Eretz-Israel* 20 [Yigael Yadin Volume] (Jerusalem: Israel Exploration Society, 1989), 253–255 [Eng. 203*–204*].

105. W. M. Flinders Petrie, *Tell el Hesy (Lachish)* (London: PEQ, 1891), 16. Frederick J. Bliss, *A Mound of Many Cities* (London: PEQ, 1894), 64–67.

106. Alfred Lucas and J. R. Harris, *Ancient Egyptian Materials and Industries*, 4th ed. (London: E. Arnold, 1962).

107. *CAD*, 5:7.

interpreted as dyeing vats; actually they are olive oil presses (see, for example, Tell Beit Mirsim). Linen and cotton were dyed before the thread was woven into cloth. Dyes were applied by the use of mordants or dye fixatives (early second millennium in Egypt). Alum was a favorite mordant. After dyeing, the excess was returned to the vats because dyes were expensive. An abundance of water was required for rinsing.

The Bible's lack of a highly developed color vocabulary keeps commentators from making clear-cut distinctions among the various hues. Nonetheless, the Bible refers often to richly colored furnishings, as well as to artisans like Bezalel and Oholiab, who were capable of embroidering them (Ex. 35:35).[108]

Purple was the most costly color in biblical times, used exclusively by the wealthy and the aristocracy.[109] It adorned the garments of the high priest (Ex. 28:6, 15, 31), as well as the inner drapery of the Tabernacle (*miškān*). In foreign cults, the images of the gods were decked in purple. "Their clothing is blue-purple (*tĕkēlet*) and red-purple (*'argāmān*)" (Jer. 10:9).

'argāmān and *tĕkēlet*[110] were used as adornments for the sanctuaries. The three colored wools alluded to in the Bible are *tĕkēlet*, *'argāmān*, and *tôla'at šānî* ("scarlet yarn"). Isaiah uses "scarlet" and "crimson" as metaphors for sinful deeds, perhaps because of their association with blood. "Though your sins are like scarlet (*šānîm*), they shall be like snow; though they are red like crimson (*tôlā'*), they shall become like wool" (Isa. 1:18). Red is a popular color because it is easily distinguished. In preparation for the building of the Temple, Solomon requested King Hiram of Tyre to furnish "an artisan skilled to work . . . in red-purple (*'argĕwān* [occurs in later Hebrew for *'argāmān*]), crimson (*karmîl*), and blue-purple (*tĕkēlet*) fabrics (2 Chron. 2:6 [E.T. 2 Chron. 2:7]). *'argāmān* and *tĕkēlet* were among the items of international trade and tribute. In the first millennium B.C.E. purple-dyed wool was brought by caravan from the west to Mesopotamia, where it was frequently used to decorate apparel intended for the wardrobe of the gods. Tiglath-pileser III's booty from the campaigns against Syria and Palestine included the following: "Multi-coloured garments, linen garments, blue-purple and red-purple wool, . . . live sheep whose wool is dyed red-purple (*'argamanu*), flying birds of the sky whose wings are dyed blue-purple (*takilte*)"[111]

---

108. Benno Landsberger, "Über Farben im Sumerisch-Akkadischen," *JCS* 21 (1967): 147–49.

109. Waldo H. Dubberstein, "Comparative Prices in Later Babylonia (625–400 B.C.)," *American Journal of Semitic Languages* 56 (1939): 29: "One price quotation for wool is two pounds of wool for one shekel. Dyed wool was much more expensive. One pound of wool dyed purple-blue cost fifteen shekels."

110. Baruch A. Levine, *Numbers 1–20*, AB (New York: Doubleday, 1993), 400–401: "Akkadian attests *takiltu*, related to the Akkadian adjective *taklu* 'consistent, fast.' This etymology reflects the fact that the dye in question maintains a highly consistent or permanent hue. The Palestinian Talmud (*Berakot* 1:5) describes this color as that of the sea, and at Ugarit it was called *uqnu*, the word for lapis lazuli."

111. Hayim Tadmor, *The Inscriptions of Tiglath-pileser III King of Assyria* (Jerusalem: Israel Academy of Sciences and Humanities, 1994), 69: Tadmor thinks this is a Phoenician king who "apparently went to great lengths to please the Assyrian emperor by inventing these extravagant presents: live red-purple sheep and blue-purple birds" (p. 70, note to line 4). See Landsberger, "Über Farben im Sumerisch-Akkadischen," *JCS* 21 (1967): 147–49, for *argamanu* (reddish-purple) and *takiltu* (bluish-purple).

The Phoenician coast was famous for the purple dye industry in antiquity. As early as 2000 B.C.E., purple dye was associated with the Phoenicians, who traded in purple-dyed fabrics. The names "Canaan" and "Phoenicia," in fact, are probably cognate terms meaning purple. The word "Canaan" may derive from the Akkadian *kinaḫḫu*, "red-purple," while "Phoenicia" probably comes from the Greek *phoinos*, "dark red." The Phoenicians produced both *tĕkēlet* and *'argāmān*. A clear-cut distinction between blue-purple (*tĕkēlet*) and red-purple (*'argāmān*) dyes is difficult to make,

Ill. 78: *Murex trunculus* (left) and *Murix brandaris* (right)

but they are not identical. In descriptions of the drapery for the Tabernacle and the Temple, *tĕkēlet* and *'argāmān* occur together (Ex. 26:1; 2 Chron. 2:6 [E.T. 2 Chron. 2:7]), as they do in descriptions of the adornments of priestly vestments (Ex. 28:4–5, 31–33).

These expensive dyes were obtained from shells of mollusks that attached themselves to the rocks of the Levantine (ancient Phoenician) coast. Heaps of these shells are the archaeological indicators of a purple dye industry. Piles of discarded shells from dye production have been found at various sites. Secretions from the hypobranchial glands of Mediterranean murex mollusks produced the dyes. The shellfish utilized for these dyes are the *Murex trunculus* and *Murex brandaris* (Ill. 78). The shellfish were crushed, boiled in salt, and placed in the sun; afterward the secretions turned purple. Eight thousand mollusks yielded one gram of purple dye.

Concentrations of murex shells have been found at several sites, such as Tyre, Sidon, Ugarit, Ashdod, and Shiqmona. Ezekiel (27:7) mentions Elishah (Cyprus) as a source of *tĕkēlet* and *'argāmān*. An important site for the production of purple dyes in antiquity was Sarepta (modern Sarafand) in Phoenicia. In the industrial sector of the city, dating to the thirteenth century, Pritchard discovered three potsherds from a storage jar covered with a purple dye, along with a spouted vat containing purple residues. He also recovered a collection of murex mollusks from a pit. Sarepta, no doubt, exported purple-dyed textiles throughout the Mediterranean basin.

Tell Keisan (Tel Qison), situated between Haifa and Acco, contains early evidence of the purple dye industry in ancient Palestine. A large vessel from the eleventh century (Iron I) was found with purple dye inside. In the Mediterranean port of Acco, large quantities of crushed murex shells as well as kilns, dating from the end of the thirteenth to the beginning of the twelfth century, point to a purple dye industry. The remains of a purple dye industry were also present at Tel Shiqmona, on the Mediterranean, southwest of the Carmel cape. A significant number of potsherds with traces of genuine purple dye were uncovered. This dye was produced at Shiqmona at least from the ninth century.[112] A pit containing crushed shells and purple-stained soil, part of a dyeing installation composed of pools and channels, was discovered at Tel Dor on the Mediterranean coast. In the Persian period (late sixth century) and probably earlier, Dor was also a producer of purple dye.[113]

In Ashkelon, and probably elsewhere, dyeing would take place in the city, but there were zoning regulations—not so much because of the smell but because of the fire. An architect from Ascalon (Ashkelon), known only from the following text as Julianus of Ascalon, set up zoning laws or customs for architects. The late Byzantine legal compiler Harmenopulus dates either to the twelfth or fourteenth century C.E. The date of Julianus of Ascalon is also uncertain, since he is known only from this text. His edict on *Thermobrochoi* (hot dyers) and *Bapheis* (dyers) reads:

> The industry of *Thermobrochoi* and *Bapheis*, since it is done in large part by fire, and that under constant application, damages the houses which overlook it. Therefore, if one man's house is low, and the house next beyond it overlooks it, the heating must not take place at their foot. For as has been said, since the application of heat is extensive and continuous, it not only creates damage to the houses that overlook it but also creates danger of fire for the same houses. Therefore, not only must these workers refrain from operating at the foot of others' houses; further, they must be distant six and two-thirds cubits [three meters] from the upper stories on every side; for the smoke is dissipated in that distance.[114]

Tanning

Tanning, the process of treating animal skins with tannins to prepare leather, consists of cleaning and soaking to remove dirt, blood, hair, fat, and flesh. Solutions from plant extracts, lime, and tree bark facilitate the process, and the removal of hair from the hide can be accomplished by steeping it in water with salt or in urine.

Tanning is an ancient art, going back to the fourth millennium, although it is not mentioned in the Hebrew Bible. The Hebrew word for "tanned" is *mě'oddāmîm*, "to

---

112. Nira Karmon and Ehud Spanier, "Remains of a Purple Dye Industry Found at Tel Shiqmona," *IEJ* 38 (1988): 184–86.

113. Ephraim Stern and Ilan Sharon, "Tel Dor, 1986," *IEJ* 37 (1987): 208.

114. Constantinus Harmenopulus, *Manuale Legum sive Hexabiblos* (Leipzig: T. O. Weigel, 1851), 247: "Edictum de Infectoribus ac Tinctoribus. Infectorum et tinctorum opificium quod per ignem plurimum et adsidue exercetur, superiores aedes laedit. Itaque si alterius aedes sint planae atque alterius illis incumbant, non oportet ignem sub his fieri. Namque, ut dictum est, frequens illa atque adsidua ustio non modo noxiam adfert superioribus, sed periculum quoque ex igne ipsis parit aedibus. Oportet ergo non solum hos non habitare sub aliorum domibus sed etiam utrimque a domibus contabulatis cubitos sex et bessem distare: dissolvetur enim fumus ante cubitos sex et bessem." For the translation, see John Pairman Brown, *The Lebanon and Phoenicia: Ancient Texts Illustrating the Physical Geography and Native Industries*, vol. 1, *The Physical Setting and the Forest* (Beirut: American University, 1969), 50.

be red"; apparently the skins reddened in the tanning process. There are references to tanning in the Intertestamental and New Testament periods, notably to Simon the tanner (*byrseus*), in whose house Peter stayed at Joppa (modern Jaffa or Yafo) (Acts 9:43; 10:6, 32). Tanners were relegated to the outskirts of town because of the unpleasant odor created by their craft.

Leather had a variety of uses. *taḥaš* ("dolphin skin") was used as the outermost curtain for the Tabernacle (Ex. 26:14). There were three other curtains: the innermost (*miškān*), linen decorated with cherubim; the curtain of goats' hair; and the curtains of sheepskin dyed red. Regarding the Ark, over the dolphin skin was a precious covering of blue-purple cloth (*tĕkēlet*) (Num. 4:6; also Num. 4:10, 12, 14).[115] It should be noted that dolphin bones have been found far inland from the Mediterranean at 'Ai as early as EB.[116]

Dolphin skin would seem to be a strange leather to use in the desert Tabernacle; however, alternate suggestions for the meaning of *taḥaš* have failed. The Hebrew word is clearly cognate with Arabic *tuḫas*, a porpoise common in the Red Sea. In Ezekiel 16:10 Yahweh puts sandals of dolphin leather on the harlot Jerusalem. G. A. Cooke notes that the Bedouin make sandals from the skin of dolphin.[117] The motif of the dolphin appears on the Canaanite (MB II) cylinder seal from Avaris in relation to Ba'al Ṣaphon skipping across the mountains (Ill. 167). A Phoenician seal of Iron II displays the dolphin as an emblem of the sailor Shem'el.[118] Phoenician votive stelae and coins feature the dolphin, symbol of the Mediterranean Sea. But why, then, did a curtain of dolphin leather adorn the desert Tabernacle? Frank Cross suggests that Yahweh's Tabernacle was patterned after the abode of the Canaanite god El, whose tent shrine "in the midst of the sea" at the "fountain of the double-deep" provides the proper aquatic setting for understanding the transposition of the mythology to a Tabernacle of dolphin skins, even if it is in the desert.[119]

Leather was also used for apparel. Parts of leather (sheepskin) garments were discovered in the Cave of the Treasure. Elijah is described as "a hairy man, with a leather belt around his waist" (2 Kings 1:8). Helmets, parts of shields, and other weaponry, and sometimes ropes and sleeping mats, were made of leather. Liquid containers consisted of "skins." Genesis 21:14 tells how "Abraham rose early in the morning, and took bread and a skin (*ḥēmet*) of water, and gave it to Hagar." Leather items in Mesopotamia extended from sandals to sieves. Sandals were made from leather, as evidenced from the Cave of the Treasure and the Cave of the Warrior. At the former

---

115. Cross, *From Epic to Canon*, 88.

116. Personal communication, Paula Wapnish.

117. G. A. Cooke, *Ezekiel*, ICC (Edinburgh: T. & T. Clark, 1936), 164.

118. N. Avigad and B. Sass, *Corpus of West Semitic Stamp Seals* (Jerusalem: Israel Exploration Society, 1997), 278; and N. Avigad, "A Phoenician Seal with Dolphin Emblem," *Sefunim* 3 (1969–71): 49–50.

119. Cross, *From Epic to Canon*, 88–89; cf. Nelson Glueck, *Deities and Dolphins: The Story of the Nabateans* (New York: Farrar, Strauss & Giroux, 1965).

were found remnants of one complete and one fragmentary sandal. At the latter a pair of sandals made of coarse leather (probably cowhide) was found.

As early as the third millennium, tanned skins were used as writing material in Egypt. The Bible does not refer to writing on leather, with the possible exception of Jeremiah 36:4: "So Jeremiah called Baruch son of Neriah; and Baruch wrote down in the scroll (*mĕgillat-sēper*), at Jeremiah's direction, all the words which Yahweh had spoken to him." It is more likely that the scroll Jeremiah dictated to Baruch was written on papyrus. Most of the manuscripts of the Dead Sea Scrolls are inscribed on leather.[120]

Metallurgy

A poem from Job 28 deals with the search for wisdom, which is transcendent and inaccessible. Humans, the sage affirms, can find precious metals but not divine wisdom; wisdom belongs to God alone:

There is a smelter (*môṣā'*) for silver, a place where gold is refined. (v. 1)
Iron is taken [extracted] from the dust/clay; copper is smelted from stone (ore). (v. 2)
Its [earth's] stones are the source of lapis lazuli, and its dust contains gold. (v. 6)
Refined gold cannot be paid as its [Wisdom's] protection (*taḥteyhā*),[121]
    nor can silver be weighed out as its [Wisdom's] price. (v. 15)
It [Wisdom] cannot be bought for gold (*ketem*) of Ophir,
    or for precious carnelian (*šōham*) and lapis lazuli. (v. 16)

The common metals used to fabricate jewelry, ornaments, and other accessories are copper/bronze, iron, gold, and silver.[122]

Copper/Bronze

Copper was the first metal used in antiquity. Arsenical copper was the primary copper alloy from the fourth through the third millennia B.C.E. Scientists have found evidence of mining at least as early as the Chalcolithic period. The Beersheba Valley was

---

120. Philip J. King, *Jeremiah: An Archaeological Companion* (Louisville, Ky.: Westminster/John Knox, 1993), 87: "Several writing surfaces were utilized in ancient Israel; among them were papyrus, animal skins in the form of leather and parchment (a refined type of leather), wooden tablets, potsherds (pieces of broken pottery), ostraca (inscribed potsherds), clay tablets, stone, and metal. . . . The more important documents would have been written on papyrus or on leather."

121. Nahman Avigad, "Two Hebrew 'Fiscal' Bullae," *IEJ* 40 (1990): 265–66. "Fiscal" bullae sealed various goods but not papyrus documents. This is a late seventh-century bulla of "Tahat (the seal owner), son of Besai (his patronymic)." The name Tahat is the biblical Taḥath, which may be translated "beneath," "instead of," or "under the protection of," as in Job 28:15.

122. The following have been especially helpful: P. Roger Moorey, *Ancient Mesopotamian Materials and Industries* (Winona Lake, Ind.: Eisenbrauns, 1999); James D. Muhly, "How Iron Technology Changed the Ancient World—And Gave the Philistines a Military Edge," *BAR* 8 (1982): 40–54; idem, "Metals," *OEANE*, 4:1–15; Paula M. McNutt, *The Forging of Israel* (Sheffield: Almond Press, 1990); R. F. Tylecote, *A History of Metallurgy* (Avon: Bath Press, 1992).

the center of copper metallurgy in the fourth millennium. At Arad, copper metallurgy dates as early as the fourth millennium, but most of the metal objects date to EB II. Evidence points to Feinan as a source for a considerable amount of the copper retrieved at EB II Arad (Levels III-II), and not the Sinai. Feinan is much closer to Arad (only seventy kilometers distance). The collection of artifacts includes axes, chisels, awls, and a lump of copper. Andreas Hauptmann reports that copper ores from Timna' (on the western side of the Arabah) and Feinan (Fenan, Phinon, Punon, on the eastern edge of the Arabah) were well known in EB and that metal was smelted there as early as the Chalcolithic period.[123]

Hauptmann[124] notes that 250 ancient mines and 150,000–200,000 tons of slag were discovered at Feinan. In PPN copper ores were used for beads and cosmetics. In the fourth millennium pyrometallurgy developed. Copper was traded to Beersheba sites, where it was smelted into various products. The Cave of the Treasure hoard (see below) in Naḥal Mishmar was probably made in such Chalcolithic settlements. One of the peak periods of mining in Feinan seems to be EB, to which twelve smelting sites have been dated.

Beno Rothenberg,[125] director of excavations at Timna', recorded copper industries dating from the fourth millennium B.C.E. to the second century C.E. The mining techniques at Timna' included shafts (some thirty-five meters deep) and galleries. Evidence of copper-smelting furnaces was also found at Timna'. In copper smelting the ore is heated over charcoal in furnaces or crucibles, while air is supplied by bellows or tuyeres (tubes for blowing air into furnaces).

Archaeologists discovered an extraordinary cache of copper objects in the Chalcolithic Cave of the Treasure in Naḥal Mishmar near the Dead Sea (Ill. 79). The hoard of more than four hundred artifacts wrapped in a straw mat included twenty copper chisels and axes, two hundred forty copper mace heads, eighty copper wands or standards, and ten copper crowns. Many of these items may have been used in religious rituals. Arsenical copper (not tin bronze) was the alloy in the Naḥal Mishmar hoard.[126]

Hebrew *nĕḥōšet* refers to either copper or bronze, the latter an alloy of copper (90 percent) and tin (*bĕdîl*) (10 percent). Tin renders the metal stronger and more resistant to corrosion. Locating the sources of tin in the ancient Near East has been a problem.

---

123. Andreas Hauptmann et al., "Copper Objects from Arad—Their Composition and Provenance," *BASOR* 314 (1999): 5: "The copper ores both from Timna' and Feinan doubtless were well known in the Early Bronze Age. They were collected and traded in the Levant as far back as the Pre-Pottery Neolithic period, and metal was smelted in the area not later than the Chalcolithic period. . . . In the area of Feinan, extensive copper mining and smelting has [sic] been dated archaeologically and by a series of radiocarbon samples to the Early Bronze Age between 3045 and 2300 B.C.E."

124. Andreas Hauptmann, "Feinan," *OEANE*, 2:310–11; Hauptmann et al., "Early Copper Produced at Feinan, Wadi Araba, Jordan: The Composition of Ores and Copper," *Archeomaterials* 6 (1992): 1–33.

125. Beno Rothenberg, Timna': *Valley of the Biblical Copper Mines* (London: Thames & Hudson, 1972).

126. Bar-Adon, *The Cave of the Treasure*; Pessah Bar-Adon, "The Naḥal Mishmar Caves," *NEAEHL*, 4:822–27.

Ill. 79: Copper artifacts from the Cave of the Treasure, Naḥal Mishmar, from fourth millennium. (Courtesy of Israel Museum; Photo: D. Harris)

Afghanistan is suggested as one source, but that remains uncertain. Tin is found only in association with granite rock, which excludes Cyprus. Recent discoveries point to the Taurus Mountains—the Bolkardag mining district on the south coast of Anatolia—as an important source of tin. The tin in this ore is stannite, in association with galena and zinc. "The slag collected from the whole area of the Bolkardag district contained considerable levels of tin. Of the 27 slag samples collected from 16 different locations, 16 of them had tin concentrations over 500 parts per million (p.p.m.) (highest at 1540 p.p.m.). There were only 6 slag samples in which no tin was detected."[127]

Tin was processed at Goltepe in the central Taurus mountain range from the third millennium. Alluvial tin (cassiterite) comes from the Eastern Desert of Egypt, but there is little evidence it was plentiful enough to be exploited. Ezekiel refers to tin coming from Tarshish: "Tarshish traded with you, so great was your wealth, exchanging silver, iron, tin, and lead for your wares" (Ezek. 27:12). Tarsus may be a more plausible location for Tarshish than Tartessus in southwest Spain, the Phoenician colony on the Guadalquivir River.[128]

Even with developments in metallurgy, copper continued to be used for certain kinds of vessels such as trays, cauldrons, and bowls. Being stronger, bronze and iron

127. K. Aslihan Yener and Hadi Ozbal, "Tin in the Turkish Taurus Mountains: The Bolkardag Mining District," *Antiquity* 61 (1987): 223–24.

128. James A. Montgomery, *Arabia and the Bible* (New York: KTAV, 1969), 177, n. 30: "'Ship of Tarshish' is technical for a large sea-going vessel. Cf. the term 'Hittite,' i.e., Syrian, which Sennacherib uses of the ships he had built for him by Phoenician craftsmen in Mesopotamian waterways for use in the Persian Gulf." H. L. Lorimer, *Homer and the Monuments* (London: MacMillan, 1950), 66: "The metals with which Ezekiel (XXVII.12) credits Tarshish (silver, iron, tin, and lead) are all abundant in East Anatolia; it was her trade in metals that made the control of Cilicia a vital matter for the Assyrians." For a solution to the *Tarsis* = *Tarsus* problem, see André Lemaire, "Tarshish—*Tarsisi*: Problème de Topographie Historique Biblique et Assyrienne," in Gershon Galil and Moshe Weinfeld, eds., *Studies in Historical Geography and Biblical Historiography* (Leiden: Brill, 2000), 44–62.

Ill. 80: Part of a bronze saw; from Ashkelon, possibly from Middle Bronze Age. (Courtesy of the Leon Levy Expedition to Ashkelon; Photo: I. Sztulman)

were better suited for weapons. According to 1 Kings 7:45–46, Solomon commissioned Hiram, a Tyrian smith, to cast the bronze pillars, the bronze sea, the ten stands, and other furnishings for the Temple. The sizes of these pillars and other accoutrements of the Temple are thought to be greatly exaggerated.

Iron

Whereas copper lies deep in the ground, iron ore deposits lie on the surface—consonant with Deuteronomy's description of Canaan: "a land whose stones contain iron (*barzel*) and in whose hills you can mine copper (*nĕḥōšet*)" (Deut. 8:9). *barzel*, the biblical designation for "iron," is a foreign word, perhaps Hittite in origin. In the twelfth and eleventh centuries, bronze and copper artifacts were more numerous than iron. Bronze was replaced by iron as the principal metal only gradually by the tenth century,[129] and bronze continued to be used later, for example, in making statues, figurines, and vessels. Because Palestine was poor in iron ore, most of its iron was imported from Syria, Asia Minor, and Gilead, a major iron-producing region. There are iron mines in the Ajlun area north of the Jabbok (Zerqa) River. Major deposits of iron ore are found at Mugharat el Wardeh and Abu Thawab in the Ajlun Hills, where Robert Coughenour excavated.[130] Iron workshops were found at Tell Jemmeh, Tell Deir 'Alla, and Tell Qasile.

Casting is the pouring of liquid metal into a mold of clay, stone, or metal. The melting point of pure iron is 1534 degrees centigrade (2793 degrees fahrenheit), which was unattainable before the nineteenth century C.E. Consequently there was no cast iron in antiquity.

---

129. Waldbaum, *From Bronze to Iron*.
130. Robert A. Coughenour, "Preliminary Report on the Exploration and Excavation of Mugharat el Wardeh and Abu Thawab," in *Annual of the Department of Antiquities, Jordan* 21 (1976): 71–77.

Ill. 81: Upper Register – Bronze Bands, Gates of Balawat. Assyrian Campaign in Phoenicia, 859 B.C.E. Phoenician tribute bearers from Tyre and Sidon. To right of ingot bearers, porters carry inverted bronze cauldrons over their heads; to right of cauldron bearers, porters carry trays with unidentified items in them. All Phoenicians wear long robes and pointed skull caps. Those of higher status have turban cloths wrapped tightly around them. Some have garments fringed at the hem. (Courtesy of the Trustees of the British Museum)

Iron is valued for its hardness and strength. Wrought iron (shaped by hammering) is softer than bronze, but it holds an edge and a point. It was used especially for smaller objects, such as axes, chisels, plowpoints, and swords. Life-size statues were cast in bronze, which would be impossible in iron. As noted in the section on "Warfare, Armies, and Weapons," the "iron chariots" of the Canaanites (Josh. 17:16) refers to the chariots' axles, which stood for the whole vehicle.[131]

> So with the smith standing near his anvil, forging crude iron. The heat from the fire sears his flesh, yet he toils away in the furnace heat. The clang of the hammer deafens his ears. His eyes are fixed on the tool he is shaping. His care is to finish his work, and he keeps watch till he perfects it in detail (Sir. 38:28; also Isa. 44:12).

Ill. 82: Upper Register – Bronze Bands, Gates of Balawat. Phoenician boatmen in *hippoi* (horse-headed boats) transport tribute from rocky island of Tyre on left, with its crenellated towers and arched gateways, to the mainland. Stevedores wade into the sea up to their knees and draw the boats to shore by ropes attached to horse-headed prows. Porters wearing shoulder pads carry the pillow-shaped metal ingots on their shoulders. (Courtesy of the Trustees of the British Museum)

---

131. Stager, "Forging an Identity," 169.

Wrought iron heated in contact with charcoal (carbon) at high temperature produces carburized iron or steel, which is more malleable than cast iron. Steel can be
hardened by quenching (practiced as early as the tenth century B.C.E.), that is, cooling off the red-hot steel by sudden immersion into a vat of cold liquid. As a result of
the quenching process, the iron object becomes hard and brittle; the hard component
is known as martensite (after German metallurgist Adolf Martens). The brittleness is
reduced by tempering or reheating. Annealing is the process of softening and rendering less brittle a metal hardened by hammering. Heating at low temperature pre-
vents cracking while hammering.

At Har Adir in Upper Galilee, a remarkably well-preserved "steel pick" with an
oak handle within the socket was found in an eleventh-century B.C.E. fortress. It was
made of carburized iron (steel) that had been quenched and then tempered. This
extraordinary artifact, one of the earliest known examples of steel tools, is a tribute
to the skill (or luck) of the artisans of ancient Palestine.[132] Taʿanach's iron artifacts,
dating from the tenth century, include both tools (sickles, plowtips, blades) and
weapons (arrowheads, armor scales). Muhly[133] notes the parallel between this inventory and a familiar biblical passage: "All Israel would go down to the Philistines to
repair any of their plowtips, mattocks, axes, or sickles" (1 Sam. 13:20).

Muhly[134] explains the shift from copper to iron as a response to the shortage of
bronze, a crisis caused by the disruption of international trade routes. Stager explains
the shift from bronze (alloy of copper and tin) to iron in terms of ecological change,
particularly deforestation. "Iron production is much more fuel-efficient than copper
smelting and processing. Copper requires two to four times as much wood charcoal
as iron."[135]

Gold

The third millennium was the "age of gold," the most valuable metal in the biblical
period. The Bible has almost four hundred references to gold, often pairing it with
silver, which is frequently mentioned first. According to the biblical account, both
were utilized in fabricating the appurtenances of the Temple; 1 Kings 6–7 emphasizes
Solomon's use of gold in the construction and appointments. Among the spoils taken
from the Temple by the conquering Babylonians were the following gold items: "the
small bowls also, the firepans, the basins, the pots, the lampstands, the ladles, and
the bowls for libation, both those of gold and those of silver" (Jer. 52:19). In the incident of the "golden calf" the Israelites were directed to contribute their golden

---

132. David Davis et al., "A Steel Pick from Mt. Adir in Palestine," *JNES* 44 (1985): 41–51.
133. Muhly, "Metals," *OEANE*, 4:4.
134. Muhly, "How Iron Technology Changed the Ancient World," 44.
135. Lawrence E. Stager, "The Archaeology of the Family in Ancient Israel," *BASOR* 260 (1985): 11.

earrings (*nizmê hazzāhāb*) from which Aaron cast an image of a calf (Ex. 32:1–6). As for crafting the ephod (at least that of later biblical sources), the apronlike vestment of the high priest, the author of Exodus describes how artisans hammered (*rāqa'*) gold to form gold leaf (*paḥê hazzāhāb*), and then cut it into threads: "Gold was first hammered into gold leaf and then cut up into threads, which were woven with the blue-purple (*tĕkēlet*), red-purple (*'argāmān*), and scarlet yarn into an embroidered pattern on the fine linen" (Ex. 39:3; 28:6).[136]

zāhāb is the common word for "gold" in Hebrew, but other designations (*paz*, *'ôpîr*, *ketem*, *tāhôr*) are used to differentiate the quality of the precious metal.[137] Isaiah reports in an oracle of hope: "I [Yahweh] will make mortals more rare than fine gold (*paz*), and humans than the gold (*ketem*) of Ophir" (Isa. 13:12). The psalmist, addressing the king, delivers an ode for the royal wedding: "At your right hand stands the queen in gold (*ketem*) of Ophir" (Ps. 45:10 [E.T. 45:9]). This "gold of Ophir" (1 Kings 9:28) was of a particularly high quality, but the geographical location of Ophir in unclear. It seems quite certain that Ophir was not legendary. A fragment of a large pottery jar found at Tell Qasile near Jaffa was inscribed: "Gold of Ophir to Beth-Horon [the temple of Horon, a Canaanite divinity] . . . 30 shekels [342 gm]." Dating to the eighth century, the inscription alludes to gold of superior quality and to its country of origin.[138]

Because gold is found in a relatively pure state in nature, it is perhaps the oldest precious metal known. Ancient Palestine, however, was very limited in mineral resources. Without a native supply, ancient Israel had to import it. Egypt was endowed with gold from mines in the Eastern and Nubian deserts. Arabia was also a prominent supplier of gold in antiquity, perhaps the source of the "gold of Ophir."[139]

Gold, as well as bdellium and red carnelian (*šōham*)[140] stones, are associated in Genesis with Havilah. References to Havilah in the Bible are so vague that it is difficult to pinpoint the location (Gen. 2:11; 10:29; 25:18). But the Bible does say that the Pishon River (in Saudi Arabia), connected with the Garden of Eden, surrounded the land of Havilah.[141] The Pishon flows around Havilah "where there is gold; and

---

136. Oppenheim, "The Golden Garments of the Gods," 172: "The present study will deal with only one aspect of this subject matter: the use of 'golden garments' as sacred vestments for the gods and, in Assyria, as *vestis regia*."

137. Benjamin Kedar-Kopfstein, "*zahab*" *TDOT*, 4: 35: "Analysis based on actual usage reveals that the use of particular terms for 'gold' does not suggest technical distinctions, but is based on stylistic considerations."

138. Benjamin Maisler (Mazar), "Two Hebrew Ostraca from Tell Qasile," *JNES* 10 (1951): 265–67.

139. Montgomery, *Arabia and the Bible*, 38–39, n. 5.

140. Jeremy Black et al., eds., *A Concise Dictionary of Akkadian* (Wiesbaden: Harrassowitz, 1999), 315: Akkadian *sâmtu* equals *šōham*, "carnelian," reddish variety of chalcedony (Chalcedon, ancient Greek city of Anatolia); root meaning of word equals "redness."

141. James A. Sauer, "The Rivers Run Dry: Biblical Story Preserves Historical Memory," *BAR* 22 (1996): 52–57, 64. Arguing that climatic changes occurred in historical periods in the ancient Near East, Sauer speculated that the dry riverbed of the Kuwait River may be the Pishon River, one of the four rivers in the Bible associated with Eden.

the gold of that land is good; bdellium and carnelian (*šōham*) are there" (Gen. 2:11–12). The recently discovered Kuwait River is adjacent to Mahd edh-Dhahab ("the Cradle of Gold"), one of the richest gold mines in Saudi Arabia. Gold, bdellium, and carnelian stones are identified with South Arabia, suggesting the gold mines of the Arabian Peninsula as the location of Havilah.

The earliest gold hoard currently known was found in the Naḥal Qanah Cave, a Chalcolithic site on the western fringe of the Samarian Hills. The gold objects, all made by casting and finished by hammering, are burial goods. The large gold rings contained thirty percent silver. Much of the gold in the ancient Near East is electrum (alloy of gold and silver).[142] The most likely source of the gold is the Nubian Desert in Egypt. The presence of these gold artifacts may mark the burial place of a prominent person.[143]

Gold from the Royal Cemetery at Ur in ancient Sumer dates to the middle of the third millennium. The vessels include a strainer, a golden goblet, fluted bowls, and spouted vessels.[144] The Neo-Assyrian royal graves in the Northwest Palace of Ashurnasirpal II at Nimrud (biblical Calah, in northern Iraq) contained more than a thousand pieces of exquisite gold jewelry, including earrings, armlets, and necklaces. Estimated to weigh twenty-two and a half kilograms, the jewelry dates to the second half of the eighth century. Among other finds are gold bowls and a gold alabastron attached to a chain.[145] Moorey speculates that Assyrian royal tableware was in gold. Probably also the tableware of the kings of Israel and Judah was in gold. In view of the extraordinary quantity of gold found among Israel's neighbors in Mesopotamia and Egypt, including the gold-plated shrine in the tomb of Egyptian king Tutankhamun (ca. 1331 B.C.E.), the quantity of gold attributed in the Bible to King Solomon was in accord with what is known about the ancient Near East.[146]

Tell el-'Ajjul, southwest of Gaza, produced large amounts of MB IIC/LB gold jewelry. Found in hoards and in tombs, it was in the form of gold crescents, pendants, earrings, toggle pins, and bracelets. Beth-Shemesh Str IV of LB II also contained a gold jewelry hoard (Ill. 83). Eight gold plaques of hammered sheet-gold, two gold rings with inlaid bezels, and three fruit-shaped gold earrings made of sheet metal were among the finds. Three unique items are given special notice: a bronze pin covered with gold foil; an Old Babylonian (seventeenth-century) cylinder seal made of hematite; and a

---

142. When gold is alloyed with lead in a special clay vessel (cupel), gold and silver remain. When silver is combined with salt, silver is removed from gold (cementation), leaving gold in the pure state.

143. Avi Gopher et al., "Earliest Gold Artifacts in the Levant," *Current Anthropology* 31 (1990): 436–43; Avi Gopher and Tsvika Tsuk, *The Naḥal Qanah Cave* (Tel Aviv: Institute of Archaeology, Tel Aviv University, 1996).

144. Moorey, *Ancient Mesopotamian Materials and Industries*, 223; C. Leonard Woolley and P. Roger Moorey, *Ur 'of the Chaldees'*, rev. ed. (Ithaca: Cornell University Press, 1982).

145. Spencer P. Harrington, "Royal Treasures of Nimrud," *Archaeology* 43 (1990): 48–53; Moorey, *Ancient Mesopotamian Materials and Industries*, 224.

146. Alan R. Millard, "Does the Bible Exaggerate King Solomon's Wealth?" *BAR* 15 (1989): 20–34.

Ill. 83: Beth-Shemesh hoard, dated Late Bronze II. Gold jewelry and precious stones found in a clay jug. (Courtesy of the Israel Museum; Photo: A. Hay)

gold chain with a pendant bead.[147] Comparable hoards of jewelry have been found at Megiddo, Beth-Shean, and elsewhere.

At Ketef Hinnom outside of Jerusalem's ancient walls, one tomb held the remains of ninety-five individuals along with a variety of artifacts. The rich collection of jewelry includes six gold items, ninety-five silver ones, and semiprecious beads. These luxury items worn by Jerusalem's wealthy attest to the affluence of the seventh- and sixth-century society. The foreign style of the objects indicates that the Judahites of Jeremiah's time had cultural contacts with neighboring nations, particularly Assyria, Babylonia, Syria, and Urartu. Besides the elaborate jewelry, the excavators found a silver amulet (talisman) inscribed with an abbreviated version of the "priestly blessing," including the divine name (Num. 6:24–26)[148] (Ill. 151, 157).

Silver

A remarkable example of silver ornamentation is the statuette of a silver calf discovered at the coastal city of Ashkelon (Ill. 84). Dating about 1600 B.C.E., the calf was once completely covered with an overleaf of pure silver in eleven pieces. Silver (*kesep*) came into greater use in the late fourth millennium and was quite common by the third millennium. It is mentioned over three hundred times in the Bible. The book of Exodus has several references to articles of silver and gold (Ex. 3:22; 11:2; 12:35), especially for the construction of the Tabernacle (Ex. 26:19; 36:24). Silver is very malleable, rendering it ideal for fabricating ornaments, jewelry, amulets, cult vessels, and fine tableware for the elite. Silver is not well preserved, however, corroding as it does in saline soils. Moreover, silver and gold are constantly being recycled.

Native silver usually occurs deep underground. Asia Minor is an important source of silver, especially the Taurus Mountains, called Silver Mountains by Sargon of

---

147. Miriam Tadmor and Osnat Misch-Brandl, "The Beth Shemesh Hoard of Jewellery," *Israel Museum News* 16 (1980): 71–79.

148. Gabriel Barkay, *Ketef Hinnom—A Treasure Facing Jerusalem* (Jerusalem: Israel Museum, 1986).

Akkad. The first use of silver in Anatolia occurred in the Chalcolithic period. In EB there are many examples of silver in Anatolia, and numerous textual references in MB. Kay Prag[149] speaks of the large number of silver objects from burials in the Eneolithic (Chalcolithic) cemetery at Byblos but the origin of the silver is unknown. Byblos may have played an important role in silver trade in the Levant. Silver mines in Laurium (modern Lavrion, near Athens) in the Aegean may have been worked as early as 1000 B.C.E. Silver mines were also located at Rio Tinto in ancient Iberia.

Seldom found in the pure state, silver is extracted from a sulphide ore of lead. Jeremiah (6:29–30) and Ezekiel (22:18–22) allude to the practice of refining impure silver from crude lead by cupellation: "The bellows blow fiercely, the lead is consumed by the fire; in vain the refining goes on, for the wicked are not removed. They are called 'rejected silver,' for Yahweh has rejected them" (Jer. 6:29–30). Here Jeremiah is figuratively describing his own failed ministry, with only dross remaining. Cupellation, which involves oxidation of the lead at temperatures of 900–1000 degrees centigrade (1632–1832 fahrenheit), is a refining process that takes place in a cupel (a shallow, porous cup, especially

Ill. 84: The silver bull calf from Ashkelon and its pottery shrine, dated around 1600 B.C.E. The calf is an example of *pesel ûmassēkâ*. The bronze body is overlaid with eleven sheets of silver, of which a few still adhere on legs and head. This is probably the emblem of the Canaanite storm god Ba'al Ṣaphon or Ba'al Ḥadad, god of the seafarers. The calf and its model shrine were found in a small temple outside the city walls of Ashkelon. (Courtesy of the Leon Levy Expedition to Ashkelon; Photo: C. Andrews)

of bone ash), used to separate the silver from the lead. Lead served as an oxidizing agent to remove the dross in refining silver. As the metals are heated in a crucible, the lead oxidizes and carries off the alloy, leaving the pure silver. Since native silver is relatively rare, cupellation was necessary to produce much of the early silver. James

---

149. Kay Prag, "Silver in the Levant in the Fourth Millennium B.C.," in P. R. Moorey and P. J. Parr, eds., *Archaeology in the Levant* (Warminster: Aris & Phillips, 1978), 36–45.

Ill. 85: Hoard of fifty-nine silver pieces found at Ekron in 604 B.C.E. destruction of Str IB, including one ingot, thirty-three pieces of *Hacksilber* and twenty-five miscellaneous pieces of broken and worn jewelry, after cleaning. (Courtesy of Tel Miqne-Ekron Excavation/Publication Project; Photo: I. Sztulman)

Muhly[150] thinks cupellation occurred as early as the late fourth millennium at Habuba Kabira, the Syrian site in the "Uruk expansion" network. Moorey,[151] however, thinks there is no definite evidence for cupellation before the sixth century B.C.E. He cites evidence from Sardis, as well as the texts of Nabonidus as the "clearest documentary evidence for refining in Mesopotamia."

Eventually silver became the primary means of exchange. Mesopotamia went on the "silver standard" about 2400–2000 B.C.E., when there was a significant increase in the amount of silver in circulation.[152] The premonetary currencies occur from LB through Iron II, with a significant increase in silver hoards in the seventh century. Before the invention of coinage, weighed metal (usually silver) was used as "money" for transactions in the ancient Near East.

Two hoards of *Hacksilber* (ca. 1100 B.C.E.), each stored in a linen pouch, were found at Philistine Ashkelon (Ill. 88). Prior to the Babylonian siege of the Philistine city of Ekron in 604 B.C.E., seventy-seven silver ingots were hidden for safekeeping in a jug nestled within another vessel (Ill. 85, 86, 87). This extraordinary silver treasure was discovered beneath the floor of a seventh-century building. Additional hoards of broken jewelry and *Hacksilber* (cut silver) dating to the seventh century were also uncovered at Ekron. They consist of broken silver jewelry, along with cut silver (*Hacksilber*), as well as intact jewelry items. For the

150. Muhly, "Metals," *OEANE*, 4: 7.
151. Moorey, *Ancient Mesopotamian Materials and Industries*, 218.
152. Muhly, "Metals," *OEANE*, 4: 9.

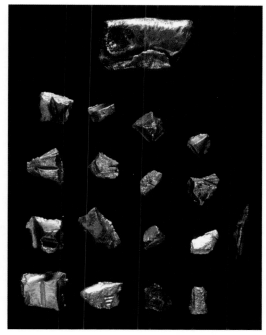

Ill. 86: Silver hoard found in a jug (within a larger jug) in the 604 B.C.E. destruction Str IB at Ekron. The hoard was composed of eighty-seven pieces including nineteen silver ingots, sixty-six pieces of *Hacksilber* and two silver fragments, as well as one silver bead. (Courtesy of Tel Miqne-Ekron Excavation/Publication Project; Photo: I. Sztulman)

Ill. 87: Part of a silver hoard from Ekron depicted in previous illustration (#86) after cleaning; one silver ingot at top and seventeen pieces of *Hacksilber*. (Courtesy of Tel Miqne-Ekron Excavation/Publication Project; Photo: I. Sztulman)

Ill. 88: Silver hoard of *Hacksilber* in linen pouch, precursor of coinage, with mass of 55 grams, found at Ashkelon. (Courtesy of the Leon Levy Expedition to Ashkelon; Photo: I. Sztulman)

most part, these hoards were found in the "elite zone" in the center of the lower city, part of the temple precinct, indicative of the affluence of the inhabitants of Ekron.[153] As noted, similar hoards have also been recovered at other sites: at Eshtemoa, the largest silver hoard discovered in ancient Palestine (tenth/ninth, possibly eighth century);[154] at 'Ein-Gedi (late seventh century); beneath a floor at Dor, a clay jar containing almost eight and one-half kilograms of *Hacksilber* (late eleventh or early tenth century), resembling small coins and stored in linen bags. The last cache may have belonged to a Phoenician merchant.[155]

TRAVEL, TRANSPORT, AND TRADE

Overland Routes

Palestine derives a great deal of prominence today from its being the land of the Bible, but many other reasons accounted for its significance in ancient times. It was "home" to many people with important heritages—the Canaanites who once ruled Egypt, the Phoenicians (as the Canaanites came to be known by the Greeks in the first millennium), Israelites, Ammonites, and more. At the same time it was a "crossroads," forming a land bridge between Egypt and Mesopotamia, linking Africa, Asia, and Europe via military and trade routes. Its location made it both strategic and vulnerable.

Topography determined the direction of the ancient roads in the biblical lands. The chief trade routes[156] lay in a north–south direction, with secondary roads running east–west. International highways traversed the northern kingdom of Israel, while the southern kingdom of Judah was largely off the beaten track. The two major international highways passing through Palestine are the Way of the Sea (Via Maris) and the King's Highway.

The Way of the Sea, along with its several branches, denotes the coastal highway connecting Egypt in the south with Phoenicia, Syria, and Mesopotamia. Originating in the Nile Delta, the Way of the Sea followed the East Mediterranean coast, turned inland at the Carmel Range, crossed the Plain of Jezreel at Megiddo, headed northward, passed along the west side of the Sea of Galilee, veered north to Hazor and

---

153. Seymour Gitin, "Philistia in Transition: The Tenth Century B.C.E. and Beyond," in Seymour Gitin, Amichai Mazar, and Ephraim Stern, eds., *Mediterranean Peoples in Transition, Thirteenth to Early Tenth Centuries B.C.E.: In Honor of Trude Dothan* (Jerusalem: Israel Exploration Society, 1998), 162–83. Amir Golani and Benjamin Sass, "Three Seventh-Century B.C.E. Hoards of Silver Jewelry from Tel Miqne-Ekron," *BASOR* 311 (1998): 57–81.

154. Ze'ev Yeivin, "The Mysterious Silver Hoard from Eshtemoa," *BAR* 13 (1987): 38–44.

155. Ephraim Stern, "Buried Treasure: The Silver Hoard from Dor," *BAR* 24 (1998): 46–51, 62.

156. David A. Dorsey, *Roads and Highways of Ancient Israel* (Baltimore: Johns Hopkins Press, 1991). This is a valuable resource.

Damascus, and terminated in Mesopotamia. The term *derek hayyām* (Via Maris) occurs only in Isa. 8:23 (9:1). The Via Maris is designated by two other names—the "Way of the Land of Philistines" and the "Way of Horus." The first is mentioned in Exodus 13:17: "When Pharaoh let the people go, God did not lead them the way of the land of Philistines (*derek 'ereṣ pĕlištîm*), although that was nearer." The phrase "Way of the Land of Philistines" is ambiguous, but it seems to be a specific route.[157] The "Way of Horus" is the Egyptian name for this route, designating "the southern section of the Via Maris connecting Egypt with Palestine."[158]

The King's Highway (*derek hammelek*) (Num. 20:17) passes through the entire length of the Transjordanian Plateau, close to the desert. Originating at the Gulf of Aqaba, it crosses Edom, Moab, Ammon, Gilead, and Bashan before continuing north to Damascus. Several transverse (east–west) routes connect the Via Maris and the King's Highway.

A third north-south route passed through the highlands of Samaria and Judah, running from Jerusalem to Bethlehem, Hebron, and points south. North of Jerusalem it connected Shechem and the Plain of Jezreel. "The yearly festival of Yahweh is taking place at Shiloh, which is north of Bethel, on the east of the highway (*mĕsillâ*) that goes up from Bethel to Shechem, and south of Lebonah" (Judg. 21:19). Also, there were roads in the Negev, Judah, the hill country of Ephraim, Lower and Upper Galilee, and Transjordan. [See Ill. 228]

Archaeology provides only limited and indirect evidence with respect to ancient roads. Open roads were not paved in the Iron Age, in contrast to the main streets of towns, which were paved with stones.[159]

Before the Roman period with its sophisticated road systems, the roads in Palestine were only tracks. On the occasion of his second journey through Palestine in 1852, American explorer and historical geographer Edward Robinson offered this typical description of the rugged road conditions:

> Leaving Saris, we descended into the head of Wady 'Aly, and fell into the Jerusalem road. This road then winds up and over a ridge on the north to the southern brow of a second Wady. . . .The road is bad; and the whole region rocky, desolate, and dreary. The badness of the road arises mainly from the great number of loose stones, which have been suffered to accumulate in the path. Were these removed, the road would be a good one for the country.[160]

Describing the road from Hebron to Jerusalem, Robinson states:

---

157. William H. C. Propp, *Exodus 1–18*, AB 2 (New York: Doubleday, 1998), 485.

158. Yohanan Aharoni, *The Land of the Bible*, rev. ed. (Philadelphia: Westminster Press, 1979), 46–47.

159. Avraham Biran, "Dan," *NEAEHL*, 1: 323–32.

160. Edward Robinson, *Biblical Researches in Palestine and the Adjacent Regions* (Jerusalem: Universitas Booksellers, 1970), 3: 156.

> This road bears every mark of having always been a great highway between Hebron and Jerusalem. It is direct; and in many parts artificially made, evidently in times of old. But wheels probably never passed here; the hills are too sharp and steep, and the surface of the ground too thickly strewn with rocks, to admit of the possibility of vehicles being used in this mountainous region, without the toilsome construction of artificial roads, such as never yet existed here.[161]

Hebrew has several words for "road"; *derek*, with a wide range of meanings, is a general term connoting "that which is trodden underfoot." This suggests a surface packed down by traffic. Virtually synonymous with *derek* are *'ōraḥ*, which occurs frequently in poetry, and *nātîb*, found only in poetry. *měsillâ* designates a major highway prepared by removing stones and by grading the rough surface. It is cognate with the verb *sll*, "to carry out road work," "to cast up a highway."[162]

Second Isaiah's several uses of *měsillâ* and *derek* in the context of the Judahites' return from Babylonian exile help to clarify the meaning of these terms. The reference is to processions carrying the statues of the deities or their emblems. Isaiah has in mind the great road Yahweh will build from Babylon to Palestine: "In the wilderness prepare the way (*derek*) of Yahweh, make straight in the desert a highway (*měsillâ*) for our God" (Isa. 40:3). Here *měsillâ* stands in synonymous parallelism with *derek*. And again in Third Isaiah: "Go through, go through the gates, prepare the way (*derek*) for the people; build up (*sōllû*), build up (*sōllû*) the highway (*měsillâ*), clear it of stones, lift up an ensign over the peoples" (Isa. 62:10; also 57:14).

Seafaring

Seagoing Vessels

Egyptian sources mention a type of craft called *kbn*, a "Byblos ship." Byblos (modern Jubayi, biblical Gebal) was known as *Kubna* in ancient Egyptian, whence *kbn*. It is an ambiguous term designating either a boat built at Byblos or built for the Byblos run. By the end of the Old Kingdom (2664–2180), *kbn* signified any large seagoing vessel, quite apart from its intended destination.[163] Since the Egyptians were at home on rivers but not on the sea, the *kbn* was probably built by the Phoenicians.[164] Of course, one of the commodities of Syria and Cilicia in great demand in Egypt, for example, was timber, especially the long lumber provided by cedars of Lebanon and

---

161. Robinson, *Biblical Researches in Palestine and the Adjacent Regions*, 1: 214–15.
162. Klaus Koch, "*derekh*," *TDOT*, 3: 278.
163. Torgny Säve-Söderbergh, *The Navy of the Eighteenth Egyptian Dynasty* (Uppsala: Lundequistska Bokhandeln, 1946), 48–49; Shelley Wachsmann, *Seagoing Ships and Seamanship in the Bronze Age Levant* (London: Chatham Publishing, 1998), 19.
164. Richard D. Barnett, "Early Shipping in the Near East," *Antiquity* 32 (1958): 223.

other conifers. Such timber could not easily be carted overland and was a natural for the ships plying the Mediterranean. Evidence of cedars in Egypt and the southern Levant suggests that ships were carrying such cargoes as early as the fourth millennium. Probably the Byblos run and the *kbn*-type ship have a history reaching at least that far back in time.[165]

The Bible seldom refers to ships and sailing, since the Israelites, despite their proximity to the Mediterranean Sea, were not a maritime people but an agrarian kingdom. Nonetheless, the Song of Deborah refers to Dan and Asher as seafaring tribes (Judg. 5:17). Commenting on this verse, Stager suggests that the Danites served as clients (*gērîm*, "economic wards") on Canaanite or Philistine ships. The Asherites, he suggests, may have been "seamen and dockworkers" at the port of Acco.[166]

Most maritime archaeologists and historians have suggested that in antiquity Mediterranean ships hugged the coast. This assumption is now being called into question by deep-sea research. For example, two eighth-century B.C.E. Phoenician ships were recently discovered some fifty kilometers west of Ashkelon, en route either to Egypt or the Phoenician colony of Carthage (Ill. 89a, b). They lie at depths of about four hundred meters.[167]

The Philistines, Phoenicians, and Syrians controlled most of the Levantine coast. The Egyptian relief in the mortuary temple of Rameses III (1182–1151) at Medinet Habu in Luxor depicts the battle between the Egyptians and the Sea Peoples at the entrance to the Nile Delta. The Philistine ships are portrayed with raised prow and stern and only one mast. "The Sea Peoples' craft have gently curving hulls ending in nearly perpendicular posts capped with bird-head devices facing outboard. Raised castles are situated at both bow and stern."[168] The Sea Peoples' vessels depicted at Medinet Habu are considered the prototypes of the Phoenician "hippos" ships, so-called by the Greeks because the prow was in the form of the head of a horse (Greek *hippos*) (See also Ill. 82).

Several maritime innovations are attributed to the Sea Peoples, including loose-footed rigging (brail), which allows the ship to tack into the wind and maneuver in unfavorable wind conditions; the crow's nest perched at the top of the mast; and the composite anchor, whose wooden flukes provide better anchorage, especially in sand.[169]

---

165. See Lawrence E. Stager, "Port Power in the Early and Middle Bronze Age: The Organization of Maritime Trade and Hinterland Production," in S. R. Wolff, ed., *Studies in the Archaeology of Israel and Neighboring Lands In Memory of Douglas L. Esse* (Chicago: Oriental Institute SAOC and ASOR, 2001), 611–24, for cedars in EB I Ashkelon.

166. Lawrence E. Stager, "The Song of Deborah—Why Some Tribes Answered the Call and Others Did Not," *BAR* 15 (1989): 63–64.

167. In 1999 a team of oceanographers and archaeologists led by Robert Ballard and Lawrence Stager found two Phoenician vessels, 2,700 years old, and their cargoes of amphoras, once filled with wine. These are two of the oldest deep-water shipwrecks ever discovered. Stone anchors, crockery, an incense stand, and a wine decanter, in addition to hundreds of amphoras, were among their cargoes.

168. Wachsmann, *Seagoing Ships and Seamanship in the Bronze Age Levant*, 171–72.

169. Avner Raban and Robert R. Stieglitz, "The Sea Peoples and Their Contributions to Civilization," *BAR* 17 (1991): 34–42, 92; Wachsmann, *Seagoing Ships and Seamanship in the Bronze Age Levant*, 175.

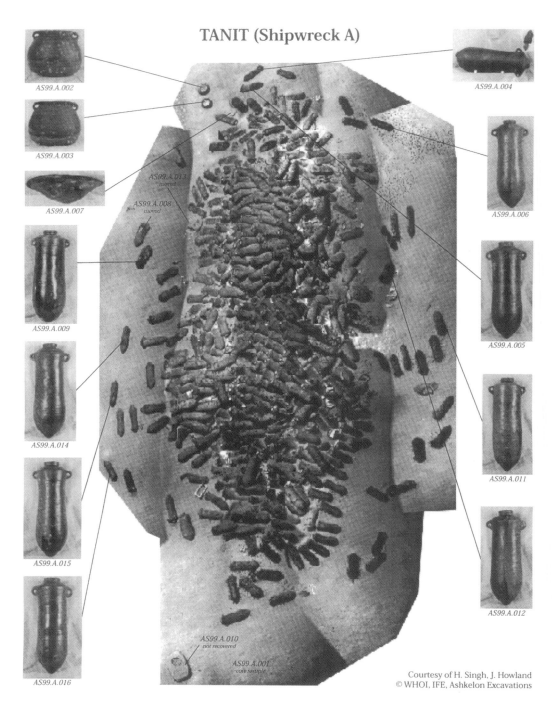

TANIT (Shipwreck A)

AS99.A.002

AS99.A.003

AS99.A.007

AS99.A.013
moved

AS99.A.008
moved

AS99.A.009

AS99.A.014

AS99.A.015

AS99.A.016

AS99.A.010
not recovered

AS99.A.001
core sample

AS99.A.004

AS99.A.006

AS99.A.005

AS99.A.011

AS99.A.012

Courtesy of H. Singh, J. Howland
© WHOI, IFE, Ashkelon Excavations

Ill. 89a: A Phoenician shipwreck now dubbed *Tanit*, latter half of the eighth B.C.E., with a cargo of wine. Retrieved artifacts are indicated in the margins. (Courtesy of H. Singh and J. Howland. © WHOI, IFE, and Ashkelon Excavations)

ELISSA (Shipwreck B)

AS99.B.020R
AS99.B.033M
AS99.B.036
AS99.B.028
AS99.B.027
AS99.B.034
AS99.B.037M
AS99.B.021R
AS99.B.022R
AS99.B.029
AS99.B.031
AS99.B.030M
AS99.B.038
AS99.B.032
AS99.B.025M
AS99.B.023R
AS99.B.024R
AS99.B.040
AS99.B.035
AS99.B.026
AS99.B.039

Ill. 89b: A Phoenician shipwreck now dubbed *Elissa*, from latter part of the eighth century B.C.E., with a cargo of wine. Retrieved artifacts are indicated in the margins. (Courtesy of H. Singh and J. Howland. © WHOI, IFE, and Ashkelon Excavations)

Ships equipped with double banks of oars were a Phoenician invention. It is hard to know whether the Sea Peoples influenced the Phoenicians in naval technology, or vice versa. The Phoenicians were outstanding navigators of antiquity, well known for shipbuilding and maritime trade. Besides the "hippos" ships, there were other types of Phoenician vessels: the "round" model with asymmetrical bow and stern on merchant ships; and the "long" model with pointed ram on warships.[170] Phoenician ships were tall, with a high mast and an upper and a lower deck. Assyrian reliefs of the late eighth and early seventh centuries depict these Phoenician merchant ships, with two banks of oars. They also have masts (Ill. 90).

Ezekiel and Tyre

In his lament over Tyre, Ezekiel compares that city to a Tyrian merchant ship whose builders select only superior materials for its construction. He describes in technical detail the kinds of timber used for the hull, mast, oars, and benches, as well as the fabrics for the sail and canopy:[171]

> They built for you the hull of juniper (*bĕrôšîm*, *Juniperus excelsa*) from Senir [Mount Hermon]. They took cedar (*'erez*) from Lebanon to make a mast over you. Of oaks (*'allônîm*) of Bashan were made your oars. They made your benches of ivory (inlaid) in cypress (*tĕ'aššurîm*) from the island of Cypriotes.

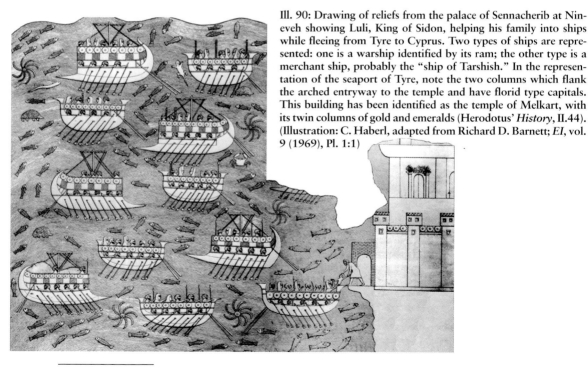

Ill. 90: Drawing of reliefs from the palace of Sennacherib at Nineveh showing Luli, King of Sidon, helping his family into ships while fleeing from Tyre to Cyprus. Two types of ships are represented: one is a warship identified by its ram; the other type is a merchant ship, probably the "ship of Tarshish." In the representation of the seaport of Tyre, note the two columns which flank the arched entryway to the temple and have florid type capitals. This building has been identified as the temple of Melkart, with its twin columns of gold and emeralds (Herodotus' *History*, II.44). (Illustration: C. Haberl, adapted from Richard D. Barnett; *EI*, vol. 9 (1969), Pl. 1:1)

---

170. Barnett, "Early Shipping in the Near East," 226.
171. Igor M. Diakonoff, "The Naval Power and Trade of Tyre," *IEJ* 42 (1992): 168–93 is the best analysis of Ezekiel 27. More than others he has confronted the textual problems of this chapter.

Byssus with embroidery(?) from Egypt was to be your sail, to be (rigged) for you to the yard (*nēs*). Bluish-purple (*tĕkēlet*) and reddish-purple (*'argāmān*) from the coasts of Cyprus [Elishah] were your canopy. (Ezek. 27:5–7)

Besides describing the naval forces of Tyre, Ezekiel discusses Tyrian commerce. To explain how the prophet acquired such detailed knowledge of Tyre as a seaport, Diakonoff suggests Ezekiel either traveled to Tyre between 588 and 585 or had access to a detailed report.[172]

Solomon's Fleet

Before Solomon's time, Israel was not known for maritime trade, and the biblical text describes how important trading by sea became for Israel during the Solomonic era: "King Solomon built a fleet of ships at Ezion-Geber, which is near Elath on the shore of the Red Sea, in the land of Edom" (1 Kings 9:26). Solomon's maritime activities centered on the Gulf of Aqaba, on the northeast arm of the Red Sea. He developed a port at Ezion-Geber, mistakenly identified with Tell el-Kheleifeh on the northern shore of the Gulf of Aqaba, which served as a base for overseas trade. Other sites have been tentatively suggested for Ezion-Geber, including Jezirat Faraun ("Pharaoh's island"), an island eleven kilometers south of modern Eilat, but this does not seem plausible.

Solomon and Hiram, king of Tyre, undertook a joint maritime venture. The fleet was Solomon's, but it was manned by Phoenicians skilled in sailing. Together Solomon and Hiram may have controlled trade from the Red Sea eastward to Africa and Arabia. "They [sailors of Solomon and Hiram] went to Ophir, and immediately imported from there four hundred twenty talents [14,400 kilograms] of gold, which they delivered to King Solomon" (1 Kings 9:28). The location of the land of Ophir, famous for its gold, remains unknown, occasioning much speculation. Arabia may be a good candidate, inasmuch as the Sheban queen is said to have had access to the gold of Arabia: "Then she [queen of Sheba] gave the king [Solomon] one hundred twenty talents [4,112 kilograms] of gold" (1 Kings 10:10). Ira Price, after eliminating sites on the east coast of Africa and in the Far East as plausible locations of Ophir, concludes: "It seems most probable that Ophir was a territory situated in south-eastern Arabia, in the region of the Gulfs of Oman and Persia."[173]

Solomon built a commercial fleet called "ships of Tarshish" (*'ŏnî taršîš*), a biblical term signifying heavy, seagoing merchantmen. From the context it is evident that these ships were able to make long voyages: "For the king [Solomon] had a fleet of ships of Tarshish (*'ŏnî taršîs*) at sea with the fleet of Hiram. Once every three years the fleet of ships of Tarshish used to come bringing gold, silver, ivory, apes, and peacocks" (1 Kings 10:22). Although "Tarshish" occurs more than thirty times in the Bible, its location is

---

172. Diakonoff, "The Naval Power and Trade of Tyre," 192.
173. Ira M. Price, "Ophir," in J. Hastings, ed., *A Dictionary of the Bible* (Peabody, Mass.: Hendrickson, 1988), 3: 628.

uncertain, prompting many scholarly suggestions.[174] Tarshish ships are frequently associated with both maritime trade and metals. Tarshish may refer to, or perhaps be the namesake for, the Phoenician colony of Tartessus in southwestern Spain, on the mouth of the Guadalquivir River north of Cádiz. The area around Tartessus is associated with metals. Albright, on the other hand, suggested that Tarshish (*taršîš*, a Phoenician loan-word) may mean "smelting plant" or "refinery," and may be related to the Akkadian *rašāšu*, "to melt," "to be smelted." This reference envisions ships delivering raw material to the refiner or conveying the purified metal from the refiner. Instead of being the identity of a specific geographical location, "Tarshish" could refer simultaneously to several sites where refining took place, among them Tartessus.[175]

Tarsus, a large commercial city on the Cydnus River in southeastern Asia Minor (modern Turkey) and the birthplace of the apostle Paul, is the most probable location of Tarshish, especially since the discovery of silver mines in the Taurus Mountains. The major trade routes from Syria to central Asia Minor passed through this coastal plain. Isaiah, in an oracle on Tyre, associates Tarshish ships with the Phoenician ports of Tyre and Sidon (Isa. 23:1–17). Tyre imported iron, lead, tin, and silver from Tarshish (Ezek. 27:12; also Jer. 10:9). As noted, Isaiah, Jeremiah, and Ezekiel refer to Tarshish in the context of metals: "For the coastlands shall wait for me, the ships of Tarshish first, to bring your children from far away, their silver and gold with them" (Isa. 60:9). "Beaten silver is brought from Tarshish, and gold from Uphaz" (Jer. 10:9). "Tarshish did business with you [Tyre] out of the abundance of your great wealth; silver, iron, tin, and lead they exchanged for your wares" (Ezek. 27:12).

Josephus made the connection between Tarshish and Tarsus (*Ant.* i.6.1 [127]). Barnett favors Tarsus as the location of Tarshish because of the city's reputation for manufacturing ships' oars.[176] Cecil Torr pointed out earlier that among the Greeks the oars of a ship are collectively called *tarsos*, the name applied to seagoing craft with multiple oars.[177] In the List of Nations in Genesis 10, Tarshish is a descendant of Javan, along with Elishah, Kittim, and Rodanim, who are associated with the East Mediterranean area (Gen. 10:4; 1 Chron. 1:7). This would point to Tarsus/Tarshish in Cilicia rather than Tartessus in Spain. In sum, it may be that the "Tarshish ships" and the "Byblos ships" shared a common extension of their original meaning (whatever it was) to signify seagoing ships—in contrast to Egyptian and Mesopotamian river craft.

King Jehoshaphat (873–849 B.C.E.) of Judah joined King Ahaziah (850–849 B.C.E.) of Israel to build Tarshish ships at Ezion-Geber for travel to Ophir, but the venture ended in shipwreck (1 Kings 22:48–49; 2 Chron. 20:35–37). Because of the close rela-

---

174. Moshe Elat, "Tarshish and the Problem of Phoenician Colonisation in the Western Mediterranean," *Orientalia Lovaniensia Periodica* 13 (1982): 55–69, gives a good survey of opinions. See also André Lemaire, "Tarshish-*Tarsisi*: Problème de Topographie Historique Biblique et Assyrienne," 44–62.

175. William F. Albright, "The Role of the Canaanites in the History of Civilization," in G. E. Wright, ed., *The Bible and the Ancient Near East* (London, Routledge & Kegan Paul, 1961), 347 and 360, n. 96.

176. Barnett, "Early Shipping in the Near East," 226.

177. Cecil Torr, *Ancient Ships* (Cambridge: Cambridge University Press, 1894), 2.

tionship between the northern kingdom of Israel and Phoenicia, Israel was more familiar with maritime commerce and shipbuilding than the southern kingdom of Judah. In biblical times the major seaports in Palestine, though seldom controlled by Israel, were located at Acco, Dor, Jaffa, Ashkelon, and Gaza. The Israelites appear to have developed Dor, already under Solomonic control according to 1 Kings 4:11, into a major seaport in King Ahab's time. Dor and Jaffa later became Phoenician territory, as they all did in the Persian period.

Phoenician Ships

Now, for the first time ever, we have recovered actual examples of Phoenician ships from the Iron Age to study. In 1999, in conjunction with the Leon Levy Expedition to Ashkelon, Robert Ballard and Lawrence Stager led a deep-sea expedition that located and surveyed two ancient ships that had sunk in waters four hundred meters deep, some fifty kilometers west of the seaport of Ashkelon. These two ships set sail from Phoenicia sometime between 750 and 700 B.C.E. From prow to stern the ships measured about sixteen meters; their width, about six meters. They were rounded and beamy and heavily laden with huge cargoes of amphoras once filled with fine wines from the Levant. Each carried more than twelve tons of wine[178] (Ill. 89a, b).

These largely single-commodity cargoes of fine wines were most likely destined for the pharaoh's table and wine cellar in Egypt, or farther west for the thirsty Tyrian colonists who had recently founded Carthage. The two ships, perhaps part of a larger fleet, apparently foundered in the same storm, most likely of the kind mentioned by Ezekiel and the Psalmist—the treacherous "east wind" (*rûaḥ qādîm*) that, on occasion, "shatters the ships of Tarshish" (Ps. 48:8 [E.T. 48:7]; cf. Ezek. 27:26). In the waterfront argot of the Greeks, these Phoenician merchantmen, now resting upright on the bottom of the Mediterranean with their bows heading west, would have been called "tubs" (Greek *gauloi*). In the harbors of the Phoenicians and the Israelites, they would have been proudly known as "ships of Tarshish."[179]

---

178. Robert D. Ballard, Lawrence E. Stager, et al., "Iron Age Shipwrecks in Deep Water off Ashkelon, Israel," *AJA* (in press). Cf. Ezekiel 27:18–19 for the fine wines from Helbon near Damascus and from Izalla near Mardin in Anatolia, which, according to cuneiform texts, produced wine "for a king." See Alan Millard, "Ezekiel XXVII. 19: The Wine Trade of Damascus," *JSS* 7 (1962): 201–3; and Diakonoff, "The Naval Power and Trade of Tyre," 188, n. "t."

179. A Hebrew scaraboid seal impression depicting a merchant ship propelled by a sail, dating to the eighth century B.C.E., has come to light. The name of the seal's owner is 'Oniyahu according to the inscription: "Belonging to 'Oniyahu Son of Merab." This sailing ship, which is the heraldic design for the seal, has, according to Nahman Avigad, a rounded hull with raised prow and stern of the same height. Avigad also called attention to the ship's horse-headed prow, steering oar, and mast with sail, as well as the lack of oars. The Hebrew name 'Oniyahu, which does not occur in the Bible, means "Yahweh is my strength"; but *'ŏnî* and *'ŏniyyâ* also mean "ship": "King Solomon built a fleet of ships (*'ŏnî*) at Ezion-Geber, which is near Elath on the shore of the Red Sea, in the land of Edom" (1 Kings 9:26; also Isa. 33:21). The owner of the seal was obviously playing on the equivocal meaning of his name when he chose the ship for his personal seal. See Nahman Avigad, "A Hebrew Seal Depicting a Sailing Ship," *BASOR* 246 (1982): 59–62.

Travel

Pedestrian travel was difficult in Palestine, because the terrain was so rugged. The Israelites had many reasons to travel—business transactions, military duty, annual pilgrim feasts (Passover, Weeks, Tabernacles), family visits, and migration in time of famine. The Bible refers frequently to messengers (*mal'ākîm*), couriers (*rāṣîm*), and traders (*sōḥărîm*), people who traveled regularly because of their work.

A day's journey in biblical times averaged between twenty-seven and thirty-seven kilometers. Marching about thirty-two kilometers a day, the Assyrian army took a little more than two months to go from Nineveh to Lachish in 701 B.C.E. Professional armies would have traveled on foot through the Palestinian highlands only after the rainy season.

As widespread as foot travel was by both day and night, lurking bandits and wild animals made walking hazardous. For security, people preferred to travel in caravans, especially to distant places. En route, travelers relied upon the hospitality of others, which was a sacred duty and a virtual necessity for the travelers' well-being (*šālôm*). Archaeology furnishes evidence of inns and caravansaries as well.

Travel on donkeyback (*ḥămôr*) was commonplace in biblical times. When David asked Mephibosheth (Meribbaal), grandson of Saul, why he had not accompanied the king (David) into exile across the Jordan, he answered: "My servant [Ziba] deceived me; for your servant [Mephibosheth] said to him, 'Saddle a donkey (*ḥămôr*) for me, so that I may ride on it and go with the king.' For your servant is lame" (2 Sam. 19:26–27). Travel on muleback was much less frequent than donkeyback, but biblical examples exist. A mule (*pered*) could travel about five kilometers an hour, forty to forty-eight kilometers a day. Apparently the mule was the mode of travel for royalty. "The king [David] said to them [Zadok, Nathan, and Benaiah], 'Take with you the servants of your lord, and have my son Solomon ride on my own mule (*pered*), and bring him down to Gihon'" (1 Kings 1:33). The Israelites apparently did not use horses for riding (see "Transport," below).

Transport

Several animals were used for both transport and travel. From Chalcolithic times, the sure-footed donkey (*Equus asinus*) was utilized as both a pack and riding animal, as well as for plowing. Evidence of the donkey's role as a pack animal comes from late Chalcolithic burial Cave One at Giv'atayim in Israel, where a donkey figurine was uncovered with two panniers on its back. As early as 3000 B.C.E. oxen were used as draft animals to draw plows, carts, and sledges.

The domestication of the camel in the Levant does not antedate the Iron Age. As mentioned, an early representation of a packed camel appears on the Lachish Reliefs (eighth century B.C.E.), installed by Sennacherib in his royal palace at Nineveh to commemorate his victory at Lachish in 701 B.C.E. A Lachishite family is being deported with their belongings placed on the camel's back[180] (Ill. 48). The Israelites appear not to have used camels for travel. The camel could travel about forty kilometers a day and was able to survive without water for three days, making possible the crossing of the Arabian desert, which in turn led to new trade routes. "A multitude of camels (*gĕmallîm*) shall cover you [Jerusalem], the young bull camels of Midian and

Ill. 91a: Horse stables at Megiddo, Str IVA, time of Ahab. Note the tethering holes at top of pillars. (Courtesy of Z. Radovan, Jerusalem)

Ephah; all those from Sheba shall come. They shall bring gold and frankincense, and shall proclaim the praise of Yahweh" (Isa. 60:6).

Horses do not appear in Palestine before the early second millennium B.C.E. They were not considered beasts of burden and were almost never used for agriculture. They were, however, utilized for military purposes. There seems to be a certain "biblical" prejudice against the use of horses and chariots in warfare, but the facts must be distinguished from the prejudice. Indicative of Israel's arrogance, in the mind of the prophet Isaiah, is that "their land is filled with horses, and there is no end to their chariots" (Isa. 2:7). The prohibition against the Israelite king's acquiring horses from Egypt results from a concern that people not be oppressed for the king's gain: "Even so, he [the king] must not acquire many horses (*sûsîm*) for himself, or return the people to Egypt in order to acquire more horses" (Deut. 17:16).

Mounted cavalry appears in the Near East initially in the first millennium B.C.E. Assyrian cavalry date to Ashurnasirpal II (883–859 B.C.E.). While there is no evidence that Israel ever had cavalry, the presence of chariotry in Israel is attested by public stables at Megiddo, where two large complexes have been excavated (Ill. 91a). Below the ninth-century stables lay the tenth-century Solomonic stables. "Solomon gathered together chariots and horses; he had fourteen hundred chariots and twelve thousand horses, which he stationed in the chariot cities and with the king in Jerusalem" (1 Kings 10:26). In the ninth-century suite, each building consisted of three rooms, with rows of pillars dividing the side rooms from the center room. Mangers formed from ashlar blocks were placed between the pillars, some of which were pierced with holes for tethering horses. These buildings are now dated to the ninth century, to the time when King Ahab reigned; however, their purpose has been much disputed. The Megiddo monumental buildings have

---

180. According to David Ussishkin, *The Conquest of Lachish by Sennacherib* (Tel Aviv: Institute of Archaeology, Tel Aviv University, 1982), 109: "The camel is one of the earliest known representations of this animal, which was still uncommon in Judea [sic] at that time."

Ill. 91b: Feeding trough between two (broken) pillars from the horse stables at Megiddo. Note crib bite on the inside of trough. (Courtesy of Z. Radovan, Jerusalem)

been designated storehouses, bazaars, and barracks.

The evidence in favor of their being stables for four hundred and fifty horses or more is now rather convincing. Megiddo was just one of several chariot cities from which King Ahab could draw his contingent of chariots that fought against King Shalmaneser III at Qarqar (in Syria) in 853 B.C.E. (*ANET*, 278–279). Ahab sent two thousand chariots and ten thousand foot soldiers into battle against the Assyrians. This was the largest contingent of chariots from any of the coalition of western kingdoms; Ahab, significantly, sent no cavalry. For that, they relied on the Aramean forces led by King Irhuleni of Hamath.

Much of the evidence for interpreting the tripartite pillared buildings of Megiddo as stables was marshaled by John S. Holladay.[181] He noted that the cobbled side aisles provided a good, solid, yet permeable, surface. The hard cobble floor toughened the hooves of the horses (horseshoes had not yet been invented). It could be easily cleaned of straw bedding and wastes daily. What was not absorbed by the straw, such as horse urine, could percolate between the cracks of the cobbles.

Deborah Contrell, a horse specialist from Tennessee and student of biblical studies at Vanderbilt University, has inspected the Megiddo buildings and brought new, incisive evidence for interpreting them as horse stables. Each stall had a limestone feeding trough set between two limestone pillars (Ill. 91b). There Contrell discovered telltale marks of horses: the stone troughs were

> clearly marked with signs of cribbing on the inner lip of the troughs. Cribbing is a common stable vice that some horses develop that involves the continuous biting and pulling with their incisor teeth against a feeding trough while sucking air. Also apparent was where the horse had paved and indented the front of the trough with its front hooves. The teeth imprints of the horse were evident on the inner edge of the troughs, which were the perfect shallow size for feeding.[182]

She also noted that the smooth plastered center aisle of the stables was wide enough

---

181. John S. Holladay, "The Stables of Ancient Israel," in L. Geraty and L. Herr, eds., *The Archaeology of Jordan and Other Studies: Presented to Siegfried Horn* (Berrien Springs, Mich.: Andrews University Press, 1986), 103–65.

182. Deborah Contrell, "Horse Troughs at Megiddo?" in *Revelations from Megiddo: The Newsletter of the Megiddo Expedition* (Nov. 2000, no. 5), 1–2.

for "a donkey and cart to deliver grain and hay to the feeding troughs on one side, turn at the end and do the same on the other side."[183] Some of the square pillars have tethering holes for grooming three horses (a typical chariot team) at once in the center aisle.

The main function of horses was to pull chariots, either four-wheeled or two-wheeled. Horse-drawn chariots were driven in the plains and valleys. The war chariots of the Philistines gave them a decisive advantage over the Israelites, because they had "chariots of iron" (*rekeb barzel*), that is, the chariot axles were of iron (Judg. 1:18–19). Two bronze linchpins for a chariot, one from Ashkelon (Ill. 46) and the other from Ekron, were found in an Iron I context. In this same Philistine context at Ashkelon another chariot fitting—a terminal for a yoke saddle—appeared. Israelite chariots do not date earlier than David. "David took from him [King Hadadezer] one thousand seven hundred horsemen, and twenty thousand foot soldiers. David hamstrung all the chariot horses, but left enough for a hundred chariots" (2 Sam. 8:4).

The Lachish Reliefs depict a Judahite chariot with its eight-spoked wheels. Similar to the Assyrian ceremonial chariot, it is being seized as booty by Sennacherib's soldiers. The differences between Sennacherib's royal ceremonial chariot and his battle chariots, both pictured on the Lachish Reliefs, are notable. To mention one feature, the ceremonial chariot has large wheels with eight spokes, whereas the battle chariot has smaller, light wheels with six spokes. Apart from warfare, ordinary travel in chariots was also common.

Drawn by oxen, donkeys, or mules, carts were used to transport goods too bulky or awkward for pack animals. Some carts were two-wheeled, others four-wheeled. As time passed, lighter wheeled vehicles were constructed. In the course of a day, one could travel about forty-five kilometers in a chariot or carriage. Covered wagons are sometimes pictured on reliefs.[184] Carts (*ăgālôt*) are depicted on the walls of the temple of Rameses III at Medinet Habu. The Lachish Reliefs in Sennacherib's palace at Nineveh portray a cart pulled by bullocks being used to deport women and children. A particularly poignant scene represents a captive woman holding a tiny child on her lap as she sits in the cart. The Bible contains frequent references to carts and wagons (Ill. 92). The Philistines yoked two milk cows to a new cart so as to return the Ark of the Covenant to Israelite territory (1 Sam. 6:7). David and the people likewise carried the Ark of the Covenant to Jerusalem on a new cart (2 Sam. 6:3).

Trade

Hebrew has several words for "merchant" or "trader," among them *sōḥēr* and *rōgēl*, but the popular term in biblical times was *kĕnaʿănî*, "Canaanite," which became a synonym for "trader." "A trader (*kĕnaʿan*), in whose hands are false balances, he loves

---

183. Ibid., 2.
184. David A. Dorsey, "Carts," *OEANE*, 1: 433–34.

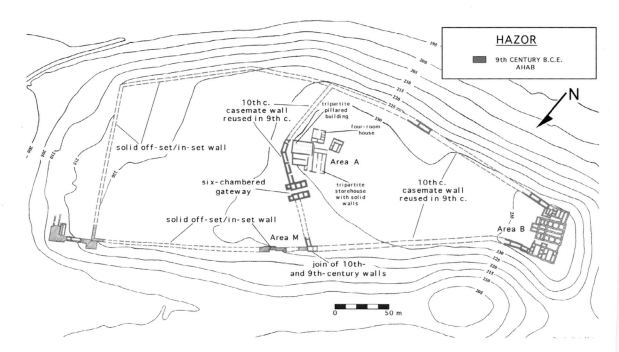

Ill. 92: Plan of Hazor at the time of Ahab (ninth century B.C.E.). City expands to twice its tenth-century size, to encompass most of the acropolis. The tenth-century wall and gate continue to be used while a solid wall is added to the east. A citadel is added in Area B. In Area A four-room houses and tripartite buildings are featured. (Courtesy of A. Ben-Tor; Drawing: A. M. Appa)

to oppress" (Hos. 12:8 [E.T. 12:7]). Originally *kĕna'an* may have referred to Phoenicians who traded in purple dye (*'argāmān*) or in purple-dyed wool. The Israelites, a primarily agrarian people, were undistinguished merchants, compared with the Babylonians, Arameans, Canaanites, Phoenicians, Greeks, and Philistines. At least in their propaganda the Israelites were condescending toward traders and commerce.

Ezekiel's lament over Tyre disparages the commercial activities of this leading Phoenician city as being the cause of its sinful pride (Ezek. 27:28–36) (Ill. 93). The prophet's negative feelings may have been incited by Phoenicia's exploitation of Judah. Attesting to extensive international trade in Ezekiel's time, this same lament lists the agricultural commodities Israel and Judah traded with Tyre: "They were your traders (*rōkĕlāyik*) in wheat of Minnith,[185] millet (*pannag*),[186] honey, olive oil, and turpentine resin [or turpentine] that they sold (*nātĕnû*) you for import (*ma'ărābēk*)"

185. Minnith was an obscure Ammonite village. Some emend the text from *ḥiṭṭê minnît*, "wheat of Minnith," to read *ḥiṭṭîm zayit*, "wheat, olives."

186. The meaning of *pannag* is uncertain; it may be a type of millet (*Panicum miliaceum*) originating in India. Oded Borowski, *Agriculture in Iron Age Israel* (Winona Lake, Ind.: Eisenbrauns, 1987), 93, states there are no archaeological remains of millet from the Iron Age in Palestine. Since the meaning of *pannag* is uncertain, Diakonoff ("The Naval Power and Trade of Tyre," 185) reads instead *dônag*, "wax."

Ill. 93: Upper Register – Bronze Bands, Gates of Balawat. Campaign in Armenia, 860 B.C.E. Booty from captured city of Urartu and a pithos carried on a cart. An example of pithoi used to transport wine overland. A ninth century B.C.E. example of *danê yayin* brought overland from Izalla in Urartu to Damascus, then transshipped to Tyre for export; compare Ezekiel 27. (Courtesy of the Trustees of the British Museum)

(Ezek. 27:17).[187] When Hiram, king of Tyre, supplied Solomon with cedar and juniper for the building of the Temple, the king of Israel reciprocated with "twenty thousand kors of wheat as food for his household, and twenty baths of virgin oil (*šemen kātît*)" (1 Kings 5:25 [E.T. 5:11]).

The marketplace was probably located at the city gate. Immediately adjacent to the gate was a large plaza that served as a bazaar where merchants traded their goods. "Elisha said, 'Hear the word of Yahweh: thus says Yahweh, Tomorrow about this time a measure of choice meal shall be sold for a shekel, and two measures of barley for a shekel, at the gate of Samaria'" (2 Kings 7:1; also 7:18). The Hebrew *ḥûṣōt* designates sections of streets set apart for a marketplace. In his elegy over Saul and Jonathan, David said: "Tell it not in Gath, proclaim it not in the streets (*ḥûṣōt*) of Ashkelon" (2 Sam. 1:20). Here *ḥûṣōt* is better understood as "bazaars," as the current excavations of Ashkelon attest. Describing the bazaar or marketplace that his excavation uncovered, Stager mentions the row of shops flanking the street. The first appears to be a wine shop, since it was littered with dipper juglets and wine jars. Another shop contained the bones of small birds. The last was the butcher shop that contained cuts of meat.[188] Ben-hadad of Syria conceded to the victorious King Ahab the right to establish bazaars (*ḥûṣōt*) in Damascus, just as Ben-hadad's father had done in Samaria. Ben-hadad said, "You [Ahab] may establish bazaars (*ḥûṣōt*) for yourself in Damascus, as my father did in Samaria" (1 Kings 20:34). Speculating that the *ḥûṣōt* in Damascus were outside the wall, Avraham Biran identifies the structures (ninth–eighth centuries) excavated outside the city wall and gate complex of Dan as *ḥûṣōt*.[189]

In classifying ancient economies, Karl Polanyi outlined three major categories of exchange, or models, by which they could be identified: reciprocity, redistribution,

---

187. The translation of this verse is based on Diakonoff, "The Naval Power and Trade of Tyre," 185.

188. Stager, "Ashkelon and the Archaeology of Destruction: Kislev 604 B.C.E.," 65*.

189. Avraham Biran, "The *ḥûṣôt* of Dan," in B. Levine et al., eds., *Eretz-Israel* 26 [Frank Moore Cross Volume] (Jerusalem: Israel Exploration Society, 1999), 25–29.

and exchange. He saw little room for market-oriented behavior in ancient society, where profit incentives were minimized. This kind of behavior, if it existed at all, was firmly embedded in other societal customs and institutions and is hardly recognizable by the criteria of modern economic theory. Nevertheless, there is evidence that all three models of exchange existed in antiquity and, probably frequently, simultaneously within many complex societies. The problem, then, is not to detect the presence of one of these modes of economic interaction, but to determine the predominant mode, or the modal character of an economy, while recognizing that other transactions can persist in other sectors of the society. According to Peter Temin, speaking of a market economy: "They acquire this attribute not by the universality of market exchanges, but by the prominence of market exchanges in transactions between unrelated private people and enterprises and by the importance of these transactions in the economy as a whole."[190]

In an agropastoralist economy, such as ancient Israel had for most of its duration, the majority of the economic activity took place within households, great and small. Barter was the norm. Householding, rather than market exchange, was paramount. And this may have been true for most of the population before and during the monarchy, to judge from the ubiquity, in both rural and urban settings, and the duration, from Iron I to Iron II, of the pillared house with three or four rooms as residential unit for the biological family, even though this unit was usually a part of a larger joint family or even lineage/clan community. With production and stabling units built into every house, the household was designed to maintain its own economic survival, even if only at a minimal level.

However, throughout the Iron Age, some households were always larger and more powerful than others. There was even a degree of specialization in some villages, where certain types of pottery, such as the collared-rim pithos of Iron I, were produced. Some highland villages produced more wine than they consumed; others, more olive oil. So there were opportunities for these communities that produced beyond subsistence levels to form communities of exchange. We can even postulate that larger communities, such as Hebron, Jerusalem, and Shechem, functioned to some degree as regional markets for village produce, which could be bought and sold in a more urban setting.

Agropastoralist villages, in which the inhabitants had a mixed economy of farming

---

190. For his final assessment of ancient economies, see Karl Polanyi, *The Livelihood of Man* (New York: Academic Press, 1977). For a good overview of the various models of economic organization, see Peter Temin, "A Market Economy in the Early Roman Empire," forthcoming in *Journal of Roman Studies*. The case for ancient Israel having a "redistributive economy" can be found in J. David Schloen, *The House of the Father as Fact and Symbol: Patrimonialism in Ugarit and the Ancient Near East*, vol. 2, Studies in the Archaeology and History of the Levant, Harvard Semitic Museum Publications (Winona Lake, Ind.: Eisenbrauns, 2001). The case against has been made in Holladay, "The Kingdoms of Israel and Judah: Political and Economic Centralization in the Iron IIA-B (ca. 1000–750 B.C.E.)." Also see Stager, "Port Power in the Early and Middle Bronze Age: The Organization of Maritime Trade and Hinterland Production."

and herding with rather small land holdings in the highlands, were dominant throughout the Iron Age, before and during the monarchy. The basic residential unit, the pillared house, whether in a rural or urban setting, persisted. The households based on agriculture remained the primary social and economic units. Through barter and marketing, these individual and collective households were the dominant economic reality of ancient Israel. In fact, they also supported the more elite households of the king, the standing army, and the priesthood through tithe or taxation. Yet there is little evidence of large-scale poverty among the tribesmen and peasants during the monarchy. Through conquest of adjoining territories and royal land grants related to this newly taken land as well as tribute tolls and taxes, the royal, military, and priestly elites skimmed off enough to maintain and sustain their institutions. But as Holladay has emphasized, Israel was not based on a redistributive economy—and, we might add, not on a predominantly market economy either. The primary productive asset of ancient Israel—namely the land—was not allocated by market forces. Land was inalienable (at least in principle) and was not a commodity but patrimony, subject to the customary rules of inheritance.

In the Diaspora, Jewish exiles could not pursue traditional agrarian ways of life, the hallmark of the Israelite kingdom. There they moved into other vocations, such as commerce and banking, which did not require much real estate. Such activities can be documented as early as the fifth century B.C.E. in the Aramaic archive of Elephantine (Egypt), where a Jewish colony was established. Some of its members became merchants and bankers. At the same time, Jews living in Babylonia are mentioned in documents of the Murashu business firm in Nippur.

Archaeological excavation and surveys have demonstrated how sparsely populated the lands west of the Jordan Valley were, following the devastation of the Neo-Babylonian army. Nevertheless, for Jewish refugees returning to Palestine after the exile, opportunities to take up farming and herding were lessened by others already having claims to the land. Among those who had not been taken into captivity were the "people of the land" ('am hā'āreṣ). During the Iron Age, these were the Israelites who comprised the notables, the landed gentry. After the exile and return, they were regarded by the returnees and their leaders as "foreigners." Ezra, the priest, exhorted the returning Jews to "make confession to Yahweh the God of your ancestors, and do his will; separate yourselves from the people of the land and from foreign wives" (Ezra 10:11; also 10:2; 9:1–2; Neh. 10:30). During New Testament times and later, the rabbis considered the 'am hā'āreṣ to be rabble, who did not fully observe the Torah (cf. John 7:49).

For Jews who returned to the province of Yehud after the Exile, available land for farming was at a premium, and so some of them took up other pursuits, such as commerce and manufacturing.[191] The once venerable "people of the land," distinguished by

---

191. For the "empty quarter" during the sixth century B.C.E., see Ephraim Stern, *Archaeology of the Land of the Bible*, vol. 2, *The Assyrian, Babylonian and Persian Periods (732–332 B.C.E.)* (New York: Doubleday, 2001), Anchor Bible Supplements. See also Stager, "The Fury of Babylon: Ashkelon and the Archaeology of Destruction"; Marvin H. Pope, "'am ha'arez," *IDB*, 1: 106–7; James L. Kugel, "Qohelet and Money," *CBQ* 51 (1989): 32–49.

their landed wealth during the Israelite monarchy (and even before), became the object of vilification of the Jewish returnees and their leaders. Their economic ideals came to resemble more closely those of the Phoenicians than those of the Israelites before the Exile.

Among the commodities Israel and Judah traded locally were barley, wheat, olives, olive oil, grapes, wine, lentils, dried peas, pomegranates, beans, raisins, dried figs, dates, and almonds. The dairy products sold on the local market included milk, cheese, and butter fat. Oxen, sheep, and goats were also traded. There can be several sectors to the economy—one controlled by royalty, others by corporate groups—and bartering can also be a part of the mix.

Included among the business ventures of Solomon are his "storage cities" ('ārê hammiskĕnôt, 1 Kings 9:19), where his royal warehouses were located. They symbolized the prosperity and power of the king, who controlled and conducted international commerce on a large scale. As noted, Solomon's fleet sailed to the Red Sea to obtain gold; he also traded in horses and chariots. The Queen of Sheba (in modern Yemen) came to Jerusalem "with camels bearing spices (bĕśāmîm), and very much gold (zāhāb), and precious stones ('eben yĕqārâ)" (1 Kings 10:2). This story is really about Solomon's trade relations with the Arabian peninsula. The kings placed tariffs on both imports and exports. Also, customs charges collected on merchandise passing through Israel provided a boost to the economy. Extant records or chits attest to commercial transactions of all kinds, including inventories of the royal storehouses, orders and receipts for goods, and payments for these commodities.

Israel's main exports were agricultural—cereals, olive oil, and wine. Other exports included dates, honey, salt, ṣŏrî (resin from the terebinth tree), textiles, leather, limestone, pine, oak, and bitumen. As noted, Israel provided Phoenicia with cereals and olive oil (1 Kings 5:25 [E.T. 5:11) and Egypt with olive oil: "And oil (šemen) is carried to Egypt" (Hos. 12:2 [E.T. 12:1]).

Israel imported tin, lead, silver, copper, and iron among the metals. Woven garments of purple-dyed wool and cedar came from Phoenicia. Egypt supplied Solomon with horses and chariots (1 Kings 10:28–29), also linen and ivory. Aromatics—frankincense and myrrh—came from Arabia.

The bartering of goods—the earliest form of trade, one commodity being exchanged for another—continued throughout history along with other forms of exchange even after coinage was introduced. Commodities that could be weighed or counted (sheep, grain, wine) were assigned a specific value and, in turn, served as the basis of exchange. Before the introduction of minted coins, pieces of copper, gold, and silver served as payment for commodities. These metal fragments, known as *Hacksilber*, were really scrap metal. *Hacksilber* is more common than ingots as precursors of money/coinage.

In Canaan, Assyria, and Babylonia, silver was used widely as the form of currency. In Israel, "silver" (kesep), later synonymous with "money," designated both the metal and the medium of exchange. Payment was always made by weight. For example, thirty shekels of silver are the prescribed amount to be paid to the owner of a slave gored by an ox (Ex. 21:32). Abraham expended four hundred shekels of silver for the purchase of Sarah's burial place (Gen. 23:15–16). Achan misappropriated booty that included two hundred shekels of silver and a bar of gold weighing fifty shekels (Josh. 7:21). David purchased the threshing floor and the oxen of Araunah for fifty shekels of silver (2 Sam. 24:24). Omri bought the hill of Samaria from She-mer for two talents of silver (ca. 6,000 shekels) (1 Kings 16:24). In 701 B.C.E. Sen-nacherib exacted tribute from Hezekiah in the amount of three hundred talents of silver and thirty talents of gold (2 Kings 18:14). Jeremiah purchased the field of Anathoth from his cousin Hanamel for seventeen shekels of silver (Jer. 32:9); Jere-miah "weighed the money on scales" in the presence of witnesses (Jer. 32:10).

Many injustices were associated with trade. Because of the temptation to falsify weights, the prophets constantly denounced merchants for fraudulence (Hos. 12:8 [E.T. 12:7]); Amos 8:5; Mic. 6:11; Ezek. 45:10). They were reflecting biblical legisla-tion governing business transactions: "You shall not cheat in measuring length, weight, or quantity. You shall have honest balances, honest weights, an honest ephah, and an honest hin" (Lev. 19:35–36).

Weight Measures

The metrological system of Israel was not an exact science. Transposing from ancient measures to modern equivalents is rendered difficult by the inaccuracy and ambigu-ity of biblical metrology, compounded by present-day ignorance of its several aspects. Furthermore, official standards of measurement were lacking in antiquity.

The basis of the monetary system was the weighing of metals, principally silver (*kesep*, also translated "money"). Silver, far more common than gold, was used in biblical transactions. There were varying standards of weight in the ancient Near East; basically, the Assyro-Babylonian, which was sexagesimal (divisible by six or sixty), and the Egyptian, which was quinquagesi-mal (divisible by five or ten). In Assyria and Baby-lonia, two standards of weight, "heavy" and "light," were in use by the end of the third mil-lennium. By Iron I the Babylonian weight stan-dard, the main source of metrology in the ancient world, became the accepted measure. The Israelite system, like the Egyptian, was quinquagesimal.

The need for standardization of weights and mea-sures is conveyed from the Yavneh-Yam ostracon, which may be a juridical document dating to the reign of Josiah. According to the text, the garment of a corvée worker was impounded by his supervisor Hashavyahu, who charged that he had failed to deliver the requisite quota of reaped grain to the gra-nary. Insisting he had complied by delivering the full

Ill. 94: Reconstruction of a scale for weighing shekels of silver or other precious metals. The balance beam from Lachish, mid-eighth cen-tury B.C.E. (Courtesy of the Expedition to Lachish, D. Ussishkin; from G. Barkay, "A Balance Beam from Tel Lachish," *TA* 23 [1996], 75–82)

Ill. 95: Metal and stone weights; arm and partial pans of scale balance, used for weighing silver. Found in 604 B.C.E. destruction layer at Ashkelon. (Courtesy of the Leon Levy Expedition to Ashkelon, Photo: I. Sztulman)

amount, the worker wanted a recount, that is, verification by weighing or measuring. The dispute arose because of the variation between the weights or vessels of the supervisor and those of the worker. The attempt was being made at that time to standardize weights and measures.[192] Metals were measured by weight. Balances (*mō'znāyim*), utilized in measuring weights, consisted of two metal pans suspended from a beam (Ill. 94). Second Isaiah refers to this mechanism: "Who has measured the waters in the hollow of his hand and marked off the heavens with a span, enclosed the dust of the earth in a measure, and weighed the mountains in scales and the hills in a balance (*mō'znāyim*)?" (Isa. 40:12).

Stager reports that in the vicinity of the Counting House (seventh century B.C.E.) at Ashkelon "a dozen scale weights of bronze and stone appeared along with two bronze pieces of pans and part of a bronze beam from a scale balance"[193] (Ill. 95, 96). Such balances were used in weighing the cut silver or silver ingots. Worked limestones (*'ăbānîm*), some inscribed with their value or symbols, served as weights. In antiquity there were also many other types of weights. A variety of zoomorphic weights was found in the Uluburun shipwreck, for example, a sphinx, cows, bulls, lions, ducks, and frogs. Archaeologists have unearthed small,

0   2 cm.

Ill. 96: Bronze cuboid scale weight, Philistine type from 604 B.C.E. destruction, Ashkelon. (Courtesy of the Leon Levy Expedition to Ashkelon, Photo: I. Sztulman)

---

192. Shemaryahu Talmon, "The New Hebrew Letter from the Seventh Century B.C. in Historical Perspective," *BASOR* 176 (1964): 29–38.

193. Stager, "Ashkelon and the Archaeology of Destruction: Kislev 604 B.C.E.," 66*.

dome-shaped limestone weights in Judah that date to the seventh–early sixth centuries B.C.E., often inscribed with Hebrew characters or hieratic Egyptian numerical symbols. Inscribed weights were marked *neṣef* (not mentioned in the Bible), *beqaʿ*, and *pîm* (Ill. 97). *pîm* appears only once in the Bible, in the passage about the Philistines sharpening the implements of the Israelites and charging a *pîm* (two-thirds of a shekel) for plowpoints, mattocks, tridents, axes, and ox goads (1 Sam. 13:21).

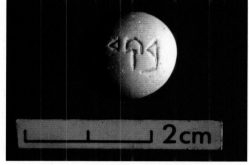

Ill. 97: *bqʿ* weight, dome-shaped; half a shekel. (Courtesy of the Leon Levy Expedition to Ashkelon; Photo: C. Andrews)

The shekel is represented by an open loop of Egyptian origin. It may be a stylized image of a small leather pouch (*ṣĕrôr*) for carrying silver pieces and stone weights.[194] The cloth bag or *kîs* suspended from the merchant's belt was used for the same purpose. Micah alludes to this practice when referring to false weights as "a bag of dishonest weights" (*kîs ʾabnê mirmâ*) (Mic. 6:11). Also, Proverbs: "All the weights in the bag (*kol-ʾabnê-kîs*) are his [Yahweh's] work" (Prov. 16:11). Deuteronomy mandates: "You shall not have in your bag (*bĕkîsĕkā*) two kinds of weights, large and small" (Deut. 25:13).

The biblical text mentions several different weights. The talent (*kikkar*, Heb. "round-shaped") is the largest unit of weight, equaling three thousand shekels or sixty minas. In descending order of value are the mina (fifty to sixty shekels), the shekel (11.4 grams [light]; 12.5 grams [heavy]), the *pîm* (7.5 grams), the *beqaʿ* (the half-shekel, from the verb "to split"), and the *gera*, the smallest unit of weight (twenty gerahs equal one shekel). Inscribed weights first came into use at the end of the eighth century. Judah had a weight system before that time, but little evidence has been uncovered from the earlier period. Only a few weights have been found in the northern kingdom and Transjordan.

Two Aramaic inscriptions from Tell Deir ʿAlla in the Jordan Valley and a Hebrew inscription from Tel Kinrot (Tell el-ʿOreme) on the shore of the Sea of Galilee, all dating to the eighth century, cast some light on metrology.[195] They refer to "the jar of the gate" (*kd hšʿr*), a formula designating the location in the town where commercial transactions took place. Such a description was clear enough in small towns like Deir ʿAlla and Tel Kinrot, but in larger cities, business would have been conducted at more than one place, such as the Fish Gate, the Sheep Gate, or the Bakers' Street (Jer. 37:21). The term "of the gate" is evidence for a local system of weights and measures in ancient Israel. Other standards were very likely in use simultaneously: the standard of the kingdom, and the imperial or international standard.

194. Robert B. Y. Scott, "Weights and Measures of the Bible," *BA* 22 (1959): 22–40.
195. Israel Ephʿal and Joseph Naveh, "The Jar of the Gate," *BASOR* 289 (1993): 59–65.

Abraham Eran, an expert on Levantine weights, has made an important study of the weights from the excavations at the City of David (Jerusalem), including the early digs.[196] In his long and detailed inventory, he lists twenty-seven Bronze Age weights and many more Iron Age weights: one from the twelfth-eleventh century (Jerusalem was still Canaanite/Jebusite); nine from the tenth century; one from the ninth century; forty-five from the eighth century; fifty-eight from the seventh–early-sixth century; twenty-four (many residual from the Iron Age) from the Persian period (Str IX).

The weights from the City of David were cuboid and spheroid in shape, produced from two kinds of stone—flint and limestone. In Judah, the weights are of basalt, diorite, and hematite. The dome-shaped limestone weights bear various inscriptions: those with a looped sign and either unit strokes or numerals; those inscribed with *pym*, *nsp*, or *bq'*; and very small ones marked with hieratic numerals. In sum, more than three hundred weights have been found up to the present in all the excavations at the City of David, the greatest yield dating to the eighth century.

Currency and Coinage

Bullion refers to gold or silver in the form of bars, plates, or ingots. An ingot is a mass of metal cast in a standard shape for storage or shipment. To facilitate negotiations, precious metals were molded into ingots of predetermined weight, each carrying a "monetary" value. Ornaments (bracelets, earrings, etc.) made of precious metal and of fixed weight, as well as cut silver pieces (*Hacksilber*), were also used as currency.

"Shekel" (*šeqel*) was first a measurement of weight and later became the term for a coin. As the basic unit of the Israelite weight system, it equaled 11.4 grams of silver. The Hebrew *šāqal* means "to weigh" in the sense "to pay." Pieces of silver were weighed by using shekel weights. Zephaniah refers to merchants as those "who weigh out silver" (*nětîlê kāsep*) (Zeph. 1:11).

A metal blank was transformed into a coin when impressed with an official stamp guaranteeing its weight. Standardizing weights and measures prepared the way for coinage, which came into use sometime after 650 B.C.E. Since the actual minting of coins in Palestine dates to the postexilic period, references to coinage in the Bible appear for the first time in the postexilic books. The earliest coins were made of electrum, a natural alloy of gold and silver. Coinage had the advantage of a determined form, a fixed weight, and a royal guarantee.[197] The use of coinage is a measure of the social and economic development of a nation. For the scholar, coins are valuable in establishing chronology and illuminating economic history.

---

196. Abraham Eran, "Weights and Weighing in the City of David: The Early Weights from the Bronze Age to the Persian Period," in D. T. Ariel and A. de Groot, eds., *Excavations at the City of David 1978–1985*, Qedem 35 (Jerusalem: Institute of Archaeology, Hebrew University, 1996) 4: 204–56.

197. John W. Betlyon, "Coinage," *ABD*, 1: 1076–89.

The earliest still extant coinage is a collection of North Syrian inscribed ingots from the Late Hittite city-state of Zincirli Huyuk (ancient Samal) in Turkey. In the mid-seventh-century B.C.E., coinage was introduced for the first time at Sardis, capital of ancient Lydia, near present-day Izmir in Turkey. The Lydians are credited with the invention of coinage. Croesus (560–546 B.C.E.), the last king of Lydia, may have been the first to issue coinage of silver and other metals. Croesus's earliest coins were struck in electrum. From Lydia the use of coins as legal tender extended to parts of the Greek world and to Persia by the mid-sixth century. By the late fifth century, foreign currency was common in Tyre, Sidon, Gaza, and Jerusalem. A coin from the island of Kos (modern Greek Cos) appeared in Jerusalem during the sixth century. Coins began to be minted in Palestine about 400 B.C.E.

Money and commerce became more important to the Jews after the exile because they were no longer as dependent on agriculture as they once were; others controlled the land. This new emphasis is evident in Ecclesiastes (Qoheleth), which dates to the Persian period, perhaps as early as the fifth century.[198] The extensive economic vocabulary of Ecclesiastes attests to the monetary preoccupations of the author's audience: *kesep* (money), *śākār* (compensation), *năḥălâ* (inheritance), *ḥešbôn* (account), *hāmôn* (wealth), and more. On the one hand, it was a time of great economic opportunity; on the other, the volatility of the economy made it an uncertain time. The people ran the risk of losing their holdings through bad investments. Despite the prosperity, everyone felt insecure and discontented. The rich could suddenly become impoverished, while the poor could suddenly become affluent. Choon-Leong Seow summarizes the unpredictable economy of Qoheleth and his contemporaries: "Theirs was a world of money, commerce, and investment. It was also a world of loans, mortgages, and foreclosures."[199]

The earliest biblical reference to money concerns contributions to the construction and furnishings of the Second Temple: "According to their resources they [heads of families] gave to the building fund sixty-one thousand darics of gold, five thousand minas of silver, and one hundred priestly robes" (Ezra 2:69). A daric is a gold coin of 8.4 grams; minas are weights of about 570 grams, fifty times the weight of a shekel (11.4 grams). Coins were already fairly common by the Persian period, and they increased in frequency thereafter. The Persians permitted the Jews to mint coins. Several bearing the Hebrew letters "YHD" (Judah) have been found. These "Yehud" (Judah) coins, inscribed in Aramaic script, date to the Persian period (mid-fifth and late fourth centuries).

Ancient Near Eastern literature attests that charging interest was practiced widely. Two Hebrew words—*nešek* and *tarbît*—are used for "interest," although

---

198. Choon-Leong Seow, *Ecclesiastes*, AB 18C (New York: Doubleday, 1997), 21–36; Kugel, "Qohelet and Money," 32–49.

199. Seow, *Ecclesiastes*, 36.

the distinction between them is unclear. To exact interest from another Israelite was prohibited, but from foreigners it was permitted (Ex. 22:24; Lev. 25:35–37; Deut. 23:20). The nonlegal sections of the Bible attest that, in fact, excessive rates of interest were imposed on all (Neh. 5:1–5).

Linear Measures

The following linear measures are based on parts of the human body. The cubit (*'ammâ*, "forearm"), the basic measure, is comparable to the shekel in the weight system. The cubit designates the distance between the point of the elbow and the tip of the middle finger. There were two values for the cubit: the short and the long cubit. The standard of cubit (short) is about 44.4 centimeters. Span (*zeret*), equal to 22.2 centimeters, is the distance between the extended fingertips, from the tip of the thumb to the tip of the little finger. *zeret* is the equivalent of half a cubit. A handbreadth (*ṭepaḥ*), equalling 7.4 centimeters, is the breadth of the hand at the base of the fingers; it is one-sixth of a cubit. A fingerbreadth (*'eṣba'*), the equivalent of 1.85 centimeters, is the smallest Israelite linear measure (Jer. 52:21).

Measures of Capacity

Foodstuffs were measured by volume, and the names are derived from the vessels containing the provisions. The standard dry measure is the *ḥōmer* (about 150 liters), derived from *ḥămôr* ("donkey") and the equivalent of a donkey load. *kōr* (or kor), equal to the *ḥōmer*, was used both for dry measure (wheat, barley, flour) and for oil (although this is disputed). *'êpâ* (ephah or three *sě'îm*), a dry measure used for cereals, is equal to a tenth of a *ḥōmer*, that is, about 15 liters. It is the Bible's most common unit of measure for solids. *bat* (or bath) (32.5 liters) is used to measure water, wine, and oil. *sě'â* (or seah) (5 liters) is a dry measure for flour and cereals. *hîn* (or hin), a liquid measure (about 5.5 liters), is used for measuring wine (Ex. 29:40) and olive oil (Ex. 30:24). *'iśśarôn* (or issaron) (a tenth part of an ephah) is a dry measure. *'ōmer* (omer) (1.5 liters), different from the *ḥōmer*, is a dry measure, the equivalent of one-tenth of an ephah.

CHAPTER 4

Patrimonial Kingdom

THE ROYAL CITY

The Acropolis

Few traces of monumental architecture have been found in premonarchic Israel.[1] And this is exactly what one might expect from a tribal-based society, with few concentrations of wealth. The Israelites' agropastoralist communities were comprised of families, many of whom were closely related. They lived in fairly simple, yet adequate, houses ranging from two to four rooms on the ground floor. The houses were subdivided by one or two rows of pillars parallel to the long axis, thus dividing the building into two or three long rooms with a transverse room along the back of the house. Most archaeologists have assumed that the main long room (the central one in a four-room plan) was an open-air courtyard, just as one of the two parallel rooms in a three-room house was thought to be. It is now clear, however, that these houses had second stories that covered the entire ground floor.[2]

The pillared house was so well adapted to Israelite life that it continued to be the most common domestic dwelling throughout the Iron Age. In fact, pillared buildings, with three long parallel rooms, built on a grand scale became the most common form

---

1. An exception could be the Fortress Temple of El-berith at Shechem. The life of this great building (Temple 1) can now be extended from MB IIC to about 1100 B.C.E. The temple was probably the focus of the Abimelech episode of Judges 9; see Stager, "The Fortress-Temple at Shechem and the 'House of El, Lord of the Covenant,'" in Prescott H. Williams Jr. and Theodore Hiebert, eds., *Realia Dei: Essays in Archaeology and Biblical Interpretation in Honor of Edward F. Campbell Jr. at His Retirement* (Atlanta: Scholars Press, 1999), 228–49.
2. See Stager, "The Archaeology of the Family in Ancient Israel," *BASOR* 260 (1985): 15–16; John S. Holladay, "House, Israelite," *ABD*, 3: 308–18; Ehud Netzer, "Domestic Architecture in the Iron Age," in A. Kempinski and R. Reich, eds., *The Architecture of Ancient Israel* (Jerusalem: Israel Exploration Society, 1992), 193–99. Evidence for second stories over the so-called open-air courtyard of these houses is found in House 1727 at Shechem and, more recently, in an Iron Age I pillared house at Tell el-'Umeiri. Larry G. Herr and Douglas R. Clark, "Excavating the Tribe of Reuben," *BAR* 27 (2001):36–47, 64–66.

of public architecture during the monarchy. Archaeologists still debate their function—whether storehouses, stables, bazaars, or barracks—without resolution. This is not surprising since the building layout tells us little about its use, but a great deal about the structural problem that the form was designed to solve: namely, how to create sizable buildings with limited materials—whether timber, stone, or mud brick—for spanning wide spaces. In the case of tripartite structures, one must look to other features and artifacts within each building to determine its use.

In Israel, monumental architecture in the form of palaces, temples, and other public buildings appears with the advent of kingship. The first example is the rusticated citadel or palace which King Saul built at Gibeah, the first capital, most probably located at the site of Tell el-Ful, north of Jerusalem.[3] This is followed by a floruit of monumental construction in the tenth century B.C.E., especially during the reign of King Solomon. Evidence of his royal cities has been discovered at Beth-Shemesh, Gezer, Megiddo, Ta'anach, Beth-Shean, Yokneam, and Hazor (see 1 Kings 4; 9:15).

Palaces

Hebrew does not have a special term for "palace," but several words are translated "palace"—*hêkāl* (generally "temple" but often "palace"), *'armôn* (perhaps the fortified section of the royal palace), *bêt hammelek* ("house of the king"), and *bayit* ("house"). The explanation for this absence of specialized vocabulary lies in the fact that the "household" was paramount at the familial, royal, and divine levels of symbolism.

According to 2 Samuel 5:11–12 and 7:1–2, David's house (*bayit*) in Jerusalem was a royal palace: When Jerusalem became the capital of the united kingdom, "King Hiram of Tyre sent messengers to David with cedar, carpenters, and builders, and they built a house (*bayit*) for David" (2 Sam. 5:11; also 7:2). The Bible (1 Kings 7:2–8) describes Solomon's large and elaborate royal palace (that is, the complex of buildings) selectively and superficially:

> (2) He [Solomon] built the *House of the Forest of Lebanon* one hundred cubits long, fifty wide, and thirty high; it was supported by four rows of cedar columns, with cedar capitals upon the columns. (3) It had a ceiling of cedar above the beams resting on the columns; these beams numbered forty-five, fifteen to a row. (4) There were three window frames at either end, with windows in strict alignment. (5) The posts of all the doorways were rectangular, and the doorways faced each other, three at either end. (6) He made the *Hall of Pillars* fifty cubits long and thirty cubits wide. There was a portico in front with pillars, and a canopy in front of them. (7) He made the *Hall of the Throne* where he was to pronounce judgment, the *Hall of Justice*, covered with cedar from floor to ceiling beams. (8) *His own house* (*bayit*) where he would reside,

3. For a convenient summary with bibliography, see Nancy Lapp, "Ful, Tell el-," *NEAEHL*, 2: 445–48.

in the other court back of the hall, was of the same construction. Solomon also made a *House for Pharaoh's Daughter*, whom he had married.

As with the Temple, no archaeological remains of the palace have survived.

According to the biblical report, seven years were required to build the Temple, but thirteen to complete Solomon's palace, which was much larger (1 Kings 7:1). The palace appears to have been built alongside the Temple, to its south, on the acropolis. The juxtaposing of palace and temple was established by the Canaanites early in the second millennium B.C.E., probably by 2000 in North Syria (e.g., Alalakh, a Syrian city-state).

In addition to his own royal residence, Solomon built, as part of the palace complex, the House of the Forest of Lebanon, the Hall of Pillars, the Hall of the Throne, and a house for Pharaoh's daughter. The House of the Forest of Lebanon (twenty-five meters by fifty meters) (1 Kings 7:2–5) was a large, detached building that may have served as a royal reception hall. The name, the House of the Forest of Lebanon, derives from the fact that its cedar pillars (*'ammûdîm*) (MT: four rows, each containing fifteen cedar pillars; LXX: three rows, each containing fifteen cedar pillars), imported from Lebanon, resembled a cedar forest (1 Kings 7:2–3). Each column was crowned with a cedar capital (*kĕrutôt*), on which the roof or ceiling beams (*sĕlā'ôt*) rested. (In the Temple, *sĕlā'ôt* designate "stories" or "side stories.") A close parallel to the House of the Forest of Lebanon appears to be the Iron II Phoenician temple (twenty-two meters by thirty-five meters) discovered at Kition in Cyprus. (The sanctuaries [temples one to five] at Kition date to LB; the Phoenicians rebuilt temples one and four in the ninth century.) Its four rows of stone bases, seven to a row, were preserved. However, comparisons are somewhat problematic, since nothing remains of the Solomonic palace.

The Hall of Pillars with its portico is sometimes described in terms of the *bît ḫilāni*, a type of palace that originated in North Syria in the second millennium and evolved in the ninth to seventh centuries, as exemplified at Tell Halaf, Zincirli, and Tell Ta'-yinat. While the provenience of this architectural structure is clear, the etymology of its name is not. The word *ḫilāni* is never used alone, always in conjunction with *bît*. The Assyrians thought *bît ḫilāni* meant "house of windows" (Hebrew *bêt ḫallônîm*), and they were probably correct. The *bît ḫilāni* is "a self-contained structure" that cannot be extended.[4] It is composed of two long, narrow rooms—a pillared portico (which is a prime feature) entered on the broad side, and an adjacent throne room entered on the long side. The pillars were extremely important and when found in Mesopotamia, where pillars were extremely uncommon, it is clear they were inspired by Syrian architectural tradition.

---

4. Henri Frankfort, "The Origin of the Bît Ḫilāni," *Iraq* 14 (1952): 120–31.

The throne room was the most important room in a palace, while the portico was an anteroom. A stairway leading to the second story was located to one side of the portico. The Hall of Pillars of Solomon's palace was the portico. Palace 6000 at Megiddo is the most relevant example.

Attempting to solve the mystery of the assassination of Eglon, king of Moab, at the hands of Ehud, Baruch Halpern suggests that Eglon's palace was a typical Near Eastern palace, modeled on the *bīt ḫilāni* plan. The reception suite consisted of a porticoed antechamber, a public audience hall, and the king's second-story quarters (*'ăliyyâ*). According to Halpern, this architectural plan helps to explain how Ehud could escape undetected after committing the murder, if the reader is convinced that Ehud exited the upper chamber through the toilet.[5]

Several other palaces were built during the divided monarchy. The most magnificent was located on the summit of the hill in Samaria, the capital of the northern kingdom, which Omri constructed in the early ninth century (1 Kings 16:24). The royal quarters on the acropolis were enclosed by a casemate wall of Phoenician-style ashlar masonry, as early as the reign of King Ahab. Archaeology attests to the affluence of this city in the First Temple period, as well as to its superb remains. The plan of the palace, begun by Omri and completed by his son Ahab, consisted of rooms grouped around a central courtyard. This lavish palace of ashlar masonry was inlaid with carved ivory. Archaeologists have recovered more than five hundred ivory fragments dating to the eighth century, including two hundred decorated pieces, from the palace debris (Ill. 196, 197). Ivory carvings appearing in the ninth and eighth centuries were the handiwork of Phoenician artisans. The Samaria ivories were Phoenician in style, drawing on Egyptian motifs. Ahab is remembered for "the ivory palace (*bêt haššēn*) that he [Ahab] built" (1 Kings 22:39). The attribution to Omri–Ahab is a literary allusion to the ivory palaces and is not attested directly by the Samaria ivories of the eighth century. For the prophet Amos, ivory inlays symbolized much of what was wrong with the luxury-loving Israelite society of the eighth century: "Alas for those who lie on beds of ivory (*miṭṭôt šēn*), and lounge on their couches" (Amos 6:4; also 3:15). Amos lived in the eighth century, but ivory inlays were already a part of the palace decor as early as Omri and Ahab.

Megiddo in northwestern Palestine had two palaces in the Solomonic period (Str VA–IVB, tenth century), constructed along lines similar to Solomon's Jerusalem palace. According to Ussishkin, Palace 6000 (the northern palace) and Palace 1723 (the southern palace) were built in the *bīt ḫilāni* manner, and most scholars would concur. Only the foundation courses that were constructed of ashlars are preserved

---

5. Baruch Halpern, "The Assassination of Eglon—The First Locked-Room Murder Mystery," *Bible Review* 4 (1988): 32–41, 44. This article has been adapted from Baruch Halpern, *The First Historians: The Hebrew Bible and History* (San Francisco: Harper & Row, 1988), 39–75.

Ill. 98: Interpretation of Jerusalem, the City of David in the time of Hezekiah, based on biblical texts and modern excavation. (Reconstruction: © L. E. Stager; Illustration: C. S. Alexander)

at Megiddo; the superstructure, too, would have been built from ashlar masonry. Quarries producing the ashlar blocks are located on the eastern slope of Megiddo. Palace 6000, which was incorporated in the peripheral fortification system (a casemate city wall) was a rectangular building (twenty-eight meters by twenty-one meters). Palace 1723, built on a square plan (twenty-three meters by twenty-three meters), stood in the middle of a large enclosure and was contiguous to a large administrative building. On the analogy of the palaces in North Syria, the northern palace (6000) was a ceremonial palace, whereas the southern palace (1723) had living quarters.

Stone capitals, erroneously designated "Proto-Aeolic," decorated the palaces. A more appropriate term for these capitals, ornamented with a central triangle separating two rising volutes, is "palmette capitals" (Ill. 100). A palmette is a stylized palm tree, with origins in the palm-tree motif of ancient Near Eastern art. In the Bible, *timōrâ* ("palmette") is applied to the palm-tree motif.[6] "He [Solomon] carved the walls of the house all around about with carved engravings of cherubim, palm trees (*timōrōt*), and rosettes (*peṭûrê ṣiṣṣîm*) in the inner and outer rooms" (1 Kings 6:29).[7] Hewn from *nari*, these capitals are distinguished by the spiral volutes. From the tenth century onward, capitals were an important element of ashlar construction. They are found at Hazor, Dan, Megiddo, Samaria, Ramat Raḥel, and Jerusalem.

Ramat Raḥel, situated on a hill midway between Jerusalem and Bethlehem, is the site where, for the first time, a palace of a Judahite king was excavated. This splendid royal palace (fifty-six meters by seventy-two meters) of dressed limestone blocks (ashlars), similar to the palace precinct of Samaria, was constructed by one of the last

Ill. 99: Limestone balustrade with palmette and petal decoration at Ramat Raḥel, from eighth or seventh century B.C.E. (Courtesy of Israel Museum)

6. Yigal Shiloh, *The Proto-Aeolic Capital and Israelite Ashlar Masonry*, Qedem 11 (Jerusalem: Institute of Archaeology, Hebrew University, 1979), 90.

7. Lawrence E. Stager, "Jerusalem and the Garden of Eden," in B. A. Levine et al., eds., *Eretz-Israel 26* [Frank Moore Cross Volume] (Jerusalem: Israel Exploration Society, 1999), 189*; David N. Freedman and M. P. O'Connor, "Kĕrub," *TDOT*, 7: 307–19.

kings of Judah, perhaps Jehoiakim (609–598 B.C.E.): "Woe to him [Jehoiakim] who builds his house by unrighteousness, and his upper stories (*ʿăliyyôtâw*) by injustice; who makes his neighbors work for nothing, and does not give them their wages; who says, 'I will build myself a spacious house (*bêt middôt*) with large upper stories,' and who cuts out windows (*ḥallônāy*) for it, paneling it with cedar, and

Ill. 100: Palmette *(timōrōt)* capital in limestone from palace at Ramat Raḥel, from eighth or seventh century B.C.E. This capital has been misnamed "Proto-Aeolic." (Courtesy of the Israel Museum; Photo: D. Harris)

painting it with vermilion" (Jer. 22:13–14). The palace was surrounded by an ashlar casemate wall. Limestone balustrades in the form of colonnades decorated with petals and voluted capitals functioned as railings in the palace windows at Ramat Raḥel (Ill. 99). They were also found in the City of David (Jerusalem).

At Lachish, the most important city in Judah after Jerusalem, the podium of the monumental palace of the Iron Age is well preserved. This massive, raised foundation structure made the palace higher than the summit of the mound. The palace had three phases: Palace A (Level V, tenth century) represents the first stage of the palace-fort; Palace B (Level IV, ninth century), the residence of the Judahite governor, was an enormous palace fort located prominently in the heart of the city; Palace C (Level III, eighth century), an eastern extension of the combined palaces A and B, was the largest building in the First Temple period, measuring thirty-six meters by seventy-six meters. Opening onto a large courtyard, it was bordered on two sides by two sets of tripartite buildings, considered storehouses by some, stables by Ussishkin. Unlike most structures in ancient Israel, this imposing palace with its several additions is still partially standing; the superstructure, of course, is not preserved. Destroyed by the Assyrians, it was rebuilt in the Persian period.

The best example from excavation of a royal temple is at Tel Dan. A massive podium constructed of ashlar blocks, dating to Iron II, was uncovered near the northern edge of the mound, as well as a monumental staircase leading to the podium (Ill. 186, 187). A major cult building once stood on this great platform. At first the excavator, Avraham Biran, assumed that this podium did not support a superstructure, but now he acknowledges the presence of a sanctuary on the podium. More likely a temple stood on the podium at Dan. The temenos at Dan was enclosed on the western side by an auxiliary room termed a *liškâ* ("chamber") by the excavator. This rectangular structure, twenty meters long, was added in the eighth century. The artifacts (altar, iron incense shovels [Ill. 191], jar of ashes, offering tables) associated with the *liškâ* attest that it was a religious sanctuary. *liškâ* designating part of a building, such as a room or chapel, occurs almost fifty times in the Bible.[8]

The Imperial Impact of Assyria on Israelite Architecture

A useful source for the study of Assyrian royal architecture is the site of Khorsabad (ancient Dur Sharrukin) in northern Iraq, founded by Sargon II, king of Assyria, to be his new capital. One of its excavators, Gordon Loud, examined Assyrian architecture based on the excavations of royal palaces, temples, and residences at Khorsabad.[9]

The invasion by the Neo-Assyrians of their neighbors to the west in the eighth and seventh centuries was followed by their domination of those lands. Those areas which were transformed into actual Assyrian provinces, such as Samerina (Samaria) and Magiddu (Megiddo), display the most Assyrian artifacts, for example, Assyrian Palace Ware (locally made), cuneiform tablets, and coffin burials. Assyrian architecture is found at Hazor, Megiddo, Tell Jemmeh, and elsewhere. Characteristic of Assyrian architecture or its influence is the "open court" style of buildings that have a large courtyard surrounded by a series of rooms on all sides.

Northeast of Hazor at nearby Ayelet ha-Shaḥar, a monumental building (Hazor, Str III, seventh century), part of an Assyrian administrative center, including a residence for the local governor, was constructed. The main audience hall was entered through a gate with double doors. A niche for the dais of the ruler was to the left of the entrance. To the right a smaller anteroom led to a room with cesspits three meters deep and lined with terracotta drainpipes. This was the lavatory or bathroom of the governor. The thick walls carried barrel vaults for the upper story. The layout and construction techniques are identical to those of Assyrian palaces in the heartland.

Megiddo III seems to be laid out according to an early form of orthogonal city planning, which Kathleen Kenyon ascribed to the Assyrians (Ill. 101).[10] At Megiddo (Str III, eighth to seventh century), Buildings 1052 and 1369 illustrate the Assyrian architectural style with their central, rectangular courtyards. Building 1052 has a court surrounded by a row of rooms. Building 1369 is erected on a podium (typical of Assyrian architecture) and has a large central courtyard surrounded by rooms on all sides. There is also a bathroom, associated with a drainage system.

At Tell Jemmeh (Yurza/Arṣa), a seventh-century building with at least six adjoin-

---

8. Avraham Biran, *Biblical Dan* (Jerusalem: Israel Exploration Society, 1994), 159–234.

9. Gordon Loud, "An Architectural Formula for Assyrian Planning Based on the Results of Excavations at Khorsabad," *Revue d'Assyriologie* 33 (1936): 156: "Common to all the buildings, whether palace, temple, or private dwelling, are two major courts about which are grouped lesser courts and the many large and small rooms."

10. Kathleen Kenyon, *Archaeology in the Holy Land* (New York: Praeger, 1960), 286.

1369

1052

490

0   25

© Ze'ev Herzog

Ill. 101: Plan of Megiddo, Level III, dated to the Assyrian period (eighth–seventh centuries B.C.E.).
(Drawing: C. S. Alexander, after Z. Herzog, *Archaeology of the City*, Fig. 5.35, p. 236)

ing rooms is evidently Assyrian in style. Its barrel vaults, made of mud bricks in a style similar to those of Dur Sharrukin (Khorsabad), suggest that this was the administrative center of a ranking Assyrian official.[11]

The King's Table

It was a great honor to be invited to sit at the king's table. The feast of the New Moon (*ḥōdeš*, derived from the verb *ḥādaš*, "make new"), the first day of the lunar month, was a time of respite and festivities (Amos 8:5). On one occasion David insulted Saul by returning to Bethlehem to be with his own family for the annual sacrifice (literally, "the sacrifice of days," *zebaḥ hayyāmîm*, 1 Sam. 20:6), instead of participating in Saul's family sacrifice at Gibeah, which lasted two or three days (1 Sam. 20:5, 18, 24–27). The prescribed sacrifices for the New Moon are detailed in Numbers 28:11–15. To assemble the people for the feast, the psalmist says: "Blow the horn (*šôpār*) at the new moon (*ḥōdeš*), at the full moon, on our solemn feast" (Ps. 81:4 [E.T. 81:3]).

David extended kindness to Mephibosheth (Meribbaal), crippled son of Jonathan, by inviting him to sit at the king's table (2 Sam. 9:1–13). Although it was a special privilege to dine at the king's table, guests had to provide their own food (1 Kings 2:7; 18:19; 2 Kings 25:27–29; Jer. 52:31–33). As an estate owner, Mephibosheth was expected to do so from the produce of his land (2 Sam. 9:10). David said to Saul's servant Ziba: "You and your sons and your servants shall till the land for him [Mephibosheth], and shall bring in the produce, so that your master's grandson may have food to eat; but your master's grandson Mephibosheth shall always eat at my table" (2 Sam. 9:10).

URBAN WATER SYSTEMS

Underground Water Systems

In the Iron Age, Israelite town planners had sophisticated engineering skills, along with knowledge of hydrology and geology, enabling them to construct their underground water systems.[12] There were two major existing types of water systems: the northern and the southern. The northern group includes Gibeon, Hazor, Gezer, and Megiddo. They cut shafts through the strata of the mound to tap the water table

---

11. Ronny Reich, "Palaces and Residences in the Iron Age," in A. Kempinski and R. Reich, eds., in *The Architecture of Ancient Israel* (Jerusalem: Israel Exploration Society, 1992), 214–22.

12. Dan P. Cole, "How Water Tunnels Worked," *BAR* 6 (1980): 8–29.

and provide water. The southern group includes Arad, Beth-Shemesh, Kadesh-Barnea, and Tel Sheva, where large cisterns or reservoirs collected water for the townspeople.

Gibeon

Two waterworks were constructed at Gibeon, one replacing the other.[13] The Gibeonite engineers discovered a source of fresh water within their city walls. Gibeon, located under the modern village of el-Jib, situated eight kilometers northwest of Jerusalem, had two adjacent but separate water systems that were fed by the same spring and water table. The first was composed of a cylindrical shaft, a stepped tunnel, and a groundwater chamber. Carved from solid rock before the tenth century, it is located at the top of the eastern slope of the tell. The large shaft (11.8 meters in diameter and 10.8 meters deep) may originally have been a large cistern for storing rainwater. A spiral staircase with a railing was hewn around its walls. About a century later, the stairway was extended below the shaft floor to a chamber on a level with the water table.

To augment the water supply, a second system was constructed, consisting of a stepped tunnel, a water chamber, and a feeder channel. The tunnel led from inside the wall to the water chamber outside the town at the base of the mound. This chamber was filled with fresh water from the spring. According to the excavator James Pritchard, the bedrock vats and cisterns at Gibeon had to be plastered to contain the water. Pritchard estimated that it took his combined labor force 23,000 hours to clear debris from the water system. More time would certainly have been required to cut the original shafts and tunnels through limestone.

A battle between the army of Ishbaal and the army of David, under the command of Abner and Joab respectively, erupted at "the pool of Gibeon" (*bĕrēkat gibʿôn*), a well-known landmark (2 Sam. 2:13). It was at "the great waters" (*mayim rabbîm*) that are in Gibeon" that Johanan defeated Ishmael in the time of Jeremiah (Jer. 41:12).

Hazor

The water system at Hazor,[14] a fortified town in northern Galilee, had four components: an entrance, consisting of crushed limestone, that sloped toward the shaft; a rock-hewn shaft, dug to the depth of thirty meters; a stepped tunnel cut in bedrock;

---

13. James B. Pritchard, *The Water System of Gibeon* (Philadelphia: University Museum, University of Pennsylvania, 1961); *Gibeon, Where the Sun Stood Still* (Princeton, N.J.: Princeton University Press, 1962), 82–83.

14. Yigael Yadin, *Hazor: The Rediscovery of a Great Citadel of the Bible* (London: Weidenfeld & Nicolson, 1975); Amnon Ben-Tor, "Hazor," in *NEAEHL*, 2: 604–5.

and a water chamber. The system appears to have been built during the reign of Ahab (Str VIII, ninth century). The engineers of King Ahab were aware of the subterranean water table at Hazor. By digging the shaft and tunnel to tap the aquifer, all situated within the city walls, they secured the city's water supply from attack. This would not have been the case if they had to dig out to the spring.

Gezer

The water system of Gezer has been variously dated, which is not surprising, in view of the erosion that inevitably occurs at the entrance to water systems. R. A. S. Macalister,[15] the original excavator, dated the water system to MB II. William Dever,[16] the second excavator of Gezer, suggested a LB date. On the analogy of Hazor's water system, Yadin[17] dated Gezer's water system "in the beginning of the first millennium." In view of the technological expertise already displayed in the water systems of Jerusalem in MB II, it is possible that the Gezer system dates to the second millennium as well. The Gezer engineers were aware of the technique for reaching the water table from within the city. Gezer's water system consisted of a rock-cut shaft connected to a sloping tunnel that extended as far as a long chamber at the water-table level.

Megiddo

Unlike the water systems at Gibeon, Hazor, and Gezer, which linked the surface with the aquifers, the system of Megiddo in the valley of Jezreel was connected to a spring, outside the fortifications, at the base of the tell (at the southwest corner), which necessitated going beyond the walls to obtain water.[18]

Megiddo's water system reflects three stages. Before the tenth century, steps that led to a natural spring were cut into the base of the tell. In Solomon's time a covered passageway was cut from inside the city wall to the exterior. It connected with the spring at the base of the mound by means of the earlier stairway. The third stage, dating to King Ahab and consisting of two elements, is more technically sophisticated than the first two stages. A large shaft with a winding staircase was cut into bedrock. A horizontal tunnel was dug, running from the bottom of the shaft to connect with

---

15. R. A. S. Macalister, *The Excavation of Gezer* (London: J. Murray, 1912).

16. William G. Dever, "The Water Systems at Hazor and Gezer," *BA* 32 (1969): 71–78; "Gezer," in *NEAEHL*, 2: 503: "It has been suggested that the water tunnel may have been dug in this [LB II] period, but the shaft was cut off from its context by Macalister and cannot now be dated. (It may belong instead, like those at Hazor, Megiddo, and Gibeon, to the Iron Age II.)"

17. Yigael Yadin, "The Fifth Season of Excavations at Hazor, 1968–1969," *BA* 32 (1969): 70.

18. Robert S. Lamon, *The Megiddo Water System* (Chicago: University of Chicago Press, 1935); Yohanan Aharoni, "Megiddo," *NEAEHL*, 3: 1003–12; Yigal Shiloh, "Megiddo: The Iron Age," *NEAEHL*, 3: 1012–23.

the spring outside the city wall. The opening of the spring was blocked by a massive wall. Through the shaft and tunnel, water could be obtained within the city wall.

The Chicago Expedition attributed the construction of Megiddo's water system to Str VI A (second half of the eleventh century B.C.E.). When Yadin's team reexamined the phases of the water system, they redated it to the ninth century B.C.E.[19]

Beth-Shemesh, Kadesh-Barnea, and Tel Sheva

At Beth-Shemesh, inhabitants obtained water from a huge underground reservoir in use during Iron II. Access was gained by a stairway leading down to the reservoir. The water system at Kadesh-Barnea was composed of a plastered channel and a cistern constructed of large stones with a plastered bottom. The channel conducted water from a spring located outside the walls to the cistern within. Tel Sheva had a water system comparable to the one at Beth-Shemesh, composed of a series of underground cisterns.

Jerusalem

The City of David (Jerusalem) has three subterranean waterworks, all issuing from a common source, the perennial Gihon Spring (Ill. 102). Located just above the floor of the Kidron Valley, the cave-spring was thought to be outside the fortifications of the city during biblical times. The recent excavations near the spring by Ronny Reich and Eli Shukron[20] have demolished that long-held notion and demonstrated that massive towers protected the Gihon Spring and the collecting pool nearby from about 1800 B.C.E. until the demise of Judah, if not later still. Thus Jerusalem's primary source of fresh water, the Gihon Spring, was always protected from enemy assault.

The Gihon (Hebrew *gîaḥ*) means "gusher," a most appropriate name for this karstic spring. During the spring season water gushes up from the underground source five-six times per day, for a total output of about twelve hundred cubic meters (ca. 316,800 gal).[21] During the dry season, freshwater gushes into the cave two or three times a day, for a total of about two hundred cubic meters (ca. 52,800 gal).

---

19. Shiloh, "Megiddo: The Iron Age," 1022: "In stratum VA-IVB [tenth century, time of Solomon, until Shishak's campaign in 925] the water system was not yet in existence. At that time, gallery 629 was built in the city wall—a long, narrow passageway, with walls built of well-dressed ashlars, similar to those in the public buildings of this level. The gallery permitted access from the city to the spring. Its construction damaged remains of strata VIA and VB [beginning of the tenth century, time of David]—yet another argument against ascribing it to a level earlier than VA-IVB."

20. Ronny Reich and Eli Shukron, "Light at the End of the Tunnel," *BAR* 25 (1999): 22–33, 72; "The System of Rock-Cut Tunnels near Gihon in Jerusalem Reconsidered," *RB* 107 (2000): 5–17.

21. Mordechai Hecker, "Water Supply of Jerusalem in Ancient Times," in M. Avi-Yonah, ed., *Sepher Yerushalayim* (Jerusalem and Tel Aviv: Bialik Institute and Dvir Publishing House, 1956), 1: 191–207 (in Hebrew).

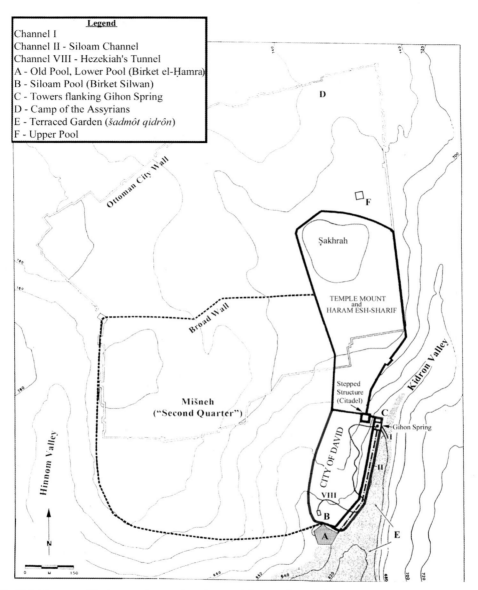

Legend
Channel I
Channel II - Siloam Channel
Channel VIII - Hezekiah's Tunnel
A - Old Pool, Lower Pool (Birket el-Ḥamra)
B - Siloam Pool (Birket Silwan)
C - Towers flanking Gihon Spring
D - Camp of the Assyrians
E - Terraced Garden (šadmôt qidrôn)
F - Upper Pool

Ill. 102: Topographical map of Jerusalem (late eighth or early seventh century B.C.E.) indicating the fortifications and water systems. (Reconstruction: L. E. Stager; Illustration: C. Haberl)

Until the recent excavations, archaeologists generally accepted the idea that the ancient Israelites lowered their water jars from the top of a thirteen-meter deep vertical shaft, named after Charles Warren, who discovered this rock-cut feature in 1867, to draw up water from the Gihon Spring, conducted to the bottom of the shaft by a feeder channel. Now, however, it is clear that Warren's Shaft is a karstic feature completely bypassed by the ancient water system. Instead, water from the spring was led by a short tunnel (Channel III, following the designations of Louis-Hugues Vincent) into a spacious basin cut in the bedrock that held as much as forty to forty-five cubic meters (ca. 10,560–11,880 gal) of water at a filling. If all the output of the Gihon were deflected into this rectangular tank, it could have been filled twenty-five to thirty times a day during the winter months and five times a day during summer. Grooves carved into the walls of the tank probably held planks of a wooden platform on which several people could stand at the same time and draw up freshwater from the basin.

The excavations of Reich and Shukron have revealed portions of a huge tower that flanked one side of the basin or pool. Very likely, another protected the other side as well. Like the even more massive tower built over the spring itself, it was made of rough-dressed cyclopean masonry, a style known from other MB cities. The towers are constructed of limestone building blocks of enormous size, some weighing about four and a half metric tons; masonry of this scale was not seen again until Herodian times.

Of course, not all the daily output of the Gihon Spring was shunted into the nearby basin, or pool. Its feeder channel (Channel III) was connected to a much larger conduit (designated Channel II), which was also built in MB II. It is a channel, not a tunnel, cut deep into the bedrock from ground level, its roof being huge boulders weighing up to two tons and lodged in the upper part of the cavity. The channel is from three to four meters deep, and its slope was slight, as it carried water for at least four hundred meters along the lower eastern flanks of Jerusalem, from the spring cave to another pool at the south end of the city, usually identified with the collecting basin known today as Birket el-Ḥamra. This is probably the Lower Pool to which the prophet Isaiah refers as he excoriates Jerusalemites and their leaders for relying on armaments rather than divine protection from enemy threats:

> On that day you looked to the weapons of the House of the Forest [the palace armory], and you saw that there were many breaches in the City of David. And you collected the water of the Lower Pool (bĕrēkâ taḥtônâ); and you counted the houses of Jerusalem and pulled houses down to fortify the wall. You built a basin (miqwâ) between the two walls for the water of the Old Pool (bĕrēkâ yĕšānâ). But you gave no thought to him [Yahweh] who did it, or took no note of him who designed it long before (Isa. 22:8–11).

The Lower Pool and the Old Pool are probably to be identified as the same bĕrēkâ into which the waters of Channel II flowed, before King Hezekiah (727–698 B.C.E.) built the tunnel (Channel VIII) and an outer wall, which put the "basin between the two walls" in position to receive the water of the Old Pool, which no longer functioned as it once had. In the days of Hezekiah's predecessor King Ahaz (743–727 B.C.E.), the waters of Channel II were still flowing into the Lower Pool, whence it was further channeled into irrigation ditches that watered the royal gardens of Jerusalem in the Kidron Valley.

Ill. 103: Wall painting of Mari, dated eighteenth century; so-called investiture of Zimri Lim. The goddess Ishtar, standing with one foot on a lion, presents him with symbols of authority. Below, two goddesses hold vases from which flow four streams of water. Flanking the building—perhaps a palace or temple—are mythological creatures—winged sphinxes, griffins, and bulls which protect the paradisiacal garden and its inhabitants. (From A. Parrot, *Mission Archéologique de Mari*)

"Waters That Flow Gently"

The prophet Isaiah referred to the "waters of the channel (*šilōaḥ*) that flow gently" (Isa. 8:6), cosmic waters emanating from the same subterranean "flow" (*'ēd*) of freshwater that "would wall up" and irrigate the garden of Eden (Gen. 2:6–8).[22] They are the eschatological waters that issue from "below the platform (*miptān*)[23] of the Temple" and become a stream (*naḥal*) in the Kidron Valley, which flows into the Dead Sea and enlivens it. Along the banks of this paradisiacal stream "fruit trees of every kind shall grow; their leaves shall not fade, nor their fruit fail. Every month they shall bear fresh fruit, for they shall be watered by the flow from the sanctuary" (Ezek. 47:12). For Isaiah, the "waters of the channel" had cosmic significance, symbolizing the quiet but sure protection of Yahweh for those who would rely on him in times of impending disaster.

Most scholars have assumed that Channel II irrigated not only gardens at the southeastern end of the City of David but also the alluvial soils of the Kidron Valley to the east, via openings (or "windows") in the east wall of the channel, which served as sluice gates.[24] At least four such openings (from 0.65 to 1.80 meters high and 0.40 to 0.60 meters wide) have been investigated by Raymond Weill.[25] The assumption that these "windows" were artificially cut into the side of Channel II has been called into question by Reich, who maintains that they are natural karstic fissures, irregularly spaced in the southern part of the channel and never used as sluice gates. Whatever the case, these apertures were blocked by the outer wall that Hezekiah built, and Channel II was partially destroyed by the tunnel that cut through it.

Nevertheless, there had to be some spring water that was channeled into the Kidron Valley from the Gihon southward. Today a series of transverse garden terraces gradually descend from north to south across the ever-widening valley. Where irrigated by the Gihon, luxuriant gardens grow. In biblical times, these wadi terraces were known as *šadmôt qidrôn*, "terraces of the Kidron." With his policy of centralization and religious reform, King Josiah desecrated this valley of sacred and royal gardens, burning "all the vessels made for Ba'al, for Asherah, and for all the host of heaven" outside Jerusalem [i.e., east of the outer wall], "on the terraces of the Kidron (*šadmôt qidrôn*)" (2 Kings 23:4). Jeremiah, however, holds out the promise that these terraces (reading *šĕdēmôt* for *šĕrēmôt*), strewn with corpses (or stelae) and ashes, as far as the Horse Gate (near the Palace or the Temple Mount), will once again be "sacred to Yahweh" (Jer. 31:40).

---

22. Stager, "Jerusalem and the Garden of Eden," 183*–194*; idem, "Jerusalem as Eden," *BAR* 26 (2000), 36–47, 66.

23. For reading "platform" rather than "threshold," see *NJPS* translation, Ezek. 9:3, passim.

24. Jan Jozef Simons, *Jerusalem in the Old Testament* (Leiden: Brill, 1952), 177.

25. Raymond Weill, *La Cité de David, II: Campagne de 1923–1924* (Paris: P. Geuthner, 1947), 144–45; Yigal Shiloh, *Excavations at the City of David, I: Interim Report of the First Five Seasons (1978–1982)*, Qedem 19 (Jerusalem: Institute of Archaeology, Hebrew University, 1984), p. 46, fig. 8; plates 39:2, 40:1.

Of course, during the winter rains the terraces of the Kidron would have received runoff water that could have been stored for irrigation later on. This, however, would have been insufficient to nurture and sustain the variety of exotic trees and plants that grew in ancient public gardens and required a permanent source of irrigation such as the Gihon provides. Therefore, if it was not the "windows" of Channel II that provided such water as far as the Horse Gate, then we should look to another viable candidate for such a purpose, perhaps the underexplored Channel I, the most easterly of the channels debouching from the Gihon. It has been explored for only fifty-four meters or so, as it rapidly descends toward the floor of the Kidron Valley in a southerly direction. Simons[26] wondered whether Channel I "ended near the King's Garden" (2 Kings 25:4; Jer. 39:4; 52:7) in a basin called the King's Pool (Neh. 3:15). Only further exploration will answer this question.

We do know that the outlet of Channel I, being the lowest in the spring-cave, had to be blocked before water could rise to the next higher outlet, that of Channel VIII, better known as Hezekiah's Tunnel. Before discussing that installation we should look briefly for the Upper Pool, which should be somewhere above and to the north of the Lower Pool.

Upper Pool

The Assyrian task force dispatched by Sennacherib to Jerusalem met Hezekiah's delegation "at the conduit of the Upper Pool (tĕ'ālat habbĕrēkâ hā'elyônâ), which is on the highway to the Fuller's Field" (2 Kings 18:17; also Isa. 36:2–3). Earlier, Isaiah and his son Shear-jashub met King Ahaz "at the end of conduit of the Upper Pool" (Isa. 7:3).

David Ussishkin has argued that the "Camp of the Assyrians" should be located on the north side of Jerusalem, and more specifically on the Northeast Hill, which faced the royal acropolis.[27] And it had to be within shouting distance if the Assyrian Rab-shakeh could address the people of Jerusalem. It is possible, although not convincingly demonstrated, that the Upper Pool could be located where the Bethesda pools of the New Testament, now on the grounds of St. Anne's Church, have been excavated. There the White Fathers[28] found an earlier collecting pool and dam, which they and Dan Bahat[29] would date to the First Temple period and identify with the Upper Pool of Isaiah's times.

---

26. Simons, *Jerusalem in the Old Testament*, 193.

27. David Ussishkin, "The Water Systems of Jerusalem during Hezekiah's Reign," in M. Weippert and S. Timm, eds., *Meilenstein: Festgabe für Herbert Donner*, Ägypten und Altes Testament 30 (Wiesbaden: Harrassowitz Verlag, 1995), 289–307.

28. Marie-Joseph Pierre and Jourdain-Marie Rousée, "Sainte-Marie de la Probatique, état et orientation des recherches," *Proche-Orient Chrétien* 31 (1981): 23–42.

29. Dan Bahat, "The Fuller's Field and the 'Conduit of the Upper Pool,'" in A. Ben-Tor, J. C. Greenfield, and A. Malamat, eds., *Eretz-Israel* 20 [Yigael Yadin Volume] (Jerusalem: Israel Exploration Society, 1989), 253–55.

The fortifications that protected Jerusalem and its waterworks, as well as the water systems themselves, were developed by the Canaanites living there in the early second millennium B.C.E. They were somewhat modified but not dramatically changed until Hezekiah responded to the Assyrian threats and the population surge into Jerusalem after the fall of the northern kingdom of Israel. At that time Jerusalem grew tenfold, with a population estimated at 15,000 inhabitants. The sixty-hectare city sprawled over the Western Hill, known as the *mišneh*, or "Second Quarter" (2 Kings 22:14), behind massive fortifications subsumed under the rubric, the "Broad Wall" (Neh. 3:8; cf. Isa. 22:9–10).

The Chronicler was often questionable as a reliable historical source, dependent as he was on other biblical sources such as the Deuteronomistic Historian(s) and the prophets. He gained some credibility, though, when Nahman Avigad discovered the "Broad Wall" and dated its construction to the late eighth century B.C.E., which the Chronicler could only have known about from preexilic sources.[30] Also to be taken seriously is the Chronicler's account of Hezekiah's construction projects done during the time of Assyrian threats. The account preserved in 2 Chron. 32:2–6, 27–30 seems to be based on an independent, extrabiblical source and appears to be supported by archaeological evidence.[31]

> And when Hezekiah saw that Sennacherib had come and intended to fight against Jerusalem, he planned with his officers and his mighty men to stopper the waters of the springs (*hā'ăyānôt*), which were outside the city; and they helped him. A great many people gathered, and they stoppered all the springs (*hamma'yānôt*) and the brook (*hannaḥal*) which flowed through the land, saying "Why should the king of Assyria come and find much water (*mayim rabbîm*)?" He set to work resolutely and built up all the wall that was broken down, and *he raised it upon the towers* (*wayya'al 'al hammigdālôt*) and outside it he built another wall; and he strengthened the Millo in the City of David. (2 Chron. 32:2–5)[32]

This same Hezekiah stoppered the upper outlet (*môṣā'*) of the waters of the Gihon and directed them underground (*lĕmaṭṭâ*)[33] to the western side of the City of David. (2 Chron. 32:30)

Hezekiah's Tunnel

There is little doubt that the last reference is to the construction of Channel VIII, better known as the Siloam, or Hezekiah's Tunnel. This tunnel superceded Channel II, as it cut through parts of the latter as it winds tortuously underground for more than

---

30. Nahman Avigad, *Discovering Jerusalem: Recent Archaeological Excavations in the Upper City* (Nashville: Thomas Nelson, 1983).

31. Sara Japhet, *I & II Chronicles*, OTL (Louisville: Westminster/John Knox, 1993), 978–79.

32. For this translation, see William H. Shea, "Jerusalem under Siege," *BAR* 25 (1999): 43–44.

33. For this translation, see NAB.

533 meters. It conducts water from the Gihon Spring to another pool at the southwest corner of the City of David, identified with Birket Silwan and the Pool of Siloam in the New Testament. According to the Gospel of John, the Pool of Siloam[34] is where the blind man washed off the mudpacks that Jesus had put on the man's eyes, saying "'Go, wash in the Pool of Siloam' (which means "Sent"). He went and washed and returned able to see" (John 9:7).[35]

At the south end of the tunnel, not far from the Pool of Siloam, a monumental Hebrew inscription was incised on a specially prepared wall panel of the tunnel. The inscription, discovered in 1880, records how the "big dig" climaxed:

> And this is the way the tunnel was cut through: while the quarriers were still wielding their pickaxes, one gang towards the other, and while there were still three cubits (1.50 meters) to be (cut through), they heard the sound of each gang calling to the other, for there was a fissure (?) in the rock to the right and to the left. So on the day the breakthrough was made, the quarriers struck, one gang towards the other, pickaxe against pickaxe; and the water flowed from the outlet (*ms'*) (?) [of the Gihon Spring] to the pool (*hbrkh*), a distance of 1,200 cubits. A hundred cubits was the height of the rock above the head of the quarriers.[36]

Surprisingly, the monumental inscription does not bear the name of King Hezekiah in whose reign the tunnel (Channel VIII) was certainly constructed.[37] It does, however, use the same word for "outlet" (*môṣā'*), referring in this case to the opening in the spring-cave to Channel VIII, which is some 2.50 meters below the "upper outlet" of Channel II, which "this same Hezekiah stoppered . . . and directed them (waters of the Gihon) underground to the western side of the City of David" (2 Chron. 32:30).

For some reason, Hezekiah decided to replace the Siloam Channel with the presumably less vulnerable Siloam Tunnel, and the Old Pool/Lower Pool (Birket el-Ḥamra) with the Siloam Pool (Birket Silwan), designated *hbrkh* in the tunnel inscription. At the same time, Hezekiah was building the "outer wall" (2 Chron. 32:5) just forty meters downslope from the "inner wall" of the City of David, thus creating a double circumvallation similar to that at contemporary Lachish. Parts of the outer wall have been discovered by the recent excavations near the Gihon Spring.[38] If the "windows" of Channel II had ever been used to irrigate the Kidron

---

34. Siloam, from the Greek '*apestalménos*, means "sent," related to Hebrew *šālûaḥ*, "sent" (root *šlḥ*, "to send"), thus signifying a channel; cf. Akkadian *šiliḥtu*.

35. In neither the New Testament nor Josephus do the writers have any knowledge about the Gihon Spring being the source of waters in the collecting pools. See Simons, *Jerusalem in the Old Testament*.

36. For translations see W. F. Albright, *ANET*, 321; John C. L. Gibson, *Textbook for Syrian Semitic Inscriptions*, I: *Hebrew and Moabite Inscriptions* (Oxford: Clarendon Press, 1971), 22–23.

37. Philip R. Davies and John Rogerson ("Was the Siloam Tunnel Built by Hezekiah?" *BA* 59 [1996]: 138–49) have attempted to redate the Siloam Tunnel inscription to the Hasmonean period. See, however, two important responses: Ronald S. Hendel, "The Date of the Siloam Inscription: A Rejoinder to Rogerson and Davies," *BA* 59 (1996): 233–37; and Jo Ann Hackett, Frank M. Cross, P. Kyle McCarter, and Ada Yardeni, "Defusing Pseudo-Scholarship: The Siloam Inscription Ain't [sic] Hasmonean," *BAR* 23 (1997): 41–50, 68.

38. Reich and Shukron, "Light at the End of the Tunnel."

Ill. 104: Garden at Nineveh from a relief at Ashurbanipal's Palace. (Illustration: A. M. Appa, based on drawing of S. Dalley, *Garden History* 21 [1993], p. 10, fig. 2)

Valley, they were certainly blocked by this outer wall from delivering such a discharge. It is not clear whether the Lower Pool, which presumably went out of commission when Channel II was blocked at the outlet and breached at the south end by Channel VIII, lay inside or outside the double walls. Clearly the Pool of Siloam, receiving water from the tunnel, lay between the outer and inner walls and might even be identified with the "reservoir (*miqwâ*) between the two walls for the water of the Old Pool" (Isa. 22:11).

Somewhere in between the double walls near the south or southeastern part of the City of David was the Fountain (or Spring) Gate (*ša'ar hā'ayin*) through which King Zedekiah and his soldiers fled Jerusalem: "They fled, going out of the city at night by way of the king's garden through the gate between the two walls; and they went toward the Arabah" (Jer. 39:4; 2 Kings 25:4). Later Nehemiah repaired the Fountain Gate and rebuilt the "wall of the irrigation pool (*běrēkat haššelaḥ*) of the King's Garden" (Neh. 3:15; 2:14). This could be the Siloam Pool, which connected with the Siloam Tunnel; or it could be the Old Pool (Birket el-Ḥamra), which once watered the royal gardens and according to some authorities remained in use as an irrigation

Ill. 105: Garden of Sargon II at Dur-Sharrukin (Khorsabad). Two Phoenician style boats with horse-head prows float on the fish pond in the palace garden. In the background is an Assyrian-styled porticoed building with columns *in antis*, with voluted capitals. To the left are two Assyrians wielding lion-headed scepters. Compare silver scepter from Tel Dan (Area T). (Drawing adapted by A. M. Appa after P. E. Botta and E. Flandin, *Monument de Ninive II* [Paris, 1849], pl. 114)

pool in the seventh century as well, receiving overflow from the pool to the west via Channels IV and VIII (which were recut by Hezekiah to reverse their flow from west to east, that is, from Birket Silwan to Birket el-Ḥamra).[39]

The Chronicler (2 Chron. 32:2), as well as the Deuteronomistic Historian (2 Kings 20:20) and Isaiah (22:11), acknowledges that all of these constructions in Jerusalem were related to the "deeds" of Hezekiah and the military threat from the Assyrians: "The rest of the deeds of Hezekiah, all his power, how he made the pool and the conduit and brought water into the city, are they not written in the Book of the Annals of the Kings of Judah?" (2 Kings 20:20).

There was probably more than one channel and irrigation pool conducting water from the Gihon Spring into the gardens and parks of the Kidron Valley before Hezekiah blocked "all the springs (*hamma'yānôt*) and the brook (*naḥal*) that flowed through the land" (2 Chron. 32:4). Since the only spring supplying the irrigation is the well-fortified Gihon—which was not outside the city but well protected, not only by the earlier enceinte of towers, but also by Hezekiah's outer wall connecting the gate towers of the Gihon—it seems unlikely that the stoppered *ma'yānôt*[40] outside the city walls were true springs. Rather, they were channels and ditches that conducted spring water into the parks and gardens of the Kidron Valley. For example, by stoppering the lowest outlet (*môṣā'*) in the spring-cave, which belongs to Chan-

39. This reuse of the Old Pool after the reign of Hezekiah, but without flow from Channel II, is discussed in Simons, *Jerusalem in the Old Testament*, and in Ussishkin, "The Water Systems of Jerusalem during Hezekiah's Reign."

40. In Proverbs 5:16 *ma'yānôt* parallel *palgê mayim* ("water channels"). See, also, the *ma'yān* that issues from the Temple (Joel 4:18).

nel II, its discharge into the Kidron Valley would be stopped and the spring water would rise to the next higher outlet, that of Hezekiah's Tunnel.

When Hezekiah stoppered the outlets of the Gihon and the irrigation channels, he also caused the brook "that flowed through the land" to dry up, because the source of its flow was the miraculous waters of the Gihon.[41] This is the same *naḥal* that Ezekiel rhapsodized about, as it flowed from the Temple, through the Kidron Valley (which becomes the Wadi en-Nar), into the Dead Sea. By damming up the cosmic waters and preventing the Assyrian army from slaking their thirst on the *mayim rabbîm* (2 Chron. 32:4), Hezekiah and the Jerusalemites were being pragmatic in the face of the military onslaught. From Isaiah's perspective, they were being perfidious, afraid to rely on the power of Yahweh and his "waters that flow gently."

WARFARE, ARMIES, AND WEAPONS

The fact that *milḥāmā*, "warfare," appears over three hundred times in the Bible attests that warfare was a prominent feature of Israel's history. When the North (Israel) and the South (Judah) were not fighting a common enemy, they were fighting each other. Several factors account for biblical Israel's frequent military encounters with neighboring peoples, among them Israel's strategic location at the crossroads of the ancient world, with Mesopotamia to the northeast and Egypt to the southwest. Israelite territory had a special appeal to imperial powers, since the primary trade routes between Egypt and Mesopotamia, connecting with the Mediterranean seaports, passed through Israel. For this reason, Assyria invested Israel and turned it into a province, but let Judah remain. Judah was not very important to Assyria until about 700 B.C.E., and even then was not worth turning into a province.

Like every other aspect of life in the ancient world, warfare was permeated by religion. Leading their armies into battle, the national deities were duly credited with the victory. Military images used in referring to Yahweh, such as "man of war" (Ex. 15:3) and "lord of hosts," are common in the Bible. Two basalt stelae bearing inscriptions from the ninth century commemorate the victories of neighboring peoples over the kingdoms of Israel and Judah.[42] The Mesha Stela from Dhiban (biblical Dibon)

---

41. For the relation of *ma'yān* to *naḥal*, see 1 Kings 18:5; Ps. 74:15; 104:10: "You [Yahweh] channel (*šlḥ*) springs [or "spring water"] into brooks (*naḥal*)."

42. The stelae bear notable resemblances to each other in terms of script, language, date, and size. In addition, both refer to the "King of Israel," and remarkably, according to André Lemaire and Émile Puech, both contain a specific reference to the "House of David." André Lemaire, "'House of David' Restored in Moabite Inscription," *BAR* 20 (1994): 30–37. Also, Émile Puech, "La stèle araméenne de Dan: Bar Hadad II et la coalition des Omrides et de la maison de David," *RB* 101 (1994): 215–41, esp. 227.

celebrates the triumph of Mesha, king of Moab, over Yahweh and his people, a victory attributed to the Moabite god Chemosh (Ill. 53). The Tel Dan Stela celebrates the triumph of Hazael, king of Damascus, over Yahweh and Israel's king Joram and Judah's king Ahaziah, a feat credited to the Aramean god Hadad[43] (Ill. 171).

Both these stelae and events recorded in the Bible concerning the prophet Elisha (who seems to be consorting with the Aramean enemy) and the Aramean king Hazael pertain to the period of about 840 B.C.E., when various kingdoms were revolting against Israel and recovering some of their lost territory. This is evident from the Mesha Stela and from the incursions Hazael made in conquering parts of northern Israel. The decline in Israel's fortunes coincides with the slayings of Ahab and Jezebel and the usurpation of the throne by Jehu.

Weapons of War

It is difficult to connect certain Hebrew terms, thought to refer to weapons, with what is actually found or can be seen in iconography. To compound the confusion for the English reader, different translations often render the same Hebrew term differently.

In warfare, the defense is ordinarily stronger than the offense. Armaments are classified essentially as offensive and defensive. On the basis of range, the offensive weapons are divided into short-, medium-, and long-range. The short-range weapons were used in hand-to-hand combat, the ordinary way of fighting in antiquity. Weapons held in the hand served for self-protection and for assault on an enemy; among these were clubs, maces, axes, spears, lances, daggers, and swords. A club is simply a piece of wood. Both maces and axes had short wooden handles. The mace, consisting of a stick with a heavy stone (sometimes metal) attached, was used to beat and smash. The axe, equipped with a stone, bronze, or iron blade, was employed for slashing and cutting.

The Bible has more than four hundred references to the sword (*hereb*), which comes in various sizes. It was worn in a sheath (*ta'ar*) and strapped to a belt about the waist. "Now Joab was wearing a soldier's garment and over it was a belt with a sword in its sheath fastened at his waist" (2 Sam. 20:8). The short sword was the dagger, usually under forty centimeters and used for stabbing. Hebrew makes no distinction between the straight sword and the sickle sword, so called because of its curved shape. The cutting edge on the outside (convex) of the curved portion of the blade was used for slashing. The sickle sword was known as *khopesh* (foreleg of an animal) in Egyptian, and perhaps *kîdôn* in Hebrew.[44] The Assyrian slingers and archers in their assault on Lachish carry straight swords. The two-edged sword is used for thrusting.

---

43. Because of the fragmentary nature of these inscriptions, their historical context can be only tentatively reconstructed. See P. Kyle McCarter, *Ancient Inscriptions* (Washington, D.C.: Biblical Archaeology Society, 1996).

44. Yigael Yadin, *The Art of Warfare in Biblical Lands* (New York: McGraw-Hill, 1963), 1: 204.

The biblical account of Ehud, the left-handed Benjaminite who slew Eglon, king of Moab, illustrates the use of the dagger (Judg. 3:12–30). The early swords were short and were designed for stabbing. Ehud's dagger was a short, two-edged sword. Since he was left-handed, he strapped the dagger onto his right thigh; a right-handed warrior wore it on the left side. Ehud's dagger went undetected by the king's guards,

Ill. 106: Iron spearpoint found in 604 B.C.E. destruction of Ashkelon. (Courtesy of the Leon Levy Expedition to Ashkelon; Photo: C. Andrews)

and by the king himself; to Eglon's surprise, Ehud drew his dagger and thrust it into the king.[45]

In the use of weapons, especially swords, iron was preferred to bronze. The sword blade required hard metal; the advantage of iron is the hardness and strength of the blade. Wrought iron (shaped by beating with a hammer) was not hard enough, so carburized iron (heating the object in contact with carbon, thereby transforming the surface into steel) was the preferred technique. Quenching (cooling hot metal by thrusting it into water or other liquid) gave the iron sword an optimal edge.

Two Hebrew words—*ḥănît* and *rōmaḥ*—refer to medium-range weapons, that is, spears, javelins, and lances; however, the words are difficult to translate precisely. Spears and lances are thrust at the enemy; javelins are hurled at medium range. The spear, a stabbing weapon, consisted of a wooden shaft with a sharp blade attached to

Ill. 107: Bronze spearpoint from Ashkelon, dated to Iron II. (Courtesy of the Leon Levy Expedition to Ashkelon; Photo: I. Sztulman)

45. Ibid., 1: 60–62, 78–80.

Ill. 108: Lachish Relief from Nineveh: Assyrian archers targeting Judahites defending the city wall. (Courtesy of the Expedition to Lachish, D. Ussishkin, Director; Photo: A. Hay)

the end. Bigger and heavier than a javelin, the spear was the main weapon of the infantry and of the chariotry. On the Lachish Reliefs, the spearmen, outfitted in helmets with earflaps, hold a round shield of wicker wood in the left hand. A javelin was lethal enough to penetrate armor (Ill. 74).

Medium-range weapons, used in both hunting and combat, are by definition discharged. A stone is the most common example; the Lachish Reliefs depict Judahite soldiers pelting the attacking Assyrians with stones. Another example is the wooden

Ill. 109: Iron arrowheads found at Lachish. Also, a few were made of bronze; note that one is made of bone. (Courtesy of the Expedition to Lachish, D. Ussishkin, Director)

missile or throwing stick, comparable to the boomerang. An Egyptian relief from the tomb of a nobleman Knumhotep (ca. 1900 B.C.E.) at Beni-Hasan portrays two men with throw sticks, as well as bows and spears.

Among long-range weapons are the bow (qešet) and arrow (ḥēṣ), as well as the sling (qelaʿ) and slingstone (ʾeben). Bows and arrows are ineffective in close quarters. The defenders at Lachish fought with bows and arrows and with slings and slingstones. They also threw down stones and firebrands; for protection the stone throwers wear a scarf wound about the head, with the free end serving as a covering for the ears. Used for both hunting and fighting, the bow is one of the most ancient long-range weapons, dating from at least 3000 B.C.E. The bow came into common use with the introduction of the chariot, about 1800 B.C.E. in the Levant.

Bows come in various shapes: the simple bow with a single convex arc, the double-convex bow, and the composite bow with its recurved shape. The composite bow, chariot, fortifications with glacis and moats, and battering ram, each in its own time, brought about a radical change in the conduct of warfare. Introduced about 2200 B.C.E., the composite bow was made of several strips of wood for resiliency, along with sections of animal horn, animal tendons and sinews, and glue. When strung, it extended from the head to the waist of the archer. This powerful bow had a range exceeding two hundred meters. For this reason, archers were the most formidable warriors in the infantry (Ill. 108). Composite bows with metal-tipped arrows were in use in the biblical period. At Lachish, both sides used composite bows.

According to the biblical account, Ahab's death at Ramoth-gilead was the result of an arrow that "struck the king of Israel between the scale armor and the breastplate" (1 Kings 22:34). Kothar-wa-Hasis confers a bow on Danel, who passes it on to his son Aqhat, and it leads to his death:

> Then he [Danel] raised his eyes and looked: a thousand fields, ten thousand acres at each step, he saw Kothar coming, he saw Hasis approaching; not only was he bringing a bow, he had also provided arrows. . . . After Kothar-wa-Hasis had arrived, he put the bow in Danel's hands, he set the arrows on his knees. . . .[46]

Arrows were tipped with points made of extremely hard material: flint, bone, bronze, or iron. Hundreds of arrowheads were recovered at Lachish; most were iron, only a few bronze (Ill. 109). The blades were leaf-shaped, averaging seven centimeters in length. The shafts were of wood or reed, with feathered tails to stabilize the arrow in flight. The bow was carried in the left hand. To free both hands for firing the bow, the archers slung a leather quiver ('ašpâ), holding twenty to thirty arrows, over the back or shoulder. In combat, archers were pro-

Ill. 110: Bronze arrowhead with tang; found in 604 B.C.E. destruction of Ashkelon. (Courtesy of the Leon Levy Expedition, Photo: C. Andrews)

---

46. Michael D. Coogan, *Stories from Ancient Canaan* (Philadelphia: Westminster Press), 35–36.

Ill. 111: Bronze trilobate arrowhead, so-called Scythian type, dated to Persian period, Ashkelon. (Courtesy of the Leon Levy Expedition to Ashkelon; Photo: C. Andrews)

tected by a full-length shield borne by a designated shield bearer.

The sling, a weapon of great antiquity, was used by both warriors and shepherds (and, without doubt, by all the youngsters). Almond-shaped sling stones and mud sling stones go back to the Neolithic era. A hollow pocket (thong) of cloth or leather large enough to hold a stone was attached to two cords. The stones found at Lachish were smooth and rounded, often of flint, measuring six or seven centimeters in diameter and weighing about 250 grams (Ill. 112). They were carried in a bag suspended from the shoulder. Placing a stone in the sling's pouch, the slinger held the ends of the cord, whirled the sling in the air and then released one cord, propelling the missile with amazing accuracy. The left-handed slingers of Benjamin were legendary: "Every one could sling a stone at a hair, and not miss" (Judg. 20:16).

In preparation for his encounter with Goliath the Philistine, David "took his (shepherd's) staff (maqlô) in his hand, and chose five smooth stones from the wadi, and put them in his shepherd's bag, in the pouch; his sling was in his hand, and he drew near to the Philistine" (1 Sam. 17:40). In striking contrast, Goliath was armed like a Mycenaean warrior—bronze helmet (kôbaʿ is non-Semitic), coat of mail (širyôn, non-Semitic), bronze greaves (miṣḥâ, non-Semitic), scimitar (kîdôn, curved sword with convex cutting edge), bronze javelin [spear] (ḥănît) with thong and ring for slinging (1 Sam. 17: 4–7).[47]

In the assault on Lachish in 701 B.C.E., the sling was used by both attackers and defenders. The slingers and archers comprised the light infantry, and at Lachish they provided the fire cover. The Lachish Reliefs depict more archers than slingers. Excavating the vulnerable gate area at Lachish, Ussishkin uncovered more arrowheads than slingstones. The reliefs show the slingers deployed farther from the wall than

---

47. Yadin, *The Art of Warfare in Biblical Lands*, 2: 265–66, 354–55; P. Kyle McCarter Jr., *I Samuel*, AB 8 (Garden City, N.Y.: Doubleday, 1980), 290–93; Stager, "Forging an Identity: The Emergence of Ancient Israel," in M. D. Coogan, ed., *The Oxford History of the Biblical World* (New York: Oxford University Press, 1988), 169.

the archers since it is impossible to sling a stone at a high angle. The sling could attain speeds of 160–240 kilometers per hour, although it lacked the range of the bow and arrow.

The Judahites and the Assyrians are variously attired in the Lachish Reliefs; there is no rigid consistency. In some cases, the two sides are outfitted similarly and also use the same kind of weapons. Some Assyrian spearmen wear helmets with earflaps, topped by a double crescent adorned with feathers. Some Assyrian archers wear conical helmets, while others have head scarves. Some Assyrian slingers are portrayed with long beards and have conical helmets outfitted with ear flaps. They are also protected with coats of mail, but are barefoot. They are holding an additional stone in the left hand for another volley. The archers and slingers at Lachish carry a

Ill. 112: Flint slingstones hurled at the enemy by means of slings in the 701 B.C.E. battle fought at Lachish. (Courtesy of the Expedition to Lachish, D. Ussishkin, Director)

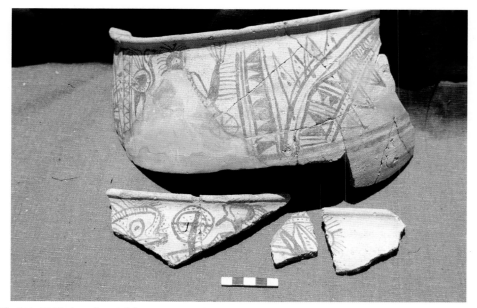

Ill. 113: Philistine pictorial krater. One side, warrior with spiked headdress holding circular shield and confronting a sea monster. On other side Philistine with spiked headdress riding in wheeled vehicle followed by a bird. Dated Iron I, Ashkelon. (Courtesy of the Leon Levy Expedition to Ashkelon; Photo: I. Sztulman)

Ill. 114: Armor scales from Lachish. (Courtesy of the Expedition to Lachish, D. Ussishkin, Director)

straight sword. The common Lachishite headdress is the scarf wound around the head, with the free end covering the ears. Some of the Judahite archers and slingers wear the conical helmet. In some cases the conical helmet is worn over the headscarf. The Israelite helmet (*qôbaʿ*, *kôbaʿ*— both words of foreign origin) was fashioned of metal or leather, modeled no doubt on the Assyrian helmet appearing on the Lachish Reliefs, which was conical in shape and fitted with earmuffs and a flap to protect the exposed neck.

The Chronicler relates that Uzziah provided the army with shields (*māginnîm*), helmets (*kôbāʿîm*), and coats of mail (*širyōnôt*) (2 Chron. 26:14). This protective gear constituted the principal defensive armament of Israel in the eighth century. The common word for "shield" is *māgēn*, designating the small, light, round-shaped buckler; the large, oblong shield is the *ṣinnâ*—the shield used by Goliath, who had his own shield bearer (*nōśēʾ haṣṣinnâ*) (1 Sam. 17:7). The small shield, worn on the forearm, covered half the body and was used in hand-to-hand combat. The round shield is associated with the Sea Peoples; in wall reliefs, Phoenician cities and ships have round shields on the battlements. The Phoenician shields from the Idaean Cave in Crete, associated with the cult of Zeus, are round. The larger, rectangular shield was used to protect the archers as they approached the wall of a besieged city. The shield consisted of a wicker, wooden, or (rarely) metal frame overstretched with leather, and a handle on the inside. The leather had to be oiled to keep it supple before battle. In his lament over Saul and Jonathan, David notes: "For there [Mount Gilboa] the shield (*māgēn*) of the mighty was defiled, the shield (*māgēn*) of Saul, anointed with oil no more" (2 Sam. 1:21). Since these materials are perishable, they lasted only a limited time. In battle array, the shield-bearing spearmen were the first line of defense while the archers were in the rear.

The Assyrian soldiers were outfitted with coats of mail, short tunics, leggings, and high boots. The coat of mail (*širyôn*), of knee or ankle length, was used to protect archers and charioteers, who could not carry shields. The coat consisted of a leather jacket covered with small scales (first, of bronze; later, of iron) secured by thongs. Armor scales are found at several sites long before the Assyrians.

Fortifications

The basic fortification consisted of an encircling wall with towers. An enclosed town was known as *'îr* or *'îr mibṣār*, "fortified town," in contrast to an open village, designated by several Hebrew words (*ḥāṣēr, kāpār, pĕrāzôt*). *'îr* and *mibṣār* are virtually synonymous. *migdāl*, "tower" or "castle," denotes a citadel, an interior stronghold built on the highest part of the city. In Iron Age I there were no true fortification systems in Israel. Contiguous houses were located along the perimeter of the village to enclose the settlement ('Izbet Ṣarṭah, Str II; Ai; Tel Sheva, Str VII; also Khirbet Raddana, Site R). In Iron Age II there were several kinds of fortification systems. Various fortifications were erected along the borders and the trade routes, and several fortresses were built in the Negev. Arad was a frontier fortress in the Negev serving as an administrative and a military outpost and controlling the main road to Edom.

Walls

The primary defensive feature was the wall (*ḥômâ*) surrounding a city on all sides. A walled city could be surmounted in a variety of ways: by scaling the walls, by breaching them with a battering ram, by tunneling below or through them. Various kinds of walls were erected in different periods consisting of stone foundations with mud brick superstructures. In the second millennium B.C.E. the primary fortification walls were built into or on top of an earthen rampart (glacis) with a revetment wall at the foot of the rampart and a dry moat on the outside of the fortification. In the Iron Age, the revetment or outer wall was known as *ḥēl*. The space between the *ḥēl* and the *ḥômâ* could be used for defensive purposes. In a song celebrating Yahweh's defense of Jerusalem, Isaiah declares: "We have a strong city; he sets up inner walls (*ḥômôt*) and outer walls (*ḥēl*) to protect us" (Isa. 26:1). Archaeologists have now identified the inner and outer walls to which Isaiah was referring.[48] Jerusalem, like Lachish, has a double wall on the east side, and on the west is a new wall surrounding the Second Quarter (Mishneh): "Yahweh marked for destruction the inner wall (*ḥômâ*) of daughter Zion: he stretched out the measuring line; his hand brought ruin, yet he did not relent—he brought grief on outer wall (*ḥēl*) and inner wall (*ḥômâ*) till both succumbed" (Lam. 2:8).

At Lachish an outer wall, three meters wide, surrounding the city halfway down the slope, protected the main wall and kept attackers from reaching it. Ussishkin identifies this outer wall as a strong revetment, commenting that it does not appear to be free-standing. Because the wall served as a revetment does not mean that it could not have been constructed high above what it was revetting. The inner wall, six meters

---

48. Hershel Shanks, "Everything You Ever Knew About Jerusalem Is Wrong (Well, Almost)," *BAR* 25 (1999): 20–29. Ronny Reich and Eli Shukron, "Light at the End of the Tunnel," *BAR* 25 (1999): 22–33, 72.

wide, was built of mud brick with a stone foundation. Between the outer and inner walls was a glacis supporting the base of the city wall.

Casemate city walls, first appearing in ancient Israel in the tenth century, continued in use until the end of the eighth century. Casemates walls in Judah lasted until the Babylonian conquest in 586 B.C.E. A casemate consisted of two parallel walls connected by short, transverse walls forming a series of rectangular compartments (casemates). These cubicles were sometimes filled with rubble to strengthen the wall; at other times they served as storage areas or were incorporated into the rear section of a residence. Casemates had an economic appeal because they required less building material and fewer laborers. In the Solomonic era, the casemate wall was integrated into the defense system, which included an inner gate with six bays or chambers formed by three piers on each side of the passageway. An outer gate with two piers was constructed on the slope of the mound.

By the ninth century, the casemates were no longer the chief fortifications in Israel and Judah because, according to Yadin, they were not adequate to withstand the devastating battering rams of the Assyrians. Consequently, they were replaced by more solid walls, costlier than casemates, and in the eighth and seventh centuries mainly solid city walls were constructed. The solid walls of offset-inset type (salients and recesses) are evident at Dan, Hazor, Megiddo, Gezer, and Tel Sheva. The face of an offset-inset wall was constructed with projecting and receding sections. The angled projections provided a better view and more control of the wall line against battering rams, scaling ladders, and sapping. Depictions on the palace walls at Nineveh of the siege of Lachish illustrate this kind of fortification system.

At Tel Sheva, a secondary administrative center in the northern Negev, the fortification systems were of two types—a solid city wall and a casemate wall. According to excavators Yohanan Aharoni and Ze'ev Herzog,[49] in Iron II four strata (Str V–II), associated with a small fortified city on the summit of the mound, are distinguished. Str V, destroyed by Shishak in 925, had a solid city wall with a four-chambered gate, and this fortification system was reused in Str IV. In Str III a casemate wall and another four-chambered gate were built on the ruins of an earlier wall. The fortifications of Str III were reused in Str II, which was destroyed by Sennacherib in 701 B.C.E.

The city wall was protected and reinforced by other installations, including earthen ramparts, moat, and towers. The glacis[50] is a massive, artificial, sloping rampart, constructed of dirt layers or lime plaster and strengthened with a core, sometimes of stone; it sloped downward from a wall on the outside. In MB II most Canaanite cities were surrounded by earthen ramparts. Yadin suggested that the ramparts or glacis were utilized to protect the base of city walls from the battering rams. However, battering rams are usually directed against gates, corners, and other vulnerable fortifications on the crest of the earthen rampart. Stager has proposed that

49. Ze'ev Herzog, "Tel Beersheba," *NEAEHL*, 1: 170–71.
50. It is important to point out that the glacis is not just MB II but was often used in the Iron Age.

earthen ramparts were intended to protect against undermining the city walls, either to cause the walls to collapse or to gain entrance and stage a surprise attack.[51]

To position the battering ram (*kar*) close to the fortification wall of a city under attack, the assailants constructed a siege ramp or mound (*sōlĕlâ*), mentioned frequently in the Bible. The glacis could be incorporated within the siege ramp. Jeremiah uttered a prophecy of judgment about the Babylonian assault on Jerusalem: "For thus says Yahweh of hosts: Cut down her trees; cast up a siege ramp (*sōlĕlâ*) against Jerusalem. This is the city that must be punished" (Jer. 6:6; also 32:24; 33:4; 52:4).

At Lachish, archaeologists uncovered two earthen ramps with logs incorporated into the upper layers of the ramps for supporting the siege machines. The Assyrian siege ramp was constructed mainly of stones covered with layers of beaten earth and consolidated with mortar. Sennacherib's army built a sloping, fan-shaped siege ramp on the vulnerable southwest corner of Lachish, near the gate. It is estimated that the Assyrian siege ramp, composed of 25,000 tons of material, required 2,400 porters working twenty-three days to construct.[52] Since captives from Philistia and Judah very likely did the actual construction, the defenders of Lachish might have been deterred from attacking them, lest they kill their own compatriots. The Lachishites responded by building a "counter-ramp" inside the inner wall directly opposite the Assyrian ramp. It consisted of debris from earlier occupational levels of the mound (including the destruction of houses of Levels IV and III) that was deposited against the inner face of the wall to function as a platform. It also served to strengthen the wall about to be battered.

The fosse is a dry moat or ditch (*ḥāpār*), dug down into bedrock outside the city wall and earthen rampart. In fact, much of the material excavated from the moat was used as fill for the adjacent ramparts. The dry moat allowed scouting parties from the besieged city to detect the tunnels of miners and sappers before they undermined the city's fortifications. The dry moat was sometimes used in combination with the glacis to augment the height of the slope and to discourage tunneling, mining, and sapping by keeping the attackers at a greater distance from the city wall. Bees and smoke were used to entrap sappers found in the sappers' tunnel.[53]

---

51. Lawrence E. Stager, *Ashkelon Discovered* (Washington, D.C.: Biblical Archaeology Society, 1991), 8.

52. Israel Eph'al, "The Assyrian Siege Ramp at Lachish: Military and Lexical Aspects," *TA* 11 (1984), 63; Israel Eph'al, *Siege Warfare and Its Ancient Near Eastern Manifestations* (in Hebrew) (Jerusalem: Magnes Press, 1996).

53. "Those who are constructing mines are to be prevented in the following manner. If you think a mine is being made you should dig the moat outside the wall as deep as possible so that the mine may open into the moat and those who are digging it may be exposed to view. And if you have a chance, a wall should also be built in the moat, of the very hardest and largest stones available. But if you have no chance to build a stone wall you should bring up logs and rubbish . . . , and if the mines at any point open into the moat, there you should dump the wood and set fire to the rubbish and cover the rest over in order that the smoke may penetrate the opening and injure those in the mine. It is even possible that many of these may be killed by the smoke. And in some instances, by releasing wasps and bees into the opening, men have worked mischief with those in the mine. One must, in a word, at whatever point the enemy are digging, construct a countermine beneath and against them, and by setting fire to [rubbish in the countermine thus destroy the] fighting force in the mine itself" [*Aeneas the Tactician*, xxxvii. 3–9].

Gates

The configuration of the gate had to accommodate opposing purposes: civic and military. In the first case, it had to be wide and accessible; in the latter, narrow and inaccessible. The city gate (ša'ar) and the adjacent square were the place of public assembly, as well as the business center where commercial and legal transactions were conducted. The prophets allude to the administration of justice at the gates, as in Amos 5:15: "Hate evil and love good, and establish justice in the gate."[54] At Dan in the Iron Age, there was a public square with a flagstone pavement located in front of the gate. The account in 2 Chron. 32:6 says that Hezekiah gathered his commanders "in the plaza (rĕḥôb) at the gate of the city" where he exhorted them to trust in Yahweh.

Stone benches lined three sides of each of the six bays in the gate in Gezer. At Dan, a bench constructed of dressed stones was located to the right of the entrance. The city elders convened in the city gate. The psalmist complained: "I am the subject of gossip for those who sit in the gate" (Ps. 69:13 [E.T. 69:12]). The question of acquiring both the land and Ruth as a wife is decided at the gate: "No sooner had Boaz gone up to the gate and sat down there than the next-of-kin (gō'ēl), of whom Boaz had spoken, came passing by. So Boaz said, 'Come over, friend, sit down here'" (Ruth 4:1).

Outside the northern gate tower at Dan in the Iron Age was an installation of limestone ashlars. At each of its corners was a pillar on a stone base. The excavator Avraham Biran suggests these pillars supported an installation for the king's throne, as in the case when David was sitting in the gate mourning for Absalom: "Then the king [David] got up and took his seat in the gate. The troops were all told, 'See, the king is sitting in the gate'; and all the troops came before the king" (2 Sam. 19:9 [E.T. 19:8]).

As a fortified passageway, the gate was the weakest part of the defense system, and consequently it needed to be well secured. At Lachish, where the gate was close to the exposed southwest corner of the mound, the only side unprotected by deep valleys, it was the first place to be assaulted. The double doors of the gates were of wood plated with metal to protect against burning by attackers. To secure the gate, there were inner gates, piers (pilasters), and flanking towers. As a result, the gate was a veritable fortress. Also, there were posterns or small gates that could be easily defended. Posterns also designate tunnels that provide escape from a besieged city.

The excavated cities with six-chambered gates are Megiddo, Hazor, Gezer, Ashdod, Lachish, and Tel 'Ira. For greater security, entry through the outer to the inner gate was gained via a dogleg right turn. In this way besiegers carrying the shield in the left hand were exposed to assaults from the defenders of the city. The Solomonic gates at Hazor, Gezer, and Megiddo were constructed on a similar plan, with one major difference. At Hazor and Gezer (Ill. 115), the gates were joined to a casemate wall. At Megiddo, however, the wall adjoining them was offset-inset in design, connecting but

---

54. Ze'ev Herzog, "Settlement and Fortification Planning in the Iron Age," in A. Kempinski and R. Reich, eds., *The Architecture of Ancient Israel* (Jerusalem: Israel Exploration Society, 1992), 231–74.

Ill. 115: Six-chambered city gate at Gezer, looking from inside city to S. Drain runs through center of gate (drain was once covered). Benches line the six chambers. This kind of Solomonic gate is alluded to in 1 Kings 9:15. (Courtesy of W. G. Dever, Hebrew Union College—The Institute of Archaeology, Jeruslaem)

not bonding with the six-chambered gate. It is generally maintained that the Solomonic gate (six-chambered) and the offset-inset wall at Megiddo are coterminous, but some (e.g., Yadin, Dever, Stager) would argue that the gate preceded the offset-inset wall. The six-chambered gateway with offset-inset wall belongs to Str VA/IVB (Solomonic period). The four-chambered gate with offset-inset wall belongs to Str IVA

Ill. 116: Upper Register – Bronze Bands, Gates of Balawat. Campaign in Syria in the Province of Hamath, 849 B.C.E. Aramean king lying on a couch surrenders to Assyrian army. Fortifications of city have crenellated towers and arched gateways. (Courtesy of the Trustees of the British Museum)

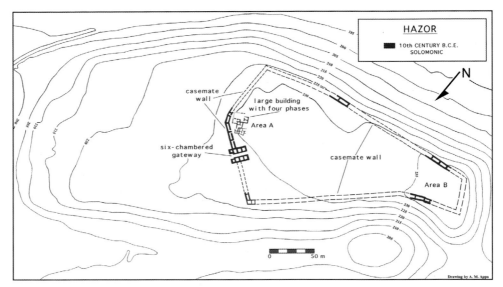

Ill. 117: Plan of Hazor at the time of Solomon (tenth century B.C.E.) with six-chambered gate, casemate wall, and a public building. (Courtesy of A. Ben-Tor; Drawing: A. M. Appa)

(Omride period). The two-chambered gateway with offset-inset wall belongs to Str III (Assyrian period).[55]

In the Iron Age, the gates were generally composed of six or four chambers, although some had only two chambers. Those with six chambers—three rows on each side of the gateway, separated from one another by an entryway probably once closed by wooden doors with bronze bands and fittings—are found at Megiddo, Hazor, and Gezer (1 Kings 9:15). They call to mind the bronze gates at Imgur-Enlil (modern Balawat), an ancient Assyrian town near Nimrud in modern Iraq. These famous palace gates from the time of Shalmaneser III were decorated with bronze strips depicting narrative scenes. The Gezer gate is the best preserved of the Solomonic gates; the gate of Megiddo, the most magnificent. The Lachish III gateway, composed of acacia doors with bronze fittings, was destroyed in 701 B.C.E. by an intense fire that also ravaged both public and domestic buildings located between the gateway and the city.

Gates had to be wide enough to accommodate chariots. This required double doors, which were barred by a heavy horizontal beam laid across the inside and held in place by slots in the doorposts. Wooden posts braced the doors, and the doors pivoted in stone sockets or in metal sockets placed inside stone sockets.

---

55. For a convenient, clear summary, see Hershel Shanks, "Where Is the Tenth Century?" *BAR* 24 (1998): 56–61. David Ussishkin and Israel Finkelstein argue that Str VA-IVB is ninth century, not tenth century (Solomonic); see "Archaeological and Historical Conclusions," in Israel Finkelstein, David Ussishkin, and Baruch Halpern, eds., *Megiddo III: The 1992–1996 Seasons* (Tel Aviv: Institute of Archaeology, Tel Aviv University, 2000), 599.

Siege Engines and Battering Rams

Siege machines with battering rams were already present in third-millennium Ebla. There are references to battering rams and siege towers in the Mari archive.[56] Siege warfare (*māṣôr*) is the term for the sustained attack on walled cities, a military operation perfected by the Assyrians, with two principal methods. Circumvallation was the complete enclosure of a fortress so as to cut off supplies. Breaching involved three phases: the siege ramp, the siege engines against the walls, battering and breaking the wall. The Assyrian annals record the attack of foot soldiers by breaches, tunneling, sapper operations, assault ladders, and wall scaling.

In siege warfare the advantage was with the defenders of a fortress. The Bible does not attribute the use of the siege engine and battering ram to Israel, but only to Israel's enemies. Siege engines have been found on excavations in Egypt and in Mesopotamia. They were already in use during the reign of Ashurnasirpal II of Assyria. The earliest representation of the battering ram, dating from 1900 B.C.E., is in Egyptian tomb reliefs of the Middle Kingdom. Siege towers from the same era are also depicted in one of the battles with the Canaanites.

While the construction of siege engines evolved in Iron

Ill. 118: A palmette capital made of limestone from the four-chambered gate of the fortress known today as Khirbet el-Mudaybiʻ. The capital is 1.00 m high and 0.50 m thick. Charred cypress beams from the gateway lined with these palmette capitals yielded radio-carbon dates around 800 B.C.E. (Courtesy of G. L. Mattingly of the Kerak Resources Project; Photo: Reuben J. Bullard, Jr.)

Ill. 119: Same as illustration 118 with capital sitting on its gate pier. (Courtesy of G. L. Mattingly, Kerak Resources Project; Photo: Reuben J. Bullard, Jr.)

---

56. Amihai Mazar, "The Fortification of Cities in the Ancient Near East," *CANE*, 3: 1527; Ephʻal, *Siege Warfare and Its Ancient Near Eastern Manifestations*.

Ill. 120: Bronze Bands, Gates of Balawat. Campaign in Syria, 854 B.C.E. (Upper Register) assault on city of Parga in Hamath; (Lower Register) male and female Syrian captives from Qarqar. The city of Parga is being attacked by archers, while a huge hog's-head battering ram makes a breach in city gate. (Courtesy of the Trustees of the British Museum)

Ill. 121: Drawing of a relief which depicts an Assyrian battering ram attacking stronghold of Gazru (Gezer?). Relief from Nimrud, Tiglath-pileser III. Residents of town who stand on turrets and walls are surrendering. (Courtesy of the Trustees of the British Museum)

Age II, the basic design consisted of a battering ram (*kar*) built on a frame and mounted on four or six wooden wheels. The covering of the frame was of wood and leather, both inflammable materials. The spearlike ram, consisting of a long wooden beam reinforced with a sharp metal blade, was equipped to bash against an unprotected mud brick wall. The beam was suspended from the siege engine by thick ropes that let it swing like a pendulum to gain momentum.

The siege engine had a high tower from which the crew could attack the enemy and at the same time protect the siege engine. Some of the crew, working within the siege engine, sprayed water on the facade and the ram to extinguish firebrands thrown down by the defenders. The Lachish Reliefs depict five siege machines deployed on the siege ramp. For protection, the siege machines were brought down from the ramp overnight and returned to the ramp each morning.

Armies

In the time of the Judges, before the Israelites organized a standing army, a people's militia was mustered to fend off the enemy. The Canaanites, Philistines, and Assyrians had standing armies. Tiglath-pileser III established the Neo-Assyrian regular army in the late eighth century. For the most part, the army comprised the infantry, including foreigners and mercenaries. Foreigners (Arameans) conquered by the Assyrians were pressed into military service. In the eighth century the Assyrian military was at the height of its power, capable of campaigning as far as five hundred kilometers from

Ill. 122: Assyrian siege ramp, approximately 70–75 m wide, 50–60 m long, from Lachish. Located in the southwest corner of the mound. (Courtesy of the Expedition to Lachish, D. Ussishkin, Director)

its base and of traveling about twenty-five kilometers per day. Besides the infantry, an Assyrian campaign included chariotry and cavalry, not to mention equipment and supplies. During a military expedition the Assyrian army carried some of its own provisions, mainly barley; otherwise, they lived off the land, commandeering supplies from the local populations en route. The biblical story about David seems to suggest that Israelite warriors were expected to provide some of their own food, in addition to their own weapons. When the men of Israel were engaged in battle with the Philistines, Jesse said to his son David: "Take for your brothers an ephah of this parched grain and these ten loaves, and carry them quickly to the camp to your brothers" (1 Sam. 17:17).

Israel's first organized army, although mainly drawn from the militia, was formed in the time of Saul: "Saul chose three thousand out of Israel; two thousand were with Saul in Michmash and the hill country of Bethel, and a thousand were with Jonathan in Gibeah of Benjamin" (1 Sam. 13:2). In David's reign, the standing army, foreign mercenaries as well as Israelites, was added to the militia, but there were still no chariots. David retained a standing bodyguard of six hundred men (1 Sam. 23:13). "All his [David's] officials passed by him; and all the Cherethites, and all the Pelethites, and all the six hundred Gittites who had followed him from Gath, passed on before the king" (2 Sam. 15:18). The Cherethites and Pelethites were mercenaries whose origin is obscure, but they are thought to be foreigners, perhaps Sea Peoples. David's loyal mercenaries captured Jebusite Jerusalem (2 Sam. 5:6–10). In the Chronicler's version, Joab, commander of David's army during most of his reign, led the attack on Jerusalem (1 Chron. 11:6). Joab was skilled in the techniques of siege warfare. When Sheba, a Benjaminite, led a revolt against David, "Joab's forces came and besieged him in Abel Beth-Maacah; they threw up a siege ramp (sōlĕlâ) against the city, and it stood against the outer wall (ḥēl)" (2 Sam. 20:15).

In addition to whatever standing army the Israelite king could afford, he also had the militia, formed on the basis of a census of the population. Primary purposes for a census have always been military conscription, levying taxes, and the corvée (forced labor). For these reasons, it is not uncommon for people, to our own day, to resist a census. When the kingdom was at its widest extent, David ordered a census to determine the militia, supplementing the standing army (2 Sam. 24:1–9). Solomon made a census to conscript a corvée of aliens for building the Temple (1 Kings 5:27; 9:21). According to Numbers 1, before the Israelites departed Sinai, a census (totaling 603,550) was taken of males twenty years and older for military service. According to Numbers 26, after the wilderness wanderings, a census (totaling 601,730) was taken in the plains of Moab for the apportionment of the land. In both instances, the numbers are unrealistically high. Among various scholarly proposals for interpreting these numbers, George Mendenhall suggested that 'elep is not always the strictly literal "thousand," but may sometimes refer to a subdivision within a tribe. Thus, 'ălāpîm (pl) may designate the number of units into which each tribe is subdivided.[57] Probably, 'elep fits into the military structure at a level comparable to that of the social unit of the mišpāḥâ within the tribal structure. The ideal size of the clan (mišpāḥâ) subdivision was about a thousand persons. From this social unit, eligible males were selected for military service, a number that would be appreciably smaller than the clan pool from which they were drafted. This interpretation would explain why a "thousand" ('elep unit = mišpāḥâ unit) is used, even though, as Mendenhall suggested, it refers to a much smaller unit than one thousand.

Roland de Vaux[58] and others have noted that the units of the Israelite militia were related to those of society. The largest of these military units was a "thousand" ('elep), which is linked to the clan (mišpāḥâ). Gideon the Abiezerite claims that his "thousand" is the weakest in Manasseh and that he is the least in his ancestral household (bêt 'āb) (Judg. 6:15). Each 'elep had a commander at its head. King Saul appointed David to the rank of śar 'ālep (1 Sam. 18:13). A contemporary bronze arrowhead was inscribed with the Phoenician equivalent rb 'lp, "commander of a thousand."[59]

The Chronicler describes military conscription under King Amaziah of Judah (2 Chron. 25:5). According to Pentateuchal regulations, everyone from twenty years of age and upward was expected to go to war (Num. 1:3). Besides priests and Levites, the following were exempted: anyone who built a new house, planted a vineyard, became engaged, was newly married, or was afraid (Deut. 20:1–9; 24:5). When soldiers were no longer engaged in warfare, they returned home to resume their usual occupations.

One of the king's duties was to lead the army. War was commonly waged in early spring, when the rains had ceased and the terrain was dry; otherwise the chariots would be mired in mud. Also, the spring season made it easier for the marching army to live off the land. "In the spring of the year, the time when kings go out to battle, David sent Joab with his officers and all Israel with him" (2 Sam. 11:1). Wars of conquest are associated especially with David. There were two kinds of warfare: open warfare and siege warfare. The infantry, backbone of Israel's military force throughout its history, was comprised of three broad units in open warfare, as indicated above: the spearmen, carrying the shield in one hand, formed a solid line and engaged in hand-to-hand fighting; the archers supported them from the rear; and the slingers operated in pairs behind the archers. The army was divided into units: 1,000 ('elep), 100 (mē'â), 50 (ḥămiššîm), and 10 ('ăśārâ). There is relatively little information about the organization of the Israelite army in the preexilic period.

57. George E. Mendenhall, "The Census Lists of Numbers 1 and 26," JBL 77 (1958): 66: "'Elef originally referred to a subsection of a tribe; the term was then carried over to designate the contingent of troops under its own leader which the subsection contributed to the army of the Federation."

58. Roland de Vaux, Ancient Israel: Its Life and Institutions (New York: McGraw-Hill, 1961), 216.

59. Frank Moore Cross, "Newly Discovered Inscribed Arrowheads of the 11th century B.C.E.," in A. Biran and J. Aviram, eds., Biblical Archaeology Today (Jerusalem: Israel Exploration Society, 1993), 533–542; photo of arrowhead in fig. 2, 535. Cf. 'el-Khaḍr arrowheads mentioned under "Writing."

The Arad Ostraca give a glimpse of military life in Judah during the final years of the kingdom. A frontier fortress located at Arad, an administrative and military outpost, guarded the road descending from the Judean hills to Edom. An archive of ostraca belonging to Eliashib, the Israelite commander, was found in a room of the fortress. The *Kittîyîm* (*ktym*, Hebrew name for Cypriots) are mentioned in ten of these Arad ostraca. Ostracon 1 reads: "To Eliashib—And (as) of now: Give the *Kittîyîm* 3 baths of wine [107.5 liters], and write the exact date. And from what is left of the old wheat, grind up one (*kor*) of wheat to make bread for them. Serve the wine in kraters" (*ANET*, 569). Albright thought that *Kittîyîm* refers to mercenaries from the Aegean, including the Cretans and the Carians, mentioned in the Bible. Yohanan Aharoni supposed that the *Kittîyîm* were Greek or Cypriot mercenaries serving in the army of Judah.[60] Na'aman suggests that the mercenaries were serving in the Egyptian army and were being provisioned by the king of Judah, as vassal to Egypt.[61]

The Lachish Letters (Ostraca) illuminate wartime activities in the vicinity of Lachish during the last days of Judah (586 B.C.E.). Most of these twenty-two ostraca are correspondence from Hoshaiah, a military officer stationed in a garrison between Lachish and Jerusalem, addressed to Yaosh, evidently the commanding officer of Lachish. Ostracon 4 is of special interest:

> May Yahweh bring my lord this very day good tidings. And now, in accordance with all that my lord hath written, so hath thy servant done. I have written on the door (*dlt*) in accordance with all that [my lord] hath directed me. And with regard to what my lord hath written about Beth-harapid [unknown outpost], there is nobody there. And as for Semakyahu, Shemayahu hath taken him and brought him up to the capital [Jerusalem], and thy servant . . . send thither. . . . And [my lord] will know that we are watching for the [fire] signals (*mś't*) of Lachish, according to all the signs which my lord hath given, for we cannot see Azekah.[62]

A corresponding reference appears in Jeremiah, who spoke to Zedekiah, "when the army of the king of Babylon was fighting against Jerusalem and against all the cities of Judah that were left, Lachish and Azekah; for these were the only fortified cities of Judah that remained" (Jer. 34:7). The fortress city of Azekah (Tell Zakariyeh), sixteen kilometers northeast of Lachish, is situated on a high hill, 365 meters above sea level.

Chariotry

The chariotry and the cavalry[63] formed the elite corps of the Assyrian army. The chief function of the chariot was as a movable firing platform for archers in open battle,

---

60. Yohanan Aharoni, ed., *Arad Inscriptions* (Jerusalem: Israel Exploration Society, 1981), 12.
61. Nadav Na'aman, "The Kingdom of Judah under Josiah," *TA* 18 (1991): 3–71.
62. D. Winton Thomas, ed., *Documents from Old Testament Times* (New York: Harper, 1958), 216.
63. Mary A. Littauer and J. H. Crouwel, *Wheeled Vehicles and Ridden Animals in the Ancient Near East* (Leiden: Brill, 1979).

Ill. 123: Lower Register – Bronze Bands, Gates of Balawat. Assyrian Campaign in Hamath, 849 B.C.E. Chariot and horsemen leaving the Assyrian camp. Royal pavilion to right with fleur-de-lis capitals. (Courtesy of the Trustees of the British Museum)

not as an offensive weapon or mode of transportation. For the most part, the chariot was confined to level terrain. It was composed of a body with a wooden frame, wheels, and a yoke attached to the forward end of a pole. Well-designed, two-wheeled chariots in the ancient Near East date from MB. The Egyptians, Assyrians, Arameans, and Philistines were adept at chariot warfare. In a famous chariot battle in the fifteenth century, Pharaoh Thutmose III defeated a large coalition of Canaanites and Syrians encamped at Megiddo under the leadership of the prince of Kadesh-on-the-Orontes.

Assyrian chariots evolved over time. By the ninth century, there was a three-horse chariot. Each chariot had a driver and an archer. The shield bearer was added later as protection for driver and archer. In the three-man chariot, all wore swords and conical helmets. Assyrian chariots of the ninth century had small, six-spoked wheels. Eight-spoked wheels on chariots were introduced by Ashurnasirpal II. Royal chariots had massive wheels with eight spokes. Sennacherib's battle chariot at Lachish had light, six-spoked wheels, whereas his ceremonial chariot was large, with eight-spoked wheels and a square driver's box. By the seventh century, chariots had eight-spoked wheels with studs for traction. These chariots were drawn by four horses, with four men in the chariot.

Archaeological evidence for the chariot is minimal: linchpins for chariot wheels were recently found at Ekron and at Ashkelon (see Ill. 46). At Ashkelon, an ivory yoke saddle finial for a chariot was found near the linchpin. The Philistines drive chariots in the Medinet Habu Reliefs and are referred to as charioteers in Egyptian texts. In LB there is evidence, too, in the form of knobs for chariots at Beth-Shean and elsewhere. These knobs were initially interpreted as pommels for knives or daggers, but Frances James recognized them as bosses and terminals of yoke saddles for chariots.[64]

---

64. Frances James, "Chariot Fittings from Late Bronze Age," in Roger Moorey and Peter Parr, eds., *Archaeology in the Levant: Essays for Kathleen Kenyon* (Warminster: Aris & Phillips, 1978), 103–15.

Despite their effectiveness, chariots had limitations. Only with the greatest difficulty could they operate in the rugged interior terrain of Palestine, especially the hilly country of the south. Also, they required ample space to maneuver. After describing in detail the modifications of the land, George Adam Smith reduces them to a simple distinction between hilly country and level country:

> This is obvious geographically; it has been of the utmost importance historically, for the mountain was fit for infantry warfare only, but the plain feasible for cavalry and chariots; and, as Palestine from her position was bound to be crossed by the commerce and the war of the two continents on either side of her, her plains would bear the brunt of these, while her mountains would be comparatively remote from them. All the central Range, and the centre of the Eastern Range, was mountain, fit for infantry only. The Maritime Plain, Esdraelon, and the Jordan Valley, along with the plateaus of the Eastern Range, Hauran, and Moab, were plains, bearing the trunk roads and feasible for cavalry and chariots.[65]

The maintenance of chariots was very costly. The chariot was made of wood, strips of leather, and metal. Iron was used for fittings and to strengthen the wood.

In its simple form, the chariot consisted of a pole to which the animals (horses, asses, oxen) were yoked, the axle connected to the two wheels with six or eight spokes each, an open frame, and fittings for the weapons. The chariot was normally drawn by two horses, sometimes four, and occasionally three, the third being an unyoked spare. The Israelite chariot, drawn by two horses, was operated by three men: a driver, whose weapon was a long spear; an archer; and a shield bearer, designated šālîš, "third."

Beginning in the eighteenth century, the horse-drawn chariot played a prominent role in warfare conducted in open terrain. The "earliest true bits" or mouthpieces of horses date to the sixteenth century B.C.E.[66] Bits dating to the fifteenth century B.C.E. were excavated at Tell el-ʿAjjul.[67] The nailed horseshoe is not attested before the ninth century C.E.; there is no firm evidence for the nailed horseshoe in the ancient Near East.[68] The stirrup first appeared in India in the late second century B.C.E.; it reached the Arab world only in the late seventh century C.E. Without stirrups, shock combat was impossible because the rider would be dismounted.[69]

Living in mountainous terrain, the Israelites did not have much use for chariots in warfare. In defeating Hadadezer son of Rehob, David hamstrung all the chariot horses, "but left enough for a hundred chariots" (2 Sam. 8:4). Solomon acquired the

---

65. George Adam Smith, *The Historical Geography of the Holy Land* (New York: Ray Long & Richard R. Smith, 1932), 54–55.
66. Paula Wapnish and Brian Hesse, "Equids," *OEANE*, 2: 255–56.
67. James R. Stewart, *Tell el-ʿAjjul: The Middle Bronze Age Remains* (Göteborg: P. Åström, 1974), 58.
68. Lynn White, *Medieval Technology and Social Change* (Oxford: Clarendon Press, 1962), 57–59.
69. Ibid., 14–25.

horse and chariot (*rekeb, merkābâ*) on a large scale, necessitated by the expansion of his empire. He imported chariots from Egypt and Cilicia. "Solomon gathered together chariots and horses; he had fourteen hundred chariots and twelve thousand horses, which he stationed in the chariot cities and with the king in Jerusalem" (1 Kings 10:26). According to 1 Kings 9:15–19, Solomon also built towns for chariots and horses.

The Omrides had their chariot corps. In time of famine, Ahab's concern was for his horses. Ahab said to Obadiah, who was in charge of the palace: "Go through the land to all the springs of water and to all the wadis; perhaps we may find grass to keep the horses and mules alive, and not lose some of the animals" (1 Kings 18:5). Ahab joined with the Arameans in the battle of Qarqar (north of Damascus) against Shalmaneser III of Assyria in 853 B.C.E. Ahab deployed two thousand war-chariots and ten thousand infantry men, but no cavalry, on the battlefield against Shalmaneser III (*ANET*, 279). At Ramoth-Gilead, a fortified city in Transjordan, Ahab purportedly died in his chariot after being wounded in battle with the Arameans (1 Kings 22:29–38).

The prophets were opposed to the use of chariots on the grounds that it compromised the power of Israel's God, upon whom the people were to depend exclusively. "I [Yahweh] will have pity on the house of Judah, and I will save them by Yahweh their God; I will not save them by bow, or by sword, or by war, or by horses, or by horsemen" (Hos 1:7).[70]

Cavalry

Cavalry, more mobile than chariotry, was introduced in the first millennium B.C.E. The Assyrian cavalry in the eighth and seventh centuries comprised both lancers and archers who were equipped with swords, helmets, and scale armor. Assyrian bas-reliefs of the ninth and eighth centuries depict cavalrymen riding in pairs: one with a long sword at his side is shooting a composite bow, while the other, with a shield to protect both, controls the reins of the two horses. Egypt and Israel did not make use of cavalry. When the Bible mentions Solomon's *pārāšîm*, "cavalry" (1 Kings 9:19, 22), the reference is to those who rode in chariots.

Like the chariot, the cavalry horse served chiefly as a movable firing platform. Limited to archers and spearmen, the cavalry engaged only in battles on the open field, never in attacks on fortified cities. The cavalry had the advantage of extraordinary mobility when compared to chariotry.

---

70. The following titles have been helpful generally, as well as specifically: JoAnn Scurlock, "Neo-Assyrian Battle Tactics," in G. D. Young et al., eds., *Crossing Boundaries and Linking Horizons* (Bethesda, Md.: CDL Press, 1997), 491–517; John Keegan, *A History of Warfare* (New York: Alfred A. Knopf, 1993).

Neo-Assyrian Warfare

The Neo-Assyrian Empire

Assyria was at its weakest point in the first half of the eighth century, when the kingdom of Urartu was enjoying its greatest power. That period coincided with the prosperous reigns of Jeroboam II in Israel and Uzziah in Judah. International commerce was an important source of revenue for Israel and Judah. By expanding the borders of his kingdom to central Syria and to the Dead Sea, Jeroboam II received tribute from conquered peoples. This newfound wealth benefited the elite but led to the exploitation of the masses in the form of social and economic abuses. At the same time, Uzziah/Azariah brought Judah to the peak of its economic and military power. He reorganized the military, extended the borders south to Elath and west to Ashdod, and developed agriculture by establishing paramilitary settlements in the Negev.

Assyria's greatest period of empire was in the Neo-Assyrian era. The classic phase of this empire began when Tiglath-pileser III usurped the throne in 744 B.C.E. His empire, which incorporated almost the whole Near East, continued to increase in power during the next half century, only to start to wane by the mid-seventh century. Despite their extraordinary military organization and power, the Assyrians could not prevail forever; their empire fell in 609 B.C.E.

Pressured by Syria and Israel to join an anti-Assyrian coalition in 734 B.C.E., Ahaz of Judah appealed to Tiglath-pileser III, who suppressed the coalition and reduced Judah to the status of Assyrian vassal. As a vassal state, Judah was allowed to retain its autonomy. Shalmaneser V conquered Samaria, the capital of the northern kingdom, in 722/721. Shortly thereafter, his successor, Sargon II, deported the inhabitants to Assyria. Samaria became an Assyrian province, deprived of its political and cultural identity and administered by Assyrian officials.[71]

Hezekiah, a vigorous king who enjoyed the confidence of both priests and prophets, stood in sharp contrast to his vacillating father, Ahaz. During his reign, prosperity returned to Judah. He gained the reputation of a reform king by centralizing sacrifice in the Jerusalem Temple and suppressing cultic practices in other parts of Judah.

Hezekiah's revolt against Assyrian rule upon Sargon II's death in 705 B.C.E. was a turning point in Judah's history. Hezekiah formed a coalition with Phoenicia and Philistia (Ashkelon and Ekron) against Sennacherib, Sargon's successor, in an effort

---

71. Mordechai Cogan and Hayim Tadmor, *II Kings*, AB 11 (New York: Doubleday, 1988), 336: Sargon II, Prism Inscription: "[The Sa]marians who had come to an agreement with a [hostile] king not to do service or to render tribute to me, did battle. In the strength of the great gods, my lords, I fought with them; 27,280 people together with their chariots and the gods in whom they trust, I counted as spoil. 200 chariots I organized as a royal unit from among them and the rest of them I settled in Assyria. I restored the city of Samaria and settled it more densely than before (and) brought there people from the lands of my conquest. I placed my eunuch over them as governor and counted them as Assyrians."

to gain political independence from Assyria, despite Isaiah's advice to shun the revolution. Breaking with Assyria, he had to contend with King Sennacherib, who laid siege to Jerusalem and almost destroyed Judah. Under the threat of Assyrian invasion by Sennacherib, Hezekiah strengthened Jerusalem's fortifications and constructed the famous Siloam Tunnel (2 Kings 20:20; 2 Chron. 32:3–4). Eventually, Hezekiah saved his kingdom by capitulating to Sennacherib, who exacted heavy tribute.[72]

Ill. 124: Level III (701 B.C.E.) pottery from Lachish. (Courtesy of the Expedition to Lachish, D. Ussishkin, Director)

As part of the preparation for Sennacherib's invasion, Hezekiah produced storage jars stamped with the letters *lmlk* ("belonging to the king") on their handles (Ill. 180–182). This would be an example of a vessel known as *nēbel*. They are associated with Sennacherib's conquest in 701 B.C.E., but scholars dispute their

Ill. 125: Level III scoops from Lachish. (Courtesy of the Expedition to Lachish, D. Ussishkin, Director)

function. Some connect them with military organization of provisions for withstanding the Assyrian attack. Others relate them to the products of royal estates, especially olive oil and wine.[73]

Sennacherib's Campaign against Lachish

Military history of the ancient Near East can be reconstructed from the encounters of Assyria with neighboring peoples, especially the Assyrian attack on Judah in 701. Royal inscriptions, annals, iconography, and archaeology provide valuable information about military tactics and weaponry. The contemporary documents of the Assyrian kings are complemented by biblical data, which are useful but selective and

---

72. Cogan and Tadmor, *II Kings*, 339: Sennacherib, Rassam Prism Inscription (see text below).
73. Amihai Mazar, *Archaeology of the Land of the Bible* (New York: Doubleday, 1990), 455–58.

incomplete. Assyrian monarchs commissioned artists to commemorate royal victories on wall reliefs and monuments. One of the best known is Sennacherib's reliefs at Nineveh celebrating his conquest of Lachish in 701 B.C.E.

In 701 Sennacherib launched an all-out attack against Judah. Forty-six of Hezekiah's fortified towns fell, and 200,150 inhabitants were taken captive, according to the annals of Sennacherib:

> As for Hezekiah, the Judahite, who had not submitted to my yoke, I besieged forty-six of his fortified walled cities, and surrounding small towns, which were without number. Using packed-down ramps and by applying battering rams, infantry attacks by mines, breaches, and siege machines, I conquered (them). I took out 200,150 people, young and old, male and female, horses, mules, donkeys, camels, cattle and sheep, without number, and counted them as spoil. Himself [Hezekiah], I locked him up within Jerusalem, his royal city, like a bird in a cage I surrounded him with earthworks, and made it unthinkable for him to exit by the city gate.[74]

> He, Hezekiah, was overwhelmed by the awesome splendor of my lordship, and he sent me after my departure to Nineveh, my royal city, his elite troops and his best soldiers, which he had brought into Jerusalem as reinforcements, with 30 talents of gold, 800 talents of silver, choice antimony, large blocks of carnelian, beds (inlaid) with ivory, armchairs (inlaid) with ivory, elephant hides, ivory, ebony-wood, boxwood, garments with multicolored trim, garments of linen, wool (dyed) red-purple and blue-purple, vessels of copper, iron, bronze and tin, chariots, siege shields, lances, armor, daggers for the belt, bows and arrows, countless trappings and implements of war, together with his daughters, his palace women, his male and female singers. He (also) dispatched his personal messenger to deliver the tribute and to do obeisance.[75]

Ill. 126: Lachish Relief from Nineveh: Sennacherib seated on throne, looking toward Lachish. (Courtesy of the Expedition to Lachish, D. Ussishkin, Director; Photo: A. Hay)

---

74. Cogan and Tadmor, *II Kings*, 338: Sennacherib, Rassam Prism Inscription.
75. Ibid., 339: Sennacherib, Rassam Prism Inscription.

Jerusalem was spared when Hezekiah paid a heavy indemnity to Sennacherib (2 Kings 18:14–16). Reconciling the disagreements between the biblical (2 Kings 18–19) and the Assyrian accounts of Sennacherib's campaign in 701 B.C.E. presents difficulties. An enormous discrepancy concerns whether Hezekiah capitulated to Sennacherib (so the Assyrian annals) or the Assyrian army suffered defeat at the hands of God and retreated (so the biblical account). Various hypotheses have been offered, including a two-campaign theory. Further, despite the similarities in the reports of 2 Kings and Isaiah 36–37, differences exist here, too. Isaiah's account is clearly secondary, depending as it does upon 2 Kings. Also, 2 Chron. 32, whose accuracy appears to be confirmed by recent excavations in the City of David, must be taken into account. Massive towers over the Gihon Spring have been uncovered, guarding Jerusalem's water supply.

The two-campaign theory, which dates to George Rawlinson in 1858,[76] has been revived by William Shea[77] who suggests, as a result of current excavations in Jerusalem (1999), that Sennacherib attacked Jerusalem twice, once in 701 B.C.E. and again in 688—contrary to Assyriologists who support the one-campaign theory, since only one is described in the Assyrian texts.

Siege of Lachish

Lachish was a royal citadel southwest of Jerusalem, strategically located on a major route linking the southern coastal plain to routes leading into the highlands toward Jerusalem and Hebron, amply supplied with water, and surrounded by fertile farmland. The city gate was near the southwest corner of the city, accessible but at the same time vulnerable. A large palace fortress commanded the center of the city.

The Assyrian army, highly skilled in military organization and maneuvers and professionally equipped, was without peer in its day. In fact, no juggernaut before it had attained such military might and power. The neighboring peoples simply imitated, but could not equal, the Assyrians in tactics, weapons, and equipment. The Assyrians were cruel warriors, slaughtering, mutilating, and flaying those whom they defeated. Were the Israelites, Arameans, and Moabites less cruel? The "biblical" slaughters by Samuel, Saul, David, Jehu, and others could probably match the Assyrians'. Only the magnitude, not the manner, of the killing distinguished the Assyrians. Probably more were taken into exile—deported—than slaughtered. Deportation and population replacement represented a new policy under the Assyrians.

---

76. Reich and Shukron, "Light at the End of the Tunnel," 22–33, 72. Following George Rawlinson, many scholars maintained the two-campaign theory, including William F. Albright, "The Date of Sennacherib's Second Campaign against Hezekiah," *BASOR* 130 (1953): 8–11; also Siegfried H. Horn, "Did Sennacherib Campaign Once or Twice against Hezekiah?" *Andrews University Seminary Studies* 4 (1966): 1–28.

77. William H. Shea, "Jerusalem under Siege," *BAR* 25 (1999): 36–44, 64. For a rebuttal of Shea and in support of a single-campaign theory, see Mordecai Cogan, "Sennacherib's Siege of Jerusalem," *BAR* 27 (2001): 40–45, 69.

Ill. 127: Lachish: four links of iron chain used to deflect the battering ram from striking the city wall. (Courtesy of the Expedition to Lachish, D. Ussishkin, Director)

The bas-reliefs in Sennacherib's Southwest Palace at Nineveh (Kuyunjik) depict the Assyrian assault of the fortified city of Lachish in the foothills of Judah in 701 B.C.E. (Ill. 48, 108, 122, 126, 128, 135, 138, 159). Austen Layard, excavator of Nineveh and Nimrud, found these reliefs at Nineveh in the mid-nineteenth century. As an indication of Lachish's importance, this is the only battle in the 701 campaign to be portrayed in stone. The reliefs are among the best example of military narrative art, capturing details of siege techniques as well as military trappings. Ashurnasirpal II, too, has some impressive reliefs showing multiple siege techniques. As David Ussishkin, the excavator of Lachish, points out, the record of the siege of Lachish is preserved in four extant sources: the biblical narrative, the Assyrian annals, the bas-reliefs at Nineveh, and the excavation itself.[78] Amihai Mazar[79] suggests that Sennacherib commemorated his conquest of Lachish in relief because of his inability to conquer Jerusalem.

During the campaign of 701, Sennacherib's headquarters were located at Lachish where he was personally present. With arrows, stones, and flaming torches, the people of Lachish tried pathetically to defend their city against formidable Assyrian battering rams, archers, spearmen, and slingers. To counter the deadly blows of the ram's shaft against the city wall, the defenders lowered an iron chain outside the wall to snare the shaft and thereby deflect it. The attackers in turn used grappling hooks to free the shaft from the clutches of the chain. Four links of such a chain, measuring about thirty-seven centimeters, were found in the debris at the base of Lachish's revetment wall[80] (Ill. 127).

Level III at Lachish, which represents the 701 B.C.E destruction, contains abundant evidence of fire and demolition. Houses and shops were reduced to ashes, while pottery vessels for domestic use, including storage jars, cooking pots, juglets, bowls, and oil lamps, were smashed. In the northwest corner of Lachish, four adjoining caves containing 1,500 disarticulated human skeletons (male, female, and children) were discovered. The excavators believe these were civilian, not military, casualties of the Assyrian attack on the city.[81] The Lachish reliefs portray some captives stripped naked and

78. Ussishkin, *The Conquest of Lachish by Sennacherib*, 11.
79. Amihai Mazar, "The Fortification of Cities in the Ancient Near East," *CANE* 3: 1535.
80. Yigael Yadin, "The Mystery of the Unexplained Chain," *BAR* 10 (1984): 65–67.
81. Ussishkin, *The Conquest of Lachish by Sennacherib*, 56–57.

Ill. 128: Lachish Relief from Nineveh: (Upper Register) Booty-bearers ; (Lower Register) deportees. (Courtesy of the Expedition to Lachish, D. Ussishkin, Director; Photo: A. Hay)

impaled on stakes, others departing the city in carts or on foot. It was the practice of the Assyrians to take prisoners of war and to deport the masses. The Lachishites wear turbans wrapped around the head and short tunics gathered at the waist with a belt.

Lachish was rebuilt and refortified later in the seventh century. Level II represents a sparsely populated Judahite city, whereas the Level III city was much larger. Level II was demolished by the Babylonians in 588/586 B.C.E., when the city was destroyed by fire.

Assyria was actively involved in the rule of the Syro-Palestinian region until 640 B.C.E. After the death of Ashurbanipal in 627, the Assyrian empire disintegrated rapidly. Then Egypt made its presence felt in the region by replacing Assyria as the imperial power. Of course, this could have happened much earlier than the death of Ashurbanipal in areas of Philistia and other areas closer to Egypt. Eventually, Neo-Babylonia (Chaldea) under Nebuchadrezzar II replaced Assyria as a leading imperial power. In 604 B.C.E. he destroyed the Philistine city-state of Ashkelon and its neighbor Ekron. In 588 B.C.E. Nebuchadrezzar laid siege to Jerusalem; the city was totally destroyed two years later.

Neo-Babylonian Warfare

The fortunes of biblical Israel would not be complete without considering the Neo-Babylonian period. *kaśdîm*, Hebrew for "Chaldea," is the biblical designation for Neo-Babylonia. Chaldea also denotes the last Babylonian dynasty (625–539 B.C.E.), inaugurated by Nabopolassar and continued by his famous son, Nebuchadrezzar II (605–562 B.C.E.). Cyrus the Great of Persia brought the Neo-Babylonian Empire to an end in 539.

Biblical Israel's location as a land bridge connecting Asia and Africa accounts for the fact that it was continuously caught between competing imperial powers, notably Assyria, Egypt, and Babylonia. In 721, the Assyrians conquered the northern kingdom of Israel. In 586, the Babylonians vanquished the southern kingdom of Judah (the tribes of Judah and Benjamin), ravaging Jerusalem and destroying the Temple. Each ruled Palestine for roughly seven decades: the Neo-Assyrians from about 715 to 640 B.C.E., and the Neo-Babylonians from about 605 to 540. The Assyrian presence in Palestine is evident in both biblical and extrabiblical texts, as well as in the archaeological remains, whereas the Babylonian presence left few traces other than destructions.

The Assyrian occupation was characterized by the establishment of provinces (e.g., Samerina and Magiddu) and the reconstruction of sites (e.g., the fortress at Tell Jemmeh [Yurza/Arṣa, according to Benjamin Mazar's identification]) along the Via Maris. After conquering Yurza/Arṣa, King Esarhaddon constructed an Assyrian vaulted building. "It preserves vaulted mud-brick ceilings that were erected with keystone-shaped bricks, or voussoirs, marking the earliest known use of voussoirs in world architecture."[82]

Until Stager's analysis, most ancient Near Eastern historians assumed that the imperial imprint of Assyria in the West, its military and administrative structure, was imitated by its successor, the Neo-Babylonian Empire. However, such was not the case. The Babylonian conquerors left far fewer traces than the Assyrians. Nebuchadrezzar's devastation of the Philistine cities of Ashkelon, Ashdod, and Ekron reflect a "scorched-earth policy,"[83] so much so that Ephraim Stern describes the period between the destruction of Jerusalem (586 B.C.E.) and the return of the exiles from Babylon (after 538 B.C.E.) as the "Babylonian gap."[84]

Nebuchadrezzar II is best known for his military exploits and expansionist policies. His first notable achievement was the utter defeat of Pharaoh Necho II in 605 B.C.E. at Carchemish, the Egyptian base on the Euphrates:

> [The twenty-first year]: The king of Akkad stayed home [while] Nebuchadnezzar (II), his eldest son (and) the crown prince, mustered [the army of Akkad]. He took his army's lead and marched to Carchemish which is on the bank of the Euphrates. He crossed the river [to encounter the army of Egypt] which was encamped at Carchemish. [. . .] They did battle together. The army of Egypt retreated before him. He inflicted a [defeat] upon them (and) finished them off completely. In the district of Hamath the army of Akkad over-

---

82. Gus W. Van Beek, "Jemmeh, Tell," *NEAEHL*, 2: 670.
83. Stager, "The Fury of Babylon: Ashkelon and the Archaeology of Destruction," *BAR* 22 (1996): 69.
84. Ephraim Stern, "The Babylonian Gap," *BAR* 26 (2000): 45–51, 76.

took the remainder of the army of [Egypt which] managed to escape [from] the defeat and which was not overcome. They (the army of Akkad) inflicted a defeat upon them (so that) a single (Egyptian) man [did not return] home. At that time Nebuchadnezzar (II) conquered all of Ha[ma]th.[85]

In the words of the prophet Jeremiah:

> Thus says Yahweh of hosts: Since you would not listen to my words, I will send for and fetch all the tribes of the north [Babylonia], and I will send for Nebuchadrezzar, king of Babylon, my servant. I will bring them against this land, against its inhabitants, and against all the neighboring nations. I will doom them, making them an object of horror, of ridicule, of everlasting reproach. (Jer. 25:8–9)

This triumph over the Egyptians gave Nebuchadrezzar control over the Assyrian Empire, including Syria and Palestine. Jeremiah urged the kings of Judah to submit to Babylon, the new imperial power, but they would not listen.

As noted, in 604 B.C.E. Nebuchadrezzar destroyed the Philistine port city of Ashkelon on the Mediterranean, and shortly thereafter Ekron, another of the five principal cities of Philistia. Both the Babylonian Chronicle and Jeremiah allude to the demise of Ashkelon: "(Nebuchadrezzar) marched to the city of Ashkelon and captured it in the month of Kislev [November/December]. He captured its king and plundered it and carried off (spoil from it . . .). He turned the city into a mound and heaps of ruins."[86]

In the words of Jeremiah, "Gaza is shaved bald, Ashkelon is reduced to silence" (Jer. 47:5). The prophets Jeremiah (25:20), Zephaniah (2:4), and Zechariah (9:6) refer also to the destruction of Ashdod in the Babylonian period.

The Leon Levy Expedition to Ashkelon confirms the details of the Babylonian sack of this city. Ashkelon's bazaars (ḫûṣôt), dating to the late seventh century B.C.E., were especially hard hit. Remains of charred wood, smashed pottery, and burnt mud brick attest to the intensity of the destruction of the bazaar and the nearby royal winery.[87] The bazaars (ḫûṣôt) of Ashkelon were made famous by the elegy of King David for Saul and his son Jonathan: "Alas, the glory of Israel, Saul, slain upon your heights [Mount Gilboa]; how can the warriors have fallen! Tell it not in Gath, herald it not in the bazaars (ḫuṣōt) of Ashkelon, lest the Philistine maidens rejoice, lest the daughters of the uncircumcised [Philistines] exult" (2 Sam. 1:19–20). A poignant witness to the destruction wrought by the Babylonians at Ashkelon is the skeleton of a woman, about thirty-five years old, found lying on her back, legs flexed, and skull fractured (Ill. 130). Anthropological evidence suggests that she was clubbed to death, and possibly also raped.

---

85. A. K. Grayson, *Assyrian and Babylonian Chronicles* (Locust Valley, N.J.: J. J. Augustin, 1975), 99, chronicle 5, obverse lines 1–8.

86. *Babylonian Chronicle*, British Museum 21946, 18–20.

87. Stager, "The Fury of Babylon," 76.

Ill. 129: Seven bronze situlae with a bronze offering stand from 604 B.C.E. destruction at Ashkelon. (Courtesy of the Leon Levy Expedition to Ashkelon; Photo: C. Andrews)

Ill. 130: Female victim of 604 B.C.E. destruction, Ashkelon—35-year old woman struck with a blunt instrument to the head. (Courtesy of the Leon Levy Expedition to Ashkelon; Photo: C. Andrews)"

From the biblical perspective, a far more devastating tragedy took place seven years later, in 597 B.C.E., when Nebuchadrezzar besieged Jerusalem, confiscating the Temple treasures, imposing heavy tribute, and deporting part of the population, perhaps as many as ten thousand, to Babylonia (2 Kings 24:14). A duplicate enumeration (2 Kings 24:16) reckons eight thousand exiles (seven thousand warriors and one thousand craftsmen and smiths). These numbers are only approximate, but there is no other accounting available. The occasion was the revolt of the Egyptian vassal, King Jehoiakim (609–598), against Babylonia. His son Jehoiachin succeeded him as king, reigning only three months in Jerusalem before surrendering to Nebuchadrezzar, who deported him to Babylon along with many of the notables.

The seventh year: In the month Kislev the king of Akkad mustered his army and marched to Hattu. He encamped against the city of Judah [*āl ia-a-hu-du*] and on the second day of the month Adar he captured the city (and) seized (its) king. A king of his own choice he appointed in the city (and) taking the vast tribute he brought it into Babylon.[88]

According to 2 Kings:

> At that time the officials of Nebuchadrezzar, king of Babylon, attacked Jerusalem, and the city came under siege. Nebuchadrezzar, king of Babylon, himself arrived at the city [Jerusalem] while his servants were besieging it. . . . He carried off all the treasures of the Temple of Yahweh and those of the palace, and broke up all the gold utensils that Solomon, king of Israel, had provided in the Temple of Yahweh, as Yahweh had foretold (2 Kings 24:10–11, 13–14).

In place of Jehoiachin, his uncle Mattaniah was enthroned by Nebuchadrezzar, who changed Mattaniah's name to Zedekiah. Thereafter, the kingdom of Judah survived for only a decade, the period when Zedekiah (597–586) ruled as a puppet of Babylonia. A vacillator by nature, he foolishly ignored Jeremiah's counsel to submit to Babylon. In fact, he was in a tight spot, caught between the pro-Egyptian and the pro-Babylonian parties: "Thus says Yahweh: See, I am giving you a choice between life and death. Whoever remains in this city [Jerusalem] shall die by the sword or famine or pestilence. But whoever leaves and surrenders to the besieging Chaldeans [Babylonians] shall live and have his life as booty" (Jer. 21:8–10).

In 594 B.C.E., by planning an anti-Babylonian conspiracy in Jerusalem with Edom, Moab, Ammon, Tyre, and Sidon, Zedekiah made a fatal error, eventually resulting in the devastation of Judah (Jer. 27:3). In 588 Nebuchadrezzar laid siege to Jerusalem, but the city held out for a year and a half. Siege walls were erected around the city to force the inhabitants into starvation: "On the ninth day of the fourth month the famine became so severe in the city [Jerusalem] that there was no food for the people of the land" (Jer. 52:6). In 586, the Babylonians breached the walls of Jerusalem, demolished the Temple and palace, and burned the city.

An unjustified myth of invincibility had grown up around Jerusalem, especially during the time of Hezekiah and the prophet Isaiah, when the mighty army of Sennacherib, for some indeterminate reason, failed to conquer Jerusalem. Many must have concluded that Yahweh would not allow his holy city and his special habitation—the Temple—to be destroyed. Nebuchadrezzar taught them a different lesson. Lamentations describes the besieged city of Jerusalem: "How lonely she [Jerusalem] is now, the once crowded city. Widowed is she who was mistress over nations. The princess among states has become forced labor (*mas*)" (Lam. 1:1).

---

88. Grayson, *Assyrian and Babylonian Chronicles*, 102, chronicle 5, obverse lines 11–13.

Zedekiah fled the city but was seized near Jericho and brought to Riblah, on the eastern shore of the Orontes, where he was forced to witness the execution of his sons. Then he was blinded and taken in chains to Babylon, where he died (2 Kings 25:4–7). Thus ended ingloriously the Davidic dynasty.

A second deportation to Babylon followed upon the destruction of 586, but Judah was nonetheless not totally depopulated during the exile. Jeremiah reports a total of 4,600 deportees exiled in 597, 586, and 582 B.C.E. (Jer. 52:28–30). The precision of Jeremiah's numbers gives them a ring of authenticity, compared to the round numbers of 2 Kings.

Although life in exile is not well documented, Ezekiel, prophesying in Babylon from 597 to 571, gives an indication of what it was like. The expatriates were free to perform their religious practices, such as circumcision and Sabbath observance. At the same time, Ezekiel's vision of the restored Temple encouraged the exiles to persevere (Ezekiel 40–44). The Psalmist attests to the understandable nostalgia the Judahites experienced in exile: "By the streams of Babylon [Tigris and Euphrates] we sat [the posture of mourners] when we remembered Zion. On the poplars (*'ărābîm*, *Populus euphratica*, 'Euphrates poplar') of that land we hung up our lyres" (Ps. 137:1–2).

Scholars differ in their interpretation of the limited textual and archaeological evidence relating to the exile. The long-standing opinion that the majority of Judahites went into exile has been modified, although some have adopted an exaggerated position characterized as "the myth of the empty land."[89] Proponents of the latter try to make the case that the majority of the population remained in the land of Judah after 586 B.C.E. Maintaining that Judah was not completely destroyed by Nebuchadrezzar, they assert that Mizpah (Tell en-Naṣbeh), Bethel, Gibeon, and the area around Bethlehem continued to be inhabited. That may be difficult to establish, since the stratigraphy at these sites is not clear.

Hans Barstad, followed by Israel Finkelstein and Neil Silberman, calls it "highly improbable" that Judah was desolate and uninhabited between 586 and 538. On the contrary, Barstad detects "clear indications of cultural and material continuity before and after 586 B.C.E."[90] While acknowledging deportation and destruction in the hill country of Judah, he asserts that the remainder of the country was left intact. Finkelstein and Silberman concur with Oded Lipschits in arguing that Tell en-Naṣbeh and sites north of Jerusalem, namely Bethel and Gibeon, continued to be populated: "Around Bethlehem, there seems to have been significant continuity from the late monarchic to the Babylonian period. Thus, to both the north and the south of

---

89. Hans M. Barstad, *The Myth of the Empty Land* (Oslo: Scandinavian University Press, 1996); Israel Finkelstein and Neil A. Silberman, *The Bible Unearthed* (New York: The Free Press, 2001).
90. Barstad, *The Myth of the Empty Land*, 78.

Jerusalem, life continued almost uninterrupted."[91] Finkelstein and Silberman deny, on the basis of both text and archaeology, that "Judah was in total ruin and uninhabited" between Jerusalem's demise (586) and Cyrus's proclamation (538).

Other scholars find no evidence of occupation at settlement sites west of the Jordan to fill the so-called "Babylonian gap." But this is not to imply that the countryside was totally uninhabited between 586 and 538. "There were undoubtedly some settlements, but the population was very small. Many towns and villages were either completely or partly destroyed. The rest were barely functioning."[92]

These positions appear to be mutually exclusive without some sort of explanation. Clearly the population of Judah was severely diminished. West of the Jordan it is difficult not only to find a settlement site that continues to be occupied during the period (586–525), but also to point to individual artifacts that fill the gap. Of course, there must have been some of the 'am hā'āreṣ who remained. Otherwise there would be little concern for reversing the definition of who is a Jew, which Ezra later dwelt on. The 'am hā'āreṣ were the landed gentry of the monarchy who were not exiled. By the time of Ezra their once honorable status had been reduced to a term of opprobrium as the unlanded returnees redefined who is a Jew, making their understanding of Torah the primary criterion. At this time there developed a greater interest in commercial activities on the part of the inhabitants of Yehud, although they also had to maintain their agrarian base to survive.

Was the rural landscape peopled or not? Where are the estates, farm houses, and the like that surface surveys should have revealed? Finkelstein and Silberman state that at least 75 percent of the population remained on the land.[93] If so, where are the archaeological remains?

Several, such as Ephraim Stern[94] and David S. Vanderhooft,[95] take issue with this statement, as do we. Stern speaks about the "Babylonian gap" as he lists the sites that were destroyed in the sixth century B.C.E., including, in addition to Jerusalem, Ashkelon, Ekron, and Tel Batash (Timnah); also, Ramat Raḥel, Lachish (II), Gezer, Beth-Shemesh, 'Ein-Gedi (V), Arad, and Tell Beit Mirsim, among others. Vanderhooft points to a "significant occupational gap" at many sites destroyed by the Babylonians.[96] He believes there was some demographic continuity, perhaps 40 percent, but administrative continuity was lacking. Because of kinship relationships, the society could still function without administrative structure.

---

91. Finkelstein and Silberman, *The Bible Unearthed*, 307; Oded Lipschits, "The History of the Benjamin Region under Babylonian Rule," *TA* 26 (1999): 155–90.

92. Stern, "The Babylonian Gap," 51.

93. Finkelstein and Silberman, *The Bible Unearthed*, 306.

94. Stern, "The Babylonian Gap."

95. David S. Vanderhooft, *The Neo-Babylonian Empire and Babylon in the Latter Prophets*, Harvard Semitic Museum Publications (Atlanta: Scholars Press, 1999).

96. Ibid., 106.

Cyrus the Great, founder of the Persian Empire who ascended the throne of Persia in 559 B.C.E., defeated the Babylonians in a decisive battle at Opis on the Tigris in 539/538. Ultimately, this victory led to the liberation of Judea and the return of the Jewish captives to their homeland. Cyrus was an enlightened leader who saw the value in respecting the culture and traditions of conquered peoples, even allowing them to govern themselves. He permitted the repatriated Jews to rebuild Jerusalem and the Temple:

> In the first year of Cyrus, king of Persia, in order to fulfill the word of Yahweh spoken by Jeremiah, Yahweh inspired King Cyrus of Persia to issue this proclamation throughout his kingdom, both by word of mouth and in writing: "Thus says Cyrus, king of Persia: All the kingdoms of the earth Yahweh, the god of heaven, has given to me, and he has also charged me to build him a house in Jerusalem, which is in Judah." (Ezra 1:1–2)

In 520 B.C.E. the Jews began construction of the Temple; in 515, at the urging of the prophets Haggai and Zechariah, the Temple was finished and rededicated under Zerubbabel and Jeshua/Joshua, the high priest.

Second Isaiah pays Cyrus a unique tribute. Only Cyrus among foreign rulers is accorded the title messiah: "anointed (*māšîaḥ*) of Yahweh" (Isa. 45:1), an instrument in the hands of Yahweh.

> Thus says Yahweh to his anointed (*mĕšîḥô*), Cyrus, whose right hand I grasp, subduing nations before him, and disarming kings, opening doors before him and leaving the gates unbarred: I will go before you and level the mountains; bronze doors I will shatter, and iron bars I will snap. I will give you treasures out of the darkness, and riches that have been hidden away, that you may know that I am Yahweh, the God of Israel, who calls you by your name. (Isa. 45:1–3)

CHAPTER 5

Culture and the Expressive Life

DRESS AND ADORNMENTS

Wearing apparel, originating as early as the Paleolithic period, not only is necessary for health and survival, but also bears considerable social significance in the life of any culture. Style of dress is often a signpost of one's ethnicity. The quality and manufacture of clothing are a gauge of one's social rank and economic position. Ornate robes and dyed garments of superior quality become a status symbol.

Apparel frequently signifies the identity of the wearer—we are what we wear—as in the case of vestments for priests and uniforms for soldiers. Raiment or what one does with clothing may carry symbolic meaning. In biblical times, to remove or tear clothes in public was a sign of either mourning or despair; for example: "Then David said to Joab and to all the people who were with him, 'Tear your clothes, and put on sackcloth, and mourn over Abner'" (2 Sam. 3:31; also Jer. 41:5). Clothes also connote the transfer of power, as in the case of Elijah, whose prophetic prerogative was consigned to Elisha by means of Elijah's mantle: "He [Elisha] took the mantle of Elijah that had fallen from him, and struck the water, say-

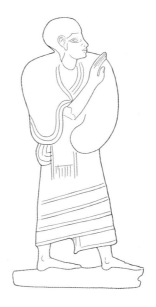

Ill. 131: Canaanite nobleman wearing skull cap, cape with fringe, wrap-around skirt, with hand raised. A bronze plaque from Hazor, from fifteenth century B.C.E. (Drawing by C. S. Alexander after Y. Yadin, *Hazor: the Rediscovery of a Great Citadel of the Bible*)

Ill. 132: Dignitary seated on a throne, from two fragments of a painted potsherd found at Ramat Raḥel, from eighth to seventh century B.C.E. (After Y. Aharoni, *Excavations at Ramat Raḥel*)

Ill. 133: Stone relief of a Canaanite/Phoenician nobleman, dated Iron Age II. (Courtesy of E. Stern, Tel Dor Excavations)

ing, 'Where is Yahweh, the God of Elijah?'" (2 Kings 2:14). King Jehoiachin's release from prison was manifested by a change of dress: when King Evil-merodach (Akkadian Amel-Marduk) of Babylon released King Jehoiachin from prison, Jehoiachin put aside his prison clothes and dined daily in the king's presence (2 Kings 25:27–29).

Despite numerous references to attire in the Bible, we lack detailed knowledge about Israelite dress. Textiles rarely survive in the Mediterranean climate of Palestine, although they may in steppe or arid environments such as the Negev, Sinai, and Judean deserts. From the Bible and other written records come the names, but not descriptions, of various garments. These designations are difficult to identify in detail, as variances in modern translations of the Bible attest. Also, because of aniconic and iconoclastic prohibitions, the portrayal of Israelite clothing depends on the art of neighboring cultures. However, while official Israelite religion prohibited images, the prohibition of representations was less rigid in the preexilic period.

The most useful sources of information about dress are representations on Near Eastern monuments, including sculptures, wall paintings, and reliefs. Scenes from the Black Obelisk (Ill. 134a-e) portray representatives of vanquished nations, including

Ill. 134a: "Black Obelisk" of Shalmaneser III (858–824 B.C.E.) found at Nimrud in 1846; height 2.02 m. Five rows of panels run around four sides of the monument. Various rulers representing their respective countries offer tribute to the Assyrian monarch. (Courtesy of the Trustees of the British Museum)

1   2   3

4   5   6   7   8

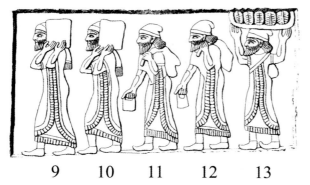

9   10   11   12   13

Ill. 134b-e: "Black Obelisk" of Shalmaneser III (858–824 B.C.E.). The second row from the top is a series of four panels in which Shalmaneser receives the tribute from "Jehu, son of Omri," who prostrates himself before the Assyrian king. Behind him are two attendants, one shading the king with a parasol. Behind Jehu stand four Assyrians who lead a procession of thirteen Israelite porters. Each porter is bearded and wears a pointed cap and pointed shoes. They wear a long garment (*kuttōnet*), over which a fringed mantle (*śimlâ*) with tassels is thrown. The Assyrian superscription reads:

ma-da-tu šá ia-ú-a DUMU ḫu-um-ri-i KÙ.BABBAR.MEŠ KÙ.GI.MEŠ sap-lu KÙ.GI zuq-u-ut KÙ.GI qa-bu-a-te MEŠ*KÙ.GI da-la-ni*MEŠ *KÙ.GI AN.NA.MEŠ* GIŠ*ḫu-tar-tú šá qāt šarri* GIŠ*pu-aš-ḫa-ti am-ḫur-šu*

and can be translated:[1]

The tribute of Jehu, son of Omri: silver, gold, a golden bowl,[2] a golden vase,[3] golden goblets, golden buckets,[4] tin,[5] a staff of the hand of the king,[6] (and) javelins,[7] I received from him.

(Illustration: K. Vagliardo; after Sir Austen Henry Layard, *The Monuments of Nineveh* [1849]).

Notes

1. See A. Kirk Grayson, *Assyrian Rulers of the Early First Millennium BC. II (850–745 B.C.)*, The Royal Inscriptions of Mesopotamia. Assyrian Period vol. 3; (Toronto: University of Toronto Press, 1996), 149: No. 88, for the standard edition of

continued

Ill. 135: Lachish Relief from Nineveh: A captive Lachishite accompanied by his two young sons. (Courtesy of the Expedition to Lachish, D. Ussishkin, Director; Photo: A. Hay)

King Jehu of Israel, presenting tribute to the Assyrian King Shalmaneser III at Nimrud (Iraq), and the Lachish Reliefs on the walls of the royal palace at Nineveh (Iraq) commemorate the victory in 701 B.C.E. of the Assyrian King Sennacherib over the Judahites at Lachish. Although dating a millennium earlier (ca. 1890 B.C.E.), the Egyptian wall paintings in the tomb of Khnumhotep III at Beni Hasan, which depict a group of Canaanite or Amorite emissaries presenting themselves to Khnumhotep, an important Egyptian official, can be instructive.

An especially valuable source is the famous Megiddo ivory plaque depicting in a composite scene a victory of a Canaanite king or prince in the twelfth century (*ANEP*, 332). Seated on a throne and drinking from a bowl, the ruler is vested in a spangled garment, resembling the robe of a Canaanite from the tomb of Rameses III. He wears an ankle-length robe, a knee-length cloak, a toga draped over one shoulder, and a tight-fitting cap or helmet over his shaved head (Ill. 136). His attendants wear ankle-length robes. A soldier dressed

(*continued from previous page*) this text. We are grateful to Peter Machinist who helped with this translation.
2. Perhaps carried by Porter #2; Akkadian *saplu*, cf. Hebrew *sēpel* (e.g., Judges 5:25; 6:38).
3. Perhaps carried by Porter #3 or #6.
4. Carried by either Porters #4, 5 or #11, 12; Neo-Assyrian *dālu/dālāni* (pl.), cf. Hebrew *dĕlî* (e.g., Num. 24:7; Isa. 40:15).
5. Porters #9 and #10 seem to be carrying metal ingots on their shoulders. Tin as well as copper and lead were transported in ingot form; however, only the word for tin, not for ingot, is mentioned here.
6. Or perhaps: "a staff used by the king." Carried by Porter #5. This is a staff made of wood.
7. Read *pu-aš-ha-ti* with wood determinative meaning "spears" or "javelins." Carried by porters #7 and #8.

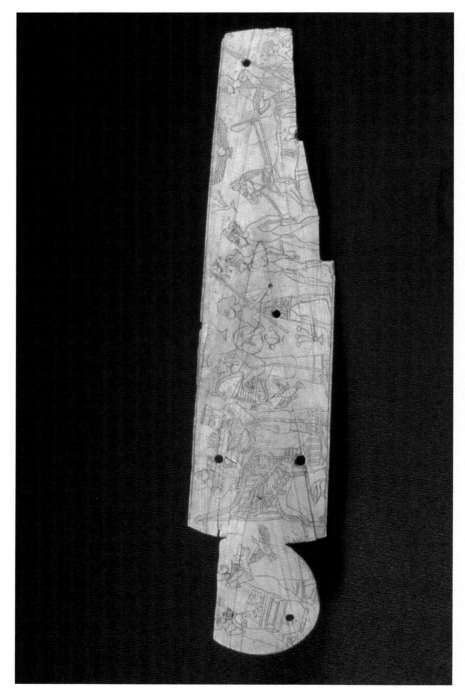

Ill. 136: Incised ivory plaque, depicting ruler of Megiddo, dated late thirteenth or early twelfth century B.C.E. (Courtesy of Israel Museum; Photo: D. Harris)

in a kilt leads two circumcised prisoners with bag-like head cloths in a procession before the king. Their nakedness, in this context, is a sign of humiliation. These prisoners are surely Shasu and not Sea Peoples, as some have maintained. A woman, probably the queen, clothed in a Syrian dress of ankle length and wearing a tiara or crown, stands before the enthroned king while presenting him with a water lily. Behind her, a female musician plays on an asymmetrical nine-stringed lyre.

Clothing

The most common Hebrew word for clothing, used over two hundred times in the Hebrew Bible, is *beged*. The term is applicable to the apparel of both women and men, both the rich and the poor. Loose-fitting clothing was manufactured primarily from wool, linen, and cotton. Wool was the main material of the Babylonian and Assyrian textile industry. In Israel, wool was the common material of clothing, because linen was much more costly. Since wool is hard to launder, it was not often cleaned.

Changing clothes was an infrequent occurrence, a luxury practically unknown to commoners. But there are several biblical examples of the elite changing their clothes. Joseph gave his brothers provisions for the journey back to Canaan: "To each one of them he gave changes of clothing (*ḥălipōt śĕmālōt*); but to Benjamin he gave three hundred pieces of silver and five changes of clothing (*ḥălipōt śĕmālōt*)" (Gen. 45:22). Samson promised his thirty wedding companions thirty linen garments and thirty changes of garments (*ḥălipōt bĕgādîm*) (Judg. 14:12). Then he killed thirty men of Ashkelon, took their suits of clothing, and gave the festal garments to those in the wedding party who guessed his riddle (Judg. 14:19). When God directed Jacob to go up to Bethel, settle there, and make an altar, Jacob said to his household, "Put away the foreign gods that are among you, and purify yourselves, and change your clothes" (Gen. 35:2). When Saul consulted a medium at Endor, he "disguised himself and put on other clothes and went there" (1 Sam. 28:8). When David learned of the death of the first child Bathsheba bore to him, he washed, anointed himself, and changed his clothes (2 Sam. 12:20). En route to Israel, seeking to be healed, Naaman took with him "ten talents of silver, six thousand shekels of gold, and ten changes of clothing (*ḥălîpôt bĕgādîm*)," which he offered to Elisha in gratitude (2 King 5:5).

Clothing was sometimes put to other uses. At the time of the Exodus, we read, "the people [Israelites] took their dough before it was leavened, with their kneading bowls wrapped up in their cloaks (*śimlōtām*) on their shoulders" (Ex. 12:34). At Gideon's request the Israelites "spread a cloak (*śimlâ*), and each threw into it an earring he had taken as booty" (Judg 8:25).[1]

Biblical law forbade weaving garments with a mixture of wool and linen: "You

---

1. Edward Neufeld, "Hygiene Conditions in Ancient Israel," *BA* 34 (1971): 53.

shall not wear cloth of two different kinds of thread, wool and linen, woven together" (Deut. 22:11). The priests were ordinarily required to wear linen vestments: "When they enter the gates of the inner court, they [Levitical priests] shall wear linen vestments; they shall have nothing of wool on them, while they minister at the gates of the inner court, and within" (Ezek. 44:17). Israelite priests wore linen underpants (*miknĕsê-bād*), "a kind of double-apron serving as a garment for the hips,"[2] as part of their ceremonial vestments (Ex. 28:42).

Among the booty taken by Tiglath-pileser III of Assyria in his campaigns against Syria and Palestine were "linen garments with multicolored trimmings, garments of their native (industries) (being made of) dark purple wool" (*ANET*, 282). These colored garments were highly prized.

Men's Dress

The undergarment worn by men next to the skin is the linen or leather *'ēzôr*, a wraparound skirt comparable to a kilt or loincloth, held in place by a belt (*ḥăgôr/ḥăgôrâ*). It was the basic garment of Israelite soldiers and laborers. One of Jeremiah's symbolic actions involved a linen loincloth: "Thus said Yahweh to me [Jeremiah], 'Go and buy yourself a linen loincloth (*'ēzôr pištîm*), and put it on your loins, but do not dip it in water'" (Jer. 13:1). Elijah is described as "a hairy man, with a leather girdle (*'ēzôr 'ôr*) around his waist" (2 Kings 1:8). Girdles and footwear were fabricated from tanned leather.

The *kuttōnet* (Greek *chiton*), which was placed over the *'ēzôr*, was similar to a tunic. Worn by both men and women, it was an ankle-length garment draped over one shoulder, with medium or long sleeves, and ordinarily made of wool. The Israelites customarily wore the *kuttōnet* while working, gathering it at the waist with a belt or sash. On the Black Obelisk of Shalmaneser III, Jehu and his attendants have fringed, ankle-length tunics with short sleeves, secured with a belt (Ill. 134b). Over this long garment is a fringed mantle with tasseled ends. On the Lachish Reliefs of Sennacherib, the Judahite leaders are delineated in two different garbs. One is a sleeveless shirt, with a fringed tassel hanging between the legs; the other, worn when the Judahites were facing the Assyrian king, is an unbelted, short-sleeved tunic reaching to the ankles. When the captive Judahites later worked on the construction of Sennacherib's palace at Nineveh, they are depicted in short garments with a fringed tassel, secured with a belt.[3]

As a sign of his special affection for Joseph, his father Jacob presented him with "a coat of many colors" (the traditional rendering based on the reading

---

2. William L. Holladay, *A Concise Hebrew and Aramaic Lexicon of the Old Testament* (Grand Rapids: Wm. B. Eerdmans Pub. Co., 1971), 194.

3. David Ussishkin, *The Conquest of Lachish by Sennacherib* (Tel Aviv: Institute of Archaeology, Tel Aviv University, 1982), 128.

Ill. 137: Limestone statue of Yeraḥʿazor from the Amman citadel, dated late eighth century B.C.E. (Courtesy of the Amman Archaeological Museum and P. Bienkowski)

of the Septuagint). The meaning of the Hebrew *kĕtōnet passîm*, now usually translated "a long robe with sleeves" (Gen. 37:3), is uncertain. The only other use of the phrase *kĕtōnet passîm* appears in the account of Amnon's rape of Tamar, where she is described as wearing "a long robe with sleeves" (2 Sam. 13:18). Perhaps "a long tunic with long sleeves" is the best attempt to translate *kĕtōnet passîm*. Joseph's costly robe, which sets him apart from his siblings, is one of the best-known examples of the role of clothes in biblical stories.

The *ḥăgôrâ* was a long, folded cloth of wool or linen, wound around the waist over the tunic, similar to a cummerbund or sash. Its folds could accommodate weapons and other items; for example, "Now Joab was dressed in his tunic (*middô*), and over it he was girded (*ḥăgôr*)

Ill. 138: Lachish relief from Nineveh: A Judahite family departing Lachish for exile. (Courtesy of the Expedition to Lachish, D. Ussishkin, Director; Photo: A. Hay)

Ill. 139: Glazed tile from Palace of Rameses III, Tell el-Yehudiyeh, depicting a bound Syrian, who wears the typical costume and hairstyle of a Canaanite of the twelfth century B.C.E. (Courtesy of the Trustees of the British Museum)

Ill. 140: Glazed tile from Palace of Rameses III, Tell el-Yehudiyeh, depicting a bound Libyan. (Courtesy of the Trustees of the British Museum)

Ill. 141: Glazed tile from Palace of Rameses III, Tell el-Yehudiyeh, depicting a Nubian. (Courtesy of the Trustees of the British Museum)

with a sword strapped to his hip in its sheath" (2 Sam. 20:8). As noted, to free the legs while working or traveling, the *kuttōnet* was sometimes tucked into the *ḥăgôrâ*. The word appears for the first time in the creation account, when Adam and Eve "sewed fig leaves together and made loincloths (*ḥăgōrōt*) for themselves" (Gen. 3:7).

When Shebna was about to be replaced by Eliakim, Yahweh said to Shebna: "[I] will clothe him with your robe (*kuttontekā*) and bind your sash ('*abnēṭĕkā*) on him" (Isa. 22:21). The priests were invested with the '*abnēṭ* at the ordination ceremony: "You shall gird them [Aaron and his sons] with sashes ('*abnēṭ*)" (Ex. 29:9). The '*abnēṭ* was made of "fine twisted linen, and of blue, purple, and crimson yarns, embroidered with needlework" (Ex. 39:29).

A general term for the male and female outer garment, resembling a cloak, is *kĕsût* (from the verb *kāsâ*, "to cover"). "You shall make tassels on the four corners of the garment (*kĕsût*) with which you cover (*tĕkasseh*) yourself" (Deut. 22:12). A more specific designation is *śimlâ/śalmâ* (Greek *himation*). Reaching just below the knee, it was sometimes simply wrapped around the body; at other times it was draped like a toga over the body and tied by a belt. In either case, it protected the wearer from the cold and rain. It was made from a square piece of cloth and could be decorated with a rather ornate hem for persons of high social standing. The Black Obelisk (Ill. 134b) portrays the prostrate King Jehu of Israel with a fringed outer garment draped over the left shoulder. Ordinarily the *śimlâ/śalmâ* was removed while working. It also doubled as a blanket during the night. An Israelite could secure a debt by handing over his *śimlâ/śalmâ*. The Covenant Code (Exodus 20–23) stipulated that a garment of a poor man used to secure a loan could not be retained overnight by the lender, because it was the poor person's only protection against the night cold: "If you take your neighbor's cloak (*śalmâ*) as a pledge, you shall restore it to him before sunset; his cloak is the only covering (*kĕsût*) he has for his body. What else has he to sleep in?" (Ex. 22:25–26 [E.T. 26–27]; also Deut. 24:10–13).

Among the accusations against Israel, Yahweh charges: "They lay themselves down beside every altar on garments taken in pledge (*bĕgādîm ḥăbulîm*)" (Amos 2:8). Traditionally commentators interpret "garments taken in pledge" in the sense of security for a loan. Recently Shalom Paul and others have rejected "garments taken in pledge," understanding the reference to confiscation of clothing as "distraint for an unpaid debt." Such appropriation was prohibited by law.[4] An Israelite letter of the seventh century concerning "garments taken in pledge" (impounded) is the best extrabiblical example of biblical law. This Hebrew ostracon was discovered inside the guardroom of a small fortress at Meṣad Ḥashavyahu on the Mediterranean coast near Yavneh-Yam. The letter was a complaint from a reaper (a corvée laborer) whose garment (*beged*) had been confiscated unjustly. Accused of inadequately performing his duties, he protests his innocence, petitioning a local official (*śar*) to intervene for the return of the garment.

The *mĕ'îl*, a royal robe, was an elegant outer garment with wide sleeves that hung loosely. This loose-fitting robe signifying rank and dignity was worn over all the other garments by the elite and by priests (Ex. 28:4, 31). As McCarter points out,[5] the *mĕ'îl* was the "characteristic robe" of Samuel: "His [Samuel's] mother [Hannah] used to make for him a little robe (*mĕ'îl*) and take it to him each year, when she went up with her husband [Elkanah] to offer the yearly sacrifice" (1 Sam. 2:19). When Saul was rejected as king, "Saul caught hold of the hem (*kānāp*) of his [Samuel's] robe (*mĕ'îl*), and it tore. And Samuel said to him, 'Yahweh has torn the kingdom of Israel from you this very day'" (1 Sam. 15:27–28). Grasping the hem of the garment is an act of entreaty traditional in the ancient Near East and evident as well in the New Testament story of the menstruating woman (Mark 5:27–28 and parallels). Samuel interprets the tearing of the garment as a symbol of the "tearing" of the kingdom from Saul; see also 1 Kings 11:29–32 for a related incident involving the symbolic rending of the whole garment.[6] Because Samuel was wrapped in his characteristic robe *mĕ'îl*, Saul was able to recognize him when the ghost of Samuel was conjured by the medium of Endor: "Saul said to her, 'What is his [Samuel's]

---

4. Shalom M. Paul, *A Commentary on the Book of Amos*, Hermeneia (Minneapolis: Fortress, 1991), 83–86.

5. P. Kyle McCarter, *I Samuel* AB 8 (Garden City, N.Y.: Doubleday, 1980), 421.

6. Ibid., 268.

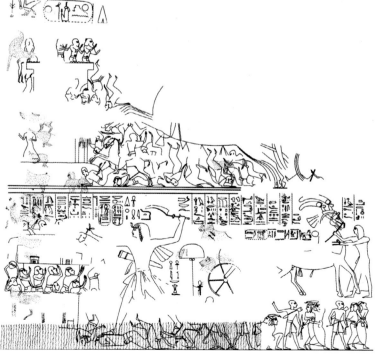

Ill. 142a-b: Reliefs of Merneptah, from late thirteenth century at Karnak. In the two lower registers to the left, not specifically identified, are Gezer and Yano'am, as mentioned on Merneptah's victory stela. This wall relief has been attributed to Rameses II, but is now dated to Merneptah. Note that Israelites in the upper register wear the same kind of costume and have the same kind of hairdos as Canaanites of Ashkelon (second register from top), who are identified in the inscription to the right of their citadel. (Drawing and reconstruction: © L. E. Stager, with F. Yurco)

Ill. 143: Bronze Bands, Gates of Balawat. Campaign in Northern Syria, 858 B.C.E. (Upper Register) Shalmaneser III receiving tribute from the Unqians; Shalmaneser III on right. The tribute includes bronze cauldrons, trays filled with unknown items, and metal ingots. (Lower Register) Syrian princess with her dowry and tribute being given to Shalmaneser III. (Courtesy of the Trustees of the British Museum)

appearance?' She said, 'An old man is coming up; he is wrapped in a robe (*mĕʿîl*).' So Saul knew that it was Samuel" (1 Sam. 28:14).

When Jonathan made a covenant with David, "Jonathan stripped himself of the robe (*mĕʿîl*) that he was wearing, and gave it to David, and his armor, and even his sword and his bow and his belt (*ḥăgōrô*)" (1 Sam. 18:4). Presenting the clothing and other items may have been intended to seal the covenant and to signify the transference of royal succession from Jonathan to David.[7] While David was hiding in a cave in the wilderness of Judah, Saul entered unaware of David's presence therein: "David arose and stealthily cut off the skirt (*kānāp*) of Saul's robe (*mĕʿîl*)" (1 Sam. 24:5 [E.T. 24:4]). David's action indicates his refusal to kill King Saul, which he could easily have done.

The *'adderet*, a rectangular cape or mantle of distinction, is identified in the Bible with Elijah: When he met God at Horeb, he wrapped his face in his mantle (*'addartô*) (1 Kings 19:13). "Then Elijah took his mantle (*'addartô*) and rolled it up, and struck the water" (2 Kings 2:8). Elijah bestowed this mantle on Elisha: "Elijah passed by him [Elisha] and threw his mantle (*'addartô*) over him" (1 Kings 19:19). The *'adderet* was the garment taken by Achan from among the spoils of Jericho (Josh. 7:21). It is also associated with the king of Nineveh. Responding to Jonah's preaching, the king of Nineveh removed his robe (*'addartô*) and covered himself with sackcloth (Jonah 3:6).

---

7. Ibid., 305.

Women's Dress

The apparel of women apparently did not differ much from men's, and the terms are similar. There must have been superficial distinctions, however, since cross-dressing was prohibited according to Deuteronomic law (Deut. 22:5). The female *śimlâ* was somewhat longer than the male garment. The woman's outer garment was draped around the body and over the left shoulder; the right shoulder was uncovered. The head and shoulders, and sometimes the face, were draped with a veil (*ṣā'îp*) on special occasions. Rebekah was veiled when she approached Isaac (Gen. 24:65), as was Tamar when she deceived her father-in-law Judah (Gen. 38:14, 19). The painting at Beni Hasan portrays three of the Amorite or Canaanite women wearing a piece of colored cloth wrapped around and draped over the left shoulder, with the right shoulder bare (Ill. 77). One woman's garment is rounded at the neck. No garment is worn over the tunic, which is colored and sleeveless. On the Lachish Reliefs, the women and girls wear an unadorned garment resembling a cloak, reaching just above the ankle. They also wear mantles pulled over the head like hoods. Over the tunic the women have a long shawl covering the head and shoulders, reaching to the ankles (Ill. 138).

In the Bronze Age clothing was fastened by a toggle pin. Resembling a needle, it had a hole in the middle for a cord to pass through. The fibula, which looks like a modern safety pin, replaced the toggle pin in the Iron Age.

In an indictment of the affluent women of Jerusalem, Isaiah and Ezekiel catalog female apparel and accoutrements, although some of the garments and jewelry were also worn by men of rank. Isaiah describes the attire of the vain and supercilious women of Israelite society who "walk with outstretched necks, glancing wantonly with their eyes, mincing along as they go, tinkling (*tě'akkasnâ*) with their feet" (Isa. 3:16). The identification of items is not completely certain, since several appear only once in the Bible. In Isaiah's list of twenty-one articles, thirteen pertain to jewelry and eight to attire, including the festive robes, the mantles, the cloaks, the handbags, the lace garments, the linen garments, the turbans, and the veils (Isa. 3:22–23).[8] Ezekiel gives a similar list of the finery of God's "faithless bride," symbolizing Jerusalem (Ezek. 16:10–13). His inventory includes fine linen, rich fabric, and embroidered cloth.

Footwear

In a detailed description of Jerusalem as a faithless spouse, Yahweh says: "I clothed you with embroidered cloth and shod you with dolphin fine leather (*'en'ălēk tāḥaš*)" (Ezek. 16:10). Sandals were the ordinary footwear for both men and women. The general term, *na'ălāyim*, occurs more than twenty times in the Bible. Made of a plain leather sole, sandals were secured to the feet at the ankle by a leather strap. The Black

---

8. Elizabeth E. Platt, "Jewelry, Ancient Israelite," *ABD*, 3: 823–34. A very useful study.

Obelisk portrays Jehu's attendants wearing shoes with turned-up toes, the footwear of the Hittites and Neo-Hittites of northern Syria (Ill. 134). The Assyrians wear sandals fitted with heel-caps. On the Lachish Reliefs, the Judahite men and women are barefooted (Ill. 48, 135, 138, 159), whereas the Judahite captives working on construction at Nineveh wear leggings and boots.

To protect the feet, the Israelites wore sandals outdoors, except the poor, who went barefoot; indoors, everyone was barefoot. Not wearing shoes was a sign of mourning or slavery. When Absalom rebelled, forcing David to abandon Jerusalem, "David went up the ascent of the Mount of Olives, weeping as he went, with his head covered and walking barefoot (*yāḥēp*)" (2 Sam. 15:30). In the reign of King Sargon II, when the Assyrians conquered Ashdod, Yahweh commanded Isaiah: "Go, and loose the sackcloth from your loins and take your sandals off your feet" (Isa. 20:2).

Sandals were removed as a sign of respect, such as when entering sacred precincts. In the account of Moses and the burning bush, Yahweh said: "Come no closer! Remove the sandals from your feet, for the place on which you are standing is holy ground" (Ex. 3:5). Joshua experienced a similar theophany (the appearance of a divine being) in the vicinity of Jericho: "The commander of the army of Yahweh said to Joshua, 'Remove the sandals from your feet, for the place where you stand is holy'" (Josh. 5:15). Today, upon entering a mosque, both Muslims and non-Muslims must remove their shoes.

Amos states in the oracle against Israel: "Thus says Yahweh: For three transgressions of Israel, and for four, I will not revoke the punishment; because they sell the righteous for silver, and the needy for a pair of sandals (*na'ălāyim*)" (Amos 2:6; 8:6). The precise connotation of *na'ălāyim* is unclear, but "a pair of sandals" may represent a "paltry sum" of money for which people are sold into slavery.[9]

Sandals were used as an instrument in legalizing contracts and treaties. Exchanging sandals signified the transfer of property rights from one party to another, as in the case of Boaz and Ruth: "Now this was the custom in former times in Israel concerning redeeming and exchanging: to confirm a transaction, the one took off a sandal and gave it to the other; this was the manner of attesting in Israel. So when the next-of-kin said to Boaz, 'Acquire it [parcel of land] for yourself,' he took off his sandal'" (Ruth 4:7–8). This practice is different from the case of the *levir* (husband's brother) who refuses to marry the widow: "Then his brother's wife shall go up to him in the presence of the elders, pull his sandal off his foot, [and] spit in his face" (Deut. 25:9).

Headdress

A headdress (*pĕ'ēr*, from *pā'ar*, "to adorn") resembling a turban was wrapped around the head or secured with string to provide protection from the sun. Contrary to mourning customs, when Ezekiel's spouse died, Yahweh instructed the prophet:

---

9. Francis I. Andersen and David N. Freedman, *Amos: A New Translation with Notes and Commentary*, AB 24A (New York: Doubleday, 1989), 312.

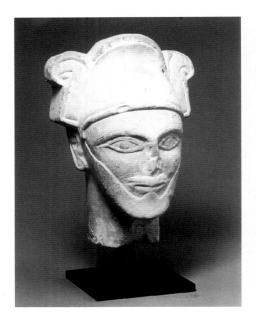

Ill. 144: Limestone head of king or deity wearing the *atef* crown from the Amman citadel, dated Iron II. (Courtesy of the Amman Archaeological Museum and P. Bienkowski)

Ill. 145: Phoenician eye-bead from Ashkelon, to avert the evil eye. (Courtesy of the Leon Levy Expedition to Ashkelon; Photo: C. Andrews)

Ill. 146: Syrians bringing tribute to an Egyptian official; Dynasty 18, Thebes. The first man has typical Canaanite beard and hairstyle, bound by a fillet; he wears a blue kilt. The second figure wears a long-sleeved garment with colored border. (Courtesy of the Trustees of the British Museum)

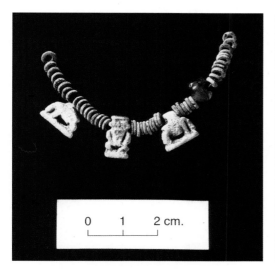

Ill. 147: Necklace of beads and amulets, found in 604 B.C.E. destruction of Ashkelon. (Courtesy of the Leon Levy Expedition to Ashkelon; Photo: I. Sztulman)

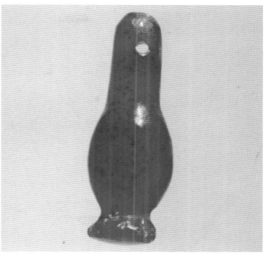

Ill. 148: Carnelian bead or pendant in form of lotus bud, from Ashkelon, dated LB II. (Courtesy of the Leon Levy Expedition to Ashkelon; Photo: I. Sztulman)

Ill. 149: Lapis lazuli amulet from Ashkelon, dated to eighth–seventh centuries B.C.E. (Courtesy of the Leon Levy Expedition to Ashkelon; Photo: I. Sztulman)

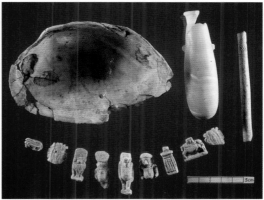

Ill. 150: Necklace of amulets, along with a shell box, an alabastron for precious oils, and an incised bone handle from the 604 B.C.E. destruction at Ashkelon. (Courtesy of the Leon Levy Expedition to Ashkelon; Photo: C. Andrews)

"Make no mourning for the dead. Bind on your turban (*pĕ'ēr*), and put sandals on your feet" (Ezek. 24:17). The Black Obelisk depicts bearded Israelite attendants with pointed caps or turbans. On the Lachish Reliefs the men wear fringed headscarves wound around the head, covering the ears and extending to the shoulders. In another scene the Judahites are pictured with short hair and beards, both tightly curled.

Ill. 152: Faience figurine of god Bes, found in 604 B.C.E. destruction of Ashkelon. (Courtesy of the Leon Levy Expedition to Ashkelon; Photo: C. Andrews)

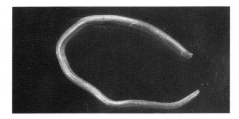

Ill. 151: Silver amulet from Ketef Hinnom, inscribed with the Priestly Benediction (Num. 6: 24–26). The first occurrence of "Yahweh" on an object excavated in Jerusalem. Dates about 600 B.C.E. (Courtesy of the Israel Museum)

Ill. 153: Gold loop earring from Ashkelon, dated to Late Bronze II. (Courtesy of the Leon Levy Expedition to Ashkelon; Photo: I. Sztulman)

Jewelry and Ornaments

In antiquity as today, both men and women wore jewelry and ornaments, which served a variety of purposes in Near Eastern society. In his lament over Saul and Jonathan, David exhorts: "Daughters of Israel, weep over Saul, who clothed you with crimson, in luxury, who put ornaments of gold (*ădî zāhāb*) on your apparel" (2 Sam. 1:24).

Jewelry was a sign of status and wealth; in addition, ornaments functioned as a form of currency. Jewelry also served religious purposes. For example, ornaments were sometimes worn around the neck as charms or amulets, whose assumed magical properties provided protection for the wearer or warded off evil spirits. While jewelry was used

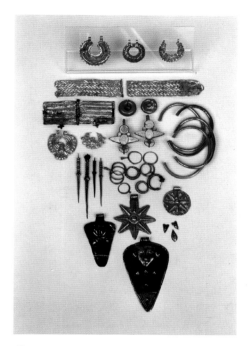

Ill. 154: Gold jewelry including pendant amulets of the goddess Asherah (bottom and lower left). Tell el-'Ajjul, dated Late Bronze I. (Courtesy of the Israel Museum; Photo: A. Hay)

Ill. 155: Philistine gold earring with granular decoration from Ashkelon, dated to tenth century B.C.E. (Courtesy of the Leon Levy Expedition to Ashkelon; Photo: I. Sztulman)

for adornment, it had a much more powerful purpose as amulets and prophylactics—to protect the wearer from the "evil eye" and every other sort of evil. This was especially true of lustrous metals like iron, which were considered to have apotropaic power.

Beads are found more frequently in burials than any other artifact. They were used for adornment and as amulets. Eye-beads to deflect the "evil eye" are common in Phoenician graves, though less so in Israelite/Judahite ones (Ill. 145). No precise Hebrew word signifies "amulet" in the Bible, but lĕḥāšîm (lāḥaš, "to charm") and bāttê hannepeš, "houses of life," probably denote amulets. The small silver amulet incised with the divine name YHWH and found at Ketef Hinnom in Jerusalem was worn as part of a necklace (Ill. 151). Jewels also adorned the high priest's garb; for example, the breastplate (ḥōšen) was bedecked with four horizontal rows of precious stones, three in each row (Ex. 28:15–21; 39:8–14).

Egypt (especially its wall paintings) is an invaluable source of information about jewelry (Ill. 39, 146, 169). Archaeological excavations in which ancient jewelry has survived also help greatly in clarifying the precise nature of jewels and ornaments. Graves, as mentioned, are especially rich in these remains buried with the deceased, as are caches of jewelry hidden for safekeeping under the floors of private dwellings or sanctuaries. Practically all the burial sites in the Iron Age have produced anklets, bracelets, earrings, and beads.

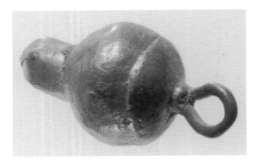

Ill. 156: Gold pendant in the shape of a plant from Ashkelon. (Courtesy of the Leon Levy Expedition to Ashkelon; Photo: I. Sztulman)

Ill. 157: Jewelry from tomb at Ketef Hinnom, dated late seventh or early sixth century B.C.E. (Courtesy of the Israel Museum)

Two biblical terms applied to jewelry have generic meanings—*kĕlî*, "jewels," and *'ădî*, "ornaments." In the prophet's description, God clothes Israel with "the garments of salvation" and "the robe of righteousness," just as "a bride adorns (*ta'deh*) herself with her jewels (*kēleyhā*)" (Isa. 61:10). Biblical catalogs of more specific terms are difficult to interpret for a variety of reasons: the meanings of many articles named are uncertain, the context is not always clear, and for us the descriptions are vague. The narrative of Abraham's servant securing a bride for Isaac in Aram-naharaim mentions several items of jewelry (Gen. 24:1–67).

The inventory of jewelry in Isaiah 3:18–21 is the most inclusive in the Bible. *'ăkāsîm* are bangles that may be worn as bracelets or anklets. *šĕbîsîm* may be head-

Ill. 158: Finger ring with a scarab setting from Ashkelon. (Courtesy of the Leon Levy Expedition to Ashkelon; Photo: I. Sztulman)

bands, but more likely they are star-disc pendants.[10] *śahărōnîm* are crescents, sometimes placed as decorations around the necks of camels: "Gideon proceeded to kill Zebah and Zalmunna; and he took the crescents (*śahărōnîm*) that were on the necks of their camels" (Judg. 8:21). "The weight of the golden earrings that he [Gideon] requested was one thousand seven hundred shekels of gold (apart from the crescents [*śahărōnîm*] and the pendants [*nĕṭipôt*] and the purple garments worn by the kings of Midian)" (Judg. 8:26). *nĕṭipôt* (*nāṭap*, "to drop") are drop-shaped pendants for the ears. *śērôt* are necklace cords; *rĕ'ālôt* are beads; *pĕ'ērîm* are headdresses; *ṣĕ'ādôt* are bracelets of the royal insignia. The Amalekite "took the diadem (*nēzer*) that was on Saul's head and the bracelet (reading: *ṣĕ'ādâ*) that was on his arm," and brought them to David (2 Sam. 1:10). McCarter suggests that the *nēzer* was an emblem worn on the forehead. *qiśśurîm* are sashes. *bāttê hannepeš* (literally, "houses of life") are in the form of small cloth bags filled with amulets and placed between the breasts.[11] *lĕḥāšîm* (*lāḥaš*, "to charm") are amulets or snake charms. *ṭabbā'ōt* are signet rings; *nizmê hā'āp* are nose rings.

Ezekiel (16:11–13) includes the following among marriage jewelry: *ṣĕmîdîm* are bangles in the form of rigid bracelets. *rābîd* designates a chain for the neck, perhaps the Egyptian beaded broad-collar presented to Joseph: "Removing his signet ring (*ṭabba'tô*) from his hand, Pharaoh put it on Joseph's hand; he arrayed him in garments of fine linen, and put a gold chain (*rĕbid hazzāhāb*) around his neck" (Gen. 41:42). *nezem* is a "nose ring" with a small mulberry pendant for ears or nose. In making the "golden calf," Aaron used *nizmê hazzāhāb*, "gold rings" (on the ears) (Ex. 32:2). *'ăgîlîm* are earrings, specifically lunates or ovoid loops. *'ăṭārâ* is a crown: "David took the crown (*'ăṭārâ*) of Milcom [the Ammonites' national god] from his [the god's] head: its weight was a talent of gold [33.75 kg], and in it was a precious

---

10. K. R. Maxwell-Hyslop, *Western Asiatic Jewellery c. 3000–612 B.C.* (London: Methuen, 1971), 241. This study is especially helpful on the whole topic of jewelry.

11. Othmar Keel, *The Song of Songs* (Minneapolis: Fortress, 1994), 65.

stone, which afterward was upon David's own head" (2 Sam. 12:30). Obviously the stone, not the heavy crown, was placed on David's head.[12]

Perfumes

That "scented oil (*šemen*) and incense (*qĕṭōret*) make the heart glad" is proverbial (Prov. 27:9). Perfumed oil was utilized in both sacral and secular contexts for anointing (oiling) the body and inanimate objects. Perfume was used in religious ritual, burial preparation, personal grooming, healing, and a variety of other circumstances. In the ancient Near East, blenders used oil as the base in the production of perfumes; today alcohol is normally used. In Palestine, olive oil (*šemen zayit*) was the liquid base for blending; in Mesopotamia, it was sesame oil.

Perfumes and cosmetics were worn by both men and women, rich and poor, in ancient Israel. Practically everyone used scented oils to mask offensive odors and to protect the skin from the dry heat and the bright sun. Naomi directed her daughter-in-law Ruth: "Bathe and oil (*sûk*) yourself and put on your best attire" (Ruth 3:3). Of course, certain luxury uses were limited to royalty and the affluent. Before young women were presented to King Ahasuerus (Xerxes I), they had to spend twelve months in cosmetic treatment, "six months with oil of myrrh (*šemen hammōr*) and six months with perfumes (*bĕśāmîm*) and cosmetics (*tamrûqîm*) for women" (Esth. 2:12). Perfume was sprinkled on clothing—myrrh, aloes, and cassia perfumed the king's robes on his wedding day: "Your [the king's] robes are all fragrant with myrrh (*mōr*) and aloes (*'ăhālôt*) and cassia (*qĕṣî'ôt*)" (Ps. 45:9 [E.T. 45:8]). The Bible narrates many stories about the use of cosmetics and perfumes in daily life. For example, after the death of Bathsheba and David's first child, the king "rose from the ground, washed and oiled (*sûk*) himself, changed his clothes, and went to the house of Yahweh to worship" (2 Sam. 12:20).

Perfumes and spices were valued as much as gold and silver. Among the luxury items Hezekiah showed to envoys from Babylon from his treasure house (*bêt nĕkōt*) were silver, gold, spices (*habbĕśāmîm*), and precious oil (*šemen haṭṭôb*) (2 Kings 20:13). For several reasons, perfumes were costly. Of course only natural materials, not synthetics, were used. Moreover, the process of extracting the product from plants was tedious, producing only small amounts of perfume. Importing plants and resins from distant places like South Arabia and Somalia added to the expense. The prophetic disdain for such luxuries in comparison to the demands of Yahweh is palpable: "Of what use to me [God] is frankincense (*lĕbônâ*) that comes from Sheba [in southwest Arabia], or sweet cane (*qāneh haṭṭôb*) from a distant land?" (Jer. 6:20). The aromatic oil from sweet cane was used in the holy anointing oil and in perfume. Only a limited number of plants, including henna (for dyeing hair), saffron, balm, and laudanum, were indigenous to Palestine. Because perfumes and cosmetics were so costly, they were dispensed in tiny containers, such as juglets and pyxides.

---

12. P. Kyle McCarter, *II Samuel*, AB 9 (Garden City, N.Y.: Doubleday, 1984), 313.

Perfumer

The common Hebrew verb meaning "to mix" or "to compound" perfumed oint-ments is *rāqaḥ* (Akkadian *ruqqu*). The perfumer's techniques in blending ointments resemble a chef's preparations for a banquet. Various procedures are used so that the odorless fats or oils will absorb the fragrance, or essence, pressed from fresh flow-ers. The process is known as enfleurage. Maceration (steeping in water) consists in crushing, boiling in oil, and stirring the raw material (bark, flowers, roots) to make it soft. Oil presses squeeze out, or express, the liquid essences.

Great skill was required to blend the ingredients of the holy anointing oil (*šemen mišḥat-qōdeš*) composed of myrrh (*mōr*), cinnamon (*qinnāmôn*), sweet cane (*qāneh*), and cassia (*qiddâ*) (Ex. 30:23–25). The holy incense consisted of four perfumes: stacte, onycha, galbanum, and frankincense (Ex. 30:34–35). In biblical tradition, an early maker of perfumes was Bezalel, a skillful and versatile craftsman (Ex. 37:29).

Cosmetics

Cosmetic eye paints were in common use among the Egyptians and Babylonians to emphasize the eyes, to protect them from the bright sun, to relieve eye ailments, and to protect the eyes from insects. Eye paint (Hebrew *pûk*) was worn in ancient Israel as well; one of Job's daughters had the name Keren-happuch ("horn of eye paint") (Job 42:14).

The eye paint was probably composed of a powdered mineral, galena (a gray lead ore) or malachite (a green copper ore). The galena was used to make black eye paint called kohl, and the malachite served to produce green eye makeup. Egyptian women painted the upper eyelids and eyebrows black and the lower eyelids green. The eye paint was stored in a small horn or vase and was applied with a stick of wood, bone, ivory, glass or bronze. Cosmetic palettes of limestone from the Iron Age have been found in Palestine.

Among the Israelites, eye paint was frequently associated with women of ill repute or evil intent: "When Jehu came to Jezreel, Jezebel heard of it; she painted her eyes with kohl (*wattāśem bappûk*), and adorned her head, and looked out the window" (2 Kings 9:30). For Jeremiah, Jerusalem can be personified as a prostitute: "And you, O deso-late one, what do you mean that you dress in crimson, that you deck yourself with ornaments of gold, that you enlarge your eyes with kohl (*tiqrĕ'î bappûk*)?" (Jer. 4:30). Similarly, Ezekiel portrays unfaithful Jerusalem as the prostitute Oholibah: "They even sent for men to come from far away, to whom a messenger was sent, and they came. For them you bathed yourself, painted (*kāḥal*) your eyes, and decked yourself with ornaments" (Ezek. 23:40). The Hebrew root *kḥl*, used only in this verse, signifies the act of applying eye paint. A kohl spoon in ivory, dating to the first half of the eighth century, was found at Hazor. An Iron II Judahite wine decanter from the Hebron area has incised on its shoulder this Hebrew inscription: "Belonging to Yaḥzeyahu, wine of Kḥl." Here *kḥl*, "to paint the eyelids," is a place-name (*koḥel*) designating a special wine named for the vineyard where it originated.[13]

Cosmetic Containers

Stone vessels were ideal perfume containers. The best known cosmetic jar is called an alabastron, made of alabaster (Ill. 150). Containers of stone and alabaster helped to keep the contents cool. Since cosmetics are very costly, small containers sufficed for the quantities in which they were sold.

Carrot-shaped perfume bottles, as well as spherical perfume containers, all dating to the sixth or fifth centuries (Persian period), have come from burial caves at Ketef Hinnom, situated west of Jerusalem. Cosmetic containers made of ivory and wood in the shape of ducks, popular in Palestine from the second half of the second millennium, have been found at Megiddo, Dan, Lachish,

Ill. 159: Lachish Relief from Nineveh: deportees departing through the city gate. (Courtesy of the Expedition to Lachish, D. Ussishkin, Director; Photo: A. Hay)

and Gezer. Also, utensils for applying cosmetics have been recovered, as well as decorated bowls for grinding and mixing cosmetics.

Several biblical texts refer to cosmetic containers. When Samuel anointed Saul, he "took a juglet (*pak*) of oil and poured it on his head" (1 Sam. 10:1). Later Yahweh said to Samuel: "I have rejected him [Saul] from being king over Israel. Fill your horn (*qarněkā*) with oil and set out" (1 Sam. 16:1). Elisha ordered a member of the company of prophets (Hebrew "sons of the prophets"): "Take this juglet (*pak*) of oil in your hand, and go to Ramoth-gilead" (2 Kings 9:1).

Grooming

One must be cautious in generalizing about hair styles, not only because our sources provide limited information, but also because considerable change can occur over

---

13. Nahman Avigad, "Two Hebrew Inscriptions on Wine-Jars," *IEJ* 22 (1972): 1–9.

time. Reliefs, sculptures, and monuments provide valuable information about hair fashions in Egypt and Mesopotamia; for ancient Israel, there are a few written sources as well as fertility figurines.

Both men and women wore long hair as a mark of beauty. Hairpins, commonly found on excavations, are made of bone, ivory, or metal and are sometimes adorned with carved heads of humans or animals. A woman's hair, hanging down the back below the shoulders, is compared to a "flock of goats, moving down the slopes of Gilead" (Song of Sol. 4:1); a man's "locks are curled, black as a raven" (Song of Sol. 5:11). On the Lachish Reliefs, the prisoners facing Assyrian King Sennacherib have short, tightly curled hair and beards.

David's son Absalom is praised for his good looks, and the text cites his long hair as one of his distinguishing attributes: When he cut his hair at the end of every year, "He weighed the hair of his head, two hundred shekels by the king's weight [about two kilograms])" (2 Sam. 14:26). Ironically his beautiful hair proved to be his undoing when it became tangled in a tree: "Absalom was riding on his mule (*pered*), and the mule went under the thick branches of a great terebinth. His head got caught in the terebinth, and he was left hanging between heaven and earth, while the mule that was under him went on" (2 Sam. 18:9). Samson was also endowed with remarkable hair; he is described as having "seven locks" on his head, which Delilah weaved into the warp on her loom (Judg. 16:13–14). Isaiah, describing the humiliation of the women of Zion, refers to their "well-coiffed hair" (*ma'ăśeh miqśeh*), which would be reduced to "baldness" (*qorḥâ*) in the day of judgment (Isa. 3:24).

Among the neighboring peoples the head and beard were shaved as a sign of mourning or impending doom. The Israelites, too, practiced such mourning rites, specifically prohibited by later Levitical injunction (Lev. 21:5). After the murder of Gedaliah the governor, "eighty men arrived from Shechem and Shiloh and Samaria, with their beards shaved and their clothes torn, and their bodies gashed, bringing grain offerings and incense to present at the Temple of Yahweh" (Jer. 41:5).

The Torah forbade the shaving of the edges of the beard. "You shall not round off the hair on your temples or mar the edges of your beard" (Lev. 19:27). To shave the beard of another was a sign of disgrace, just as to expose another's buttocks was an act of humiliation. Hanun, king of the Ammonites, suspected David's envoys: "So, Hanun seized David's envoys, shaved off half the beard of each, cut their skirts in half up to the buttocks, and sent them away" (2 Sam. 10:4). McCarter interprets these two acts as "symbolic castration."[14]

Mirrors

Mirrors are ordinarily associated with Egypt. Handheld mirrors (Heb. *mar'ōt*), known as early as the mid-third millennium in Egypt, were greatly valued. When

---

14. McCarter, *II Samuel*, 270.

monarchs exchanged gifts, mirrors were often included. They were made of highly polished metal, often bronze, copper, silver, gold, and electrum. Typically the mirrors were circular in shape, and the handles were of decorated metal, bone, or ivory. Glass mirrors did not appear until the Roman period.

An obsidian mirror dating as early as the sixth millennium (Neolithic) was discovered in a tomb at Tell Kabri in the foothills of Lower Galilee. An Egyptian bronze mirror fitted with a handle in the shape of a nude woman was found among the funerary offerings in Grave B3 of a LB cemetery north of Acco (Ill. 160). Mirrors from LB were unearthed in Palestine at Tell el-'Ajjul, Megiddo, Deir el-Balaḥ, and elsewhere. The bronze mirror from Tell el-'Ajjul near Gaza, with its handle designed like a lotus flower, was probably an Egyptian import during the Eighteenth Dynasty.

Ill. 160: Egyptian bronze mirror from Acco, dated fourteenth century B.C.E. Handle in form of Egyptian deity. (Courtesy of the Israel Museum)

Aromatics

The hot climate of 'Ein-Gedi, an oasis in the desert of Judah above the west shore of the Dead Sea, supports the growth of tropical plants. While we know the names of the tropical plants growing there, scientists are not sure that they correspond to the biblical names for aromatics. The words *bāśām*, *bōśem*, and *beśem* are used more than forty times in the Bible.[15] *bōśem* is a general term for spices. "She [the queen of Sheba] came to Jerusalem with a very great retinue, with camels bearing spices (*běśāmîm*)" (1 Kings 10:2). "The traders of Sheba and Raamah traded with you [Tyre]; they sold you the best of the balsam (*bōśem*), every precious stone, and gold for your storehouses/warehouses (*'izbônāyik*)" (Ezek. 27:22).[16] Balsam (*opobalsamum*), a viscous liquid with a pleasing fragrance, was very precious. *bōśem* is identified with *opobalsamum* (literally, "balsam sap"), a shrub or small tree whose bark is incised to obtain resin used in the preparation of balm. This process corresponds to the method for obtaining frankincense and myrrh. Note that, in the contemporary Ezekiel 27:22 passage, balsam (of highest quality) comes from Sheba and Raamah (in Najran, situated today in southwestern Saudi Arabia).

The most prominent site at 'Ein-Gedi is Tel Goren. The first permanent settlement

---

15. Michael Zohary, *Plants of the Bible* (Cambridge: Cambridge University Press, 1982), 198.
16. Igor M. Diakonoff, "The Naval Power and Trade of Tyre," *IEJ* 42 (1992): 182–84.

(Str V) dates to the Late Iron Age (630–582 B.C.E.). On the basis of the layout of the buildings and courtyards, as well as the arrangement of the various pottery vessels and tools, Benjamin Mazar conjectured that the settlement was a commercial center, under royal auspices, for the production of perfume balm. The workshops contained large ceramic barrels, which may have served as furnaces. Set close together in rows and surrounded by charcoal and ashes, these vessels may have been stills for the distillation of balsam products.

MUSIC, SONG, AND DANCE

Music and Its Functions

The importance of music in the life of ancient Israel is seen in the legend of Genesis that lists musician among the three primary professions, along with herdsman and metal worker: Jubal "was the ancestor of all those who play the lyre (*kinnôr*) and pipe (*'ûgāb*)" (Gen. 4:21). Although professional musicians emerged in Israel only in the time of David and Solomon, music has a much longer history in the Near East, traceable to at least 3000 B.C.E. Music, song, and dance were an integral part of daily life in antiquity, just as today. They were closely associated with Israelite religion, society, and culture, particularly Temple worship, warfare, festivals of every kind, and the life of the court.

For the postexilic period (after 538 B.C.E.), Chronicles and the Psalter, the hymn-book of the Second Temple, illuminate the development of Israelite music in the Persian period. However, many psalms antedate the Second Temple period. Dating individual psalms is far from an exact science and has undergone major shifts. Since seventy-three psalms have superscriptions or "titles" attributing them to David, scholars dated them and several others early. Critical scholarship eventually questioned this assumption and dated them late, some even to the third and second centuries B.C.E.

The excavations at Ugarit (modern Ras Shamra), an ancient Syrian city, recovered a literature (fourteenth to twelfth centuries B.C.E.) that has striking affinities with the Bible, especially the Psalter. The mythology of the storm god Ba'al and his consort Anat in the Ba'al cycle at Ugarit, for example, has influenced the composition of the Psalter. As a result of these and other links, many scholars today do not hesitate to date certain psalms to the period of the monarchy.

There are several preexilic psalms, most likely Psalms 18, 29, and 68, at the least. Psalm 18, a royal hymn of thanksgiving, is almost identical with a version in 2 Samuel 22, prompting scholars to date the psalm in the early part of the preexilic period.[17] Psalms 29 and 68 bear similarities with literature from Ugarit. The evidence is clearer with Psalm 29 than with Psalm 68, which is somewhat obscure because of its textual

---

17. Frank M. Cross and David N. Freedman, "A Royal Song of Thanksgiving: II Samuel 22 = Psalm 18a," *JBL* 72 (1953): 15–34.

uncertainties. Psalm 29, a hymn praising the power of God, is considered one of the oldest psalms in the Bible, dating as early as the tenth century. It is an adaptation of an ancient hymn to the Canaanite god Ba'al.

Although the Hebrew vocabulary of music is extensive, some of the technical terminology in the Bible, especially designations for musical instruments, is not well understood today. The uncertainty of identification is evident in the variety of nomenclature employed, as translators tend to choose designations familiar to them. The titles of the psalms contain many musical notations (technical terms, musical arrangements, and the like), the meanings of which are also elusive. Nonetheless it is clear that music (including string, wind, and percussion instruments), song, and dance figured prominently in the psalms, especially in the hymns of praise, and consequently in worship.

In dealing with literature of any era, ancient or modern, it is necessary to identify the literary form the author is using. As a result of the form-critical studies (*Formgeschichte*) of Hermann Gunkel and others,[18] it is possible to categorize the psalms, determine their type and characteristics, and trace their historical development, thereby gaining limited insight into biblical song. The major types are hymns of praise, enthronement psalms, laments, royal psalms, and songs of thanksgiving.

Egyptian and Mesopotamian evidence, both literary references and pictorial representations, supplement the somewhat meager data on music in Israelite life. An account of Sennacherib's siege of Jerusalem in 701 B.C.E. includes "male and female musicians" among the prized tribute which Hezekiah sent to Nineveh, capital of Assyria. Since they were listed among "all kinds of valuable treasures," musicians were obviously held in high regard [*ANET*, 288]. Likewise, Babylonian administrative documents in the time of Jehoiachin, king of Judah, record deliveries of oil for the sustenance of prisoners of war. Among them is included the "director of the singers from Ashkelon" whom Nebuchadrezzar deported to Babylon [*ANET*, 308]. Assyrian reliefs from the first millennium are especially informative, as are Egyptian and Mesopotamian wall paintings, figurines, and painted or coroplastic decorations on pottery vessels. Meanwhile, archaeologists continue to discover remains of musical instruments in Palestine.

The Psalter contains more references to the performance of music than any other biblical book. Music is to be understood as both vocal and instrumental. As for song, most biblical references are to religious singing, especially as part of Temple worship, but song was also a prominent feature of other celebrations. Several of the psalms describe both vocal and instrumental music in the Temple: "Your solemn processions

---

18. See, e.g., Hermann Gunkel, *Introduction to Psalms: The Genres of the Religious Lyric of Israel*, completed by Joachim Begrich (Macon: Mercer University Press, 1998; German original in 1933); and Sigmund Mowinckel, *The Psalms in Israel's Worship*, with a foreword by Robert K. Gnuse and Douglas A. Knight (Sheffield: JSOT Press, 1992; Norwegian original in 1951).

are seen, O God, the processions of my God, my King, into the sanctuary—the singers (*šārîm*) in front, the musicians (*nōgĕnîm*) last, between them girls playing tambourines (*tôpēpôt*)" (Ps. 68:25–26 [E.T. 68:24–25]). "Raise a song (*zimrâ*), sound the tambourine (*tōp*), the sweet lyre (*kinnôr*) with the harp (*nābel*). Blow the ram's horn (*šôpār*) at the new moon, at the full moon, on our festal day (Ps. 81:3–4 [E.T. 81:2–3]; also Ps. 98:4–6). The Bible has a great variety of songs both in the Psalter and elsewhere. The earliest song—the twelfth-century victory hymn of Judges 5, better known as the "Song of Deborah"—describes the defeat of a coalition of Canaanite kings under Sisera. It is sung by both Deborah and Barak, commander of the Israelite militia, who was Deborah's subordinate (Judg. 5:1).

Despite the Psalter's title—*seper tĕhillîm*, "Book of Praises"—songs of lament outnumber hymns of praise. Outside the Psalter, David's lament (*qînâ*) over Saul and his son Jonathan, occasioned by their death on Mount Gilboa, is one of the Bible's earliest and best known (2 Sam. 1:17–27). David instructed the people of Judah to learn this dirge (funeral song), technically classified as *qînâ*. Jeremiah admonished the people of Judah to lament over the imminent destruction of the nation. Women served as professional mourners when personal tragedies or national calamities struck. Their loud laments prompted the community to participate in the mourning. "Hear, O women, the word of Yahweh, and let your ears receive the word of his mouth; teach your daughters a dirge (*nehî*), and each to her neighbor a lament (*qînâ*)" (Jer. 9:19 [E.T. 9:20]).

Music and Prophecy

Music was often associated with prophecy in antiquity. Playing music was sometimes used to induce prophetic ecstasy, attributed to possession by the spirit of Yahweh. This ecstatic state was often accompanied by dancing, trances, and self-mutilation. After Samuel anointed Saul, he told the new king:

> You will meet a band of prophets coming down from the shrine (*habbāmâ*) [of Gibeah] with harp (*nēbel*), tambourine (*tōp*), flute (*ḥālîl*), and lyre (*kinnôr*) playing in front of them; they will be in a prophetic frenzy (*mitnabbĕ'îm*). Then the spirit of Yahweh will possess you, and you will be in a prophetic frenzy (*hitnabbîtā*) along with them and be turned into a different person. (1 Sam. 10:5–6)

These prophets were engaged in a form of ecstatic practice induced by music.

A terracotta cult stand, dating to the tenth century and decorated with figures of musicians playing instruments, was found at the Philistine city of Ashdod (Ill. 161). Roughly contemporary with the event described in 1 Samuel 10:5–6, the figures, resembling a Philistine-type quartet, are depicted as playing cymbals, double pipe, lyre, and tambourine. This scene is reminiscent of the prophets' orchestra, coming down from the shrine at Gibeah, whom Saul met.

In the course of Elisha's mission, music was also used to induce a prophetic ecstasy during the military campaign that King Jehoram of Israel was waging against the Moabites. Failing to find water for the army and the animals, the king appealed to Elisha, who responded: "'Get me a musician.' Then, while the musician was playing, the power of Yahweh came on [overtook] him [Elisha]. And he said, 'Thus says Yahweh, I will make this wadi full of pools'" (2 Kings 3:15–16).

David the Musician

The Bible credits David with laying the foundation for Temple music, and by reason of his association with music, Hebrew tradition assigns many of the psalms to David, although authorship cannot be proved. In his younger years David is described as "a son of Jesse the Bethlehemite [1 Sam. 16:18] who is skillful in playing (*yōdēaʿ naggēn*) the lyre (*kinnôr*)" (1 Sam. 16:16). Reputed to be a professional musician, David was summoned to the court of Saul on several occasions to soothe the king's depression: "And whenever the evil spirit from God came upon Saul, David would take the lyre (*kinnôr*) and play it; Saul would be relieved and feel better, and the evil spirit would depart from him" (1 Sam. 16:23).

From the reign of Saul onward, music was part of court life. David and several other musicians frequented the palace. Barzillai, the influential Gileadite, supported David during the time of Absalom's rebellion. So David invited him to join the courtiers in Jerusalem, but he declined because of his advanced age, saying, "Can I discern what is pleasant and what is not? . . . Can I still listen to the voice of singing men (*šārîm*) and singing women (*šārôt*)?" (2 Sam 19:36 [E.T. 19:35]). According to McCarter's analysis of Barzillai's rhetorical questions, "He has outgrown his sexual powers . . . and his other sources of pleasure; consequently, he could not enjoy court life."[19] On the occasion of Solomon's accession to the throne, David ordered, "Then blow the ram's horn (*šôpār*), and say, 'Long live King Solomon!' . . . And all the people went up after him [Solomon], playing flutes (*měḥallělîm baḥălilîm*) and rejoicing so much as to split open the earth with their shouting" (1 Kings 1:34, 40).

Music and Revelry

Music also played a role in high society. In the prophet Amos's denunciation of the dissolute behavior of the wealthy upper echelons in Samaria at sumptuous banquets (*marzēaḥ*), he describes these revelers as those "who sing idle songs (*happōrěṭîm*) to the sound of the harp (*nābel*), and like David improvise (*ḥāšěbû*) on musical instruments (*kělê-šîr*)" (Amos 6:5). In this verse Amos is ridiculing those who

---

19. McCarter, *II Samuel*, 422.

compare themselves with David.[20] In a comparable oracle against social injustice, Isaiah refers to those "whose feasts consist of lyre (*kinnôr*) and harp (*nebel*), tambourine (*tōp*) and flute (*ḥālîl*) and wine, but who do not regard the deeds of Yahweh" (Isa. 5:12).

Music also accompanied ordinary domestic events, as when Jacob departed stealthily with his family and flocks from the house of Laban. Laban complained that, had he known in advance, "I [Laban] would have sent you away with mirth (*śimḥâ*) and songs (*šîrîm*), with tambourine (*tōp*) and lyre (*kinnôr*)" (Gen. 31:27).

Music and song were an integral part of wedding festivities. Jeremiah alludes to this custom in his indictment of the people of Judah who violate their covenant with God. The punishment is meted out: "I [Yahweh] will bring to an end the sound of mirth and gladness, and the voice of the bride and bridegroom in the cities of Judah and in the bazaars (*ḥuṣôt*) of Jerusalem; for the land shall become a waste" (Jer. 7:34; also 16:9). Psalm 45 is a song for the marriage of the king, and music is an integral part of the festivities: "From ivory palaces stringed instruments (*minnî* [for *minnîm*]) make you [the king] glad" (Ps. 45:9 [E.T. 45:8]). "Ivory palaces" refers to the halls and furnishings within the palace decorated with ivory inlays.

Music, song, and dance were an essential part of vintage festivals, which could easily take on sexual overtones. Isaiah's famous song about the unfruitful vineyard begins: "Let me sing for my beloved my love-song (*šîrat dôdî*) concerning his vineyard" (Isa. 5:1). In Israelite poetry "vineyard" is the usual metaphor for "lover," as the Song of Solomon attests. As well as being a love song, Isaiah's unique poem is also a judgment oracle. In a lament over the destruction of the vineyards of Moab, Isaiah says: "Joy and gladness are taken away from the fruitful field; and in the vineyards no songs are sung (*lō'-yĕrunnān*), no shouts are raised. . . . Therefore my heart throbs like a lyre (*kinnôr*) for Moab" (Isa. 16:10–11).

Music accompanied an annual festival that resulted in abduction. The author of Judges describes how the Benjaminites, survivors of internecine warfare, were allowed to acquire new wives from non-Benjaminite land, lest they become extinct. They secured wives by abduction, perhaps while under the influence of alcohol. This took place at Shiloh (modern Seilun) in the central mountain range, about thirty kilometers north of Jerusalem. The occasion was an unspecified annual feast. The Benjaminites were instructed: "Go and lie in wait in the vineyards, and watch; when the young women of Shiloh come out to dance in the dances (*lāḥûl bammĕḥōlôt*), then come out of the vineyards and each of you carry off a wife for himself from the young women of Shiloh, and go to the land of Benjamin" (Judg. 21:20–21).

---

20. Shalom M. Paul, *Amos: A Commentary on the Book of Amos*, Hermeneia (Minneapolis: Fortress, 1991), 207.

Music and Warfare

Music, song, and dance played a part in warfare, particularly with the victory celebration after battle. Women, especially Miriam, Deborah, and Jephthah's daughter, are associated with these victory odes. After Israel's safe crossing of the Reed Sea (*yam sûp*), Miriam sang a victory song: "Then the prophet Miriam, Aaron's sister, took a tambourine in her hand; and all the women went out after her with tambourines (*tuppîm*) and with dancing (*měḥōlōt*). And Miriam sang to them: 'Sing to Yahweh, for he has triumphed gloriously; horse and chariot he has thrown into the sea' " (Ex. 15:20–21). Deborah, after the victory over a coalition of Canaanite kings, sang: "Hear, O kings; give ear, O princes; to Yahweh I will sing (*'āšîrâ*), I will make melody (*'ăzammēr*) to Yahweh, the God of Israel" (Judg. 5:3).

And, finally, the fateful meeting of Jephthah and his daughter: "Then Jephthah came to his home at Mizpah; and there was his daughter coming out to meet him with tambourines (*tuppîm*) and with dancing (*měḥōlôt*)" (Judg. 11:34).

Musical Instruments

Musical instruments were frequently played in ensemble, and scholars are able to identify a good number of them in the Bible. In Psalm 150, a fitting conclusion to the Psalter, every section of the orchestra is invited to join in the crescendo of praise for the marvelous works of God: "Praise him [God] with the blast of the horn (*šôpār*); praise him with harp (*nēbel*) and lyre (*kinnôr*); praise him with tambourine (*tōp*) and dance (*māḥōl*); praise him with strings (*minnîm*) and pipe (*'ûgāb*); praise him with resounding cymbals (*ṣilṣělê-šāma'*); praise him with clashing cymbals (*ṣilṣělê-těrû'â*) (Ps. 150:3–5).

Musical instruments, all apparently dating from early times (harps, lyres, and lutes to the third millennium B.C.E.), are divided into three basic categories—string, wind, and percussion,

Ill. 161: Terracotta cult stand of musicians, from late eleventh or early tenth century B.C.E. Ashdod. (Courtesy of Israel Museum; Photo: D. Harris)

although some cannot be satisfactorily identified. Musical instruments were constructed of bronze, iron, gold, silver, and sometimes pottery. Bone was used at times in crafting wind and percussion instruments.

Unfortunately, we are entirely too little informed about the tonal systems of the ancient Near East, and we cannot know what was considered pleasing to the ear. Quite possibly, though, these bands and orchestras dominated by strings and percussion and flutes might have sounded rather much like some Middle Eastern music today, at least from a Westerner's perspective.

Stringed Instruments

In ancient Israel, singing was generally accompanied by musical instruments. The *kinnôr*, the most frequently mentioned stringed instrument in the Bible, is often translated "lyre"

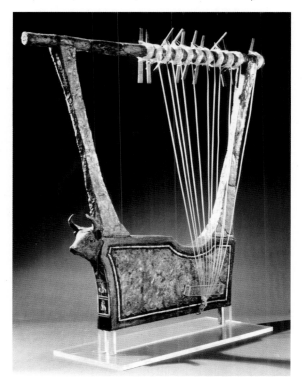

or "harp," but "lyre" is more accurate. The lyre consists of a rectangular soundbox, two asymmetrical arms, and an oblique yoke. A basic distinction between the two is the yoke or crossbar which the harp lacks. Bo Lawergren,[21] who has made an exhaustive study of lyres in the ancient Near East, distinguishes between "thin" and "thick" lyres. The former, which he identifies as "Eastern," has four to eight strings and is struck with a plectrum. "Thick" lyres have ten to thirteen strings and are plucked with the fingers. He identifies the thin lyre with the *kinnôr*, and the thick lyre with the *nēbel*. He observes that no thick lyres have been found in Palestine.

The strings of the lyre are approximately the same length. Josephus specifies that the lyre was an instrument of ten strings, sounded with a plectrum [*Ant.* 7,12,3], but the number of strings is uncertain. Like all stringed instruments, the

Ill. 162: Reconstructed royal lyre from Ur; Early Dynastic III, twenty-fifth century B.C.E. It is a typical Sumerian "bull-lyre" of the third millennium, with the sound box terminating in the head of a bearded bull. The crossbar is attached to the uprights. (Courtesy of the Trustees of the British Museum)

21. Bo Lawergren, "Distinctions among Canaanite, Philistine, and Israelite Lyres, and Their Global Lyrical Contexts," *BASOR* 309 (1998): 41–68.

lyre is ordinarily plucked with the right hand and fingered with the left. The Hebrew *nāgan* means "to play a stringed instrument," as in the statement: "Whenever the evil spirit from God came upon Saul, David took the lyre and played (*niggēn*) it with his hand" (1 Sam. 16:23). The lyre, like the harp, is a wooden instrument, fashioned from *'almug* (wood) (1 Kings 10:12). The parallel passage in 2 Chronicles has *'algum* (wood). "Almug" and "algum" are names for the same tree; in the case of "algum," the letters "m" and "g" have been transposed, as is apparent from the Ugaritic *'almg*. Botanists have made several conjectures about the tree in question, but without evidential support.

Sometimes "lyre" and "harp" appear in the same verse: "You [Saul] will meet a band of prophets coming down from the shrine with harp (*nēbel*), tambourine, flute, and lyre (*kinnôr*) playing in front of them" (1 Sam. 10:5; also Isa. 5:12). This verse is the earliest reference to *nēbel*. The *nēbel*, commonly translated "harp" (although there is room for doubt), comes from a Hebrew root meaning "skin-bottle" or "jar"; it has a waterskin-shaped sound box. The *nēbel*, according to Josephus [*Ant.* 7,12,3], has twelve strings and was plucked with the fingers. The psalmists from an earlier era state that the instrument had no more than ten strings (*nēbel 'ăśôr*, "the harp of ten strings" (Ps. 33:2; 92:4; 144:9). The strings of the *nēbel*, which was larger than the *kinnôr*, were of unequal length.

Both *kinnôr* and *nēbel* are associated with joyous occasions. Homesick, the people of Judah refused to sing the "songs of Zion" when requested by their Babylonian captors: "On the poplars there [in Babylon] we hung up our lyres (*kinnōrôtênû*). For there our captors asked us for songs . . . saying, 'Sing us one of the songs of Zion!'" (Ps. 137:2). The *nēbel* was most often played in religious contexts, whereas the *kinnôr* was employed on both religious and nonreligious occasions.

Many representations of lyres have been discovered. Remains of nine lyres dating from the Early Dynastic Period (ca. 2500 B.C.E.) were found in the Sumerian royal cemetery at Ur. Among them was an eleven-stringed wooden instrument encased entirely in silver, with a wooden sounding box terminating in a bearded bull's head (Ill. 162). It has two uprights and a crossbar.[22] The earliest depiction of an Amorite/Canaanite lyre player entering Egypt with his clan is found on a wall painting at Beni Hasan in Egypt, dating about 1900 B.C.E. He plucks his eight-stringed, thin lyre with a plectrum. The lyre is not a native instrument in Egypt.[23] One of the best illustrations comes from twelfth-century Megiddo: an ivory plaque depicting a female musician playing a nine-stringed asymmetrical lyre with the fingers of the left hand before an enthroned Canaanite king who is drinking from a bowl. This instrument may have been the prototype of the biblical *kinnôr*.

The "Orpheus" strainer-spout jug, dating to the eleventh century, was also found at Megiddo (Str VI A), a time when it was a Canaanite city with some Philistine pottery (Ill. 163). In bichrome decoration, it depicts a bearded musician playing a stringed instru-

---

22. Joan Rimmer, *Ancient Musical Instruments of Western Asia* (London: British Museum, 1969).
23. Nahman Avigad, "The King's Daughter and the Lyre," *IEJ* 28 (1978): 151.

Ill. 163: Philistine pictorial jug; the so-called "Orpheus vase" from eleventh century B.C.E. Megiddo. A lyre player and a procession of animals. Compare the rendering of the eye and beard with that of Ill. 114. (Courtesy of the Israel Museum; Photo: D. Harris)

ment (possibly a thin lyre) amid a procession of animals, among them a lion, gazelle, dog, and horse, as well as water birds, fish, crabs, and scorpions. The instrument's sounding box is square, and its two arms asymmetrical. Moving toward a stylized palm tree, the animals are not facing the musician. The scene suggests to some scholars the legend of Orpheus, the Greek hero skilled in music, who played to the animals. However, according to Benjamin Mazar,[24] the Orpheus motif was unknown in Greek art and poetry before the sixth century B.C.E. Trude Dothan[25] points out earlier parallels on seals from Tarsus and Mardin in southern Turkey. As Lawergren notes: "The *topos* of 'animals and music' began in the East long before Orpheus saw the light of day."[26]

There are several other depictions worth noting. At Kuntillet 'Ajrud (Ḥorvat Teiman), a wayside shrine in northeastern Sinai, the picture of a seated woman playing an asymmetrical, horizontal lyre (*kinnôr*) was painted on the shoulder of an eighth-century B.C.E. storage jar.[27] An alabaster relief in the palace of Sennacherib at

24. Benjamin Mazar, "The 'Orpheus' Jug from Megiddo," in F. M. Cross et al., eds., *Magnalia Dei: The Mighty Acts of God* (Garden City, N.Y.: Doubleday, 1976), 188.
25. Trude Dothan, *The Philistines and Their Material Culture* (New Haven, Conn.: Yale University, 1982), 78, 138, 149–53.
26. Lawergren, "Distinctions among Canaanite, Philistine, and Israelite Lyres," 53.
27. Pirhiya Beck, "The Drawings from Ḥorvat Teiman (Kuntillet 'Ajrud)," *TA* 9 (1982): 35–36.

Nineveh shows three lyre players followed by an Assyrian soldier. The three figures are plucking their five-stringed, oblique lyres with a plectrum. This scene was considered by some scholars to commemorate the capture of Lachish in 701 B.C.E., but the assumption is questionable.[28] From the seventh century comes a beautifully crafted seal of brown jasper, bearing the inscription "(Belonging) to Ma'adanah, the king's daughter." On the seal of Ma'adanah a twelve-stringed asymmetrical lyre (*kinnôr*) is depicted. The sound box of the lyre is elaborately decorated with a string of pearls around its outer edge and a rosette in the center.[29]

Wind Instruments

Numbered among the wind instruments are the *ḥālîl*, "flute," *qeren*, "horn," *ḥăṣōṣĕrâ*, "trumpet," and *šôpār*, "ram's horn." The *ḥālîl* (plural, *ḥălilîm*), derived from the Hebrew root *ḥll* ("to pierce," "to bore," with reference to the hollow reed from which it is made), was composed of two separate pipes of reeds, metal, or ivory, each with its own mouthpiece. Some prefer to translate *ḥālîl* as "clarinet" in place of "flute," but "double-pipe" may be best. The *ḥālîl*, occurring six times in the Bible, was ordinarily played in a joyous context, such as festivals and banquets, but it is also associated with mourning services.

When Solomon was anointed king, the common people, not only the professional musicians, played the *ḥălilîm* (1 Kings 1:40). Isaiah denounces the social injustice of the people of Judah "whose feasts consist of lyre and harp, tambourine and flute (*ḥālîl*) and wine" (Isa. 5:12). Elsewhere Isaiah mentions the *ḥālîl* in the context of a procession to the "mountain of Yahweh" (Mount Zion/Temple Mount) (Isa. 30:29). In Jeremiah's long oracle against Moab the *ḥālîl* is associated with a funeral dirge: "Hence the wail of flutes (*ḥălilîm*) for Moab is in my heart; for the people of Kîr-ḥereś [modern Kerak, capital of Moab] the wail of flutes (*ḥălilîm*) is in my heart: the wealth they acquired has perished" (Jer. 48:36). A clay Edomite figurine of a flute player with a double-stemmed flute was discovered at Tel Malḥata in the Negev, indicative of the Edomite encroachment on Judah from the late seventh to the early sixth century[30] (Ill. 165). An ivory trumpet in the form of a ram's horn was found on the Uluburun shipwreck (1300 B.C.E.).

The *qeren*, a kind of trumpet, is the general word for "horn." The *ḥăṣōṣĕrâ*, made of beaten silver or bronze, was a long straight trumpet with a limited range of notes. Perhaps "bugle" would be a better translation than "trumpet," as the trumpet, unlike the bugle, has valves that depress to give a wide range of notes. The first reference to

---

28. Rimmer, *Ancient Musical Instruments*, 34; Lawergren, "Distinctions among Canaanite, Philistine, and Israelite Lyres," 49.

29. Avigad, "The King's Daughter and the Lyre," 146–51.

30. Itzhaq Beit-Arieh, "Edomites Advance into Judah—Israelite Defensive Fortresses Inadequate," *BAR* 22 (1996): 4 (note), 28–36.

Ill. 164: Satirical papyrus from New Kingdom Egypt. Various animals engaged in human activities. To the left, an antelope and lion play the board game *senet*; the lion seems to be winning. To the right, a fox plays the double flute as he herds a small flock of goats (?), and another fox and a cat drive a flock of geese. At far right, a lion stands upright at the end of a bed and copulates with an ungulate. (Courtesy of the Trustees of the British Museum)

Ill. 165: Terracotta figurine of musician playing double flute from Tel Malhata, dated around 600 B.C.E. Approximately 10 cm high. (Courtesy of I. Beit-Arieh)

the trumpet and a summary of its uses appear in Numbers 10:2–10, where Moses is directed to make two bugles of beaten silver (ḥăṣōṣĕrōt kesep miqšâ) for the journey from the wilderness of Sinai. The bugle was blown during sacred functions, including the daily offering of sacrifice and at coronations. It was also sounded to summon the congregation, to break camp, and to signal the alarm in the time of war. In religious contexts the ḥăṣōṣĕrâ was the priests' instrument exclusively; only Aaron's descendants had the privilege of sounding the bugle, according to Numbers 10:8. On nonreligious occasions, however, those who were not priests blew the bugle. The account of the dethronement of Athaliah and the subsequent restoration of the Davidic monarchy mentions that "all the landed gentry ('am hā'āreṣ) were rejoicing and blowing bugles (ḥăṣōṣĕrôt)" (2 Kings 11:14).

The šôpār (shofar), originally a "ram's horn" and so translated, is the most frequently mentioned musical instrument in the Bible. It is probably identical with the qeren. The account of Joshua's capture of Jericho mentions repeatedly "seven priests bearing seven rams' horns (šôpĕrôt hayyôbĕlîm) before the Ark" (Josh. 6:4; šôpār and yôbēl describe the ram's horn). Translators who frequently fail to distinguish between the "ram's horn" (šôpār) and the "bugle" (ḥăṣōṣĕrâ) cause confusion by rendering these terms arbitrarily.

Strictly speaking, the shofar, while related to the bugle, is not a musical instrument; it simply emits a loud sound. A long horn with an upturned end and piercing tone, the shofar was used in both religious and military contexts (Judg. 3:27; 6:34) and in national celebrations. When Solomon was anointed king, David ordered the ram's horn (šôpār) to be blown (1 Kings 1:34). The shofar was a signaling instrument used to summon people and to alert them to danger. When launching his rebellion, Absalom prompted his "secret messengers" (mĕraggĕlîm) to shout "Absalom has become king at Hebron" upon hearing the sound of the ram's horn (šôpār) (2 Sam. 15:10). When the Ark was transported to Jerusalem, only the šôpār ("horn") accompanied the procession, according to 2 Samuel 6:15; both the šôpār ("horn") and the ḥăṣōṣĕrôt ("bugles"), according to 1 Chronicles 15:28.

The diversity of translations for 'ûgāb illustrates the difficulty of determining the nature of this musical instrument. Some even think it is a stringed instrument. On the basis of a parallel construction with minnîm, "strings" in the Psalter, it appears to be a collective, not a specific, term for wind instruments. "Praise him [Yahweh] with strings (minnîm) and pipe (*ʿûgāb*)!" (Ps. 150:4). *ʿûgāb*, derived from the Hebrew root *ʿāgab* "to love passionately," was a secular instrument and was not used in the Temple. Marvin Pope[31] suggested that *ʿûgāb* designates the single pipe or true flute, and *ḥālîl* the double pipe.

Percussion Instruments

The *mĕṣiltayim* (a dual form meaning a pair of cymbals) and *ṣelṣĕlîm* (related to *mĕṣiltayim*) are synonymous terms [*ANEP*, 202] derived from the Hebrew root *ṣll* "to ring," "to resound." Translated "cymbals," they are copper or bronze (*nĕḥōšet*) (1 Chronicles 15:19) percussion instruments found in Egypt, the Levant, and Assyria. Representations of cymbals date as early as the end of the third millennium B.C.E. Bronze finger cymbals from LB were found in the vicinity of the *migdāl* temple (2048) at Megiddo. Additional examples date to Iron I. Bronze cymbals (fourteenth century B.C.E.) measuring ten centimeters in diameter were discovered in a Canaanite shrine located in the lower city of Hazor. A tiny wire affixed to the center of the cymbal slipped over the musician's finger. Bronze cymbals are frequently found in tombs as well as in temples. The earliest biblical reference to *ṣelṣĕlîm* appears at the transfer of the Ark to Jerusalem: "David and all the house of Israel were dancing before Yahweh with all their might, with songs, lyres, harps, tambourines, sistrums, and cymbals (*ṣelṣĕlîm*)" (2 Sam. 6:5). The only other occurrence of *ṣelṣĕlîm* is in Psalm 150. Cymbals seem to be used in the context of ritual. *mĕṣiltayim*, the exilic and postexilic term, appears only in 1 and 2 Chronicles, Ezra, and Nehemiah.

The *tōp* (plural, *tuppîm*) designates all kinds of hand drums or tambourines. The small, shallow, handheld frame drum is a simple instrument frequently played by women, as in the case of Miriam, and associated with the dance. It was struck with the hand, not with sticks. In the Bible, the frame drum is associated with joyous occasions and with worship. When David returned from slaying the Philistine, the women greeted King Saul and David "with tambourines (*tuppîm*), with songs of joy, and with musical instruments" (1 Sam. 18:6; also Ex. 15:20; 2 Sam. 6:5). A comparable instrument, called *duf* in Arabic, consists

Ill. 166: Rasp made from incised bone scapula, with perforation at one end, dated to Iron Age I. (Courtesy of the Leon Levy Expedition to Ashkelon; Photo: I. Sztulman)

---

31. Marvin Pope, *Job*, AB 15 (Garden City, N.Y.: Doubleday, 1965), 196.

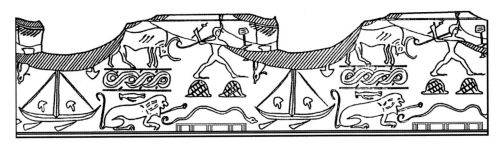

Ill. 167: Cylinder seal impression from Avaris. Ba'al Ṣaphon striding from mountain to mountain. Dated to first half of eighteenth century B.C.E. (Courtesy of M. Bietak)

of goatskin stretched over a frame of wood, about twenty-five centimeters in diameter and five centimeters deep.

A clay mold for the manufacture of terracotta figurines of the "lady with the tambourine" was discovered in a tenth-century cultic structure at Ta'anach. She holds a disc over the left breast. Delbert Hillers[32] identified her as a goddess; if not, she does seem to represent a temple/sanctuary female musician. Many figurines of women holding flat circular objects have come to light in the Levant and in Mesopotamia. Scholars differ in the interpretation of this object, but most agree that it is a tambourine, not a loaf of bread (see also Ill. 220).

Dance

Although the biblical writers do not describe dancing in detail, it is a form of religious praise that goes hand in hand with music.[33] The Bible has a dozen verb roots to designate dance, among them *rqd* "to skip," *krr* "to hop," *pzz* "to leap," and *ḥwl* "to whirl."

maḥôl and *mĕḥôlâ* (from *ḥwl*) signify the "round dance" commonly, but not exclusively, performed by women. Women accompanied Miriam in her victory song "with tambourines and with dancing (*mĕḥōlōt*)" (Ex. 15:20). When Jephthah returned from battle to Mizpah, he was greeted by his daughter "with tambourines and with dancing (*mĕḥōlôt*)" (Judg. 11:34). When David came back from slaying the Philistine, women met King Saul and David with singing and dancing (*mĕḥōlôt*) (1 Sam. 18:6). Jeremiah cites a salvation oracle about the return from Babylonian exile: "Then shall the young women rejoice in the dance (*māḥôl*)" (Jer. 31:13). After Aaron had fashioned the "golden calf" during Moses's prolonged absence on Mount Sinai, the Israelites celebrated with dancing (*mĕḥōlōt*) and revelry (Ex. 32:19). It is not possible from the Hebrew syntax to determine who were dancing—men, women, or both. Religious and secular feasts were joyful occasions celebrated with music and

---

32. Delbert Hillers, "The Goddess with the Tambourine," *Concordia Theological Monthly* 41 (1970): 606–19.
33. Yosef Garfinkel, "Dancing and the Beginning of Art Scenes in the Early Village Communities of the Near East and Southeast Europe," *Cambridge Archaeological Journal* 8 (1998): 207–37.

dance. On the occasion of the yearly festival at Shiloh, the young women came out "to join in the dances (*lāḥûl bammĕḥōlôt*)" (Judg. 21:21).

As the Ark of the Covenant was being brought to the royal city of Jerusalem to be installed in the sanctuary:

> David danced (*mĕkarkēr*) before Yahweh with all his might; David was girded with a linen ephod. So David and all the house of Israel brought up the Ark of Yahweh with shouting, and with the sound of the (ram's) horn (*šôpār*). As the Ark of Yahweh came into the city of David, Michal daughter of Saul looked out of the window, and saw King David leaping (*mĕpazzēz*) and dancing (*mĕkarkēr*) before Yahweh. (2 Sam. 6:14–16)

This may be the only specific biblical reference to a male dancing. Since the "linen ephod" was a priestly garment, David may have been performing the ritual dance as a priest. The *šôpār* would have served to assemble the people rather than to make music.

At Mount Carmel the name of Ba'al is associated with a hopping dance: "They [prophets of Ba'al] took the bull that was given them, prepared it, and called on the name of Ba'al from morning until noon, shouting, 'O Ba'al, answer us.' But there was no voice, and no answer. So they performed a hopping dance (*waypassĕḥû*) about the altar that had been set up" (1 Kings 18:26). A "hopping dance" designates a ritual dance. In his comments on this verse, John Gray observes: "A local manifestation of Ba'al in Lebanon was Ba'al Marqad ('Ba'al of the Dance')."[34] There are other references to dancing deities. A cylinder seal from MB II Avaris depicts Ba'al Ṣaphon "skipping" (*rqd*) from mountain to mountain[35] (Ill. 167).

Dancing in Israel, unlike the Egyptian practice, was not associated with mourning or burials. The Psalmist juxtaposes mourning and dancing: "Your face turned my mourning into dancing (*māḥôl*); you have taken off my sackcloth and clothed me with joy" (Ps. 30:12 [E.T. 30:11]). So, too, the author of Ecclesiastes, who states that everything has an appointed time: "A time to weep, and a time to laugh; a time to mourn, and a time to dance (*rĕqôd*)" (Eccl. 3:4). The Psalter contains several refer-

Ill. 168: "Dancer from Dan"; a clay plaque depicting a male dancer who is playing a lute-like instrument, from Late Bronze Age. (Courtesy of Tel Dan Excavations, Hebrew Union College, Jerusalem; Photo: Z. Radovan)

---

34. John Gray, *I and II Kings*, OTL (Philadelphia: Westminster, 1963), 353. Roland de Vaux, "Les prophètes de Baal sur le Mont Carmel," *Bulletin du Musée de Beyrouth* 5 (1941): 9, concurs with the interpretation of a ritual dance around the altar: "ils dansaient en pliant le genou devant l'autel."

35. Edith Porada, "The Cylinder Seal from Tell el-Dab'a," *AJA* 88 (1984): 485.

Ill. 169: (Upper Register) Banquet scene from Nebamun, Thebes, Egypt; eighteenth dynasty. A nude girl wearing amulets, bracelets, and a hip girdle serves a drink to a guest. (Lower Register) To the right, a stack of wine jars for the banquet. A musician plays the double flute accompanied by three women clapping hands while two nude young girls, wearing hip girdles, perform an erotic dance. (Courtesy of the Trustees of the British Museum); see also Ill. 21 for female musicians.

ences to dancing in association with religious observance, for example: "Let them praise his [God's] name with dancing (*māḥôl*), making melody (*yĕzammĕrû*) to him with tambourine and lyre" (Ps. 149:3). A molded clay plaque found at Tel Dan was aptly dubbed by the excavator, Avraham Biran, as "the dancer from Dan." Dating to LB it depicts a man playing a stringed instrument resembling a lute, his right foot raised in a dancing posture[36] (Ill. 168).

LITERACY AND SCHOOLS

Evidence of Writing

The earliest writing, confined to elite scribes, was found at Uruk (biblical Erech, modern Warka) on the Euphrates and dates about 3100 B.C.E. Shortly thereafter, writing appeared in the Nile Valley. Cuneiform and hieroglyphic writing flourished for the next three millennia. This is not to suggest, however, that the Mesopotamians and the Egyptians

---

36. Avraham Biran, *Biblical Dan* (Jerusalem: Israel Exploration Society, 1994), 120–21.

1500	13th	1200	12th	1100	11th	1000	10th	ca.770	ca.600

Ill. 170: "Script chart" showing the evolution of the alphabet from 1500–600 B.C.E. To left are the pictographs which represent the rebus principle. (Courtesy of Frank Moore Cross)

were literate on a grand scale. With regard to the Egyptians, John Baines proposes that, most often, not more than one percent of the population was literate.[37]

The alphabet was invented by the Canaanites early in the second millennium B.C.E. The first alphabetic system, consisting of the twenty-two-letter Phoenician script (also in the standard Hebrew-Aramaic alphabet), materialized about 1100 B.C.E.[38] The presence of alphabetic writing in ancient Israel does not mean the populace was literate at that time. Determining the spread of literacy in ancient Israel is a difficult undertaking.

Among the earliest examples of alphabetic writing were the Proto-Sinaitic inscriptions written in a linear alphabetic script. In 1905, W. M. Flinders Petrie discovered eleven inscriptions at modern Serābît el-Khâdem in the southern Sinai Peninsula. These inscriptions, incised on rock and on stone, may have been carved by Canaanite laborers working the Egyptian turquoise mines in the area. Petrie dated the Proto-Sinaitic inscriptions to the early fifteenth century B.C.E. and suggested the script represented a linear alphabet. Albright dated them provisionally between 1525 and 1475 B.C.E. Egyptologist Alan Gardiner dated them to the eighteenth century (MB IIA), corresponding with the Middle Kingdom of Egypt, and he seems to be correct. The total number of these inscriptions now exceeds forty-five.[39] A new discovery of alphabetic writing, carved in limestone cliffs in Wadi el-Hol, across from the royal city of Thebes in Upper Egypt, dates between 1900 and 1800 B.C.E. It seems likely that the Serābît el-Khâdem writing, which is typologically similar, should be dated that early as well. Detailed study remains to be done.

A small corpus of Canaanite alphabetic inscriptions from good archaeological contexts suggests that the Canaanite alphabet was in use by the MB II period. MB IIC storage jars, excavated at Gezer by Joe D. Seger, bear a probable series of letter signs incised on their shoulders. These seem to be early Canaanite alphabetic symbols consisting of twelve different signs, which resemble closely the Early-Canaanite alphabet from Serābît el-Khâdem.[40] Additional examples of Old Canaanite alphabetic inscriptions of the MB II period are the following. A bronze dagger blade retrieved from Tomb 1502 (MB IIB) at Lachish bears the vertical inscription *trnz*, which, on the basis of the tomb contents, Albright dated about 1600–1550 B.C.E. and speculated it might be a name.[41] A bowl fragment with an Old Canaanite inscription, to be read *boustrophedon* (lines inscribed alternately from right to left and left to right), was discovered in Pit 3867 of

37. John Baines and O. J. Eyre, "Four Notes on Literacy," *Göttinger Miszellen* 61 (1983): 65–72.

38. Joseph Naveh, *Early History of the Alphabet* (Jerusalem: Magnes Press, Hebrew University, 1982), 30–31: At Ugarit, thirty letters were used; the original number was twenty-seven, the last three being added later; the Phoenician alphabet omits five letters, thus consisting of twenty-two characters, adopted by Hebrew and Aramaic.

39. W. M. Flinders Petrie, *Researches in Sinai* (London: J. Murray, 1906); Alan H. Gardiner, "The Egyptian Origin of the Semitic Alphabet," *Journal of Egyptian Archaeology* 3 (1916): 1–16; William F. Albright, *The Proto-Sinaitic Inscriptions and Their Decipherment* (Cambridge: Harvard University Press, 1966), 1–3.

40. Joe D. Seger, "The Gezer Jar Signs: New Evidence of the Earliest Alphabet," in C. L. Meyers and M. O'Connor, eds., *The Word of the Lord Shall Go Forth* (Philadelphia: ASOR, 1983), 477–95.

41. Albright, *The Proto-Sinaitic Inscriptions and Their Decipherment*, 10; Émile Puech, "The Canaanite Inscriptions of Lachish and Their Religious Background," *TA* 13 (1986): 13–14.

Level VI at Lachish. Ussishkin dates it about 1200 B.C.E. or even earlier, while Cross prefers the first half of the thirteenth century. Reading *'il'ib*, the "divine ancestor" (line 1), Cross compares the 'Aqhat Epic, "who sets up the stele of his divine ancestor, in the sanctuary, the marker (?) of his clansman" (*CTA* 17.1.27f.).[42]

A MB IIA/B (ca. 1800–1750 B.C.E.) "Canaanite Jar" with two snakes incised on the shoulder was found at Ashkelon. The snakes look very much like the pictograph for *nûn* on the Lachish bronze dagger represented by *nāḥāš*. The Ashkelon exemplar has a vertical stroke (representing presumably a unit of some sort) in front of one of the snakes—another reason to suggest that this is an Old Canaanite letter for *nûn* rather than iconography, in which case the Ashkelon jar letters are a century or two earlier than the Gezer jar letters and not far removed from the Wadi el-Hol epigraphs. An inscription from Tell Nagila (twenty-eight kilometers east of Gaza) is incised on a potsherd from MB IIC. Cross prefers to read the inscription as a hypocoristic (pet name) personal name, Lahwiya.[43]

The following are examples of LB inscriptions. A fragmentary Old Canaanite inscription on the outside rim of a bowl (LB II/Iron I) was recovered from Qubūr el-Walaydah in the northwest Negev. Cross reads the inscription "Šimī-paʻal (son of) 'Iyya-'El 10 (?) [sheep (or sheqels)]."[44] A ewer or offering vessel (44.25 centimeters high), found at Lachish in rubble outside the so-called Fosse Temple, dates to the second half of the thirteenth century B.C.E. An eleven-letter, red-painted inscription on the shoulder of the vessel reads, "Mattan: an offering to my lady 'Elat," who was consort of the Canaanite god 'El (Ill. 43). A group of stylized animals (goats, stag, lion, bird) surround the inscription.[45]

An inscribed jar handle from Raddana dating to Early Iron I (1200 B.C.E. is a minimal date) was found in a stratified context of the Early Israelite period. This three-letter inscription—*'alep, ḥet, lāmed*—written vertically may be a personal name.[46]

Inscriptions dating to LB suggest there were scribal schools for the elite in that period, namely, scribes versed in international languages of the day. There is a (multilingual) cuneiform lexical text from Ashkelon with a Canaanite column, dating from about the thirteenth century. John Huehnergard and Wilfred van Soldt observe that apprentice scribes learned their profession by copying lexical texts.[47] A trilingual list with Canaanite

---

42. Frank M. Cross, "An Old Canaanite Inscription Recently Found at Lachish," *TA* 11 (1984): 71–76; David Ussishkin, "Excavations at Tel Lachish 1978–1983: Second Preliminary Report," *TA* 10 (1983): 155–57.

43. Cross, "An Old Canaanite Inscription Recently Found at Lachish," 74.

44. Frank M. Cross, "Newly Found Inscriptions in Old Canaanite and Early Phoenician Scripts," *BASOR* 238 (1980): 1–4.

45. Frank M. Cross, "The Evolution of the Proto-Canaanite Alphabet," *BASOR* 134 (1954): 15–24; Puech, "The Canaanite Inscriptions of Lachish and Their Religious Background," 17–18.

46. Frank M. Cross and David N. Freedman, "An Inscribed Jar Handle From Raddana," *BASOR* 201 (1971): 19–22.

47. John Huehnergard and Wilfred van Soldt, "A Cuneiform Lexical Text from Ashkelon with a Canaanite Column," *IEJ* 49 (1999): 186: "The string of UGU signs in the right-hand column suggests that we are dealing with a lexical text, that is, a text in which Sumerian signs in one column are explained by syllabically-written words in another."

words from Tel Aphek was published by Anson Rainey.[48] This trilingual lexical text (Sumerian, Akkadian, Northwest Semitic) illuminates scribal practices in LB Canaan.

Among the LB literary texts is the fragment from the Epic of Gilgamesh found at Megiddo.[49] The deathbed scene of Enkidu, close friend of Gilgamesh, king of the Sumerian city of Uruk, is the subject of this Megiddo fragment, which dates to the fourteenth century B.C.E. As McCarter notes, the Megiddo tablet is evidence that Mesopotamian literature was known in the West already in the pre-Israelite period.

Writing Materials

Archaeology casts light on the writing materials employed in ancient Israel. Among the common writing surfaces were stone, metal, clay, potsherds, wood, papyrus, and leather (sheep, goat, and calf hides). It was customary to coat rough stone surfaces of stelae or walls with plaster before writing on them in ink (děyô). The Bible attests that the Israelites were directed, after crossing over the Jordan into the land of Canaan, to set up large stones and cover them with plaster, and "You shall write on them all the words of this law" (Deut. 27:3).

Ill. 171: The famous "House of David" (byt dwd) inscription from Tel Dan. (Courtesy of Tel Dan Excavations, Hebrew Union College, Jerusalem; Photo: Z. Radovan)

Archaeologists uncovered an ink inscription, written by a non-Israelite group, fallen from a once-plastered wall or stela in a temple at Deir 'Alla (biblical Succoth) in the Jordan Valley. Dating about 700 B.C.E., this plaster text contains the sayings of Balaam, son of Beor, identified with the non-Israelite prophet whom the Israelites met on their way to the land of Canaan before crossing the Jordan River (Numbers 22–24). The language of the inscription is neither Ammonite nor Aramaic but an unknown local dialect.[50]

---

48. Anson F. Rainey, "A Tri-Lingual Cuneiform Fragment from Tel Aphek," *TA* 3 (1976): 137–40.

49. McCarter, *Ancient Inscriptions*, 18–19.

50. McCarter, *Ancient Inscriptions*, 96–98; Jo Ann Hackett, *The Balaam Text from Deir 'Alla* (Chico, Calif.: Scholars Press, 1984).

Several ink-on-plaster inscriptions were found on the walls and doorways of the main building at Kuntillet 'Ajrud, a caravanserai for pilgrims from Israel and Judah on their way to Mount Sinai/Horeb in Midian. Dated to the first half of the eighth century B.C.E., one of these inscriptions is a two-line blessing in the Hebrew language and script. In addition, inscriptions and drawings adorned two pithoi in the "bench room" of the main building. One has the now-famous phrase "Yahweh and his asherah" written in Hebrew; the other includes abecedaries.[51]

Major lapidary inscriptions include the Tel Dan Stela, the Moabite Stone, the Amman Citadel Inscription, and the Siloam Inscription. At Tel Dan in Upper Galilee Avraham Biran recovered in 1994 two new fragments from a large basalt monument incised in Aramaic and dating to the mid-ninth century, the time of King Hazael of Damascus (Ill. 171). The inscription refers to Joram son of Ahab, king of Israel, and Ahaziah son of Jehoram, king of the "House of David." A king of Damascus, probably Hazael, erected this stela.[52]

At Dhiban (biblical Dibon) in Moab a basalt stela with a thirty-four-line inscription was found in 1868. Known as the Moabite Stone, it commemorates a victory of Mesha, king of Moab, over Israel (Ill. 53). Dating to the second half of the ninth century, the inscription is written in Moabite. By substituting Yahweh for Chemosh, one could almost read the stela as Israelite, the language and motifs of the Moabite Stone being so similar to 1 and 2 Kings.[53] The Amman Citadel Inscription, dating to the second half of the ninth century, may be the dedication of the public building to the Ammonite god Milcom. The language of the inscription is Ammonite, and the script is Aramaic.[54] The Siloam Inscription, dating to the late eighth century and written in Hebrew, was carved on the wall of Hezekiah's Tunnel in Jerusalem, also known as the Siloam Tunnel. This tunnel connects the Gihon Spring, which was already fortified as early as MB II, with the Pool of Siloam, also inside the southwestern wall of the city (2 Kings 20:20; 2 Chron. 32:30). We assume the purpose of the new waterworks was to ensure protection of Jerusalem's water supply during Sennacherib's siege.[55]

A chisel was used to write on stone surfaces. To incise on metal, a stylus, a tool with a pointed metal tip made of iron or other hard substance, was employed. As Jeremiah proclaimed: "The sin of Judah is written with an iron stylus; with an adamant (*šāmîr*) point it is engraved on the tablet of their hearts, and on the horns of their altars" (Jer. 17:1).

The Copper Scroll (3Q15) from Qumran Cave 3 is engraved in Hebrew on two copper sheets. The date of this scroll, which contains a list of buried treasure, is uncertain, probably between the third or early second century B.C.E. and 66–73 C.E. Two

---

51. The best exposition of the inscriptions and of the use of the buildings is in Othmar Keel and Christoph Uehlinger, *Gods, Goddesses, and Images of God in Ancient Israel* (Minneapolis: Fortress, 1998).

52. Biran, *Biblical Dan*, 274–78. The interpretation of this find has occasioned considerable debate among scholars. Baruch Halpern, "The Stela from Dan: Epigraphic and Historical Considerations," *BASOR* 296 (1994): 63–80. William M. Schniedewind, "Tel Dan Stela: New Light on Aramaic and Jehu's Revolt," *BASOR* 302 (1996): 75–90.

53. Andrew Dearman, ed., *Studies in the Mesha Inscription and Moab* (Atlanta: Scholars Press, 1989).

54. McCarter, *Ancient Inscriptions*, 93.

55. Ronny Reich and Eli Shukron, "Light at the End of the Tunnel," *BAR* 25/1 (1999): 22–33, 72.

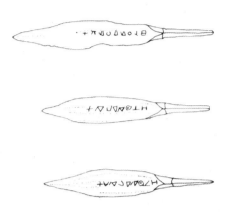

Ill. 172: Incised bronze arrowheads with tangs, probably twelfth or early eleventh century. (Courtesy of F. M. Cross and S. Moussaieff)

small, rolled silver plaques incised with the Priestly Benediction (Num. 6:24–26), including the divine name Yahweh, were discovered in the Ketef Hinnom cemetery in Jerusalem (Ill. 151). This is the first occurrence of "Yahweh" on an object excavated in Jerusalem. These amulets date to either the late seventh or early sixth century B.C.E.[56] An engraved metallic bottle was found at Tell Siran in Amman (Jordan). Dating to the late seventh or early sixth century, the inscription is composed of 92 letters written in the Ammonite script. The name of an Ammonite king Amminadab is mentioned, as well as his public works including orchards, vineyards, parks, and underground reservoirs.[57]

Ill. 173: The Ekron royal dedicatory inscription from the cella of the sanctuary of Temple Complex 650, found in Str IB and destroyed in 604 B.C.E. Inscription tells how *IKAUSU* (Achish), a ruler of Ekron, built the sanctuary and dedicated it to his goddess *PTGYH*. (Courtesy of Tel Miqne-Ekron Excavation/Publication Project; Photo: Z. Radovan)

56. Gabriel Barkay, "News from the Field: The Divine Name Found in Jerusalem," *BAR* 9/2 (1983): 14–19; idem, *Ketef Hinnom: A Treasure Facing Jerusalem's Walls*, Catalog No. 274 (Jerusalem: Israel Museum, 1986).

57. McCarter, *Ancient Inscriptions*, 98–99.

Earlier examples of inscriptions on bronze are the 'el-Khaḍr arrowheads (twelfth and eleventh centuries) (Ill. 172). The arrowheads are of great importance for the history of the alphabet. Besides those purportedly found in the Judean hills in the vicinity of 'el-Khaḍr, others came from Lebanon or southern Syria. Of the five 'el-Khaḍr arrowheads "from the same quiver," four are inscribed vertically (one horizontally) along one side of the blade with the legend "arrow of 'Abdilabi'at" ("servant of the Lioness," a [Canaanite goddess]), who was their owner.[58] More than forty inscribed arrowheads have been published. McCarter deciphered two additional, eleventh-century bronze arrowheads with archaic alphabetic inscriptions (from a private collection). One reads (obverse) "Arrow of Yataṛṣidq," and (reverse) "man of 'Ummi'a" (a personal name). The second arrowhead reads (obverse) "Arrow of Yakkiba'l," and (reverse) "brother of Shumba'l."[59]

The Phoenician inscription on a bronze spatula from Byblos (eleventh century) consists of a puzzling six-line text. The background of the inscription is the custom of granting property to loyal subordinates. The author of the text disavows any obligation to make a grant to 'Izriba'l, a faithless subordinate.[60] The question remains, however: how can one make a *naḥălâ* land grant if it is patrimonial or inherited property?

Clay was a common writing material that could be used in a variety of ways, including tablets, bullae (seal impressions in clay), and ostraca (inscribed potsherds). Ostraca bear both ink and incised inscriptions. Availability and cheapness made ostraca (akin to scrap paper) the standard means of written communication. Well-known ostraca in ink circulated at Samaria, Lachish, and Arad.

A large number of seal impressions on clay date to the late eighth and especially the seventh century, and later. Jerusalem's City of David excavations yielded a hoard of fifty-one bullae; the site of the find is appropriately dubbed the "House of the Bullae," which was burned during the Babylonian destruction of Jerusalem in 586 B.C.E. Bullae were used to seal documents written on papyrus or leather. After the document was rolled and secured with string, a glob of soft clay was applied to the knot and then sealed. The obverse of the bulla was impressed with a seal; the reverse bears the markings of the papyrus fibers and the strings to which the bulla was attached. The intense fire destroyed the scrolls stored in the House of the Bullae, but baked and thereby preserved the bullae.[61]

---

58. McCarter suggests the name was engraved to facilitate the division of spoils after victory, to reward a marksman whose arrow had struck a fatal blow. Cross proposes that the arrowheads were inscribed for use in archers' contests. Samuel Iwry suggested the signed arrowheads were used in belomancy (divination by arrows or drawing of lots by arrows). McCarter, *Ancient Inscriptions*, 78–79; Frank M. Cross, "Newly Discovered Inscribed Arrowheads of the 11th Century B.C.E.," *Biblical Archaeology Today, 1990: Proceedings of the Second International Congress on Biblical Archaeology* (Jerusalem: Israel Exploration Society, 1993), 533–42; Samuel Iwry, "New Evidence for Belomancy in Ancient Palestine and Phoenicia," *JAOS* 81 (1961): 32–34.

59. P. Kyle McCarter, "Two Bronze Arrowheads with Archaic Alphabetic Inscriptions," in B. A. Levine et al., eds., *Eretz-Israel*, 26 [Frank Moore Cross Volume] (Jerusalem: Israel Exploration Society, 1999), 123*–28*.

60. P. Kyle McCarter and Robert B. Coote, "The Spatula Inscription from Byblos," *BASOR* 212 (1973): 16–22.

61. Yigal Shiloh, *Excavations at the City of David I*, Qedem 19 (Jerusalem: Institute of Archaeology, Hebrew University, 1984).

Ill. 174a: Clay bulla of King Hezekiah with winged scarab. (Courtesy of F. M. Cross and S. Moussaieff)

Ill. 174b: Drawing of clay bulla. "Belonging to Hezekiah, (son of) 'Ahaz, King of Judah" *lḥzqyhw 'ḥz mlk/yhdh*. (Courtesy of F. M. Cross and S. Moussaieff)

Ill. 175: Copy of a seal "Belonging to Shemaʿ servant of Jeroboam II" *lšmʿ ʿbd yrbʿm*, from eighth century B.C.E. Megiddo. Original missing. (Courtesy of Israel Museum)

Ill. 176: "Belonging to Gemaryahu ben Shaphan" *(l) gmr yhw [b]n špn*. From seventh or sixth century B.C.E. City of David. (Courtesy of Israel Museum)

Writing was also done on wood. Ezekiel was instructed by Yahweh to write on a "piece of wood" (*ʿēṣ*), perhaps a wooden writing board (Ezek. 37:16). There is evidence from Assyria of wax-coated, wooden writing-board sets hinged together forming a diptych. The waxed surfaces faced each other to protect them when closed. Assyrian reliefs show scribes with wooden tablets taking head counts. "Wax-covered tablets could also make books. A high-class set of twelve ivory leaves, with gold hinges at alternate edges, was prepared for Sargon II of Assyria and recovered from a well at Nimrud. Enough wax remained to reveal that the book had apparently contained over 7,500 lines of an encyclopedia of omens."[62]

62. Piotr Bienkowski and Alan Millard, eds., *Dictionary of the Ancient Near East* (Philadelphia: University of Pennsylvania Press, 2000), 56–57.

A good example of a writing-board set comes from the late fourteenth-century (ca. 1300 B.C.E.) wreck of a merchant ship off the Turkish peninsula of Uluburun near Kaç (Ill. 177). Besides the raw materials, which included ten tons of ingots of Cypriot copper, a ton of terebinth resin, as well as fruits and spices, there was an ivory-hinged wooden writing-board set. The wax no longer adhered to the surface of the boards, and the stylus used to inscribe the wax was not recovered. It is known from reliefs that one end of the stylus was pointed for incising, the other was flat for erasing. The writing-board sets were so ornate that only the rich could afford them. The wood of the Uluburun diptych was boxwood (*Buxus*) from the Amanus mountain range in coastal northern Syria. The Uluburun writing-board set was the first LB example of its kind from the ancient Near East.[63]

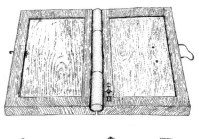

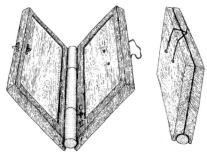

Ill. 177: Wooden writing board with ivory hinges. When the board was coated with beeswax, the writer inscribed his message into the wax. Found in Uluburun shipwreck, about 1300 B.C.E. (Courtesy of Çemal Pulak)

Papyrus, which flourishes in an arid climate, was commonly used as a writing surface in Egypt, dating as early as the first Egyptian dynasty (ca. 3100 B.C.E.). Papyrus is not mentioned in the Bible, but from the seventh century onward papyrus documents appear. A Hebrew papyrus palimpsest (written on twice) from the seventh century was found in a cave in the Wadi Murabba'at (about eighteen kilometers south of Qumran) near the Dead Sea. The documents, dating to the first half of the seventh century B.C.E., contain a letter and a list of names. A cache of Aramaic papyri (known as the Samaria papyri), dating from the fourth century B.C.E., was discovered in a cave in the Wadi ed-Daliyeh. Among them are legal or administrative documents. That a large quantity of writing was apparently committed to perishable papyrus may explain the paucity of extant Iron Age inscriptions.

Leather was the primary material from which *mĕgillat sĕpārîm*, "scrolls," were made, especially sacred documents such as the Dead Sea Scrolls (Qumran). It is much more durable than flimsy papyrus. The Dead Sea Scrolls were written, for the most part, on tanned leather, not on parchment, a fine processed leather produced in Pergamum which came into use only in the fourth century C.E.

---

63. Robert Payton, "The Ulu Burun Writing-Board Set," *Anatolian Studies* 41 (1991): 99–106; Peter Warnock and Michael Pendleton, "The Wood of the Ulu Burun Diptych," *Anatolian Studies* 41 (1991): 107–10.

Ill. 178: Assyrian scribes; seventh century B.C.E. relief from the Southwest Palace at Nineveh. Two scribes recording booty; one is writing on a hinged, waxed, wooden tablet; the other, on a papyrus scroll. (Courtesy of the Trustees of the British Museum)

Either black or red ink (*děyô*) was used to write on leather and papyrus. The initial words of the Balaam inscription at Deir 'Alla are in red ink, literally a "rubric," (from Latin *ruber*, "red"). Baruch, Jeremiah's secretary, reported: "He [Jeremiah] dictated all these words to me, and I wrote them with ink (*děyô*) on the scroll" (Jer. 36:18). The black ink was a form of charcoal mixed with gum, oil, or other substance. The red ink was made from red ocher or iron oxide and gum. The stylus used on these surfaces was a reed fashioned to function as a brush.

Literacy

In the ancient world, and to a lesser degree in the modern world, determining literacy is difficult, because reliable statistics are not available, nor are there objective criteria for assessing literacy. Even defining what is meant by popular literacy is complex; hence ambiguous terms like "limited" (McCarter) or "widespread" (Millard) literacy are proposed by scholars. What constitutes a literate society? Does it involve the ability only to read or to write, or both? In his discussion of functional literacy, Sean Warner[64] cites the definition of Everett Rogers: "the ability to read and write written symbols at a level of competence adequate for carrying out the functions of the individual's role in his customary social system."[65]

As already noted, the history of alphabetic Canaanite begins even earlier than had been previously thought, now stretching back to the beginning of the second millennium B.C.E. However, the one-time invention of this simplified system of writing and reading, which could be learned in a matter of days rather than the lifetime of those struggling with syllabic cuneiform and hieroglyphic writing, did not necessarily guarantee that the bulk of the populace was literate.

Some scholars conjecture that the relative simplicity of the Hebrew alphabet, compared to the complex cuneiform and hieroglyphic scripts of neighboring peoples, was responsible for the rapid spread of literacy. But, as Warner points out, certain societies such as the Chinese, have attained a high degree of literacy despite their complex script. Also, in countries using the alphabet, literacy has not always taken hold immediately. Other influences must be taken into consideration, such as the sociological, religious, political, and economic factors. Paleographic studies alone are inadequate.

As Susan Niditch has argued, orality and literacy should be regarded not as opposites, but as points along a spectrum, and they can coexist and continue to influence each other even after written texts have come into existence.[66] Without doubt the Israelite tradition was handed down orally from adults to children through stories, songs, poems, and proverbs repeated around the hearth, whether in the home or shrine, and at religious festivals or other public gatherings. The Israelite Epic known as "JE," after its two traditions "J" (Yahwist) and "E" (Elohist) were joined, began to take form orally. Its many early poems may have been common fare for youths to learn, sing, and recite. At the same time there could have been those who wrote down oral traditions at an early date, even if the texts continued for some time to remain in a rather fluid state.

Documents from the kingdoms of both Israel and Judah, but not the neighboring kingdoms, of the eighth and seventh centuries contain Egyptian hieratic signs (cursive hieroglyphic) and numerals that had ceased to be used in Egypt after the tenth century. Orly Goldwasser states: "The fact that the hieratic numerals appear in both Israel and Judah points to an earlier date of adoption, probably the age of David and Solomon."[67] Nadav Na'aman makes the point that literacy was prevalent among the elite of Jerusalem during the united monarchy.[68] There is evidence that some level of

---

64. Sean Warner, "The Alphabet: An Innovation and Its Diffusion," *VT* 30 (1980): 81–90.

65. Everett M. Rogers, *Modernization among Peasants: The Impact of Communication* (New York: Holt, Rinehart & Winston, 1969), 73–74.

66. Susan Niditch, *Oral World and Written Word: Ancient Israelite Literature*, LAI (Louisville, Ky.: Westminster John Knox, 1996).

67. Orly Goldwasser, "An Egyptian Scribe from Lachish and the Hieratic Tradition of the Hebrew Kingdoms," *TA* 18 (1991): 251.

68. Nadav Na'aman, "The Contribution of the Amarna Letters to the Debate on Jerusalem's Political Position in the Tenth Century B.C.E.," *BASOR* 304 (1996): 22.

Ill. 179: "Private" seal: Meshullam/Aḥimelech, from Lachish. (Courtesy of the Expedition to Lachish, D. Ussishkin, Director)

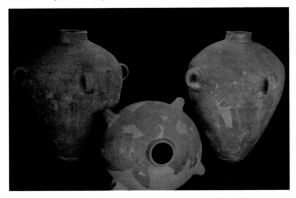

Ill. 180: *lmlk* storage jars from a storeroom near the city gate, found in Level III, at Lachish. (Courtesy of the Expedition to Lachish, D. Ussishkin, Director)

Ill. 181: *lmlk* storage jar, with the four-winged symbol and the name Hebron. (Courtesy of the Expedition to Lachish, D. Ussishkin, Director)

literacy began to become widespread in the eighth century, in effect trickling down from courtier to commoner. The majority of texts date from the late eighth to the sixth centuries B.C.E. Still, this does not mean that a great number of Israelites were literate.

Clay bullae, inscribed personal seals, seal impressions, inscriptions on vases, ostraca, and inscribed weights date from the eighth and seventh centuries, and later. All these and the thousands of *lmlk* ("belonging to the king") seal impressions on jar handles attest to the role literacy played in the economy during the eighth century.

Literacy, at least among the elite, is attested by the Samaria Ostraca, the Arad Ostraca, the Ḥorvat ʿUza Ostracon, the Yavneh-Yam Ostracon, and the Lachish Ostraca (Ill. 183). The Samaria Ostraca represent one of the most important collections of inscribed documents from Israel. One hundred and two ostraca, many of them dating to the time of King Jeroboam II (789–748 B.C.E.), were found at Samaria, the capital of the northern kingdom of Israel. This corpus consists mainly of Hebrew inscriptions in black ink.[69]

Several suggestions have been made about the function of the Samaria inscriptions. The answer hinges on the role of the person whose name is preceded by the Hebrew prepositional *lāmed*, that is, the "*l*-man/men." (*lāmed* has a variety of meanings: "to," "belonging

69. Baruch Rosen, "Wine and Oil Allocations in the Samaria Ostraca," *TA* 13 (1986): 39–45.

to," "for.") Yigael Yadin, Frank Cross, and Ivan Kaufman[70] identify the "*l*-men" as the tax gatherers who collected the commodities from their respective districts and forwarded them to the royal city of Samaria. The ostraca are receipts, written by a court official, for the shipment of vintage wine, virgin olive oil, and grain. According to Anson Rainey,[71] the "*l*-men" ("servants of the crown"), who actually resided in Samaria and ate "at the king's table," consumed the produce from their family estates, which was shipped to the capital as a subsidy. Commensality in the palace is reminiscent of Mephibosheth, son of Jonathan, to whom David accorded the privilege of eating "at the king's table" (2 Sam. 9:7–13).

Ill. 182: *lmlk* storage jar, with the two-winged emblem and the name Sochoh. (Courtesy of the Expedition to Lachish, D. Ussishkin, Director)

Stager would prefer to understand the "*l*-men" not as bureaucratic officials such as tax collectors from various administrative districts around Samaria but as notables representing various clans in and about the capital. Sometimes the commodities of olive oil and vintage wine arriving in the capital, which are attributed to one "*l*-man," come from more than one village in different (so-called) "administrative districts." Whether these "*l*-men" were delivering goods to the king or consuming them "at the king's table" themselves, it seems

Ill. 183: Ostracon XXI, from Lachish; inscribed in ancient Hebrew, no later in date than the beginning of Level II (seventh century B.C.E.). (Courtesy of the Expedition to Lachish, D. Ussishkin, Director)

70. Yigael Yadin, "Recipients or Owners: A Note on the Samaria Ostraca," *IEJ* 9 (1959): 184–87; "A Further Note on the Samaria Ostraca," *IEJ* 12 (1962): 64–66. Frank M. Cross, "Epigraphic Notes on Hebrew Documents of the Eighth–Sixth Centuries B.C.: I. A New Reading of a Place Name in the Samaria Ostraca," *BASOR* 163 (1961): 12–14. Ivan T. Kaufman, "The Samaria Ostraca: A Study in Ancient Hebrew Palaeography, Text and Plates" (Diss., Harvard University, 1966); "The Samaria Ostraca: An Early Witness to Hebrew Writing," *BA* 45 (1982): 229–39.

71. Anson F. Rainey, "The Samaria Ostraca in the Light of Fresh Evidence," *PEQ* 99 (1967): 32–41; and "The *Sitz im Leben* of the Samaria Ostraca," *TA* 6 (1979): 91–94.

clear that they were the notables, the leading heads of households, lineages, or clans, who received these commodities from their kinsmen, whose gifts and obligations were to their patrimonial leaders, not to some government bureaucrats. The "*l*-men," in turn, delivered the goods to their patrimonial overlord, the king. As J. David Schloen has summarized the evidence:

> However we interpret the Samaria ostraca, these texts make clear the continuing importance in ancient Israel, well into the monarchic period, of cohesive clans as the basic economic and social units responsible for organizing resources and providing goods and services to overlords. This arrangement was much simpler than the alternative, which would have involved close supervision of dispersed settlements by a large core of royal officials. It was also congruent with a long standing mode of traditional patrimonial authority by which political leaders acquired surpluses and pooled resources in all periods in the Levant, regardless of the spatial scale of the overarching political regime, ranging from tiny 'chiefdoms' consisting of a few villages to larger kingdoms or 'states' spanning wide areas.[72]

Arad controlled the main road to Edom. An Iron Age frontier fortress at Arad served as both an administrative and a military outpost. About two hundred ostraca were found at the site; over half were inscribed in Hebrew and date to the late seventh or early sixth century B.C.E. Eighteen ostraca are addressed to Eliashib, commander of the fortress, authorizing him to provide rations (wine, oil, flour) to the *Kittîyîm* (*ktym*), probably Cypriot or Greek mercenaries in the army of Judah. Ostracon 18 refers enigmatically to the "House of Yahweh," the Temple in Jerusalem. There was a temple at Arad, but it may have been demolished about 700 B.C.E., well before the Arad Ostraca.

At Ḥorvat ʿUza in the eastern Negev, about ten kilometers southeast of Arad, a Judahite fortress was constructed in the seventh century. Excavators discovered twenty-eight ostraca in Hebrew, one in Edomite, and one in Aramaic. These documents consist of "a military directive, name lists, the distribution of supplies or inventories, a literary-legal document, and fragmentary lists."[73] A Hebrew ostracon found in the front guardroom of the fortress gate was addressed to a certain Aḥiqam, probably commander of the fort. This ostracon may be an administrative document dealing with military organization in Judah in the early sixth century.[74] The sole Edomite ostracon at Ḥorvat ʿUza, dating to the early sixth century and inscribed with six lines in cursive script, appears to be addressed to the commander of the fort by his superior, who gives instruction concerning the distribution of food. More important, this ostracon is evidence that the Edomites had established themselves in the Negev before the Babylonian destruction of 586 B.C.E.[75]

---

72. J. David Schloen, *The House of the Father as Fact and Symbol: Patrimonialism in Ugarit and the Ancient Near East*, Studies in the Archaeology and History of the Levant, 2 (Cambridge: Harvard Semitic Museum, 2001), 165.

73. Itzhaq Beit-Arieh, "'Uza, Ḥorvat," *NEAEHL*, 4: 1496.

74. Itzhaq Beit-Arieh, "The Ostracon of Aḥiqam from Ḥorvat ʿUza," *TA* 13 (1986): 32–38.

75. Itzhaq Beit-Arieh and Bruce Cresson, "An Edomite Ostracon from Ḥorvat ʿUza," *TA* 12 (1985): 96–101; Itzhaq Beit-Arieh, "New Light on the Edomites," *BAR* 14 (1988): 28–41.

The Yavneh-Yam (Meṣad Ḥashavyahu) ostracon, written in Biblical Hebrew in the late seventh century B.C.E., is an official complaint by a reaper whose garment was unjustly confiscated for apparently not meeting his quota of grain. He appeals to Hoshaiah (Yahwistic name), the military governor, for the return of the garment. This is one of the few extrabiblical allusions to biblical laws (Ex. 22:25–26; Deut. 24:10–13; see also Amos 2:8).[76]

Lachish was the most important city in Judah after Jerusalem. Because of its strategic location, it was targeted by Sennacherib during the siege of 701 B.C.E., and by Nebuchadrezzar in 586 B.C.E. The twenty-one Lachish Ostraca (Lachish Letters) were written during the reign of King Zedekiah, the last king of Judah. They deal with military activities underway at the southwestern frontier of Judah just before the Babylonian siege of the city. Presumably the military had personnel who could read (and write) orders and lists.

With respect to the biblical text, Isaiah refers to the ability to read and write: "The vision of all this has become for you like the words of a sealed document. If it is given to those who can read, with the command, 'Read this,' they say, 'We cannot, for it is sealed'" (Isa. 29:11). "Then Yahweh said to me [Isaiah], Take a large tablet and write on it in common characters, 'Belonging to Maher-shalal-hash-baz'" (Isa. 8:1). Several references to a basic knowledge of writing also appear in Jeremiah. The prophet was directed by Yahweh: "Take a scroll and write on it all the words that I have spoken to you against Israel and Judah and all the nations" (Jer. 36:2; also 29:1; 30:2–3; 32:10). Jeremiah did not write; his scribe Baruch did.

Schools

André Lemaire[77] suggests that some form of schools existed in Israel from the time of the monarchy, especially in Judah during the eighth and seventh centuries B.C.E. He argues from the analogy of Egypt and Mesopotamia, where schools date from the third millennium. Such schools were informal, consisting of a small number of students who gathered around a teacher. Schools in the strict sense did not come into existence in Palestine until the postexilic period. Most references to education are found in the Wisdom literature. The only mention of "school" (bêt midrāš) appears in Sirach: "Draw near to me, you who are uneducated, and lodge in the house of instruction (bêt midrāš)" (Sir. 51:23). Since knowledge about education in biblical times is fragmentary and evidence from the Bible for the presence of schools is slight,

76. Frank M. Cross, "Epigraphic Notes on Hebrew Documents of the Eighth-Sixth Centuries B.C.: II. The Murabba'ât Papyrus and the Letter Found near Yabneh-yam," BASOR 165 (1962): 34–46.

77. André Lemaire, "Education (Israel)," ABD, 2: 305–12; Les écoles et la formation de la Bible dans l'ancien Israël (Fribourg: Editions universitaires; Göttingen: Vandenhoeck & Ruprecht, 1981). See also Alan R. Millard, "An Assessment of the Evidence of Writing in Ancient Israel," in J. Aviram et al., eds., Biblical Archaeology Today (Jerusalem: Israel Exploration Society, 1985), 301–12; James L. Crenshaw, Education in Ancient Israel: Across the Deadening Silence (New York: Doubleday, 1998); Ian M. Young, "Israelite Literacy: Interpreting the Evidence," VT 48 (1998), 1:239–253; 2:408–422.

Lemaire has recourse to Palestinian inscriptions to support his argument. He appeals to abecedaries (the alphabet written in traditional sequence), but it is uncertain whether they were written by children or adults.

Ostraca inscribed with abecedaries from the First Temple period have been discovered in both towns and villages. The oldest, complete abecedary (twenty-two letters constitute line five) was found at 'Izbet Ṣarṭah, a small village near Aphek. Dating to the early part of the twelfth century B.C.E., this five-line abecedary contains eighty-three alphabetic signs, with most letters written from left to right. The alphabet appears in the traditional sequence, with the exception of pê-'ayin (in contrast to the standard 'ayin-pê). This unusual order is also found in the abecedaries inscribed on a pithos (large storage jar) at Kuntillet 'Ajrud and in the acrostics of Lamentations 2–4. The 'Izbet Ṣarṭah abecedary was written in Old Canaanite characters by a scribe who may have been Israelite. McCarter refers to this ostracon as a "practice tablet."[78]

The tenth-century Gezer Calendar, one of the earliest Hebrew inscriptions, consists of a seven-line inscription dividing the year into eight agricultural seasons (Ill. 33). Because of the similarity between Phoenician and Hebrew in the tenth century, it cannot be determined with certainty whether the script is Phoenician or Hebrew. It may have been a schoolboy exercise for the teaching of scripts, but this is far from certain. On the basis of Egyptian and Mesopotamian parallels, Albright described the Gezer Calendar as a "school exercise," commenting that the scribe's hand was slow and awkward.

Seeing no connection between abecedaries and schools, Menahem Haran[79] completely disagrees with Lemaire's thesis that abecedaries attest to the existence of schools in ancient Israel. He points out that some of the obscure sites (both First and Second Temple periods) where these abecedaries have appeared were inappropriate for schools. Khirbet el-Qom is an Iron II cemetery on a hilltop site twenty kilometers west of Hebron. Among the inscriptions found there are the Uriyahu Epitaph (upon whom a blessing is invoked) from Tomb II and a stonecutter's inscription calling forth a blessing upon the one who cut the tomb.[80] At Lachish, the first five letters of the early Hebrew alphabet (late ninth or early eighth century) are inscribed in order on the rise of the steps of Palace C. This exercise was hardly accessible for the instruction of students.[81]

---

78. McCarter, *Ancient Inscriptions*, 77; Frank M. Cross, "Newly Found Inscriptions in Old Canaanite and Early Phoenician Scripts," *BASOR* 238 (1980): 8–15.

79. Menahem Haran, "On the Diffusion of Literacy and Schools in Ancient Israel," in J. A. Emerton, ed., *Congress Volume*, VTSup 40 (Leiden: E. J. Brill, 1988), 81–95. Graham Davies, "Were There Schools in Ancient Israel?" in J. Day et al., eds, *Wisdom in Ancient Israel* (Cambridge: Cambridge University Press, 1995), 210: "But even after allowances have been made for the different interests of the biblical writers and the chances of archaeological discovery, there is at present insufficient evidence for envisaging such a widespread educational system as that sketched by Lemaire."

80. McCarter, *Ancient Inscriptions*, 111–12.

81. Olga Tufnell, *Lachish III: The Iron Age* (London: Oxford University Press, 1953), 118, 357–59. Ussishkin ("Excavations at Tel Lachish—1973–1977, Preliminary Report," 81–83) describes a few short inscriptions, dating to Level II, which was destroyed in 588/586 by Nebuchadrezzar, king of Babylon. Inscription XXIV is an abecedary, composed of the first four letters of the Hebrew alphabet, found on a complete storage jar with two handles and a pointed base.

Lemaire offers an additional argument in support of instruction of scribal elite in the First Temple period. Solomon's administrative officers are listed in 1 Kings 4, indicating the extent to which the kingdom has enlarged to become an imperial state. Administrative duties required more scribal expertise, and hence training, than priestly duties. The early activity in court by the tenth century entailed the adaptation of Egyptian hieratic, which according to Na'aman had ceased to be used in Egypt by that period but appeared in Israel/Judah later as numerals. Lemaire contends that once the Temple was built in Jerusalem, instruction was imparted for the training of priestly personnel in the conduct of religious services and sacrificial rites.[82]

Edward Lipinski[83] maintains that royal and state scribes (*sōpĕrîm*) in Jerusalem performed a variety of tasks presupposing special training that exceeded knowledge of the alphabet and the ability to write and count. These royal scribes managed international relations, state affairs, and palace administration. They were trained by their fathers, who were also scribes, as in the case of Gemariah, son of the scribe (*sōpēr*) Shaphan: "Then, in the hearing of all the people, Baruch read the words of Jeremiah from the scroll, in the house of Yahweh, in the chamber of Gemariah son of Shaphan the scribe (*sōpēr*), which was in the upper court" (Jer. 36:10). But this points only to elite scribal writing among the courtiers, not the commoners.

---

82. In her discussion of royal officials and court families, Nili Fox ("Royal Officials and Court Families: A New Look at the *yĕlādîm* in 1 Kings 12," *BA* 59 [1996]: 225–32) looks for evidence in 1 Kings 12 dealing with the northern kingdom's petition to King Rehoboam to lighten the burden of taxes and forced labor imposed by his father Solomon. In reaching his decision Rehoboam consulted the court *zĕqēnîm* ("elders") and *yĕlādîm* ("young men") "who had grown up with him" (1 Kings 12:8). Ignoring the wisdom of the former, he followed the advice of the latter; he imposed harsher demands than his father. On the basis of Egyptian analogies, Fox argues that *yĕlādîm* is a technical term designating sons of royal officials brought up in the palace together with the princes.

83. Edward Lipinski, "Royal and State Scribes in Ancient Jerusalem," in J. A. Emerton, ed., *Congress Volume*, 157–64.

CHAPTER 6

Religious Institutions

Cults today are widely considered to be fringe groups or new religious movements. Dictionary definitions of "cult" often point to religious sects, their extremism, and their idiosyncratic teachings; cult is, in other words, commonly used in a pejorative sense. In the biblical context, cult is a broader term than worship and includes rituals, prayers, pilgrimages, and sacrifices.[1] Roland de Vaux defined cult as "all those acts by which communities or individuals give outward expression to their religious life, by which they seek and achieve contact with God."[2] Briefly, cult may be defined as a formal means of expressing religious reverence.

Hebrew has two elemental terms signifying the act of worship: 'ābad, "to serve" (as well as the noun 'ăbōdâ, "service"), and hištaḥăwâ (root, ḥwh), "to prostrate oneself." Just as one renders service to the king, it is incumbent upon a subject to do homage to the deity. The external gesture must be linked with an internal attitude, both compatible with the proper service of God. In a judgment speech on fasting, Second Isaiah defines true worship in terms of the biblical doctrine of righteousness: "This, rather, is the fasting that I [Yahweh] wish: releasing those bound unjustly, untying the thongs of the yoke; setting free the oppressed, breaking every yoke; sharing your bread with the hungry, sheltering the oppressed and the homeless; clothing the naked when you see them, and not turning your back on your own" (Isa. 58:6–7).

Integral to Israelite religious practice were local places of worship in a variety of forms, including mountains, portable shrines like the Ark or tabernacle, provincial sanctuaries, and bāmôt (singular, bāmâ), conventionally rendered "high places."

---

1. Two very helpful sources are Rainer Albertz, *A History of Israelite Religion in the Old Testament Period* (London: SCM Press, 1994), and Patrick D. Miller, *The Religion of Ancient Israel*, LAI (Louisville: Westminster John Knox, 2000).
2. Roland de Vaux, *Ancient Israel* (New York: McGraw-Hill, 1961), 271.

SACRED SITES

"High Places"

The *bāmôt* are mentioned more than a hundred times in the Bible. Their nature, appearance, and architecture are disputed, and scholars disagree about the definition and translation of *bāmâ*. In ancient Israel and Judah, many sanctuaries, situated in both towns and countryside, were identified as *bāmôt*. These cult installations are traditionally envisioned as raised platforms, built in the open air, where religious rituals were performed. *bāmâ* as a cultic term can refer to a sacred site that is elevated naturally (as on a hill) or artificially (as on a platform) (Ill. 184).

The idea of an elevated platform probably derives from the reference to Samuel and Saul ascending and descending the *bāmâ* where Samuel offered a sacrifice the day before he anointed Saul as king: "Samuel answered Saul, 'I am the seer; go up before me to the shrine (*'ălēh lĕpānay habbāmâ*), for today you shall eat with me' " (1 Sam. 9:19). "When they came down from the shrine (*wayyērdû mēhabbāmâ*), a bed was spread for Saul on the roof, and he lay down to sleep" (1 Sam. 9:25). The Bible's most detailed description of a *bāmâ* appears in the context of Samuel's anointing of Saul (1 Sam. 9:1–10:16). Associated with the *bāmâ* was a *liškâ*, the room used for dining (1 Sam. 9:22), where sacrificial meals were eaten. Elsewhere in the Bible,

Ill. 184: Reconstruction of *bāmâ* ("high place") in city gate at Bethsai'da, with stela of Ba'al Ḥadad on dais. Dated Iron II. (Drawing: C. S. Alexander, after Rami Arav et al., "Bethsaida Rediscovered," BAR 26/1 (2000): 48–49, and O. Keel, *Goddesses and Trees, New Moon and Yahweh*, 1998, fig. 106)

lĕšākôt (pl.) refers to rooms serving a variety of functions in the Jerusalem Second Temple. *bāmôt* were adorned with cult objects, including altars (*mizbĕḥôt*), stone pillars (*maṣṣēbôt*), and groves of trees (*'ăšērîm*).

A *bêt bāmâ* was a kind of sanctuary building where a priest was required to serve. "He [Jeroboam I] also made house(s) on high places (*bêt bāmôt*), and appointed priests from among all the people, who were not Levites" (1 Kings 12:31). In the reigns of David and Solomon, *bāmôt* existed as legitimate cultic places in the Israelite countryside. Both David and Solomon patronized the *bāmâ* at Gibeon. Chronicles describes sacrificial activities conducted at the *bāmâ* of Gibeon under the aegis of David: "He [David] left the priest Zadok and his kindred the priests before the tabernacle of Yahweh in the high place (*bāmâ*) that was at Gibeon, to offer burnt offerings to Yahweh on the altar of burnt offering regularly, morning and evening, according to all that is written in the law of Yahweh that he commanded Israel"

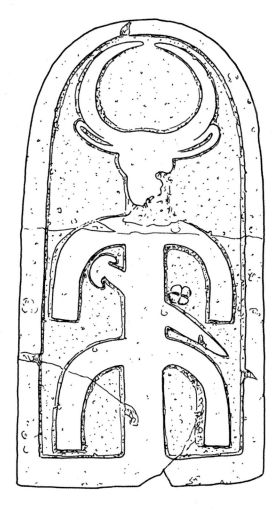

Ill. 185: Close-up of the stela of Ba'al Ḥadad, with bull's head; armed with sword or dagger. (Drawing: C. S. Alexander, after "Bethsaida Rediscovered," 50)

(1 Chron. 16:39–40). Solomon, too, offered a sacrifice at the *bāmâ* at Gibeon: "Solomon loved Yahweh, walking in the statutes of his father David; only, he sacrificed and offered incense at the high places (*bāmôt*). The king went to Gibeon to sacrifice there, for that was the principal high place (*habbāmâ haggĕdôlâ*)" (1 Kings 3:3–4). Isaiah alludes to worship at the *bāmôt* in Moab: "Dibon [modern Dhiban] has gone up to the temple, to the high places (*bāmôt*) to weep; over Nebo and over Medeba Moab wails" (Isa. 15:2; also 16:12).

Only at the end of the eighth century, in the reign of Hezekiah, were there claims that the high places were demolished: "He [Hezekiah] removed the high places (*habbāmôt*), broke down the pillars (*hammaṣṣēbōt*), and cut down the sacred pole (*hā'ăšērâ*)" (2 Kings 18:4). As a consequence of Josiah's reform (622/621 B.C.E.), religious worship was centralized in Jerusalem. He abolished the local shrines, purified worship in Jerusalem, and eliminated the *bāmôt* throughout the land: "[Josiah] defiled the high places (*habbāmôt*) where the priests had made offerings, from Geba [north of the Dead Sea] to Beer-sheba" (2 Kings 23:8).

The writers of the Deuteronomistic History (the biblical books, Joshua through Kings, influenced by Deuteronomy) comment negatively on the *bāmôt*. In Deuteronomic theology, the high places were considered illicit sanctuaries after the building of the Temple, since thereafter worship was to be conducted only at the central sanctuary in Jerusalem. Amos prophesied, "The high places (*bāmôt*) of Isaac shall be made desolate" (Amos 7:9). Hosea foretold that God would punish Israel's idolatry by destroying the cult places and transforming them into a wilderness: "The high places (*bāmôt*) of Aven [Bethel], the sin of Israel, shall be destroyed. Thorn and thistle shall grow up on their altars" (Hos. 10:8).

In recent years archaeologists have uncovered several cult sites that may qualify as *bāmôt*. Integral to these *bāmôt* or local shrines, where syncretistic worship was practiced, are the *'ăšērîm* (sacred poles), *maṣṣēbôt* ("pillars"), and altars.

Bull Site

The oldest known cultic site considered to be Israelite is located on the summit of a range near Dothan in northern Samaria. In the early 1980s a bronze statuette of a young bull was found there. Although its precise archaeological context is unknown, this finely rendered but awkward-looking animal appears to have been associated with an open-air cultic site, described by the excavator, Amihai Mazar,[3] as an elliptical area paved with flat stones and containing a large standing stone, possibly a *maṣṣēbâ*, as well as fragments of an incense burner and animal bones. Some scholars question the Israelite provenience of this cultic site, inasmuch as it is difficult to distinguish between Canaanite and Israelite material culture in the Early Iron Age. Evidence for identifying the "bull site" as cultic is not compelling, according to Michael Coogan.[4]

The bull, prominent in the Canaanite cultic tradition, is identified with the Canaanite god El; the bull calf, with Ba'al. This discovery calls to mind King Jeroboam I, who placed a golden calf in the sanctuaries of Dan and Bethel to discourage the people of the northern kingdom of Israel from traveling south to worship in the Jerusalem Temple (1 Kings 12:26–33). The account of the infamous "golden calf"

---

3. Amihai Mazar, "The 'Bull Site': An Iron Age I Open Cult Place," *BASOR* 247 (1982): 27–42.
4. Michael D. Coogan, "Of Cults and Cultures: Reflections on the Interpretation of Archaeological Evidence," *PEQ* 119 (1987): 1–8.

(Exodus 32), fashioned by Aaron for the Israelites to worship, may have been intended as a subtle attack on Jeroboam I for setting up the bull cult in the northern kingdom.

Sacred Precinct at Dan

After Solomon's reign, the united monarchy split in two. The much larger and wealthier sector became the northern kingdom of Israel, while the smaller, landlocked sector became the southern kingdom of Judah. The regal-ritual city Jerusalem remained Judah's capital, whereas in Israel the political capital was separate from the two main religious centers, Dan in the north and Bethel in the south. The secessionist king Jeroboam I, who was not of the Davidic dynasty, established the complementary centers of worship and pilgrimage at the far reaches of his kingdom, in order to offset the attraction of Jerusalem for his subjects. According to the Deuteronomistic historian, Jeroboam I was guilty of setting up illicit cults featuring golden calves as the focus of their idolatry:

> So the king [Jeroboam] took counsel and made two calves of gold. He said to the people, 'You have gone up to Jerusalem long enough. Here is your God [or gods], O Israel, who brought you up from the land of Egypt.' He set one in Bethel, and the other he put in Dan. And this thing became a sin. . . . He also built temples on the high places [reading *bāttê habbāmôt*][5] and appointed priests from among the people who were not Levites (1 Kings 12:28–31).

As our reading of the iconography of the cult stand from Ta'anach (Ill. 211), Solomon's provincial center and a Levitical city, indicates, the bullock was a perfectly acceptable icon or emblem associated with the deity Yahweh before the schism between north and south. It was only later that the cherubim iconography of the Jerusalem Temple prevailed and the bull-calf iconography of Dan and Bethel was condemned as idolatry.

In choosing dual national shrines, Jeroboam was not only making pilgrimage to those sites easier for his subjects; he was also catering to two great priestly families: those priests who traced their lineage from Aaron and those who counted Moses as their ancestor. In this respect he was following the lead of David, who earlier had appointed both of these leading (and at the time rivalrous) clans over sacerdotal matters in Jerusalem.

The etiological origins of the Danite shrine mark it clearly as a Mosaic, or Mushite, enterprise. As the Danites move up north to their new home at Laish (renamed Dan after its capture), they take with them a Levitical priest (cf. 1 Kings 12:31 above) from Bethlehem in Judah, then serving in the household of Micah, in the hill country of Ephraim. The young Levite accompanies them and brings along his

---

5. See 1 Kings 13:32 for *bāttê habbāmôt*; LXX and Vulgate for pl. in 1 Kings 12:31.

Ill. 186: Sacred precinct at Tel Dan with the steps, dated to Jeroboam II. (Courtesy of Tel Dan Excavations, Hebrew Union College, Jerusalem; Photo: A. Biran)

Ill. 187: Sacred precinct at Tel Dan from the days of Ahab. (Courtesy of Tel Dan Excavations, Hebrew Union College, Jerusalem; Photo: A. Biran)

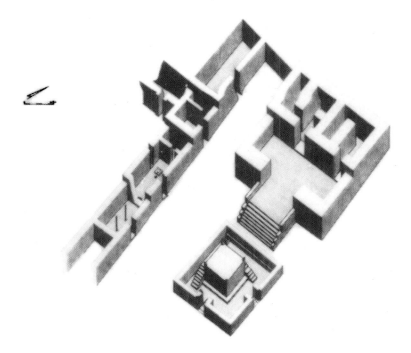

Ill. 188: Isometric drawing of the Dan sacred precinct, from eighth century B.C.E., time of Jeroboam II. The great four-horned altar stands in the courtyard before the stairway leading up to the temple. The side rooms to the west may be part of the *liškâ* or *bêt marzēaḥ*. (Illustration: C. Haberl, adapted from A. Biran, *Biblical Dan*, p. 203, fig. 163)

cultic paraphernalia, including an ephod, teraphim, and a *pesel* of silver (perhaps in the form of a bull-calf). Before they depart for the north, however, they ask the priest to "inquire of God that we may know whether the mission we are undertaking will succeed" (Judg. 18:5). The cultic specialist consults the media, probably the sacred lots Urim and Thummim stored in the ephod[6] by which he divines the will of the deity and replies to the Danites: "Go in peace. The mission you are on is under the eye of Yahweh" (Judg. 18:6). In this etiological tale, the religious center of Dan is founded and legitimated by a Levitical priest, a Judahite from David's hometown of Bethlehem. "Then the Danites set up the idol (*pesel*) for themselves. Jonathan son of Gershom, son of Moses,[7] and his sons were priests to the tribe of

---

6. In the more archaic biblical material, the ephod is not the linen garment worn by the high priest, but rather a box in which the Urim and Thummim are stored (see 1 Sam. 14:1–3, 41–42). Note also that in this pericope it is the Shilonite-Mushite priests who are in charge of the ephod. See also Cornelis Van Dam, *The Urim and Thummim: A Means of Revelation in Ancient Israel* (Winona Lake, Ind.: Eisenbrauns, 1997).

7. Read *mšh*. The MT reading "Manasseh" is a later insertion, as Julius Wellhausen noted long ago in his *Prolegomena to the History of Israel* (Atlanta: Scholars Press, 1994; German original in 1878), 142; see also Frank M. Cross, *Canaanite Myth and Hebrew Epic* (Cambridge: Harvard University Press, 1973), 197 n. 18. Cross reads *mšh* with the Lucianic Recension of the Old Greek and with the Vulgate.

the Danites until the time the land went into captivity. So they maintained as their own Micah's idol that he had made, as long as the temple of God was at Shiloh" (Judg. 18:30–31). Thus, to avoid rivalries between the two great priestly clans, Jeroboam I appointed Mushites over the temple at Dan and Aaronids over the temple at Bethel.[8] Both priestly houses were condemned for golden calf iconography by later interpreters, although in some circles it was the Aaronids who bore the brunt of that "apostasy" (cf. Exodus 32).

In contrast to the situation in Jerusalem, for which there are only biblical descriptions of the Solomonic Temple (as well as comparative archaeological evidence from Syria), the excavations of Biran at Tel Dan have revealed a cultic structure and its surroundings that beg to be identified with the sacred precinct of Dan, established by King Jeroboam at the end of the tenth century B.C.E. and continued as a sacred center through the Roman period. And although the archaeological evidence is yet lacking, the biblical traditions lead one to expect even pre-tenth-century B.C.E. cultic associations with this most prominent area of Tel Dan, situated in the northwest quarter of the city near freshwater springs and an awesome view of snow-capped Mount Hermon to the north. In its tenth to ninth century B.C.E. phase, the sacred precinct of Dan (Area T) was set apart from the rest of the site by a temenos wall, which encompassed about 2,700 meters (45 meters by 60 meters).

The archaeology and history of the sacred precinct are difficult to unravel because of its continuous use for a millennium or more. The most prominent feature—a beautifully built podium of ashlar blocks—occupies the northern quarter of the temenos (Ill. 187). In its mature phase, the podium was about 18.5 meters square and 3 meters high. Its ashlar blocks were laid header-stretcher style. A deep groove was cut along the lower courses of ashlars for the insertion of wooden beams (now rotted away), just as in Solomon's Temple and palace complex in Jerusalem where, according to the biblical description, they were built "with three courses of dressed stone to one course of cedar beams" (1 Kings 6:36; cf. 1 Kings 7:12 and Ezra 6:4). Wooden sleeper beams in stone foundations cushioned shockwaves and made buildings more resilient to earthquakes. On the south side of the square platform, or podium, an eight-meter-wide monumental staircase led to the top. Biran has interpreted the great podium as an open-air sanctuary and identified it with a biblical *bāmâ*, usually translated "high place." The whole precinct, in his estimation, may constitute a *bêt bāmôt* (1 Kings 12:31).[9]

---

8. For a detailed discussion of the Mushite and Aaronide traditions, see initially Wellhausen, *Prolegomena*, 121–51; and more recently Cross, *Canaanite Myth and Hebrew Epic*, 195–215. It is somewhat difficult to believe, however, that the polemic against the "golden calf" originated with the Mushites of Shiloh, since presumably this Ephraimite center and its traditions were conveyed to Dan, where the bull-calf iconography was on full display.

9. Avraham Biran, *Biblical Dan* (Jerusalem: Israel Exploration Society, 1994), 181; idem, "Sacred Spaces: Of Standing Stones, High Places, and Cult Objects at Tel Dan," *BAR* 24 (1998): 40.

Ill. 189: Base of canopied podium with two colocynth bases for the columns, in the city gate at Tel Dan. (Courtesy of Tel Dan Excavations, Hebrew Union College, Jerusalem; Photo: A. Biran)

The Deuteronomistic Historian, who uses "temples and high places" (*bāttê bāmôt*) as a term of opprobrium for illicit sanctuaries, does not specifically designate Dan as such. However, his condemnation of the golden calves of Dan and Bethel in the same context leaves little doubt as to his intent. We, then, think that Biran is correct in associating the term *bêt bāmôt* with the sacred precinct of Area T at Dan (Ill. 188). But we go further and suggest that the precinct was so designated precisely because the temple stood atop the great square podium (Ill. 187). There stone socles for a sizable public building have been discerned. The monumental staircase leads to a broadroom at the top of the square podium. From the broadroom, separate doorways lead into two square rooms in the north half of the podium, each with stairways winding up to a second story.[10] There it seems likely that the golden calf, the animal emblem and mount of Yahweh, was displayed.

---

10. See especially the reconstruction by Biran in *Biblical Dan*, Fig. 163, the upper half of the plate; cf. Figs 149 and 176. Although we know of no exact architectural parallel for this building, its archaeological context, the cultic paraphernalia within the temenos, and the faunal assemblage leave no doubt about its cultic character. Attempts to erect insubstantial tent shrines on the ashlar podium at Dan, supposedly in keeping with Mushite "Tabernacle" traditions, are no more convincing than leaving it an open-air *bāmâ*. Cf. Frank M. Cross, "The Priestly Tabernacle in the Light of Recent Research," in Avraham Biran, ed., *Temples and High Places in Biblical Times* (Jerusalem: Hebrew Union College—Jewish Institute of Religion, 1981), 169–80, esp. 178 n. 34; Edward F. Campbell, "Jewish Shrines of the Hellenistic and Persian Periods," in F. M. Cross, ed., *Symposia Celebrating the Seventy-Fifth Anniversary of the Founding of the American Schools of Oriental Research (1900–1975)* (Cambridge: American Schools of Oriental Research, 1979), 159–67.

Ill. 190: Four-horned limestone altar for small burnt offerings, such as incense, found at Tel Dan. (Courtesy of Tel Dan Excavations, Hebrew Union College, Jerusalem; Photo: A. Biran)

In front of the Dan temple was another precinct within the precinct—an enclosure, 12.5 meters by 14 meters, separated from the rest of the courtyard by walls of impressive ashlar masonry. This court was entered by one of two gates, one on the east and the other on the south. A small limestone incense altar, with four horns, was found in the northwest corner of the court (Ill. 190). Its top had been calcined from the fires that burned the aromatics. In the center of the court stood an enormous four-horned altar (only one horn, .5 meter high and .39 meter at the base, survives), about six meters square. Like the temple podium to the north, an ashlar staircase led to the top of the great altar, some three meters above its surroundings.

It is tempting to compare the great open-air altar at Dan with the four-horned altar hearth (*har'ēl*, literally "mountain of El") located in the courtyard of Ezekiel's restored temple in Jerusalem (Ezekiel 43). According to his vision (informed to some degree by the Temple in Jerusalem), the *har'ēl* is to be twelve cubits (about six meters) square, with a staircase leading to the top from the east. On it shall be offered bullocks, rams, and (male) goats, all "without blemish." The list of burnt animal offerings in Ezekiel and other Priestly sources is remarkably similar to the animal remains found in the sacred precinct of Dan. There in Area T, Paula Wapnish and Brian Hesse[11] identified sheep, goat, and cattle bones. The faunal remains in the sacred precinct were much younger than those found elsewhere at Dan. Sixty percent of the sheep/goat bones and forty percent of the cattle showed signs of slaughter. Many of the animals were less than a year old, very probably victims of animal sacrifice.[12]

Side rooms built into the outer perimeter wall of the Dan temenos provided further evidence of cultic activities. In one room an altar, about one meter square and .27 meter high, was built of limestone blocks and apparently used for animal sacrifice. Nearby a sunken jar was found filled with bone ash.[13] Three iron shovels (Ill. 191), as well as a beautiful bowl with omphalos base, were also found in the same room.

---

11. Paula Wapnish and Brian Hesse, "Faunal Remains from Tel Dan: Perspectives on Animal Production at a Village, Urban and Ritual Center," *Archaeozoologia* 4 (1991): 9–86.

12. *'ōlâ*, translated "holocaust" (meaning, "wholly burnt"), signifies a sacrifice in which the entire victim is burnt, leaving nothing for the presenter or the priest, e.g., 2 Kings 16:15; Ex. 29:38–42; Num. 28:3–8; Lev. 1:3–9.

13. Avraham Biran, "The Dancer from Dan, the Empty Tomb and the Altar Room," *IEJ* 36 (1986): 168–87.

Ill. 191: Three iron incense shovels found near the incense altar at Tel Dan. (Courtesy of Tel Dan Excavations, Hebrew Union College, Jerusalem; Photo: A. Biran)

Ill. 192: Bronze and silver scepter head found under the stones of the incense altar at Tel Dan. (Courtesy of Tel Dan Excavations, Hebrew Union College, Jerusalem; Photo: Z. Radovan)

The bowl is of a type associated with drinking at *marzēaḥ* rituals. The shovels, although made of iron, are similar to those made of bronze and part of the appurtenances of Solomon's Temple (1 Kings 7:40, 45), known as *yāʿîm*. At Dan the shovels were no doubt used by priests to remove ashes and coals from the altars. Another cultic item appeared buried just below the altar in the side room. Part of a bronze and silver scepter, decorated with animal heads (perhaps lions), it was probably an emblem of priestly authority (Ill. 192).

Near the altar room lay other cultic objects, among them a large die made of blue frit or faience (Ill. 193). Like dice today, the dots on opposing facets add up to seven.[14] Of course, seven as a sacred number is already attested at least a millennium earlier at the temple and "high place" at Nahariyah, where many composite vessels with seven cups were found.[15] Seven-spouted oil lamps on stands are known from the Dan precinct. The findspot of the die and its sacred number seven suggest that dice

14. Biran, *Biblical Dan*, 199.
15. Lawrence E. Stager and Samuel R. Wolff, "Production and Commerce in Temple Courtyards: An Olive Press in the Sacred Precinct at Tel Dan," *BASOR* 243 (1981): 95–102.

Ill. 193: Faience die which may have been used in divination, found in the sacred precinct at Tel Dan. (Courtesy of Tel Dan Excavations, Hebrew Union College, Jerusalem; Photo: Z. Radovan)

were an important part of the priestly paraphernalia at the Danite sanctuary, where, as we have seen, Moses is viewed as founder, especially in the epic traditions (J–E) and in the archaic hymn in Deuteronomy 33:8: "Give to Levi your Thummim, your Urim to your faithful one, whom you tested at Massah, whom you tried at Meribah."[16]

The Mushite household of Eli at Shiloh was known for divination using the sacred lots of Urim and Thummim (see above). The Levitical priest, removed from Micah's household shrine to the sanctuary at Dan, was also skilled in divination using the sacred lots housed in the ephod. Is it possible that Urim and Thummim were sacred dice similar to the exemplar from the Dan precinct, cast by priests to divine the will of Yahweh?

Temples and Shrines

"Temple" ordinarily, but not exclusively, in the Bible designates an architectural structure intended for divine worship. Considered to be the earthly dwelling of the deity, it was also part of the administrative organization of Jerusalem and the state. The Jerusalem Temple was first and foremost the dwelling place or house of Israel's God. Secondarily, the Temple was the king's chapel, situated next to the Solomonic palace complex. The Temple was not a place of public cult; worshipers were limited to the courts of the Temple. The temple-palace complex was a fundamental institution in the ancient Near East, serving as the economic, cultural, civic, and ritual center of the state.

Two Hebrew words are used frequently for "temple": *bayit* (literally "house") and *hêkāl* ("great house"), signifying the house of a god (temple) or the house of a king (palace). The Temple in Jerusalem is *bêt YHWH*, "house of Yahweh," in conjunction with *bêt hammelek*, "house of the king," and with *bêt 'āb*, "house of the father"—all structural analogues in the social, political, and theological spheres of ancient Israel. This three-tiered hierarchy—the deity's house, the king's house, and the family house, along with their respective households—constitutes the order of being in the cosmion (that is, the meaning that a particular society ascribes to the elements of its world or cosmos).

hêkal may denote the temple as a whole or simply its large central room or nave. Designations for the Jerusalem Temple include *bêt YHWH* ("house of Yahweh"), *bêt*

16. See Ex. 17:2–7, and Cross, *Canaanite Myth and Hebrew Epic*, 197.

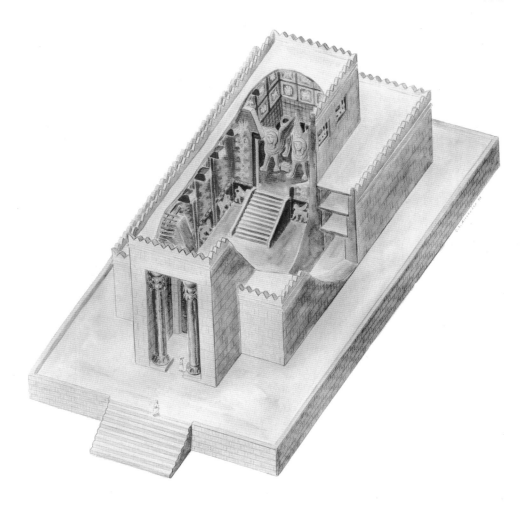

Ill. 194: Interpretation of Solomon's Temple based on biblical texts and comparative temple architecture and iconography. (Reconstruction: © L. E. Stager; Illustration: C. S. Alexander)

'ĕlōhîm ("house of God"), and *miqdāš* ("sanctuary," "shrine"). While the Bible furnishes an elaborate description of the construction of the Temple and its appurtenances, much of the technical terminology of its architecture eludes us. The depiction of the Temple in 1 Kings 6–7 is more reliable than 2 Chronicles 2–4. The final editing of Kings took place sometime early in the exile (586–539 B.C.E.), whereas the Chronicles were written probably in the fourth century B.C.E. Ezekiel 40:1–43:12 is the prophetic vision of the restored Temple, of which several references resonate with the description of the First Temple. Discrepancies exist in these descriptions. Since nothing remains of the Solomonic Temple, architectural reconstruction is based on evidence from the biblical texts (1 Kings 6:1–7; 2 Chron. 3:1–10; Ezekiel 40–43), as well as from analogous Near Eastern temples, especially the tripartite temples in North Syria.

Ill. 195: Three eight-spoked wheels from a bronze stand, similar to the *mĕkônôt*, a bud and a corner of the stand (lower left in photo) found in Bldg. 350, Str V, eleventh B.C.E., Tel Miqne-Ekron. The wheels and the square stand supported a basin or laver. The decorative bud once hung down from the decorative stand. (Courtesy of Tel Miqne-Ekron Excavation/Publication Project; Photo: I. Sztulman)

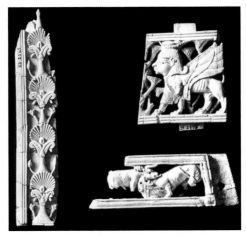

Ill. 196: Ivory plaques from Samaria, dated eighth century B.C.E. (Upper right) winged sphinx in a sacred garden; compare cherubim of Genesis 3. (Lower right) lion and bull in combat. (Left) sacred tree of palmette style. (Courtesy of the Israel Museum)

Solomon's magnificent Temple was situated on the East Hill, north of the City of David, close to the present site of the Dome of the Rock (Qubbet eṣ-Ṣakhra), which was built in 691 C.E. The Temple edifice measured approximately 10 meters wide by 35 meters long by 15 meters high. Constructed of hewn stone prepared at the quarry (1 Kings 6:7) and surrounded by two courtyards (inner and outer) in front, the Temple was a long-room building, laid out on an east-west axis, with the entrance to the east, toward the rising sun (Ill. 194). A four-horned wooden altar covered with bronze for burnt offerings was located in the inner courtyard. There also was a huge, round laver (ceremonial basin) of cast bronze for priestly ablutions, with a capacity of about 40,000 liters. Known as *yām*, literally "sea," it was supported on the backs of a dozen bronze oxen, arranged in groups of three facing in the four cardinal directions of the compass. Near the Temple's entrance stood ten (five on the north and five on the south) bronze *mĕkônôt*, "wheeled stands," each holding a large water basin (*kiyyōr*) (Ill. 195).

Rectangular and tripartite, the Temple included the '*ûlām* or portico (ten meters wide by five meters deep) (1 Kings 6:3); the *hêkāl* or main room (ten meters wide by twenty meters long by fifteen meters high); and the *dĕbîr* or innermost chamber, known as the Holy of Holies, a cube measuring twenty cubits (ten meters) on each side. Two hollow, cast-bronze columns (nine meters high) with double capitals flanked the entrance to the '*ûlām*. The columns, probably engaged, were designated "Jachin" ("he establishes") and "Boaz" ("in strength"), perhaps referring to the Temple and the royal dynasty established by God.

Imported cedar panels, adorned with carvings of sacred trees (palmettes), gourds, rosettes, and cherubim, all overlaid with gold, covered the walls of the *hêkāl* or main room from floor to ceiling, concealing the masonry. There, most of the priestly functions took place. The elaborately decorated *hêkāl* contained the internal furnishings of the Temple. Among these sacred appurtenances, all inlaid with gold, were an incense altar directly in front of the entrance to the Holy of Holies (*dĕbîr*), a table for the showbread (twelve loaves of unleavened bread as an offering to God, replaced every *šabbāt*), and ten lamp stands, five on the north side and five on the south. The *dĕbîr* was overlaid with pure gold. The doors to the entrance of the *dĕbîr* were made of pine, with carvings of cherubim, sacred trees (palmettes), and rosettes, covered with gold leaf. Within, two gigantic cherubim (five meters tall), carved from pine ('*ēṣ šemen*) and overlaid/sheathed with gold foil/leaf (1 Kings 6:23–31), flanked the Ark of the Covenant with their outstretched wings. The cherubim formed the throne of the Deity; the Ark, his footstool.

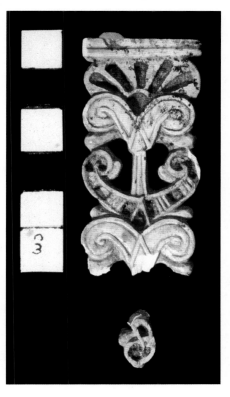

Ill. 197: Ivory palmette with stone and glass inlay from Samaria, from eighth century B.C.E. (Courtesy of L. E. Stager)

Ill. 198: Phoenician ivory from Salamis (Tomb #79) of a gilded and inlaid openwork panel from a throne depicting a winged sphinx and sacred tree (palmette); eighth century B.C.E. (Courtesy of V. Karageorghis, Cyprus Museum, Nicosia)

Ill. 199: Salamis throne; ivory inlay over wood. Dated 800 B.C.E. (Courtesy of V. Karageorghis, Cyprus Museum, Nicosia)

Iron Age Temple at 'Ain Dara'

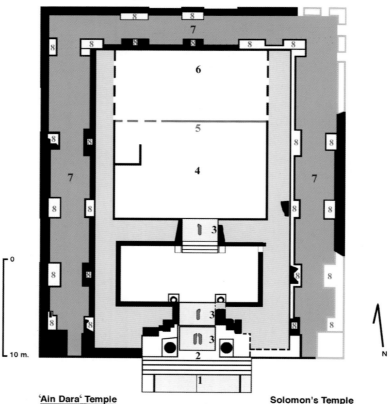

'Ain Dara' Temple	Solomon's Temple
1. Monumental Stairway	1. *sullām* (Gen. 28.12) and *ma'alōt* (Eze. 40.49)
2. Portico with engaged columns	2. Portico with engaged columns Jachin and Boaz (*'ammûdîm ba-'ûlām*, I Kgs. 7.19)
3. Deity's footprints	3. Unshod deity of Israel enters temple via main portal (Eze. 43.4)
4. Central room	4. *hêkāl*
5. Podium base with mountain deities	5. Raised *dĕbîr* and cherubim (throne) "The place of my throne....the place for the soles of my feet" (*kappôt raglay*, Eze. 43.7)
6. Throne room	6. *dĕbîr*, or "Holy of Holies"
7. Side corridors	7. *ṣĕlā'ôt*
8. Sculpted stelae/pilasters	8. *migrā'ôt*

Ill. 200: Reconstruction of Iron Age temple at 'Ain Dara', with legend comparing this Neo-Hittite temple with Solomon's. (Reconstruction: © L. E. Stager; Drawing: A. M. Appa)

The Temple's ground plan was relatively modest in size. Three stories of rooms (*šĕlā'ôt*) surrounded the two long sides and the rear of the Temple. At 'Ain Dara' (in Syria) the side rooms of the temple are a kind of ambulatory decorated with reliefs. Since King Hiram of Tyre supplied the artisans and the building materials for the Jerusalem Temple, the result was a typical Phoenician (Canaanite) temple. Solomon sent word to Hiram: "Command that cedars from the Lebanon be cut for me. My servants will join your servants, and I will give you whatever wages you set for your servants; for you know that there is no one among us who knows how to cut timber like the Sidonians" (1 Kings 5:20). In return for supplying timber and other construction materials, Hiram received wheat and oil (1 Kings 5:25). These exchanges were part of the commerce conducted between Israelite and Phoenician royalty in the Iron Age.

Two of the closest parallels to the Jerusalem Temple are found at Tell Ta'yinat (ancient Hattina, eighth century B.C.E.) in the 'Amuq Valley at the northern Orontes (Syria), and at 'Ain Dara' (tenth to eighth centuries B.C.E.), northwest of Aleppo (Syria) (Ill. 200). 'Ain Dara', much better preserved than Ta'yinat, is larger than Solomon's Temple, measuring thirty-two meters by thirty-eight meters. Ta'yinat is smaller, the temple (Bldg. II) being 11.75 meters by 25.35 meters. These are long-axis temples, oriented with entrances on the short side, and the innermost sanctuary at the opposite end of the building. This temple type has a long history, beginning about 2000 B.C.E.

The Ta'yinat temple is approached from the east and entered through a portico with two columns *in antis* (*antae*: pilaster-like doorjambs), situated on twin lion bases. The nave was a long central room "separated by wing walls from a shallow sanctuary (*dĕbîr*) with an offering table and altar at the rear."[17] The temple used wood-crib construction. Like the Jerusalem Temple, the Ta'yinat temple is located adjacent to the

Ill. 201: Overview of the 'Ain Dara' temple (looking northeast) showing the portico with engaged columns (largely broken) flanked by basalt orthostats carved in relief of lions and winged sphinxes (see partially excavated area to the west of entrance). Monumental in-the-round sculptures of basalt lions (largely defaced) sit above and behind the orthostats supporting the entrance facade. To the north of the portico one enters the anteroom, behind which is the central room paved with flagstones and behind that the throne room. The entrance to one of the three side corridors can be seen in foreground of photo.

17. Richard C. Haines, *Excavations in the Plain of Antioch* (Chicago: University of Chicago Press, 1971), 53.

palace, which measures twenty-nine meters by fifty-eight meters. Such juxtaposition will also characterize the acropolis at 'Ain Dara' when it is more completely excavated. The entrance columns of the large temple of Neo-Hittite style at 'Ain Dara' are engaged with the roof of the portico. This supports the assumption that Jachin and Boaz of the Jerusalem Temple were engaged, and not freestanding columns. The surrounding rooms of the Jerusalem Temple are well illustrated at 'Ain Dara', where on the first floor are corridors with windows and carved stelae or orthostats.

The recent excavations at Ekron, directed by T. Dothan and S. Gitin, have revealed a magnificent temple with a pillared forecourt, located in the heart of the city. According to the royal dedicatory inscription found in the cella, King Achish built the temple precinct and dedicated it to the goddess *PTGYH*, a Philistine deity of probable Hellenic orgin (Ill. 173). This seventh-century B.C.E. temple has several features in common with Syro-Palestinian sacred architecture, such as a long axis, rooms on three sides, and a cella at the end of the main hall, opposite the entrance that opens to the east (cf. Jerusalem Temple) onto a large pillared courtyard. From our perspective the Ekron temple precinct has little in common with Neo-Assyrian architecture.

Ill. 202: 'Ain Dara': carved basalt orthostats of a winged sphinx and a lion guarding the entrance on right to the 'Ain Dara' temple.

Ill. 204: Meter-long footsteps carved in limestone threshold of the tenth through eighth centuries B.C.E. temple at 'Ain Dara' (Syria). The deity strides from the portico toward the throne room of the inner sanctum.

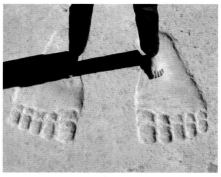

Ill. 203: Deity's footprints compared with feet of mortal at entrance of 'Ain Dara' temple.

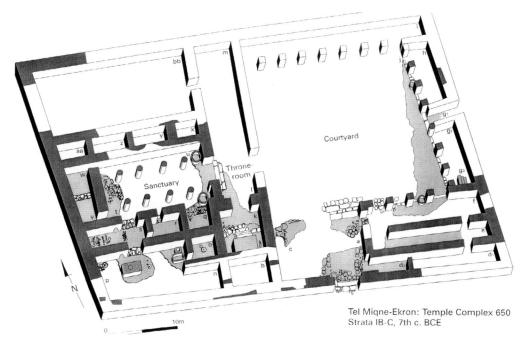

Tel Miqne-Ekron: Temple Complex 650
Strata IB-C, 7th c. BCE

Ill. 205: Plan of Temple Complex 650 with sanctuary, Tel Miqne-Ekron, Str IB, seventh century B.C.E. (late Philistine period). (Courtesy of Tel Miqne-Ekron Excavation/Publication Project; Drawing: J. Rosenberg)

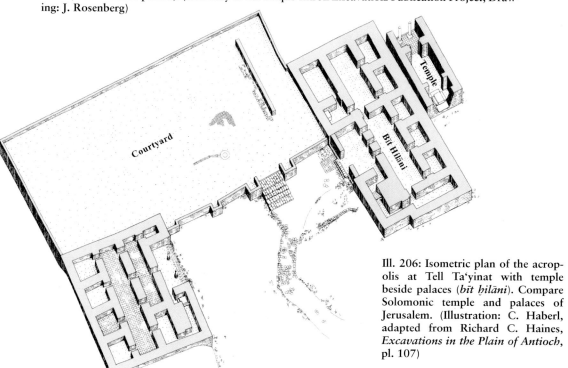

Ill. 206: Isometric plan of the acropolis at Tell Ta'yinat with temple beside palaces (*bīt ḫilāni*). Compare Solomonic temple and palaces of Jerusalem. (Illustration: C. Haberl, adapted from Richard C. Haines, *Excavations in the Plain of Antioch*, pl. 107)

Ill. 207: At the stairway leading into ʿAin Daraʿ temple, looking east. Many of the treads of the stairway have been robbed out. One of the two columns is clearly visible in background left of center where, also, the stairway is intact. Compare Jachin and Boaz.

Ill. 208: Defaced winged sphinx guarding entrance on left, with larger basalt lions above, with only their paws remaining; ʿAin Daraʿ.

Sanctuary at Arad

Yohanan Aharoni uncovered what he considered to be the only Israelite temple to come to light in the course of an archaeological excavation.[18] It is located on the eastern hill of Arad, a Judahite border sanctuary in the valley of Beersheba. The temple, dated to Iron II and dedicated to the God of Israel, is situated in the northwest corner of a royal fortress. Unlike the long-room Jerusalem Temple, the Arad temple is a broad-room type, with the entrance on the long side. This tripartite structure consists of a forecourt, main hall, and Holy of Holies. A large, unhewn altar was located in the open forecourt. The main hall, or *hêkāl*, was in the form of a broad room. The Holy of Holies, or *děbîr*, was located in the center of the wall opposite the entrance of the *hêkāl*. Three steps led upward to the *děbîr*, whose entrance was flanked by two small limestone incense altars without horns, separating the *děbîr* from the *hêkal*. A standing stone (*maṣṣēbâ*) was situated on a small platform within the *děbîr*. It still remains unclear when the Arad temple came to an end.

---

18. Miriam Aharoni, "Arad: The Israelite Citadels," *NEAEHL*, 1: 82–85. This, of course, excludes *bāmôt*, some of which were probably full-fledged temples.

RITUAL OBJECTS

Altars

The altar was the exclusive domain of the priests. The primary Hebrew word for "altar" is *mizbēaḥ*, appearing four hundred times in the Bible. It is derived from the root *zbḥ*, "to slaughter," "to sacrifice," indicating that the altar is the place where animal offerings were slain. There, too, liquids are poured out and grains are burnt. Altars were not restricted to the Temple area but were also used in other sanctuaries. Horns (*qěrānôt*) are a prominent feature of altars, although the significance of these projections from the altars' four corners is uncertain. They may be stylized representations of *maṣṣēbôt*, symbolizing the deity. The horns were considered the holiest part of the altar; to remove them was tantamount to desecrating the altar, as Amos attests: "I [Yahweh] will punish the altars of Bethel, and the horns (*qarnôt*) of the altar shall be cut off and fall to the ground" (Amos 3:14).

The Covenant Code specifies the materials for the construction of altars. Two are mentioned in particular: "altar of earth" (*mizbaḥ 'ădāmâ*) (Ex. 20:24), an ambiguous term that may connote a mound of dirt, and "altar of stones" (*mizbaḥ 'ăbānîm*) (Ex. 20:25), which must be unhewn. Altars of earth and stones have been found, as well as bronze altars. Steps are normally an integral part of an altar. Altars of holocaust (i.e., burnt offerings) usually stood in the courtyard at the front of the Temple, but they are also found elsewhere. Altars of incense stood in the *hêkāl* of the Temple, in front of the *děbîr*.

Apparently the rooftops of houses served as cultic places in the late monarchy. Jeremiah alludes to the practice of making offerings on rooftops: "And the houses of Jerusalem and the houses of the kings of Judah shall be defiled like the place of Topheth—all the houses upon whose roofs offerings have been made (*qṭr*) to the whole host of heaven, and libations have been poured out (*nsk*) to other gods" (Jer. 19:13; also 32:29). In these two verses from Jeremiah, *qṭr* (*pi'el*) and *nsk* occur together with reference to rituals that take place on roofs. The meaning of the root *qṭr* is uncertain, so the cultic activity to which it refers is likewise uncertain. *qṭr* in pi'el does not mean "to offer incense" in all cases; it may also mean "to offer a meal-offering." Of course, the *minḥâ*, or cereal offering, was an offering that combined incense, libations, and flour (Lev. 2:1). *qṭr* in hiph'il can mean "to burn incense."[19]

In accordance with Josiah's reform, "the altars on the roof of the upper storey of Ahaz" were destroyed (2 Kings 23:12). While the priesthood of Jerusalem condemned the practice, at Ashkelon the Philistines offered incense on rooftop altars. When Stager excavated the Babylonian destruction levels of Ashkelon dating to 604 B.C.E., he uncovered the remains of a stone altar used for burning incense. It was found in the destruction debris resting on top of a collapsed roof (Ill. 213, 214).

---

19. Kjeld Nielsen, *Incense in Ancient Israel*, VTSup 38 (Leiden: E. J. Brill, 1986), 54–59.

Altar at Tel Sheva

Excavating at Tel Sheva, Yohanan Aharoni found almost half the stones of a monumental horned altar, dating from the eighth century, reused in constructing a storehouse wall.[20] Three of the four horns of the altar were found intact; the top of the fourth had been broken off. The stones are of ashlar masonry, contrary to the biblical prescription that the altar be of unhewn stones ('ăbānîm šĕlēmôt) (Deut. 27:6; Josh. 8:31). This altar was probably intended for burnt offerings. Its dismantling and subsequent reuse appear to coincide with Hezekiah's religious reform requiring that worship be centralized in Jerusalem.

Cult Stands

"Cult stand" is a generic category embracing a variety of small, portable offering stands. They are characteristic of Iron I and II Palestine. Late Iron II stands were found at the Edomite roadside shrine at Ḥorvat Qitmit in the biblical Negev and at 'En Ḥaṣeva (biblical Tamar) on the road to Edom. Pirhiya Beck divided the stands at Qitmit into two categories: cylindrical stands, open at both ends, with applied animal or anthropomorphic figures, and cylindrical stands without application. The stands are all wheel-made, with handmade applications. The upper part of the stands were composed of the neck and shoulders of a store jar, and the lower part, a wide, hollow cylinder.[21] At 'En Ḥaṣeva, forty-five kilometers southeast of Qitmit, the Edomite shrine from the First Temple period is located outside the fortress walls. The anthropomorphic and cylindrical stands are similar to the assemblage at Qitmit.[22] Cult stands in the coastal plain and in the northern valleys were painted; in the hill country, stands had relief and incised decoration.[23] Materials used in constructing these stands include bronze, clay, limestone, and basalt. Cult stands were used to hold various offerings for the deity, such as incense, water libation, vegetables, and unleavened cakes.

Two cult stands from Iron II were recovered at Ta'anach, one by Ernst Sellin in 1902 and the other by Paul Lapp in 1968. Sellin identified his as an "incense altar," and Lapp called his a "cultic stand." These cult stands from Ta'anach are the only ones in Palestine on which lions and winged sphinxes appear together. The two Ta'anach cult stands, both dating from the tenth century, bear strong resemblance to

0   1   2 cm.

Ill. 209: Shaved/polished astragalus of sheep or goat, perhaps used as gaming piece or for divinatory purposes. From 604 B.C.E. destruction at Ashkelon. (Courtesy of the Leon Levy Expedition to Ashkelon; Photo: I. Sztulman)

---

20. Ze'ev Herzog, "Beersheba," *NEAEHL,* 1: 170–72.

21. Pirhiya Beck, "Catalogue of Cult Objects and Study of the Iconography," in I. Beit-Arieh, ed., *Ḥorvat Qitmit: An Edomite Shrine in the Biblical Negev* (Tel Aviv: Institute of Archaeology, Tel Aviv University, 1995), 28–43.

22. Rudolph Cohen and Yigal Yisrael, "The Iron Age Fortress at 'En Ḥaṣeva," *BA* 58 (1995): 223–35.

23. Pirhiya Beck, "The Cult-Stands from Ta'anach: Aspects of the Iconographic Tradition of Early Iron Age Cult Objects in Palestine," in I. Finkelstein and N. Na'aman, eds., *From Nomadism to Monarchy* (Jerusalem: Israel Exploration Society, 1994), 352.

Ill. 210: Cache of astragali of sheep or goat found in 604 B.C.E. destruction, Ashkelon. (Courtesy of the Leon Levy Expedition to Ashkelon; Photo: C. Andrews)

each other, but at the same time differ from all others. The Sellin stand consists of five superimposed pairs of winged sphinxes and lions. The cult stands were found in a cistern next to the Cultic Structure, destroyed by Shishak in 925, that was part of the Levitical city and provincial capital of Solomon's kingdom (1 Kings 4). Very likely they were legitimate cult objects with legitimate iconography—both the bull-calf (later symbolizing the emblem of Yahweh in the northern kingdom) and the winged sphinxes, an emblem of Yahweh in the southern kingdom.

Similarities between the Taʿanach Cultic Structure and the public shrine at Megiddo within Building 2081, in Str VA, have been noted. Yigal Shiloh among others linked Megiddo and Taʿanach "cult corners" (chapels).[24] Bowls of sheep/goat astragali (ankle bones) were found in both Megiddo and Taʿanach "cult corners." These astragali, like dice at Dan, may have served divinatory purposes (Ill. 209, 210).

Taʿanach Cult Stand

Lapp's Israelite cult stand in clay, slipped and burnished, was meant to resemble shiny copper (Ill. 211). The four-sided stand, with ajouré (cut out or cut away) decoration, was a cheap version of the copper stands so well known from LB Cyprus (and now, in part, from Iron I Ekron, namely the wheels). When on wheels, the copper stands have been very rightly compared with the *měkônôt* in the courtyard of the Solomonic Temple.[25] That the bronze four-sided cult stands continue throughout the Iron Age (and the Mediterranean area) can be seen from examples that appear in ninth–eighth

---

24. Yigal Shiloh, "Iron Age Sanctuaries and Cult Elements in Palestine," in Cross, *Symposia Celebrating the Seventy-Fifth Anniversary,* 149–52. Here Shiloh discusses the small "cultic corners" (chapels) from the Israelite period. At Megiddo, in Building 2081 of Str VA, near the city gate in the front corner of a court-yard, excavators found a group of cult objects, including limestone and pottery cult stands, a selection of bowls and juglets, and two horned limestone altars. At Israelite Lachish, comparable cult places were dis-covered. The principal component of these tenth-century "cultic corners" were the horned limestone altars.

25. For the most comprehensive recent treatment of this comparison, see Helga Weippert, "Die Kessel-wagen Salomos," *ZDPV* 108 (1992): 8–41.

Ill. 211: Cult stand from the Levitical city of Ta'anach, dated tenth century B.C.E. (height=50 cm).
Slipped and burnished to imitate bronze or copper stand; ajouré technique. Read iconography from
bottom to top and from the outer to the inner precinct of the sanctuary. (Bottom Register) nude "Mistress of Animals" flanked by standing lions. (2nd from bottom) winged sphinxes (cherubim). (3rd
from bottom) sacred or cosmic tree flanked by goats nibbling from it and lions. (Top Register - inner
sanctum) a bull calf flanked by voluted columns with winged sun disc on the back of the calf, probably symbol of Yahweh as in the "sun of righteousness shall rise with healing in its wings" (Mal. 4:2).
(Courtesy of the Israel Museum)

Ill. 212: Part of a four-sided bronze stand in ajouré technique from Idaean Cave (Crete), dated Iron II. A ship is represented with five oarsmen and a standing warrior with a round shield. The continuation of the tradition of making four-sided bronze stands with or without wheels provides contemporary parallels with the *měkônôt* of the Solomonic Temple. (Courtesy of N. Stampolidis)

century Crete. The *měkônôt* of the Jerusalem Temple inspired the vision of Ezekiel 1 and 10, not the *markābôt* designated in later tradition as the throne of God.[26]

As one "reads" the Ta'anach Cult Stand from bottom to top, one moves to more sacred space, until one reaches the top register, where the winged sun disc (Yahweh symbol) rides on the back of the bull-calf. The bull-calf is the beast of Yahweh, not Yahweh himself. Reading the stand from bottom to top,[27] we have "Mistress of Animals" standing naked and en face between two lions. Some have identified her as Asherah, but this is by no means certain. In the next register from the bottom, stand two winged sphinxes, commonly identified with the cherubim of the Bible. They guard entrances to palaces and temples throughout the ancient Near East. Much has been made of the empty space between the winged sphinxes. It could possibly represent the outer entrance of the portal or be a part

26. Lawrence E. Stager, "Jerusalem and the Garden of Eden," in B. A. Levine et al., eds., *Eretz-Israel* 26 [Frank Moore Cross Volume] (Jerusalem: Israel Exploration Society, 1999), 83–88.

27. Beck, "The Cult-Stands from Taanach," 375: "The top panel represents the cella of a shrine, as in the top panel from Mari, while the lower panels (tree and goats, vanquisher of lions), like the bottom panel in Mari, represent the statues or reliefs in the entrance. The lions and sphinxes are the guardians of the shrine's facade." Thus the calf is located in the inner sanctum of the Holy of Holies.

of the ajouré technique of modeling in clay and forging in metal. On the back side of the stand are rectangular windows. The side panels are also "cut out" in the shape of the figures being represented. What should not be read into the opening of the second register, contra Taylor, is the "invisible deity" Yahweh "enthroned (between) the cherubim" throne.[28] Yahweh is enthroned on, not between, the cherubim, which in terms of the Solomonic Temple is in the inner sanctum, the *děbîr*, or Holy of Holies.

On the third tier, or register, another two roaring lions flank two goats, standing on their hind legs, nibbling on the sacred tree. As we move from lower to higher registers, we move from outside or from the entrance to the sanctuary, through the doorway flanked by the guardian cherubim, into the main hall of the building, decorated with lions and goats and cosmic trees. At the top tier, we reach the most sacred part of the building, the cella or "holy of holies," where the symbol or image of the deity resides. In the Ta'anach stand, a young, prancing animal stands, side view, between two voluted columns representing ornamental trees. Mounted on the back of the bull-calf (we doubt that it is a colt) is the symbol of the deity: the winged sun disc, the solar symbol of Yahweh. This is the abstract symbol of the deity Yahweh mounted on the bull-calf or *ʿēgel*. This is a "legitimate" cult stand for the provincial and Levitical city of Ta'anach in the time of Solomon.

Both the bull-calf *and* the cherubim were sanctioned symbols of the Yahwistic cult before the split into north and south, after which point the bull-calf became identified with the deity himself, in order to discredit the temple centers of Dan and Bethel. Not only the South with its cherubim iconography, but certain prophetic groups in the North, belittled the bull-calf icon and declared it an "idol." Hosea disparaged the Israelite shrine at Bethel because of its association with the golden calf fashioned by Jeroboam I, calling it by the derogatory name "Beth Aven," meaning "house of iniquity." Twice Hosea calls the place "Bethel" (10:15; 12:5); thrice he calls it "Beth Aven" (4:15; 5:8; 10:5). In the same scornful spirit Amos cautioned: "Bethel shall become 'Aven' ('iniquity')" (5:5).

Incense Altars

Prominent among cult stands are stone incense altars, which played a substantial role in the Israelite cult of the Iron Age, especially during the seventh and sixth centuries. Typical incense altars stood twenty-five to forty centimeters high, were square in shape, and were crafted from soft limestone. They appear ordinarily in houses and domestic industrial installations. Incense altars have been found at sites in Israel[29] and Judah, as well as in the Philistine cities of Ashkelon and especially Ekron. At least twelve incense

---

28. J. Glen Taylor, *Yahweh and the Sun: The Biblical and Archaeological Evidence for Sun Worship in Ancient Israel*, JSOTSup 111 (Sheffield: JSOT Press, 1993), 29, 36.

29. Seymour Gitin, "Incense Altars from Ekron, Israel, and Judah: Context and Typology," in A. Ben-Tor et al., eds., *Eretz-Israel* 20 [Yigael Yadin Volume] (Jerusalem: Israel Exploration Society, 1989), 55*–56*. A corpus of Iron II incense altars was found at Megiddo; most were horned.

altars have come to light at Ekron, ten with horns and two without, dating to the late seventh century. These altars vary in size from fifteen to sixty-five centimeters in height. Most are made from limestone and a few from basalt, and they are modeled on types from the northern kingdom of Israel. Since horned altars are characteristic of Israelite religious practice, Seymour Gitin, co-excavator of Ekron, suggests that Israelites may have been employed as artisans at Ekron.[30]

The altars at Ekron were not used in a typical Israelite cultic context. They were found, according to the excavator, in industrial, domestic, and elite zones. Each olive-oil building contained at least one four-horned altar. The combination of cult and industry is evident at Ekron, but there is precedent elsewhere. Owing to the large number of altars in the industrial zone, Gitin suggests that it may have been administered by a priestly class. Incense may have been burnt in these altars both to dispose the gods and to mask the odors from the industrial area; in the latter case, it served as a sweet-smelling fumigant that also helped ward off unwanted insects and vermin attracted to the olive oil industry.

Ill. 213: Sandstone incense altar without horns from 604 B.C.E. destruction, Ashkelon. (Courtesy of the Leon Levy Expedition to Ashkelon; Photo: C. Andrews)

Ill. 214: Incense altar without horns (*in situ*) from 604 B.C.E. destruction of Ashkelon. Altar found on a collapsed roof. (Courtesy of the Leon Levy Expedition to Ashkelon; Photo: C. Andrews)

Menaham Haran[31] disagrees with the "incense altar" interpretation proposed by Gitin and others. Haran maintains that a less costly offering than incense was more fitting for these small altars. He would restrict the burning of incense to the Temple in Jerusalem. Remarking that few excavated altars show signs of burning, Haran claims there is no proof that incense altars were used in Israelite cult practice. In his estimation these altars were used for grain offerings, which were not always burnt.

---

30. Seymour Gitin, "Incense Altars from Ekron, Israel, and Judah: Context and Typology," 61*: "Under the influence of the Assyrian economic and population movement policies, northern Israelite artisans could have brought the tradition of altar making to Ekron."

31. Menaham Haran, "'Incense Altars'—Are They?" in A. Biran and J. Aviram, eds., *Biblical Archaeology Today, 1990* (Jerusalem: Israel Exploration Society, 1993), 237–47. The biblical evidence, according to Haran, indicates the cultic use of incense was limited to the Temple in Jerusalem. Therefore, the Iron II four-horned altars outside Jerusalem could not have been incense altars.

Haran maintains that altars outside of the Temple were intended for simple, in-expensive offerings, probably grain offering (*minḥâ*) rather than incense. Haran's view must be countered; Gitin's[32] critique is convincing. Haran's thesis goes up in smoke when it is recalled that quite often the altars (at Arad, Tel Sheva, and else-where) show no signs of burning. They could have put smaller vessels in/on the four-cornered space and burnt incense there. Furthermore, if incense functions as a fumigant in the olive-oil industry, then a grain offering would do a poor job of fumi-gation.

Like the tabernacle, Solomon's Temple had two altars: one for burnt offering, and one for incense. The courtyard altar of acacia wood was the altar for burnt offering (Ex. 27:1–8). The altar for incense stood in the "holy place"; it was located in front of the veil at the entrance to the Holy of Holies (Ex. 30:6). This altar was constructed, like a courtyard altar, of acacia wood but overlaid with pure gold. "On it [altar of incense] Aaron shall burn (*hiqṭîr*) fragrant incense (*qěṭōret sammîm*). Morning after morning, when he prepares the lamps, and again in the evening twilight, when he lights the lamps, he shall burn incense" (Ex. 30:7–8).

Incense

Incense was used in the religious practice of Israel during the First Temple period. The burning of incense was a priestly prerogative whose ritual use was confined to official worship in the Temple. *qěṭōret* ("that which goes up in smoke"), the most common word in the Bible for incense, has several connotations, embracing the incense material, the incense offering, the smoke or fragrance from the offering, and the sacrifice in general.[33] Incense was considered to have certain apotropaic (evil-averting) qualities. It had a variety of uses, both profane and religious. In addition to celebrations, incense was employed in spicing wine, in concocting medicine, in ritu-als of magic, in preparing corpses for burial, and as a cosmetic for perfuming the body. It also served to dispel unpleasant odors and to rid the sanctuary of annoying flies and persistent mosquitoes.

Regarding the religious use of incense, Jeremiah describes the proper activities on the sabbath, which include: "People shall come from the towns of Judah and the places around Jerusalem . . . bringing burnt offerings and sacrifices, grain offerings and frank-incense (*lěbônâ*)" (Jer. 17:26). Incense was also utilized during the annual festivals. On the Day of Atonement (Yom Kippur), Aaron was directed as follows: "He [Aaron] shall

---

32. Seymour Gitin, "New Incense Altars from Ekron: Context, Typology and Function," in E. Stern and T. Levy, eds., *Eretz-Israel* 23 [Avraham Biran Volume] (Jerusalem: Israel Exploration Society, 1992), 47*: "The archaeological evidence is undeniably consistent with the consensus that the four-horned altar was used to burn incense, while also accommodating the possibility that other substances may have been burned on some of the altars."

33. Nielsen, *Incense in Ancient Israel*, 54.

take a censer full of coals of fire from the altar before Yahweh, and two handfuls of crushed sweet incense, . . . and put the incense (*haqqĕṭōret*) on the fire before Yahweh, so that the cloud from the incense covers the mercy seat (*hakkappōret*) that is over [the Ark of] the Covenant, lest he die" (Lev. 16:12–13).[34] The ascent of smoke from the burning incense, according to Nigel Groom,[35] suggests the upward movement of prayer to the heavens, thus equating the offering of incense with worship.

The Bible has specific directives about the composition of incense and the ceremonies regulating its use. Incense used in Israelite worship consisted of frankincense and several other ingredients, including sweet spices, stacte, onycha, and galbanum (Ex. 30:34–38). Stacte, onycha, and galbanum are plants, but more precise identification is uncertain. Both frankincense (*lĕbōnâ*) and myrrh (*mōr*)[36] are obtained by tapping shrubs native to only two parts of the world: southern Arabia and northern Somaliland (comprising present-day Somalia, Djibouti, and southeastern Ethiopia). Hatshepsut transplanted myrrh trees from Punt (location uncertain) to Egypt. Transplantations to Palestine were also possible, although not on any great scale. In the Song of Solomon (4:13–14) the *pardēs* ("orchard") has frankincense and myrrh trees.

Frankincense[37] is a costly, fragrant, whitish gum resin extracted from the trunk of Boswellia (named after John Boswell) trees. *lĕbōnâ*, signifying whiteness, may be an allusion to the milky color of the fresh juice. Frankincense, the main ingredient of the incense burnt on the altar (Ex. 30:7–8), produced the fragrant smoke of incense. It was also added to certain meal offerings (Lev. 2:1–3). In the secular realm, frankincense was compounded in medicines and perfumes. Frankincense was imported to Palestine by caravans from Sheba in southern Arabia: "A multitude of camels shall cover you, the young camels of Midian and Ephah; all those from Sheba [South Arabic "Saba"] shall come. They shall bring gold and frankincense (*lĕbônâ*), and shall proclaim the praise of Yahweh" (Isa. 60:6). Sheba is usually identified with Saba located in modern Yemen, in the southwestern part of the Arabian peninsula. Midian, Ephah, and Sheba designate the nomadic inhabitants of the Syrian and Arabian deserts. Camel caravans traversed the incense routes running the length of the Arabian peninsula, which is connected by land with Sinai, Syria-Palestine, and Mesopotamia.

Myrrh (*mōr*),[38] a gum resin reddish in color, occurring as a solid and as a liquid, is derived from the Semitic root *mrr*, "to be bitter," because of its taste. Already attested in the Amarna Tablets, it, too, was used in incense, but less so than frankincense. The incense produced from myrrh and other aromatic substances served ritual

---

34. de Vaux, *Ancient Israel*, 509: "There is no mention of the feast [Day of Atonement] in any pre-exilic text, either historical or prophetical."

35. Nigel Groom, *Frankincense and Myrrh: A Study of the Arabian Incense Trade* (London: Longman, 1981), 2.

36. Gus W. Van Beek, "Frankincense and Myrrh," *BA* 23 (1960): 69–95.

37. D. Kellermann, "*lĕbōnâ*, Frankincense," *TDOT*, 7: 441–47.

38. J. Hausmann, "*mōr*, Myrrh," *TDOT*, 8: 557–60.

purposes, especially in the Temple cult. In addition, myrrh was used as a perfume, cosmetic, and medicine, as well as for embalming and anointing the deceased. The ingredients of the "anointing oil" were liquid myrrh (*mor-dĕrôr*) and spices (Ex. 30:23). The Bible refers to the fragrance of myrrh as a symbol of luxury and beauty. Myrrh was used to perfume royal garments. The ode for a royal wedding describes the king's raiment as "fragrant with myrrh (*mōr*) and aloes and cassia" (Ps. 45:9 [E.T. 45:8]). In extolling a woman's beauty, the Song of Solomon alludes metaphorically to her breasts: "I will hasten to the mountain of myrrh (*hammôr*) and the hill of frankincense (*hallĕbônâ*) (Song of Sol. 4:6).

Cult Figurines

Archaeologists have found thousands of terracotta figurines, both anthropomorphic and zoomorphic, in Israel dating between the tenth and sixth centuries B.C.E. Clay figurines were common in Judah, including Jerusalem. Hoards of fertility figurines have come to light in the excavations of Jerusalem's Jewish Quarter and the City of David. Pillar-shaped figurines from the eighth and seventh centuries appeared in Jerusalem mainly in the debris of private homes, not in sanctuaries. This discovery was not a surprise, in view of the prophets' condemnation of such images: "They shall be turned back and utterly put to shame—those who trust in carved images, who say to cast images, 'You are our gods'" (Isa. 42:17; 44:9–17; Jer. 44:15–25). The figurines were among the "other gods" (*'ĕlōhîm 'ăḥērîm*) whom "the people of Judah and the inhabitants of Jerusalem" worshiped (Jer. 11:9–10).

Ill. 215: Three deities, two male on right and one female on left, with offering cups on their heads. From the Edomite shrine at 'En Ḥaṣeva, from seventh or sixth century B.C.E. (Courtesy of the Israel Museum; Photo: A. Hay)

The traditional fertility goddesses are depicted naked and supporting prominent breasts with their hands. The exaggerated sexual features of the pillar-base figurines suggest they relate to the

Ill. 216: Head of terracotta female figurine, probably a Philistine goddess from Ashkelon, dated Iron II. (Courtesy of the Leon Levy Expedition to Ashkelon; Photo: I. Sztulman)

Ill. 217: Terracotta female figurine, probably a Philistine goddess from Ashkelon, dated Iron II. (Courtesy of the Leon Levy Expedition to Ashkelon; Photo: C. Andrews)

cult of the mother goddess, who provides life and nourishment, and were talismans abetting conception and childbirth. "Pillar figurines" have three characteristics: conical bodies, heavy breasts, and head (Ill. 218). The pillar base and breasts were shaped by hand; the head, molded or shaped by hand. The "pillar" is not a stylized tree but a way of manufacturing these figures.[39] Ephraim Stern, excavator of Dor, describes a new technique beginning in the sixth century, imported from the west, probably Greece, for fashioning "pillar figurines": "a hollow body molded in front, with the back sealed with smooth strips of clay."[40] This Western type was the most common at Dor. Some argue these "pillar figurines" are associated with the cult of Asherah or Ashtoreth, but this remains unclear. Ashtoreth (pl. Ashtaroth) is the biblical designation of the Canaanite goddess more commonly known as Astarte (Astarte [Greek], Ishtar [Akkadian]), the goddess of both war and sex. Astarte was the local consort of Ba'al, the Canaanite god of both the storm and fertility.

---

39. Othmar Keel and Christoph Uehlinger, *Gods, Goddesses, and Images of God in Ancient Israel* (Minneapolis: Fortress, 1998) 331–32.

40. Ephraim Stern, "What Happened to the Cult Figurines?," *BAR* 15 (1989): 27.

Ill. 218: Votive terracotta pillar figurines of either the goddess (Asherah) or the female dedicant, Iron II, from Judah. (Courtesy of Israel Museum)

In the cult of the "Queen of Heaven" described by Jeremiah, determining the identity of the goddess is not simple, and scholars have proffered a variety of suggestions. Hurrian Ishtar/Palestinian Astarte/Heavenly Aphrodite may be the goddess for whom the women of Judah made cakes, burned incense, and poured drink offerings (see Ill. 23). Others suggest that Asherah or Anath was the object of this cult.[41] "The children gather wood,

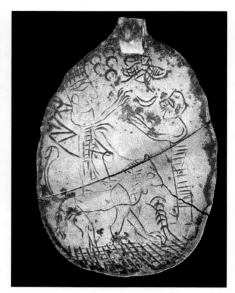

Ill. 219: Silver medallion depicting worshiper with arms raised, praying to the goddess Ishtar standing on a lion. Above is the crescent moon, a winged solar disc, and seven circles (the constellation Pleiades). Part of a silver hoard found in 604 B.C.E. destruction, Tel Miqne-Ekron, Str IB. (Courtesy of Tel Miqne-Ekron Excavation Publication Project; Photo: I. Sztulman)

the fathers kindle fire, and the women knead dough, to make cakes for the queen of heaven (*lĕmalkat haššāmayim*);[42] and they pour out drink offerings to other gods, to provoke me [Yahweh] to anger" (Jer. 7:18; 44:17–25).

The well-known terracotta figurines depicting a female with a disc-shaped object in hand have occasioned much discussion over two issues: whether the figure is a goddess or human, and whether the object is a frame drum (*tōp*), round loaf, plate, or sun disc (Ill. 220). Carol Meyers, who has made a detailed study of this type of figurine, concludes that the female figure is a musician playing a frame drum. Delbert

---

41. Walter Rast, "Cakes for the Queen of Heaven," in A. L. Merrill and T. W. Overholt, eds., *Scripture in History and Theology* (Pittsburgh: Pickwick Press, 1977), 167–80. Vassos Karageorghis and Lawrence E. Stager, "Another Mould for Cakes from Cyprus," A. "The Mould and Its Interpretation" (Karageorghis); B. "In the Queen's Image" (Stager), *Rivista di Studi Fenici* 28/1 (2000): 3–13. Philip J. King, *Jeremiah: An Archaeological Companion* (Louisville, Ky.: Westminster John Knox, 1993), 102–7.

42. For this reading, see William L. Holladay, *Jeremiah 1*, Hermeneia (Philadelphia: Fortress, 1986), 251. Ze'ev Meshel, *Kuntillet 'Ajrud: A Religious Centre from the Time of the Judean Monarchy on the Border of Sinai*, Catalog 175 (Jerusalem: Israel Museum, 1978), unnumbered page.

Hillers identified the figure from Ta'anach as "the goddess with the tambourine."[43]

Shrine at Kuntillet 'Ajrud

Ze'ev Meshel discovered remarkable remains at a remote caravanserai, dating about 800 B.C.E., in northeastern Sinai near the Negev border.[44] The site is known in Arabic as Kuntillet 'Ajrud, "the solitary hill of the water-wells" (Heb., Ḥorvat Teman). The inscriptions and drawings found at this cultic installation are of considerable importance. Hebrew and Phoenician inscriptions decorated the plaster walls of the building, two large pithoi, and stone vessels. Crude drawings appear on the walls and storage jars, although the connection, if any, between the iconography and the inscriptions is uncertain. Othmar Keel distinguishes between the well-rendered wall paintings and the rather sloppy graffiti. One pithos is decorated with two drawings, one on either side. There is a sacred tree flanked by ibexes along with a lion. These motifs parallel tier two (from the top) of the

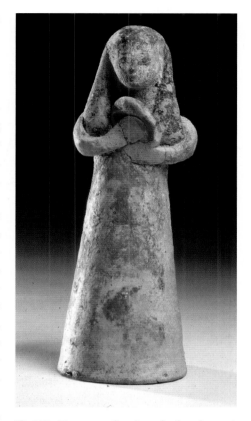

Ill. 220: Terracotta figurine of a female musician playing hand drum (tōp); dated Iron II. (Courtesy of the Harvard Semitic Museum)

Ta'anach cult stand. Also depicted are two standing figures and a seated woman (not a goddess), playing a lyre (kinnôr). The standing figures represent the Egyptian god Bes and his consort Bastet (Beset), identified by their grotesque features as well as by the feathered headdress, lion skin, and akimbo position of their arms.[45]

The accompanying inscription, which has occasioned endless scholarly discussion, reads: "I bless you by Yahweh of Samaria and by his asherah." Scholars disagree

---

43. Carol L. Meyers, "A Terracotta at the Harvard Semitic Museum and Disc-holding Female Figures Reconsidered," *IEJ* 37 (1987): 116–22, pl. 7; idem, "Of Drums and Damsels: Women's Performance in Ancient Israel," *BA* 54 (1991): 21–22; Delbert Hillers, "The Goddess with the Tambourine," *Concordia Theological Monthly* 41 (1970): 609–19.

44. Meshel, *Kuntillet 'Ajrud: A Religious Centre from the Time of the Judean Monarchy on the Border of Sinai*, unnumbered pages.

45. Keel and Uehlinger, *Gods, Goddesses, and Images of God in Ancient Israel*, 219: "The two figures from Kuntillet 'Ajrud are not to be treated as a heterosexual pair, in the sense of Bes and Beset, but it is rather more likely that they are two Bes variants, one masculine and one bisexual-feminized."

about the meaning of "his asherah"—whether it refers to the Canaanite goddess, Asherah, to her wooden cult symbol, or to her sanctuary. It is unlikely that "his asherah" refers to the goddess, since personal names are not found with pronominal suffixes in biblical Hebrew. Apparently the wooden symbol of the goddess is intended.

The Canaanite goddess Asherah[46] is mentioned at least forty times in the Bible. The tree and tree trunk are symbols of the goddess. When Ahab married Jezebel, he built a temple to Ba'al for his Tyrian wife and set up therein Asherah (*'ăšērâ*) (1 Kings 16:33). Manasseh erected an image of Asherah in the Temple (2 Kings 21:7). In his accusations against Judah, Jeremiah adds, "while their children remember their altars and their sacred poles (*'ăšērêhem*), beside every green tree, and on the high hills" (Jer. 17:2). "Asherah" may signify an image representing the goddess herself, or the wooden pole symbolizing the goddess, or a sacred tree or grove. Some argue that the asherim were not living trees but were made by human hands. The verbs describing their origin are inappropriate for living trees but pertinent for wooden objects: *'āśâ*, "to make," *bānâ*, "to build," *hiṣṣîb* (*hiphil*), "to erect," *gāda'*, "to fell," *kārat*, "to cut," *śārap*, "to burn."[47] It could be a combination of a natural tree bedecked with artificial elements—a kind of "Christmas tree." Stager believes they were actual trees growing in the courtyards and surroundings of temples and high places. Deuteronomic legislation seems to share that understanding: "You shall not plant (*nāṭa'*) any tree as an Asherah beside the altar that you make for Yahweh your God" (Deut. 16:21). *nāṭa'* is used for "natural" trees.[48]

The religion of ancient Israel appropriated several aspects of the Canaanite cult, including the identification of Yahweh as El, the chief god of the Canaanite pantheon, whose consort was Asherah. The implication may be that Asherah was the consort of Yahweh.[49]

Votives

Petitioners presented votive offerings (also known as *ex voto*) in the hope that a request would be granted. Votive figurines or statuettes, fabricated from metal, stone, or clay,

---

46. Judith M. Hadley, "Yahweh and 'His Asherah': Archaeological and Textual Evidence for the Cult of the Goddess," in W. Dietrich and M. A. Klopfenstein, eds., *Ein Gott Allein?* OBO 139 (Göttingen: Vandenhoeck & Ruprecht, 1994), 235–68.

47. Hadley, "Yahweh and 'His Asherah,'" 238.

48. Stager, "Jerusalem and the Garden of Eden," 83–88.

49. P. Kyle McCarter, "Aspects of the Religion of the Israelite Monarchy: Biblical and Epigraphic Data," in P. D. Miller et al., eds., *Ancient Israelite Religion* (Philadelphia: Fortress, 1987). Discussing the phenomenon of the personification of Yahweh's asherah at Kuntillet 'Ajrud, McCarter comments: "The asherah of the Yahweh of Samaria ought to be a wooden cult object associated with the worship of Yahweh in that city. We seem to have a case, therefore, of the personification of a cult object as a goddess" (147). He concludes his remarks on hypostatic personality by stating that Yahweh's asherah (the Israelite, not the Canaanite, asherah) is "the personification of a hypostatic form of Yahweh" (149).

have been found by the hundreds and from almost every archaeological period. Votives may be anthropomorphic and theriomorphic, as well as nonzoomorphic. Many were relegated to a prescribed pit (*favissa*), since their sacred character prevented them from simply being cast out.

Votives in the form of inscribed ceramic vessels have been found at Hazor, el-Qom, Arad, Tel Sheva, and Kuntillet 'Ajrud. The stone bowls from Kuntillet 'Ajrud were incised with inscriptions in early Hebrew script. They read: *l'bdyw bn 'dnh brk h' lyhw*—"(Belonging) to 'Obadyau son of 'Adnah, may he be blessed by God"; and *sm'yw bn 'zr*—"Shema'yau son of 'Ezer." "The wording of the inscriptions," according to Meshel, "shows that the stone bowls were dedicated to this place by the donors, who asked for divine blessing."[50]

RELIGIOUS PRACTICES

Feasts

The weekly observance of the sabbath, the seventh day of the week, commemorates both creation (Ex. 20:8–11) and Israel's liberation from slavery (Deut. 5:12–15). The sabbath grew in importance over time, but Israelite law gives the impression that its observance was ancient: "Six days you shall do your work, but on the seventh day you shall rest (*tišbōt*), so that your ox and your donkey may have relief, and your homeborn slave and the sojourner (*gēr*) may be refreshed" (Ex. 23:12; also 34:21). "Sabbath" is related to the root *šbt*, "to rest," "to cease," appearing over a hundred times in the Bible. Amos implies that commerce was prohibited on both the sabbath and the New Moon. Corrupt merchants, eager to prey on the needy, inquired, "When will the New Moon be over so that we may sell grain; and the sabbath, so that we may offer wheat for sale?" (Amos 8:5). Included in the book of Jeremiah is an oracle exhorting the people of Judah to honor the sabbath as a matter of life and death (Jer. 17:19–27). This sermon, however, may be later than Jeremiah, dating more likely to the postexilic period.

The New Moon (*ḥōdeš*, Num. 28:11–15) celebrates the first day of the lunar month. Like the sabbath, it was a day of rest and feasting. The prescribed holocaust offering consisted of two bullocks, one ram, and seven unblemished yearling lambs (Num. 28:11). Especially important is the observance of the New Moon on the seventh month, Tishri (September/October).

ḥaggîm (plural form) designate the annual feasts of pilgrimage. Only three holy days are included among the *ḥaggîm*: "the festival of Unleavened Bread" (*ḥam-*

---

50. Meshel, *Kuntillet 'Ajrud: A Religious Centre from the Time of the Judean Monarchy on the Border of Sinai*, unnumbered page.

maṣṣôt), later combined with Passover (*pesaḥ*); "the festival of Harvest" (*qāṣîr*), also called "the festival of Weeks" (*šābuʿôt*); and "the festival of Ingathering" (*ʾāsîp*), also known as "the festival of Booths" (*sukkôt*) (Ex. 23:14–17). These feasts underwent historical development and became associated with major events in Israel's religious history.[51] According to Exodus 23:14–17 (Elohist Code), Exodus 34:18–23 (Yahwist Code), and Deuteronomy 16:1–17 (Deuteronomic Code), all males are to present themselves before Yahweh annually on these three occasions.[52] However, references to "your sons and your daughters, your male and female slaves, the Levites resident in your towns, as well as the strangers, the orphans, and the widows who are among you" (Deut. 16:11, 14) participating in the *ḥaggîm* indicate that observance was not restricted to males. Perhaps the centralization of the cult in Jerusalem influenced this change.[53]

The feast of Unleavened Bread (*maṣṣôt*) is a combination of two feasts: the evening of the first day is Passover (*pesaḥ*), commemorating the exodus from Egypt; and the feast of Unleavened Bread (*maṣṣôt*), observed for the following seven days, marks the festival, in the month of Abib, when the barley ripened. The festival of Weeks (*šābuʿôt*) or Pentecost, falling between the barley and wheat harvests, is the feast of the wheat harvest. The feast of Booths (*sukkôt*) or Tabernacles derives its name from the Israelite practice of dwelling temporarily in booths (*sukkôt*) to protect the olive orchards during the month of harvest (September). *Sukkôt*, also known as Ingathering (*ʾāsîp*), is a seven-day autumn festival of thanksgiving celebrated in mid-October (Tishri), when the agricultural work was finished.

Eschatological Banquet

When the prophets of Israel envision a new age of peace and righteousness, they picture Yahweh hosting a lavish banquet for all people. Besides the family banquet hosted by the paterfamilias and the royal banquet hosted by the king, there is the eschatological (messianic) banquet hosted by Yahweh in which the elect are invited to participate.

Isaiah describes two such joyous banquets with abundant food. The first: "On this mountain Yahweh of hosts will make for all peoples a feast (*mištēh*) of rich food (*šĕmānîm*), a feast of vintage wines (*šĕmārîm*), of rich food filled with marrow, of vintage wines strained clear" (Isa. 25:6). This festive meal prepared for the redeemed nations is set on Mount Zion and is accompanied by vintage wine that was strained before being poured. The second: "Everyone who thirsts, come to the waters; and you

---

51. de Vaux, *Ancient Israel*, 484–506.
52. Leviticus 23:1–44 (Priestly Collection) makes no mention of exclusive male participation.
53. Menahem Haran, *Temples and Temple-Service in Ancient Israel* (Winona Lake, Ind.: Eisenbrauns, 1985), 293.

that have no money, come, buy and eat! Come, buy wine (*yayin*) and milk (*ḥālāb*) without money and without price. Why do you spend your money for that which is not bread (*leḥem*), and your labor for that which does not satisfy? Listen carefully to me, and eat what is good, and delight yourselves in rich food (*dešen*)" (Isa. 55:1–2). This invitation is extended to the exiles in Babylon to return to Zion, the shrine of Yahweh. The free banquet consists of the choicest foods.[54]

Ill. 221: Decorated bronze bowl, Tel Dan. Type used in a *marzēaḥ* festival, found inside room near altar in the sacred precinct. (Courtesy of Tel Dan Excavations; Photo: R. Novick)

Marzēaḥ

The two biblical references to *marzēaḥ* are Amos 6:7 and Jeremiah 16:5, often mistranslated "revelry" in Amos and "mourning" in Jeremiah:

> They lie on beds of ivory (*miṭṭôt šēn*), and sprawl on their couches, eating lambs from the flock, and calves from the stall (*'ăgālîm miṭṭôk marbēq*). They sing to the tune of the harp (*nābel*), and like David improvise song. They drink wine from bowls (*mizrĕqê yayin*), and smear (*yimšāḥû*) themselves with choicest oils (*rē'šît šĕmānîm*). They are not grieved over the ruin of Joseph [northern kingdom]. Therefore they shall be the first to go into exile, and the "revelry" (*mirzaḥ sĕrûḥîm*) of the loungers shall pass away. (Amos 6:4–7)

The *marzēaḥ* (LXX *thiasos*), the Semitic equivalent of the Greek symposium, has a long history, attested from the fourteenth century B.C.E. through the Roman period. The *marzēaḥ* took the form of a social and religious association. Sometimes the *marzēaḥ* was the setting for mourning rites that consisted of eating, drinking, and sexual intercourse comparable to a bacchanalian banquet. Whether sacred repasts or memorial meals, these feasts lasted several days and were accompanied by indulgence, particularly inordinate consumption of wine.

The *marzēaḥ* consisted of five elements, all mentioned by Amos. The "beds of ivory" were couches decorated with ivory inlays on which the guests reclined during the festivities. The gourmet meal consisted of lambs from the flock and calves

---

54. Richard J. Clifford, "Isaiah 55: Invitation to a Feast," in C. L. Meyers and M. O'Connor, eds., *The Word of the Lord Shall Go Forth* (Winona Lake, Ind.: Eisenbrauns, 1983), 27–35.

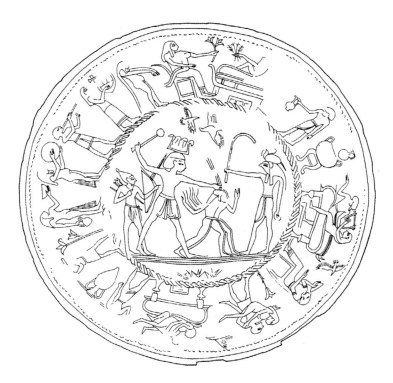

Ill. 222: Banquet scene on Phoenician bronze bowl from Salamis (Cyprus), dated Iron II. In center of bowl pharaoh smites his enemies; on the circumference of the bowl, musicians in procession, nursing mothers, banqueters and couples engaged in sexual intercourse are depicted. (Drawing: S. Bird; Greek and Roman Antiquities, the British Museum; in Vassos Karageorghis, "*Erotica* from Salamis," *Rivista di Studi Fenici* 21 [1993])

from the stall, that is, stall-fattened, tender calves, equivalent to veal. The meal was eaten to the accompaniment of songs and music from the harp, and the drinking of wine from bowls. Among the other indulgences of the luxury-loving participants, Amos calls attention to the anointing (oiling) with the "choicest oils." The first crushing of the olives, done in a vat before the pressing process, yields oil of the finest quality. The prepressed oil is the best and most expensive oil, known today as "virgin oil."

The erotic scene engraved on the interior of the Salamis bronze bowl is reminiscent of the biblical *marzēaḥ* (Ill. 222). It depicts a ritual banquet feast with musicians, dancer, persons drinking, and figures carrying wine. A nude woman seated across a bearded man's lap plays a lyre; a second woman plays a tambourine or hand drum. A male in a loincloth plays a double flute; a woman in a long robe plays the lyre. Another nude woman appears to be dancing. A man carries a nude woman. Three couches are depicted; on one a couple is engaged in sexual intercourse, she with raised legs and he kneeling between her legs. Two men in loincloths carry a wine jar on a pole.

A woman drinks from a bowl. Five human figures approach a woman seated on a chair and holding a child on her lap, a scene identified by some scholars as Isis with Horus. The ritual feast appears to be held in her honor. This erotic banquet scene surrounds the medallion of a pharaoh smiting captives. There is a strong Egyptianizing motif in all of these depictions. The Salamis bronze bowl typical of the Phoenicians may possibly date to the ninth century B.C.E. on the basis of comparison with a bowl from Lefkandi (Boeotia) of that date.[55]

A fluted bronze bowl (*phiale*) with a Phoenician dedicatory inscription, which may have been used as a cup in the *marzēaḥ*, dates to the fourth century B.C.E. Measuring 18.1 centimeters in diameter and only 3.6 centimeters high, it has a sixteen-petaled rosette at bottom center. Like other bowls depicted in libation scenes, this *phiale* lacks handles, reminiscent of two well-known scenes of royalty holding cups—Ashurbanipal and his queen feasting in their garden, and a Canaanite king or prince seated on a throne celebrating a victory feast. The significant aspect of this *phiale* is the one-line inscription in dotted lettering: "we offer two cups to the *marzēaḥ* of Shamash."[56]

At Dan a carinated bronze bowl with an omphalos base was found southeast of the altar in the Dan sanctuary, specifically in the *liškâ*, or chamber, where the priests officiated in the time of King Jeroboam II (793–753). This bowl, 16 cm in diameter and 5 cm deep, is richly adorned with a lotus leaf decoration and was probably used as a wine cup in the banquets there (Ill. 221).[57]

Sacrifices and Offerings

The chief references to the sacrificial system occur in Leviticus (1–7) and Numbers.[58] "Offerings" is the genus, "sacrifices" the species. *zebaḥ*, the basic biblical term for sacrifice, is an oblation burnt, in whole or in part, on the altar; it includes *ʿōlâ*, *sělāmîm*, *ḥaṭṭāʾt*, and *ʾāšām*.

The *ʿōlâ*, derived from the Hebrew root *ʿlh*, "to go up," was so called because its smoke (odor) ascended to the deity who "inhaled" it. This sacrifice, in which an unblemished male animal or a bird was entirely burnt on the altar, was offered twice daily, morning and evening. The synonym *kālîl* also designates a whole burnt offering.

šělāmîm (almost always in the plural) or *zebaḥ sělāmîm*, "peace offering," was an animal sacrifice in which only a portion was burnt on the altar, and the remainder

55. Vassos Karageorghis, "*Erotica* from Salamis," *Rivista di Studi Fenici* 21 (1993): Supplement, 7–13; Glenn Markoe, *Phoenician Bronze and Silver Bowls from Cyprus and the Mediterranean* (Berkeley, Calif.: University of California, 1985), 174, 251.

56. Nahman Avigad and Jonas C. Greenfield, "A Bronze *phiale* with a Phoenician Dedicatory Inscription," *IEJ* 32 (1982): 118–28.

57. Biran, *Biblical Dan*, 196.

58. Gary A. Anderson, *Sacrifices and Offerings in Ancient Israel*, HSM (Atlanta: Scholars Press, 1987); Jacob Milgrom, *Leviticus 1–16*, AB 3 (New York: Doubleday, 1991).

consumed by donor and family at a festive meal. As Gary Anderson notes, the *ʿōlâ* nourished the deity, the *šĕlāmîm* nourished the people. The "peace offering" does not serve as expiation or atonement.

It is practically impossible to distinguish between *ḥaṭṭāʾt* and *ʾāšām*. *ḥaṭṭāʾt* is a purification offering (not a "sin offering") pertaining to inadvert violations of purity; it cleansed the altar and sanctuary of impurity. *ʾāšām* is a reparation offering imposed for trespassing on a holy thing. The offense in question was not moral but ceremonial.

minḥâ connotes either a "cereal offering" (exclusively in P) or a "gift" (in non-Priestly texts). "Cereal offering" and "gift" are closely associated, because in Israel's agricultural economy, grain was the common gift (tithe) to the Temple.

While sacrifice was a central element in the religion of Israel, its significance is complex and difficult to define. As Roland de Vaux observed, "Sacrifice is one act with many aspects."[59] It has many meanings at many levels, including gift, communion, and expiation. The prophets, notably Amos, Isaiah, and Jeremiah, inveighed vehemently (rhetorically?) against Israelite religious worship offered as a substitute for community responsibility: "I [Yahweh] hate, I despise your festivals, and I take no delight in your solemn assemblies. Even though you offer me your burnt offerings (*ʿōlôt*) and grain offerings (*minḥôtêkem*), I will not accept them; and the offerings of well-being (*šelem*) of your fatted animals I will not look upon. . . . But let justice roll down like waters, and righteousness like an ever-flowing stream" (Amos 5:21–22, 24; also Isa. 1:10–17; Jer. 7:21–23).

The Bible refers to another sacrifice—*zebaḥ hayyāmîm* (lit. "the sacrifice of days"). David absented himself from the king's (Saul) table on the feast of the New Moon to go to Bethlehem to participate with his whole clan (*kol-hammišpāḥâ*) in the *zebaḥ hayyāmîm*, often translated "clan sacrifice" (1 Sam. 20:6). Later it was referred to as *zebaḥ mišpāḥâ*, "kinship sacrifice" (1 Sam. 20:29). Elkanah, father of Samuel, went up to Shiloh with his whole household (*kol-bêtô*) to offer the "annual sacrifice" (*zebaḥ hayyāmîm*) to Yahweh (1 Sam. 1:21).[60]

Firstfruits

An ancient and common form of sacrifice was the offering of firstfruits (*bikkûrîm*, *rēʾšît*) of animals and vegetables. They were ordinarily offered on the occasion of the feast of Weeks (*šābuʿôt*), the harvest festival. Deuteronomy 26:5–10 is a confession of faith that the Israelite makes when presenting the firstfruits of the harvest at the sanctuary. The purpose was to acknowledge that the land and its produce belonged

---

59. de Vaux, *Ancient Israel*, 451.
60. Haran, *Temples and Temple-Service in Ancient Israel*, 304–7.

to God as creator. The firstfruits were considered the best yield of the harvest. Such offerings symbolized the donor's gratitude to and dependence upon Yahweh; at the same time, they were considered a guarantee of future productivity. A portion of the firstfruits was contributed to the priests for their support. Through the covenant, Israel was Yahweh's firstborn. Jeremiah describes Israel as the "firstfruits" of Yahweh's harvest, proclaiming: "Israel was holy to Yahweh, the first fruits (*rē'šît*) of his harvest. All who ate of it were held guilty; disaster came upon them" (Jer. 2:3).

Firstborn

The firstborn, the firstfruits, and the firstlings all belong to God: "You shall give me [Yahweh] the firstborn (*běkôr*) of your sons" (Ex. 22:28 [E.T. 22:29]). There is no mention here of redemption of the firstborn by a sheep or other means. The Levites as a group, by substituting for the firstborn of all the Israelites, free them of their obligation to Yahweh. As Martin Noth expressed it, "Yahweh accepts the Levites as compensation for his right to the first-born."[61] "Yahweh said to Moses, 'It is I who have chosen the Levites from the Israelites in place of every firstborn that opens the womb among the Israelites. The Levites, therefore, are mine, because every firstborn is mine. When I slew all the firstborn in the land of Egypt, I made all the firstborn in Israel sacred to me, both of man and of beast. They belong to me; I am Yahweh'" (Num. 3:11–13; also 8:15–16). It may be that the firstborn were originally not meant to be sacrificed but were to serve in the role of priests before the priesthood was established.

Human Sacrifice

Roland de Vaux,[62] among others, questioned whether the sacrifice of the firstborn was regularly practiced. He doubted the literal reading of the biblical text and thought they were to be redeemed. The Bible attests that two kings of Judah, Ahaz (2 Kings 16:3) and Manasseh (2 Kings 21:6), offered their sons and daughters as human sacrifices at the Tophet, the cultic installation on the south side of Jerusalem where children were sacrificed. On at least two occasions Jeremiah pronounces harsh judgment on the Tophet: "They [the Judahites] built the high places of Ba'al in the valley of the sons of Hinnom, to offer up (*lěha'ăbîr*) [literally, 'to pass through (the fire)'] their sons and daughters in the *mulk*-sacrifice,[63] though I [Yahweh] did not command them, nor did it enter my mind that they should do this abomination, causing Judah to sin" (Jer.

---

61. Martin Noth, *Numbers*, OTL (Philadelphia: Westminster, 1968), 40.
62. Roland de Vaux, *Studies in Old Testament Sacrifice* (Cardiff: University of Wales, 1964), 71.
63. MT *lammolek*, "to Molech"; LXX *tō basilei*, "to the king."

Ill. 223a: The Carthage "Tophet" or the "Precinct of Tanit," looking W. across a field of monuments from the seventh through sixth centuries B.C.E., beneath which lie the remains of cremated (sacrificed) infants buried in ceramic urns. (Courtesy of L. E. Stager; Photo: J. Whitred)

Ill. 223b: Sacrificial urns in a stratigraphic sequence from the earliest period (Tanit I, eighth through sixth centuries) at Carthage. See red burnished urn in the foreground, above which lie urn burials from sixth through fifth centuries B.C.E. (Courtesy of L. E. Stager; Photo: J. Whitred)

Ill. 223c: Carthage Tanit I, from eighth century. Sacrificial urn burial with lid in place, located in a pit cut in the bedrock of the tophet. (Courtesy of L. E. Stager; Photo: J. Whitred)

Ill. 223d: Same urn as above with charred remains of the human infant visible in the jar. (Courtesy of L. E. Stager; Photo: J. Whitred)

32:35; also 7:31–32; 19:5–6; 2 Kings 23:10). Instead of reading *mōlek*, Paul Mosca[64] like Otto Eissfeldt[65] before him prefers *mulk*, a technical term designating a live sacrifice of child or animal in fulfillment of a Tophet vow. Mosca contends that *mōlek* is a strictly sacrificial term in the Bible, and not the name of a deity, Molech. Others, such as George Heider,[66] assert that *mōlek* represents a West Semitic deity in all usages.

Scholars differ regarding whether these Tophet texts refer literally to child sacrifice. In a desire to tone down the idea of burning children as a sacrifice in biblical Israel, Moshe Weinfeld[67] and others argue that such expressions as "to burn their sons and daughters in the fire" and "to offer up their sons and daughters" either envision a nonsacrificial initiation rite, or are meant figuratively, or are prophetic hyperbole. Children interred in the Tophet, they claim, died of natural causes and not as victims of sacrifice. Other scholars insist that the texts mean what they say, especially when corroborated by nonbiblical texts and artifactual evidence.[68]

Stager's[69] excavations in the open-air precinct of the goddess Tanit at Carthage illuminate the practice of child sacrifice. Artifacts (urns, cremated remains, and grave goods), combined with inscriptions on stelae indicating that the vows made by the offerants were being fulfilled, attest that child sacrifice took place at Carthage[70] (Ill. 223a–d). Phoenicians elsewhere also practiced human sacrifice. Archaeologists have recovered the gruesome evidence not only at the great Phoenician city of Carthage (in modern Tunisia), but also in Sicily, Sardinia, and Cyprus.

For Jon Levenson, child sacrifice in the Bible would be a "norm" rather than a "deviation." He interprets the positive response to the directive—"You shall give me [Yahweh] the firstborn of your sons" (Ex. 22:28b)—as a theological ideal of sacrifice, that is, parents offering to Yahweh what is most precious to them. As already indicated, this Exodus text does not indicate redemption by substitution.[71] The Akedah (Gen. 22:1–19) is unmistakable about Yahweh's mandating Abraham to

---

64. Paul G. Mosca, "Child Sacrifice in Canaanite and Israelite Religion: A Study in Mulk and *molek*" (Ph.D. diss., Harvard University, 1975).

65. See Otto Eissfeldt, *Molk als Opferbegriff im Punischen und Hebräischen und das Ende des Gottes Moloch* (Halle: Max Niemeyer, 1935). From his study of Punic inscriptions, he contended that *mlk* is a type of sacrifice (votive offering).

66. George C. Heider, *The Cult of Molek: A Reassessment*, JSOTSup 43 (Sheffield: University of Sheffield, 1985).

67. Moshe Weinfeld, "The Worship of Molech and of the Queen of Heaven and Its Background," *UF* 4 (1972): 133–54.

68. Morton Smith, "A Note on Burning Babies," *JAOS* 95 (1975): 477–79.

69. Lawrence E. Stager, "Carthage: A View from the Tophet," in H. G. Niemeyer, ed., *Phönizier im Westen*, Madrider Beiträge 8 (Mainz am Rhein: Philipp von Zabern, 1982), 155–66; Lawrence E. Stager and Samuel R. Wolff, "Child Sacrifice at Carthage—Religious Rite or Population Control?" *BAR* 10 (1984): 30–51.

70. King, *Jeremiah: An Archaeological Companion*, 136–39.

71. Jon D. Levenson, *The Death and Resurrection of the Beloved Son; the Transformation of Child Sacrifice in Judaism and Christianity* (New Haven, Conn.: Yale University Press, 1993).

offer up Isaac as a holocaust (‘ōlâ) on the hill. Levenson[72] cites Mosca's reading of the progression that moves "from valuable to more valuable to most valuable" concerning Micah's famous "What Yahweh Requires":[73]

> With what shall I come before Yahweh, and bow myself before god on high? Shall I come before him with burnt offerings (‘ôlôt), with calves a year old? Will Yahweh be pleased with thousands of rams, with ten thousands of rivers of oil? Shall I give my firstborn (bĕkôrî) for my transgression, the fruit of my body for my sins? He has showed you, O man, what is good; what does Yahweh require of you but to do justice and to love kindness (ḥesed), and to walk humbly with your God? (Micah 6:6–8)

This text signifies that at one time child sacrifice was part of the official cult. Levenson states: "Only at a particular stage rather late in the history of Israel was child sacrifice branded as counter to the will of YHWH and thus ipso facto idolatrous."[74]

"Clean" and "Unclean"

Leviticus 11–15 is concerned with legal purity; specifically, clean and unclean food, uncleanness of childbirth, leprosy, and personal uncleanness.[75] Cleanness meaning freedom from physical, moral, and cultic contamination is prerequisite for participating in a cultic act. When David absented himself from the royal table on the feast of the New Moon, King Saul assumed he was not ṭāhôr ("clean") (1 Sam. 20:26). Ritual impurity would prevent him from participating in the meal.

The terms "clean" and "unclean" have little to do with hygiene and sanitation, or morality. Uncleanness is not a moral but a ritual state. "Clean" and "unclean" are to be considered in relation to the "holy." "Holy" and "clean" are intimately related; "holy" and "unclean" are polar opposites. What is unclean cannot be brought into contact with the holy. "Put on your beautiful garments, O Jerusalem, the holy (qōdeš) city; for the uncircumcised and the unclean (ṭāmē’) shall enter you no more" (Isa. 52:1; also 35:8). The common term designating "to be ritually clean" is ṭāhēr; the opposite is ṭāmē’, "to be unclean." Purification rites were enjoined when ritual impurity was contracted.

The concepts of "clean" and "unclean" pertain to four categories rendering individuals ritually unclean: eating prohibited foods, skin diseases (ṣāra‘at) of persons, contact with a corpse or certain dead animals, and involuntary genital discharges of both men and women. As for animals, the classification is not scientific but popular (Lev. 11:1–47): those with cloven hoofs who chew the cud are considered clean. Fish are deemed clean if they have fins and scales. The meaning of ṣāra‘at (wrongly trans-

---

72. Levenson, *Death and Resurrection of the Beloved Son*, 11.
73. Mosca, "Child Sacrifice in Canaanite and Israelite Religion," 225.
74. Levenson, *Death and Resurrection of the Beloved Son*, 5.
75. Mary Douglas, *Purity and Danger* (London: ARK Books, 1984); *Leviticus as Literature* (New York: Oxford University Press, 1999). Helmer Ringgren, "ṭāhar," *TDOT*, 5: 287–96. G. André and Helmer Ringgren, "ṭame’," *TDOT*, 5: 330–42. See also David P. Wright, *The Disposal of Impurity* (Atlanta: Scholars Press, 1987).

lated "leprosy") is uncertain; included in the category of "leprosy" (Lev. 13:1–14:57) are a number of skin diseases, "leprosy" being the worst. Contact with corpses or certain dead animals and touching, carrying, or eating an animal carcass (clean or unclean) rendered one unclean. Involuntary genital discharges were unclean, that is, male emission of semen and the female menstrual cycle.

DEATH, BURIAL, AND AFTERLIFE

The proper interment of the dead was a fundamental concern in the ancient Near East, and especially in Palestine, as the Bible, other ancient texts, and thousands of tombs attest. For a corpse to remain unburied was a disgrace and a sign of divine judgment. Recent textual and archaeological discoveries have given new insights into burial practices and customs in the biblical world. They also illuminate Israelite belief about the afterlife, a concept that underwent substantial development during the first millennium B.C.E. Certain ideas prevalent in the preexilic period about the cult of the dead were modified or even rejected by religious officialdom in the exilic and post-exilic periods.

Tomb Types and Burial Customs

At several points, the biblical text conveys a sense of the Israelite abhorrence of improper burial. The corpse of the loathed King Jehoiakim of Judah was not to receive proper burial: "With the burial of a donkey (*ḥămôr*) he [Jehoiakim] shall be buried—dragged off and thrown out beyond the gates of Jerusalem" (Jer. 22:19; 36:30). Jezebel, too, was denied proper burial: "Concerning Jezebel Yahweh said, 'The dogs shall eat Jezebel within the bounds of Jezreel'" (1 Kings 21:23). Frequently Jeremiah threatened the people of Judah with the ignominious punishment of being unburied: "Both great and small shall die in this land; they shall not be buried, and no one shall lament for them" (Jer. 16:6; also 7:33; 8:2; 9:21; 15:3).

Biblical texts describing preparation for burial, as well as ornaments and jewelry found with the corpse, attest that the deceased were clothed when their remains were placed on the benches/floors of grave and tomb. Like King Asa, the royalty of Byblos lay in their coffins with costly perfumes and wearing specific apparel: a king is covered with myrrh and bdellium (aromatic gum resin resembling myrrh); a queen wears her robes, tiara, and a gold mask. Frank Cross's translation of a Phoenician inscription of the Persian period from Byblos reads: "I [PN and titulary] lie in this sarcophagus, I alone, and here, behold I lie prepared for burial in myrrh and bdellium . . . and if anyone seeks to open this sarcophagus or to disturb my mouldering bones, seek him out O (Ba'l) Addir and with all the assembly of the gods."[76]

Burial (*qĕbûrâ*) took place on the same day as death, so as to prevent the corpse from becoming carrion. As for the burial of a hanged (not crucified) criminal: "His corpse must not remain all night upon the tree; you shall bury him that same day, for anyone hung on a tree is under God's curse" (Deut. 21:23). The embalming of Jacob and Joseph in Egypt according to Egyptian custom was exceptional for the Israelites and was performed to allow their bodies to be transported to Canaan for burial.

The Phoenicians introduced cremation, but the Israelites considered it an act of desecration. Excavated burials of Israelites during the First Temple period show no signs of cremation. When by exception cremation occurred, the remains were placed in urns and jars covered with an inverted bowl. The inhabitants of Jabesh-gilead "took the body of Saul and the bodies of his sons from the wall of Beth-Shean. They came to Jabesh and burned them there. Then they took their bones and buried them under the tamarisk tree in Jabesh, and fasted seven days" (1 Sam. 31:12–13).

Primary and Secondary Burials

Successive generations were interred in the family tomb, which was either a natural cave or a rock-cut type. Entrance to these family tombs was gained by a short, sloping shaft carved in the limestone rock. The book of Judges records the burials of Gideon and Samson, each interred in his father's tomb located in the vicinity of the hometown: "[Gideon] was buried in the tomb of his father Joash at Ophrah of the Abiezrites" (Judg. 8:32). Samson was interred between Zorah and Eshtaol in the tomb of his father Manoah (Judg. 16:31).

Two main types of burials, designated primary and secondary, were practiced among the Israelites. In primary burials the deceased was placed permanently in the burial site and not moved after decomposition. Primary burials were usually in graves or cists and often single. In secondary burials, the corpse was placed in a grave or tomb only temporarily, until the flesh decomposed; afterward the skeletal remains were transferred to a pit or repository. When additional space was needed to accommodate new burials in a "family tomb," the bones were collected and placed in a heap on the floor or deposited in a pit designated for that purpose. Multiple family tombs may contain both primary and secondary burials. In Hellenistic and Roman times, sarcophagi (stone coffins often inscribed and decorated) and ossuaries (receptacles resembling urns for holding the bones of the deceased) were commonly used, but not among Israelites during the Iron Age.

---

76. Brian Peckham, "Phoenicia and the Religion of Israel: The Epigraphic Evidence," in P. D. Miller et al., eds., *Ancient Israelite Religion*, 86–87; Frank M. Cross, "A Recently Published Phoenician Inscription of the Persian Period from Byblos," *IEJ* 29 (1979): 41.

Most Israelites were buried in family caves and bench tombs. Family tombs often consisted of several chambers for multiple burials, each surrounded with elevated rock benches upon which the deceased were placed temporarily. The biblical expressions "to sleep with" and "to be gathered to one's fathers" refer to secondary burials within the family tomb. According to Huldah's prophecy to Josiah, "I [Yahweh] will gather you to your fathers, and you shall be gathered to your grave in peace" (2 Kings 22:20). These references are to be understood in terms of the continuing relationship existing between the living and the deceased. Family burials had important implications for the maintenance of that relationship. The deceased's well-being in the afterlife depended upon the descendants' preservation of the patrimonial estate.

The afterlife of the ancestors, according to Herbert Brichto,[77] was contingent upon the association of parents, posterity, and property. The fifth commandment, "Honor your father and your mother that you may long endure on the land that Yahweh your God is giving you" (Ex. 20:12), has serious implications both here and hereafter, making the possession of the land dependent upon dutiful behavior toward one's forebears. The purpose of the cult of the dead was to perpetuate the patrimony. In the case of Joshua, "they buried him in his own patrimony (*naḥălātô*) at Timnath-serah, which is in the hill country of Ephraim" (Josh. 24:30). In the period of the settlement (LB and Iron I) family burial secured title to the patrimony (*naḥălâ*), inasmuch as the inheritance was held to pass through the ancestral dead. These traditions later served Israel's claims to *naḥălâ*.

Several texts illustrate the continuing relationship that existed between the living and deceased family members, as well as the connection between burial and ownership of land. According to the Deuteronomist, Rachel's tomb is clearly in Ephraim [Benjamin] (1 Sam. 10:2; Jer. 31:15). The Priestly account, a later tradition, moves her tomb to Ephrath in Judah ("that is, Bethlehem") in Genesis 35:19. Again, according to the Priestly source, Sarah, Jacob, and Joseph were buried in Hebron, in the cave of Machpelah. Abraham purchased the field of Ephron the Hittite in Machpelah as a burial site for Sarah (Gen. 23:1–20), and he also was eventually buried there. In response to Jacob's wish, Joseph traveled from Egypt to Canaan to bury his father's bones in the cave of Machpelah (Gen. 50:4–14). Moses in turn transported the bones of Joseph on his journey from Egypt to the promised land, as Joseph had requested (Gen. 50:25; Ex. 13:19). Jacob and Joseph's tombs were not in Judah but at Shechem (see Gen. 50:5 [cf. 33:19]; Josh. 24:32). These verses express different traditions. As with Rachel in Ephraim and in Ephrath, the ancestral stories and associated burials served apologetic purposes of later Israelites laying claim to land.

---

77. Herbert C. Brichto, "Kin, Cult, Land, and Afterlife—A Biblical Complex," *HUCA* 44 (1973): 1–54.

Ill. 224: Anthropoid clay sarcophagi for Egyptian burials from Deir el-Balah, from fourteenth or thirteenth century. (Courtesy of Israel Museum; Photo: N. Slapak)

Tomb Types

In LB the two main tomb types were burial caves for multiple, successive burials and pit graves.[78] The burial caves of the Coastal Plain were abandoned and replaced with simple dug-out pits for individuals. The MB II burials at Tell el-ʿAjjul were cut into the soft sandstone. The LB II tombs at Tell el-ʿAjjul were constructed of stones and had a *dromos* (corridor) approach to them. Stone-built tombs with roofs appear in LB II at Megiddo, Dan, and Aphek. One might also compare the more elegantly built tombs from Ugarit.

Pits lined with stone slabs or mud brick are known as cist graves. MB II stone-lined, capped pits are found at Ugarit, Megiddo, and Aphek. These individual graves were intended for the affluent.[79]

In LB there were multiple burials in caves and in shaft tombs throughout the highlands; a number of the largest caves accommodated hundreds of corpses. Some of the most extensive rock-cut necropoleis, with chambers radiating from a central room entered by a vertical shaft or stepped ramp, are located in the Coastal Plain, for example, at Tell el-ʿAjjul, Rishon Leziyyon,[80] and Ashkelon in the second millennium.

Anthropoid coffins, constructed of clay, wood, or stone, are easily recognized by their lids, which are sculpted to depict the human face and upper torso (Ill. 224). Egyptian in origin, anthropoid coffin burials may contain as many as six bodies. During LB and Iron I in Egyptian-controlled territories in Canaan, these coffins pertained to Egyptians and were not used to bury Sea Peoples. They were popular among the Phoenicians in the Persian period.[81]

Bench tombs, found in the highlands beginning in the tenth century, are caves or chambers with burial benches, on which the corpses were laid; the benches were carved or built of boulders along three side walls. Skeletal remains from earlier

---

78. Elizabeth Bloch-Smith, *Judahite Burial Practices and Beliefs about the Dead* (Sheffield: Academic Press, 1992); Amihai Mazar, *Archaeology of the Land of the Bible* (New York: Doubleday, 1990).

79. Elizabeth Bloch-Smith, "Cist Graves," *OEANE*, 2: 13–14.

80. Daphna Ben-Tor, "The Relations between Egypt and Palestine in the Middle Kingdom as Reflected by Contemporary Canaanite Scarabs," *IEJ* 47 (1997): 162–89.

81. Lawrence E. Stager, "The Impact of the Sea Peoples (1185–1050 B.C.E.)," in T. E. Levy, ed., *The Archaeology of Society in the Holy Land* (New York: Facts on File, 1995), 341: "From the Middle Kingdom to the Roman period, anthropoid clay coffins were used to bury Egyptians, both at home and abroad."

burials in the tomb were gathered up and placed in a repository cut into the floor of the cave. The earliest bench tombs, dating to the thirteenth and twelfth centuries B.C.E., are found at Tell el-Far'ah (S) where they were used for interring not "Philistines" (as usually maintained because of the presence of anthropoid coffins) but Egyptians. From the tenth to the seventh century, bench tombs became popular in Israel and Judah, with the majority in Judah, especially Jerusalem. The tombs were located in cemeteries adjacent to settlements.

The Tomb of Dothan

Chamber Tomb I at Dothan, a town in Manassite territory north of Shechem, contained the remains of at least 288 individuals. In this rock-cut "family" tomb with multiple burials over many generations, no coffins were used; instead the corpses were placed in an extended position on the floor or upon the debris of earlier burials. Described by the excavator Robert Cooley as "a successive multiple-burial tomb," five distinct levels of stratification are represented (LB II to Iron I). The burials in the tomb date from the fourteenth to the end of the twelfth century. Included are 3,000 artifacts for the needs of the deceased in the netherworld, among them a thousand whole pots, pyxides, lamps, bowls, pottery vessels, clothing, jewelry, bronze daggers, and household articles. Items deemed important in this life were considered serviceable in the afterlife.[82] Tomb I's five strata of continual burial, ranging from LB II to Iron I, suggest that this multigenerational family bridged the transition from "Canaanite" to "Israelite" at Dothan. Were they like the Shechemites, forging a new identity while retaining many of their earlier customs?

The architecture of Tomb I consisted of a vertical shaft leading to a stepped entryway that led into a central chamber. It was rectangular with a domed roof. Also, there were six niches for burials. Cooley observed an opening or window above one of the chamber niches, as well as two large storage jars, each with a dipper juglet, located outside the chamber and below the opening. This phenomenon led him to speculate that water was poured into the chamber through the window to slake the thirst of the deceased. However, it is just as likely that these jars held wine.

In a study of the Iron Age animal bones from the tombs of Dothan, Justin Lev-Tov suggests that "the majority of the faunal remains found within the tombs were intentionally placed there as offerings."[83] The practice of food offerings appears to have been continuous from MB to at least Iron I. Of the identified bones, six were definitely goats and five definitely sheep. There are clear indications of sheep and goat, as well as *Bos* offerings, in the Dothan tomb. It is not so clear how much

---

82. Robert E. Cooley, "Gathered to His People: A Study of a Dothan Family Tomb," in M. Inch and R. Youngblood, eds., *The Living and Active Word of God* (Winona Lake, Ind.: Eisenbrauns, 1983), 47–58.

83. Justin Lev-Tov, "Iron Age Animal Bones from the Tombs of Tell Dothan: Identification and Evaluation of Ritual Offerings" (unpublished manuscript).

is LB and how much Iron I. It is probably not critical, since the tomb was used continually from LB II to Iron I. And no one is suggesting that "Canaanites" occupied it in LB and "Israelites" in Iron I (if they are not one and the same here).

Iron II Tombs

In Iron II, rock-hewn tombs took the form of a square or rectangular room with a small square entrance that could be closed with a large stone. Rock-cut benches were located on three sides of the chamber. The headrests on the benches resembled a horseshoe in shape or a "Hathor headdress." This feature characterizes only some of the Jerusalem tombs.[84] Bones and offerings of earlier burials were placed in a repository to make room for new burials. The plan of these tombs is reminiscent of the "four-room house," which may indicate belief in an afterlife. As many as 250 rock-cut caves and bench tombs, dating from the tenth to seventh centuries, have been investigated in Judah, particularly in the vicinity of Jerusalem. The majority were bench tombs, the prime examples being the tombs in St. Etienne and those at the Silwan Village.

In the Second Temple period, bench burials were replaced by loculi (*kokhim*), long, narrow burial niches hewn into walls on three sides. Ossuaries containing the bones were placed in the *kokhim* for permanent burial. Family tombs consisted of several chambers, each with a number of loculi in the walls.

Clay coffin burials resembling "bathtubs" were used for interment in Iron II (e.g., at Dothan). These "bathtub" coffins measured one to one and a half meters in length. (Most are one meter in length, but the coffin of Adoni-Nur in Amman is about one and a half meters long.) The coffins have one rounded and one squared end and were sometimes fitted with handles around the sides. They date no earlier than the late eighth century and originated in Mesopotamia with the Assyrians. The Mesopotamian practice was to bury the dead inside the settlement walls and below the floors of buildings in "bathtub" coffins. As the Assyrian empire expanded to the West, this form of burial spread. There is evidence for such coffins at Tell Abu Hawam, Tell en-Naṣbeh, Tell Dothan, Tell el-Farʿah (N), Tell el-Mazar, Megiddo, and Shechem—all in the north, which unlike Judah, became a part of the Assyrian provincial system.[85]

---

84. The "Hathor" headdress is so called because it resembles the wig typically worn by the Egyptian goddess Hathor. The horseshoe-shaped headrest is much simpler. This is the opinion of Gabriel Barkay and Amos Kloner ("Jerusalem Tombs from the Days of the First Temple," *BAR* 12 [1986]: 36). Othmar Keel denies this interpretation, suggesting instead that the headrest may depict return to the womb ("Peculiar Tomb Headrests May Depict Return to the Womb," *BAR* 13/4 [1987]: 50–53).

85. Jeffrey R. Zorn, "Mesopotamian-Style Ceramic 'Bathtub' Coffins from Tell en-Naṣbeh," *TA* 20 (1993): 216–24; idem, "More on Mesopotamian Burial Practices in Ancient Israel," *IEJ* 47 (1997): 214–19; P. L. O. Guy, *Megiddo Tombs* (Chicago: University of Chicago Press, 1938), 74–81.

A complete Mesopotamian-style "bathtub" coffin from the late Iron Age, containing an intact burial, was uncovered at Jezreel (Grave 2000). The excavators report that Grave 2000 was cut through the floor of an Iron Age building. The coffin had no lid, nor were there grave goods within. The body lay on its left side in a flexed position, with the hands positioned in front of the face.[86] The intramural "bathtub" coffins at Megiddo and Dothan appear to be modeled on Assyro-Babylonian burial customs. The "bathtub" coffin from Megiddo (Tomb 37) has thick, vertical walls and a heavy rim, as well as a raised band with finger indentations midway on the wall.[87] The coffin is 67 centimeters wide and 57 centimeters deep at the rim.

The Israelites followed Canaanite burial practice of providing the deceased with a miscellany of pottery vessels for food and drink. Organic remains of offerings including a lamb or goat chop and a small bird (dove or partridge) have been found in an LB I tomb at Ashkelon.[88] Food offerings of parts of sheep, goats, and birds have accompanied burials in the large (intramural?) necropolis there, dating from 1800–1200 B.C.E. Tomb I at Beth-Shemesh, originally a natural grotto, stems from the late tenth to early ninth century. The excavator, Duncan Mackenzie, reported that "an artificial funnel opening was pierced through the roof," which may have been used to provide food and drink for the nourishment of the deceased.[89]

R. A. S. Macalister mentioned that Cave Tomb 8I (LB–Iron IA) at Gezer contained a "great pile of bones, human and animal (sheep, goat, and cow), indiscriminately heaped up under the southern roof entrance, through which they had evidently been cast."[90] He referred to another Iron Age tomb at Gezer in which "an earthenware bowl contained some decayed matter in which a few mutton bones were mingled. A bronze knife lay in the midst, for cutting the meat; and a second bowl was inverted over the deposit."[91] Elizabeth Bloch-Smith cites other tombs and graves of the Iron Age with food remains. Human and animal bones were found in Lachish Cave Tomb 218. Pits associated with Samaria Cave Tomb 103 were interpreted by the excavators as receptacles for offerings related to the cult of the dead. There are other examples, but not in great abundance.[92]

---

86. Ussishkin and Woodhead, "Excavations at Tel Jezreel 1994–1996: Third Preliminary Report," *TA* 24 (1997): 36–40.

87. Jeffrey Zorn describes this as "perhaps the most diagnostic feature of such coffins." See note 85 for reference.

88. Lawrence E. Stager, *Ashkelon Discovered* (Washington, D.C.: Biblical Archaeology Society, 1991), 9.

89. Duncan Mackenzie, *Excavations at 'Ain Shems* (London: Palestine Exploration Fund, 1912–1913), 53.

90. R. A. S. Macalister, *The Excavation of Gezer, 1902–1905 and 1907–1909* (London: J. Murray, 1912), 1: 81.

91. R. A. S. Macalister, *A Century of Excavation in Palestine* (London: Religious Tract Society, 1925), 260.

92. Bloch-Smith, *Judahite Burial Practices and Beliefs about the Dead*, 108: "Although there are relatively few instances of actual foodstuffs preserved in burials, the ubiquitous jar and bowl indicate that food and liquids were provided for the dead."

Articles of everyday life were supplied for the welfare of the deceased in the after-life. Archaeologists have found a range of objects, including ceramics, jewelry, tools, weapons, and other items (e.g., toggle pins [Bronze Age], fibulae, combs, mirrors, and seals). Among the pottery vessels were pilgrim flasks, pyxides, craters, bowls, chalices, store jars, cooking pots, and dipper juglets. A variety of both male and female figurines have also been uncovered. A large number of oil lamps were deposited in Iron Age tombs, apparently intended to illuminate the way to the after-life in the darkness of Sheol.

Rock-cut Tombs in Jerusalem

In Iron II, Jerusalem was surrounded by a city of the dead. More than a hundred chamber and cave tombs have been discovered on the north, east, and west sides of the city. Since most burials had to be outside the city walls, they effectively defined the perimeter of Jerusalem during Iron II.

North of Jerusalem, two impressive tomb complexes were uncovered at St. Etienne Convent on Nablus Road, just north of the Old City's Damascus Gate.[93] Each tomb complex was part of a much larger necropolis. The famed "Garden Tomb" outside the Old City wall, erroneously identified by General Charles Gordon in 1883 as the tomb of Jesus, is part of this northern complex of tombs. On the basis of their plan and archi-tecture, these magnificent bench tombs are to be dated to the First Temple period. The two tombs are similar, consisting of a central entrance chamber surrounded by addi-tional burial chambers. The entrance to the first complex is about two meters high, and the chamber itself measures five meters by four meters and is three meters high. Six bur-ial chambers radiate from the entrance chamber. Each contains rock-hewn burial benches located along three of the walls. The benches have an elevated parapet to hold the body in place. They are also equipped with a rock-hewn headrest shaped like a horseshoe. The remains of the deceased reposed on these benches. These chambers were also provided with repositories for collecting the skeletal remains of previous genera-tions after the corpses had decomposed on the benches. These burial benches were typ-ical of the First Temple period, in contrast to the Second Temple period, when benches were replaced by burial niches (*kokhim*). These tombs are so elaborate that they may have been intended as the resting place for the last kings of Judah. Also, the St. Etienne tombs and their architecture may bear a relationship to the *bayit* ("house") in Sheol and on earth. Sheol was regarded as a *bayit* or residence for the dead. In his prayer for relief, Job asks: "If I look for Sheol as my house (*bêtî*), . . . where then is my hope?" (Job 17:13–15). Also, Job declares, "I know that you [God] will bring me to death, and to the house (*bêt mô'ēd*) appointed for all living" (Job 30:23).

The Silwan Village necropolis, dating to the eighth and seventh centuries, is situated

---

93. Barkay and Kloner, "Jerusalem Tombs from the Days of the First Temple," 22–39.

Ill. 225: Tomb of Shebna, the royal steward in court of Hezekiah, dated eighth century B.C.E. The inscription incised in the facade above the tomb's entrance reads: "This is the tomb of [*šbn*] *yahû* who is over the house [an official of high rank at the court]. There is no silver and no gold here, only his bones and the bones of his slave wife [who is] with him. Cursed be the one who will open this." See Isaiah 22:15-16, which parallels the inscription. (Courtesy of Z. Radovan, Jerusalem; translation: N. Avigad)

on the steep east slope of the Kidron Valley, opposite the City of David. In this cemetery of more than forty monumental rock-cut tombs furnished with headrests, the tomb entrances were cut into the Silwan cliffs.[94] Most have only one burial chamber. All of these tombs were subsequently robbed of both offerings and skeletons. Prominent citizens of Jerusalem may have been buried in these tombs. Kings and other leaders were ordinarily buried in their capital cities. Both David (1 Kings 2:10) and Solomon (1 Kings 11:43) were interred in the City of David. Because of his personal fidelity and the profound respect in which he was held, Jehoiada the high priest was buried among the kings: "They buried him [Jehoiada] in the city of David among the kings, because he had done good in Israel, and for God and his house" (2 Chron. 24:16).

Architecturally, several kinds of tombs can be distinguished in the Silwan Village cemetery. Some had gabled ceilings, reflecting Phoenician influence; others had flat ceilings. The entrance led into a rectangular burial chamber. The bench with its headrest was hewn in the chamber's long wall. Some of these tombs consisted of two or three burial chambers. The above-ground monolithic tombs with pyramid-shaped roofs were located at the north end of the Silwan Village. The Silwan tombs paralleled the classic bench tombs, consisting of a chamber with burial places along the sides. Some of the cube-shaped tombs had Hebrew inscriptions on the facade. One of the most elaborate is known as the "tomb of the royal steward," according to the inscription above the tomb's entrance (Ill. 225). It reads: "This is the tomb of [Sheban] yahû who is over the house [title of a high-ranking court official—hence, the royal steward]. There is no silver and no gold here, only his bones and the bones of his slave wife [who is] with him. Cursed be the one who will open this."[95] This may be the

94. David Ussishkin, "The Necropolis from the Time of the Kingdom of Judah at Silwan, Jerusalem," *BA* 33 (1970): 34–46.

95. Nahman Avigad, "The Epitaph of a Royal Steward from Siloam Village," *IEJ* 3 (1953): 137–52.

same Shebna, royal steward (literally, "one who is over the house" [*'ăšer 'al hab-bayit*]) of King Hezekiah, whom Isaiah at the direction of Yahweh upbraided for carving such an elaborate tomb for himself in the cliff for all to see: "What right do you [Shebna] have here? Who are your relatives here, that you have hewn out a tomb here for yourself, cutting a tomb on the height, and carving an abode for yourself in the cliff?" (Isa. 22:16). Just as with the Temple and royal palace in Jerusalem, so, too, the architecture of these tombs reflects Phoenician influence. Excellent examples of Iron II Phoenician tombs carved out of the bedrock have also been discovered in the cemetery at Achzib on the Mediterranean coast in northern Israel.

A series of rock-cut burial caves on the slopes of the Hinnom Valley have come to light at Ketef Hinnom ("Shoulder of Hinnom"), located on the grounds of the St. Andrew's Scottish Hospice.[96] These caves, dating to the end of the First Temple period and later, were hewn into the limestone cliff; they served as family tombs for successive generations. Nine of these burial caves have been excavated, most having only one chamber. Like other burial caves in Jerusalem, repositories were dug under the burial benches as receptacles for the bones of the deceased and associated funeral offerings after they were removed to make room for new burials. One cave (Number 25) contained the remains of ninety-five corpses. Among the artifacts in the repository were pottery, iron arrowheads, and objects of bone and ivory, as well as precious and semiprecious jewelry (Ill. 157). Archaeologists recovered close to three hundred intact vessels from Ketef Hinnom, including oil lamps, perfume bottles, and small juglets. Two small, rolled silver amulets or ornaments were also found. These silver talismans are incised with the personal name of the God of Israel, the earliest occurrence of "Yahweh" on an object excavated in Jerusalem (Ill. 151). The Priestly Benediction inscribed on the amulets is almost identical to Numbers: "Yahweh bless you and keep you; Yahweh make his face to shine upon you, and be gracious to you; Yahweh lift up his countenance upon you, and give you peace" (Num. 6:24–26).

Mourning

The announcement of death was followed by lamentation. When Saul's death was reported to David, he "took hold of his clothes and tore them; and all the men who were with him did the same. They mourned and wept, and fasted until evening for Saul and for his son Jonathan" (2 Sam. 1:11–12). Besides fasting, the traditional ritual of mourning involved putting on sackcloth, as happened at the funeral of Abner.

---

96. Barkay, *Ketef Hinnom: A Treasure Facing Jerusalem's Walls,* catalog no. 274 (Jerusalem: Israel Museum, 1986).

Sackcloth (*śaqqîm*) is a coarse material woven from camel or goat hair. The rough sackcloth was placed next to the skin, without benefit of undergarment. "Then David said to Joab and to all the people who were with him, 'Tear your clothes, and put on sackcloth, and mourn over Abner.' And King David followed the bier" (2 Sam. 3:31). Also, the mourners transformed their physical appearance by tearing the hair and beard (Jer. 7:29) and rolling in ashes (Jer. 6:26). They also might sit on the ground (Lam. 2:10). Gashing, however, was not to be done, according to Deuteronomic law (Deut. 14:1).

Despite the fact that intentional baldness was prohibited (Lev. 19:27; Deut. 14:1), shaving the head was sometimes practiced as a sign of mourning. "Make yourselves [Judahites] bald and cut off your hair for your pampered children; make yourselves as bald as the eagle, for they have gone from you into exile" (Micah 1:16). Describing the plight of the refugees from Moab who were in mourning, Isaiah says: "Dibon [modern Dhiban] has gone up to the temple, to the high places to weep; over Nebo [a Moabite city] and over Medeba [a Moabite city] Moab wails. On every head is baldness, every beard is shorn" (Isa. 15:2).

Mourning was part of the burial rite, a way of honoring the deceased. In addition to family members, professional mourners, generally women, were paid to lament during a funeral. In proclaiming doom, Jeremiah states: "Thus says Yahweh of hosts: Consider, and call for the mourning women to come; send for the skilled women to come; let them quickly raise a dirge over us" (Jer. 9:16–17). Mourning continued for a period of seven days. In connection with Jacob's death and burial, it is reported: "When they came to the threshing floor of Atad, which is beyond the Jordan, they held there a very great and sorrowful lamentation; and he [Joseph] observed a time of mourning for his father seven days" (Gen. 50:10). In his celebrated lament over Tyre, Ezekiel describes the city metaphorically as a great cargo ship manned by skilled mariners from the Phoenician coastal cities north of Tyre. Considered invulnerable, the ship is destroyed in a storm on the high seas. The prophet describes the general lament: "The mariners and all the pilots of the sea stand on the shore and wail aloud over you, and cry bitterly. They throw dust on their heads and wallow in ashes; they make themselves bald for you, and put on sackcloth, and they weep over you in bitterness of soul, with bitter mourning. In their wailing they raise a lamentation for you, and lament over you" (Ezek. 27:29–32).

Belief in the Afterlife

There existed in biblical Israel a belief in some form of afterlife, considered to be basically an extension of earthly life, even though Job 14:12 and the book of

Ecclesiastes raise some doubts about what comes after death. Three Hebrew texts are often cited as describing physical resurrection of the dead.[97] Ezekiel's (37:1–14) famous vision of the dry bones scattered over the plain is thought by some scholars to support a belief in bodily resurrection, while most believe that the dry bones, representing Judah's destruction at the hands of the Babylonians, refer not to a general resurrection of the deceased but to the restoration of Judah in the postexilic period.

Many understand a text from the Isaiah Apocalypse to refer to a physical resurrection of all the faithful Jews, while others maintain it is a national restoration: "Your dead shall live, their corpses shall rise. O dwellers in the dust, awake and sing for joy! For your dew is a radiant dew, and the earth will give birth to those long dead" (Isa. 26:19). This text was probably composed earlier than the well-known text of Daniel 12:1–4, dating to about 165 B.C.E., which appears to be an explicit statement of belief in the resurrection of the dead for the righteous Jews: "Many of those who sleep [are dead] in the dust of the earth shall awake [shall come back to life], some to everlasting life, and some to shame and everlasting contempt" (Dan. 12:2). The interpretation of this text is extremely complex, connected as it is to developments in religious notions and sectarian movements. For his part, Herbert Brichto argues that one should distinguish between afterlife and resurrection; biblical belief prior to Daniel was limited to afterlife, while after Daniel the biblical credo embraced resurrection to eternal life.[98]

Sheol, Abode of the Dead

The Israelites developed their own ideas on death from concepts associated with Mesopotamian and Canaanite culture. Although death marked the end of life on earth, the deceased continued an ethereal existence in Sheol or in the family tomb. In other words, death is not extinction but transition to another kind of existence in Sheol, as Brichto has shown. Sheol, the Semitic Hades, is practically a proper name designating the gloomy underworld where the departed spirits descend. Used sixty-six times in the Bible, "Sheol" is not found in other Semitic languages. Its etymology is uncertain, but it may be related to the Hebrew šā'al, "to ask," in the sense of consulting the spirits of the dead. Some think Sheol originally meant the place of interrogation. Other Hebrew words denoting the abode of the dead are bôr and šaḥat, both translated "pit."

In the book of Jonah, Sheol is associated with water imagery; the abode of the dead is located beneath the floor of the sea (Jonah 2:3–6). Sheol is a place of dust and

---

97. Robert Martin-Achard, "Resurrection," ABD, 5: 680–84.

98. Brichto, "Kin, Cult, Land, and Afterlife—A Biblical Complex," 53; William W. Hallo, "Royal Ancestor Worship in the Biblical World," in M. Fishbane and E. Tov, eds., "Sha'arei Talmon" (Winona Lake, Ind.: Eisenbrauns 1992), 381.

darkness (*ḥōšek*): "If I [Job] look for Sheol as my house, if I spread my couch in darkness (*ḥōšek*), if I say to the pit (*šaḥat*), 'You are my father,' and to the maggot (*rimmâ*), 'you are my mother and my sister' . . ." (Job 17:13–14). Sheol is a place of dim lighting and darkness. No wonder that oil lamps were among the most common offerings found in Iron Age tombs.

A classic passage on Sheol is Isaiah's taunt ridiculing the Assyrian king Sargon II:

> Sheol beneath is stirred up to meet you [Sargon] when you come; it rouses the shades (*rĕpā'îm*) to greet you, all who were leaders of the earth; it raises from their thrones all who were kings of the nations. All of them will speak and say to you: "You too have become as weak as we! You have become like us!" Your pomp is brought down to Sheol, and the sound of your harps; the couch beneath you is the maggot (*rimmâ*), your covering, the worm." (Isa. 14:9–11)

Tranquillity of the dead in Sheol was of primary importance both in Phoenician and Israelite thought. Brian Peckham compares the two cultures and notes similarities between royal Phoenician-Syrian inscriptions and the Bible.[99] In the Sidonian royal inscriptions, the tranquillity of the dead meant sleeping with the rephaim (the shades). To open the coffin or to remove the coffin from its resting place was tantamount to disturbing the rest of the dead. To discourage such disruption, assurance was given in advance that the tombs contained nothing of value; also, would-be perpetrators were cursed. Concepts expressed in the Sidonian royal inscriptions on death and burial are also found in Isaiah 14. The punishment visited upon Sargon was unseemly burial and death for all his children: "All the kings of the nations lie in glory, each in his own tomb; but you are cast out, away from your grave, like loathsome carrion, clothed with the dead, those pierced by the sword, who go down to the stones of the Pit, like a corpse trampled underfoot. You will not be joined with them in burial, because you have destroyed your land, you have killed your people" (Isa. 14:18–20; also Ezek. 32:17–32). Since the bones of the dead were not to be disturbed, Moses took the bones of Joseph with him upon departing Egypt (Ex. 13:19). Later, David took the bones of Saul and Jonathan from the people of Jabesh-Gilead and buried them in the land of Benjamin (2 Sam. 21:12–14).

Sheol is not a place of punishment in the sense of torment and torture; rather, it represents an exile from God, which in itself is a deplorable fate. In Israelite belief the essence of life is the ability to praise God; for the dead in Sheol that was impossible because they had no contact with the divine presence. In the words of King Hezekiah after recovering from illness: "For Sheol cannot thank you, death cannot praise you; those who go down to the Pit cannot hope for your faithfulness" (Isa. 38:18).

---

99. Peckham, "Phoenicia and the Religion of Israel: The Epigraphic Evidence," 82–83.

Cult of the Dead

Cult of the dead, which was a feature of Israelite society, designates rituals performed by the living for the benefit of deceased family members. In ancient Israel "official Yahwism" condemned any form of contact with the dead, whereas "popular religion," under the influence of Canaanite practice, condoned ancestor worship. In folk religion, the cult of the dead was a common way of obtaining favors from the deceased or of placating them.[100] Furnishing the deceased with personal objects implied that these would be useful in the afterlife. Nurturing the dead was a way for family members to maintain the relationship between one generation and the next. In other words, cult of the dead emphasized the continuity of kinship.

The authoritative teaching of the Deuteronomists and the Priests was vehemently opposed to such a cult: "Do not turn to mediums or wizards; do not seek them out, to be defiled by them. I am Yahweh your God" (Lev. 19:31). "No one shall be found among you . . . who consults ghosts or spirits, or who seeks oracles from the dead" (Deut. 18:10–11). The fact that the Bible legislates against such a cult argues for its continuous practice: "I [Israelite worshiper] have neither transgressed nor forgotten any of your commandments: I have not eaten of the sacred portion (*qōdeš*, tithed offering) while in mourning; I have not removed any of it while I was unclean; and I have not offered any of it to the dead" (Deut. 26:13–14). Commenting on this verse, G. Ernest Wright denied there was a reference to offering sacrifices to the dead because, in his view, such a custom did not exist in Israel. He interpreted food and drink offerings as symbolic not real, noting the absence of cooking pots at burial sites. Yehezkel Kaufmann and Roland de Vaux shared Wright's skeptical opinion.[101] New evidence from Mesopotamia, and especially from Ugarit, has prompted a reconsideration of afterlife in Israelite religion, changing this negative appraisal.

Both textual and archaeological evidence point to a developed cult of the dead at Ugarit (Ras Shamra), in present-day Syria. Methodologically one begins with the textual evidence from Ugarit, to which can be added the available archaeological evidence. The LB tombs at Ras Shamra and elsewhere, including Palestine, were so poorly excavated and their contents so badly recorded that they can be understood only in light of pertinent texts.

The architectural structure of certain tombs made it easy to provide offerings to the deceased. Grandiose vaulted tombs constructed of ashlar masonry were found under all the houses in the upper city of Ugarit, in the residential quarters south and

100. Theodore J. Lewis, *Cults of the Dead in Ancient Israel and Ugarit* (Atlanta: Scholars Press, 1989), passim.

101. Lewis, *Cults of the Dead in Ancient Israel and Ugarit,* 1; G. Ernest Wright, *Deuteronomy, IB* (New York: Abingdon, 1953), 486–87; Yehezkel Kaufmann, *The Religion of Israel,* trans. M. Greenberg (New York: Schocken, 1960), 312; de Vaux, *Ancient Israel,* 60.

east of the palace. Stepped shafts led down from the first floor. The family tombs situated under the floor were built at the same time as the houses.

Scholars have not achieved a consensus with regard to the funerary nature of some key texts from Ugarit. Two in particular require comment: "The Ugaritic Funerary Text" (*KTU* 1.161; RS 34.126) and "The Duties of an Ideal Son" (*CTA* 17.1.26–34). The first is a mortuary ritual for a recently deceased king (Niqmaddu III); its purpose is to provide services to the dead and to obtain, in turn, blessings for this life.[102] The second, from the 'Aqhat epic, deals only indirectly with the funerary rite. The text lists six chores, cultic and profane, that a dutiful son accomplishes for his father. Two of the tasks are clearly cultic: "One who sets up the stele of his divine ancestor (*škn ilibh*)"; and "One who eats his grain offering in the temple of Ba'al, his portion in the temple of El." Marvin Pope's view of the funerary imagery in this passage contrasts sharply with Brian Schmidt's conclusion that there is no "supernatural beneficent power of the dead" in this literature.[103]

Corrupt Rulers, Apostate People

Scholars continue to debate the meaning of Isaiah 56:9–57:13, especially regarding allusions to the Canaanite-Israelite cult of the dead. According to Lewis,[104] this passage from Third Isaiah, dating to the late sixth century B.C.E., is an interweaving of the cult of the dead and the cult of sex. The initial verses (Isa. 56:9–57:2) are a scathing tirade against Israel's religious leaders for neglect of duty:

> (56:9) All you beasts of the field, come to eat, all you beasts in the forest. (10) My watchmen (*ṣōpāy*) are all blind, they lack knowledge. They are all mute dogs, they cannot bark. The seers (*ḥōzîm*) recline, they love to slumber. (11) Dogs, gluttons! They never have enough. And they are the shepherds! They have no understanding. They all turn to their own way, each seeks his own gain. (12) "Come, let me get some wine, let us guzzle grappa (*šēkār* [not "beer"]). Tomorrow will be like today, or even better yet." (57:1) The righteous one perishes, but no one takes it to heart. Devout men are "gathered" (= they die), but no one gives it a thought. (The righteous one) is "gathered." (2) The just one enters (the grave) in peace. They rest on their biers (*miš-kĕbôtām*), those who walk uprightly.

---

102. Lewis, *Cults of the Dead in Ancient Israel and Ugarit*, 5–46, 53–71. Lewis's careful analysis of the Ugaritic texts is a valuable resource.

103. Marvin H. Pope, "The Cult of the Dead at Ugarit," in G. D. Young, ed., *Ugarit in Retrospect* (Winona Lake, Ind.: Eisenbrauns, 1981), 159–61. Brian B. Schmidt, *Israel's Beneficent Dead* (Winona Lake, Ind.: Eisenbrauns, 1996), 121: "The belief in the supernatural beneficent power of the dead as expressed in ancestor worship or veneration and necromancy is not documented in the texts from Ugarit."

104. Lewis, *Cults of the Dead in Ancient Israel and Ugarit*, 143–58; idem, "Death Cult Imagery in Isaiah 57," *Hebrew Annual Review* 11 (1987): 267–84; Susan Ackerman, *Under Every Green Tree* (Atlanta: Scholars Press, 1992), 101–63. The translation of Isa. 56:9–57:13 is T. J. Lewis's, with very minor changes.

Ill. 226: Bronze situla with ithyphallic god Min, found in 604 B.C.E. destruction. (Courtesy of the Leon Levy Expedition to Ashkelon; Photo: C. Andrews)

The remaining verses (Isa. 57:3–13) are a prophetic condemnation of the wicked, whose identity is difficult to determine:

(57:3) But you, draw near, you sons of a conjurer (*'ōnĕnâ*), offspring of an adulterer and a whore (*zōnâ*). (4) Over whom do you delight (at the prospect of eating), over whom do you open wide your mouth, and stretch out your tongue? Are you not children of sin, the offspring of lies. (5) Comforting yourselves with the dead spirits, in light of these things, should I be comforted? Slaughtering your children in the wadis (*nĕḥālîm*), under the rocky cliffs. (6) Among the dead of the wadi (*ḥallĕqê-naḥal*) is your portion (*ḥelqēk*), they, they're your lot. Even to them have you poured libations, and brought offerings. (7) On a high and lofty mountain you have placed your bed/grave (*miškābēk*). There too you have gone up to offer sacrifice. (8) Behind the door and the doorpost you have put your indecent symbol/mortuary stela (*zikrônēk*). You tried to discover (oracles) from me (by) bringing up (spirits), you have made wide your bed/grave (*miškābēk*). You have made a pact for yourself with them (the dead). You have loved their bed/grave (*miškābām*), you have gazed on the phallic symbol/mortuary stela (*yād*). (9) You lavished oil on the (dead?) king, you multiplied your perfumes. You sent your envoy afar, you sent them down to Sheol. (10) You were wearied by your travel, but you did not say, "It is hopeless." You found new strength (*ḥayyat yādēk*), so that you did not weaken. (11) Whom did you dread and fear so that you were false? You did not remember (*zākart*) me, you did not give me any thought. Was I to remain silent forever, so that you would not have me to fear? (12) I will tell of your "righteousness," your deeds will not help you. (13) When you cry out, will your dead (*qibbûṣayik*) deliver you? The wind will carry all of them away, a breeze shall take them. But he who takes refuge in me will inherit (*yinḥal*) the land (*'ereṣ*), he will possess my holy mountain.

The sexual imagery contained here has been recognized by many scholars, but not the death-cult imagery. Lewis sees them as intertwined. Among the terms under consideration are *nĕḥālîm*, "wadis" > "burial sites"; *ḥallĕqîm*, "smooth (stones)" > "the dead"; *miškāb*, "bed" > "grave"; *zikkārôn*, *yād*, "sign," "phallus" > "memorial monument."[105] For example, the biblical author plays on the various meanings of

---

105. Brian B. Schmidt, *Israel's Beneficent Dead* (Winona Lake, Ind.: Eisenbrauns, 1996), 255–56.

miškāb, namely, "grave," "resting place," and "bed" (Isa. 57:2, 7, 8). *miškāb* designates a resting place in a tomb (v. 2) as well as a harlot's bed (vv. 7, 8). A parallel to the first use appears in the Chronicler's description of the burial of Judah's King Asa (913–873 B.C.E.). "They laid him on his resting place (*miškāb*) that had been filled with various kinds of spices prepared by the perfumer's art" (2 Chron. 16:14). Isaiah 57:6 is a critical but ambiguous verse: "Among the dead of the wadi is your portion (*bĕḥallĕqê-naḥal ḥelqēk*); they are your lot. Even to them have you poured libations and brought offerings." Lewis comments: "The death imagery is overpowering. The ritual being described is that of a cult of the dead where offerings and libations were being brought to the deceased."[106]

Marzēaḥ and Kispu

The word *marzēaḥ* occurs only twice in the Bible: in Amos 6:4–7 (vocalized *mirzaḥ*), where it signifies a luxurious banquet accompanied by sensuous excesses; and in Jeremiah 16:5–9, where it describes a mourning rite consisting of food and drink.

> For thus says Yahweh: Do not enter a house of mourning (*bêt marzēaḥ*); do not go to mourn; do not lament for them. For I have withdrawn my favor from this people, my kindness and compassion. Great and small alike shall die in this land. They shall not be buried. None shall mourn or lament. There shall be no gashing, no shaving of the head for them. None shall break bread for the mourner, to offer comfort for the dead. Nor shall anyone give them the cup of consolation to drink for their fathers or mothers. You shall not go into the house of feasting (*bêt mišteh*) to sit with them, to eat and drink. For thus says Yahweh of hosts, the God of Israel: I am going to banish from this place, in your days and before your eyes, the sound of mirth and gladness, the voice of bridegroom and bride. (Jer. 16:5–9)

The *marzēaḥ* was frequently associated with the cult of the dead. Practiced from North Africa to Syria, the *marzēaḥ* was known from Ugarit in LB to Palmyra in the third century C.E. The *marzēaḥ*, both a religious and a social institution, denoted the association or guild sponsoring the banquet or designated the location of the banquet. The occasion could be either joyful or sorrowful.

The *bêt marzēaḥ* ("house of mourning") and the *bêt mišteh* ("house of feasting") appear to be synonymous in Jeremiah 16. Yahweh forbade Jeremiah to enter the *bêt marzēaḥ* ("house of mourning") to participate in memorial meals associated with mourning the dead and consoling the mourners. The *bêt marzēaḥ* was the site of the funerary cult. Partaking of food and drink, an integral part of the *marzēaḥ*, was a means of consoling the bereaved. The funerary ritual was at the heart of the *marzēaḥ*

---

106. Lewis, *Cults of the Dead in Ancient Israel and Ugarit*, 157.

described by Jeremiah, whereas the *marzēaḥ* depicted by Amos lacks funerary imagery.[107]

Pope maintained that the West Semitic *marzēaḥ* corresponded to the Mesopotamian *kispu*, a ritual banquet for the deceased.[108] This term also refers to funeral or memorial rites conducted at a family tomb. But the *kispu*, unlike the *marzēaḥ*, had a royal focus. In the Mari texts, the *kispu* ritual consisted of three parts: invocation of the deceased's name, presentation of food, and libation of water.[109] The *kispu* ceremony, known from the time of Mari and down to the Neo-Babylonian period, also involved eating and drinking in memory of the dead. With respect to the memorial rites for departed ancestors, King Panammu expresses the hope that his son and successor will invoke the soul/spirit of Panammu before Ḥadad, the head of the Aramaic pantheon: "May the soul of Panammu eat with you, and may the soul of Panammu drink with you" (*KAI* 214.16–22). This eighth-century invocation expresses the wish for a life of feasting with Ḥadad in the afterlife.

Necromancy

The practice of necromancy, consulting the dead, usually with the help of a medium, was roundly condemned in Israel. The classic case of necromancy in the Bible is Saul's request of the medium at Endor (north of Mount Gilboa) to conjure Samuel from the dead (1 Sam. 28:3–25). Saul was desperate to seek Samuel's counsel about the impending battle with the Philistines. In disguise, Saul approached the necromancer (*'ēšet ba'ălat-'ôb*) at night, the preferred time for conducting this chthonic ritual. He made two requests: "Consult a spirit (*'ôb*) for me, and bring up for me the one whom I name to you" (1 Sam. 28:8). At Saul's direction the woman raised a divine being (*'ĕlōhîm*) from the dead whom she described as "an old man who is wrapped in a robe (*mĕ'îl*)." Saul recognized Samuel by his distinctive garment (*mĕ'îl*) (1 Sam. 28:14; also 2:19; 15:27). The necromancer is designated as *ba'ălat-'ôb*, literally "possessor of a pit," that is, she who officiates at such a pit. It may be significant that sorcery was practiced chiefly by women, perhaps to compensate for the fact they had no role in the official cult. According to Harry Hoffner,[110] *'ôb* may refer to the ritual pit itself, the spirit (ghost) of the deceased, or the necromancer. The pit provided the ghosts with access to the world, and ladders were extended into the pit to help the

---

107. Note that the *liškâ* and *bêt marzēaḥ* may be the same. Some have suggested that what Avraham Biran calls an eighth-century *liškâ* at Dan is a *bêt marzēaḥ*. In that context, though, how "funerary" would it be?

108. Pope, "The Cult of the Dead at Ugarit," 176: "There is scant reason to doubt that the West Semitic Marzeah was a feast for and with the departed ancestors, corresponding to the Mesopotamian *kispu*."

109. Hallo, "Royal Ancestor Worship in the Biblical World," 394–96.

110. Harry A. Hoffner, "*'ôbh*," *TDOT*, 1: 133.

shades (*rĕpā'îm*) to get out. Sometimes food offerings were deposited in the pit. In this story, Samuel chided Saul: "Why have you disturbed me (*hirgaztanî*) by bringing me up?" (1 Sam. 28:15). *hirgîz* (the basic meaning of *rgz* is "to shake, disturb") is a technical term, referring to the interruption of the deceased's tranquillity.[111]

In a prophetic oracle about Yahweh's siege of Jerusalem, Isaiah states scornfully: "Then deep from the earth you [Jerusalem] shall speak, from low in the dust your words shall come. Your voice shall be like a ghost's (*'ôb*) from the earth, and your speech like chirping from the dust" (Isa. 29:4). Compare the prophetic warning against necromancy: "When they say to you, 'Inquire of mediums and fortune-tellers who chirp and mutter,' should not a people inquire of their gods, apply to the dead on behalf of the living?" (Isa. 8:19). In these verses "chirp" and "mutter" refer derisively to necromancers.

---

111. Jonas C. Greenfield, "Scripture and Inscription: The Literary and Rhetorical Element in Some Early Phoenician Inscriptions," in H. Goedicke, ed., *Near Eastern Studies in Honor of William Foxwell Albright* (Baltimore: Johns Hopkins Press, 1971), 258–59.

Epilogue

After the fall of Judah and the destruction of Jerusalem in 586 B.C.E., the cosmion of the ancient Israelites—that creative analogue of the cosmos that mediates between the finite and the infinite—was shattered.[1] All levels of their three-tiered hierarchy of order—the nested households of patrimonial authority from paterfamilias to king to deity—were severely disrupted.

At the base of this hierarchy were the agropastoralists in the towns and villages of the countryside, organized into joint families, lineages, and clans, who either died during the Babylonian onslaught, or fled as refugees into other countries, or were deported to Babylonia. The kingdom of Judah governed by the dynasty of David had become but a memory or, at best, an eschatological hope. The palace complex that stood on Mount Zion next to the Temple was in ruins, never to be rebuilt. The "house of Yahweh," a symbol of the inviolability of Jerusalem, also lay in ruins, abandoned by the Deity, according to Ezekiel; but this same prophet also had a vision of restoration and the return of the "glory" of God to the holy mount.

Without a king, without a permanent abode for Yahweh, and without landed patrimony, the condition of the exiles from Judah resembled, at least superficially, that of their ancestors in Egypt, as related in epic tales of the distant past. The pragmatic conditions of existence in exile required their drawing on a reserve stock of symbols, many of them from the formative period of Israel's history, before Yahweh dwelt in a permanent house in Jerusalem.

The contingencies of history, as well as the resilience of the patrimonial structure of society in which kingship was not essential, gave the Jewish exiles room to create

---

1. The political philosopher Eric Voegelin developed the idea that human society "is as a whole a little world, a cosmion, illuminated with meaning from within by the human beings who continuously create and bear it as the mode and condition of their self-realization. It is illuminated through an elaborate symbolism . . . from rite, through myth, to theory. . . . The self-illumination of society through symbols is an integral part of social reality . . . for through such symbolization the members of a society experience it as more than an accident or a convenience; they experience it as of their human essence" (Eric Voegelin, *The New Science of Politics* [Chicago: University of Chicago Press, 1952], 27).

a new cosmion. The new vision was built as much as possible on the past but evoked in new ways the symbolization of ordered relationships that took into account the new circumstances and reality in which they found themselves. The relationship between ruler and ruled had to be reassessed, and two important differences in imperial policy between the Assyrian and the Babylonian empires opened opportunities for this reassessment.

First, Judah was spared the fate of Samaria, in that Nebuchadrezzar did not try to transform it into a province, as Assyria had done with the northern kingdom. There, portions of the local population were deported to other parts of the empire, and foreign deportees were moved in beside those who remained. The Assyrians engaged in a large-scale plan of forced acculturation and assimilation of conquered peoples, which broke up families, traditions, and customs. Their policy was to homogenize and "Assyrianize" exiled populations.[2]

Second, rather than impose an effective imperial bureaucracy on the petty kingdoms of the West, Nebuchadrezzar implemented a "scorched earth" policy there, leaving whole regions severely underpopulated. Many of the deportees were taken to Babylonia to strengthen the core of his empire, which had suffered a great depletion of manpower as a consequence of earlier wars with Assyria.[3] This left some areas, such as Judah and Philistia, veritable wastelands.

After a thorough review of most of the archaeological evidence in Palestine between 604 and 539 B.C.E., Ephraim Stern concluded that "there is virtually no clearly defined period that may be called 'Babylonian,' for it was a time from which almost no material finds remain."[4] There were scattered populations in the countryside, but these were quite small when compared with Iron Age II and the Persian period. International trade was minimal. Only two regions showed a few signs of prosperity during Babylonian rule: northern Judah (the region of Benjamin) and the land of Ammon.

The Jews were just one of many western minorities deported to Babylonia. There were also Egyptians, Greeks, Phoenicians, and Philistines still living there in the Persian period. And, although the Jews are the best-known group to return to their homeland, other communities returned as well. A cuneiform archive of the Nusku-gabbē family found in the town of Neirab, southeast of Aleppo (Syria), covers the period of about 560–520 B.C.E., when members of this family or lineage were exiles in Babylonia. They, with their archive in hand, returned to their hometown some time later. In many ways their return resembles that of the Jews, who "returned to

---

2. Israel Eph'al, "The Western Minorities of Babylonia in the 6th–5th centuries B.C.: Maintenance and Cohesion," *Orientalia* 47 (1978): 83.

3. Lawrence E. Stager, "Ashkelon and the Archaeology of Destruction: Kislev 604 B.C.E.," in A. Biran et al., eds., *Eretz-Israel* 25 [Joseph Aviram Volume] (Jerusalem: Israel Exploration Society), 61*–74*.

4. Ephraim Stern, *Archaeology of the Land of the Bible*, vol. 2, *The Assyrian, Babylonian, and Persian Periods (732–332 B.C.E.)*, (New York: Doubleday, 2001), 350.

Jerusalem and Judah, each to his own town" (Ezra 2:1; Neh. 7:6).[5] Clearly, memories of their homelands, hometowns, and family estates remained very much alive in some Diaspora communities. The "elders," who would have been leaders in this regard, continued to represent various segments of kin-based society as they had done throughout Israelite and Judahite history. Both Jeremiah and Ezekiel refer to this significant body in Babylonia as the "elders of the exiles" (Jer. 29:1), the "elders of Judah" (Ezek. 8:1), and the "elders of Israel" (Ezek. 14:1; 20:1, 3).

The Philistines, however, were not so fortunate. Their homeland, largely depopulated under Babylonian military policy, was repopulated during the Persian period not by Philistines returning from Babylonia but by Phoenicians moved south from Tyre and Sidon by the Persian authorities. The Persians preferred a Phoenician maritime presence in these coastal communities to that of the Philistines.[6] Thus historical contingencies resulting from different treatments by the Assyrians and the Babylonians to subject populations and a Persian policy of "enlightened self-interest"[7] played a significant role in the successful repatriation of Jewish exiles from Babylonia.

Under the edict of 538 B.C.E.[8] issued by Cyrus the Great of Persia, the founder of the largest empire the world had ever seen, Jews began returning to their homeland, less than half a century after the fall of Judah. Cyrus also granted the returnees permission to rebuild the Temple in Jerusalem. He even ordered the return of the gold and silver sacred vessels, which Nebuchadrezzar had plundered from the First Temple.

Although many preferred to remain in the Diaspora, the return of some of the Jewish exiles to Judah to restore their community and rebuild the Temple was greeted with hostility by the landowners of Judah who were not exiled ('am hā'āreṣ) as well as by unfriendly neighbors all around: the Samarians, led by Sanballat, to the north; the Ammonites, led by the Tobiad family, to the east; the Edomites and Arabs to the south; and the "Ashdodites" (actually Phoenicians) to the west.

Work on the Temple in Jerusalem, however, began in earnest after 520 B.C.E., when another wave of Jewish returnees arrived with Zerubbabel, a "governor of Judah" and the last descendant of the Davidic dynasty mentioned in the Bible. With the encouragement of two prophets, Haggai and Zechariah, the Second Temple was completed in five years (by 515 B.C.E.). However, Haggai's hopes that Zerubbabel would restore kingship as a Davidic dynasty went unfulfilled (cf. Haggai 2:20–23).

The Second Temple was built over the foundations of the Solomonic Temple,

---

5. Eph'al, "The Western Minorities of Babylonia in the 6th–5th centuries B.C.," 84–87.

6. Lawrence E. Stager, *Ashkelon Discovered* (Washington, D.C.: Biblical Archaeology Society, 1991), 22–23, 30–31.

7. Mary Joan Leith, "Israel among the Nations: The Persian Period," in M. D. Coogan, ed., *The Oxford History of the Biblical World* (New York: Oxford University Press, 1998), 378–79.

8. See Ezra 1:2–4; 6:3–5.

which, although it lay in ruins after 586 B.C.E., was still revered as a holy site to which pilgrimage was made (cf. Jer. 41:5). The new edifice was constructed on Mount Zion within a square fortified enclosure, about 250 meters (500 cubits) on each side, with elaborate gates leading into the courtyards of the acropolis complex. Unlike Mount Zion of the monarchy, there were no palaces next to the "house of Yahweh." The Temple stood alone in the fortified enclosure, known as *bîrâ* in the Persian period.[9] And for those who could remember or who had been told what the Solomonic Temple had looked like before its destruction, the Second Temple was but a pale reflection of its splendor: "Many of the priests and Levites and heads of patriarchal houses [*rāʾšê hāʾābôt*], the old men [*hazzĕqēnîm*] who had seen the first house, cried out in sorrow as they watched the founding of this house" (Ezra 3:12; cf. Haggai 2:3).

Jerusalem and the province of *Yehud* (Judah) in the Fifth Satrapy of the Persian Empire[10] were also pale reflections of what they had been during the last century of the monarchy. The province now was only a portion of one of the twenty satrapies into which the Persian Empire was divided. The Fifth Satrapy, known as "Beyond the River" (Heb. *ʿēber hannāhār*, Aramaic *ʿăbar nahărâ*; i.e., west of the Euphrates), was composed of Palestine, Phoenicia, and Cyprus.

The province of Samaria (Samerina) greatly declined during the Babylonian era. Of the major tells excavated there—Dothan, Samaria, Shechem, Tell el-Farʿah (N), and Gezer—not one has yielded material remains that can be definitely assigned to that time.

By the Persian period, however, the demographic and economic fortunes of Samaria province were on the upswing. In the northern and western parts, archaeological surveys show about the same density of settlements as in Iron Age II; many of these were villages with 500–600 inhabitants. Their prosperity seemed to be linked to that of the rich Phoenician coastal communities that flourished from Sidon to Ashkelon. In contrast, the southern part of Samaria province shows a sharp decline in number and size of settlements during the Persian period from what had been there in Iron Age II.[11]

---

9. See Benjamin Mazar, "The Temple Mount from Zerubbabel to Herod," in Shmuel Ahituv, ed., *Biblical Israel: State and People* (Jerusalem: Magnes Press, Hebrew University; Israel Exploration Society, 1992), 111–12. Nehemiah worked in the citadel of Susa (*bĕšûšan habbîrâ*) before going to Jerusalem; cf. also the acropolis of Carthage known in Greek as *byrsa*, probably borrowed from an as yet unattested Phoenician **brt*, which, like Hebrew *bîrâ* and Aramaic *bîrtā*, derives from Assyrian *birtu*, meaning "citadel."

10. See the overview of Israel Ephʿal, "Syria-Palestine under Achaemenid Rule" in John Boardman, N. G. L. Hammond, D. M. Lewis and M. Ostwald, eds., *Cambridge Ancient History*, vol. 4, *Persia, Greece and the Western Mediterranean* (Cambridge: Cambridge University Press, 1988), 139–64; Ephraim Stern, "The Archaeology of Persian Palestine," in W. D. Davies and Louis Finkelstein, eds., *The Cambridge History of Judaism*, vol. 1, *Introduction: The Persian Period* (Cambridge: Cambridge University Press, 1984), 88–114; and Leith, "Israel among the Nations: The Persian Period."

11. Stern, *Archaeology of the Land of the Bible*, 2:428.

Personal names reveal a heterogeneous population living in Samaria during the Persian period. The Wadi ed-Daliyeh papyri (fourth century B.C.E.) mention names composed of the divine element: Qaus (Edomite), Chemosh (Moabite), Ba'al (Phoenician), Sahar (Aramaic), and Nabu (Babylonian). But the most common names are Yahwistic. Even Governor Sanballat, portrayed in the Bible as archenemy of Nehemiah and the Jews who rebuilt Jerusalem, gave his sons Yahwistic names, indicating that a variant of Yahwism was very much alive among the ruling circles of Samaria. Like the Jews of Elephantine in Egypt and the 'am hā'āreṣ of Judah, the Samarians represented a variant of Yahwism considered anathema by Ezra and Nehemiah, who were developing very exclusivist views about "who is a Jew" in the province of *Yehud*. As Mary Joan Leith has aptly noted, "reassessments of sectarian Samaritanism have demonstrated that its feasts, its conservatism toward the Torah, and its version of the Pentateuch indicate more derivation than deviation from Judaism of the Second Temple period."[12]

Perhaps we can see architectural derivation in the great "temple-city," which crowns the top of Mount Gerizim, recently unearthed by the revealing excavations of Yitzhak Magen. Atop this holy mountain, rival to Mount Zion, stands a temple site surrounded by a large fortified enclosure with gates and monumental stairway.[13] This magnificent complex built in the Persian and Hellenistic periods gives a much better impression of what the Jerusalem temple citadel (*bîrâ*) probably looked like than what can be gleaned from the excavations in Jerusalem.

Yehud province can be roughly delimited by the distribution of coins and seal impressions inscribed with the name of the province. This evidence puts its northern boundary at Tell en-Naṣbeh, ancient Mizpeh, its southern border at Beth-Zur, its western one near Keilah, and its eastern one as far as the Jordan River and the Dead Sea, along a line from Jericho to 'Ein-Gedi.[14] All of these towns were called upon to supply corvée labor for rebuilding the fortifications in Jerusalem (Neh. 3:15–17). *Yehud* province, then, incorporated no more than three thousand square kilometers, making it less than half the size of the former kingdom of Judah.

According to the biblical census, almost 50,000 exiles returned to *Yehud* during the century following Cyrus's edict of 538 B.C.E.[15] For the most part, these Jews lived outside Jerusalem in this small impoverished province, surrounded by a mosaic of more prosperous cultures and communities. Excavations in the Phoenician cities of Dor and Ashkelon have revealed rich cosmopolitan cultures. These coastal communities, as well as Samaria and its surroundings, contrast sharply with contemporary

---

12. Leith, "Israel among the Nations," 385–86 (quotation on 386).
13. Yitzhak Magen, "Mt. Gerizim—A Temple City," *Qadmoniot* 33/2 (2000), 74–118.
14. Stern, *Archaeology of the Land of the Bible*, 2:430–31 and map III.6, p. 375.
15. The list in Ezra 2 seems to be the same one cited in Nehemiah 7, although the details differ slightly. Both report 42,360 laity and 7,337 servants. Ezra lists 200 singers; Nehemiah, 245.

sites in *Yehud* province.[16] When Nehemiah, Jewish cupbearer to Artaxerxes I and governor of *Yehud*, arrived in Palestine about 445 B.C.E., he was appalled by many economic hardships caused by heavy taxation from the Persian crown[17] and debt servitude:

> Some said, "Our sons and daughters are numerous; we must get grain to eat in order that we may live!" Others said, "We must pawn our fields, our vineyards, and our homes to get grain to stave off hunger." Yet others said, "We have borrowed money against our fields and vineyards to pay the king's tax. Now we are as good as our brothers, and our children as good as theirs; yet here we are subjecting our sons and daughters to slavery—some of our daughters are already subjected—and we are powerless, while our fields and vineyards belong to others." (Neh 5:2–5, NJPS)

Nehemiah censured several of the notables of the Jewish community, accusing them of "pressing claims on loans made to [their] brothers." He then instituted sweeping reforms by ordering them to "give back at once their fields, their vineyards, their olive trees, and their homes, and [abandon] the claims for the hundred pieces of silver, the grain, the wine, and the oil that you have been pressing against them!" (Neh 5:11, NJPS) From these grievances it seems clear that most of the Jewish returnees were engaged in some form of agriculture, although there was a trend in some quarters toward more commercial activities.

As governor, Nehemiah had extensive authority over social, religious, and economic matters in the province of *Yehud*. From his first-person "memoirs" (Neh. 1:1–7:72 and 11:1–13:31), we see that he had the power to call for the remission of debts and for the fallowing of fields every seven years, to curtail commerce on the Sabbath, to prohibit Jews from marrying "foreign wives," to organize Temple funds and funding, to call up corvée labor from the countryside, and to compel, by an act of synoecism, part of the rural population to move to the city.

Nehemiah was also appalled at the desolate condition of Jerusalem: "the city was quite wide and spacious, but its population was small, and none of the houses had been rebuilt" (Neh. 7:4). The "wide and spacious" city that Nehemiah saw was the ruins of the metropolis of the monarchy that spread over the Western Hill, or the Mishneh Quarter, which once included more than 12,000 inhabitants.[18]

Artaxerxes I had dispatched Nehemiah to Palestine with an escort of cavalry and documents authorizing his safe passage from Susa to Judah and the procurement of

---

16. See Stern, "The Archaeology of Persian Palestine," 88–114; and for an up-to-date summary see Stern, *Archaeology of the Land of the Bible*, 2:385–443; also Leith, "Israel among the Nations: The Persian Period," 383–87, and Stager, *Ashkelon Discovered*, 20–33.

17. See Eph'al, *Cambridge Ancient History*, 158–59. The Jews of *Yehud* paid a "king's tax" (*middat hammelek*, Neh. 5:4; a "land tax" (in kind) (*bĕlô* related to Akkadian *biltu*, Ezra 4:13, 20; 7:24), and a "poll tax" (*hălāk*, Ezra 4:13, 20; 7:24).

18. Nahman Avigad, *Discovering Jerusalem: Recent Archaeological Excavations in the Upper City* (Nashville: Thomas Nelson, 1983), 62.

timber (probably cedar) from Asaph, keeper of the royal park (*pardēs*), that "he may give me [Nehemiah] wood to timber the gates of the Temple citadel (*ša'ărê habbîrâ 'ăšer-labbayit*), the city wall, and the house that I am to occupy" (Neh. 2:8).[19]

After a three-day rest from his long journey, Nehemiah and a small group went out at night to conduct a secret survey of the dilapidated defenses of Jerusalem in order to assess the damage and plan for the restoration of the city. Nehemiah rode his mount (probably a donkey), starting along the remnants of the western wall of the City of David and continuing south, in a counterclockwise manner, until he reached the Fountain Gate and the King's Pool,[20] where, he says, "there was no room for the beast under me to continue. So I went up the wadi [Nahal Kidron] by night, surveying the wall, and, entering again by the Valley Gate, I returned" (Neh. 2:14–15).

What Nehemiah encountered along the east slope of the City of David that caused him to proceed farther down in the Kidron Valley was an avalanche of stone and debris from houses and from the inner and outer fortification walls, which had tumbled down the slope. This scree of rubble from preexilic Jerusalem was discovered in the excavations of Kathleen Kenyon (Site A)[21] and, later, of Yigal Shiloh (Area G, Str 9). The debris was so dense and heavy that Nehemiah and his builders gave up on reclaiming the east slope of the City of David altogether and instead built a north-south fortification wall (ca. 2.5 meters thick) along its crest. Since none of the modern excavations has detected settlement on the Western Hill during the Persian period,[22] we can conclude that postexilic Jerusalem was limited to the confines of the City of David (4.4 hectares, excluding the Temple Mount) and was probably only half that size, with a few hundred inhabitants.

Nehemiah completed the repairs and restoration of the gates and fortifications in just fifty-two days, all the while working under adverse conditions because of hostile neighbors. For the construction he recruited task forces and their supervisors from towns in *Yehud* province. The term *pelek* is better translated "task force" than the more customary "territory" or "district."[23] It is clearly related to Akkadian *pilku*, already attested at Ugarit, where it refers to "service owed by landholders to their overlord. . . . In all cases it refers to the regular service obligation of the landholder (like *ilku*), not to the landholding itself."[24] The builders recruited from the towns and

---

19. From this description it is clear that the Second Temple was built within the citadel enclosure with gates and courtyard(s), and not south of the *bîrâ*; cf. Leith, "Israel among the Nations," 396.

20. This is probably the "Lower Pool" known today as Birket el-Hamra. See Avigad, *Discovering Jerusalem*, 60.

21. Kathleen Kenyon, *Digging Up Jerusalem* (New York: Praeger Publications, 1974), 108–10.

22. Stern, *Archaeology of the Land of the Bible*, 2:581; Avigad, *Discovering Jerusalem*, 62.

23. See Eph'al, "Syria-Palestine under Achaemenid Rule," 159, citing A. Demsky, "Pelekh in Nehemiah 3," *IEJ* 33 (1983): 242–44.

24. J. David Schloen, *The House of the Father as Fact and Symbol: Patrimonialism in Ugarit and the Ancient Near East* (Cambridge: Harvard Semitic Museum, 2001), 246.

hamlets of the countryside were mostly farmers who left their property ('ăḥuzzâ, Neh. 11:3) or their landed patrimony (naḥălâ, Neh. 11:20) to work for the state for a couple of months.

When their work was completed, Nehemiah then had to recruit people to live permanently in Jerusalem. He held a lottery. Besides the "leaders of the people" (śārê-hā'ām) who settled there, the "rest of the people cast lots for one out of ten to come and settle in Jerusalem, the holy city, and the other nine-tenths to stay in towns" (Neh. 11:1–2).

The exile and the return of the Jews to their homeland and the restoration of Jerusalem necessitated many changes in their cosmion. Their Deity once again had a permanent abode in the holy city, but the royal line of the Davidic household no longer reigned. Instead, political and religious leadership was represented by the governors and the priests, respectively. At the culmination of the restoration of Jerusalem, with the governor Nehemiah at his side, Ezra, the priest and scribe, read from the Torah, the "scroll of the law of Moses," to men and women assembled in the square before the Water Gate (Neh. 8:1–8).

There have been many explanations as to why the Jews survived the exile and returned to their homeland. It is significant, we think, that the exiles returned "each to his own town"; even after Jerusalem was reconstituted as a ritual center, 90 percent of the populace lived in towns and hamlets in the countryside. Even though some of the kinship terminology changed between the preexilic and postexilic periods,[25] joint families under the authority of the paterfamilias constituted a sizable portion of the population of the province of Yehud. The resilience and restorative power of familial organization helped the Jews survive the exile, even when deprived of their landed patrimony.

Although an "archaeology of the family" in postexilic Palestine remains to be written, we would imagine that the seasonal and diurnal activities of most of the inhabitants resembled those of Micah's household, which we introduced in chapter one.

---

25. See David Vanderhooft, "The Israelite mišpāḥâ in the Priestly Writings: An Elite Reconstruction of Social Organization" in Baruch Halpern, Gary Knoppers, and Alex Joffe, eds., Rival Communities in the Ancient Near East, Studies in the Culture and History of the Ancient Near East (Leiden: E. J. Brill, forthcoming). The term for "clan" (mišpāḥâ) seems to be replaced by bêt 'abôt in the postexilic period.

Maps

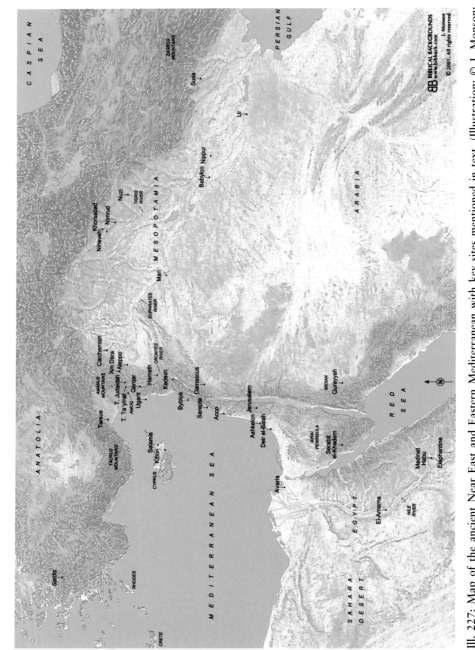

Ill. 227: Map of the ancient Near East and Eastern Mediterranean with key sites mentioned in text. (Illustration: © J. Monson; www.bibback.com)

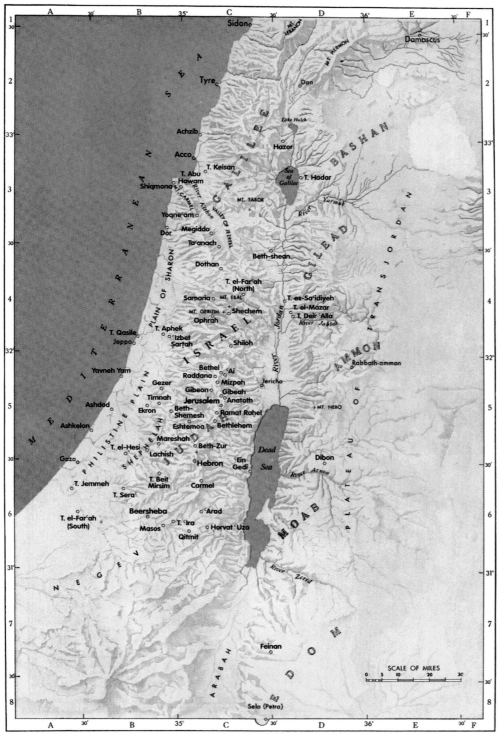

Ill. 228: Map of Palestine with key sites mentioned in text. (Illustration: C. Haberl after G. E. Wright and F. V. Wilson)

Bibliography

Ackerman, Susan. *Under Every Green Tree.* Atlanta: Scholars Press, 1992.

Aharoni, Miriam. "Arad: The Israelite Citadels." *NEAEHL,* 1: 82–85.

Aharoni, Yohanan. *The Land of the Bible.* Rev. ed. Philadelphia: Westminster Press, 1979.

———. "Megiddo." *NEAEHL,* 3: 1003–12.

Aharoni, Yohanan, ed. *Arad Inscriptions.* Jerusalem: Israel Exploration Society, 1981.

Albertz, Rainer. *A History of Israelite Religion in the Old Testament Period.* London: SCM Press, 1994.

Albright, William F. "The Date of Sennacherib's Second Campaign against Hezekiah." *BASOR* 130 (1953): 8–11.

———. "The Gezer Calendar." *BASOR* 92 (1943): 16–26.

———. *The Proto-Sinaitic Inscriptions and Their Decipherment.* Cambridge: Harvard University Press, 1966.

———. "The Role of the Canaanites in the History of Civilization." In *The Bible and the Ancient Near East,* edited by G. E. Wright, 328–62. Garden City, N.Y.: Doubleday, 1961.

———. *Yahweh and the Gods of Canaan.* Garden City, N.Y.: Doubleday, 1968.

Amiran, Ruth, and Ornit Ilan. "Arad." *NEAEHL,* 1: 75–82.

Andersen, Francis I., and David N. Freedman. *Amos: A New Translation with Notes and Commentary.* AB 24A. New York: Doubleday, 1989.

Anderson, Gary A. *Sacrifices and Offerings in Ancient Israel.* HSM 41. Atlanta: Scholars Press, 1987.

Anderson, William P. "The Kilns and Workshops of Sarepta (Sarafand, Lebanon): Remnants of a Phoenician Ceramic Industry." *Berytus* 35 (1987): 41–66.

André, G., and Helmer Ringgren. "ṭame'." *TDOT,* 5: 330–42.

Ariès, Philippe. *Centuries of Childhood: A Social History of Family Life.* Translated by Robert Baldick. New York: Vintage Books, 1962.

Avalos, Hector. *Illness and Health Care in the Ancient Near East.* HSM 54. Atlanta: Scholars Press, 1995.

Avigad, Nahman. *Discovering Jerusalem: Recent Archaeological Excavations in the Upper City.* Nashville: Thomas Nelson, 1983.

———. "The Epitaph of a Royal Steward from Siloam Village." *IEJ* 3 (1953): 137–52.

———. "A Hebrew Seal Depicting a Sailing Ship." *BASOR* 246 (1982): 59–62.

———. "The King's Daughter and the Lyre," *IEJ* 28 (1978): 146–51.

———. "Two Hebrew 'Fiscal' Bullae." *IEJ* 40 (1990): 263–66.

———. "Two Hebrew Inscriptions on Wine-Jars." *IEJ* 22 (1972): 1–9.

Avigad, Nahman, and Jonas C. Greenfield. "A Bronze *phiale* with a Phoenician Dedicatory Inscription." *IEJ* 32 (1982): 118–28.

Avigad, Nahman, and Benjamin Sass. *Corpus of West Semitic Stamp Seals*. Jerusalem: Israel Exploration Society, 1997.

Bahat, Dan. "The Fuller's Field and the 'Conduit of the Upper Pool.'" In *Eretz-Israel* 20 [Yigael Yadin Volume], edited by A. Ben-Tor, J. C. Greenfield, and A. Malamat, 253–56. Jerusalem: Israel Exploration Society, 1989.

Baines, John, and O. J. Eyre. "Four Notes on Literacy." *Göttinger Miszellen* 61 (1983): 65–72.

Ballard, Robert D., and Lawrence E. Stager, et al. "Iron Age Shipwrecks in Deep Water off Ashkelon, Israel." *AJA*. In press.

Bar-Adon, Pessah. "The Nahal Mishmar Caves." *NEAEHL*, 4: 822–827.

———. *The Cave of the Treasure*. Jerusalem: Israel Exploration Society, 1980.

Barber, Elizabeth W. *Prehistoric Textiles: The Development of Cloth in the Neolithic and Bronze Ages with Special Reference to the Aegean*. Princeton, N.J.: Princeton University Press, 1991.

———. *Women's Work: The First 20,000 Years*. New York: W. W. Norton, 1994.

Barkay, Gabriel. *Ketef Hinnom: A Treasure Facing Jerusalem*. Catalogue No. 274. Jerusalem: Israel Museum, 1986.

———. "News from the Field: The Divine Name Found in Jerusalem," *BAR* 9/2 (1983): 14–19.

Barkay, Gabriel, and Amos Kloner. "Jerusalem Tombs from the Days of the First Temple." *BAR* 12/2 (1986): 22–39.

Barnett, Richard D. "Early Shipping in the Near East." *Antiquity* 32 (1958): 220–30.

———. "Lachish, Ashkelon, and the Camel: A Discussion of Its Use in Southern Palestine." In *Palestine in the Bronze and Iron Ages* [OLGA Tufnell Festschrift], edited by J. N. Tubb, 15–30. London: Institute of Archaeology, 1985.

Barr, James. *History and Ideology in the Old Testament: Biblical Studies at the End of a Millennium*. New York: Oxford University Press, 2000.

Barstad, Hans M. *The Myth of the Empty Land*. Oslo: Scandinavian University Press, 1996.

Bar-Yosef, Ofer, Tamar Schick, and David Alon. "Nahal Hemar Cave." *NEAEHL*, 3: 1082–84.

Barzun, Jacques, and Henry F. Graff. "A Medley of Mysteries: A Number of Dogs That Didn't Bark." In *The Historian as Detective: Essays on Evidence*, edited by R. W. Winks, 213–31. New York: Harper, 1970.

Beck, Pirhiya. "Catalogue of Cult Objects and Study of the Iconography." In *Ḥorvat Qitmit: An Edomite Shrine in the Biblical Negev*, edited by I. Beit-Arieh, 28–43. Tel Aviv: Institute of Archaeology, Tel Aviv University, 1995.

———. "The Cult-Stands from Taanach: Aspects of the Iconographic Tradition of Early Iron Age Cult Objects in Palestine." In *From Nomadism to Monarchy*, edited by Israel Finkelstein and Nadav Na'aman, 352–81. Jerusalem: Israel Exploration Society, 1994.

———. "The Drawings from Ḥorvat Teiman (Kuntillet 'Ajrud)." *TA* 9 (1982): 35–36.

Beek, Gus W. Van. "Frankincense and Myrrh." *BA* 23 (1960): 69–95.

———. "Jemmeh, Tell." *NEAEHL*, 2: 667–674.

Beit-Arieh, Itzhaq. "Edomites Advance into Judah—Israelite Defensive Fortresses Inadequate." *BAR* 22/6 (1996): 28–36.

———. "New Light on the Edomites." *BAR* 14/2 (1988): 28–41.

———. "The Ostracon of Ahiqam from Ḥorvat 'Uza." *TA* 13 (1986): 32–38.

———. "'Uza, Ḥorvat." *NEAEHL*, 4: 1496.

Beit-Arieh, Itzhaq, and Bruce Cresson. "An Edomite Ostracon from Ḥorvat 'Uza." *TA* 12 (1985): 96–101.

Ben-Tor, Amnon. "Hazor." *NEAEHL*, 2: 604–605.

Ben-Tor, Daphna. "The Relations between Egypt and Palestine in the Middle Kingdom as Reflected by Contemporary Canaanite Scarabs." *IEJ* 47 (1997): 162–89.

Betlyon, John W. "Coinage." *ABD*, 1: 1076–89.

Bier, Carol. "Textile Arts in Ancient Western Asia." *CANE*, 3: 1567–88.

Bietak, Manfred. *Avaris: the Capital of the Hyksos: Recent Excavations at Tell el-Dab'a*. London: British Museum Press, 1996.

Biran, Avraham. *Biblical Dan*. Jerusalem: Israel Exploration Society, 1994.

———. "Dan." *NEAEHL*, 1: 323–32.

———. "The Dancer from Dan, the Empty Tomb and the Altar Room." *IEJ* 36 (1986): 168–87.

———. "The *ḥuṣôt* of Dan." In *Eretz-Israel* 26 [Frank Moore Cross Volume], edited by B. Levine et al., 25–29. Jerusalem: Israel Exploration Society, 1999.

———. "Sacred Spaces: Of Standing Stones, High Places and Cult Objects at Tel Dan." *BAR* 24/5 (1998): 38–45, 70.

Bird, Phyllis A. "Women (OT)." *ABD*, 6: 951–57.

Black, Jeremy, et al., eds. *A Concise Dictionary of Akkadian*. Wiesbaden: Harrassowitz, 1999.

Blenkinsopp, Joseph. "The Family in First Temple Israel." In *Families in Ancient Israel*, edited by Leo G. Perdue et al. Louisville, Ky.: Westminster John Knox, 1997.

Bliss, Frederick J. *A Mound of Many Cities*. London: A. P. Watt, 1894.

Bloch-Smith, Elizabeth. "Cist Graves," *OEANE*, 2: 13–14.

———. *Judahite Burial Practices and Beliefs about the Dead*. Sheffield: Academic Press, 1992.

Bloch-Smith, Elizabeth, and Beth Alpert Nakhai. "A Landscape Comes to Life: The Iron Age I." *NEA* 62 (1999): 62–92, 101–27.

Boessneck, Joachim, and Angela von Den Driesch. "Preliminary Analysis of the Animal Bones from Tell Hesban." *Andrews University Seminary Studies* 16 (1978): 259–87.

Borowski, Oded. *Agriculture in Iron Age Israel*. Winona Lake, Ind.: Eisenbrauns, 1987.

Braudel, Fernand. *The Mediterranean and the Mediterranean World in the Age of Philip II*. Translated by Siân Reynolds. Revised edition. New York: Harper & Row, 1972.

Brichto, Herbert C. "Kin, Cult, Land, and Afterlife—A Biblical Complex." *HUCA* 44 (1973): 1–54.

Burckhardt, Jacob. *The Greeks and Greek Civilization*. Translated by Sheila Stern. Edited, with an introduction, by Oswyn Murray. New York: St. Martin's Press, 1998.

Cahill, Jane, et al. "It Had to Happen—Scientists Examine Remains of Ancient Bathrooms." *BAR* 17/3 (1991): 64–69.

Campbell, Edward F. "Archaeological Reflections on Amos's Targets." In *Scripture and Other Artifacts* [Philip J. King Festschrift], edited by M. D. Coogan et al., 32–52. Louisville, Ky.: John Knox Press, 1994.

———. "Jewish Shrines of the Hellenistic and Persian Periods." In *Symposia Celebrating the Seventy-Fifth Anniversary of the Founding of the American Schools of Oriental Research (1900–1975)*, edited by Frank M. Cross, 159–67. Cambridge: American Schools of Oriental Research, 1979.

Cancik, Hubert. "Ikonoklasmus." In *Handbuch religionswissenschaftlicher Grundbegriffe*, vol. 3, edited by H. Cancik et al., 3: 217–21. Stuttgart: W. Kohlhammer, 1993.

Childs, Brevard S. *Book of Exodus*. OTL. Philadelphia: Westminster Press, 1974.

Clifford, Richard J. "Isaiah 55: Invitation to a Feast." In *The Word of the Lord Shall Go Forth* [David Noel Freedman Festschrift], edited by C. L. Meyers and M. O'Connor, 27–35. Winona Lake, Ind.: Eisenbrauns, 1983.

Clutton-Brock, Juliet. *A Natural History of Domesticated Mammals*. Cambridge: Cambridge University Press, 1987.

Cogan, Mordechai. "Sennacherib's Siege of Jerusalem." *BAR* 27/1 (2001): 40–45, 69.

Cogan, Mordechai, and Hayim Tadmor. *II Kings*. AB 11. New York: Doubleday, 1988.

Cohen, Rudolph, and Yigal Yisrael. "The Iron Age Fortress at 'En Ḥaṣeva." *BA* 58 (1995): 223–35.

Cole, Dan P. "How Water Tunnels Worked." *BAR* 6/2 (1980): 8–29.

Coogan, Michael D. "Of Cults and Cultures: Reflections on the Interpretation of Archaeological Evidence." *PEQ* 119 (1987): 1–8.

Coogan, Michael D., ed. and trans. *Stories from Ancient Canaan*. Philadelphia: Westminster Press, 1978.

Cooley, Robert E. "Gathered to His People: A Study of a Dothan Family Tomb." In *The Living and Active Word of God*, edited by M. Inch and R. Youngblood, 47–58. Winona Lake, Ind.: Eisenbrauns, 1983.

Coughenour, Robert A. "Preliminary Report on the Exploration and Excavation of Mugharat el Wardeh and Abu Thawab." *Annual of the Department of Antiquities, Jordan* 21 (1976): 71–77.

Craven, Toni. "Women Who Lied for the Faith." In *Justice and the Holy: Essays in Honor of Walter Harrelson*, edited by Douglas A. Knight and Peter J. Paris, 35–59. Atlanta: Scholars Press, 1989.

Crenshaw, James L. *Education in Ancient Israel: Across the Deadening Silence*. New York: Doubleday, 1998.

Cross, Frank M. *Canaanite Myth and Hebrew Epic*. Cambridge: Harvard University Press, 1973.

———. "Epigraphic Notes on Hebrew Documents of the Eighth–Sixth Centuries B.C.: I. A New Reading of a Place Name in the Samaria Ostraca." *BASOR* 163 (1961): 12–14.

———. "Epigraphic Notes on Hebrew Documents of the Eighth–Sixth Centuries B.C.: II. The Murabbaʿat Papyrus and the Letter Found near Yabneh-yam." *BASOR* 165 (1962): 34–46.

———. *From Epic to Canon: History and Literature in Ancient Israel*. Baltimore: Johns Hopkins University Press, 1998.

———. "Newly Found Inscriptions in Old Canaanite and Early Phoenician Scripts." *BASOR* 238 (1980): 8–15.

———. "An Old Canaanite Inscription Recently Found at Lachish." *TA* 11 (1984): 71–76.

———. "The Priestly Tabernacle in the Light of Recent Research." In *Temples and High Places in Biblical Times*, edited by A. Biran, 169–80. Jerusalem: Hebrew Union College—Jewish Institute of Religion, 1981.

———. "A Recently Published Phoenician Inscription of the Persian Period from Byblos." *IEJ* 29 (1979): 40–44.

Cross, Frank M., and David N. Freedman. "An Inscribed Jar Handle from Raddana." *BASOR* 201 (1971): 19–22.

———. "A Royal Song of Thanksgiving: II Samuel 22 = Psalm 18a." *JBL* 72 (1953): 15–34.

Crowfoot, Grace M. "Textiles, Basketry, and Mats." In *A History of Technology*, edited by C. J. Singer, E. J. Holmyard, and A. R. Hall, 1: 413–55. Oxford: Clarendon Press, 1954.

Curtis, Robert I. *Ancient Food Technology*. Leiden: Brill, 2001.

Dahood, Mitchell. *Psalms I*. AB 16. Garden City, N.Y.: Doubleday, 1966.

Dalley, Stephanie. *Mari and Karana: Two Old Babylonian Cities*. London: Longman, 1984.

Dalman, Gustaf Hermann. *Arbeit und Sitte in Palästina*. 8 volumes. Gütersloh: C. Bertelsmann, 1928–42.

Dauphin, Claudine. "Leprosy, Lust, and Lice: Health Care and Hygiene in Byzantine Palestine." *Bulletin of the Anglo-Israel Archaeological Society* 15 (1996–1997): 55–80.

Davies, Graham. "Were There Schools in Ancient Israel?" In *Wisdom in Ancient Israel*, edited by J. Day et al. Cambridge: Cambridge University Press, 1995.

Davies, Philip R. *In Search of "Ancient Israel."* JSOTSup 148. Sheffield: Sheffield Academic Press, 1992.

Davies, Philip R., and John Rogerson. "Was the Siloam Tunnel Built by Hezekiah?" *BA* 59 (1996): 138–49.

Davis, David, et al. "A Steel Pick from Mt. Adir in Palestine." *JNES* 44 (1985): 41–51.

Dayagi-Mendels, Michal. *Perfumes and Cosmetics in the Ancient World*. Israel Museum Catalogue 395. Jerusalem: Israel Museum, 1993.

Dearman, Andrew, ed. *Studies in the Mesha Inscription and Moab*. Atlanta: Scholars Press, 1989.

Deetz, James. *In Small Things Forgotten: An Archaeology of Early American Life*. New York: Doubleday, 1996.

Dever, William G. "Gezer." *NEAEHL*, 2: 496–506.

———. "The Water Systems at Hazor and Gezer." *BA* 32 (1969): 71–78.

———. *What Did the Biblical Writers Know and When Did They Know It?: What Archaeology Can Tell Us about Ancient Israel*. Grand Rapids: Wm. B. Eerdmans Pub. Co., 2001.

Diakonoff, Igor M. "The Naval Power and Trade of Tyre." *IEJ* 42 (1992): 168–93.

Dorsey, David A. "Carts." *OEANE*, 1: 433–34.

———. *Roads and Highways of Ancient Israel*. Baltimore: Johns Hopkins University Press, 1991.

Dothan, Trude. *The Philistines and Their Material Culture*. New Haven, Conn.: Yale University, 1982.

Dothan, Trude, and Seymour Gitin. "Miqne, Tel (Ekron)." *NEAEHL*, III, 1051–59.

Douglas, Mary. *Purity and Danger*. London: ARK Books, 1984.

Dubberstein, Waldo H. "Comparative Prices in Later Babylonia (625–400 B.C.)." *American Journal of Semitic Languages and Literature* 56 (1939): 20–43.

Eissfeldt, Otto. *Molk als Opferbegriff im Punischen und Hebräischen und das Ende des Gottes Moloch*. Halle: Max Niemeyer, 1935.

Elat, Moshe. "Tarshish and the Problem of Phoenician Colonisation in the Western Mediterranean." *Orientalia Lovaniensia Periodica* 13 (1982): 55–69.

Eph'al, Israel. "The Assyrian Siege Ramp at Lachish: Military and Linguistic Aspects." *TA* 11 (1984): 60–70.

———. *Siege Warfare and Its Ancient Near Eastern Manifestations*. Jerusalem: Magnes Press, 1996 (Hebrew).

———. "Syria-Palestine under Achaemenid Rule." In *The Cambridge Ancient History*, Vol. IV: *Persian, Greece and the Western Mediterranean c. 525–479 B.C.*, edited by John Boardman, N. G. L. Hammond, D. M. Lewis, M. Oswald, 139–64. Cambridge: Cambridge University Press, 1988.

———. "The Western Minorities in Babylonia in the 6th–5th Centuries B.C.: Maintenance and Cohesion." *Orientalia* 47 (1978): 74–90.

Eph'al, Israel, and Joseph Naveh. "The Jar of the Gate." *BASOR* 289 (1993): 59–65.

Epstein, Claire. *The Chalcolithic Culture of the Golan*. Report 4. Jerusalem: Israel Antiquities Authority, 1998.

Eran, Abraham. "Weights and Weighing in the City of David: The Early Weights from the Bronze Age to the Persian Period." In *Excavations at the City of David 1978–1985*, edited by D. T. Ariel and A. de Groot, 204–56. Qedem 35. Jerusalem: Institute of Archaeology, Hebrew University, 1996.

Eras, Vincent J. M. *Locks and Keys throughout the Ages*. New York: Lips' Safe and Lock Manufacturing Co., 1957.

Finkelstein, Israel. "A Few Notes on Demographic Data from Recent Generations and Ethnoarchaeology." *PEQ* 122 (1990): 47–52.

Finkelstein, Israel, and Neil A. Silberman. *The Bible Unearthed*. New York: Free Press, 2001.

Finkelstein, Israel, and David Ussishkin. "Archaeological and Historical Conclusions." In

Megiddo III: The 1992–1996 Seasons, edited by Israel Finkelstein, David Ussishkin, and Baruch Halpern, 576–602. Tel Aviv: Institute of Archaeology, Tel Aviv University, 2000.

Fischer, David Hackett. *Albion's Seed: Four British Folkways in America*. New York: Oxford University Press, 1989.

Fox, Nili. "Royal Officials and Court Families: A New Look at the *yeladîm* in 1 Kings 12." *BA* 59 (1996): 225–32.

Frankfort, Henri. "The Origin of the Bīt Ḫilāni." *Iraq* 14 (1952): 120–31.

Freedman, David N. "Kingly Chronologies: Then and Later (with an Appendix by A. Dean Forbes)." In *Eretz-Israel* 24 [Avraham Malamat Volume], edited by S. Ahituv and B. A. Levine, 41*–65*. Jerusalem: Israel Exploration Society, 1993.

———, ed. *The Anchor Bible Dictionary*. 6 vols. New York: Doubleday, 1992.

Freedman, David N., and M. P. O'Connor. "*kĕrûb*." *TDOT*, 7: 307–19.

Friedman, Richard E. *Who Wrote the Bible?* San Francisco: Harper, 1987.

Galili, Ehud. "Prehistoric Site on the Sea Floor." *NEAEHL*, 1: 120–22.

Gardiner, Alan H. "The Egyptian Origin of the Semitic Alphabet." *Journal of Egyptian Archaeology* 3 (1916): 1–16.

Garfinkel, Yosef. "Dancing and the Beginning of Art Scenes in the Early Village Communities of the Near East and Southeast Europe." *Cambridge Archaeological Journal* 8 (1998): 207–37.

———. *Neolithic and Chalcolithic Pottery of the Southern Levant*. Qedem 39. Jerusalem: Hebrew University, 1999.

Gibson, John C. L. *Textbook for Syrian Semitic Inscriptions I: Hebrew and Moabite Inscriptions*. Oxford: Clarendon Press, 1971.

Gitin, Seymour. "Ekron of the Philistines, Part II: Olive Oil Suppliers to the World." *BAR* 16/2 (1990): 32–42, 59.

———. "Incense Altars from Ekron, Israel, and Judah: Context and Typology." In *Eretz-Israel* 20 [Yigael Yadin Volume], edited by A. Ben-Tor et al., 52*–67*. Jerusalem: Israel Exploration Society, 1989.

———. "New Incense Altars from Ekron: Context, Typology and Function." In *Eretz-Israel* 23 [Avraham Biran Volume], edited by Ephraim Stern and Thomas Levy, 42*–49*. Jerusalem: Israel Exploration Society, 1992.

———. "Philistia in Transition: The Tenth Century B.C.E. and Beyond." In *Mediterranean Peoples in Transition, Thirteenth to Early Tenth Centuries B.C.E.: In Honor of Professor Trude Dothan*, edited by S. Gitin, A. Mazar and E. Stern. Jerusalem: Israel Exploration Society, 1998.

———. "Seventh Century B.C.E. Cultic Elements at Ekron." In *Biblical Archaeology Today, 1990: Proceedings of the Second International Congress on Biblical Archaeology, Jerusalem, June–July 1990*, edited by A. Biran and J. Aviram, 248–58. Jerusalem: Israel Exploration Society, 1993.

———. "Tel Miqne: A Type-Site for the Inner Coastal Plain in the Iron Age II Period." In *Recent Excavations in Israel: Studies in Iron Age Archaeology*, edited by S. Gitin and W. G. Dever, 23–58. AASOR 49. Winona Lake: Eisenbrauns, 1989.

Gitin, Seymour, Trude Dothan, and Joseph Naveh. "A Royal Dedicatory Inscription from Ekron." *IEJ* 47 (1997): 9–16.

Golani, Amir, and Benjamin Sass. "Three Seventh-Century B.C.E. Hoards of Silver Jewelry from Tel Miqne-Ekron." *BASOR* 311 (1998): 57–81.

Goldwasser, Orly. "An Egyptian Scribe from Lachish and the Hieratic Tradition of the Hebrew Kingdoms." *TA* 18 (1991): 248–53.

Gopher, Avi, et al. "Earliest Gold Artifacts in the Levant." *Current Anthropology* 31 (1990): 436–43.

Gopher, Avi, and Tsvika Tsuk. *The Naḥal Qanah Cave*. Tel Aviv: Institute of Archaeology, Tel Aviv University, 1996.

Gray, John. *I and II Kings*. OTL. Philadelphia: Westminster Press, 1963.

Grayson, A. K. *Assyrian and Babylonian Chronicles*. Locust Valley: J. J. Augustin, 1975.

Greenberg, Moshe. *Ezekiel 1–20*. AB 22. Garden City, N.Y.: Doubleday, 1983.

Greenfield, Jonas C. "Scripture and Inscription: The Literary and Rhetorical Element in Some Early Phoenician Inscriptions." In *Near Eastern Studies in Honor of William Foxwell Albright*, edited by H. Goedicke, 253–68. Baltimore: Johns Hopkins Press, 1971.

Grigson, Caroline. "Plough and Pasture in the Early Economy of the Southern Levant." In *The Archaeology of Society in the Holy Land*, edited by T. E. Levy, 245–68. New York: Facts on File, 1995.

Groom, Nigel. *Frankincense and Myrrh: A Study of the Arabian Incense Trade*. London: Longman, 1981.

Gruber, Mayer I. "Breast-Feeding Practices in Biblical Israel and in Old Babylonian Mesopotamia." *JANES* 19 (1989): 61–83.

Gunkel, Hermann. *Introduction to Psalms: The Genres of the Religious Lyric of Israel*. Completed by Joachim Begrich. Macon, Ga.: Mercer University Press, 1998; German original in 1933.

Gutmann, Joseph. "The 'Second Commandment' and the Image of Judaism." In *No Graven Images*, edited by J. Gutmann, 3–14. New York: KTAV, 1971.

Guy, P. L. O. *Megiddo Tombs*. Chicago: University of Chicago Press, 1938.

Hackett, Jo Ann. *The Balaam Text from Deir ʿAlla*. Chico, Calif.: Scholars Press, 1984.

Hackett, Jo Ann, et al. "Defusing Pseudo-Scholarship: The Siloam Inscription Ain't [sic] Hasmonean." *BAR* 23 (1997): 41–50, 68.

Hadley, Judith M. "Yahweh and 'His Asherah': Archaeological and Textual Evidence for the Cult of the Goddess." In *Ein Gott Allein?*, edited by W. Dietrich and M. A. Klopfenstein. OBO 139. Göttingen: Vandenhoeck & Ruprecht, 1994. 235–68.

Haines, Richard C. *Excavations in the Plain of Antioch*. OIP 61, 95. Chicago: University of Chicago Press, 1971.

Hallo, William W. "Royal Ancestor Worship in the Biblical World." In *"Shaʿarei Talmon,"* edited by M. Fishbane and E. Tov, 381–401. Winona Lake, Ind: Eisenbrauns, 1992.

Halpern, Baruch. "The Assassination of Eglon: The First Locked-Room Murder Mystery." *Bible Review* 4/6 (1988): 32–41, 44.

———. *The First Historians: The Hebrew Bible and History*. San Francisco: Harper & Row, 1988.

———. "The Stele from Dan: Epigraphic and Historical Considerations." *BASOR* 296 (1994): 63–80.

Haran, Menahem. "On the Diffusion of Literacy and Schools in Ancient Israel." In *Congress Volume*, edited by J. A. Emerton, 81–95. VTSup 40. Leiden: E. J. Brill, 1988.

———. *Temples and Temple-Service in Ancient Israel*. Winona Lake, Ind.: Eisenbrauns, 1985.

Hareuveni, Hogah. *Nature in Our Biblical Heritage*. Kiryat Ono: Neot Kedumim, 1980.

Harmenopulus, Konstantinus. *Manuale Legum sive Hexabiblos*. Leipzig: T. O. Weigel, 1851.

Harrington, Spencer P. "Royal Treasures of Nimrud." *Archaeology* 43 (1990): 48–53.

Harris, J. Gordon. "Old Age." *ABD*, 5: 10–12.

Harris, Marvin. *Cows, Pigs, Wars, and Witches: The Riddles of Culture*. New York: Random House, 1975.

Hauptmann, Andreas. "Feinan." *OEANE*, 2:310–11.

Hauptmann, Andreas, et al. "Copper Objects from Arad—Their Composition and Provenance." *BASOR* 314 (1999): 1–17.

————. "Early Copper Produced at Feinan, Wadi Araba, Jordan: The Composition of Ores and Copper." *Archeomaterials* 6 (1992): 1–33.

Hausmann, J. "*mōr*, Myrrh." *TDOT*, 8: 557–60.

Hecker, Mordechai. "Water Supply of Jerusalem in Ancient Times." In *Sepher Yerushalayim* (Hebrew), edited by M. Avi-Yonah, 191–218. Jerusalem and Tel Aviv: Bialik Institute and Dvir Publishing House, 1956.

Heider, George C. *The Cult of Molek: A Reassessment*. JSOTSup 43. Sheffield: University of Sheffield, 1985.

Hendel, Ronald S. "The Date of the Siloam Inscription: A Rejoinder to Rogerson and Davies." *BA* 59 (1996): 233–37.

Hepper, F. Nigel. *Baker Encyclopedia of Bible Plants*. Grand Rapids: Baker Book House, 1992.

Herr, Larry G. "Tripartite Pillared Buildings and the Market Place in Iron Age Palestine." *BASOR* 272 (1988): 47–67.

Herr, Larry G., and Douglas R. Clark. "Excavating the Tribe of Reuben." *BAR* 27/2 (2001): 36–47, 64–66.

Hershkovitz, Israel. "Trephination: The Earliest Case in the Middle East." *Mitekufat Haeven* N.S. 20 (1987): 128*–35*.

Herzog, Ze'ev. *Archaeology of the City*. Tel Aviv: Yass Archaeology Press, Institute of Archaeology, Tel Aviv University, 1997.

————. "Beersheba," *NEAEHL*, 1: 167–73.

————. "Building Materials and Techniques." *OEANE*, 1: 360–63.

————. "Settlement and Fortification Planning in the Iron Age." In *The Architecture of Ancient Israel*, edited by A. Kempinski and R. Reich, 231–74. Jerusalem: Israel Exploration Society, 1992.

Hesse, Brian. "Animal Husbandry and Human Diet in the Ancient Near East." *CANE*, 1: 203–22.

Hestrin, Ruth. "The Lachish Ewer and the 'Asherah." *IEJ* 37 (1987): 212–23.

Hiebert, Theodore. *The Yahwist's Landscape: Nature and Religion in Early Israel*. New York: Oxford University Press, 1996: 212–23.

Hillers, Delbert. "The Goddess with the Tambourine." *Concordia Theological Monthly* 41 (1970): 606–19.

Hoffner, Harry A. "'ôbh." *TDOT*, 1: 130–34

Holladay, John S. "House, Israelite." *ABD*, 3: 308–18.

————. "The Kingdoms of Israel and Judah: Political and Economic Centralization in the Iron IIA-B (ca. 1000–750 B.C.E.)." In *The Archaeology of Society in the Holy Land*, edited by T. E. Levy, 368–98. New York: Facts on File, 1995.

————. "The Stables of Ancient Israel." In *The Archaeology of Jordan and Other Studies: Presented to Siegfried Horn*, edited by L. Geraty and L. Herr, 103–65. Berrien Springs, Mich.: Andrews University Press, 1986.

Holladay, William L. *A Concise Hebrew and Aramaic Lexicon of the Old Testament*. Grand Rapids: Wm. B. Eerdmans Pub. Co., 1971.

————. *Jeremiah 1*. Hermeneia. Philadelphia: Fortress, 1986.

Horn, Siegfried H. "Did Sennacherib Campaign Once or Twice against Hezekiah?" *Andrews University Seminary Studies* 4 (1966): 1–28.

Huehnergard, John, and Wilfred van Soldt. "A Cuneiform Lexical Text from Ashkelon with a Canaanite Column." *IEJ* 49 (1999): 184–92.

Hulse, E. V. "The Nature of Biblical 'Leprosy' and the Use of Alternative Medical Terms in Modern Translations of the Bible." *PEQ* 107 (1975): 87–105.

Hurvitz, Avi. "The Evidence of Language in Dating the Priestly Code." *RB* 81 (1974): 24–56.

————. "The Usage of *šeš* and *buṣ* in the Bible and Its Implication for the Date of P." *HTR* 60 (1967): 117–21.

Jackson, Kent P. "The Language of the Mesha' Inscription." In *Studies in the Mesha Inscription and Moab*, edited by Andrew Dearman, 96–130. Atlanta: Scholars Press, 1989.

Jacobsen, Thorkild. *Toward the Image of Tammuz and Other Essays on Mesopotamian History and Culture*, edited by W. L. Moran. Cambridge: Harvard University Press, 1970.

James, Frances. "Chariot Fittings from Late Bronze Age." In *Archaeology in the Levant: Essays for Kathleen Kenyon*, edited by Roger Moorey and Peter Parr, 103–15. Warminster: Aris & Phillips, 1978.

James, Peter, and Nick Thorpe. *Ancient Inventions*. New York: Ballantine Books, 1994.

Japhet, Sara. *I & II Chronicles*. OTL. Louisville: Westminster/John Knox Press, 1993.

Johnston, Robert H. "The Biblical Potter." *BA* 37 (1974): 86–106.

Jones, Richard N. "Paleopathology." *ABD*, 5: 60–69.

Karageorghis, Vassos. "*Erotica* from Salamis." *Rivista di Studi Fenici* 21 (1993) Supplement, 7–13.

———. "Another Mould for Cakes from Cyprus: The Mould and Its Interpretation." In *Rivista di Studi Fenici* 28/1 (2000): 1–5, Tavola I, II.

Karmon, Nira, and Ehud Spanier. "Remains of a Purple Dye Industry Found at Tel Shiqmona." *IEJ* 38 (1988): 184–86.

Kaufman, Ivan T. "The Samaria Ostraca: An Early Witness to Hebrew Writing." *BA* 45 (1982): 229–39.

———. "The Samaria Ostraca: A Study in Ancient Hebrew Palaeography, Text and Plates." Diss., Harvard University, 1966.

Kaufmann, Yehezkel. *The Religion of Israel*. Translated by Moshe Greenberg. New York: Schocken, 1960.

Kedar-Kopfstein, Benjamin. "*zāhāb*." *TDOT*, 4: 32–40.

Keegan, John. *A History of Warfare*. New York: Alfred A. Knopf, 1993.

Keel, Othmar. "Peculiar Tomb Headrests May Depict Return to the Womb." *BAR* 13/4 (1987): 50–53.

———. *Jahwe-Visionen und Siegelkunst*. Stuttgart: Verlag Katholisches Bibelwerk, 1977.

———. *The Song of Songs*. Minneapolis: Fortress, 1994.

Keel, Othmar, and Christoph Uehlinger. *Gods, Goddesses, and Images of God in Ancient Israel*. Minneapolis: Fortress, 1998.

Kellermann, D. "*lĕbōnâ*, Frankincense." *TDOT*, 7: 441–47.

Kelso, James L. "The Ceramic Vocabulary of the Old Testament." *BASOR* Supplementary Studies. New Haven: ASOR, 1948.

Kenyon, Kathleen. *Archaeology in the Holy Land*. New York: Praeger, 1960.

———. *Digging Up Jericho*. London: Ernest Benn, 1975.

———. *Digging Up Jerusalem*. New York: Praeger Publications, 1974.

King, Philip J. *Jeremiah: An Archaeological Companion*. Louisville, Ky.: Westminster/John Knox Press, 1993.

Kletter, Raz. *Economic Keystones: The Weight System of the Kingdom of Judah*. JSOTSup 276. Sheffield: Sheffield Academic Press, 1998.

Koch, Klaus. "*derek*." *TDOT*, 3: 270–93.

Kochavi, Moshe. "Divided Structures Divide Scholars," *BAR* 25/3 (1999): 44–50.

———. "The Eleventh Century B.C.E. Tripartite Pillar Building at Tel Hadar." In *Mediterranean Peoples in Transition* [Trude Dothan Festschrift], edited by S. Gitin, A. Mazar, and E. Stern, 468–78. Jerusalem: Israel Exploration Society, 1998.

Koehler, Ludwig, and Walter Baumgartner. *Hebräisches und aramäisches Lexikon zum Alten Testament*, Lieferung 2. 3d ed. Leiden: E. J. Brill, 1974.

Kugel, James L. *The Great Poems of the Bible*. New York: Free Press, 1999.

———. "Qohelet and Money." *CBQ* 51 (1989): 32–49.

Lamon, Robert S. *The Megiddo Water System*. Chicago: University of Chicago Press, 1935.

Landsberger, Benno. *The Date Palm and Its By-Products according to the Cuneiform Sources.* Graz: Weidner, 1967.

———. "Über Farben im Sumerisch-Akkadischen." *JCS* 21 (1967): 139–73.

Lapp, Nancy L. "Ful, Tell el-." *NEAEHL,* 2: 445–48.

———. "Pottery Chronology of Palestine." *ABD,* 5: 433–44.

Lapp, Paul W. "The 1963 Excavations at Ta'annek." *BASOR* 173 (1964): 4–44.

———. "The 1966 Excavations at Tell Ta'annek." *BASOR* 185 (1967): 2–39.

———. "The 1968 Excavations at Tell Ta'annek." *BASOR* 195 (1969): 2–49.

———. "Taanach by the Waters of Megiddo." *BA* 30 (1967): 2–27.

Lawergren, Bo. "Distinctions among Canaanite, Philistine, and Israelite Lyres, and Their Global Lyrical Contexts." *BASOR* 309 (1998): 41–68.

Layard, Austen H. *Discoveries in the Ruins of Nineveh and Babylon.* New York: Harper & Bros., 1853.

Leith, Mary Joan Winn. "Israel among the Nations: The Persian Period." In *The Oxford History of the Biblical World,* edited by Michael D. Coogan, 366–419. New York: Oxford University Press, 1998.

Lemaire, André. *Les écoles et la formation de la Bible dans l'ancien Israël.* Fribourg: Editions universitaires; Göttingen: Vandenhoeck & Ruprecht, 1981.

———. "Education (Israel)." *ABD,* 2: 305–12.

———. "'House of David' Restored in Moabite Inscription," *BAR* 20/3 (1994): 30–37.

———. "Tarshish-*Tarsisi*: Problème de Topographie Historique Biblique et Assyrienne." In *Studies in Historical Geography and Biblical Historiography* [Zechariah Kallai Festschrift], edited by G. Galil and M. Weinfeld, 44–62. Leiden: Brill, 2000.

Lemche, Niels Peter. "Early Israel Revisited." *Currents in Research: Biblical Studies* 4 (1996): 9–34.

———. "The History of Ancient Syria and Palestine: An Overview." *CANE* 2: 1195–1218.

———. *Prelude to Israel's Past: Background and Beginnings of Israelite History and Identity.* Peabody, Mass.: Hendrickson, 1998.

Lernau, Hanan, and Omri Lernau. "Fish Remains." In *City of David Excavations Final Report III,* edited by Alon de Groot and Donald T. Ariel, 131–148. Qedem 33. Jerusalem: Institute of Archaeology, Hebrew University, 1992.

Levenson, Jon D. *The Death and Resurrection of the Beloved Son.* New Haven, Conn.: Yale University Press, 1993.

———. *Sinai and Zion.* Minneapolis: Winston, 1985.

Levenson, Jon D., and Baruch Halpern. "The Political Import of David's Marriages." *JBL* 99 (1980): 507–18.

Levine, Baruch A. *Numbers 1–20.* AB 4A. New York: Doubleday, 1993.

Lev-Tov, Justin. "Iron Age Animal Bones from the Tombs of Tell Dothan: Identification and Evaluation of Ritual Offerings." Unpublished manuscript.

Lewis, Theodore J. *Cults of the Dead in Ancient Israel and Ugarit.* Atlanta: Scholars Press, 1989.

———. "Death Cult Imagery in Isaiah 57." *Hebrew Annual Review* 11 (1987): 267–84.

Lewy, Hildegard. "On Some Old Assyrian Cereal Names." *JAOS* 76 (1956): 201–4.

Liphshitz, Nili, and Gideon Biger. "Cedar of Lebanon (*Cedrus libani*) in Israel during Antiquity." *IEJ* 41 (1991): 167–75.

Liphschitz, Nili, Simcha Lev-Yadun, and Ram Gophna. "The Dominance of *Quercus calliprinos* (Kermes Oak) in the Central Coastal Plain in Antiquity." *IEJ* 37 (1987): 43–50.

Lipinski, Edward. "Royal and State Scribes in Ancient Jerusalem." In *Congress Volume,* edited by J. A. Emerton, 157–64. VTSup 40. Leiden: E. J. Brill, 1988.

Lipschits, Oded. "The History of the Benjamin Region Under Babylonian Rule." *TA* 26 (1999): 155–90.

Littauer, Mary A., and J. H. Crouwel. *Wheeled Vehicles and Ridden Animals in the Ancient Near East*. Leiden: E. J. Brill, 1979.

Lloyd, Seton. "Excavating the Land between the Two Rivers." *CANE*, 4: 2729–41.

Loud, Gordon. "An Architectural Formula for Assyrian Planning Based on the Results of Excavations at Khorsabad." *Revue d'Assyriologie* 33 (1936): 153–60.

———. *Megiddo II: Seasons of 1935–39*. Chicago: Oriental Institute, University of Chicago Press, 1948.

Lowenthal, David. *The Past Is a Foreign Country*. Cambridge: Cambridge University Press, 1985.

Lutfiyya, A. M. *Baytin, A Jordanian Village: A Study of Social Institutions and Social Change in a Folk Community*. The Hague: Mouton, 1966.

Macalister, R. A. S. *A Century of Excavation in Palestine*. London: Religious Tract Society, 1925.

———. *The Excavation of Gezer, 1902–1905 and 1907–1909*. 3 vols. London: J. Murray, 1912.

MacDonald, John. "The Status and Role of the Na'ar in Israelite Society." *JNES* 35 (1976): 147–70.

Macdonald, M. C. A. "North Arabia in the First Millennium B.C.E." *CANE*, 2: 1355–69.

Mackenzie, Duncan. *Excavations at 'Ain Shems*. London: Palestine Exploration Fund, 1912–13.

Magen, Yitzhak. "Mt. Gerizim- A Temple City" (Hebrew). *Qadmoniot* 33/2 (2000): 74–118.

Maisler (Mazar), Benjamin. "Two Hebrew Ostraca from Tell Qasile." *JNES* 10 (1951): 265–267.

Markoe, Glenn. *Phoenician Bronze and Silver Bowls from Cyprus and the Mediterranean*. Berkeley, Calif.: University of California, 1985.

Martin-Achard, Robert. "Resurrection." *ABD* 5: 680–84.

Matthews, Victor H., and Don C. Benjamin. *Social World of Ancient Israel 1250–587 B.C.E.* Peabody, Mass.: Hendrickson, 1993.

Matthiae, Paolo. "Princely Cemetery and Ancestors Cult at Ebla during Middle Bronze II." *UF* 11 (1979): 563–69.

Maxwell-Hyslop, K. R. *Western Asiatic Jewellery c. 3000–612 B.C.* London: Methuen, 1971.

Mazar, Amihai. *Archaeology of the Land of the Bible*. New York: Doubleday, 1990.

———. "The 'Bull Site': An Iron Age I Open Cult Place." *BASOR* 247 (1982): 27–42.

———. "The Fortification of Cities in the Ancient Near East," *CANE* 3: 1523–37.

Mazar, Benjamin. *Biblical Israel: State and People*. Edited by Samuel Ahituv. Jerusalem: Magnes Press, Hebrew University, Israel Exploration Society, 1992.

———. "The 'Orpheus' Jug from Megiddo." In *Magnalia Dei: The Mighty Acts of God* [G. Ernest Wright Festschrift], edited by Frank M. Cross et al., 187–92 Garden City, N.Y.: Doubleday, 1976.

McCarter, P. Kyle. *Ancient Inscriptions*. Washington, D.C.: Biblical Archaeology Society, 1996.

———. "Aspects of the Religion of the Israelite Monarchy: Biblical and Epigraphic Data." In *Ancient Israelite Religion* [Frank Moore Cross Festschrift], edited by Patrick D. Miller et al., 137–55. Philadelphia: Fortress, 1987.

———. *I Samuel*. AB 8. Garden City, N.Y.: Doubleday, 1980.

———. *II Samuel*. AB 9. Garden City, N.Y.: Doubleday, 1984.

———. "Two Bronze Arrowheads with Archaic Alphabetic Inscriptions." In *Eretz-Israel 26* [Frank Moore Cross Volume], edited by Baruch A. Levine et al., 123*–28*. Jerusalem: Israel Exploration Society, 1999.

McCarter, P. Kyle, and Robert B. Coote. "The Spatula Inscription from Byblos." *BASOR* 212 (1973): 16–22.

McGovern, Patrick E., and Garman Harbottle. "'Hyksos' Trade Connections between Tell el-Dab'a (Avaris) and the Levant: A Neutron Activation Study of the Canaanite Jar." In *The*

Hyksos: New Historical and Archaeological Perspectives, edited by E. D. Oren, 141–57. Philadelphia: University Museum, 1997.

McNutt, Paula M. *The Forging of Israel: Iron Technology, Symbolism, and Tradition in Ancient Society.* Sheffield: Almond Press, 1990.

———. *Reconstructing the Society of Ancient Israel.* LAI. Louisville, Ky.: Westminster John Knox; London: SPCK, 1999.

Mendenhall, George E. "The Census Lists of Numbers 1 and 26." *JBL* 77 (1958): 52–66.

Meshel, Ze'ev. *Kuntillet 'Ajrud: A Religious Centre from the Time of the Judean Monarchy on the Border of Sinai* (addendum: Sheffer, Avigail, *"The Textiles"*). Catalogue 175. Jerusalem: Israel Museum, 1978.

Mettinger, Tryggve. *No Graven Image?* Stockholm: Almqvist & Wiksell International, 1995.

Meyers, Carol. *Discovering Eve: Ancient Israelite Women in Context.* New York: Oxford University Press, 1988.

———. "Of Drums and Damsels: Women's Performance in Ancient Israel," *BA* 54 (1991): 16–27.

———. "A Terracotta at the Harvard Semitic Museum and Disc-holding Female Figures Reconsidered." *IEJ* 37 (1987): 116–22.

———. "Threshold." *ABD,* 6: 544–45.

Meyers, Eric M., ed. *Oxford Encyclopedia of Archaeology in the Near East.* 5 vols. New York: Oxford University Press, 1997.

Milgrom, Jacob. *Leviticus 1–16.* AB 3. New York: Doubleday, 1991.

Millard, Alan R. "An Assessment of the Evidence of Writing in Ancient Israel." In *Biblical Archaeology Today,* edited by J. Aviram et al., 301–12. Jerusalem: Israel Exploration Society, 1985.

———. "Does the Bible Exaggerate King Solomon's Wealth?" *BAR* 15/3 (1989): 20–29, 31, 34.

———. "Ezekiel XXVII. 19: The Wine Trade of Damascus." *JSS* 7 (1962): 201–3.

———. "The Temple Mount from Zerubbabel to Herod." In *Biblical Israel: State and People,* ed. Samuel Ahituv, 109–15. Jerusalem: Magnes Press, Hebrew University and Israel Exploration Society, 1992.

Miller, Patrick D. *The Religion of Ancient Israel.* LAI. Louisville, Ky.: Westminster John Knox Press, 2000.

Moldenke, Harold N., and Alma L. Moldenke. *Plants of the Bible.* New York: Ronald Press, 1952.

Montgomery, James A. *Arabia and the Bible.* New York: KTAV, 1969.

Moorey, P. Roger. *Ancient Mesopotamian Materials and Industries.* Winona Lake, Ind.: Eisenbrauns, 1999.

Moran, William L. *The Amarna Letters.* Baltimore: Johns Hopkins University Press, 1992.

Mosca, Paul G. "Child Sacrifice in Canaanite and Israelite Religion: A Study in Mulk and *molek.*" Ph.D. diss., Harvard University, 1975.

Mowinckel, Sigmund. *The Psalms in Israel's Worship.* With a foreword by Robert K. Gnuse and Douglas A. Knight. Sheffield: JSOT Press, 1992; Norwegian original in 1951.

Muhly, James D. "How Iron Technology Changed the Ancient World—And Gave the Philistines a Military Edge." *BAR* 8/6 (1982): 40–54.

———. "Metals." *OEANE,* 4: 1–15.

Mumcuoglu, Kostas, and Joseph Zias. "How the Ancients De-Loused Themselves." *BAR* 15/6 (1989): 66–69.

Na'aman, Nadav, "The Contribution of the Amarna Letters to the Debate on Jerusalem's Political Position in the Tenth Century B.C.E." *BASOR* 304 (1996): 17–27.

———. "The Kingdom of Judah under Josiah." *TA* 18 (1991): 3–71.

Naveh, Joseph. *Early History of the Alphabet.* Jerusalem: Magnes Press, Hebrew University, 1982.

Netzer, Ehud. "Domestic Architecture in the Iron Age." In *The Architecture of Ancient Israel,* edited by A. Kempinski and R. Reich, 193–201. Jerusalem: Israel Exploration Society, 1992.

Neufeld, Edward. "Hygiene Conditions in Ancient Israel." *BA* 34 (1971): 42–66.

Niditch, Susan. *Oral World and Written Word: Ancient Israelite Literature*. LAI. Louisville: Westminster John Knox, 1996.

Nielsen, Kjeld. *Incense in Ancient Israel*. VTSup 38. Leiden: E. J. Brill, 1986.

North, Robert. *Medicine in the Biblical Background*. AnBib. Rome: Editrice Pontificio Istituto Biblico, 2000.

Noth, Martin. *Numbers*. OTL. Philadelphia: Westminster, 1968.

Oppenheim, A. Leo. *Ancient Mesopotamia: Portrait of a Dead Civilization*. Rev. ed. Chicago: University of Chicago, 1964.

———. "The Golden Garments of the Gods." *JNES* 8 (1949): 172–93.

Oren, Eliezer D. "The 'Kingdom of Sharuhen' and the Hyksos Kingdom." In *The Hyksos: New Historical and Archaeological Perspectives*, edited by E. D. Oren, 253–83. Philadelphia: University Museum, University of Pennsylvania, 1997.

———. "Sera', Tel." *NEAEHL*, 4: 1329–35.

Parker, Simon B., ed. *Ugaritic Narrative Poetry*. SBLWAW 9. Atlanta: Scholars Press, 1997.

Paul, Shalom M. *Amos: A Commentary on the Book of Amos*. Hermeneia. Minneapolis: Fortress, 1991.

Payton, Robert. "The Ulu Burun Writing-Board Set." *Anatolian Studies* 41 (1991): 99–106.

Peckham, Brian. "Phoenicia and the Religion of Israel: The Epigraphic Evidence." In *Ancient Israelite Religion* [Frank Moore Cross Festschrift], edited by P. D. Miller, P. D. Hanson, and S. D. McBride, 79–99. Philadelphia: Fortress, 1987.

Pedersen, Johannes. *Israel: Its Life and Culture*. 4 vols. London: Oxford University Press, 1926–1940.

Petrie, W. M. Flinders. *Researches in Sinai*. London: J. Murray, 1906.

———. *Explorations in Palestine*. London: Palestine Exploration Fund, 1890: 159–166.

Pierre, Marie-Joseph, and Jourdain-Marie Rousée. "Sainte-Marie de la Probatique: État et orientation des recherches." *Proche-Orient Chrétien* 31 (1981): 23–42.

Platt, Elizabeth E. "Jewelry, Ancient Israelite." *ABD*, 3: 823–34.

Polanyi, Karl. *The Livelihood of Man*. New York: Academic Press, 1977.

Pope, Marvin H. "'am ha'arez." *IDB*, 1: 106–7.

———. "The Cult of the Dead at Ugarit." In *Ugarit in Retrospect*, edited by G. D. Young, 159–79. Winona Lake, Ind.: Eisenbrauns, 1981.

———. *Job*. AB 15. Garden City, N.Y.: Doubleday, 1965.

Porada, Edith. "The Cylinder Seal from Tell el-Dab'a." *AJA* 88 (1984): 483–88.

Post, George. "Oil Tree." In *A Dictionary of the Bible*, edited by J. Hastings, 3: 592–93. Edinburgh: T. & T. Clark, 1898. Reprint, Peabody, Mass.: Hendrickson, 1988.

Powell, Marvin A. "Wine and the Vine in Ancient Mesopotamia: The Cuneiform Evidence." In *The Origins and Ancient History of Wine*, edited by P. E. McGovern, S. J. Fleming, and S. H. Katz, 97–122. Amsterdam: Overseas Publishers Association, 1995.

Prag, Kay. "Silver in the Levant in the Fourth Millennium B.C." In *Archaeology in the Levant* [Kathleen Kenyon Festschrift], edited by P. R. Moorey and P. J. Parr, 36–45. Warminster: Aris & Phillips, 1978.

Price, Ira M. "Ophir." In *A Dictionary of the Bible*, edited by J. Hastings, 3:626–28. Edinburgh: T. & T. Clark, 1898. Reprint, Peabody, Mass.: Hendrickson, 1988.

Pritchard, James B. *Gibeon, Where the Sun Stood Still*. Princeton, N.J.: Princeton University Press, 1962.

———. *Recovering Sarepta, a Phoenician City*. Princeton, N.J.: Princeton University Press, 1978.

———. *The Water System of Gibeon*. Philadelphia: University Museum, University of Pennsylvania, 1961.

Propp, William H. C. *Exodus 1–18*. AB 2. New York: Doubleday, 1998.

Provan, Iain W. "Ideologies, Literary, and Critical: Reflections on Recent Writing on the History of Israel." *JBL* 114 (1995): 585–606.

Puech, Émile. "The Canaanite Inscriptions of Lachish and Their Religious Background." *TA* 13 (1986): 13–25.

———. "La stèle araméenne de Dan: Bar Hadad II et la coalition des Omrides et de la maison de David." *RB* 101 (1994): 215–41.

Pulak, Çemal. "The Uluburun Shipwreck." In *Res Maritimae: Cyprus and the Eastern Mediterranean from Prehistory to Late Antiquity*, edited by S. Swiny, R. L. Hohlfelder, and H. W. Swiny, 233–62. Atlanta: Scholars Press, 1997.

Raban, Avner, and Robert R. Stieglitz. "The Sea Peoples and Their Contributions to Civilization." *BAR* 17/6 (1991): 34–42, 92–93.

Rainey, Anson F. "The Samaria Ostraca in the Light of Fresh Evidence." *PEQ* 99 (1967): 32–41.

———. "The *Sitz im Leben* of the Samaria Ostraca." *TA* 6 (1979): 91–94.

———. "A Tri-Lingual Cuneiform Fragment from Tel Aphek." *TA* 3 (1976): 137–40.

Rast, Walter. "Cakes for the Queen of Heaven." In *Scripture in History and Theology: Essays in Honor of J. Coert Rylaarsdam*, edited by A. L. Merrill and T. W. Overholt, 167–80. Pittsburgh: Pickwick Press, 1977.

Reich, Ronny. "Building Materials and Architectural Elements in Ancient Israel." In *The Architecture of Ancient Israel from the Prehistoric to the Persian Periods*, edited by A. Kempinski and R. Reich, 1–16. Jerusalem: Israel Exploration Society, 1992.

———. "Palaces and Residencies in the Iron Age." In *The Architecture of Ancient Israel from the Prehistoric to the Persian Periods*, edited by A. Kempinski and R. Reich, 202–22. Jerusalem: Israel Exploration Society, 1992.

Reich, Ronny, and Eli Shukron. "Light at the End of the Tunnel." *BAR* 25/1 (1999): 22–33, 72.

———. "The System of Rock-Cut Tunnels near Gihon in Jerusalem Reconsidered." *RB* 107 (2000): 5–17.

Reisner, George A., Clarence S. Fisher, and David G. Lyon. *Harvard Excavations at Samaria*. Cambridge: Harvard University Press, 1924.

Rimmer, Joan. *Ancient Musical Instruments of Western Asia*. London: British Museum, 1969.

Ringgren, Helmer. "*ṭahar.*" *TDOT*, 5: 287–96.

Robinson, Edward. *Biblical Researches in Palestine and the Adjacent Regions*. 1856. Reprint, Jerusalem: Universitas Booksellers, 1970.

Rogers, Everett M. *Modernization among Peasants: The Impact of Communication*. New York: Holt, Rinehart & Winston, 1969.

Rosen, Baruch. "Wine and Oil Allocations in the Samaria Ostraca." *TA* 13 (1986): 39–45.

Rothenberg, Beno. *Timna': Valley of the Biblical Copper Mines*. London: Thames & Hudson, 1972.

Sakenfeld, Katharine D. *Ruth*. Interpretation. Louisville: John Knox Press, 1999.

Sasson, Jack M. "Circumcision in the Ancient Near East." *JBL* 85 (1966): 473–76.

Sasson, Jack M., ed. *Civilizations of the Ancient Near East*. 4 vols. New York: Charles Scribner's Sons, 1995.

Sauer, James A. "The River Runs Dry: Biblical Story Preserves Historical Memory." *BAR* 22/4 (1996): 52–57, 64.

Säve-Söderbergh, Torgny. *The Navy of the Eighteenth Egyptian Dynasty*. Uppsala: Lundequistska Bokhandeln, 1946.

Schaub, R. Thomas. "Bab edh-Dhra'." *NEAEHL*, 1: 130–36.

Schick, Tamar. *The Cave of the Warrior*. Jerusalem: Israel Antiquities Authority, 1998.

Schloen, J. David. *The House of the Father as Fact and Symbol: Patrimonialism in Ugarit and the Ancient Near East*. Studies in the Archaeology and History of the Levant, 2. Cambridge: Harvard Semitic Museum, 2001.

Schmidt, Brian B. *Israel's Beneficent Dead*. Winona Lake, Ind.: Eisenbrauns, 1996.

Schniedewind, William M. "Tel Dan Stela: New Light on Aramaic and Jehu's Revolt." *BASOR* 302 (1996): 75–90.

Scott, Robert B. Y. "Weights and Measures of the Bible." *BA* 22 (1959): 22–40.

Scurlock, JoAnn. "Neo-Assyrian Battle Tactics." In *Crossing Boundaries and Linking Horizons*, edited by G. D. Young et al. Bethesda, Md.: CDL Press, 1997: 491–517.

Seger, Joe D. "The Gezer Jar Signs: New Evidence of the Earliest Alphabet." In *The Word of the Lord Shall Go Forth* [David Noel Freedman Festschrift], edited by C. L. Meyers and M. O'Connor, 477–95. Philadelphia: ASOR, 1983.

Selbie, John A. "Terebinth." In *A Dictionary of the Bible*, edited by J. Hastings, 4: 718–19. Edinburgh: T. & T. Clark, 1898. Reprint, Peabody, Mass.: Hendrickson, 1988.

Seow, Choon-Leong. *Ecclesiastes*. AB 18C. New York: Doubleday, 1997.

Shanks, Hershel. "Everything You Ever Knew about Jerusalem Is Wrong (Well, Almost)." *BAR* 25/6 (1999): 20–29.

———. "Where Is The Tenth Century?" *BAR* 24/2 (1998): 56–61.

Shea, William H. "Jerusalem under Siege." *BAR* 25/6 (1999): 36–44, 64.

Shepard, Anna O. *Ceramics for the Archaeologist*. Washington, D.C.: Carnegie Institution, 1956.

Shiloh, Yigal. *Excavations at the City of David, I: Interim Report of the First Five Seasons (1978–1982)*. Qedem 19. Jerusalem: Institute of Archaeology, Hebrew University, 1984.

———. "Iron Age Sanctuaries and Cult Elements in Palestine." In *Symposia Celebrating the Seventy-Fifth Anniversary of the Founding of the American Schools of Oriental Research (1900–1975)*, edited by Frank M. Cross, 147–57. Cambridge: American Schools of Oriental Research, 1979.

———. "Megiddo: The Iron Age." *NEAEHL*, 3: 1012–23.

———. *The Proto-Aeolic Capital and Israelite Ashlar Masonry*. Qedem 11. Jerusalem: Institute of Archaeology, Hebrew University, 1979.

Simons, Jan Jozef. *Jerusalem in the Old Testament*. Leiden: E. J. Brill, 1952.

Smith, George Adam. *The Historical Geography of the Holy Land*. 26th ed. London: Harper, 1937.

Smith, Morton. "A Note on Burning Babies." *JAOS* 95 (1975): 477–79.

Smith, Patricia. "The Trephined Skull from the Early Bronze Age Period at Arad." In *Eretz-Israel* 21 [Ruth Amiran Volume], edited by A. Eitan, R. Gophna, and M. Kochavi, 89*–93*. Jerusalem: Israel Exploration Society, 1990.

Snell, Daniel C. *Life in the Ancient Near East 3100–332 B.C.E.* New Haven, Conn.: Yale University Press, 1997.

Speiser, Ephraim A. *Genesis*. AB 1. Garden City, N.Y.: Doubleday, 1964.

Stager, Lawrence E. "Another Mould for Cakes from Cyprus: In the Queen's Image." In *Rivista di Studi Fenici* 28/1 (2000): 6–11.

———. "The Archaeology of the Family in Ancient Israel." *BASOR* 260 (1985): 1–35.

———. "Ashkelon and the Archaeology of Destruction: Kislev 604 B.C.E." In *Eretz-Israel* 25 [Joseph Aviram Volume], edited by A. Biran et al., 61*–74*. Jerusalem: Israel Exploration Society, 1996.

———. *Ashkelon Discovered*. Washington, D.C.: Biblical Archaeology Society, 1991.

———. "Carthage: A View from the Tophet." In *Phönizier im Westen*, edited by H. G. Niemeyer, 155–66. Madrider Beiträge 8. Mainz am Rhein: Philipp von Zabern, 1982.

———. "Forging an Identity: The Emergence of Ancient Israel." In *The Oxford History of the Biblical World*, edited by M. D. Coogan, 123–75. New York: Oxford University Press, 1998.

———. "The Fortress-Temple at Shechem and the 'House of El, Lord of the Covenant.' " In *Realia Dei: Essays in Archaeology and Biblical Interpretation in Honor of Edward F.*

Campbell, Jr., at His Retirement, edited by Prescott H. Williams Jr., and Theodore Hiebert, 228–49. Atlanta: Scholars Press, 1999.

———. "The Fury of Babylon: Ashkelon and the Archaeology of Destruction." *BAR* 22/1 (1996): 56–69, 76–77.

———. "Haggling over Leviathan" (unpublished manuscript).

———. "The Impact of the Sea Peoples (1185–1050 B.C.E.)." In *The Archaeology of Society in the Holy Land*, edited by T. E. Levy, 332–48. New York: Facts on File, 1995.

———. "Jerusalem and the Garden of Eden." In *Eretz-Israel* 26 [Frank Moore Cross Volume], edited by B. A. Levine et al., 183*–94*. Jerusalem: Israel Exploration Society, 1999.

———. "Jerusalem as Eden." *BAR* 26/3 (2000): 36–47, 66.

———. "Painted Pottery and Its Relationship to the Weaving Crafts in Canaan during the Early Bronze Age I." In *Eretz-Israel* 21 [Ruth Amiran Volume], edited by A. Eitan et al., 83*–88* Jerusalem: Israel Exploration Society, 1990.

———. "Port Power in the Early and the Middle Bronze Age: The Organization of Maritime Trade and Hinterland Production." In *Studies in the Archaeology of Israel and Neighboring Lands: In Memory of Douglas L. Esse*, edited by Samuel R. Wolff, 611–24. Chicago: Oriental Institute of the University of Chicago and the American Schools of Oriental Research, forthcoming.

———. "The Song of Deborah—Why Some Tribes Answered the Call and Others Did Not." *BAR* 15/1 (1989): 50–64.

———. "Why Were Hundreds of Dogs Buried at Ashkelon?" *BAR* 17/3 (1991): 26–42.

Stager, Lawrence E., and Samuel R. Wolff. "Child Sacrifice at Carthage—Religious Rite or Population Control?" *BAR* 10/1 (1984): 30–51.

———. "Production and Commerce in Temple Courtyards: An Olive Press in the Sacred Precinct at Tel Dan." *BASOR* 243 (1981): 95–102.

Stern, Ephraim. *Archaeology of the Land of the Bible*. Vol. 2, *The Assyrian, Babylonian, and Persian Periods (732–332 B.C.E.)*. AB Supplements. New York: Doubleday, 2001.

———. "The Babylonian Gap," *BAR* 26/6 (2000): 45–51, 76.

———. "Buried Treasure: The Silver Hoard from Dor." *BAR* 24/4 (1998): 46–51, 62.

———. "What Happened to the Cult Figurines?" *BAR* 15/4 (1989): 22–29, 53–54.

———. "The Persian Empire and the Political and Social History of Palestine in the Persian Period." In *The Cambridge History of Judaism*, Vol. I: *Introduction: The Persian Period*, edited by W. D. Davies and Louis Finkelstein, 70–87. Cambridge: Cambridge University Press, 1984.

———. "The Archaeology of Persian Palestine." In *The Cambridge History of Judaism*, Vol. I: *Introduction: The Persian Period*, edited by W. D. Davies and Louis Finkelstein, 88–114. Cambridge: Cambridge University Press, 1984.

Stern, Ephraim, ed. *The New Encyclopedia of Archaeological Excavations in the Holy Land*. Jerusalem: Israel Exploration Society & Carta; New York: Simon & Schuster, 1993.

Stern, Ephraim, and Ilan Sharon. "Tel Dor, 1986," *IEJ* 37 (1987): 201–11.

———. "Tel Dor, 1992: Preliminary Report." *IEJ* 43 (1993): 126–50.

Stewart, James R. *Tell el-'Ajjul: The Middle Bronze Age Remains*. Göteborg: P. Åström, 1974.

Stronach, David. "The Imagery of the Wine Bowl: Wine in Assyria in the Early First Millennium B.C." In *The Origins and Ancient History of Wine*, edited by P. E. McGovern, S. J. Fleming, and S. H. Katz, 175–95. Amsterdam: Overseas Publishers Association, 1995.

Sweet, Louise E. *Tell Toqaan: A Syrian Village*. Ann Arbor, Mich.: University of Michigan, 1974.

Tadmor, Hayim. *The Inscriptions of Tiglath-pileser III, King of Assyria*. Jerusalem: Israel Academy of Sciences and Humanities, 1994.

Tadmor, Miriam, and Osnat Misch-Brandl. "The Beth Shemesh Hoard of Jewellery." *Israel Museum News* 16 (1980): 71–79.

Talmon, Shemaryahu. "The New Hebrew Letter from the Seventh Century B.C. in Historical Perspective." *BASOR* 176 (1964): 29–38.

Taylor, J. Glen. *Yahweh and the Sun: The Biblical and Archaeological Evidence for Sun Worship in Ancient Israel.* JSOTSup 111. Sheffield: JSOT Press, 1993.

Temin, Peter. "A Market Economy in the Early Roman Empire." Forthcoming in *Journal of Roman Studies.*

Thomas, D. Winton, ed. *Documents from Old Testament Times.* New York: Harper, 1958.

Thompson, Henry O., and Fawzi Zayadine. "The Tell Siran Inscription." *BASOR* 212 (1973): 5–11.

Thompson, Thomas L. *The Mythic Past: Biblical Archaeology and the Myth of Israel.* New York: Basic Books, 1999.

Torr, Cecil. *Ancient Ships.* Cambridge: Cambridge University Press, 1894.

Trible, Phyllis. *Texts of Terror: Literary-Feminist Reading of Biblical Narratives.* Philadelphia: Fortress Press, 1984.

Tsuk, Tsvika. "Hydrology." *OEANE,* 3: 132–33.

Tufnell, Olga. *Lachish III: The Iron Age.* London: Oxford University Press, 1953.

———. *Lachish IV: The Bronze Age.* London: Oxford University Press, 1958.

Tylecote, R. F. *A History of Metallurgy.* Avon: Bath Press, 1992.

Ussishkin, David. *The Conquest of Lachish by Sennacherib.* Tel Aviv: Institute of Archaeology, Tel Aviv University, 1982.

———. "Excavations at Tel Lachish—1973–1977, Preliminary Report." *TA* 5 (1978): 1–97.

———. "Excavations at Tel Lachish—1978–1983, Second Preliminary Report." *TA* 10 (1983): 97–175.

———. "Lachish." *NEAEHL,* 3: 897–911.

———. "The Necropolis from the Time of the Kingdom of Judah at Silwan, Jerusalem." *BA* 33 (1970): 34–46.

———. "The Water Systems of Jerusalem during Hezekiah's Reign." In *Meilenstein: Festgabe für Herbert Donner.* Ägypten und Altes Testament 30, edited by M. Weippert and S. Timm, 289–307. Wiesbaden: Harrassowitz Verlag, 1995.

Ussishkin, David, and John Woodhead. "Excavations at Tel Jezreel 1994–1996: Third Preliminary Report." *TA* 24 (1997): 6–72.

Van Dam, Cornelis. *The Urim and Thummim: A Means of Revelation in Ancient Israel.* Winona Lake, Ind.: Eisenbrauns, 1997.

Vanderhooft, David S. "The Israelite *mišpāḥâ* in the Priestly Writings: An Elite Reconstruction of Social Organization." In *Rival Communities in the Ancient Near East,* edited by B. Halpern, G. Knoppers, and A. Joffe. Leiden: Brill, forthcoming.

———. *The Neo-Babylonian Empire and Babylon in the Latter Prophets.* HSM 59. Atlanta: Scholars Press, 1999.

Vaux, Roland de. *Ancient Israel.* New York: McGraw-Hill, 1961.

———. "Les prophètes de Baal sur le Mont Carmel." *Bulletin du Musée de Beyrouth* 5 (1941): 7–20.

———. *Studies in Old Testament Sacrifice.* Cardiff: University of Wales, 1964.

Voegelin, Eric. *The New Science of Politics.* Chicago: University of Chicago Press, 1952.

Vogt, Ernest. "The 'Place in Life' of Ps 23." *Biblica* 34 (1953): 195–211.

Wachsmann, Shelley. *Seagoing Ships and Seamanship in the Bronze Age Levant.* London: Chatham Publishing, 1998.

Waldbaum, Jane C. *From Bronze to Iron: The Transition from the Bronze Age to the Iron Age in the Eastern Mediterranean.* Studies in Mediterranean Archaeology 54. Göteborg: Paul Åströms Förlag, 1978.

Walsh, Carey Ellen. *The Fruit of the Vine: Viticulture in Ancient Israel.* HSM 60. Winona Lake, Ind.: Eisenbrauns, 2000.

Wapnish, Paula, and Brian Hesse, "Equids." *OEANE,* 2: 255–56.

———. "Faunal Remains from Tel Dan: Perspectives on Animal Production at a Village, Urban and Ritual Center." *Archaeozoologia* 4 (1991): 9–86.

Warner, Sean. "The Alphabet: An Innovation and Its Diffusion." *VT* 30 (1980): 81–90.

Warnock, Peter, and Michael Pendleton "The Wood of the Ulu Burun Diptych." *Anatolian Studies* 41 (1991): 107–10.

Weill, Raymond. *La Cité de David, II: Campagne de 1923–1924*. Paris: P. Geuthner, 1947.

Weinfeld, Moshe. *Deuteronomy 1–11*. AB 5. New York: Doubleday, 1991.

———. "The Worship of Molech and of the Queen of Heaven and Its Background." *UF* 4 (1972): 133–54.

Weippert, Helga. "Die Kesselwagen Salomos." *ZDPV* 108 (1992): 8–41.

Wellhausen, Julius. *Prolegomena to the History of Israel*. Atlanta: Scholars Press, 1994; German original in 1878.

Wheeler, Margaret. "Loomweights and Spindle Whorls." In *Excavations at Jericho*, edited by K. M. Kenyon and T. A. Holland, 4: 622–37. London: British School of Archaeology in Jerusalem, 1982.

White, Lynn. *Medieval Technology and Social Change*. Oxford: Clarendon Press, 1962.

Wolff, Hans Walter. *Anthropology of the Old Testament*. Philadelphia: Fortress Press, 1974.

Woolley, C. Leonard, and P. Roger Moorey. *Ur 'of the Chaldees'*. Rev. ed. Ithaca: Cornell University Press, 1982.

Wright, G. Ernest. *Biblical Archaeology*. Philadelphia: Westminster, 1957.

———. *Deuteronomy*. IB. New York: Abingdon, 1953.

———. "The 'New' Archaeology." *BA* 38 (1975): 104–15.

Wright, G. Ernest, ed. *The Bible and the Ancient Near East* [W. F. Albright Festschrift]. Garden City, N.Y.: Doubleday, 1961.

Wright, J. H. Christopher. "Family." *ABD*, 2: 761–69.

Yadin, Yigael. *The Art of Warfare in Biblical Lands*. New York: McGraw-Hill, 1963.

———. "Excavations at Hazor, 1968–1969: Preliminary Communiqué." *IEJ* 19 (1969): 1–19.

———. "The Fifth Season of Excavations at Hazor, 1968–1969." *BA* 32 (1969): 50–70.

———. "A Further Note on the Samaria Ostraca," *IEJ* 12 (1962): 64–66.

———. "Goliath's Javelin and the *menor 'orgîm*." *PEQ* 86 (1955): 58–69.

———. *Hazor: The Rediscovery of a Great Citadel of the Bible*. London: Weidenfeld & Nicolson, 1975.

———. *Hazor II*. Jerusalem: Hebrew University, 1960.

———. "The Mystery of the Unexplained Chain." *BAR* 10/4 (1984): 65–67.

———. "Recipients or Owners: A Note on the Samaria Ostraca." *IEJ* 9 (1959): 184–87.

Yeivin, Ze'ev. "The Mysterious Silver Hoard from Eshtemoa." *BAR* 13/6 (1987): 38–44.

Yener, K. Aslihan, and Hadi Ozbal. "Tin in the Turkish Taurus Mountains: The Bolkardag Mining District." *Antiquity* 61 (1987): 223–24.

Zeist, Willem van, and Johanna A. Heeres. "Paleobotanical Studies of Deir 'Alla, Jordan." *Paléorient* 1 (1973): 21–37.

Zias, Joseph. "Health and Healing in the Land of Israel—A Paleopathological Perspective." In *Illness and Healing in Ancient Times*, edited by O. Rimon, 13*–19*. Reuben and Edith Hecht Museum Catalogue 13. Haifa: University of Haifa, 1996.

———. "Three Trephinated Skulls from Jericho." *BASOR* 246 (1982): 55–58.

Zias, Joseph, and Kostas Mumcuoglu. "Pre-Pottery Neolithic B Head Lice from Naḥal Ḥemar Cave." *'Atiqot* 20 (1991): 167–68.

Zimmerli, Walther. *Ezekiel 2*. Hermeneia. Philadelphia: Fortress Press, 1983.

Zohary, Michael. *Flora Palaestina*. Jerusalem: Israel Academy of Sciences and Humanities, 1966.

———. *Plants of the Bible*. Cambridge: Cambridge University Press, 1982.

Zorn, Jeffrey R. "Mesopotamian-Style Ceramic 'Bathtub' Coffins from Tell en-Naṣbeh." *TA* 20 (1993): 216–24.

———. "More on Mesopotamian Burial Practices in Ancient Israel." *IEJ* 47 (1997): 214–19.

Index of Biblical Passages and Ancient Sources

413

Index of Modern Authors

Index of Subjects

Boldface numbers indicate the more important references. Page numbers in italics refer to captions of illustrations.

426